INSIGHT AND INFERENCE:
DESCARTES'S FOUNDING PRINCIPLE AND
MODERN PHILOSOPHY

MURRAY MILES

Insight and Inference: Descartes's Founding Principle and Modern Philosophy

UNIVERSITY OF TORONTO PRESS
Toronto Buffalo London

© University of Toronto Press Incorporated 1999
Toronto Buffalo London
Printed in Canada

ISBN 0-8020-4315-1

Printed on acid-free paper

Toronto Studies in Philosophy
Editors: James R. Brown and Calvin Normore

Canadian Cataloguing in Publication Data

Miles, Murray Lewis
  Insight and inference

  (Toronto studies in philosophy)
  Includes bibliographical references and index.
  ISBN 0-8020-4315-1

  1. Descartes, Rene, 1596–1650 – Contributions in metaphysics.
  2. Metaphysics.   3. Metaphysics – History – 17th century.   I. Title.
  II. Series.

  B1878.M5M54 1998   194   C98-931119-8

University of Toronto Press acknowledges the financial assistance to its publishing
program of the Canada Council for the Arts and the Ontario Arts Council.

This book has been published with the help of a grant from the Canadian Federation for
the Humanities, using funds provided by the Social Sciences and Humanities Research
Council of Canada. Additional funding was provided by the Office of the Dean of
Humanities, Brock University.

ISABELAE FILIAE
in memoriam

Have I caught thee?

By 'thinking' you mean that you understand and will and imagine and have sensations; and that you think in such a way as to contemplate and consider your thought by a reflexive act, thus thinking or knowing and considering that you are thinking (which is what it is to be conscious ...). This, you claim, is a property of a faculty that is superior to matter and wholly spiritual ... But while *sound*, this is nothing *new*, since we all heard it from our teachers long ago, and they from their teachers, and so on, I would think, right back to Adam ... (AT VII 533f.: CSM II 364)

The Jesuit Pierre Bourdin berates the Father of Modern Philosophy for his want of originality.

Contents

Preface

Mais les textes ont leurs exigences, même si les interprétations ont leurs habitudes.
(J.-L. Marion)

The present volume is the first book-length study devoted specifically to Descartes's founding principle, *cogito, ergo sum*. It deals in the main with three themes: the precise sense of *cogitare* in the word *cogito* (Part One); the certainty or necessary truth of *sum* or *existo* (Part Two); and the nature of the inference marked by the presence of the logical particle *ergo* (Part Three). What it seeks to establish in respect of each is stated briefly in the chapter outline of the Synopsis (section 5.1) and argued at length in the corresponding chapter. Nevertheless, a brief confession of its principal heresies may not be out of place here at the outset.

Descartes's most lasting philosophical achievement is the elaboration of a metaphysics in a sense of that term largely (though not entirely) continuous with the oldest metaphysical tradition. While his early epistemological, scientific, and methodological preoccupations still play a great role in his mature thought, metaphysical and theological concerns are clearly paramount. Despite marked departures from the epistemological and metaphysical outlook of his Scholastic predecessors, the still fundamentally realist character of Descartes's thought is everywhere apparent. The now justly decried doctrines that all we can perceive and know immediately or with perfect certainty are ideas in the mind, and that the knowing subject is ontologically as well as epistemologically prior to the things known, were never espoused by Descartes himself, who is therefore blameless in their elevation to the status of unchallengeable dogmas at various points in the subsequent history of modern thought. Behind these misunderstandings lies a widespread neglect of two fundamental distinctions. The first is between the order of knowing and the order of being. It calls for careful attention to a variety of different dimensions broadly classifiable as 'ontological' rather than 'epistemological.' The other is the distinction between thought and consciousness. Appreciation of this latter distinction is greatly facilitated by the Husserlian analysis of the intentional structure of consciousness (*Bewußtsein*). Both distinctions are discussed within the Introduction and Part One.

Contrary to another very widespread misconception about Descartes, there is simply no difference between 'certainty' and 'truth' in that primary sense of the word relevant to *first* truths like *cogito, ergo sum*. There is, of course, another meaning of 'truth' in Descartes (roughly, the standard realist notion common to correspondence theories), a sense consistently mistaken for the sole or basic meaning of 'truth' by the majority of commentators. As for the derivation of the truth of *sum* from *cogito*, it clearly involves a transition of the mind and therefore an inference of sorts, though this distinctive movement of thought unfolds within the confines of intuition itself. Called 'analytical reflexion,' 'reflexive analysis,' and 'intuitive induction' in Part Three, it has little to do with any discursive or ratiocinative process, still less with a 'performance' of any sort, being rather a hitherto unrecognized form of direct intuitive apprehension comprising a sequence of temporally discrete stages. To this the term *deductio* is applied in Descartes's early *Regulae*, though it is also described as an *intuitus mentis* in that work; it forms the heart of the "analytic method of discovery" described in the Replies to the Second Set of Objections to the *Meditations*. If this is correct, *deductio* and its cognates cannot be equated, as they often are, with direct or indirect logical inference based on the forms of valid arguments – though these are no doubt among the many meanings of 'deduction' in Descartes. Nor can deduction simply be opposed to intuition. In one little-noticed use, 'deduction' refers to that intuitive movement of thought in analytical reflexion upon innate concepts and principles by which all that is immediately though only implicitly intuited in the first truths is rendered explicit, i.e., clearly and distinctly known. This is precisely the movement of thought involved in the *cogito, ergo sum*. Truth and certainty are the subject of the second, reflexion and inference of the third and final part. Here the centuries-old puzzle regarding the *ergo* – insight or inference? – receives a new solution based on a detailed re-examination of Descartes's theory of the mind.

Likely to spark some resistance (if not indignation) are the implications of all this for the time-honoured rationalist mantle that still adorns Descartes despite the re-tailoring efforts of numerous (mainly English-speaking) commentators over the last two or three decades. The crux of the matter has always been clearly seen. Whether or not Descartes can be legitimately called a 'rationalist' depends on the extent to which he subscribed to a fairly robust doctrine of innateness and a model of the logical structure of science patterned after that of formal axiomatizable systems. The findings of this study suggest that he did both to an extent seldom acknowledged nowadays, though the theory of innateness and the paradigm of mathematical deduction are interpreted in a new way, resulting in fairly extensive revision of the familiar rationalist stereotype of the past.

In elaborating these new or unfashionable perspectives it proved necessary to take a fresh look at most of the standard topics of Cartesian scholarship: Cartesian method and doubt, clear and distinct perception, analytic and synthetic method, innate ideas, the 'Cartesian circle,' the divine creation of the eternal truths, and virtually every central theme except (mercifully!) the proofs of the existence of God and the details of Cartesian physics. The result falls short of a complete reinterpretation of Descartes's system of thought, though not by much. By leaving out the proofs of God's existence the present study falls short even of a comprehensive treatment of Cartesian metaphysics. The omission comes of deviating from the standard order of presentation, which has long been that of the *Meditations* themselves. Since here the three words of Descartes's founding principle form the guiding thread of the exposition, the proofs, like the basic laws of Descartes's defunct science, fall outside its scope.

Apart from those mentioned already, the matters that have occasioned most discussion among interpreters of the *cogito*, beginning with contemporaries of Descartes like Bourdin and Arnauld, are mainly historical. As for the historical antecedents of Descartes's founding principle, what little I have to add to the already voluminous literature on the subject is confined largely to incidental comment in the Introduction. The question of Descartes's posterity, his role as Father of Modern Philosophy and alleged founder of modern idealism, receives more attention. It is taken up first in the Introduction and then, more fully, in the Conclusion. In both places Descartes's philosophy is portrayed in a new light: not just as one of the two "great types of possible philosophies" (Russell) the Western tradition has brought forth so far, but as *the* leading philosophy of transcendence in the modern era and the principal target of all broadly 'naturalistic' philosophies from neo-Scholasticism to the latest forms of empiricism. These two portions of the work provide what justification there may be for the ambitious-sounding (not to say pretentious) subtitle. Looked at differently, though, the task envisaged in the subtitle is quite modest: neither to provide a critical exposition of Descartes's system as a whole, nor to point out the bearing of some parts of it on contemporary philosophical debates (especially about the mind), but to set in a clear light Descartes's signal contribution to the framework of metaphysical and epistemological ideas that evolved over the next three centuries of European philosophy – with rather more attention to twentieth-century Continental developments than is customary among those writing in English. A key element in this task is obviously to determine what Descartes is *not* responsible for among the more dubious departures from realism and sound common sense prevalent in the later modern tradition and regularly ascribed to the Father of Modern Philosophy himself. But the task is equally to bring out the genuinely new and arguably progressive in Descartes's analysis of the mind. That is the direction in which the main title points. Thus, in its three main parts, the work is a detailed reinterpretation of the theories of intuition and deduction or reflexion elaborated by Descartes as part of his metaphysics: insight and inference.

The key sections of this study were written during the second of two leaves granted by Brock University and spent mainly in France. Thanks are due to the former dean of the Faculty of Humanities (now rector and vice-chancellor of the University of the Western Cape, Cape Town, South Africa), Dr Cecil Abrahams, and to the past chair of the Department of Philosophy, Dr Martha Husain, for their support in obtaining leave from teaching duties. To my wife, Silvia, I am deeply grateful for frequent leaves from my responsibilities as husband and father, including a three-month stay in France, without which this book would probably not have been written.

Finally, it is a pleasure to record my indebtedness to those colleagues and friends who kindly consented to read earlier drafts of portions of this work, providing detailed comments and suggestions, many of which are reflected in the version published here: Professors Lawrence Dewan, O.P. (Ottawa), Graeme Hunter (Ottawa), Martha Husain (St Catharines), Thomas Lennon (London, Ontario), Robert McRae (Toronto), James C. Morrison (Toronto), Joseph Owens, C.S.s.R (Toronto), and Thomas Vinci (Halifax). Mr Scott Stapleford provided invaluable assistance with the proofs.

Abbreviations used in source citations throughout the text and notes are explained on pages 531–4 of the References.

Murray Miles
St Catharines, Ontario

INTRODUCTION

And observing that this truth "*I am thinking, therefore I exist*" was so firm and sure that all the most extravagant suppositions of the sceptics were incapable of shaking it, I decided that I could accept it without scruple as the first principle of the philosophy I was seeking. (AT VI 32: CSM I 127)

1

The "Twin Pillars" of Cartesianism

Over three decades have elapsed since Hintikka remarked (1962, 108): "Thirty years ago Heinrich Scholz wrote that there not only remain many important questions concerning the Cartesian dictum [*cogito, ergo sum*] unanswered but that there also remain important questions unasked." Scholz (1931) divided the outstanding issues into two classes, "external" questions regarding Descartes's relationship to major thinkers before and after him, and "internal" matters. Heading the list of the former is the "Aristotelian question" whether the first principle of philosophy is the axiom "the same attribute cannot at the same time belong and not belong to the same subject and in the same respect" or Descartes's *cogito, ergo sum*.[1] Next comes the "Augustinian question" whether modern philosophy should continue to be regarded as having begun with Descartes when St Augustine apparently anticipated Descartes's founding principle and all its chief uses.[2] Finally, there is the "Kantian question" whether Descartes "proved too much" in claiming to have demonstrated the existence of a thinking substance, and not just of thinking itself ("Paralogisms"), while proving "too little" in claiming to have established the existence of thoughts ordered successively in time but not that of an external object of thought ordered both temporally and spatially ("Refutation of Idealism").[3]

As for the internal questions, these are reducible to a single pair: In what precise sense is *cogito, ergo sum* the *first* principle of Descartes's metaphysics? and How is the relation expressed in the *ergo* to be understood in a manner at once both faithful to Descartes's express pronouncements on the subject (that is, non-syllogistically) and consonant with the principles of Aristotelian and modern logic?[4] Deliberately leaving the historical questions aside, Scholz nevertheless scrutinizes the answers given the systematic questions by a great many prominent historical figures. Spinoza, Leibniz, Pascal, Wolff, Kant, Hegel, Schopenhauer, and Heidegger all figure at some point in his own attempt to shed fresh light on the internal questions.[5] Any list of the major philosophical figures who have pronounced on either subject should probably include Descartes's illustrious contemporaries Arnauld, Hobbes, and Gassendi as well. Among twentieth-century figures it should certainly include Husserl. The reflections of these distinguished thinkers, together with the abundant work of an army of philosophical scholars, amount to an almost grotesquely disproportionate expenditure of philosophical talent and energy on the interpretation of three little words. Yet if the view of the matter to be set out in the present work is even roughly correct, the significance of Descartes's founding principle was a good deal clearer at various times in the past than it is today.[6]

1.1 Augustine, Kant, and logic

The allure of historical parallels may be one reason why a better understanding of Descartes's founding principle eludes us today more than ever. While certain similarities to St Augustine may have misled Descartes's contemporaries, a number of obvious affinities with Kant, as well as a preoccupation with logic, have created new obstacles since.

As the "Augustinian question" implies, it is not the formulation of principles *like* the *cogito, ergo sum* that is original with Descartes. Nor is it the recognition that whenever we think, we are aware that we are thinking and that we who are thinking must therefore exist. Gilson (1951, 191–201 and 1947a, 295f.) has shown that St Augustine was fully seized of this point and of its importance for the refutation of scepticism, for the establishment of a real distinction between body and soul, and even for the demonstration of God's existence by a new proof. Descartes, of course, thought otherwise. Augustine, he writes,

does use it [the *cogito, ergo sum*] to prove the certainty of our existence. He goes on to show that there is a certain likeness of the Trinity in us, in that we exist, we know that we exist, and we love the existence and the knowledge we have. I, on the other hand, use the argument to show that this *I* which is thinking is *an immaterial substance* with no bodily element. (AT III 247: CSMK 159)

But so, Gilson insists, did Augustine, who at times comes remarkably close to Descartes's own wording of the principle.[7] This Augustinian teaching, moreover, was "never forgotten" in the Middle Ages; an unbroken tradition links it to the seventeenth century and Descartes. Hoenen (1937, 470f.) has traced a similar principle back from St Thomas, for whom it was only one principle among others, to Aristotle's formulation of a clearly recognizable prototype in the ninth book of the *Nicomachean Ethics*.[8] This much can be conceded. Yet if the theory of the mind to be described here is in fact Descartes's, no earlier formulation expressed either the precise *insight* or the exact *inference* embodied by Descartes in his classic formula, *cogito, ergo sum.*

In that case, the originality of Descartes's founding principle cannot be said to consist merely in the elevation of a long-familiar principle to the status of *the* first principle of philosophy, an "Archimedean point" (cf. Hoenen 1937, 465n, 470; also Marion 1986, §11); despite a family resemblance to classical predecessors, the principle itself is new. Moreover, its distinctively modern employment brought about a radical reversal in the traditional order of knowing. Henceforth the immaterial soul was to come before ordinary sensible things in the order of cognition.[9] At the same time, a profound change was introduced into the traditional order of being. Without altering the mind's dependence on God, Descartes made the activity of thinking independent of material things both for its existence and for its logical, mathematical, and metaphysical ideas and first principles. If this were all there were to the talk of the 'subjective' or 'epistemic turn' in modern philosophy, little could be said against it, historically; but not infrequently the reversal in the order of knowing is taken as grounds for regarding Descartes as the first modern idealist and intellectual forebear of all subsequent metaphysical idealisms, especially Kant's.[10]

Gilson has observed that the historical role of Descartes in fostering varieties of metaphysical idealism as disparate as Berkeley's and Kant's involves a "déformation de la pensée de Descartes lui-même, dont l'inspiration réaliste est évidente" (1947a, 301). Hamelin at bottom concurs: having anointed Descartes "le fondateur authentique de l'idéalisme moderne," he adds (somewhat ruefully): "Mais dans le dernier pas qu'il va faire" – Hamelin presumably means the proof of the existence of the external world in the Sixth Meditation – "les habitudes réalistes ... vont reprendre le dessus" (1921, 128).[11] Even Gueroult shows himself acutely aware of the fundamentally realist tendency of Descartes's thought: "Descartes n'a jamais admis que l'esprit humain pût définir et poser la réalité des choses en vertu de ses propres nécessités à lui. Il n'a jamais cru pouvoir faire reposer la certitude sur l'esprit humain seul, dont il sent l'imperfection. En ce sens il diffère entièrement de Kant" (1968, I, 32). Here Gueroult may only be alluding to the role of the divine guarantor in Descartes's philosophy (on this, see below, section 13.6); elsewhere, however, he elaborates the most sustained argument to be found in the literature that the consciousness of whose existence Descartes becomes absolutely certain in the Second Meditation is a *conscience intellectuelle* rather than ordinary empirical consciousness, *conscience psychologique*.[12] In a similar vein, Gilson remarks (1947a, 301): "Si donc on veut rapprocher ici Descartes de Kant, la seule analogie que l'on puisse légitimement établir est celle du *Cogito* avec le: *Je pense*, accompagne toutes mes représentations." Though cautiously worded, this too introduces the Kantian notion of a pure *ego* into Descartes's analysis of mind, a temptation to which both Hamelin (1921, 131) and Gueroult succumb as well. The latter echoes Gilson's sentiment almost verbatim (cf. 1968, I, 53 n. 5): "Le rapprochement s'impose ... avec le *Ich denke* kantien : « Le « je pense » doit pouvoir accompagner toutes mes représentations »." Such was the hold exercised by neo-Kantianism on the minds of European scholars in the early part of this century.

If the absorption in historical parallels was a factor in the failure of these distinguished European scholars to recognize what Descartes's founding principle is all about, the prestige of logic has misled a different set of commentators. The temptation to misconstrue the formula *cogito, ergo sum* either as enthymematic or as embodying a logical operation simpler and more perspicuous than any deductive inference was already strong among Descartes's contemporaries; but recent advances in logic leading to more sophisticated logical analyses of the statements *cogito, sum,* and of the relation between them have exacerbated the problem.[13] Behind the deceptively logical façade of Descartes's formula lies a subtle and complex analysis of the formal structure of thought as the principal attribute of mind. The analysis is set squarely within a framework of metaphysical concerns traditionally grouped together under the title 'first philosophy.' Apart from the usual queries about what is consistent or inconsistent with what, what presupposes or entails what, purely logical considerations play no special role in Descartes's enquiry. Even epistemological issues are subordinate to the primarily metaphysical objectives pursued in the expressly so titled *Meditationes de prima philosophia* but no less central to Descartes's other philosophical writings.

1.2 Ontological and epistemological direct realism

The analysis of knowledge and the mind is the first pillar of Descartes's revolutionary dualistic metaphysics. As will become more evident later (cf. chapter 7), it derives its properly metaphysical significance from the knowledge of the essence of something actually existent to which it gives rise: from *ego existo* (AT VII 25: CSM II 17) and *sum res cogitans* (AT VII 27f.: CSM II 18f.). Descartes was after all no philosopher of mind or philosophical psychologist in the contemporary sense. He analysed the structure and classified the chief varieties of the mental as a metaphysician. Philosophical psychology, like the primacy of epistemology within philosophy, is a post-Kantian, nineteenth- and twentieth-century outgrowth of the revolution in philosophy pioneered by Descartes.

The other pillar of Descartes's dualistic system is the analysis of matter as a substance whose principal attribute is extension in length, breadth, and depth and the sole modes of which are figure and motion.[14] It is a commonplace nowadays to speak of the theory of Ideas and doctrine of immortality as the "twin pillars" of Platonism. Although it is by no means customary to do so, one could with equal justice speak of the analysis of matter and the theory of the mind as the twin pillars of Cartesianism. But here a special problem arises. The philosophy of physics and philosophical psychology have become relatively autonomous subdisciplines of philosophy, separated and even estranged from their roots in traditional metaphysics. The trouble is that critics for whom 'metaphysics' has largely pejorative connotations tend to advocate a similar separation of Descartes's strictly analytic insights regarding matter and the mind from their properly metaphysical setting. Those insights may still be regarded as 'metaphysical,' but usually in some special, contemporary sense of the word, cleansed of negative associations (see chapter 2, n. 16). The aim of this Introduction is to show that this approach leads inevitably to distortion, given the marked continuity of Descartes's concept of metaphysics with that of the older, Aristotelian tradition of philosophy. The next section traces in broad historical outline the familiar features of that idea of metaphysics which defines the Aristotelian mainstream of philosophy right down to Descartes. This is followed in chapter 3 by a sketch of Descartes's philosophical project, substantially in his own words. The aim is to show that the main features of the Scholastic-Aristotelian concept of metaphysics are preserved, relatively intact, in Descartes's own statements of his aims and intentions in the *Meditations*.

This raises the much larger question of the fundamental *dis*continuity in epistemological and metaphysical outlook between Descartes and his Aristotelian predecessors despite the overlap in their understanding of metaphysics itself. It is another commonplace that the transition from medieval to modern philosophy involves a radical change in philosophical starting point (see Gilson 1947b, 176–97 and 1947c, *passim*). This, given its profound significance for later philosophy, amply warrants the designation of Descartes as the Father of Modern Philosophy. However, as the testimony cited earlier shows, Descartes's philosophical outlook is often seen as subverting the epistemological and metaphysical realism of Scholastic-Aristotelian philosophy. Though something of the sort undoubtedly took place in the subsequent course of the development of modern philosophy, it is an outgrowth rather than the aim of the revolution in philosophy brought about by Descartes. Distinguishing the order of being from the order of knowing and, within the latter, knowledge of essence from knowledge of existence, Des-cartes's philosophical standpoint can be contrasted with that of his Scholastic-Aristotelian predecessors in roughly the following terms.

In the order of being, the transition from Scholastic-Aristotelian hylomorphism to Cartesian dualism is nothing like a reversal. While the absolute primacy of the uncreated being (God) is retained, the relative priority of material *vis-à-vis* immaterial created things is replaced by two autonomous domains of beings or substances, minds and sensible things, each dependent on the absolutely First Being but independent of the other. There is no priority of the mental here, let alone a reductive analysis that makes the being of the non-mental dependent on ideas in the mind. To that extent Cartesian metaphysical dualism is an ontological realism (see section 22.1). Still, the basic realism of the Aristotelian view that perception of sensible things is a necessary condition of *all* thinking about such things, which are therefore ontologically as well as epistemologically prior, is clearly abandoned by Descartes. *Some* thought originates in this way; but thinking does not depend for its existence on sensible things. Although thinking is always thinking *of* something, and primarily of sensible objects, and although *what* we think is largely determined by the action of such sensible objects on the mind, the existence of thinking as such does not depend for Descartes, as it did for Aristotle, upon the existence of any sensible things whatever, even our own bodies. Moreover, much of what we think does not in fact derive from such objects, but is innate in the mind itself. Examples are "the simple notions which are the basic components of our thoughts" (AT VIII-1 22: CSM I 208), such as 'substance,' 'duration,' 'order,' 'number,' 'perception,' 'volition,' 'size,' 'shape,' 'motion,' 'position,' 'divisibility' of parts "and the like" (ibid.). To these must be added the ideas of thinking, perfection, the infinite, an infinite thinking thing (God), and the ideas of truth and freedom. Innate are also the "common notions or axioms" (AT VIII-1 24: CSM I 209) like 'nothing comes from nothing,' 'nothing has no properties,' 'what is done cannot be undone,' and 'the same thing cannot both be and not be at the same time in the same respect.' Thus, the existence of thinking is independent of that of sensible things, while, conversely, the existence of sensible things does not depend upon the existence of the human mind. The ontological priority of sensible things in the Aristotelian tradition is modified rather than reversed by Descartes.[15]

In the order of knowing, on the other hand, Descartes effected a radical reversal by asserting that the knowledge of the human mind is prior to the knowledge of sensible things. The slightest reflection on the Cartesian *cogito* reveals that the *existence* of the mind is not just independent of that of any sensible thing but also prior in the order of cognition. One reason for this is that the existence of the mind is immediately and intuitively known, while knowledge of the existence of sensible things is not intuitive but inferential, based on a formal process of reasoning from ideas in the mind to their extra-mental causes. All this has been well understood. It is with regard to the knowledge of the *essence* of mind and body that confusion is apt to arise. For this is often taken to involve a similar opposition of immediate or intuitive to inferential knowledge. Descartes indeed reversed the order of knowing in respect of the essences of minds and things; but he never espoused the view that our knowledge of essences other than that of the mind is acquired by reasoning or inference. The order of precedence is rather an order *within* intuitive knowledge itself. The mind knows the nature of things other than itself (both God and material bodies) immediately and intuitively *in and through* reflection upon its own nature and upon "those simple notions which are basic components of our thought."[16]

The tendency to read back into Descartes shades of the later reversal in the order of being in the philosophies of Berkeley and Kant stems in part (1) from the failure to distinguish the order of being from the order of knowing, in part also (2) from neglect of the distinction between the knowledge of existence and of essence within the order of knowing itself. But the main reason for it is (3) the ascription to Descartes of the theory known as 'representationalism.' From this stems a widely held account of why thought does not depend on the existence of the extra-mental for Descartes: to think is indeed to think *of* something, an object, but that object is only an idea in the mind, never the thing itself.

Owing largely to these three factors the choice between Scholastic-Aristotelian hylomorphism and Cartesian dualism is apt to be seen in some such distorting way as this. On the one side we have a metaphysical and epistemological outlook according to which things exist in themselves and are immediately accessible to thought as they are in themselves. Over against this allegedly naive view stands the self-styled critical attitude of Descartes and modern philosophy. According to the latter the *only* objects of thought that are immediately accessible are ideas. The objects of ideas are the things themselves. The things are therefore accessible, but only mediately, via ideas. On this model, which interposes a realm of ideas between the thoughts and the things of the 'naive' model, it is difficult to see how one can ever get beyond ideas to the things at all. Descartes's manner of doing so is widely held to involve an inference the reliability of which is guaranteed by God's veracity.[17] The proof of the existence of a veracious God, however, has been regarded as circular. If the interpretation to be developed here is correct, this account of the role of the divine guarantor is misleading and the charge of circularity misplaced. Nevertheless, both suggested themselves quite naturally to Descartes's contemporaries and successors. Once seized of the divide across which (it was thought) Descartes had illicitly constructed a theological bridge, subsequent thinkers strove to devise better solutions. Retaining some form of the dualism of thought and things, some resorted, if not to Descartes's, then to another version of the *deus ex machina*. (This is at least a common interpretation of occasionalism and pre-established harmony.) Short of abandoning dualism, the only alternative to such theological solutions appeared to be scepticism, whether acknowledged, as in Hume, or unacknowledged, as in Locke, the latent scepticism of whose doctrine of unknowable "real essences" Berkeley was quick to grasp and point out. The other main strategies, reductive materialism and idealism, involve abandoning the irreducible duality of thought and things. Both are perhaps best understood as pre-emptive strikes, though idealism is often presented as a solution to the problem to which the model of interposed ideas gives rise. According to Berkeley, the problem of how to get beyond ideas to the things themselves is based on a misconception. There is no need to get beyond ideas in order to retain a concept of real existence, truth, and knowledge perfectly satisfactory for the purposes of 'the learned,' even if strangely remote from the notions of 'the vulgar': the agreement among ideas supplants that between thought and material things.[18] A similar solution has been ascribed, *mutatis mutandis*, to Kant. The choice, in short, is between a metaphysical dualism that, in the epistemological arena, is either dependent on God or vulnerable to scepticism and a metaphysical idealism that manages to avoid these pitfalls but is almost wildly at variance with ordinary experience and common sense.

These are the alternatives to 'naive' realism at the one extreme and reductive materialism at the other. The first of them is widely held to be a reasonable facsimile of Descartes's historical position. Behind it lurks the model of knowledge via interposed ideas, necessitating the resort to God. But the model represents a serious distortion of Descartes's view of the order of knowing. Not only is the role of God in Cartesian philosophy different from that usually assigned it (cf. section 13.6); so is the dualistic metaphysical picture of minds and things that Descartes set in opposition to Aristotelian hylomorphism (cf. section 22.1). Once the role of God is clarified, the problem of the circle can be laid to rest once and for all (cf. chapter 14).

Before pursuing the question of the new order of knowing and the doctrine commonly called 'representationalism' further (cf. section 4.1 below), we must try to make some headway on the other task described earlier. The aim of the next two chapters is to show that Descartes's express aim in the *Meditations* is to elaborate a metaphysics in a sense of the term largely, if not in all points, continuous with the Aristotelian tradition.

2

Scholastic-Aristotelian Metaphysics

We begin with a brief and necessarily impressionistic sketch of the concept of metaphysics in Aristotle and the medievals, to be followed by a discussion of Descartes's concept of metaphysics and the purpose of his *Meditations*. The immediate aim is to develop a background idea or working definition of 'metaphysics' as it was understood, with some variations, in the Aristotelian mainstream of philosophy before Descartes.[1]

2.1 Aristotle: The name and subject matter of metaphysics[2]

The exact origins of the word 'metaphysics' are obscure, but it may go back as far as the direct pupils of Aristotle, though Aristotle himself never used it. Literally, the Greek expression *ta meta ta physika* means 'the things after (or beyond) the physical things,' the Greek preposition *meta* having both meanings, 'after' in a temporal sequence and 'beyond' in a spatial arrangement. These strands of meaning (in Latin, *post* and *trans* or *ultra*) are interwoven in the long history of the concept. In the Aristotelian *corpus* the title is ambiguous in two ways.

Those who first coined it were long thought to have used the term 'metaphysics' solely as an editorial designation for that group of Aristotelian treatises that Aristotle himself called, not 'metaphysics,' but (variously) 'first philosophy,' 'the most divine science,' 'theology,' or simply 'wisdom.' These treatises were placed by the earliest Greek editors of Aristotle's writings *after* the treatises dealing with the principles and causes of the material or physical universe (which Aristotle called *ta physika*, 'physics'). Hence, 'metaphysics' was taken to mean the treatises 'after the physical treatises.'

This view of the origin of the term 'metaphysics' is now no longer defended.[3] It is generally agreed that 'metaphysics' was used from the first as a designation for the subject matter of the treatises in question. The reason why they were placed after the physical treatises by the editors was that their starting points were the conclusions or end points of physics, while their own end points lay 'beyond the physical,' that is, beyond the material or sensible world in the realm of the immaterial or supersensible. Hence, 'metaphysical' is now generally taken to have meant, from the outset, going beyond the physical (material, sensible) universe, transcending the world of sense toward the insensible, the supersensible.[4]

That is the first ambiguity: metaphysics has been understood both as an editorial designation and as a designation for the subject matter of a science. But even as the designation for the subject matter of what Aristotle called 'first philosophy,' the term 'metaphysics' proves ambiguous in a second way. It designates both (1) the most universal science, or 'ontology' (as it came later to be called) and (2) the highest science, 'theology' (as Aristotle himself called it).

As the study of being qua being or 'ontology,' metaphysics studies the "first principles and highest causes" of all beings universally (Aristotle 1924 [*Met.*, 1003a 32; also 981b 28ff.]). Metaphysics, in other words, is that strictly universal science which treats of both material and immaterial beings (sensible and insensible or supersensible being), including those beings that are 'substances,' that is, capable of existing in their own right, and those which are not, for instance, the properties and relations of substances that can only exist 'in' another. Thus, first philosophy or metaphysics as the all-encompassing universal science differs from those particular sciences that hive off some compartment of reality for separate study.[5] It differs, for example, from physics, which studies only the changing things that exist in their own right, as substances; and it differs from mathematics, which studies only unchanging things (attributes and relations) that do not exist in their own right, but in something else that is a substance (ibid. [*Met.*, 1026a 17; also 1064a 31ff.]). While 'first' or 'primary philosophy' is Aristotle's own coinage, 'ontology' is a term first employed in the early seventeenth century by a number of German philosophers and applied to the study of 'being as being,' or 'being in general' (cf. Vollrath 1962, 265f.).

This is the first sense of the term 'metaphysics' as a designation for the subject matter of a science. This most universal science is, however, at the same time the study of that particular being which 'is' in the fullest sense, the primary or divine being. Metaphysics, in short, is theology. The first cause of the sensible, material, or changing things has no matter, no principle of change; as pure form it is eternal or unchanging, like the objects of mathematics; but unlike the objects of mathematics, it is a substance capable of existing in its own right, an Unmoved Mover. First philosophy or metaphysics, so understood, is not so much the universal as the highest science, the science which goes beyond (*trans*cends) the sensible toward the non-sensible or supersensible eternal or divine (Aristotle 1924 [*Met.*, 1026a 19f.; cf. 1064a 38 – 1064b]).

For Aristotle himself, the universal science of being as being is unproblematically included in theology. In other words, the study of a particular kind of being, primary immaterial being (theology), *just is* the universal science that treats of *all* beings with respect to their being (ontology); and it is universal *because* it is first:

> The question might be raised as to whether the science of being qua being should be regarded as universal or not. Each of the mathematical sciences deals with some one class of things which is determinate, but universal mathematics is common to all alike. If, then, natural substances are the first of existing things, physics will be the first of the sciences; but if there is some other nature and substance which exists separately and is immovable [i.e., the divine], then the science which treats of it must be different from and prior to physics, *and universal because of its priority.* (ibid. [*Met.*, 1064b 7–14] e.a.; cf. also ibid. [*Met.*, 1026a 31])

What for Aristotle was unproblematic has been thought profoundly puzzling by his interpreters.

So much for the double ambiguity of the term 'metaphysics.' To round out this account of the conception of metaphysics that was to dominate the Aristotelian tradition, we must briefly consider what else is included in this science.

Metaphysics includes, in the first place, the study of the axioms, notably the so-called principle of contradiction, which are in some sense primary as well as unchanging (ibid. [*Met.*, 1005a 19ff.; also 1061b 19ff. and 1061b 34 – 1062b 12]). It includes also the study of unchanging formal and relational determinations like unity and plurality, sameness and otherness, similarity and contrariety, equality and inequality, perfection and imperfection, earlier and later, genus and species, whole and part, and so on (ibid. [*Met.*, 1004b 5ff.; also 1055a 3 – 1059a 3 and 1061a 18ff.]). It does not, however, include the study of accidental attributes (ibid. [*Met.* 1026b 4ff.]) or of being in the special sense of 'truth' (ibid. [*Met.*, 1027b 17 – 1028a 6]). In addition to the foregoing, metaphysics comprises the study of changing sensible substances in so far as *one* principle, namely form, is unchanging even in them and exists as separate and unchangeable (without matter) in divine substances. This is no doubt at least part of the explanation why, for Aristotle, the study of perfect being without potency or matter is ipso facto the study of *universal* being. But sensible substances are also those that are immediately known. For this reason, too, the study of material substance belongs to metaphysics. Finally, metaphysics includes the study of all the different varieties of beings, the different ways in which beings are what they are and the different senses of the word 'to be,' that is, of the categories.

Exactly how this all fits together into a single unified conception of a science is a difficult question.[6] To some it has seemed that these strands can be drawn together without divorcing the science that treats of being universally from the science of the primary being at all: Aristotle merely characterizes one and the same science from different points of view, now from that of its most universal object (being qua being, the universal 'ontology' of the programmatic statements in the early books), now from that of its highest object (God and the separate Intelligences, the 'theology' of the later books), now with a view to that of which 'being' is said in the first instance (sensible substance, the 'ousiology' of the middle books). But as the Aristotelian *Metaphysics* was absorbed into the thought-world of medieval Europe, the theological wisdom of the pagan Greeks, handed down via the Islamic culture, confronted an already existing Christian theology. For the Christian thinkers of the period, theology proper was revealed wisdom, the science of Sacred Scripture. The *theological* character of the study of the first causes and principles of being qua being thus posed a special problem. To this problem the thinkers of the twelfth and thirteenth centuries provided at bottom two solutions: it belongs to metaphysics to investigate God either (1) as falling under its subject matter or (2) as lying outside its subject matter, being in general, of which it is the first cause. Here we can only consider one form of the latter solution in any detail, that of St Thomas, and only as far as may serve to highlight the fundamental continuity of Descartes's conception of metaphysics with that of the tradition.[7]

2.2 Medieval views of the subject matter of metaphysics

In fact, by introducing a further division into the first category it is possible to distinguish three solutions to the problem of the subject matter of metaphysics: (i) God, the highest being and sole object of revealed theology, is *a* subject of metaphysics alongside its *proper* subject, being qua being. (Some who advocate this solution single out 'substance,' as a third principal subject matter, since substances instantiate 'being' more fully than other sorts of beings.) (ii) God is *not* the subject, but the *cause* of the subject, of metaphysics. This is the view envisaged by Albert the Great but only fully worked out by St Thomas. (iii) God is neither *a* subject alongside *ens commune*, nor the first cause of being in general, but a *part* of the proper subject of metaphysics: God falls under the general concept 'being' in a sense broad enough to encompass both created and uncreated being. This is the view of Siger of Brabant, subsequently taken up, with some variations, by Scotus and Suarez, from whom it passed to Descartes and the seventeenth century.[8]

Aquinas's treatment of metaphysics is thus pivotal in the history of the medieval discussion of its nature and names. It provides a suitable vantage point from which to look ahead to Scotus and Suarez as well as back over the history of the onto-theological problem. The *Disputationes Metaphysicae* (1597) of Suarez were used at the Jesuit school of La Flèche where Descartes was educated, and Descartes is known to have had the work at hand while composing the Replies to the Fourth Objections to the *Meditations* (cf. AT VII 235: CSM II 164). Following a brief account of the *Varia metaphysicae nomina*, the first section of the first *disputatio* treats *De Natura Primae Philosophiae seu Metaphysicae*, reviewing the medieval history of the debate right back to the Arabian commentators. Thus, Descartes probably knew something of the history of the debate concerning the *subjectum* of metaphysics, at least to the extent that it was accessible through Suarez's work – a very imperfect source (cf. Zimmermann 1965, 86 n. 3).

Thomas comments on the nature of metaphysics in many places, the most sustained and technical treatment being the fifth and sixth questions of the early incomplete *Expositio super librum Boethii De Trinitate* (before 1259), the most succinct the Prooemium of the commentary on Aristotle's *Metaphysics* (1269–72).[9] Despite the titles, neither work is just an exposition of someone else's thought (cf. Wippel 1983, 25).

The division of the speculative sciences into metaphysics, physics, and mathematics came down to the Middle Ages from Aristotle via Boethius. In his commentaries Aquinas elaborates the doctrine in a way that goes well beyond both Boethius and Aristotle himself. The *corpus articuli* of art. 1, qu. 5 sets out the rationale for the division and explains the different names given metaphysics as one of the three speculative sciences:

Now there are [A] some objects of speculation that depend on matter for their being, for they can exist only in matter. And these are subdivided. [A1] Some depend on matter both for their being and for their being understood, as do those things whose definition contains sensible matter and which, as a consequence, cannot be understood without sensible matter. For example, it is necessary to include flesh and bones in the definition of man. It is things of this sort that physics or natural science studies. On the other hand, there are [A2] some things that, although dependent upon matter for their being, do not depend upon it for their being understood, because sensible matter is not included in their definition. This is the case with lines and numbers – the kinds of objects with which mathematics deals. There are still [B] other objects of speculative knowledge that do not depend upon matter for their being, because [B1] they can exist without matter, as in the case of God and the angels, or [B2] they exist in matter in some instances and not in others, as in the case of substance, quality, being, potency, act, one and many, and the like. The science that treats of all these is theology or divine science, which is so called because of its principal object; by another name it is called metaphysics; that is to say *beyond physics*, because it comes to us after physics among the subjects to be learned; for we have to proceed from sensible things to those that are non-sensible (*ex sensibilibus ... in insensibilia*). It is also called first philosophy, inasmuch as all the other sciences, receiving their principles from it, come after it. (Aquinas 1986, 14f. [*BDT*, 5.1])

The basis of this division of the speculative sciences is the degree to which the object of each is matter-free.[10] According as it can (A1) neither be nor be understood, (A2) be understood but not be, or (B) both be and be understood apart from sensible matter and the qualities that inhere therein, an object belongs either to physics, mathematics, or to what Thomas, following Boethius, calls 'divine science,' alias 'first philosophy,' 'metaphysics,' or 'theology.' Though the division is threefold, the underlying distinction is (A) 'dependent on matter' versus (B) 'independent of matter,' (A1) and (A2) being just subdivisions of the former. The latter, too, is subdivided into (B1) those objects "never" found in matter, such as God and other "separate substances," and (B2) those that exist in matter "in some instances" but not always, for instance, 'substance,' 'quality' (and the other categories), 'being' (*ens*), one and many, potency and act, and so on, that is, *ens et ea quae ens consequuntur*, as Thomas says in the Prooemium.[11]

The onto-theological character of the science here described leaps to the eye: the science of the highest being, that is, of *a* being (God) is at the same time the science of 'being in general,' *ens commune*, the totality of what is, all beings, and all that belongs to them in themselves *as* beings. Without in any sense posing the problem, Thomas attempts to solve it by distinguishing the subject matter of this science (*subjectum*) from its end or goal (*finis*). 'Subject' here is a technical term; it does not mean 'everything that comes within the purview of a science in any way,' whether as its subject matter or an element, property, principle, or cause of its subject matter, be it an internal, constitutive principle or an external, efficient cause (cf. Zimmermann 1965, 88 and passim). Rather, the Prooemium explicitly confines the subject of a science to that "whose causes and properties (*causas et passiones*) we seek," excluding thereby "the causes themselves of any kind of thing investigated." But since, as noted just before this passage, "it belongs to one and the same science to consider both the proper causes of some genus and the genus itself," it must "belong to one and the same science to consider separate substances and *ens commune*, which is the genus of which the aforesaid substances are the common and universal causes."[12] Natural, rational, or philosophical knowledge of God (theology) thus belongs to metaphysics in virtue of its goal: to understand the first principles and causes of being in general, of everything that *has* being. Unlike the created separate Intelligences, however, God himself is not encompassed under the concept *ens* or *esse commune*; he is *supra ens*. He does not *have* being; he *is* (self-subsisting) being according to St Thomas.[13] There is, however, another "divine science" that is indeed devoted to

God as its proper *subjectum*; in it he is considered, not as cause or principle, but as a nature. That is the science of Sacred Scripture.[14]

The initial part of this solution derives from Avicenna, the first to champion the 'ontological' interpretation of the subject of metaphysics (cf. Zimmermann 1965, 108ff.). Avicenna rejects the idea that God is the subject of this science on the grounds that no science investigates the existence of its own subject matter; since first philosophy plainly investigates the existence of God, it follows that God cannot be its subject. In his critique of Avicenna, Averroës revived the 'theological' interpretation favoured unanimously by the Greek commentators, arguing that God's existence is known prior to metaphysical enquiry, namely in physics.

Thus, the parameters had already been set when the debate was enkindled afresh in the thirteenth century.[15] Up to this point the view that God was the subject of first philosophy had been almost universally accepted (cf. Zimmerman 1965, 106). Beginning early in the century, with Roger Bacon, however, the ontological interpretation to which Thomas subscribes became the dominant one. It prevailed still in Suarez's time and until supplanted by the division of metaphysics into 'general metaphysics' (or ontology) and three varieties of 'special metaphysics': rational cosmology, rational psychology, and rational or natural theology. This division, prefigured in late Scholasticism but only firmly established in the German Protestant *Schulphilosophie* of the seventeenth and eighteenth centuries (cf. Vollrath 1962), was quite wrongly considered the traditional view by Kant, maintaining itself as such throughout the nineteenth and well into the neo-Kantian phase of twentieth-century philosophy.[16]

As for the latter part of the solution, the relation of God to the subject matter of metaphysics, here Thomas parts company with Avicenna, who took *ens* in a sense so broad that God, the first cause and necessary being, was included under it (cf. Zimmermann 1965, 112f. and Wippel 1993, 86). This Thomas rejected, elaborating a counter-position already tentatively sketched by Albert the Great (Zimmermann, 154ff. and 180). To those, like Siger of Brabant, who followed Avicenna in regarding God as *a* being, Thomas's distinction between the subject and goal of metaphysics seemed incoherent: the notion of a 'first cause or principle of *all* beings' entails that every being, including God, has a cause, that is, that no being is *first* cause; yet without a first cause there can be no other causes.[17] So Thomas's notion of God as cause of the subject of metaphysics, being qua being, seemed unintelligible to Siger – as indeed it is on the assumption of a univocal rather than analogical sense of 'being' applicable to both God and creatures (ibid., 183ff.). Scotus argues in a similar way: since God falls *under* the subject of metaphysics, he cannot be the cause or principle of being in general, but only of *created* being. The concept of being in general is articulated into finite and infinite, created and uncreated being, much as later in Descartes, whereby Scotus maintains explicitly that a univocal sense of 'being' applies to both (cf. ibid., 272ff.), something Descartes expressly denies.[18]

With a view to Descartes's philosophical enterprise, three aspects of Thomas's conception of metaphysics are of particular note. The first is the perfectly obvious and characteristic subordination of natural to revealed theology. It may be among the sources of the distinction of subject and goal of metaphysics. If so, it probably accounts for Thomas's approach to the onto-theological problem to a far greater extent than the combined influence of Avicenna and Albert. The second point is the marked emphasis on 'first principles' in Thomas. These are *principia essendi*, principles of the being of entities, both in the order of formal and of efficient causality. Finally, in the body of the *Metaphysics* commentary Thomas introduces the following division into the *subjectum* of metaphysics: "since this science investigates as its proper subject being in general, and this is divided into substance and the nine classes of accidents, and a knowledge of accidents depends upon substance ... it follows that this science is principally concerned with substances (*Principalis intentio huiusmodi scientiae sit circa substantias*)." Thus, the 'ousiological' strand, too, is preserved and given a certain prominence here and everywhere that Thomas develops the theory of the 'analogy of being' at the 'horizontal' (substance-accident) level (cf. Wippel 1993, 89).[19]

As for Descartes, he too subordinates natural to revealed theology, while insisting, unlike Thomas, that the philosopher's concern is with natural, not with revealed, theology or theology proper (see section 3.4). However, Descartes belongs to that anti-Thomistic movement that understands God as *an* entity and hence as falling *under* the concept of being. This is true of Suarez, who fixes the *objectum adaequatum* of metaphysics or first philosophy as *ens inquantum ens reale*, adding: "For it has been shown that the adequate object of this science ought to encompass God and other immaterial substances." According to Suarez, this "is the opinion of Aristotle ..., St. Thomas, Alexander of Hales, Scotus, Albert, Alexander of Aphrodisias ... Avicenna ..., Soncinas ..., Aegidius Romanus ... *et reliqui fere scriptores*."[20] Suarez, it appears, was simply unaware of the range and diversity of medieval opinion on this subject, and of the fact that his own conclusion was actually at odds with that of St Thomas. So too, probably, Descartes. By the sixteenth century the differences among proponents of the three views outlined earlier were so faint that (iii) – God as *part* of the subject of metaphysics – could pass for the only view.[21] So despite the sharp division between natural and revealed theology that unites Descartes with Thomas, the priority assigned the former as regards philosophy and the approach taken to the onto-theological question are indicative of quite radical change.

Concerning the second point, the place accorded *principia prima*, this too is sometimes thought to betoken change of a very significant order, such principles being only *principia cognoscendi* in Descartes but *principia essendi* for St Thomas (next subsection) and the entire Peripatetic tradition. This, as we shall see (cf. section 3.2), is a gross exaggeration, though it is true that the order of knowing, gradually eclipsed in Aquinas's successive discussions of metaphysics, takes on new and decisive importance in Descartes.

As for the ousiological strand within Thomistic metaphysics, the third point noted above, this is, if anything, accentuated by Descartes's prominent *substance* dualism. Of course, Descartes still pays lip service to the peculiarly Christian notion of substance in the definition of *Principles*, I, 51: "there is only one substance which can be understood to depend on no other thing whatsoever, namely God." But the concept of substance really *functions* at the level at which substance and mode (or accident) are juxtaposed – as they cannot be in the case of God (cf. *Principles*, I, 56).[22] It is true that the term 'dualism' is most frequently applied to Descartes's philosophical anthropology, where it designates the theory that the human being is a composite of two complete substances, mind and body.[23] However, the term can also be used to designate the *general* ontological position according to which everything that is is *either* a thinking substance *or* an extended substance, *or* an attribute of such a substance, *or* a mode of such an attribute. Thus, Descartes's 'dualistic' substance-attribute-mode ontology is primarily a thesis about the *kinds* of beings there are, not about the number.[24]

So all three aspects of the Thomistic conception of metaphysics find a distinctive echo in Descartes's philosophical enterprise. One final point regarding Descartes's substance-attribute-mode ontology: the notion of substance qua substantiality is dismissed as an empty abstraction by Descartes, who notes that "it is much easier for us to have an understanding of extended substance or thinking substance than it is for us to understand substance on its own, leaving out the fact that it thinks or is extended. For we have some difficulty in abstracting the notion of substance from the notions of thought and extension" (AT VIII-1 31: CSM I 215). 'Substance' figures among the abstract universals that do not represent any complete thing or nature (cf. section 10.8f). There is more to this than the simple rejection of a key Thomistic doctrine, the analogy of being; in denying the notion of substantiality any real content of its own, rendering it a *nescio quid* (cf. section 7.3), Descartes unwittingly paves the way for the devastating attack of Locke and company on the substance-accident distinction and on metaphysics itself.[25]

2.3 Aquinas on the *varia metaphysicae nomina*

We turn next to St Thomas's account of the various names given this branch of knowledge. The cited passage from the Boethius commentary differentiates the underlying notion of the immaterial (insensible, intelligible) in three respects: (a) with regard to the *praecipuum cognitorum*, the chief among the intelligible objects known by this science, *deus* (hence 'theology'); (b) with respect to the pedagogically appropriate order in which to learn the sciences, beginning with the sensible and proceeding beyond (*trans*) to the *insensibilia* (thus, 'metaphysics'); and finally, (c) with respect to the natural hierarchy of the sciences themselves inasmuch as the lower depend upon the highest or first science for their principles or starting points (*'prima philosophia'*). Which principles Thomas has in mind is not spelled out here, but apart from such concepts as 'being' and 'nonbeing,' 'cause' and 'effect,' 'similarity' and 'difference,' 'substance,' 'accident,' 'relation,' 'whole and part,' 'existence,' and 'essence,' the other sciences apparently derive general principles of knowledge, like those of non-contradiction, identity, and excluded middle, from 'first philosophy.'[26]

The notion of the intelligible is articulated rather differently in the Prooemium to the *Metaphysics* commentary, and it is worth pausing to consider the differences. Thomas takes his initial cues from Aristotle's *Politics*, whence he derives the notion of a *scientia regulatrix*, but also from the discussion of wisdom (*sapientia*) in Book I of the Aristotelian *Metaphysics*.[27] That science deserves the titles *'rectrix aliarum'* and 'wisdom,' he explains, which is *maxime intellectualis*, that is, concerned with the things that are in themselves *maxime intelligibilia*. Intelligibility is then interpreted in terms of (i) certitude, (ii) universality, and (iii) immateriality, from which the names of this science ('first philosophy,' 'metaphysics,' and 'theology') are derived. This account involves a considerable measure of straight revision of Thomas's earlier explanation of the names of this science in the Boethius commentary.

First of all, that of which the intellect achieves certainty is considered 'more intelligible.' Certainty, however, is acquired from the knowledge of causes. "Hence that science which considers first causes also seems to be the ruler of the others in the highest degree." This science is called 'first philosophy' since the science of the first or highest causes is the source of certainty of all others.

The 'first causes' in question are the *primae causae essendi*, the first efficient causes of the *esse* or existence of things. Not only is this inspired by the biblical idea of creation *ex nihilo* and hence patently un-Greek; it is a marked departure from Thomas's own earlier statement that this science is 'first' because it furnishes the others with their principles. The difference can be explained (cf. Wippel 1983, 59–65) with the help of two distinctions developed in qu. 6, art. 1 of the Boethius commentary and presupposed in the Prooemium: (1) between the order of external or efficient and internal or formal causes or principles, and (2) between the analytic and the synthetic orders, the *via resolutionis* and *via compositionis* or *inventionis*.

Where, in the Boethius commentary, Aquinas designates this science 'first philosophy' because it gives the others their principles, the *principia* are understood as starting points in the synthetic order of intrinsic or formal causality, that is, the downward path of composition or discovery from the known 'cause' to the as yet unknown 'effects,' from universal concepts like *ens, potentia, actus*, and so on, and principles like identity and contradiction, to certain generic or specific forms constituting the quiddity of things and the specific principles employed in the particular sciences. 'First philosophy' here is the science of *ens et ea quae consequuntur ens, ut unum et multa, potentia et actus*; all the special sciences, receiving their concepts and principles from this science, come *after* it.

In the Prooemium, by contrast, Aquinas explains the name 'first philosophy' with a view to the upward path of analysis in the order of efficient causes of the existence of things, terminating in the First Cause: "it is called *prima philosophia* in so far as it considers the *primae rerum causae.*" Thus, not only does the creator God or First Cause supplant the First Mover of Aristotelian metaphysics in Thomas's Prooemium account of the first name; the ascending order of external causes is substituted for the descending order of internal causes envisaged in the Boethius commentary. Not that the consideration of formal causality simply vanishes from the scene; it recurs in the explanation of the second of the three names, 'metaphysics.'

This science is called 'metaphysics,' namely, as the most universal science, the science whose subject matter comprises the most universal concepts or principles, *ens* and the rest. It is *maxime intellectualis* and hence *rectrix* because these concepts or principles are *maxime universalia.* At the end of the Prooemium Thomas states that this science is called 'metaphysics' because the metaphysical concepts are "things which transcend the physical order *in via resolutionis,* just as the more common are discovered after the less common." So although consideration of the order of formal causality is preserved, that order is analytic rather than synthetic; the *via inventionis,* the order of discovery, drops out of the Prooemium account altogether.

Finally, this science is also called 'theology' as the science of the most immaterial being. Those things are *maxime intelligibilia* that are *maxime a materia separata.* Here Thomas reintroduces his earlier distinction between the mathematicals, which are separate from matter only *secundum rationem,* and the metaphysicals, which are separate *secundum rem* as well. The latter, however, are often found in matter, while *Deus et intellectuales substantiae* are by nature incapable of existing in matter. Maximally intelligible, therefore, are these last, for which further reason this science deserves the title *scientia regulatrix.* It is called divine or *theologia* "inasmuch as it considers the aforementioned substances."

The explanation of the third name represents no change at all from the Boethius commentary, the latter having already designated this science 'theology' with reference to the highest of its three objects, God. As for the name 'metaphysics,' the earlier work is ambiguous. In the passage from qu. 5, art. 1 cited earlier, Thomas writes: "by another name it is called metaphysics; that is to say *beyond physics*, because it comes to us after physics among the subjects to be learned." This apparently refers to the order of learning or discovery. Yet qu. 6, art. 1 of the same work takes *meta* in the sense of *trans*, interpreting *trans* as *post*, 'later': this science, writes Thomas, "is learned after physics and the other sciences ... For this reason it is called 'metaphysics,' as if to say *beyond physics* (*trans physicam*), for in the process of analysis (*resolvendo*) it comes after (*post*) physics" (Aquinas 1986, 73 [*BDT* 6.1]). If this also explains Thomas's mind in qu. 5, art. 1, then nothing really changes in the transition from the Boethius commentary to the Prooemium, which similarly refers to the *via resolutionis* in explaining the name 'metaphysics.' The only question is whether in the earlier work Thomas might not have had both orders of causes in mind, external and internal, leading to God and *ens commune*, respectively, whereas in the Prooemium only the latter series is envisaged. This is probably undecidable. Against Wippel's (1983, 66) argument that since the later work is clear enough, it is probably the best interpretation of the earlier one as well, stands the fact that Thomas altered his perspective on the first title, *prima philosophia*, quite radically. A change in rationale for the name 'metaphysics' might well indicate that by the time of the Prooemium Thomas had come to associate the second name exclusively with the order of formal causality and the study of being qua being, having come to identify 'first philosophy' with the order of efficient causes leading to the First Cause.

2.4 Conclusion

In Thomas's treatment of metaphysics, the synthetic order of the sciences *quoad nos* gives way to exclusive consideration of their order *naturaliter* based on the ontological status of their objects. Where, in the Prooemium, Thomas seeks to justify the *meta* as *trans* and *post*, he does so with reference to the *via resolutionis* rather than *inventionis*. The *via resolutionis* figures in the explanation of the designation 'first philosophy' as well. While the order of knowing and the sciences can be considered in two ways, *naturaliter* and *quoad nos*, the ontological order actually branches into two distinct causal series: the series of internal or formal and that of external, efficient causes. The natural order of the sciences corresponds to this branching ontological order from the highest things, the things first 'in themselves' (the objects of metaphysics), down to the lowest and last, reversing the order in which the sciences must be learned.

This concludes the examination of the concept of 'metaphysics' or 'first philosophy' in the Peripatetic tradition broadly conceived. The aim of the chapter as a whole has been to develop a working definition of 'metaphysics' or 'first philosophy' as understood in the broadly Aristotelian mainstream of philosophy before Descartes. As such a working definition, adequate for present purposes, we retain the following: metaphysics is the philosophical study of being in general, as existence and as essence, of substantial as well as accidental being, but principally of substance and the supersensible as well as first principles or axioms.

Equipped with this definition, we turn now to Descartes.

3

Cartesian Metaphysics

Of the twin pillars described in chapter 1, Descartes's analysis of knowledge and the mind was by far the more enduring, setting the agenda for philosophical discussion and debate right down to the present day.[1] By contrast, the philosophy of nature, though a powerful shaping force, especially in France, for the remainder of seventeenth and well into the next century, was gradually supplanted with the advent of Newtonian science only a few decades later.[2] On Descartes's own understanding of metaphysics, a consideration of thinking and its modes figures centrally within *prima philosophia* on three separate counts.

First, as one of the two principal species of the supersensible (God being the other), the mind is a *meta*physical theme in the quite literal sense that it lies 'beyond the physical.' Thus, in the famous Letter to Picot that was to serve as preface to the latter's translation of the *Principles of Philosophy*, Descartes speaks of the "immaterial *or metaphysical* things" (AT IX-2 10: CSM I 184 e.a.), as though these terms were simply convertible. In rendering Descartes's Latin *res Metaphysicas* as "les choses *immaterielles ou metaphysiques*" (AT IX-1 104 e.a.), Clerselier, who translated the Objections and Replies into French, was in fact just inserting a phrase Descartes himself had employed in the preface to the *Principles*.[3]

In the first place, then, the analysis of thought and its modes belongs to metaphysics as the science of *super*sensible being. Aristotle, to be sure, treated of the *theos* within first and *peri psuchēs* within second philosophy, or physics. For him, animated corporeal beings, even those endowed with a rational soul, belong straightforwardly to the realm of nature (*physis*). The promotion of the rational soul from an object of second or natural to one of the two principal objects of first philosophy or metaphysics is thus a departure from Aristotelian naturalism. As a body, man is still part of nature for Descartes; but as a soul he transcends it. For this there is plenty of precedent, not only in Plato, but in the Christian philosophy and theology of the Middle Ages, with its focus on the salvation (immortality) of the human soul; a more immediate inspiration for Descartes's retracing of the boundary between physics and metaphysics may have been Spanish Scholastic thought in the preceeding century.[4] Still, Descartes's manner of redrawing the boundary between the sensible and the supersensible is dictated not so much by the dominant Christian theological and philosophical tradition as by his own analysis of mind: as for the Scholastics God and *ens commune* are (though in different senses) separable from matter, 'trans-physical,' so for Descartes the soul of man, rightly conceived, is separable, not just *per rationem*, but *per essentiam* (cf. Vollrath 1962, 267). This reassignment of the analysis of mind to metaphysics is announced with a certain fanfare in the full title of the *Meditations: Meditationes de Prima Philosophia, in qua Dei existentia et animae Immortalitas demonstratur* (or, in the second edition: ... *In quibus Dei existentia, & animae humanae a corpore distinctio, demonstantur*).[5]

Second, in respect of both essence and existence, the mental and the supersensible generally (the soul and God) are on an entirely different evidential footing from the world of sensible things. According to a further connotation of 'metaphysics' in the Aristotelian tradition, knowledge of being (existence and essence) is properly metaphysical knowledge.[6] Moreover, the consideration of substance belongs to this science to a pre-eminent degree. Descartes's preoccupation with questions of the existence and essence of substances is clear on the most cursory reading of the *Meditations.* After the regimen of doubt in the First, the existence and essence of the mind form the subject matter of the Second Meditation: the mind exists as a substance whose essence is thinking. Next come the existence and essence of the infinite substance, God, which are, as Descartes remarks, "almost the same thing" (AT III 396: CSMK 186). They are examined first in the Third and then again in the Fifth Meditation. The work concludes with a proof of the existence of the external world in the Sixth Meditation, the essence of material substances having been considered briefly at the outset of the Fifth and in the famous wax example of the Second. True, the main emphasis lies on the greater certainty of the knowledge of the existence and essence of mental (non-sensible) substance. But for Thomas, too, as we have seen (chapter 2.3), certitude figures prominently in the delineation of the subject matter of metaphysics.

There is, in addition, a third connotation of the term 'metaphysics' according to which this science deals, as Aristotle says, with "the truths which in mathematics are called axioms," notably the axiom that "the same attribute cannot at the same time belong and not belong to the same subject and in the same respect" (Aristotle 1924 [*Met.*, 1005a 20f.]). This is "the starting-point even for other axioms," notes Aristotle. Such axioms are not only the "best known" and hence "non-hypothetical"; they are also "the most certain" (ibid., [*Met.*, 1005b 14ff.]). As with the first connotation, there may be a Platonic *motif* in evidence here as well, though Aristotle's notion of the *anhupotaton* reflects Descartes's conception of a first principle better than does Plato's (cf. below chapter 7 n. 1). It was no doubt this feature of metaphysics that was uppermost in Descartes's mind when, in a letter of 11 November 1640 to Mersenne, he proposed as a title for his recently completed work *Meditationes de prima philosophia*, "because I do not confine my discussion to God and the soul, but deal in general with *all the first things* to be discovered by philosophising" (AT III 235: CSMK 157 e.a.). Recalling in the Preface to the Reader that precedes the *Meditations* that he had "briefly touched on the topics of God and the human mind" (AT VII 7: CSM II 6) in an earlier publication (the *Discourse*), Descartes points out that his treatment of the subject there was merely preliminary, adding: "But now that I have, after a fashion, taken an initial sample of people's opinions, I am again tackling the same questions concerning God and the human mind; and this time I am also going to deal with the foundations of first Philosophy *in its entirety*" (AT VII 9: CSM II 8 e.a.). The last three words correspond to "all the first things" of the letter to Mersenne. The allusion in both places is to the treatment of axioms, principles, or "common notions" within the work. This, however, forms a key part of the discussions of the existence and essence of God, the human soul, and material bodies. Whether such common notions are 'first things' in virtue of the place occupied by their objects in the ontological hierarchy, or solely on the basis of epistemic considerations, is not said here; the matter will be discussed below (section 3.1). But that the consideration of 'simple' or 'primary notions,' among them that of the mind, is included under 'first things' is perfectly clear. Hence, there is a third reason why the analysis of mind was primarily a metaphysical undertaking on Descartes's understanding of that science.

3.1 Epistemo-ontology and metaphysical physics

Against the straight continuity of Descartes's concept of metaphysics with that of his predecessors, Marion (1986, §4) has urged that the 'general science of being,' later dubbed *ontologia* by Clauberg, Calov, and Göckel (the latter two wrote the word only in Greek letters), was surpassed and supplanted by a new *science universelle*: the science of the *ens qua cognitum* (see also Vollrath 1962). To the extent that the traditional *ens qua ens* is replaced by the *ens qua cognitum*, Cartesian metaphysics is at best an *ontologie grise*: it seeks to establish a new ontological order solely by reversing the old epistemological order of things.[7]

It is no doubt true that, beginning with Descartes, metaphysics no longer considers beings simply qua beings, but chiefly as the objects of various branches of knowledge or sciences (cf. Heidegger 1994, passim). Still, Marion is among those interpreters who tend to privilege the order in which God, the soul, and material things are known at the expense of the order – that is, the relations of dependence, independence, interdependence, or inter-independence – in which they actually stand as entities. Looking ahead as it does to Kant's conception of metaphysics, this approach represents an advance on the older neo-Kantian interpretation of epistemological 'critique' as (roughly) 'overcoming metaphysics through epistemology' (see the quotation from Hartmann in n. 16 of the previous chapter); for it recognizes clearly the primarily metaphysical thrust of the 'critique of knowledge' (cf. Heidegger 1973). By contrast, the neo-Kantian view, while providing a tolerably accurate picture of Kant's attitude toward the subdisciplines of the *Schulmetaphysik* of his day, overlooks the sense in which the very *Critique of Pure Reason* is itself at once both (a) a "metaphysics of metaphysics"[8] and (b) a regional ontology of nature as the object of natural science.

While Marion and others take their cue chiefly from (a), a much more prevalent approach draws inspiration from (b). Stressing the discontinuity of Cartesian with traditional metaphysics on rather different grounds, advocates of this approach see as Descartes's overriding concern the task of laying secure foundations for the new natural science of his day; Cartesian metaphysics replaces the old medieval synthesis of Greek science and Christian theology with a new synthesis of modern mathematical physics and metaphysics, that is, a "metaphysical physics" (cf. Garber 1992, 1f.).[9]

This approach privileges the philosophy of nature, the physics and metaphysics of matter in motion, at the expense of metaphysical knowledge of God and the soul. Yet if Descartes's own testimony is authoritative, as it must be, the latter are the chief fruits of his efforts as a metaphysician. Metaphysics, to be sure, encompasses the totality of what is, all being; it corresponds, moreover, to the roots of the tree of knowledge, whose trunk is physics and whose branches are all the other sciences. Varying the metaphor, Descartes likens himself now to Archimedes (see below, section 11.3), now to an architect who "wants to build a house which is stable on ground where there is sandy topsoil over underlying rock" (cf. AT VII 536f.: CSM II 366; cf. also AT VI 29: CSM I 125, AT X 509: CSM II 407, and the opening sentences of the *Meditations*). The intent of these metaphors is plain. And yet knowledge of the non- and supersensible has an intrinsic importance for Descartes far exceeding its instrumental value within the foundational enterprise so described. Immaterial substances can be known directly and intuitively through simple reflexion upon the mind itself; even God can be so known, that is, his complete concept or nature grasped (though not comprehended) as he is in himself – and not just through his works by rational inference from effect to cause. In Descartes there is little scope, therefore, for anything like the pure 'underlabourer' conception of philosophy memorably formulated by Locke. Perhaps no one would wish to father quite this Lockean creed on Descartes; still, the temptation to see Descartes as primarily concerned with natural philosophy, a philosophical physicist, is strong among scientifically-minded philosophers and historians of science today.[10]

The present chapter attempts to counter these two interpretive tendencies by highlighting the metaphysical dimension of Descartes's analysis of mind. Some further considerations will be added when we return to the question of the role of the new science in the Cartesian revolution in the Conclusion (chapter 22.3).

3.2 Metaphysics and theory of knowledge

Without suggesting that Descartes is an epistemologist in the contemporary sense, Marion credits him nonetheless with already having effected the transition from the perspective of medieval Scholasticism to that of the German *Schulphilosophie* of the seventeenth and eighteenth centuries (1986, 2f.). For the former, as for Aristotle, metaphysics is both the universal science and the science of the highest being; for the latter, as for Kant, it is the "science of the first principles of human knowledge" (cf. Baumgarten 1963, §1). For Aristotle, metaphysics is the most universal science *because* it is the science of the highest being (cf. above section 2.1); for Kant, his immediate predecessors, and his successors, metaphysics is *first* philosophy because it treats of the most universal principles of all things generally (or of all things within a certain object-domain).[11]

That Descartes understood metaphysics in something like the latter of these two ways is no doubt true; to this the title of Part I of the *Principles* (*De principiis cognitionis humanae*) clearly attests. But that he abandoned or even subordinated the older ontological perspective is true only in one limited perspective, to be explained presently. Even for Kant the principles of the pure understanding are still metaphysical or ontological principles of things – if not of things as they are in themselves, then at least as appearances. The first to have made the principles of "metaphysics" pure *principia cognoscendi* – fundamental truths regarding the nature of the human mind as knowing subject, first in the order of knowing but not principles of being at all – is Hume. For the medievals, as for Descartes, the words 'first principles,' when used to characterize the science called 'metaphysics' or 'first philosophy,' were ambivalent as between 'first principles of knowing' (*causae sciendi*) and 'first principles of being' (*causae essendi*). Scotus weighed both options in interpreting Aristotle's definition of first philosophy as 'the science of the first principles of being qua being' (cf. Zimmermann 1965, 248). And with good reason, given that this science furnishes the others with their first principles.[12]

The ambiguity of Descartes's use of the term *principium* will be fully docu-
mented below (see chapter 7, n. 1). Here we must consider Marion's argument
that the order of being is either subordinated to or simply supplanted by the order
of knowing. From this arises an alleged split between metaphysics and first philosophy: the former, as the study of the *ens qua cognitum*, gains ascendency over
the latter, the *ego cogitans* supplanting God as the *summum ens*. Along with this
idiosyncratic interpretation we must briefly consider the more straightforward
view that Descartes's chief preoccupation as a philosopher is not metaphysics at
all but epistemology in something like the now familiar sense.[13]

Marion's view is either partly warranted or sheerly anachronistic, depending
on how 'ontological order' is understood. Earlier the order of being was described
in a 'top-down' perspective as comprising (1) the relations of dependence, independence, interdependence, and inter-independence in which actually existing
entities stand to one another. Thus, for Descartes, finite minds and bodies are
independent of each other but alike dependent for their being on the supreme
being, God. But the ontological order can also be viewed in a 'bottom-up' perspective in terms of (2) the ultimate principles of composite things (atoms, form
and matter, simple natures, monads, and so on). Thus, when Röd (1971, 58),
for example, opposes the order of knowing and of being ("Erkenntnis- und
Seinsordnung"), he has in mind the *Regulae* conception of simple natures as the
absolutely first *principia* of things themselves. These are *also* the first things
known clearly by the human mind. Finally, the order of being may be regarded in
what might be called (3) the 'horizontal' or 'lateral' perspective, that is, with a
view to the relation of a substance to its own accidents or modes.

Now with respect to (3), the substance-attribute-mode ontology of Descartes,
and its relation to the metaphysical doctrine of categories stemming from Aristotle, Marion's general view of the two orders does seem warranted.[14] The old order
of formal causality, with accidents or forms dependent on other accidents or forms
and all such accidents in the secondary categories dependent on substance or
being in the first category, is indeed supplanted in the *Regulae* (and thereafter) by
a new order: that of clear and distinct perception (cf. Marion 1975, §15; also
Menn 1995; and Röd 1971, 58f.). But to conclude on this basis that the *principia*
are only *principia cognoscendi* is to give very short shrift to the key top-down and
bottom-up vertical dimensions of the order of being. Regarding the latter, (2),
Röd points out that it would be wrong to suggest even that the order of being
follows (let alone is supplanted by) the order of knowing, were this taken to mean
that the mind simply *invents or imposes* the order of things, as though there were
no mind-independent order to be *discovered*.[15] Those things first in the order of
knowing – the simple natures of mind and body and the common notions – are
first 'in the things themselves' as well. Nevertheless Röd rightly regards it as a

key goal of Cartesian metaphysics to establish the "parallelism" or "conformity" of the two orders (1971, 58f.). In the case of (1), the top-down perspective, on the other hand, the one order *actually reverses* the other. For what is first and absolutely independent ontologically is the uncreated being, God, whereas what is first in the order of knowing is the created, dependent human mind.

Such textual support as Marion provides for the thesis of a transition to a new conception of metaphysics as an *ontologie grise* is drawn mainly from the explanation given Mersenne on 11 November 1640 of the proposed title of the *Meditations*. He cites it at the outset of his study and thereafter repeatedly: "I do not confine my discussion to God and the soul, but deal in general with all the first things to be discovered by philosophizing" (AT III 235: CSMK 157).[16] The phrase "je ne traite point en particulier de Dieu et de l'Ame, mais en général de toutes les premières choses" recurs almost verbatim in a second letter to Mersenne of the same date: "car je n'y traite *pas seulement* de Dieu et de l'Ame, mais en général de toutes les premières choses qu'on peut connaître en philosophant *par ordre*" (AT V 239: CSMK 158 e.a.). The words "pas seulement" make clear the inclusive sense of "je ne traite point en particulier ... mais en général": *not only* God and the soul, *but equally* all other 'first things.' Yet the addition of "par ordre" suggests to Marion a fairly restrictive interpretation of "the first things," and a corresponding terminological distinction between 'metaphysics' and 'first philosophy.' Metaphysics, he maintains, is the science of those objects entirely separate from matter and so first in the order of being, while first philosophy is the science of the things first in the order of knowing, "dans l'ordre établi pour leur mise en évidence."[17] As Marion sees it, it is *only* the order of knowing to which Descartes refers in speaking of other "first things" in the letter to Mersenne; since it is the knowing subject that is absolutely first in this order, the significance of Descartes's remark to Mersenne is clear: "La primauté passe, ici, résolument de l'étant premier (à connaître) [i.e., God] à la connaissance elle-même (éventuellement fixée en un étant) [i.e., to the *ego cogitans*]; inversement, l'étant comme tel [being qua being] (et même le premier) [God] disparaît" (1986, 4).[18]

A closer look suggests a different conclusion. The meaning of "toutes les premières choses" is clearer in the letter to Picot that was to become the preface to the French translation of the *Principles*. There Descartes refers to "la Métaphysique, qui contient les Principes de la connaissance, entre lesquels est l'explication des principaux attributs de Dieu, de l'immatérialité de nos âmes, *et de toutes les notions claires et simples qui sont en nous*" (AT IX-2 10: CSM I 184 e.a.). This is taken from the famous passage describing the order of the sciences by analogy with a tree. If "toutes les premières choses" refers to all the "clear and simple notions" (principally, those of God and the soul), and if these are identical with the "Principes de la connaissance," then this reference to principles may shed valuable light on the sense of *principia cognitionis humanae* in the title of Part I of the *Principles* as well. That sense cannot plausibly be confined to 'first in the order of knowing,' first according to 'the method,' in the new 'epistemological' as opposed to the old 'ontological' order. This would be to assign the principles a purely functional status within the epistemic order, irrespective of the nature of their objects, whereas it is precisely the ontological status of their objects that motivates Descartes's interest in establishing – against both the materialistic and the Scholastic metaphysical systems of his day – the new epistemic order. If one considers the principles actually introduced and deployed in the course of the *Meditations* by Descartes, *principia* will be seen to refer to the basic concepts and axioms through which a knowledge of the *existence* and *essence* of *immaterial* substance is attainable prior to and independently of knowledge of the existence of sensible things. Should the latter exist, they can only be known to exist and their natures reliably grasped on the basis of prior knowledge of the existence of the non- or supersensible. If this is what Descartes is out to show by investigating "les Principes de la Connaissance" or *principia cognitionis humanae*, then the order of knowing itself is of very little interest apart from that 'top-down' ontological order of things that Descartes was careful to preserve as a Christian philosopher.

In itself the talk of philosophizing "par ordre" and of *cognitionis principia* provides scant support for the alleged ascendancy of epistemological over ontological concerns in Descartes. The ascendancy of 'first philosophy' over 'metaphysics' that Marion detects in Descartes he finds also in the latter's immediate predecessors (Pereira, Fonseca, Raconis, Eustache, Dupleix, and Suarez). Yet the sense of 'first philosophy' – or "protologie" as Marion dubs it – is different in Descartes, he alleges: "Descartes rompt ... avec ce courant, majoritaire avant et après lui, puisque l'instance universelle qui surpasse la métaphysique réduite à la théologie rationelle n'est plus, pour lui, la science de l'étant en tant que tel (future *ontologia*) mais la disposition en ordre de la connaissance, c'est-à-dire la connaissance selon l'ordre de la mise en évidence" (1986, 58; cf. 68). Although the "protologie *épistémique* de Descartes" (55, 60 e.a.), the science of "l'étant en tant que connu" (59 and passim), supplants the traditional science of the *ens inquantum ens*, Descartes, Marion suggests, is a metaphysician nevertheless – one is tempted to add "*malgré lui*" – by the criterion implicit in Heidegger's thesis concerning "the onto-theo-logical constitution of metaphysics." It is in this perspective that he makes the more extravagant claim that the *ego cogitans* supplants God as the *summum ens* or "*étant par excellence*" of Descartes's metaphysics (cf. ibid., 103 and 110, and Heidegger 1957, 31ff.).[19]

Behind the thesis that Descartes "refuse de penser la métaphysique selon les deux principales voies qui s'offraient à lui – la théologie, l'*ontologia*" (Marion

1986, 59) lies a failure to separate two questions: the *subject matter* of metaphysics and the selection of a *starting point* and *order* of metaphysical knowledge. Granted, Descartes's choice of the cognizing subject as first in the order of *knowing* was a radical departure from his predecessors; that did not prevent him from retaining "un concept de la métaphysique" as a doctrine of *being* that was in important respects continuous with the oldest Aristotelian tradition. The claim that the new order of knowing is the "unique détermination correcte de l'antérieur et du postérieur, du principe et du dérivé" fails to take account of the three sorts of ontological order distinguished above. Viewed in the light of that distinction, the claim that the order of knowing either supplants or determines the order of being in Descartes's conception of first philosophy or metaphysics is true in one sense but otherwise anachronistic. In particular, the claim that the *ego cogitans* supplants God as the *summum ens* simply glosses over the fact that a creation story, and hence a definite order of being, commencing with God, the creator, still stands at the very heart of Descartes's metaphysics.

For all its erudition, Marion's argument goes almost no way at all toward establishing either that metaphysics is supplanted by first philosophy as 'onto-epistemology,' or that the hierarchy of being is simply inverted, with the *ego cogitans* henceforth at the summit. No one seriously disputes the fact that the epistemic order takes on a new measure of importance in Descartes; yet the full significance of this becomes apparent only when the various dimensions of the new ontological order are given their full weight as well.

Of course, there are those who see in Descartes's project the outlines of an epistemological enterprise not unlike that described in a famous passage of the "Epistle to the Reader" that begins Locke's *Essay*.[20] Of this there are clear echoes in the *Regulae*.[21] Against the temptation to believe that Descartes abandoned the science of being qua being and of the first principles of knowledge in favour of epistemology in something like Locke's sense stand the same considerations adduced against Marion's subtler thesis regarding 'epistemo-ontology.' There is no denying either that such matters come first in the order of knowing or that the study of the order of knowing itself precedes that of the order of being – whence the centrality of *method* in Descartes's philosophy (see sections 15.6 and 15.7). But that the discovery of the true order of knowing supplants or renders the investigation of the order of being and the nature of things themselves otiose or even secondary in importance will be difficult to square with the evidence.

The requirement that the various dimensions of the new ontological order be considered together with the epistemic order can only be satisfied gradually in the course of this study. Consideration of the new order and guiding idea of being in Descartes will be postponed until the Conclusion (chapter 22). Before turning once more to the revised order of knowing in the next chapter, a different misinterpretation of Descartes's philosophical intentions must be considered briefly.

3.3 Metaphysics and physics

The second pillar of Descartes's dualistic system is the analysis of matter as a substance whose principal attribute is extension in length, breadth, and depth, and the sole modes of which are figure (shape) and motion. The analysis of matter, undertaken with a view to the foundation or reformation of science, is frequently regarded as the philosophical task nearest Descartes's heart.[22] But despite the early and profound impact of the new science upon his thought, Descartes was no more a methodologist or philosopher of science in anything like the contemporary sense than he was a philosopher of mind or epistemologist. It is true that in the letter to Mersenne cited twice already Descartes writes: "the little book which I sent you [i.e., the *Meditations*] contains all the principles of my physics" (AT III 233: CSMK 157; cf. also AT VII 602: CSM II 397). And it is no less true that, as Belaval has put it (1960, 19), "Descartes avait séparé la philosophie de la théologie pour mieux l'unir à la science." But in thus liberating philosophy from the (as he believed) antiquated world-picture of Scholastic-Aristotelian natural science and theology, Descartes's primary aim was to re-forge the link between philosophy and *natural* theology, the latter understood as knowledge of God and the soul demonstrated "by natural reason" (AT VII 2: CSM II 3). Only secondarily was it his purpose to furnish a conception of body that might banish all trace of the Aristotelian forms and thus serve to underpin the mathematico-mechanistic world-picture of modern science.[23] It is difficult to doubt the sincerity of the sentiment fervently expressed in the dedication of the *Meditations* to the "Dean and Doctors of the sacred Faculty of Theology":

I have always thought that two topics – namely God and the soul – are prime examples of subjects where demonstrative proofs ought to be given with the aid of philosophy rather than theology. For us who are believers, it is enough to accept on faith that the human soul does not die with the body, and that God exists; but in the case of unbelievers, it seems that there is no religion, and practically no moral virtue, that they can be persuaded to adopt until these two truths are proved to them by natural reason ... Moreover, I have noticed both that you and all other theologians assert that the existence of God is capable of proof by natural reason, and also that the inference from Holy Scripture is that the knowledge of God is easier to acquire than the knowledge we have of many created things ... Hence I thought it was quite proper for me to enquire ... how God may be more easily and more certainly known than the things of this world. (AT VII 2: CSM II 3f.)

Faced with this, it is hard to question the primacy of the study of the supersensible over the physical.[24]

None of this alters the fact that the striking contrast between warring schools of metaphysicians on the one hand and the seemingly incontestable findings of the new physico-mathematical science on the other must have seemed to Descartes, as later to Kant, highly prejudicial to the proud pretensions of the science of being and the supersensible. That he was disheartened by the state of philosophy as he found it in his early years is attested by this remark from the *Discourse*:

Regarding philosophy, I shall say only this: seeing that it has been cultivated for many centuries by the most excellent minds and yet there is still no point in it which is not disputed and hence doubtful, I was not so presumptuous as to hope to achieve any more in it than others had done. And, considering how many diverse opinions learned men may maintain on a single question – even though it is impossible for more than one to be true – I held as well-nigh false everything that was merely probable. (AT VI 8: CSM I 114f.)

Yet years later, upon completion of his *Meditations*, the same Descartes was to observe:

It is very striking that metaphysicians unanimously agree in their descriptions of the attributes of God (at least in the case of those which can be known solely by human reason). You will find that there is much more disagreement among philosophers about the nature of anything which is physical or perceivable by the senses, however firm or concrete our idea of it may be. (AT VII 138: CSM II 99)[25]

This astonishing claim is in perfect accord with Descartes's teaching that the idea of God is "utterly clear and distinct":

[F]or whatever I clearly and distinctly perceive as being real and true, and implying any perfection, is wholly contained in [that idea]. It does not matter that I do not grasp (*non comprehendam*) the infinite, or that there are countless additional attributes of God (*alia innumera*) which I cannot in any way grasp (*nec comprehendere*), and perhaps cannot even be reached (*attingere*) by my thought; for it is in the nature of the infinite not to be grasped (*non comprehendatur*) by a finite being like myself. It is enough that I clearly understand (*intelligere*) the infinite, and that I judge that all the attributes which I clearly perceive (*percipio*) and in which I know (*scio*) there to be some perfection – and perhaps countless others of which I am ignorant – are present in God either formally or eminently. This is enough to make the idea that I have of God the truest and most clear and distinct (*maxime clara et distincta*) of all my ideas. (AT VII 46: CSM II 32)[26]

Elsewhere Descartes insists that he means "by the idea of God nothing but what all men habitually understand when they speak of him" (AT III 393:CSMK 185). And passing immediately to the soul, he remarks that here the case is "even clearer" (AT III 394: CSMK 186).[27]

Contrary to a widely prevalent view, Descartes's aim was not merely to place a reformed metaphysics in the service of, or on an equal footing with, mathematical physics; he sought to place metaphysics on a much higher plane. For apart from the manifest inferiority of its objects, he set out to prove that the widely admired new physics was vastly inferior in point of certainty to metaphysics, and that the knowledge of sensible things ultimately owed whatever reliability it possessed to metaphysical knowledge of the supersensible. This is plain from the *mens notior corpore* doctrine of the Second Meditation, the doctrine succinctly expressed in the *Principles* as "our knowledge of our thought is prior to, and more certain than, our knowledge of any corporeal thing" (AT VIII-1 7: CSM I 195). As for the other domain of the supersensible, the dedication of the *Meditations*, cited above, leaves little doubt concerning the primacy of our knowledge of God vis-à-vis that of the physical universe.

The precise sense in which all other knowledge (*scientia*) depends for its certainty upon the metaphysical knowledge of God will be discussed briefly below and more fully in Part Two. It may, however, be worth quoting the final sentences of the "Synopsis" with which Descartes prefaced his *Meditations*, for they provide as clear a statement of his intentions in that work as one could wish for. After reviewing the arguments of the Sixth and final Meditation, Descartes closes with the words:

> The great benefit of these arguments is not, in my view, that they prove what they establish – namely that there really is a world, and that human beings have bodies and so on – since no sane person ever seriously doubted these things. The point is that in considering these arguments we come to realise that they are not as solid or as transparent as the arguments which lead us to knowledge of our own minds and of God, so that the latter are the most certain and evident of all possible objects of knowledge for the human intellect. Indeed, this is *the one thing that I set myself to prove* in these Meditations. (AT VII 16: CSM II 11 e.a.)

The view this suggests of the relation of metaphysics to physics has steadily lost ground among English-speaking commentators in recent years.[28] However, there are at least three separate primacy questions to be carefully weighed in assessing the relative importance of the metaphysics of the sensible and of the supersensible in Descartes's thought: (1) the respective places of each in the system of the sciences; (2) the place accorded their respective object-domains in the hierarchical order of being; and (3) the place of each in Descartes's own intellectual development and the extent to which they absorbed his intellectual and literary energies.

The last part of (3) is straightforward enough. Moreover, Gilson's thesis ("action réciproque de la métaphysique et de la physique," Gilson 1951, pt. I, chap. 2, esp. 167) provides a balanced view of the first part, Descartes's intellectual development. However, there would seem to be compelling reasons for regarding (1) and (2) as decisive in any overall assessment of the "raison d'être of Descartes's philosophical program" (Hatfield). And here the primacy of metaphysics is plain. What has led to confusion on both points is to some extent the mistaken model of cognition frequently ascribed to Descartes. Before examining that model and the associated account of the order of knowing in chapter 4, something should be said of the ambiguity of 'theology' in Descartes.

3.4 Natural and revealed theology

There is obviously one sense of the word in which it was clearly Descartes's aim to separate sharply the "province" of philosophy from that of theology, very much as Belaval suggests. Descartes uses 'theology' in this sense in the Dedication of the *Meditations*, and in another letter to Mersenne, written some ten years before that already cited (15 April 1630), it is even designated the 'strict' sense of 'theology': "Your question of theology is beyond my mental capacity," he writes, "but it does not seem to me outside my province, since it has no concern with anything dependent upon revelation, which is what I call 'theology' in the strict sense (*ce qui dépend de la révélation, ce que je nomme proprement Théologie*); it is a metaphysical question which is to be examined by human reason" (AT I 135: CSMK 22).

The operative distinction here is obviously the familiar one between revealed and natural theology. That the science of Sacred Scripture is theology in the strict sense is confirmed by the *Discourse* (AT VI 6; cf. also 8: CSM I 113f.). Theology as knowledge attainable through the natural light of reason, on the other hand, belongs to metaphysics or first philosophy, one of whose two principal objects – Aristotle would say simply: 'whose principal object' – is God. The "metaphysical question" which Descartes here describes as beyond his mental capacities concerns the origin of the eternal truths.[29] Though beyond *his* capacity, as he claims, this question is not beyond the powers of unassisted human reason as such. That is why it is not outside his province, which is that of philosophy. The answer to Mersenne's query, as developed both in this letter and in about a dozen other places in Descartes's writings, is the notorious doctrine of God's creation of the eternal truths, a doctrine that forms part of natural theology as a branch of metaphysics or the science of the supersensible.[30] Interestingly, in another letter to Mersenne of later the same month Descartes declines to reply to a question concerning the doctrine of the Holy Trinity, remarking: "I do not want to involve myself in theology" (AT I 150: CSMK 25). The theology to which he refers here can, of course, only be revealed theology. In the earlier of the two letters to Mersenne Descartes is as clear as possible about the intrinsic importance of metaphysics, even while stressing its instrumental value for physics:

I think that all those to whom God has given the use of this reason have an obligation to employ it principally in the endeavour to know him and to know themselves [i.e., their souls]. That is the task with which I began my studies; and I can say that I would not have been able to discover the foundations of physics if I had not looked for them along that road. It is the topic which I have studied more than any other and in which, thank God, I have not altogether wasted my time. At least I think that I have found how to prove metaphysical truths in a manner which is more evident than the proofs of geometry. (AT I 135: CSMK 22)

Other matters of revealed theology touched upon by Descartes, aside from the doctrine of the Holy Trinity, just mentioned (cf. also *Principles*, I, 25), are the mystery of the Incarnation (ibid., and AT VIII-2 353: CSM I 300) and the doctrines of the Resurrection (cf., for example, AT V 53: CSMK 320) and Transubstantiation (for example, AT VII 248ff.: CSM II 173ff. and espcially the correspondence with Mesland between 1644 and 1646). Damnation for eternity belongs here as well (AT I 153: CSMK 26). The case of immortality is more complex. While the Dedication of the *Meditations* states unequivocally that the proof of the immortality of the soul belongs to the province of natural human reason (AT VII 2f.: CSM II 3f.), the "Synopsis" of the Second Meditation opens a wide gap between immateriality and immortality (AT VII 12f.: CSM II 9f.). This may seem to be bridged by the distinction between a "pure substance" like the human soul and "a certain configuration of limbs and other accidents" (ibid.) like the human body; for pure substances, once created by God, cannot perish "unless they are reduced to nothingness by God's denying his concurrence to them," whereas the human body "loses its identity merely as a result of a change in the shape of some of its parts" (ibid.). According to the Second Set of Replies, however, this fails to close the gap entirely: "you go on to say that it does not follow from the fact that the soul is distinct from the body that it is immortal, since it could still be claimed that God gave it such a nature that its duration comes to an end simultaneously with the end of the body's life. Here I admit that I cannot refute what you say. For I do not take it upon myself to try to use the power of human reason to settle any of those matters which depend on the free will of God" (AT VII 153: CSM II 108f.). So the decision on the soul's immortality lies with God: "if your question concerns the absolute power of God, and you are asking whether he may have decreed that human souls cease to exist precisely when the bodies which he joined to them are destroyed, then it is for God alone to give the answer. And since God himself has revealed to us that this will not occur, there remains not even the slightest room for doubt on this point" (AT VII 154: CSM II 109). The certainty to which Descartes alludes here is not that of the natural light of reason in intuition and demonstrations, but "a certain inner light which comes from God, and when we are supernaturally illumined by it we are confident that what is put forward for us to believe has been revealed by God himself. And it is quite impossible for him to lie; this is more certain than any natural light, and is even more evident because of the light of grace" (AT VII 148: CSM II 105).

Thus, while the distinction between two senses of 'theology' undoubtedly gives some point to Belaval's observation, quoted earlier, it only serves to confirm a rank ordering of physics and metaphysics within Descartes's philosophical project that is quite the reverse of that frequently assigned them in the apologetics of the commentators.

3.5 Conclusion

Given the extent and obviousness of Descartes's preoccupation with questions regarding the being (existence and essence) of substances, their attributes, and the modes of those attributes, two concluding remarks may be in order.

The first is terminological. There is a loose yet perfectly legitimate sense (that is, one sanctioned by contemporary and traditional usage) in which 'metaphysics' or 'ontology' is simply 'the study of the being of beings.' In this sense, metaphysics is clearly the central preoccupation of those works for which Descartes is best remembered. Whatever the significance of his contributions to mathematics and natural science, methodology and epistemology, philosophical psychology, and the metaphysical foundations of physics, the proper parameters in which to make sense of the revolution in philosophy brought about by Descartes are metaphysical or ontological.

The final comment harks back to Locke's 'underlabourer theory' of philosophy, briefly evoked at an earlier stage. The Welsh poet Dylan Thomas (1964, vii) recalls having "read somewhere of a shepherd who, when asked why he made ... ritual observances to the moon to protect his flocks, replied: 'I'd be a damn' fool if I didn't.'" Like his Greek and medieval predecessors, Descartes elaborated a metaphysical understanding of the totality of what is within the framework of a new guiding idea of being. And (*pace* Locke et al.) he'd have been a damn' fool if he hadn't.

4

The New Order of Knowing

Before considering the order of knowing itself, it is necessary to examine more closely a widely held account of the model of cognition instituted by Descartes. In section 1.2 the doctrine known as 'representationalism' was cited as one of the principal roadblocks to understanding Descartes's founding principle. For attributing this doctrine to Descartes obscures the new order of knowing implicit in that principle.

4.1 The model of cognition

An influential proponent of the ascription to Descartes of the model of the mind on which the only immediate objects of knowledge are ideas is Gewirth: "The direct object of the mind's act of perception is for Descartes always an idea ... The total cognitive situation as conceived by Descartes thus contains three elements: perceptive act, idea (the direct content or object perceived), and the thing purportedly represented by the idea" (1987a, 3f.; cf. 1968, 252f. as well). In support of his analysis Gewirth cites this from the letter to Gibieuf, 19 January 1642: "I am certain that I can have no knowledge of what is outside me except by means (*par l'entremise*) of the ideas I have within me" (AT III 473: CSMK 201). Whatever this sentence may seem to express, it does not mean that only ideas are perceived directly, while extra-mental objects are perceived indirectly, via interposed ideas. It is perfectly possible to assert that one cannot know objects except by means of one's ideas, that is, by thinking of them, and to insist nevertheless that one thinks and knows those objects directly.[1] The "total cognitive situation" that Gewirth here misdescribes involves only two elements, (1) the idea *or* perceptive act (these two are the same) and (2) its direct or intentional object, the extra-mental thing represented. But the total cognitive situation "as Descartes conceives it" involves a further element as well: (3) the consciousness (*conscientia*) of the act or idea itself. The object of self-conscious awareness (*conscientia*) is indeed an idea; yet the idea is not the object of the perceptive act of which one is self-consciously aware. It is identical with that act. Typically, that is, unless the act in question is a second- or higher-order act directed upon an act, the intentional object of the perceptual act or idea is an extra-mental, usually a sensible, thing. None of this differs significantly from Aristotle or the Scholastics, though the vocabulary, in particular the carefully drawn distinction between *cogitatio* and *conscientia*, is new.[2]

Almost thirty years later (1987b, 88), Gewirth renewed the claim that Descartes "upholds a doctrine of representative perception according to which the mind perceives only ideas directly." Kenny is another who takes it for granted that "Descartes believed that the direct object of the mind's perception was always an idea" (1968, 197). However, what we *think*, for instance, perceive, for Descartes, are things outside the mind. These we perceive directly. What we are immediately *conscious of*, on the other hand, are our acts of perceiving as acts of perceiving something. To say 'I perceive x' entails 'I am immediately conscious of an act of perceiving x (directly).' In ordinary usage, as within Scholastic-Aristotelian philosophy, 'I perceive x (by means of the senses)' entails the actual existence of x outside the mind no less than its intentional existence within it. Descartes was well aware of the difference between "I am now seeing light, hearing a noise, feeling heat" (AT VII 29: CSM II 19) and "I *seem* to see, to hear, to be warmed" (ibid.). Yet the knowledge of things existing outside the mind is always direct knowledge.

Confusion on this point is more widespread than might be thought. Marion (1986, 172) may be expressing the same point of view when he writes: "de l'*ego* aux *cogitationes* se déploie la relation épistémique immédiate." From this it would appear to follow that the cognitive relation to things is indirect. Gilson clearly subscribes to this view (1947a, 318ff. and 1951, chap. III, esp. 206), as does Maritain (1937, 41); and so too most of those who have been influenced by them.[3] According to McRae, "what remains basic for the earlier Descartes, for the later Descartes, for Malebranche and for Locke, is that ideas are the immediate objects of perception" (1965, 179), even if this is only part of the story in Descartes's case. Yolton (1975b, 149ff.) points out that Alquié is a firm adherent. Some commentators have taken strong exception to the ascription of representationalism to Descartes.[4] The claim here, then, is not that no previous commentator has got Descartes's view essentially right, but that there is still lingering confusion on this point. This is perhaps enough to warrant a fresh look at Descartes's understanding of the order of knowing. Certainly, the distinction between thought and consciousness (to be elaborated in Part One) is an important piece of the puzzle that has been largely absent from the discussion thus far. This alone would warrant re-examination of the whole question.

4.2 The epistemic difference

On the account of Descartes's philosophical intentions given in the preceding chapter a key facet of the Cartesian revolution in philosophy is the attempt to fix once and for all the proper starting point of knowledge. To Descartes a new point of departure seemed imperative, the metaphysical systems of the Schools having been largely discredited, he believed, by the new mathematical science of nature with which they were inconsistent.[5] Whereas the till then dominant metaphysical outlook involved taking for granted the existence and immediate givenness of material things possessing sensible properties, Descartes began his metaphysical enterprise with the analysis of certainty and of the structure and varieties of the mental. He stressed above all the difference between knowledge of the existence of one's own mental states and knowledge of the existence of entities outside the mind, especially of material things known through the senses. He first doubted and then, on mature reflection, denied that metaphysical knowledge of the nature or essence of material things involves perception of their sensible properties. But that we can and do know their natures by means of the pure intellect he either never doubted or doubted only in order to dispel such doubts in a manner he naively believed would banish all forms of scepticism regarding the intellect once and for all. Only the *existence* of the material universe, like that of God, remained, upon careful examination, a matter for inference from the existence of the intellectual or sensible ideas of such entities in the mind. Knowledge of their existence, being inferential, differs from the mind's immediate apprehension of the simple *natures* of all things, mental and extra-mental, and of its own *existence* and that of its states. But knowledge of the existence of God and the external world is none the less certain for being inferential. Whereas the "true and immutable natures" of all things, the axioms or principles of the natural light, and even the existence of the mental neither require nor admit of demonstration, being immediately intuitable and known with perfect certainty as soon as we direct our attention to them, the existence of entities outside the mind, both of God and of material things, must and can be proved, Descartes held, with perfect certainty. The starting points of such proofs are (1) the corresponding ideas, whose existence in the mind we apprehend immediately, and (2) the principles of the natural light (in particular Descartes's causal principles). The latter, too, are immediately intuitable through reflexive attention to what is implicit in our very thinking, that is, innate.

While others were to suggest that this *epistemic difference* between the intuitive knowledge of one's own existence and the inferential knowledge of the existence of non-mental things rendered all knowledge of the existence of anything apart from the mind and its ideas precarious, it did not seem to Descartes that the difference between immediate intuition and knowledge based on inference had any such sceptical consequence at all. Of course, he accorded the knowledge of the mental as a department of the supersensible a distinct priority, seeing in this a means of reasserting the traditional primacy of metaphysics within the domain of human knowledge. However, in insisting upon the gap separating knowledge of the existence of the mind and its states from knowledge of the existence of material things, Descartes by no means manoeuvred himself into the preposterous position that it can only be the ideas of things rather than the things themselves that we perceive and know immediately and with perfect certainty.[6]

The difference between the immediate intuitive certainty one has of the existence of one's thinking and inferential knowledge of the existence of things outside the mind cannot be construed as that between (1) those modes of thinking in which the mind is intentionally related to its own ideas, which it knows immediately and with perfect certainty, and (2) other modes of thought in which the mind is intentionally related to extra-mental objects, though only mediately, by precarious inference from its ideas. It is true that, for Descartes, we are immediately *conscious* only of our own thoughts or mental states and of our own existence as minds, as substances to which such thoughts belong. But while the only things immediately *present* to consciousness are intentionally structured acts of thinking and the self that thinks, such acts *represent* extra-mental things immediately; the things themselves are not immediately present to consciousness, that is, literally in the mind; nor are thoughts of such things themselves *re*presented (except in rare second- and higher order acts of thinking about thinking).[7] Even acts that are 'ideas' only in the broad sense, like judging, volition, and emotion, are intentionally related to extra-mental objects in an immediate fashion. However, their being so related to an object is due to the properly representational acts (ideas in the strict sense) contained within them. Though such objects are only *mediately* present *to consciousness*, via the acts of thinking in which they are intended, they are nonetheless *immediately* represented by those acts *of thinking*. This difference between thought (*cogitatio*) and consciousness (*conscientia*) has been regularly overlooked or underestimated. As a consequence, what is *im*mediately present to *consciousness* is mistaken for an *im*mediate object of *thought*, as in (1). Conversely, what is the *mediate* object *of consciousness*, namely the intentional object of those ideas or thoughts of which we are *immediately* conscious, is frequently mistaken for the *mediate* object *of thought*, as in (2). The knowledge of the objects of thought, it is assumed, involves inferences from ideas. But, as we have just seen, this is no more true of the immediate intuitive knowledge of the "true and immutable nature" (AT VII 64: CSM II 44) or essence of extra-mental objects than it is of the essence of the mind or, for that matter, the mind's existence.

Where, for Descartes, there *is* inferential knowledge is at the level of the *exist-*

ence of extra-mental objects – though even here the difference is one of immediacy, not certainty. In the case of extra-mental objects, the direct objects of thought, the knowledge that such objects actually exist outside the mind as well as intentionally in it is inferential, an inference from ideas to the things that are their causes. Thus, (a) knowledge of the essence or nature of extra-mental things is just as immediate as (b) knowledge of the essence or nature of the mind, both being innate ideas of "true and immutable natures" immediately intuitable in reflection on the thinking of which one is immediately conscious. On the other hand, (c) knowledge that there exist outside the mind objects corresponding to the ideas of material objects in it differs from (d) knowledge of the existence of thinking and of the mind itself as a thinking thing. While (c) involves an inference from ideas to their causes, (d) is just as immediate and intuitive as (a) and (b). For (d) requires nothing more than attention to the innate idea of truth or certainty of which we become immediately aware as soon as we attend to the fact that it is true that we think and that we therefore exist. By contrast, (c) demands an inference from our knowledge of the existence of ideas of objects to their causes outside the mind. Herein lies the primacy of (b) and (d), the knowledge of the essence and existence of the mental as a department of the supersensible. It resides also in the fact that knowledge of the mind (and God) must be acquired *first* if the inference to the existence of material things is to go through at all. But it does not reside in any higher degree of certainty accorded (a), (b), and (d) vis-à-vis (c), for all four are perfectly certain, at least every time I actually bring the grounds of their truth within the compass of a single intuition or clear and distinct perception. And once God's existence and veracity have been definitively proved, *all* are perfectly certain at any subsequent time as well, provided I remember having once clearly and distinctly perceived the grounds for their truth and having likewise perceived that God exists and is no deceiver.

Thus, what we have termed the 'epistemic difference' between the knowledge of the mind and of extra-mental reality is not the difference between knowledge that is perfectly certain and knowledge that is not. Nor is it simply a distinction between knowledge that is intuitive and that which is inferential – unless we restrict our view to existence alone, in which case it is. Nor, finally, is it (without the same restriction) a distinction between two types of object, the one immediately, the other only mediately knowable, by inference. These are the misunderstandings that have done most to skew the picture of the transition from the old metaphysics and theory of knowledge to the new metaphysical and epistemological outlook of Descartes. We will examine them more fully in chapter 16.

To sum up: in the order of cognition we have, on the one hand, knowledge that is intuitive, immediate insight, as we might say. Such is the mind's knowledge of its own nature and existence, but also of the natures, though not the existence, of extra-mental immaterial (God) and material things (body). Descartes refers to a *simplex mentis intuitus* (AT VII 140f.: CSM II 100), to *conscientia, testimonium internum,* and *experientia* (AT X 524: CSM II 418), and *cognitio interna quae reflexam semper antecedit* (VII 422: CSM II 285) when speaking of the knowledge of the mind (cf. chapter 15 below). As for the mind's knowledge of the nature of body, he uses such expressions as *mente percipere* and *inspectio mentis* (AT VII 31: CSM II 21) to convey the intuitive character of such knowledge, while in the case of God he speaks of the "natural light" of reason (for example, AT VII 52: CSM II 35). On the other hand, we have knowledge of the existence of extra-mental things. This involves inference from the intuitively certain existence of ideas in the mind. Such objects, however, are the immediate objects of intentionally structured acts of thinking, be it sense-perception of their accidental properties or purely intellectual knowledge of their "true and immutable natures." Inferential is the knowledge that those extra-mental objects, clear and distinct ideas of which exist in the mind, exist *actually* ('really') outside the mind as well as *intentionally* ('objectively') in it; the knowledge, in other words, that we indeed have immediate, intuitive knowledge of the essential nature of something actually rather than just possibly existent. The model of perceiving and knowing on which an impenetrable 'veil of ideas' hangs between the knowing mind and extra-mental things cannot be fathered on Descartes, who, despite important differences, was much closer to the 'epistemological direct realism' of the Scholastics than is generally supposed.[8]

5

Synopsis

So much for the similarities and differences of metaphysical and epistemological outlook between Descartes and his medieval predecessors. Further discussion of these general themes must await the renewed consideration of the order of knowing to be undertaken, together with an analysis of the order and idea of being or existence, in the Conclusion. Much of the scholarly discussion of Descartes's founding principle revolves around three specific issues: the precise sense of *cogitare* in the word *cogito*; the necessity and certainty of *sum*; and the nature of the inference marked by the word *ergo*. These form the subject matter of the individual parts of this study. The second turns crucially on Descartes's doctrine of divine creation of the eternal truths. We conclude this Introduction, therefore, with a brief outline of the study's main parts and a rapid survey of the principal controversies surrounding the eternal truths.

5.1 Outline

Part One, "Thought and Consciousness," is focused upon the terminological and philosophical distinction between *cogitatio* and *conscientia*. The first three chapters (6 through 8) examine what may be called, following Husserl, the 'phenomenological reduction' of the complex whole 'thought-of-an-extra-mental-object' to its phenomenologically pure kernel. This kernel consists in the intentionally structured, that is, object-representing modes or acts of thinking that are the sole immediate objects of consciousness as opposed to thought. To the extent that Descartes himself speaks expressly of 'reduction' in this regard, the Husserlian vocabulary is employed without obvious anachronism.[1] But there is a further justification for it. The sense of 'clear and distinct' in Descartes has as marked affinities with Husserl's use of 'pure' (roughly, 'purged of naive positings of extra-mental existents') as it has with Kant's ('purged of sensory elements').

Of course, Descartes's use of 'pure' in speaking of *intellectio pura* and *pura &
incorrupta ratio* (see section 10.1) is closer to Kant's sense of the term; but while
all pure or sense-free intellection is necessarily clear and distinct, the converse is
not true: not everything clearly and distinctly perceived is pure in the Kantian
sense. Even an internal sensation like pain may be clearly and distinctly perceived by those who take care to inhibit their customary "judgement ... concerning the nature of something which they think exists in the painful spot [outside
the mind] and which they suppose to resemble the sensation of pain" (AT VIII-A
22: CSM I 208). And so too in the case of external sensation or what we ordinarily call 'sense-perception.' Admittedly, the relevance of Husserl's sense of 'pure'
to Descartes's reductive analysis of thought depends upon a somewhat different
interpretation of clarity and distinctness from that usually given (on this see section 7.1).

Part One concludes (cf. chapter 9) with an examination of Gueroult's attempt
to read the Kantian sense of 'pure consciousness' (*conscience intellectuelle*) back
into Descartes's *cogito*. At bottom, what is asserted by the first word of the *cogito,
ergo sum* is nothing other than the immediate presence to consciousness of
certain purely mental existents, that is, acts of thinking that are pure in the
phenomenologically reduced, though not in the Kantian, sense. It is a mistake to
suggest that the subject of the statements *cogito* and *sum* is anything other than
the empirical or psychological self of everyday experience, though it is true that
the presence of such existents is not *empirically* ascertained in simple introspection, but involves the intellectual faculty. To this extent Gueroult's point has some
force after all.

Part Two, "Certainty and Truth," addresses a cluster of problems, much mooted
by the commentators, touching the certainty and necessary truth of the *sum*. The
first two chapters (10 and 11) offer an analysis of the degrees and kinds of certainty distinguished by Descartes. On this basis, chapter 12 then undertakes an
examination of various and sundry interpretations of the *sum*, beginning with
logical interpretations of the necessity of *sum* or *existo* as that of a self-referential
statement or as a logical consequence of *cogito*. Next come those normative and
psychological interpretations that have largely supplanted the logical in the recent literature. On the positive view of the matter developed over the course of
Part Two, the impossibility of denying one's own existence is not primarily logical, normative, or psychological, but rather metaphysical. It can, with a certain
justice, be termed 'psychological' as well, though Descartes construed the mind's
inability to withhold assent from the clearly and distinctly perceived as a limitation upon the freedom of the will. To call this necessity 'psychological' may
therefore obscure the metaphysical point at issue. But psychological or metaphysical, the necessity in question at least does not lay Descartes open to the

charge of 'psychologism.' The standard forms of psychological interpretation might better be termed 'psychologistic,' since most assume that Descartes committed the fallacy of collapsing objective truth into (the) subjective (feeling of) certainty. However, for Descartes, certainty *just is* truth in the primary sense and the only one relevant to the task of discovering a first truth as the foundation on which to rebuild the edifice of human knowledge. This is not to deny that there is a further sense of 'true' in Descartes, one indistinguishable from the straightforward realist conception embodied in the traditional correspondence theory of truth. (This is the subject of chapter 13.) The point is rather that this latter sense of 'truth,' although extremely important in the sequel, is quite irrelevant to the quest for a first principle of knowledge.

If *nothing* is strictly beyond the possibility of a metaphysical doubt, not even the axioms of the natural light employed in the proof of God's existence, the charge of circularity traditionally brought against Descartes's validation of reason by reason has prima facie overwhelming force (cf. chapter 14). That is why so many are drawn to the normative and psychological interpretations of the certainty and necessity of the *sum*. The validation of reason, they argue, aims only at showing the clearly and distinctly perceived to be *certain* either beyond the descriptive psychological or beyond any normatively reasonable possibility of a doubt. Once this is shown for the axioms and principles employed in the proof of God's existence and veracity, the knowledge of God can be used to guarantee the truth of this and all other knowledge. Both interpretations, however, assume a gap between certainty and truth that simply does not exist for the special sense of 'truth' relevant to the *cogito* and the metaphysical axioms and principles associated with it.

In a notorious passage of the Third Meditation, Descartes suggests that even the clear and distinct perception that I exist depends for its certainty on the prior knowledge of God and his veracity. More than anything else this passage is responsible for fostering the misconception that it is psychological or normative certainty Descartes is after. Seldom noticed is the fact that this dependence of *sum* on the knowledge of God holds only for *sum* considered as an item of knowledge within *vera & certa scientia*, not as the expression of that immediate certainty of one's own existence of which everyone is capable through simple reflexion upon his actually occurring thoughts. The latter Descartes terms *persuasio*. *Persuasio* has nothing at all to do with that inferior grade of certainty that we today call 'persuasion'; it is a different kind, not a lesser degree, of certainty. It differs from *scientia* as 'perfect certainty now' differs from 'perfect certainty now and at all subsequent times.' It encompasses all such simple intuitions and demonstrations as are either immediately present to consciousness or evident through simple reflexion on what we are conscious of, as well as all such mathematical or metaphysical demonstrations as are capable of being brought within the compass of a single intuition. As *persuasio*, the certainty of *sum* does not depend upon the knowledge of God's existence and veracity; the same holds for all other clear and distinct perceptions of simple natures, axioms, and demonstrations, be it in logic, mathematics, or metaphysics. Only as *scientia* does all knowledge depend upon that of a veracious God. But *persuasio* is that *truth* sought for first principles, just as *vera et certa scientia* is the truth sought for the whole edifice of human knowledge, including first principles, but unattainable without the knowledge of God. On careful examination, the distinction between *scientia* and *persuasio* (cf. section 11.2) proves entirely effective against the charge of circularity traditionally brought against Descartes's alleged attempt to validate reason by reasoning.

A recurring theme of Part Two is accordingly the doctrine of divine immutability and the creation of the eternal truths. If the knowledge of a divine guarantor itself required a guarantee in order to become *scientia*, the problem of the circle would be postponed rather than averted. Fortunately, the knowledge of God himself forms an exception to the rule that clear and distinct *scientia* depends for its certainty upon knowledge of God's existence and veracity. God's immutability ensures that *persuasio* of which he is the object is on an entirely different footing from the remainder of the so-called eternal truths. As created, the latter are the issue of a decree of the divine will; but the instants of time being entirely "separable from each other" (AT VII 78: CSM II 78), "the distinction between preservation and creation is only a conceptual one": creation and preservation are but one and the same power or action considered in different ways (AT VII 49: CSM II 33). It follows that the eternal truths, once created, must be preserved in their sameness at each subsequent moment of time by the very power by which they were originally produced; and hence that even truths regarding those simple natures termed "true and immutable" (AT VII 64: CSM II 44) are not strictly eternal or immutable at all. For though not subject to alteration by *our* will or dependent on our intellect, the divine intellect could have conceived them otherwise and the divine will have ordained, for example, that two plus two *not* equal four. Thus, all such truths, though clearly and distinctly perceived by us *now*, may yet be altered without our knowledge at any instant of time at which we are not actually attending to them; that is, they *would* be so alterable, unbeknownst to us, if the creator of all things could be a deceiver. God himself, however, is an uncreated necessary or eternal being whose nature is strictly immutable. Hence, unlike other inferences, the proofs of God's existence and veracity, once clearly and distinctly perceived, require no guarantee in order to take their place within the system of human *scientia*; the conclusions of sound arguments concerning God remain unalterably true, even when their premises and the logical relations among them are no longer immediately before the attentive mind. Theological knowledge alone among the eternal truths is not subject to doubt at any subsequent time. Thus, in its primary employment, as a faculty of clear and distinct *persuasio*, human reason is entirely autonomous or self-validating, even if the validation of reason as the source of *vera et certa scientia* depends on the knowledge of God (cf. section 14.9).

While the theory known as 'representationalism' and the notion of truth as 'correspondence' are addressed through the interpretation of the *cogito* and *sum* in the first two parts, the chief problem facing the interpreter of Descartes's founding principle is clearly, In what sense is *sum* inferred from *cogito*? The logical particle *ergo* suggests that it is inferred in some sense, and Descartes repeatedly resorts to the language of logical inference in this regard.[2] A solution to this problem is proposed in chapter 17 of Part Three, "Reflexion and Inference." To the various logical conceptions of direct and indirect inference it opposes the notion of a *transition of the mind from implicit to explicit knowledge* through selective focusing of attention on those elements within thinking that are naturally recessive in pre-philosophic experience and that only philosophical reflexion can bring luminously to the fore. It is this notion of 'inference' that finds expression in the *ergo*: neither discursive logical analysis nor ratiocinative inference, direct or indirect (syllogistic), but reflexive attention to what is implicit in the thinking we are immediately conscious of but do not normally attend to. To this kind of intuition or insight the label 'intuitive induction' may be applied, partly for lack of a better term, but partly in quite deliberate allusion to one of Aristotle's chief uses of epagōgē.[3] Despite a marked affinity in their conceptions of the process itself, there is, however, a crucial difference between Descartes's and Aristotle's views of that experience on the basis of which intuitive induction is practised: ordinary outer experience for Aristotle, inner experience for Descartes. This gives a distinctively modern, quite un-Aristotelian flavour to Descartes's analysis of mind. Apart from the concept of experience, the elaboration of Descartes's theory of intuitive induction (chapter 20) requires detailed consideration of his theory of innateness and model of the mind (chapters 18 and 19).

Part Three is introduced by two preparatory chapters, the first devoted to the relation among consciousness, thought, and reflexion (chapter 15). Here a number of stages within *persuasio* as the process of analytical reflection on the pre-reflexively conscious are distinguished. These correspond to successive phases in the mind's transition from implicit to explicit knowledge in intuitive induction. This provides the key to Descartes's conception of the analytic and synthetic methods and to the nature of mathematical reasoning as the universal method. The other chapter deals with Descartes's distinction between the formal and objective reality both of ideas and of things. There are two senses in which thought, itself the object of consciousness, has objects of its own: either only intentionally (or 'objectively,' as Descartes says), or both intentionally and really. This distinction is vital to the theme of this study if only because it establishes that the intentional object is, as the real object is not, part of the structure of thought itself and therefore included in the sphere of absolute certainty of the Cartesian *cogito* (cf. chapter 16).

Finally, a word on the the Conclusion and this Introduction itself. The preceding chapters have sought to establish that, unlike present-day epistemologists and philosophers of mind, Descartes undertakes the analysis of knowledge and the mind within the framework of a *metaphysics* in a sense largely continuous with the preceding tradition. The scope of the Introduction has, however, been confined to consideration of Descartes's *reversal of the order of knowing*. Consideration of his metaphysics proper, that is, the *new guiding idea* and *order of being* has been left for the Conclusion. Only once the three main parts have set out Descartes's metaphysical analysis of knowledge and the mind in some detail (chapters 6 through 20) can the result of the entire study – a portrait of Descartes as Father of Modern Philosophy in many ways very different from the standard one – be set in a clear light in the Conclusion, where others of the "great types of possible philosophies" (Russell) will be contrasted with the new epistemological, metaphysical, and methodological outlook of modern philosophy, and with the new guiding idea of being or existence inaugurated by Descartes.

5.2 The eternal truths

From the foregoing summary it is plain that Descartes's doctrine of the creation of the eternal truths by God, first set out in three letters to Mersenne of 1630, plays a pivotal role in the extended argument of Part Two. This doctrine is the subject of a number of scholarly controversies. One of the oldest concerns (1) the precise identity of the opponent(s) against whom Descartes's criticisms are directed. On the face of it, it is just not clear that anyone ever held the view that there exists anything eternal – truths in this case – apart from God.[4] Puzzling in a different way is (2) the paucity of references to so central a doctrine in Descartes's chief published writings.[5] Apart from these historical matters, there are more basic questions about (3) what the doctrine actually asserts. Some have taken it for a radical thesis about the modality of *all* propositions: since even 'necessary' truths depend on the divine will, and since God, being free, could have decreed otherwise, all truths are ultimately contingent. Against this 'voluntarist' reading (as it is sometimes called) stands Descartes's remark to Mesland: "even if God has willed some truths should *be* necessary, this does not mean that he willed them necessarily; for it is one thing to will that they be necessary, and quite another to will this necessarily, or to be necessitated to will it" (AT III 118: CSMK 235 e.a.). From this it appears that Descartes had no wish to deny that some truths are necessary, but only that such necessary truths are *necessarily* so; though all truths depend on God, some were willed freely as necessary, others as contingent. Since it follows from this that '□ p' ('it is necessary that p') does not entail '□ □ p,' this reading clashes with our standard modal intuitions almost as starkly as the competing voluntarist interpretation. On yet another reading, Descartes's doctrine is the antithesis of voluntarism (understood as a doctrine of 'universal contingency'), pointing rather in the direction of the universal necessity of all truths, as in Spinoza. This, too, of course, runs right counter to all our standard modal assumptions.[6]

Another issue is (4) whether Descartes drew a distinction between created and uncreated eternal truths, or between "absolute" and "relative" impossibility and necessity.[7] Even among those who acknowledge such a distinction there are several areas of disagreement. One concerns (5) the precise nature of the distinction and the extension of the class of the absolutely eternal truths.[8] Another is (6) whether its extension coincides with those first principles perfectly immune from all, even a metaphysical, doubt. If so, such absolutely necessary principles could be employed without circularity to prove God's existence, thus validating the remainder of the eternal truths.[9] A further issue is (7) whether the Cartesian theory of modal concepts is purely epistemic, modality being a function of our contingent psychological make-up and limitations (*à la* Hume); or whether it is a function of the divinely ordained nature of universal human reason (as in Kant); or whether, finally, it is in some sense ontological (as in Leibniz), grounded not only in the divinely ordained nature of the human mind but also in the (for Descartes, created) natures of mind-independent 'possibles' themselves.[10] Finally, there is some question about (8) whether the eternal truths decreed by God are also alterable by him (cf. section 14.7).

On the view of these matters developed in Part Two, the effect of divine omnipotence (beneficent or maleficent) is by no means to annul the distinction between necessary and contingent truth or to render it solely mind-dependent. Of course, the familiar distinction between necessary and contingent truth is curiously overlaid with a theological one. The result is indeed a further distinction between absolute and relative necessity. Even in the straightforwardly logical perspective, the usual boundary between necessary and contingent truth shifts so as to include the most basic laws of physics among those necessary truths the denials of which cannot be conceived without contradiction (cf. section 18.9). But if the familiar distinction is undeniably blurred, there are yet compelling reasons why it cannot be said to be obliterated entirely.

The formal criterion by which Descartes distinguishes logically necessary (eternal) from contingent truths looks much like the familiar one: the denials of the former involve contradiction. Though inconceivable to us, it cannot be asserted *absolutely*, however, that their denials cannot be conceived – or indeed made true – by a sheerly omnipotent intellect and will. Superimposed on the familiar logical distinction is thus another between *metaphysically* contingent and necessary truths. Drawn along purely theological lines, it entails that (a) some logically contingent truths are metaphysically necessary. Once God's existence and veracity are known, such truths are *certain* beyond the possibility even of a metaphysical doubt; till then they are both metaphysically and logically contingent. The contrapositive of (a) holds as well: (b) some logically necessary truths are metaphysically contingent unless and until we know God. For though we can never comprehend *how* the denials of such truths could be true, we understand well enough *that* a sheerly omnipotent Deceiver could make them so (unbeknownst to us). That is why they are subject to a metaphysical doubt (and hence, metaphysically speaking, *not* necessarily true, that is, contingent), even though logically necessary.

This conjunction of theological and logical perspectives leads Descartes to lump logically contingent truths, including the *cogito, ergo sum*, together with the logically necessary principles of mathematics, metaphysics, and morals as truths all of which are metaphysically necessary once God's existence and veracity are known. This accounts in part for the appearance of necessitarianism in his system. And since even logically necessary truths of the kinds already mentioned are dependent for their existence and preservation on God's will, the converse appearance, universal contingency, can also arise. Still, given that the logically necessary or eternal truths created by God and implanted in the human mind include not just the simple truths of mathematics and the metaphysical principles of the natural light, but even the most basic laws of physics, Descartes clearly shifts the familiar boundary between logically necessary and contingent truth in a way that raises legitimate questions about the *radix contingentiae* (Leibniz) of things within the created physical universe.[11]

This and the overlapping of logical and theological considerations are the principal reasons why the familiar distinction between the contingent and the necessary is blurred. However, two facts assure us that it has not in fact been obliterated entirely. (a) The semblance of a thoroughgoing necessaritarianism is dispelled by the logical contingency of the first metaphysically necessary truths, *cogito* and *sum*. And (b) the appearance of universal contingency is belied by the fact that, while some logically necessary truths may depend on God's will, being created by him, there is (*pace* Ishiguro) at least one class of absolutely necessary uncreated truths, namely those concerning God himself.

Since only the created among logically necessary truths are subject to God's will, they are on a different epistemological footing from uncreated eternal truths. As items of *persuasio*, both are utterly immune even from the most radical doubt. Yet the former are open to a metaphysical doubt at such times as I no longer attend to them. It requires God's goodness and veracity to guarantee that what I have once perceived clearly and distinctly is still necessarily true even when I no longer attend to it. It is a peculiarity of *un*created eternal truths about God himself that there can never be any subsequent doubt once they are perceived clearly and distinctly. To know God, therefore, nothing more is required than *persuasio*. And once he is so known, this and all other *persuasio* becomes *scientia*.[12] The answer to issue (4), then, is that the class of uncreated eternal truths does not correspond to that of metaphysically indubitable truths since some of the principles employed in the proof of God's existence are both subject to God's will and yet known to be true while I actually attend to them. But if the distinction between two classes of eternal truths is not the key to avoiding circularity in proving God's existence and veracity, it is nonetheless crucial in avoiding a second circle concerning the knowledge of God at such times as the proofs of his existence are no longer under the mind's direct scrutiny. It therefore provides the key to the problem of circularity after all (see chapter 14).

PART ONE:
THOUGHT AND CONSCIOUSNESS

[W]e cannot have any thought (*cogitatio*) of which we are not conscious (*conscii*) at the very moment when it is in us. (AT VII 246: CSM II 171f.)

The Latin and French terms *conscientia* and *conscience* are frequently regarded as equivalents of *cogitatio* and *pensée.* So, for example, by Gilson (1947a, 293), Laporte (1950, 78), and Alquié (ALQ, II, 586n.). Moreover, certain translators of Descartes's works have instituted the practice of rendering even the latter pair by the English word 'consciousness,' notably Anscombe and Geach. In a short but incisive discussion of both points, McRae warns that while the translation of 'thought' by 'consciousness' has obvious merits, it leaves the problem of "what to do with Descartes's own use of the word *conscientia*, in particular, how to translate Descartes's definition of thought without making it a definition of consciousness by consciousness, together with the loss of what Descartes means by consciousness" (McRae 1976, 8ff.).[1]

There are two reasons why Descartes's definition of 'thought' cannot entail that 'thought' is a synonym for 'consciousness.' First, Cartesian definitions are not concerned with the meanings of words (McRae 1976, 9). Moreover, thought and consciousness "do not, as the definition shows, have the same objects" (10). Both points will be borne out by the investigations of Part One. We begin with an examination of Descartes's formal definitions of 'thought' (chapter 6), to be followed by a consideration of 'clarity' and 'distinctness' and of the relation of 'thought' and 'consciousness' to the first of three senses of 'the *cogito*' (chapter 7). Couched in this sense (the others will be explained in Part Two) is a minute analysis of the formal structure of thought in general (cf. chapter 8). It is therefore more than a terminological point to insist that what Descartes understands by 'thought' corresponds to 'consciousness' in the now customary sense of that word, that is, to pure or phenomenologically reduced consciousness or *Bewußtsein* in Husserl's sense. Consequently, efforts to see in the *cogito* a *conscience intellectuelle* that is pure in something like Kant's sense distort Descartes's fundamental insight into the structure of thinking (cf. chapter 9).

6

Descartes's Definition of 'Thought'

'Thought' (*cogitatio*), writes Descartes in the Replies to the Second Set of Objections, is a word that covers "everything that is within us in such a way that we are immediately conscious (*immediate conscii simus*) of it. Thus all the operations of the will, the intellect, the imagination and the senses are thoughts. I say 'immediately' so as to exclude the consequences of thoughts (*ea quae ex iis consequuntur*); a voluntary movement, for example, originates in a thought, but is not itself a thought" (AT VII 160: CSM II 113). Descartes here defines 'thought' in part by illustrating the extension of the term. As the illustrations show, the functions or operations of the mind are not confined to the *actions* of the soul in Descartes's technical sense of that term, but correspond to what we should call 'mental acts,' 'psychic experiences (phenomena),' or 'states of consciousness' in the widest sense. Thus, in the *Passions of the Soul* Descartes distinguishes "two principal kinds" of thoughts (*pensées*), "some being actions of the soul and others its passions. Those I call its actions are all our volitions ... On the other hand, the various perceptions or modes of knowledge present in us may be called its passions, in a general sense" (AT XI 342: CSM I 335). The *Principles of Philosophy* detail the chief varieties of actions and passions: "Sensory perception, imagination and pure understanding are simply various modes of perception; desire, aversion, assertion, denial and doubt are various modes of willing" (AT VIII-1 17: CSM I 204). According to the formal definition of *cogitatio* in the *Principles*, 'thought' designates "everything of which we are conscious (*consciis*) as taking place within us insofar as there is a consciousness (*conscientia*) of it in us. And that is why not only understanding, willing, and imagining but also sensing (*sentire*) is the same as thought" (AT VIII-1 7: CSM I 195).[1] In saying that these are "the same (*idem*)" as thought, Descartes means that they are specific varieties or modalities of thought; that the full extension of the term 'thought' embraces all the "operations of the soul" (AT II 36: CSMK 97), actions or passions, of which we are immediately conscious.[2]

The explanation given *immediate* in the passage from the Second Replies deserves close attention. There is nothing here to suggest that the immediate objects of our mental operations (thoughts) are themselves something mental, that is, ideas rather than things. Nor is anything of the kind entailed by the definition of 'idea' in the Third Set of Replies: "by an 'idea' I mean whatever is *immediately* perceived by the mind (*quod immediate a mente percipitur*)" (AT VII 181: CSM II 127 e.a.). The distinction drawn is not between ideas and things as the direct and indirect objects *of thinking* but as the immediate and mediate objects *of consciousness*. In other words, it is a distinction between (a) that which is immediately *present* to consciousness, as are all acts of thinking, including ideas, whether as a proper subset of or as synonymous with 'thoughts' (cf. chapter 16 below) and (b) that which is not thus present to consciousness, for instance, the voluntary or involuntary motions of the limbs that are directly *represented* in sense-perception but, unlike volition itself, are only indirectly *present* to consciousness via a thought.

Nevertheless, in the definition of 'idea' Descartes designates consciousness itself by the word *percipere*; and he does so again in a later passage of the same Replies (to Hobbes): "I have frequently pointed out that I use the term 'idea' to apply to what is established by reasoning *as well as anything else that is perceived in any manner whatsoever*" (AT VII 185: CSM II 130 e.a.). But though occasionally designated a form of *perceptio*, consciousness is not a mode of perceiving (in Descartes's technical sense) on an equal footing with sensation, imagination, or intellection. It is rather the formal structure of these and all other acts or operations of the mind, owing to which I cannot but be immediately *conscious* of (or 'perceive' in this Pickwickian sense) my act of perceiving (in the ordinary signification) extra-mental things whenever I do so. Referred to as a *perceptio* here, *conscientia* is also designated both an *idea* and *cognitio* (*savoir*) elsewhere (cf. AT III 295: CSMK 172). But again, care must be taken not to assimilate this act-structure to those acts normally designated 'ideas' or 'knowledge' of my thoughts by Descartes. Thus, it cannot be assumed that 'I am conscious that I am thinking' entails 'I know that I am thinking,' since knowledge of the ongoings in the mind ordinarily involves some degree of reflexion upon what we are immediately conscious of as well as a judgment about the object of reflexion. These are rather uncharacteristic uses of 'know' and 'idea'; though apt to spawn confusion, they are without question to be met with in Descartes's writings.[3]

6.1 Seventeenth-century and Scholastic usage

The stress repeatedly laid on the inclusion of sensing suggests that in Descartes's day, as in modern usage, 'seeing,' 'hearing,' or 'feeling' something were generally opposed to just 'thinking' of it, whether in the sense of 'imagining' it or of 'conceiving' it according to its strict definition. Similarly, 'desire' and 'holding in aversion' designate states of mind not now ordinarily regarded as having anything to do with thinking and not so regarded in Descartes's day either. This is confirmed by Anscombe and Geach (A/G, xlvii), at least as far as contemporary English usage is concerned: "Now, as may be seen e.g. from the Oxford English Dictionary *think* and *thought* have always had a predominantly intellectual reference; thought is naturally taken to be a cognitive process; and it would be most unnatural to call an act of will, and still more a fit of anger or a toothache, a 'thought'." However, they go on to assert (ibid.) that in "everyday XVIIth-century French, *pensée* had a rather wider application than in modern French; it was then natural, as it would not now be, to call an emotion *une pensée*." A similar claim is made about the use of *cogitatio* in philosophical Latin. Malcolm (1968, 317 n. 22) has cast doubt on both claims, and Cottingham (1978b, 209) openly contests them, pointing out that when Mersenne objected that if man were simply a thinking being it would follow that he had no will, Descartes had to make it clear that thinking included willing: "I do not see that this follows; for willing, understanding, imagining and sensing and so on are just different ways of thinking (*façons de penser*)" (AT I 366: CSMK 56). To say so would hardly have been necessary were this already standard usage.[4] The matter is quickly settled by a glance at Randle Cotgrave's *Dictionarie of the French and English Tongues* (1611), which gives under the entry "Penser" the following English equivalents: "To thinke, weene, deeme, judge, imagine, suppose, conjecture, surmise; have an opinion, or be of opinion, that; also, to studie, muse, mediate, consider of; pause, or deliberate upon; examine, weigh, ponder, perpend, revolve, or cast, in mind" (Cotgrave 1970). Thus far the correspondence with twentieth-century French usage is quite close. Most of the remainder of the entry ("dresse, tend, looke unto, have a care of, provide for, furnish with all necessaries; also, to dress, Physicke, applie medecines unto") belongs properly under "Panser" (which is indeed cross-referenced with "penser").

Apropos of seventeenth-century English usage, we also have Locke's testimony that thinking, "in the propriety of the *English* tongue, signifies that sort of operation in the mind about its *ideas*, wherein the mind is active, where it, with some degree of voluntary attention, considers anything" (Locke 1977, 65). This may reflect a conception of thinking not unlike Mersenne's understanding of *cogitare* and *penser*. However, it did not prevent Locke from actually using 'thinking' in what is clearly Descartes's extended sense to cover perceptions and volitions alike, the ample extension of the term being by then well established. But while Descartes's use of 'thought' may be broader than both contemporary and older English and French usage alike, that of the "operations" or "functions of the soul" (AT XI 342: CSM I 335) is nonetheless narrower than one particular usage still common in seventeenth-century thought. Deliberately excluded are various phenomena proper to living bodies, notably the nutritive, appetitive, sensitive, and locomotive functions customarily ascribed to the soul in Scholastic-Aristotelian philosophy and in popular thought as well (see below). In Descartes's view, "voluntary movements," nutrition, and being "aware (*animadvertere*) of bodily things as it were through the senses" (AT VII 29: CSM II 19) are just so many physical operations ascribable to the complex bodily organism or machine to which the soul is conjoined, not to the soul itself.[5]

Interestingly, it is not that Descartes regarded the Scholastic-Aristotelian doctrine of the soul as having trickled down into popular thought; just the reverse is the truth. In the Second Meditation he sets about answering the question 'what am I?' by asking what he formerly believed himself to be (cf. AT VII 25f.: CSM II 17f.). 'A rational animal' is the time-hallowed response that immediately suggests itself. This Scholastic definition by genus and specific difference is rejected out of hand, for "I should have to enquire what an animal is, what rationality is, and in this way one question would lead down the slope to other harder ones" (AT VII 25: CSM II 17), for example, what a living and sentient being is, what an animate body is, what a body is, and so on (cf. also AT X 515f.: CSM II 410). Instead Descartes proposes "to concentrate on what came into my thoughts spontaneously and quite naturally whenever I used to consider what I was" (AT VII 25: CSM II 17). The second item in the ensuing enumeration of his pre-philosophical beliefs is "that I was nourished, that I moved about, and that I engaged in sense-perception ...; and these actions I attributed to the soul" (ibid.). In the next paragraph, reviewing these beliefs in the light of the doubts of the First Meditation, he remarks: "Nutrition or movement? Since now I do not have a body, these are mere fabrications. Sense-perception? This surely does not occur without a body" (AT VII 26f.: CSM II 17f.). In short, it is Descartes's view that the Scholastic doctrine is the philosophical but still naive expression of a pre-philosophical tendency that is natural and spontaneous in mankind.[6]

This is especially clear in *The Search for Truth* (AT X 510: CSM II 407). Descartes's mouthpiece, Eudoxus, addresses Polyander, the spokesman of plain common sense (while Epistemon, embodiment of the learning of 'the Schools,' stands by): "So please join me in considering which, of all the truths men can know, are the most certain and the easiest to become acquainted with." To this Polyander replies: "Is there anyone who can doubt that things that are perceivable by the senses – by which I mean those that can be seen and touched – are much more certain than all the others? I for one would be quite astonished if you were to make me see just as clearly any of the things which are said about God or the soul." This is exactly the viewpoint of plain common sense. Eudoxus rejoins:

"That is just what I hope to do," that is, reverse the so-called natural standpoint of pre-philosophical experience.[7]

That Descartes was convinced of the essential continuity of the Scholastic with our everyday way of thinking about the self is also plain from his observations on the concept of the soul held by "primitive man":

[P]rimitive man probably did not distinguish between, on the one hand, the principle by which we are nourished and grow and accomplish without any thought all the other operations which we have in common with the brutes, and, on the other hand, the principle in virtue of which we think. He therefore used the single term 'soul' to apply to both; and when he subsequently noticed that thought was distinct from nutrition, he called the element which thinks 'mind,' and believed it to be the principal part of the soul. I, by contrast, realising that the principle by which we are nourished is wholly different – different in kind – from that in virtue of which we think, have said that the term 'soul', when it is used to refer to both these principles, is ambiguous. If we are to take 'soul' in its special sense ... then the term must be understood to apply only to the principle in virtue of which we think; and to avoid ambiguity I have as far as possible used the term 'mind' for this. For I consider the mind not as a part of the soul but as the thinking soul in its entirety. (AT VII 356: CSM II 246)

On this showing, both Aristotle and Aquinas are "primitive men" par excellence. Both would presumably have regarded this sort of naïveté as a mark of a sound naturalism and thus of philosophical sophistication. The persistent notion, stemming in one form from Plato, but given new and wider currency in the modern era by Descartes, that the "door of reason" (AT IX-1 212: CSM II 275) opens on a material world and an immaterial self totally unlike the things and persons of everyday experience will be discussed at greater length in the Conclusion. There it will be argued that as Scholastic philosophy is continuous with and derives from common sense in one signification of the expression, so Cartesian metaphysics is intended as the extension of common sense (*le bon sens*) in another.[8]

So much for the extension or denotation of the term 'thought' in Scholastic, seventeenth-century, and contemporary usage. If we wish to find a contemporary English translation of the words *pensée* and *cogitatio* as Descartes applied them, the best rendering is undoubtedly 'consciousness.' Nevertheless, the Latin and French equivalents of 'thought' and 'consciousness' are by no means synonyms for Descartes, who employs *conscius* and *conscientia* in his definitions of *cogitatio* without the slightest circularity. In deference to Descartes's own practice, the translation of *cogitatio* and *pensée* by 'thought' or 'thinking' should be retained, despite the obvious clash with current English usage.[9] Detailed consideration of the exact difference between thought and consciousness in Descartes will be postponed till the next chapter. A few preliminary remarks on the subject may still be in order here as we turn to the intensional meaning of 'thought,' examining Descartes's definition in the context of his general theory of definition.

6.2 Thought and consciousness

Beyond illustrating the extension of the term by means of examples, Descartes's various definitions all highlight one basic feature of anything designated as 'thought': *immediate presence to consciousness*. It is with the intensional meaning of the word 'thought' that each of the two definitions begins: "everything that is within us in such a way that we are immediately conscious of it"; and "everything of which we are conscious as taking place within us insofar as there is a consciousness of it in us." Circularity aside, it is difficult to see what, if anything, this might mean, unless thought and consciousness differ in respect of their objects. To put McRae's first point differently: If 'thought' and 'consciousness' were simply synonymous, then 'I think x' would trivially entail 'I am conscious of x,' and vice versa; whereas in fact 'I think x' non-trivially entails 'I am conscious that I think x,' thought of an object being itself the proper or immediate object of consciousness.[10]

Consciousness belongs to the complex inner structure of thought itself; it is not a 'thought of a thought,' either simultaneous with or subsequent to the thought that is its object, but a constitutive feature of every thought as such. Thus, not only is there "nothing in the mind ... of which it is not conscious (*conscia*)," according to Descartes; this fact is "self-evident (*per se notum*)" (AT VII 246: CSM II 171). Yet while necessarily conscious of whatever it thinks, the mind does not always perceive its own states with sufficient clarity to be able to remember what it thought or even that it was thinking. Thus, when Arnauld raised an objection to the doctrine Descartes had put to Caterus this way (AT VII 107: CSM II 77): "there can be nothing within me which I am in no way conscious of (*nihil in me cuius nullo modo sim conscius, esse posse*)," pointing out that "an infant in its mother's womb has the power of thought, but is not conscious of it" (AT VII 214: CSM II 150), Descartes replied: "we cannot have any thought of which we are not conscious (*conscii*) at the very moment when it is in us. In view of this I do not doubt that the mind begins to think (*cogitare*) as soon as it is implanted in the body of an infant, and that it is immediately conscious of its thought (*suae cogitationis conscia*), even though it does not remember this afterwards because the impressions (*species*) of these thoughts do not remain in the memory" (AT VII 246: CSM II 171f.).[11]

Two separate questions are addressed in this brief passage: whether the mind always thinks and whether it can think without being to any degree conscious that it is thinking. The latter has to do with the intensional meaning of 'thought,' our concern here, the former with Descartes's definition of 'mind' as "a thinking thing" (AT VII 27f.: CSM II 18f.) To Locke's characteristic retort[12] that it is for empirical investigation rather than definition to determine whether the mind always thinks and whether thinking can occur without consciousness of it, Descartes would have rejoined that his defining 'thought' as he does is neither arbitrary nor simply a matter of linguistic convention. Like other explicit definitions he provides, that of thought does not merely elucidate the meaning of the term 'thought'; it serves to circumscribe the "true and immutable nature" (AT VII 64: CSM II 44) of thought itself, at least to the extent that *any* definition can make this clearer than it already is to the reflective individual who "wants to examine things for himself, and to base his judgements about them on his own conceptions" (AT X 523: CSM II 417). What thought is, like what a thing is, or what truth is, is an innate idea for Descartes (cf. AT VII 38: CSM II 26), an immediate deliverance of the "natural light" of reason.

Can then any sort of definition render the meaning of 'thought' clearer? Certainly, logical definitions cannot. In the *Principles*, Descartes writes: "Matters which very simple and self-evident are only rendered more obscure by logical definitions, and should not be counted as items of knowledge which it takes an effort to acquire" (AT VIII-1 8: CSM I 195).[13] By 'logical definitions' Descartes means Scholastic definitions by genus and specific difference. The moratorium on these obviously does not preclude defining 'thought' in another way, as Descartes himself does, in fact, in the immediately preceding article. But just how necessary he took even such a definition as this to be is hard to say. In a letter of August 1641 to Hyperaspistes he writes: "I utterly deny that we do not know ... what thought is, or that I need to teach people this. It is so self-evident that there is *nothing* which could serve to make it any clearer (*ut nihil habeatur per quod clarius explicetur*)" (AT III 426: CSMK 192 e.a.). Of course, since Descartes's definitions begin, "By the word 'thought' (*cogitationis nomine*)," and since they clarify, as we have seen, both the extension and intensional meaning of the term, it will be hard to agree entirely with McRae that they are not concerned with the meaning of the term 'thought' *at all*. But that definitions, on Descartes's theory, are not concerned *only* with meanings is undoubtedly correct, and this is perhaps McRae's point after all.

Because anyone not blinded by prejudice and whose judgment is not perverted by habit must have an "adequate knowledge" of what thought is "whenever he attends to the question" (AT X 523: CSM II 417), Descartes sees no need to define 'thought' in the *Meditations*. Instead, he simply directs attention to what can be immediately understood by anyone who thinks and reflects upon his own thinking so as to attend to what thinking is. This is the strategy pursued throughout the Second Meditation, as Descartes himself attests:

All our ideas of what belongs to the mind have up till now been very confused and mixed up with the ideas of things that can be perceived by the senses. This is the first and most important reason for our inability to understand with sufficient clarity the customary assertions about the soul and God. So I thought I would be doing something worthwhile if I explained *how the properties or qualities of the mind are to be distinguished from the qualities of the body.* Admittedly, many people had previously said that in order to understand metaphysical matters [like the distinction between mind and body] the mind must be drawn away from the senses; but no one, so far as I know, had shown how this could be done. The correct, and in my view unique, method of achieving this is contained in my Second Meditation. (AT VII 131: CSM II 94 e.a.)

This method of "drawing the mind away from the senses" *just is* the explanation of "how the properties or qualities of the mind are to be distinguished from the qualities of the body": turning one's reflexive gaze away from sensible things and directing it back upon what is immediately present to consciousness. The procedure actually followed in the Second Meditation is, of course, embodied in the 'definitions' of the *Principles* and the Second Replies as well; for in addition to the illustrations intended to clarify the extension of 'thought,' the intensional meaning of the term is expressly defined in both places in terms of *immediate presence to consciousness*. It is this that makes them 'definitions' in a distinctively Cartesian sense, quite different from the 'logical definitions' of the Scholastics.[14]

6.3 Cartesian definitions

Turning one's gaze back upon that which is immediately present to consciousness makes possible reflexive attention to what the natural light of reason reveals. This, the principal piece in "detaching the mind from the senses" (cf. section 10.1), is the key to Cartesian definitions as well. At this stage, the point can perhaps be best illustrated by the concept of a cause.

Like the concepts of thought, mind, existence, and so on, the concept 'cause' is an innate idea of a "true and immutable nature" directly disclosed by the natural light of reason. When Caterus urges that for anything to derive its existence 'from itself' in the manner considered in the second version of the Third Meditation proof of God's existence (AT VII 48ff.: CSM 33ff.) it would have to exist prior to itself, Descartes grants that this is indeed how efficient causality is conventionally understood. Thus, it is "impossible for something to be the efficient cause of itself ... when the term 'efficient' is taken to apply only to causes which are prior in time to their effects" (AT VII 108: CSM II 78). Yet "*the natural light does not establish* that the concept of an efficient cause requires that it be prior in time to its effect. On the contrary, the concept of a cause is, *strictly speaking*, applicable only for as long as the cause is producing its effect, and so is *not* prior to it" (ibid., e.a.). The point is reiterated in the Fourth Replies, where the same passage elicited from Arnauld a "sombre warning that 'it will scarcely be possible to find a single theologian who will not object to the proposition that God derives his existence from himself *in a positive sense and as it were causally*'" (AT VII 237: CSM II 166 e.a.). Descartes replies that "the restriction 'prior in time to' can be deleted from the concept while leaving the notion of an efficient cause intact ... the notion of a cause is applicable only during the time when it is producing its effect" (AT VII 240: CSM II 167). In thus defining 'efficient cause' in accordance with the natural light, Descartes understands himself to be furnishing a 'real' definition of a "true and immutable nature," that is, of a cause as something positive; his is not one of the familiar types of 'nominal' definitions (for example, 'stipulative,' 'lexical,' or 'operational'). The latter may indeed be merely negative, that is, derive from the weakness of the human mind. Thus, the negative definition sanctioned by established usage involves (a) temporal priority of the cause to the effect and (b) their non-identity. Surprisingly, Descartes elsewhere calls this the "literal and strict meaning of the phrase 'efficient cause'" (AT VII 109: CSM II 79; cf. also AT VII 239f.: CSM II 167) and the "proper meaning" (AT VII 240: CSM II 167). But, he adds, were those who use 'efficient cause' in this way to "*look at the facts rather than the words*, they would readily observe that the negative sense of the phrase 'from itself' comes merely from the imperfection of the human intellect and has *no basis in reality*" (AT VII 110: CSM II 79 e.a.). So 'strict' means, 'the strict *nominal* definition' as opposed to the true or *real* definition of 'efficient cause' immediately accessible in reflexion on that which is present to consciousness.

In sum, then, there are two definitions of a cause, one nominal, the other real, one negative, the other positive, one based on usage, the other on the natural light:

[I]f we think that a given body derives its existence from itself, we may simply mean that it has no cause; but our claim here is not based on any positive reason, but merely arises in a negative way from our ignorance of any cause. Yet this is a kind of imperfection in us ... Similarly when we say that God derives his existence 'from himself,' we can understand the phrase in the negative sense, in which case the meaning will simply be that he has no cause. But if we have previously enquired into the cause of God's existing or continuing to exist, and we *attend to the immense and incomprehensible power that is contained within the idea of God*, then we will have recognised that this power is so exceedingly great that it is plainly the cause of his continuing existence, and nothing but this can be the cause. And if we say as a result that God derives his existence from himself, we will not be using the phrase in its negative sense but in an *absolutely positive sense*. (AT VII 110: CSM II 79f. e.a.)

If anything, Cartesian real definitions of key metaphysical concepts ('thinking,' 'thing' or 'substance,' 'mind,' 'truth,' 'existence,' 'God,' 'cause,' and so on) are akin to *ostensive* definitions – though the 'pointing' in question is to the immediate datum of intuition, of inner experience, that is, to what is immediately disclosed in reflexive self-awareness when, for example, I think and attend to the fact that I am thinking and that I therefore exist; or when I reflect upon the fact that I am an imperfect, finite, dependent thinking thing, discovering thereby in me the idea of a being whose power is so great "that it can preserve something situated outside itself" and "must *a fortiori* preserve itself by its own power, and hence derive its existence from itself" (AT VII 111: CSM II 80). I can fail to attend to the ideas present to consciousness whenever I think; but if I attend to them sufficiently, I cannot fail to recognize what is contained in them unless blinded by prejudice or enslaved by habit or prevented from doing so by the influence of my body, so that I carelessly misdescribe what is immediately given.[15]

All such concepts being completely self-evident, Descartes makes no attempt to define them in the *Meditations*, but tries instead to effect the appropriate redirection of the intellectual gaze *inward* upon the objects of consciousness. Of the general concept 'cause,' for example, he remarks that those "who follow the sole guidance of the natural light ... spontaneously form a concept ... that is common to both an efficient and a formal cause: that is to say, what derives its existence 'from another' will be taken to derive its existence from that thing as an efficient cause, while what derives its existence 'from itself' will be taken to derive its existence from itself as a formal cause – that is, because it has the kind of essence which entails that it does not require an efficient cause. Accordingly, I did not explain this point in my *Meditations*, but left it out, assuming it was self-evident" (AT VII 238f.: CSM II 166f.). And so too, at bottom, with all the innate ideas just mentioned, whether or not anything approaching a formal definition is to be found in the text.[16]

6.4 Conclusion

The recognition of the inherently self-reflexive character of thinking, the concomitant self-awareness in all object awareness, is a commonplace in philosophical psychology before and after Descartes. It goes back at least as far as Aristotle.

Nor, apparently, was Descartes the first to recognize its potential in putting the sceptics to rout. But epistemology and philosophical psychology aside, Descartes was the first to give the 'epistemic difference' between thought and consciousness its distinctively modern employment in establishing a starting point for a new brand of metaphysics. Within that metaphysics the bearing of the epistemic difference extends beyond the absolutely certain first principle; it underpins a new order of being whose chief feature is the mutual independence of mind and matter ('Cartesian dualism'). As for its subsequent history, 'immediate presence to consciousness,' as Descartes understood it, does not even figure among the five criteria of "the distinction between mental and physical phenomena" painstakingly elaborated by Brentano and culled from the rich resources of nineteenth-century British and German philosophical or "descriptive psychology." The closest Brentano comes to it is his fourth criterion of the mental: "We ... define the mental phenomena as the *exclusive object of inner perception*; they alone, therefore, are perceived with immediate evidence" (Brentano 1973, 97). As it is usually understood, this definition renders the act of thinking the object of another, higher-order act, in direct opposition to Descartes's theory of the mind. Only through meticulous criticism of this doctrine does Brentano find his way to something closely resembling the doctrine of Descartes – whom he does not even mention. The comparison with Brentano is all the more interesting as another feature of thought to which Descartes attached great importance, "*intentional in-existence*, or reference to something as an object" (ibid.), is singled out by Brentano as the "best" criterion (ibid., 98) of all.[17]

These preliminary remarks on Descartes's definition of 'thought' and Cartesian definitions generally have an important bearing upon Descartes's concept of truth (see chapter 12), innateness generally (chapter 18), and 'intuitive induction' (chapter 20). We shall therefore have frequent occasion to return to the subject of Cartesian definitions in what follows.

7

Thought, Consciousness, and 'the *Cogito*'

Talk of 'the *cogito*' as opposed to *cogitatio* or 'thought' places Descartes's analysis of mind squarely within the metaphysical setting described in the Introduction. Since *cogito, ergo sum* is the first item or *principle* of knowledge, since it concerns the *actual existence* of something, and since it is the existence of a *supersensible* or *immaterial* thing that is in question, a substance, the *cogito* is properly *metaphysical* knowledge in that fairly loose sense of 'metaphysics' taken over from the Aristotelian tradition by Descartes. When scholars speak of 'the *cogito*,' they generally have in mind this founding principle of Descartes's metaphysics, in particular the conclusion *sum* or *existo*. The *locus classicus* of 'the *cogito*' in this sense is Descartes's proof of his own existence within the Second Meditation, a passage in which the famous dictum of the *Discourse* and the *Principles* does not even occur. Without quarrelling with the practice of using 'the *cogito*' to designate the principle *cogito, ergo sum* as a whole, it is possible to isolate the first part of Descartes's formula from the rest. This will be done throughout Part One. *Cogito* in this restricted sense is an existential proposition, the first item of absolutely certain knowledge concerning the existence of anything whatever. *Sum*, by contrast, is the first item of knowledge asserting the existence *of a substance*, a thinking *thing*. Thus, the answer to what Scholz termed the "Aristotelian question" (cf. chapter 1 above) is not far to seek. As Descartes explains to Clerselier:

[T]he word 'principle' can be taken in several senses. It is one thing to look for a *common notion* so clear and so general that it can serve as a principle for proving the existence of all the beings, or entities, to be discovered later; and another thing to look for a *being* whose existence is known to us better than that of any other, so that it can serve as a *principle* for discovering them.

In the first sense, it can be said that 'It is impossible for the same thing both to be and not to be at the same time' is a principle which can serve in general, not properly speaking to make known the existence of anything, but simply to confirm its truth once known ...

In the second sense, the first principle is *that our soul exists*, because there is nothing whose existence is better known to us. (AT IV 444: CSMK 290)[1]

The present chapter considers the way in which the *cogito* differs from *cogitatio* generally and the relation of both to what Descartes calls *conscientia*. It accordingly takes 'the *cogito*' as a variable whose values are all members of the class of judgments asserting the actual existence of one's own mental acts or modes of thinking: 'I see,' 'I hear,' 'I feel,' 'I affirm,' 'I doubt,' 'I deny,' and so on. To distinguish this *cogito* from 'the *cogito*' as a designation for Descartes's founding principle as a whole, we shall adopt the convention of using the phrase 'the *cogito* principle' whenever the latter is meant.

7.1 Clear and distinct perception

To determine how the *cogito* differs from *cogitatio* and *conscientia*, a useful starting point is the notion of clear and distinct perception.

According to a number of well-known passages, truth, for Descartes, resides only in judgments.[2] By 'judgment' (*judicium*) Descartes usually means the act of judging (asserting or denying), the psychological or mental phenomenon or event; nevertheless, sometimes – for example, when the conditions of *vera & certa scientia* are in question – he takes 'judgment' in the sense of 'that which is judged,' that is, as the *proposition* asserted or denied, *a truth* within the ordered system of truths he calls *scientia*.[3] To judge truly about anything is at bottom to perform not one but two mental acts, corresponding to the two "principal kinds" of thought distinguished in the *Passions of the Soul*: clear and distinct *perception* (AT VII 35: CSM II 24) and *assent* to all and only that which is clearly and distinctly perceived (AT VII 61f.: CSM II 43). Nevertheless, Descartes applies the term 'judgment' more particularly to the act of assenting, the "determination of the will."[4]

As for the clarity of clear and distinct *perception*, this is above all a matter of what we *attend* to:

I call a perception 'clear' when it is present and accessible to the *attentive* mind – just as we say that we see something clearly when it is present to the eye's gaze and stimulates it sufficiently strongly and openly. I call a perception 'distinct' if, as well as being clear, it is so sharply separated from all other perceptions that it contains within itself only what is clear. (AT VIII-1 22: CSM I 207f. e.a.)

This is from the *Principles*. In the *Meditations* Descartes does not define 'clear' or 'distinct.' That is because he believes that one has only to reflect on one's perception of one's own thought and existence in order to know what 'clear and distinct' means much better than any definition could explain it. Clarity itself counts as one of those things that must be immediately obvious to everyone upon the slightest reflexion: "Some of the things I clearly and distinctly perceive are obvious to everyone, while others are discovered only by those who look more closely and investigate more carefully" (AT VII 68: CSM II 47). But though neither 'clear' nor 'distinct' is defined in the *Meditations*, what reflexion reveals is spelled out rather fully, in a form roughly resembling a definition, in the article of the *Principles* partially cited already.

According to the cited passage, an object is perceived clearly if we are aware of it at all; and the greater our awareness of it, both intensively and extensively, the more clearly we perceive it. Just as an object that is very small or very distant may not stimulate our sense organs sufficiently to produce changes in the bodily organs affected (eye, optic nerve, brain, and so on), so there is a threshold of physiological sensation below which we are simply not consciously aware of those objects whose physical presence impinges on our sense organs via the media of air and light. Above that threshold we may be aware of them only very unclearly (or 'obscurely,' as Descartes says), and so on up, with ever-increasing degrees of clarity, all the way to an awareness that is so very clear that it occupies almost the whole of our attention. It is similar for the ideas of non-sensory objects, like simple mathematical or metaphysical natures. There is a threshold below which even innate ideas are merely latent in our thinking and not actually present to consciousness at all. Though not actually, that is, *explicitly* conscious, they are nevertheless immediately *accessible to consciousness*; they may therefore be called '*unconscious*' in this sense: they are 'potentially' rather than actually, implicitly rather than explicitly, present to consciousness. (On the identity of 'being in the mind *potentiâ* and 'being *implicitly* present to consciousness,' cf. section 18.5 below.) To the extent and degree that we actually become aware of them, such ideas, like our sensible ideas, become clear or clearer.[5] It is a peculiarity of the simple among our mathematical and metaphysical ideas that we cannot attend to them at all without understanding them completely. Like the nature of clarity itself, therefore, such ideas are "obvious to everyone."[6]

So much for clarity. A clear perception is distinct only if (1) *all* the individual perceptions or 'parts' included in it are themselves clear (the objects of actual rather than merely potential conscious awareness); and (2) *nothing* is merely presumed to be thus included in it that is not in fact immediately present to consciousness. The second of these conditions has to do with passing judgment on, the first with attending closely to, what is immediately present to consciousness.[7] When both requirements are fulfilled, the perception is not only clear but sharply distinguished from all others, that is, perfectly distinct.[8] To take a mathematical example employed by Descartes in a related context (cf. AT VII 73: CSM II 51), the perception of a chiliagon is clear to the extent that all (even the remoter geometrical) properties of such a figure are to some degree present to the attentive mind, while it is distinct in so far as it is sharply distinguished from that of a myriagon, say, or any other polygon. We possess clear ideas of both chiliagon and myriagon to the extent that we understand what the words 'chiliagon' and 'myriagon' mean at all, that is, that the one means 'a thousand-sided figure' the other 'a ten-thousand-sided figure.'[9] "For we cannot express anything by our words, when we understand what we are saying, without its being certain thereby that we have in us the [clear] idea of the thing which is signified by our words" (AT III 393: CSMK 185). On the other hand, when we try to picture or imagine them, our perceptions of chiliagon and myriagon are confused. We end up imagining a many-sided figure that could be either of the two (or any of a host of other polygons). The perception, therefore, while somewhat clear, is not distinct. Nevertheless, *parts* of the chiliagon or myriagon can be both clear and distinct even in imagination, just as can parts of material objects given in sense-perception:

[I]f we look from a distance so that our vision almost covers the entire sea at one time, we see it only in a confused manner, just as we have a confused picture of a chiliagon when we take in all its sides at once. But if we fix our gaze on some part of the sea at close quarters, then our view can be clear and distinct, just as our picture of a chiliagon can be, if it is confined to one or two of the sides. (AT VII 113: CSM II 81)

Unlike the chiliagon and geometrical figures generally, many things that we understand clearly and distinctly we just cannot imagine at all. Examples are the ideas of God, of the mind, the 'I' or self that thinks, of 'volition,' 'perception,' and the like.

From these considerations it is plain why "a perception can be clear without being distinct, but not distinct without being clear" (AT VIII-1 22: CSM I 208).[10] The illustration Descartes gives here is a sensation of pain in the foot. The pain is clear but not distinct because, in addition to the acute awareness of the sensation now actually occurring in my mind (which is therefore very clear, flooding my consciousness), I am apt to suppose or judge that there is something in an extramental object, my body, specifically, my foot, which causes this pain and resembles it somehow. So as long as I attend only to my sensation, I perceive the pain very clearly; but when I form a judgment about my foot something unclear creeps in, something that is not actually part of my sensation properly understood, that is, not immediately present to consciousness. As a result, my perception of pain is not distinct but confused. On the other hand, if I refrain from any such judgment, the perception of pain is distinct as well as clear. That is why even sensory ideas can be made clear and distinct through attention to what is actually contained in them and by withholding judgment on all else.

Despite Descartes's choice of this example to illustrate distinctness, the use of the example of a chiliagon or myriagon as understood and as imagined makes an additional point worth noting. For Descartes, most of our clear and distinct perceptions are innate ideas, that is, conceptions of the intellect or reason rather than sensations like pain, colour, texture, and the like. Maximally clear and distinct are mathematical ideas (e.g., square, triangle, chiliagon) and metaphysical ideas (e.g., mind, matter, God, truth), as well as certain 'common notions' or 'axioms,' that is, truths like the mathematical axiom that 'if equals are added to equals the sums are equal' (cf. AT VIII-1 9: CSM I 197), or the metaphysical axioms 'what is done cannot be undone' and 'something cannot come from nothing.' By contrast, the perceptions of the senses have to be *made* clear and distinct by careful attention and by inhibiting the natural tendency to judge that objects somehow resembling those sensations or perceptions exist actually outside the mind and cause the ideas in it. Even then, though, such attention functions not so much as a means of discovering truth as of avoiding error; it is clear and distinct ideas innate in the mind that form the starting points of the "search for truth."

From the perspective of the *cogito* Descartes's example of sensory ideas (like 'pain') made clear and distinct by what the mind attends to and judges is ideally suited to drive home a crucial point. Thought, for Descartes, has a complex structure within which what one thinks and what one is conscious of are different. When we think or perceive things obscurely and confusedly, we attend chiefly to what we are thinking of, extra-mental objects. From infancy on, owing to a "spontaneous impulse" (AT VII 38: CSM II 26) later reinforced by habit and teaching, what arrests our attention are the objects of thinking, principally of sense-perception. But when we think clearly and distinctly about these same things, we turn our attention from what we are thinking of to what we are immediately conscious of; that is, to the actually occurring "operations of the soul" (AT II 36: CSMK 97) or acts themselves of seeing, doubting, judging, desiring, willing, hoping, fearing, and so on. Hence, to think clearly and distinctly about such things is to think in such a way that (1) there is nothing of which we are immediately conscious that we do not also attend to; and that (2) we pass judgment on nothing of which we are not immediately conscious. "There are, however," notes Descartes, "few people who correctly distinguish between what they in fact perceive and what they think they perceive; for not many people are accustomed to clear and distinct perceptions" (AT VII 511: CSM II 348). When we assent to the existence of all and only that of which we are immediately conscious, we judge truly and certainly. The *cogito* of the formula *cogito, ergo sum* stands for any judgment of this kind.[11]

7.2 The sphere of certainty of 'the *cogito*'

Inscribed within judgments of the form *cogito* are four things, each of which is perfectly certain.

First, in thinking anything I am conscious of the actual existence of *the act or operation of the mind*, of the occurrence of thinking, its "actual or formal reality" (AT VII 41: CSM II 28). I am conscious, in other words, of an idea "taken materially, as an operation of the intellect" (AT VII 8: CSM II 7). We have already quoted the remark from the Fourth Replies that "there can be no thought in us of which, at that moment in which it is in us, we are not conscious (*conscii non simus*)" (AT VII 246: CSM II 171). The same point is made in the First Replies: "there can be nothing within me of which I am not in some way conscious (*conscius*) (AT VII 107: CSM II 77). Although 'that which is directly present to consciousness' conveys the strict intensional meaning of the term 'thought,' it is not what we are conscious of that usually engages our attention when we think; for the most part, we do not attend to our thoughts nearly as much as to what we are thinking about, the extra-mental things that are the direct objects of our thinking. But this comparison only provides reason the more for insisting that we are and must always be to some slight degree conscious of our acts whenever we think about objects; for this fact is apt to be overlooked due to a powerful natural propensity of the mind.

Second, I am conscious of the peculiar *act-character* of my act as an act of doubting, of knowing, of willing, or the like. In the dialogue *The Search for Truth*, Descartes's spokesman, Eudoxus, remarks that "in order to know what doubt and thought are, all one need do is to doubt or to think" (AT X 524: CSM II 418). Polyander continues in the same vein: "I can say for sure that I have never doubted what doubt is, though I only began to recognise it, or rather *to give my attention to it*, when Epistemon tried to cast doubt on it" (ibid., e.a.). Earlier on Polyander had defined doubt by asking: "what is doubt if not thinking in a certain kind of way?" (AT X 521: CSM II 415). It is this that Epistemon had attempted to place in question, calling for demonstrations based on definitions. In the *Regulae* Descartes makes a similar point: "it is impossible to form any corporeal idea which represents to us what knowledge or doubt or ignorance is, or the action of the will which may be called 'volition,' and the like; *and yet we have real knowledge of all of these* (*quae tamen omnia revera cognoscimus*), knowledge so easy that in order to possess it all we need is some degree of rationality (*sufficiat, nos rationis esse participes*)" (AT X 419: CSM I 44f. e.a.). According to this, we know what knowledge, doubt, and volition are the moment we actually know, doubt, or will anything, thereby experiencing inwardly, that is, becoming *conscious* of, volition, for example, be it the peculiar spontaneity of the will in assenting to the clearly and distinctly perceived in knowledge, or the will's peculiar 'indifference,' its wavering, in doubt and ignorance. The fact that we have no corporeal idea of the imagination that *represents* it is no reason to suppose that we do not know exactly what volition is at the precise moment when an act of volition is *present* to consciousness.[12]

In section 9.2 fuller consideration will be given the almost casual way in which Descartes links self-awareness and rationality in this passage of the *Regulae*. Two items remain in the enumeration of all that is contained within the sphere of certainty of the *cogito*.

Thus far we have seen that in every mental act I am immediately conscious of (1) the occurrence of an act and of (2) its specific act-character. Third, I am immediately conscious of the occurrence of such an act *as taking place 'in me,'* that is, that *I* am thinking, of the *ego* as thinking 'subject': "Is it not one and the same 'I' who is now doubting almost everything, who nonetheless understands some things, who affirms that this one thing is true [viz., 'I exist'], denies everything else, desires to know more, is unwilling to be deceived, imagines many things even involuntarily, and is aware of many things that apparently come from the senses (*multa etiam tanquam a sensibus venientia animadverto*)?" (AT VII 28: CSM II 19). The answer is not long in coming: "The fact that it is I who am doubting, understanding and willing is *so evident that I see no way of making it any clearer*. But it is also the case that the 'I' who imagines is the same 'I' ... Lastly, it is also the same 'I' who has sensory perceptions, or is aware of bodily things as it were through the senses (*qui res corporeas tanquam per sensus animadverto*)" (AT VII 28: CSM II 19 e.a.). And in the Sixth Meditation: "it is one and the same 'I' who has sensory perceptions, or is aware of bodily things as it were through the senses (*qui res corporeas tanquam per sensus animadverto*)" (AT VII 29: CSM II 19 e.a.). This distinction between the modes of thinking and the 'I' that thinks is simply self-evident for Descartes: "hence I perceive that the distinction between them [the modes of imagination and sensory perception] and myself corresponds to the distinction between the modes of a thing and the thing itself" (AT VII 78: CSM II 54). This latter distinction is self-explanatory. Although the first use of the word 'substance' in the *Meditations* is in reference to a material substance (and a rather lowly one at that), Descartes as quickly applies it to the 'I':

For example, I think that a stone is a substance, or is a thing capable of existing independently, and I also think that I am a substance. Admittedly I conceive of myself as a thing that thinks and is not extended, whereas I conceive of the stone as a thing that is extended and does not think, so that the two conceptions differ enormously; but they seem to agree with respect to the classification 'substance.' (AT VII 44: CSM 30)

A little later he hints broadly at the subjective origin of the very concept of substance: "It is true that I have the idea of substance in me in virtue of the fact that I am a substance" (AT VII 45: CSM II 31), that is, in virtue of the fact that I am immediately conscious of myself as existing independently, as a thinking *thing*.

We shall return to the third after adding a fourth and final item to the list of things immediately given as included in the *cogito*: whenever I think anything I am conscious of *what* I am thinking of, that I am thinking *of x*, the intentional object of my act. Although "there can be no ideas that are not as it were of things" (AT VII 44: CSM II 30), this is true primarily of those ideas that Descartes describes as *tanquam rerum imagines*, "images of things, as it were." To these alone "the term 'idea' is strictly appropriate – for example when I think of a man, or a chimera, or the sky, or an angel, or God" (AT VII 37: CSM II 25). The intentional objects of such ideas are for the most part *res*, that is, either actually existing or non-existent (but possible) objects of representational acts of sense-perception, imagining, and conceiving. But the objects of such ideas may also be *non res* (AT VII 43; 44: CSM II 30), 'unreal things,' for example, cold, rest, darkness, ignorance, and the like; for the latter, though perhaps merely privations rather than anything real or positive, are nevertheless represented as though they were something positive. From this it is clear that 'unreal' has a meaning quite different from 'non-existent.' Reflecting on the idea of God, for example, Descartes remarks that "although perhaps one may imagine that such a being does not exist, it cannot be supposed that the idea of such a being represents something unreal (*nihil reale exhibere*), as I said with regard to the idea of cold" (AT VII 46: CSM II 31f.).[13] Yet some of our sensory ideas are so obscure and confused that we cannot even be sure that *what* they represent is really something positive rather than nothing, a mere absence of something; that is why Descartes distinguishes them in the *Meditations* from those sensory ideas like colours, odours, tastes, and so on, which clearly represent something positive that at least could exist really outside the mind as it exists intentionally in it.[14]

The acts by which objects – real or unreal, existing or non-existent – are represented may involve *imagines*, as does the act of representing a chimera (part lion, part goat, part serpent) by means of visual imagery. Or such acts may be only *tanquam rerum imagines*, for instance, the act of conceiving God by means of the pure intellect, in which no mental imagery of any kind is involved, though the acts in question are still 'representational,' that is, directed toward an intentional object. Both are accordingly 'ideas' in Descartes's strict sense. However, even those acts that are not ideas in this sense still *involve* representation of an intentional object: "thus when I will, or am afraid, or affirm, or deny, there is always a particular thing which I take as the object of my thought (*aliquam rem ut subiectum mei cogitationis apprehendo*)" (AT VII 37: CSM II 26). Here it is worth noting

Descartes's use of the word *repraesentare* (or, synonymously, *exhibere*) in the Third Meditation passage where he takes stock of his ideas with a view to the proof of God's existence: "Among my ideas, apart from the idea which gives me a representation of myself (*quae me ipsum mihi exhibit*) [as a man or human being], ... there are ideas which variously represent (*repraesentant*) God, corporeal and inanimate things, angels, animals and finally other men like myself. As far as concerns the ideas which represent (*exhibent*) other men, or animals, or angels ... etc." (AT VII 42f.: CSM II 29). 'Representation,' for Descartes, has nothing to do with the formation of an image and everything to do with the intentional relatedness of thought to an object.[15]

The fourth item can briefly be circumscribed as follows. Representation of an object belongs to all thought as such in virtue of that specific class of thoughts, termed 'ideas' in the strict sense, that are basic to volitions, emotions, and judgments, bestowing on them their intentional relatedness to an object. Consciousness (*conscientia*), by contrast, does not represent anything; thought that represents objects is not itself the object of representation but is immediately *present* to consciousness. Being thus present to consciousness, thinking *can* also be represented; for example, an idea or thought of myself as a substance or mind (and not just as a human being, a psycho-physical entity) *can* be derived from the immediate consciousness that I have of myself as a thinking thing simply by attending to what I am in the first instance immediately or non-representationally aware of. Nevertheless, the non-representational consciousness of myself and the representational idea of myself are, for Descartes, distinct modes of self-awareness.[16]

7.3 *Istud nescio quid mei*

This completes the list of everything contained within the sphere of certainty of the *cogito*. Most of these points have been made in two separate studies by McRae (1972b, 57f. and 1976, 10ff.). In the later of the studies, McRae takes Furth (1967) and others to task for failing to appreciate fully the complex inner structure of the *cogito*. Furth echoes a familiar criticism (found, McRae notes, in sources as disparate as Russell and Sartre) when he asserts that the third of these elements, the *ego*, cannot properly belong to the Cartesian *cogito*, adding that the distinction between act and intentional object is likewise one that Descartes can no longer consistently maintain after the pervasive doubt of existence in the First Meditation. This is entirely mistaken. McRae probably singled Furth out among many who have criticized Descartes in both ways because Furth developed a notation for the analysis of the structure of the Cartesian *cogito* that McRae wished to employ against these and similarly misplaced criticisms. Below (section 8.1) an alternate notation will be introduced, adapted from Husserl and Heidegger; it may prove better suited to McRae's purpose. In this and the next section we consider Furth's two criticisms in detail, starting with the inclusion of the *ego* within the sphere of certainty.[17]

In several Latin formulations, notably in the *Principles* and the Second Replies, Descartes expressly includes the *ego* in the statement of the first principle of his philosophy: *ego cogito, ergo sum* (AT VIII-1 7 and 8: CSM I 195 and 196; AT VII 140: CSM II 100), though its inclusion is grammatically unnecessary. Whoever prepared the Latin translation of the *Discourse* that appeared in 1644 was probably aware of these passages, for the famous *je pense, donc je suis* is translated in just this way. Gilson is surely right in remarking that the *ego* is not so much added in this Latin translation (AT VI 558) as suppressed in the original French version of the *Discourse*; for to make the force of the Latin *ego* comparably perceptible to the French ear Descartes would have had to resort to something as clumsy as "*Moi, qui pense, je suis*" (1947a, 292). This is precisely what the context calls for and what the Latin expresses so well. For considering next what exactly he knew this 'I' to be, he continues: "I knew I was *a substance* (*une substance*; Latin: *rem quandam sive substantiam*) whose whole essence or nature is solely to think."[18]

In a letter to Mersenne of July 1641, Descartes again makes a point of the absence of any corporeal idea of the imagination, this time in reference to the *ego* or the soul that thinks rather than the act-character of its acts:

> [T]he soul is nothing but a thing which thinks, and so it is impossible for us ever to think of anything without at the same time having the idea *of our soul as a thing* capable of thinking of whatever we think of. It is true that a thing of such a nature cannot be imagined, that is, cannot be represented by a corporeal image ... But that does not make it any less *conceivable* ... (AT III 394: CSMK 186 e.a.)

Here 'conceivable' means 'directly intuitable as immediately given,' 'immediately present to consciousness' along with the act and its act-character.

For Descartes, in short, it is no less immediately conceivable or intuitively evident that it is a thing or substance that is now doubting, now willing, and so forth, than that this operation of the mind called 'doubting' differs markedly from that called 'volition.' Nevertheless, the notion of an *ego* or 'I,' an immaterial self that is immediately given in and with every act of thinking, has drawn the fire of Descartes's critics almost from the start. There were those who pressed the objection that what does the thinking might be corporeal in some important respect. This is Hobbes's response: "it may be that the thing that thinks is the subject to which mind, reason or intellect belong; and this subject may thus be something corporeal. The contrary is assumed, not proved" (AT VII 173: CSM II 122).

Gassendi voices a similar objection: "You say: 'I know I exist; and knowledge (*notitia*) of this thing taken strictly cannot depend on that of which I am unaware (*quod non novi*).' Fair enough; but remember that you have not yet made certain that you are not air or a vapour or something else of this sort" (cf. AT VII 265: CSM II 185; cf. also AT IX-1 207: CSM II 272).[19] Gassendi is perfectly satisfied that the existence of the mind is established by its changing perceptions; this, "at all events, is something which no one questions" (AT VII 275: CSM II 192). But not only has its alleged incorporeality not been demonstrated, its "internal substance" has not been characterized in any *positive* manner at all:

I do not see how you can deduce or 'know plainly' that anything more can be perceived concerning your mind beyond the fact that it exists ... what, after all your efforts, have you told us about yourself? You are not a bodily structure, you are not air, not a wind, not a thing which walks or senses, you are not this and not that. Even if we grant these results ..., they are not what we are waiting for. They are simply negative results; but the question is not what you are not, but what you are ... What we are unclear about, what we are looking for, is that inner substance of yours whose property is to think ... Your conclusion should ... tell us not that you are a thinking thing, but what sort of thing this 'you' who thinks really is ... You should carefully scrutinise yourself and conduct a kind of chemical investigation of yourself, if you are to succeed in uncovering and explaining to us your internal substance. (AT VII 275ff.: CSM II 192f.)

Just who is begging the question here should be obvious enough.[20]

Coming at the alleged givenness of the *ego* from the later wax example, Gassendi voices a further objection. Descartes himself pointed the way for this perennial criticism when he spoke, in a patently ironic mode, of *istud nescio quid mei, quod sub imaginationem non venit* (AT VII 29).[21] Writes Gassendi: "just as your conclusions about the wax merely establish your perception of the existence of your mind and not its nature, so all your other considerations will fail to establish any result beyond this. If you aim to deduce anything further from your perception of the substance of the wax or other things, your only valid conclusion will be that since our conception of this substance [i.e., the wax] is merely a confused perception of something, we know not what (*quemadmodum substantiam illam confuse solum & nescio quid concipimus*), the same applies to our conception of the mind. Hence you may well repeat your earlier phrase *illud nescio quid tui*" (AT VII 275: CSM II 191f.) Later he applies this directly to the mind: "although you recognise that you are thinking, you still do not know what kind of thing you, who are thinking, are. And since it is only this operation that you know (*nota sit*), the most important element is still hidden from you (*lateat*), namely the substance which performs this operation" (AT VII 338: CSM II 234). Locke and company were to echo Descartes's reference to a certain 'I know not what' with an irony very different from Descartes's, applying it, as had Gassendi, to the notion of corporeal substance as well:

> [I]f any one will examine himself concerning his *Notion of pure Substance in general,* he will find he has no other *Idea* of it at all, but only a Supposition of *he knows not what* support of such Qualities as are commonly called Accidents. If any one should be asked, what is the subject wherein Colour or Weight inheres, he should have nothing to say, but the solid extended parts: And if he were demanded, what is it, that that Solidity and Extension inhere in, he would not be in a much better case, than the *Indian* ... who, saying that the World was supported by a great Elephant, was asked, what the Elephant rested on; to which his answer was, a great Tortoise: But being again pressed to know what gave support to the broad-back'd Tortoise, replied, something, *he knew not what.*[22]

For both sorts of critic of the givenness of an *ego* whose nature is self-evident great importance attaches to a consideration ('unimaginability') that Descartes treats with veiled derision, sometimes with open scorn: "to say 'I will use my imagination to get to know more distinctly what I am' would seem to be as silly as saying 'I am now awake, and see some truth; but since my vision is not yet clear enough, I will deliberately fall asleep so that my dreams may provide a truer and clearer representation' (*ut hoc ipsum mihi somnia verius evidentiusque repraesentent*)" (AT VII 28: CSM II 19). As the letter to Mersenne makes clear, this 'I know not what,' though not picturable in the imagination, is nevertheless very distinctly "conceivable" by the pure intellect; and cognitively speaking, the conceivable is to the imaginable roughly as waking experience is to the phantasms of dreams. Or so, at least, maintains Descartes.[23]

Criticism of the inclusion of the 'I' in the *cogito* ('*I* think' rather than 'there are thoughts' or 'there is thinking') has by no means been confined to materialists like Hobbes and Gassendi or empiricists like Locke and Hume.[24] Among contemporary commentators, some have retreated from this interpretation of Descartes altogether, while others regard Descartes's position as unclear. Yet from the earliest formulations of the argument for the immateriality of the soul in the *Discourse* and the letter to Silhon of May 1637, Descartes treats the givenness of the thinking self as an incorporeal substance as an irrefragable datum no less intuitively certain in the highest degree than the occurrence of the modes of thinking themselves.[25]

7.4 Intentional and real objects

Descartes's analysis of thinking may seem less open to attack on the last item included within the sphere of certainty of the *cogito*, the intentional object, than the third. Furth is certainly mistaken about the scope of the apparently all-corroding doubt of the First Meditation. It is true that the mind that is immediately conscious of its thinking typically thinks something other than it is conscious of. Along with what is in the mind and immediately present to consciousness we are usually aware of things not literally in the mind at all, namely material objects, including our own bodies. Though we may speak figuratively even of physical objects as that which we have 'in mind,' only what is in the mind actually or 'formally' is immediately present to consciousness in Descartes's sense; everything else, if anything else exists, is 'outside' the mind ('extra-mental'). Hence, only what is in the mind literally, as an actual mode of thinking, may be asserted to exist with that degree of certainty which distinguishes the *cogito* from other existential statements. But this is undeniably true of the intentional though not of the real or extra-mental object of thinking – provided 'intentional object' is understood in the sense of what Descartes, following traditional usage, calls the 'objective reality' of the act (or idea) itself. What the universal doubt of the First Meditation calls into question are the things themselves as *res*, actually existing things and essences outside the mind, not the intentional relatedness of acts to these same *res* as intentional objects (*cogitata*).[26]

While it plainly follows from Descartes's definition of thought that the things we think of, the objects of sense-perception, for example, are only mediately present to consciousness, this cannot mean that we do not perceive them directly but only through the intermediary of our perceptions. Rather, to say of something, x, the immediate object of sense-perception, that it is only mediately present to consciousness is just another way of saying that a sensory perception having x as its intentional object is immediately present to consciousness, that is, really exists in the mind. The notion that we cannot think of or perceive objects existing outside the mind directly, but only indirectly, via our ideas, is one of the most serious obstacles to a correct understanding of Descartes's analysis of mind. Descartes himself is by no means blameless in fostering this misconception (cf. section 16.1ff., where the attempt is made to unravel his confusing use of the term 'idea'); but despite certain indications to the contrary he quite clearly never espoused the view so frequently ascribed to him.[27]

7.5 'The *cogito*' as *cogitatio* in the phenomenologically reduced sense

Because thought has the complex structure 'I am conscious that I am thinking something,' it is possible, by turning attention away from external things, to become certain of the existence and nature of one's own thoughts as modes of an immaterial substance. That is why all species of thought are equally capable of occupying the place of the *cogito* in Descartes's formula, even those having external or extra-mental objects. Still, when, for example, instead of "I am now seeing light, hearing a noise, feeling heat" (AT VII 29: CSM II 19), I say "I *seem* to see, to hear, and to be warmed" (ibid.), the original judgment undergoes a change in meaning. The modified judgment bears, not on the object of thought, but on the object of attention to what is immediately present to consciousness. By his own admission, Descartes does not always "distinguish the two" (AT VII 33: CSM II 22), does not always distinguish, for example, between 'I see the wax' and 'I think I see the wax' (ibid.). But that is because, from the Second Meditation on, the "blind impulse" (AT VII 40: CSM II 27) to refer our ideas, volitions, emotions and judgments to things or causes outside the mind is methodically held in check.[28]

This suspension or inhibition of the perfectly natural though philosophically naive belief in the existence of objects outside the mind has been termed *epochē* (cf. Husserl 1970). To the extent that Descartes practises something like *epochē* in the Second through Fifth Meditations, all other judgments are 'phenomenologically reduced' to the form *cogito*.

It might be objected that the *cogito* cannot stand for a form of judging since, as was just observed, any mode of thought, whether judging, perceiving, willing, or holding in aversion, can occupy the place of the *cogito* without altering the sense of the formula, *cogito, ergo sum*. This objection correctly stresses the fact that the *cogito* of Descartes's founding principle has the function of a variable. While it is true that the values of the variable can belong to any of the categories of thinking instanced in Descartes's definition of thought, the variable itself ('I am conscious that I am thinking x') belongs to that of judgments or acts of judging: for every assigned value of 'thinking x,' *cogito* asserts the actual existence of just that mode of thought. Since x (an object that exists or may exist outside the mind) may include the movements of one's own body, 'I think that I am seeing, breathing, walking, etc.' are possible values of *cogito* too, though 'I am seeing,' 'I am breathing,' 'I am walking,' and so on are not. Thus, in *Principles*, I, 9, Descartes writes:

[I]f I say 'I am seeing, or I am walking, therefore I exist,' and take this as applying to vision or walking as bodily activities, then the conclusion is not absolutely certain. This is because, as often happens during sleep, it is possible for me to think I am seeing or walking, though my eyes are closed and I am not moving about; such thoughts might even be possible if I had no body at all. But if I take 'seeing' or 'walking' to apply to the actual sense or consciousness (*conscientia*) of seeing or walking, then the conclusion is quite certain, since it relates to the mind, which alone has the sensation or thought that it is seeing or walking. (AT VIII-1 7f.: CSM I 195)

In a letter to Reneri (for Pollot) of April 1638 Descartes makes what is essentially the same point, while underscoring the *reducibility* of all other judgments to the form of the variable *cogito*: "When someone says 'I am breathing, therefore I am,' if he wants to prove he exists from the fact that there cannot be breathing without existence, he proves nothing" (AT II 37f.: CSMK 98). He proves nothing because, though the inference is formally valid, the premise 'I am breathing' is subject to doubt. "But," Descartes continues,

if he wants to infer his existence from the feeling or opinion (*du sentiment ou de l'opinion*) he has that he is breathing, so that he judges that even if the opinion was untrue he could not have it if he did not exist, then his inference is sound. For in such a case *the thought of breathing is present to our mind* [i.e., engages our attention] before the thought of our existing, and we cannot doubt that we have it while we have it. To say 'I am breathing, therefore I am' in this sense [i.e., I *think, believe, feel that I* am breathing, therefore I am], is *nothing other than* saying 'I think, therefore I am'; and if one pays attention, one finds that all other propositions from which we can thus prove our existence *reduce to* (*reviennent à*) this same one [i.e., *cogito*]. (ibid., e.a.)

'I am breathing' (and so on) can (and, if certainty is to be achieved regarding something's existence, must) be reduced to 'I think that I am breathing,' where breathing is an operation of the body and hence an external object of thought, while the thought that I am breathing is an "operation of the soul" immediately present to consciousness. Since all statements about external objects are thus reducible – though not 'without remainder,' that is, not without a profound shift in meaning – to statements about *cogitationes* of one kind or another, the *cogito* is a variable whose possible values are the reduced forms of all such statements; that is, a variable whose values are statements about thoughts of all the different varieties distinguished in Descartes's definition of thought. Consequently, the range of mental phenomena whose actual existence is expressible in judgments of the form *cogito* coincides exactly with that designated by the substantive *cogitatio*.

Hintikka claims that the *cogito* "cannot be replaced by any arbitrary verb" (1962, 123), say, *ambulo* or *video*. This much is borne out by the letter to Reneri just cited, but also by a well-known passage of the Replies to the Fifth Set of Objections: "When you say that I 'could have made the same inference from any one of my other actions,'" writes Descartes to Gassendi,

you are far from the truth, since I am not wholly certain of any of my actions, with the sole exception of thought ... I may not, for example, make the inference 'I am walking, therefore I exist,' except in so far as the consciousness of walking is a thought (*nisi quatenus ambulandi conscientia cogitatio est*). The inference is certain only if applied to this consciousness, and not to the movement of the body which sometimes – in the case of dreams – is not occurring at all, despite the fact that I seem to myself to be walking. Hence from the fact that I think I am walking I can very well infer the existence of a mind that has this thought, but not the existence of a body that walks. (AT VII 352: CSM II 244)

For Hintikka, in so far as the *cogito, ergo sum* is (1) "an expression of the logical truth of sentences of the form" B(a) $\supset$ (Ex)(x = a), the "word *cogito* may ... be replaced by any other word which refers to one of my acts of consciousness" (ibid., 131f.), that is, of thinking. But in so far as the *cogito* serves (2) "to express the existential self-verifiability of the sentence 'I exist'" (ibid.), it "cannot ... be an instance of arbitrary mental activity, say of willing or of feeling," since these do not involve "an attempt to think in the sense of making myself believe" (ibid., 123); in other words, *cogito* "cannot be replaced by any arbitrary verb which refers to some act of one's immediate consciousness" (ibid., 136). On this, the "most interesting interpretation" (121) of Descartes's insight, the verb *cogitare* must be "interpreted rather narrowly. The word *cogito* may still be replaced by such 'verbs of intellection' as *dubito* (or *profero*), but not any longer by verbs referring to arbitrary mental acts, such as *volo* or *sentio*" (132).[29]

Other difficulties aside, this sense of *cogito* is difficult to square with the examples most frequently given (which include, *inter alia*, volitions and feelings), both in the key passages of the Second Meditation (AT VII 28f.: CSM II 19) and elsewhere, including the reply to Gassendi just cited.[30] However, it remains open to Hintikka to treat all such counter-examples as instances of the first and broader sense of *cogito*, so that his position, however mistaken, may be irrefutable on textual grounds.

7.6 Descartes's 'table of judgments'

The foregoing interpretation of the extension of the *cogito* might be contrasted with Hintikka's in this way: *cogito* stands for all *first-person singular* judgments having as their referents the *now actually occurring* mental acts, states, or experiences of some mind in so far as they are *clearly and distinctly perceived*. Being in their phenomenologically reduced form, such judgments differ in a crucial respect from the following classes of judgments about entities outside the mind:

(a) second- and third-person singular and plural mental-act judgments ('you think,' 'he sees,' 'God wills,' and so on);[31]
(b) first-person singular judgments about mental acts not now actually occurring ('I thought,' 'felt,' 'shall conceive,' and so on);[32]

(c) first-person singular judgments about acts other than mental acts ('I walk,' 'I breathe,' 'I see the table,' where 'seeing' is something I do with my bodily sense organs rather than the mind alone;[33]

(d) all judgments concerning material things, whether understood as predicative, existential, or both ('the table is round,' 'the table exists').[34]

By his own admission, Descartes, in the Second through Fifth Meditations, does not distinguish any longer between judgments of type (a) to (d) like 'I see the wax' or 'the wax is hard' and corresponding judgments of the form *cogito*, 'I think I see the wax' or 'the wax feels hard to me,' thanks to a standing phenomenological reduction of all judgments to the basic form *cogito*.[35] This is the point of the comment in the Replies to the Fifth Set of Objections: "I was not here [that is, in the Second Meditation] dealing with sight and touch, which occur by means of bodily organs, but was concerned solely with the thought of seeing and touching, which, as we experience every day in our dreams, does not require these organs" (AT VII 360: CSM II 249). Note that here Descartes does not say that he was "not distinguishing" the two. Putting the point less ambiguously, he says that he was dealing only with the latter (to which the former had been reduced). Later in the same set of Replies he responds favourably to Gassendi's observation that even in "cases where doubt is permissible, at least we may not doubt that the things appear to us in such and such a way: it cannot but be wholly true that they appear as they do ... Reason may indeed persuade us not to accept much of what nature impels us to believe, but at least it cannot take away the truth of the appearances or the *phenomena*" (AT VII 333f.: CSM II 231 e.a.). Although prone to contemptuousness where Gassendi is concerned, Descartes can only commend him for this observation, which aptly embodies the spirit of the phenomenological reduction: "But when you come round to saying that 'at least we may not doubt that things appear as they do,' you are back on the right road: I made this very assertion in the Second Meditation" (AT VII 386: CSM II 264f.).[36]

To arrive at a complete classification of all types of judgment or truth at least tacitly recognized by Descartes we need only add the following to (a) through (d):

(e) the axioms or simple truths of logic and mathematics as well as the most basic laws of nature and the metaphysical principles of the 'natural light' (that is, the 'eternal truths' in the sense of *Principles*, I, 48); and

(f) first-person singular mental-act judgments of the type *cogito*.

While Leibniz, Hume, and Kant concerned themselves with the classification of truths or judgments in the sense of propositions, Descartes focuses upon the truth of the various judgment-types distinguished here primarily as *acts* of asserting or denying, that is, as statements, though 'statements' construed as thought-rather than speech-acts. This peculiarity of the type of judgment for which the *cogito* stands has attracted a good deal of attention and been made the focus of certain influential interpretations of the *cogito, ergo sum* as embodying an insight into the logical behaviour of *cogito* or *existo* as a self-referential or "existentially self-verifying" statement or "performance" (cf. Ayer 1956, Hintikka 1962, Williams 1962). For convenience in the Cartesian context, we may at times employ the term 'assertion' and its cognates rather than 'statement.' Descartes focuses upon the truth of judgments primarily as statements rather than propositions, but not exclusively. As noted earlier, he conceives *scientia* as consisting of propositions. The truths of mathematics as well as the metaphysical principles of the natural light can be taken either as *scientia* or as what Descartes calls *persuasio* (on this distinction, see section 11.2ff.). The same is true of the *cogito, ergo sum.* As we shall see later, this is of great importance in assessing the certainty of the *sum* and the force of the charge of circularity brought against Descartes's use of the truth rule.[37]

Admittedly, Descartes nowhere differentiates among judgments in terms corresponding exactly to the 'table of judgments' just elaborated. Still, it is by classes rather than individually that, in the First Meditation, he examines and rejects the types of opinion formerly held to be "most true" (AT VII 18: CSM II 12). The two broad classes of judgments considered there correspond to the two *principia* (ibid.) on which all his former beliefs rested: the senses and the intellect. Within the domain of the intellect he considers and rejects, first, the propositions of pure physics concerning "corporeal nature in general, and its extension; the shape of extended things, the quantity or size and number of these things; the place in which they may exist, the time through which they may endure, and so on" (AT VII 20: CSM II 14). He then rejects the propositions of "arithmetic, geometry, and other subjects of this kind, which deal only with the simplest and most general things, regardless of whether they really exist in nature" (ibid.). As for the belief in an omnipotent benevolent God, this falls within the sphere of beliefs "acquired either from the senses or through the senses (*per sensus*)," the senses being the source of all that has been learned "through hearsay" (*per auditum*).[38] Corresponding to Descartes's two *principia*, items (a) through (e) fall into two broad categories: empirical truths that are contingent and knowable only through sense-experience and reliance on the memory (a–d); and necessary truths, knowable by the intellect alone (e). Among the latter, theological truths have a special status. The *sum* (f), or *cogito, ergo sum*, on the other hand, represents a third and distinctive class of truths, being logically contingent and yet in certain sense necessary. Necessary truth is the subject of Part Two.[39]

8

The Structure of Thought

The extension of *cogitatio* in its original and phenomenologically reduced senses marks out the domain of the certainly existent within the larger totality of the putatively so. The question of the precise intensional meaning of 'thought' is again a metaphysical rather than merely terminological matter for Descartes: by the use to which he put the terms 'thought' and 'consciousness,' Descartes articulates the essential structure of thought as the principal attribute of thinking substance. In the previous chapter the constitutive elements within the structural totality of thinking were only enumerated as distinct items within the sphere of absolute certainty of the *cogito*. The chief task of this chapter is to present them as Descartes in fact conceived them, within the unity of a single embracing structure. For this a suitable notation is required, one more apt than Furth's to consolidate the distinctions drawn above and to forestall the errors pointed out by McRae.

Such a notation is in fact readily available. Husserl's term for Descartes's generic *cogitatio* or *pensée* is *Bewußtsein*, 'consciousness,' while *cogitationes* or *modi cogitandi* are, in Husserl's vocabulary, *Akte* or *Erlebnisse*, mental 'acts' or 'act-experiences.'[1] Equivalences between other items in Husserl's and Descartes's vocabularies can be readily established once the basic structure of thought has been elaborated with the help of the later notation. The immediate task is to set out clearly, in terms other than Descartes's own, four fundamental distinctions first drawn by Descartes but fully developed only much later by Husserl and his school. In Part Three (chapters 15 and 16) we shall consider the way in which Descartes formulated these same distinctions using the traditional terminology at his immediate disposal. While this should allay any misgivings about possible anachronism (see section 8.3 below), some textual obstacles to the interpretation developed in this and the previous chapter will still have to be faced (section 8.4).

8.1 A notation

In a course of lectures on Nietzsche held in 1940, Heidegger remarks that for Descartes *"cogito* is *cogito me cogitare"*: 'I think that I am thinking' (Heidegger 1961, II, 158; cf. also 1994, 132, 255, 261). In *Being and Time* (1927) the same formula occurs in somewhat expanded form: *cogito me cogitare rem* (Heidegger 1977, 572). Modifying this slightly in accordance with a suggestion of Husserl (1960, 33 and 1964, 12), *cogito* may be taken as shorthand for *ego cogito me cogitare cogitatum*: 'I think that I am thinking something (thought of).' Descartes's inclusion of the *ego* in the sphere of certainty of the *cogito* has been discussed already. As for the amplifying phrase *me cogitare,* this does not refer to a complete mental act upon which another, higher-order act supervenes; that, as Descartes clearly recognized, could lead to an infinite regress. It merely sets off one constitutive element within the complex internal structure of the mental act or event. Any such event is an act of self-conscious awareness of one's *thinking (cogitare)* as that of an *ego (me)* as well as of the act-character of the act (for example, *me percipere, dubitare,* and so on) and of something thought (*cogitatum*). This is so even without reflecting upon our experiences, as we sometimes do, in special, higher-order acts. Moreover, it is a necessary condition of our ability to attend explicitly to what is in the mind, for only that of which one is already implicitly conscious can be made an explicit object of reflexive awareness through expressly attending to it.[2]

Even when the first-order mental acts or experiences of which I am self-consciously aware in 'living' a particular segment of my conscious life are not made the objects either of higher-order acts or of heightened reflexive attention, they remain immediately present to consciousness. The object in this Pickwickian sense, the first-order act of thinking, must be sharply distinguished from the objects of thinking in the everyday reach-me-down sense in which we speak of a variety of other things, but not usually our now actually occurring psychic states, as objects. Each actually occurring mental act in which an object is represented is itself, as act, *present* to consciousness; it is not *re*presented by another, higher-order act, and this in turn by another, and so on ad infinitum. Nor, however, does the chain simply stop, inexplicably, at the second-order act; though they *can* become the objects of other acts, mental acts are not in the first instance represented but simply present to consciousness. As thus immediately present to consciousness they are objects in a special sense. With a view to that subclass of mental acts that Descartes designates as 'ideas' in the strict sense,[3] we can say: representational acts (ideas) represent; their objects are represented; the acts themselves are not represented but immediately present to consciousness, while their extramental objects are represented but not immediately present to consciousness.

Take, for example, seeing the table. Seeing is a representational act. It represents (in this case) the table. It is not itself *re*presented (say, by another act), but is immediately present to consciousness. The table, on the other hand, is not present to consciousness (in the mind) at all, but only represented.

Of course the represented object or *cogitatum*, that about which I am thinking, need not be an actually existing material object like the table. It may be some other, now no longer actual, bit of my own conscious experience; or it may be the actual or possible experience of another mind; it may, as in the example, be an actually existing or a merely possible material thing; or, finally, it may be something physically or even logically impossible. This represented object has been called, following Husserl (who borrows the term from Brentano and the Scholastics), the 'intentional object' of the act. To say that such an object is 'in the mind' is simply equivalent to saying that an act that represents it is in the mind in the literal sense in which an actually occurring item or bit of conscious experience is really there. But to say of the object *as distinct from* the act that it is 'in the mind' can only mean that it is the intentional object, not a constitutive state, of conscious experience; in other words, that, although not a real constituent of the mind's current state, it is the thing *intended* (sensed, imagined, thought about, doubted, desired, willed, and so on) in such acts or such experiences as *do* constitute the actually occurring parts, episodes, and phases within the 'stream of consciousness.'

That intentional existence (or 'inexistence') in the mind in no way implies actual existence outside it is plain from the fact that the intentional object of an act may not actually exist at all, may not even be physically possible, or may be logically impossible. Regardless of whether the object is actual, however, the act at least exists: "as I have noted before, even though the objects of my sensory experience and imagination may have no existence outside me, nonetheless the modes of thinking which I refer to as cases of sensory perception and imagination, in so far as they are simply modes of thinking, do exist within me – of that I am certain" (AT VII 34f.: CSM II 24). Should the object of the act exist actually, then we may say it exists 'really' outside the mind as well as 'intentionally' in it. If not, it exists only intentionally, not really. But even at that, such objects are not simply nothing. They still exist in the mind, and their intentional existence is no less immediately present to consciousness and certain than the real existence of the acts themselves. That is what was meant when it was said that the intentional object is included within the sphere of certainty of the *cogito*. As for the real existence of such objects outside the mind, this can never be immediately present to consciousness in Descartes's sense, though it can sometimes be inferred with a certainty so perfect that it leaves nothing to be desired.

8.2 Descartes and Husserl

What this characterization of the structure of thought owes to the fifth of Husserl's *Logical Investigations* should be clear without detailed acknowledgment. Apart from the absolutely fundamental distinction between act and intentional object, Husserl would by no means have accepted all of Descartes's analysis. In 1900 he would certainly not have accepted the notion of an *ego* to which all acts are referable, though in various addenda to the second edition of the work (1913) he recanted on this point, admitting a pure or transcendental *ego* while still rejecting the empirical *ego* of Descartes (cf. below, chapter 9). Accordingly, Husserl's name must be added to the list of prominent thinkers who, at one time or another, denied the immediate presence to consciousness of anything corresponding to the Cartesian 'I,' 'subject,' or 'self.'[4]

Nor would Husserl have accepted the characterization of the act itself as an immediate 'object,' that is, two objects, the intentional object of thought in Descartes's sense, whose real existence outside the mind is at least open to doubt, and the intentionally structured act (the object of 'consciousness' in Descartes's sense), the existence of which is indubitably certain. With one notable exception (see next note), Descartes does not designate thoughts as *objecta*, and there are two problems with distinguishing *conscientia* and *cogitatio* on the grounds that they have different objects (as was done, following McRae, in chapter 6). First, the term 'object' is customarily employed in contradistinction to a correlative notion of 'act.' Thus, different acts of the same type, different types of act of the same order, or acts of thinking of an entirely different order may be said to have the same object or else to differ in respect of their objects. 'Having different objects' accordingly suggests a comparison between acts, whereas what Descartes has in view with the term *conscientia* is not an act at all but a feature or *act-structure* common to all acts. The talk of two objects is apt to obscure this crucial difference. That is the first difficulty. Second, talk of two different 'objects' may obscure the quite different senses in which acts generally and their objects are *in* the mind. Descartes lays considerable stress on this difference – explicitly in the Replies to the First Set of Objections (see section 16.5) – while in effect treating acts as a different order of objects nevertheless. Provided these caveats are borne in mind, there is no insuperable objection to speaking of consciousness and thought as having two different objects – or, if this seems preferable, of thought as having two different objects according as one focuses attention primarily upon what one thinks or on what one is conscious of. This is in any case quite different from the sort of 'dual object theory' associated with the infamous 'veil-of-perception' theory, since the objects are the *immediate* objects of thought and consciousness respectively.[5]

There is a further respect in which Husserl would have found Descartes's analysis wanting. Among the various kinds of intentional object listed above is the class of those that are logically impossible. While this reflects Husserl's attitude well enough, it appears that Descartes would deny that finite minds can think such objects at all (for instance, a mountain without a valley, a supremely perfect being who does not exist). On the whole, his view seems to be that if the description of an object involves a contradiction, we are not thinking and cannot think of it; we are merely employing meaningless signs – for example, uttering gibberish or performing in thought whatever mental act or acts may correspond to uttering in speech words without meaning. There is and can be, for Descartes, no idea in the mind, no act that can correctly be said to be intentionally related to the object designated by a term or concept that involves a contradiction – not even an obscure and confused idea. When Descartes says "it is just as much of a contradiction to think of God (that is a supremely perfect being) lacking existence (that is lacking a perfection) as it is to think of a mountain without a valley" (AT VII 66f.: CSM II 46), he is apparently placing a restriction, not just on what we can *think without contradiction*, but on what we can correctly be said to *think at all*.[6] Husserl's view differs significantly from this, since for him the thought or concept of (say) a round square or a mountain without a valley is none the less a real thought, an intentionally structured act of thinking, for being patently self-contradictory and hence incapable of being instantiated.

And yet, the distance separating Descartes and Husserl is perhaps not as great as this suggests. At issue is the nature of the intentional relation between act and object. This is the relation described in the foregoing as 'representing an object' as opposed to 'being present to consciousness.' There is an important qualification to be added to the preceding account of Descartes's views on this subject.

As noted earlier, Descartes makes it perfectly clear that the intentional relatedness of thought to an object may (but need not) involve the occurrence of mental imagery. Thus, I can 'picture' a triangle, though I need not picture it in order to understand the concept 'triangle'; and though I cannot picture a chiliagon clearly, I nevertheless have as clear and distinct an understanding of what is meant by 'a thousand-sided figure' as I have of 'a figure bounded by three straight lines.' Descartes's formal definition of the term 'idea' in the Second Replies (see below section 16.4) places it beyond doubt that one's having the idea or concept of x in one's mind *is* entailed by one's correctly understanding the ideal sense of expressions in which the word 'x' is correctly employed.[7] So while Descartes's views on thinking the logically impossible appear naively psychologistic in the Fifth Meditation, as though the inability to form a mental image of a mountain without a valley quite simply entailed that no such idea or concept existed in the mind, the distance separating him from Husserl is in fact less than might be inferred from that context alone. It is after all a small step from the claim of the Second Replies that understanding the sense of an expression entails having the idea of the thing(s) designated by it to admitting that since I understand the expression 'round square' as well as I understand the words 'round' and 'square,' and since I understand 'a mountain without a valley' as well as I understand 'mountain' and 'valley,' I must have the ideas of a round square and a mountain without a valley, even though neither is capable of being instantiated *in rerum natura*. Yet Descartes does not appear to have taken this step, persisting in the view that such concepts and the expressions in which they are employed are simply meaningless for us (though not for God!) and that there can exist in the human mind no ideas of the objects they purport to designate. So a certain discrepancy between him and Husserl remains.[8]

8.3 Anachronism

To speak of the First and Second Meditations as carrying out a 'reduction' having marked affinities with the later phenomenological *epochē* of Husserl is not obviously anachronistic. For one thing, Descartes himself not infrequently uses 're- duction' and its cognates in the relevant contexts (see above, section 5.1, n. 1). For another, Husserl specifically acknowledges Descartes's *Meditations* as hav- ing had a decisive influence on the formation of the phenomenological method practised in the *epochē* (Husserl 1960). Not only does Descartes himself speak of 'reduction' in discussions of his own method as early as the *Regulae* (for ex- ample, AT X 379: CSM I 20); to do so in connection with the regimen of doubt is fairly common among interpreters, even those who have no thought of Husserl (for instance, Gewirth 1968, 268f.). Whatever justification there may be for it, however, the practice may still obscure at least one very important facet of reduc- tion as Descartes understood it. In the Second Replies he writes: "When you ask me to 'add something further which lifts us up to an incorporeal or spiritual plane,' I cannot do better than refer you to my Second Meditation ... *which was designed with this sole aim in mind*" (AT VII 137: CSM II 98 e.a.). Obviously, the religious motif of elevating the soul from the contemplation of material to that of immate- rial (supersensible) things – a vestige of Descartes's spiritual training at La Flèche, or only a concession to the theologian-authors of this set of objections? – has no analogue in the later phenomenological reduction of Husserl.

   If this does not make the talk of 'reduction,' even 'phenomenological reduc- tion,' unacceptably anachronistic, neither does the fact that the First and Second Meditations come up far short of a Husserlian *epochē* in other key respects. On the contrary, the contrast helps make the precise character of the Cartesian reduc- tion clearer.[9] But if the talk of 'reduction' is unobjectionable, it appears to be quite another matter to identify a whole range of subtle phenomenological dis- tinctions, loosely adapted from Husserl and Heidegger, as present in Descartes's analysis of the embracing formal structure of thought, as has been done in the present chapter.

Faced with the charge of anachronism, it is well to consider Curley's apt rejoinder to an objection against interpreting another prominent seventeenth-century figure with the help of a contemporary theory (Hobbes 1994, xxiv): "Surely it is no more anachronistic [to invoke game theory to interpret Hobbes]," he writes, "than supposing that, long before Aristotle constructed a formal theory of the syllogism, people argued in ways capable of being analyzed by that theory." Anachronism, in short, arises not simply from applying the distinctions of a later age to the thought of an earlier one, but from ascribing one's own *tools of analysis* to those whose ideas and theories are made clearer by them – sometimes much clearer than they could have been to their first discoverers. Thus, to take a rather different example (cf. Robinson 1991, 182f.), it is hardly anachronistic to distinguish a 'descriptive' and a 'prescriptive' side of the Heraclitean *logos* – though this distinction was, by general agreement, first sharply drawn much later, and though the terms 'descriptive' and 'prescriptive,' now generally in use, are of still more recent origin. By contrast, it would be grossly anachronistic to suggest that Heraclitus himself actually drew, or would have seen any need for, a distinction of this kind.

In the present work, it is true, both types of claim go together: that certain Husserlian distinctions are invaluable tools of analysis in the Cartesian context; and that Descartes himself was fully seized of them. The Introduction and this part confine themselves to the first claim. Only in Part Three (chapters 15 and 16) is the attempt made to actually *show* that Descartes himself drew precisely these distinctions in the cumbersome Scholastic terminology that was his. Therefore, final judgment on the analysis provided here should be postponed till that part.

Anachronism, of course, is not confined to reading the ideas, distinctions, and methods of a later age back into an earlier one. It is not uncommon for historians of thought to hunt down antecedents for new ideas, sometimes to the point of obscuring what is genuinely new, perhaps even revolutionary, in them. Because of his Scholastic training and vocabulary, Descartes has come in for a good deal of interpretation of this kind. There is indeed very little for which some important precedent cannot be (and has not been) found somewhere between the fourth and sixteenth centuries.[10] Of this there are many examples in the literature, though the interpreter who deserves most credit for pointing out the Scholastic baggage of the Father of Modern Philosophy (Gilson) is as free of this particular prejudice as he is mired in anachronism of the first sort: reading the later evolution of modern philosophy (certainly Kant, possibly Malebranche) back into the Cartesian revolution in philosophy. Danger of still another sort of anachronism lurks in the attempt to identify an unnamed interlocutor or unstated theory of an earlier age as the object of a point-by-point examination and critique in a work that purports to be a systematic treatise. Marion's efforts to read the *Regulae* as Descartes's *Auseinandersetzung* with Aristotle through unrelenting *remise en situation aristotélicienne* (cf. Marion 1975, 35) may constitute anachronism of this kind.

8.4 Some textual difficulties

Apart from anachronism, there may appear to be certain purely textual obstacles standing in the way of the sharp distinction between *cogitatio* and *conscientia* drawn in this and the preceding chapter. We conclude with two that seem important.

In the Third Replies Descartes writes: "There are other acts which we call 'acts of thought,' such as understanding, willing, imagining, having sensory perceptions, and so on: these all fall under the common concept of thought or perception or consciousness (*sub ratione communi cogitationis, sive perceptionis, sive conscientiae*)" (AT VII 176: CSM II 124). The French translation reads: "tous lesquels conviennent entre eux en ce qu'ils ne peuvent être sans pensée, ou perception, ou conscience et connaissance." Similarly, in a letter to Gibieuf of 19 January 1642, Descartes writes: "Pour ce qui est du principe par lequel il me semble connoistre que l'idee qu i'ay de quelque chose, *non redditur a me inadaequata per abstractionem intellectus*, ie ne le tire que *de ma propre pensée ou conscience*" (AT III 474: CSMK 201 e.a.). In these passages, surely, Descartes simply equates thought (*cogitatio*, 'pensée') and consciousness (*conscientia*, conscience).[11]

That depends on the sense to be given *sive* and 'ou' in these contexts. To the suggestion that both mean 'or (in other words),'[12] it can be replied that *sive* certainly cannot mean this in the case of *cogitationis, sive perceptionis*. The "perceptions of the understanding" are only one species of thought, with sensing, imagining, and pure intellection as subspecies; the other is volition or the "operations of the will."[13] So unless Descartes is giving the term *perceptio* an uncharactertistically sweeping extension here, it cannot be a synonym for *cogitatio*, and the first occurrence of *sive* is not intended to suggest otherwise. Nor should the second *sive* be understood as implying synonomy of *cogitatio* and *conscientia* – although *conscientia*, as that universal and necessary structural feature that sets *cogitatio* apart from all non-mental acts (*ambulo* and so on), serves just as well as *cogitatio* to pick out the mental among our acts or actions. Still, Descartes is not using 'conscience' and *conscientia* synonymously with '*pensée*' and *cogitatio* in these passages, but rather metonymically. The 'part' or structure *conscientia* is essential to the whole and therefore suited to stand for it in some contexts.

If *conscientia* indeed stands *pars pro toto* for *cogitatio* here, then the first use of *sive* may well be similar. We saw earlier (chapter 6 *in initio*) that in the same set of Replies (to Hobbes) Descartes in fact designates *conscientia* by the word *percipere*. Thus, it is at least understandable (though nonetheless confusing) that he should write *cogitationis, sive perceptionis, sive conscientiae* here, assuming that both *perceptio* and *conscientia* can be used metonymically for *cogitatio*. So too if one of them, *perceptio*, is used for the genus of which both *conscientia* and *cogitatio* are species. Either usage would be awkward, since *perceptio* is normally used to designate one species of *cogitatio*, while *conscientia* refers to the essential structure, as distinct from all particular modes, of thought. But neither usage is sheerly beyond the pale. (For further documentation of the metonymic use, see section 16.3.) In an early letter Descartes uses – again misleadingly – both *cogitare* and *sentire* instead of *percipere* to designate *conscientia*.[14]

The other problematic passage is found in the Sixth Meditation proof of the existence of the external world. Descartes begins by going "back over all the things which I previously took to be perceived by the senses and reckoned to be true" (AT VII 74: CSM II 51). Passing in review the ideas of the qualities of bodies "which presented themselves to my thought," he remarks that "although the ideas were, strictly speaking, the only immediate objects of my sensory awareness, it was not unreasonable for me to think that the items which I was perceiving through the senses were things quite distinct from my thought, namely bodies which produced the ideas" (AT VII 75: CSM II 52). This certainly suggests that the direct objects of sense-perception are not things but the ideas of things; in that case, the sharp distinction between thought and consciousness will be difficult to sustain, as will the denial that Descartes holds any form of representationalism.

A look at the Latin text, however, suggests otherwise.

Nec sane absque ratione, ob ideas istarum omnium qualitatum quae cogitationi meae se offerebant, & quas solas proprie & immediate sentiebam, putabam me sentire res quasdam a mea cogitatione plane diversas, nempe corpora a quibus ideae istae precederent.

The translation followed above takes the relative pronoun *quas* to refer to *ideas*, whereas, grammatically, the referent could just as well be *qualitates*. If it is indeed the latter, then the distinction is not between *ideae* in the mind and extramental *res* as the immediate and mediate objects of sense-perception, respectively; immediately perceived are the qualities, not the ideas of the qualities, and the passage should be translated accordingly.

At least some indication that this is indeed the way the comments in the Sixth Meditation are to be understood and translated is provided by the frequently cited Second Meditation passage in which Descartes warns of the misleadingness of ordinary language:

We say that we see the wax itself, if it is there before us, not that we judge it to be there from its colour or shape; and this might lead me to conclude without more ado that knowledge of the wax comes from what the eye sees, and not from the scrutiny of the mind alone (*solius mentis inspectione*). But then if I look out the window and see men crossing the square, as I just happen to have done, I normally say that I see the men themselves, just as I say that I see the wax. Yet do I see more than hats and coats which could conceal automata? I *judge* that they are men. And so something which I thought I was seeing with my eyes is in fact grasped solely by the faculty of judgement which is in my mind. (AT VII 32: CSM II 21).

To paraphrase: for most purposes ("normally") we do not distinguish between 'seeing' the colours and shapes of things and 'seeing' objects like hats and coats or men. We say we 'see' the men, even though this is in fact what we *judge* and all we really *see* (looking down on the square from above) are hats and cloaks in motion, or rather the qualities of things we *judge* to be hats and cloaks. In the same way we ordinarily say we *see* the wax even though (as Descartes has just demonstrated) we in fact *understand* (*mente percipere*) the nature of body as "something extended, flexible, and changeable" not by means of the faculty of sight at all, but by "the scrutiny of the mind (*inspectio mentis*)."

Interpreted in this light, the Sixth Meditation passage merely points out that we normally say we sense things, that is, bodies, which we take to be the causes of the sensory ideas in the mind, when in fact all we immediately *sense properly speaking* are qualities of those bodies (*quas solas proprie & immediate sentiebam*). These "present" or "offer themselves" (without our consent and even against our will) by means of, that is, are *represented* by, ideas. As for the bodies whose qualities they are, these we *judge* to possess such qualities and to be the causes of the ideas of those qualities in the mind. Distinguishing between (1) the sensory qualities of things, (2) those corporeal things themselves, and (3) the ideas of their sensory qualities in the mind (the objects of sensation, perceptual judgments, and consciousness, respectively), we can now retranslate the above passage correctly as follows: "And [it was] not without reason that, on account of the ideas of all those qualities [Descartes has just mentioned 'hardness, heat, and other tactile qualities,' 'light and colour and odours and tastes and sounds'] that presented themselves to my thought ['without my consent,' as Descartes is soon to add], they [these qualities] being all I was sensing properly and immediately [i.e., the sole immediate objects of my sensory ideas], I believed myself to be sensing things altogether distinct from my thought, namely bodies from which those ideas proceeded." So translated, there is nothing here to compel us to believe that the immediate objects of sensation or thought are ideas in the mind rather than extra-mental things or to commit Descartes to representationalism. Nor is there anything to suggest that the distinction between thought and consciousness cannot be maintained.

9

Pure and Empirical Thought

We noted in passing the almost casual way in which Descartes links self-awareness with rationality in the passage from the *Regulae* quoted earlier: "we have real knowledge of all of these ['what knowledge or doubt or ignorance is, or the action of the will'], knowledge so easy that in order to possess it *all we need is some degree of rationality*" (AT X 419: CSM I 44f. e.a.). This link provides the key to Descartes's novel conception of innateness as well as to the *imago Dei* doctrine in his writings. Reason, long understood as the faculty of innate ideas and principles in the broadly Platonic tradition,[1] is here grasped for the first time as that faculty by which I am always immediately conscious of my thinking and capable of reflecting on what I am thus conscious of; through reflexion I can understand what thinking is, what existence is, what a thing or substance is, what truth is (since it is true that I am a thing that thinks and exists), thus furnishing my mind with these ideas as well as the founding principle of knowledge: I who am thinking exist. The same reflexive act is involved in the innate idea of freedom; for it is by reflecting on those truths from which I am not free to withhold assent that I understand, not just what truth is, but what freedom is as well. This is what it means to say that these ideas and that principle – along with a host of others – are 'innate.' For Descartes *innatum*, 'in-born,' means literally, 'born of the mind's reflexion on its own thinking.' Pre-reflexively and hence only implicitly conscious of these "common notions" whenever I think, I am able – even disposed – to become explicitly aware of them through attention to my thinking. This is no Lockean conception of innateness, opposing the inborn to the acquired; instead it juxtaposes ideas acquired through reflexion on inner experience and ideas acquired through ordinary non-reflexive outer experience. While the former are termed 'innate,' ideas acquired through representation of external objects are usually called 'adventitious.'[2] Yet the ideas so juxtaposed have little if anything in common with Locke's ideas of sensation and reflection, involving as they do a radically different model of the mind and conception of human reason (cf. chapter 19).

The conception of human reason implicit in this doctrine of innateness is at the heart of the *imago Dei* doctrine of Descartes. The doctrine of innate ideas will be studied in detail in chapter 18. In the present chapter, the liaison between self-consciousness and rationality will be explored in its bearing on Descartes's conception of human reason and on the *imago Dei* doctrine. For the latter, too, there is ample precedent in the tradition.[3] Nevertheless, Descartes at least adumbrated an account of human reason as the image of the divine intellect or reason that was not simply taken over from any earlier source. Examination of this theme will shed further light on the exact nature of that thinking designated by the term *cogito*, in particular on what is to be the principal question here: whether it is pure or empirical 'consciousness' (in the contemporary sense of the word) to which Descartes refers.

9.1 *Imago Dei*

At the conclusion of the Third Meditation Descartes notes that the idea of God is "innate in me, *just as* the idea of myself is innate in me" (AT VII 51: CSM II 35 e.a.). The parallel with the idea of myself is the striking thing here: "the mere fact that God created me is a very strong basis for believing that I am somehow made in his image and likeness, and that *I perceive that likeness*, which includes the idea of God, *by the same faculty which enables me to perceive myself*" (AT VII 51: CSM II 35 e.a.). The faculty in question is reflexion, which, for Descartes, presupposes consciousness; the idea of God is innate in precisely the same way as the ideas of thinking, existence, substance, and so on mentioned above: "*when I turn my mind's eye upon myself*, I understand that I am a thing that is incomplete and dependent upon another ... but I also understand *at the same time* that he on whom I depend has within him all those greater things, not just indefinitely and potentially but actually and infinitely, and hence that he is God" (AT VII 51: CSM II 35 e.a.; cf. also AT VII 53: CSM II 37). Of course, it "is not in the nature of an image to be identical in all respects with the thing of which it is an image, but merely to imitate it in some respects. And it is quite clear that *the wholly perfect power of thought* which we understand to be in God is represented by means of that less perfect faculty which we possess" (AT VII 373: CSM II 256f. e.a.).

In the light of the *Regulae* passage quoted above, a plausible preliminary account of this is the following. Through exercising my faculty of attending to the mental states of which I am immediately conscious I become reflexively aware, not just that I am a thinking thing, that is, of what thinking and existence are and that I, who think, exist; I become aware also that I am pre-reflexively conscious of my thinking; and this is what it is to become aware that I possess the faculty of reason or rational knowledge, resembling in this God, the creator, though only remotely, since he possesses actually and infinitely all that I possess only indefinitely and potentially through my finite and seldom exercised capacity or disposition to reflect upon my thinking.

If this is correct, then Marion (1986, §8, esp. 106ff.) is right to insist that there is no strictly univocal sense in which the attribute of thought belongs both to God and to "our mind, which is finite" (AT VII 119: CSM II 85). However, in discounting the divine attribute of thought altogether (ibid., 108f.) he goes too far, all but eliminating the basis of the *imago Dei* doctrine that Descartes took over from the theological tradition, modifying it in accordance with his own principles. The doctrine is prominent in two places within the *Meditations*. The first is the passage at the end of the Third Meditation quoted above; the other is the Fourth Meditation passage (AT VII 57: CSM II 39f.) in which it is urged that it is "above all in virtue of the will that I understand myself to bear in some way the image and likeness of God."[4] Here "above all (*praecipue*)" implies 'not only'; in what *other* respect I resemble God is stated in the sequel: "If, for example, I consider the faculty of understanding, I immediately recognise that in my case it is extremely slight and very finite, and I at once form the idea of an understanding which is much greater – indeed supremely great and infinite ... etc." Unfortunately, this misleadingly suggests that the idea of myself as a finite thinking thing makes possible the formation of the idea of God – when "in reality," as Descartes explains to Burman, "the infinite perfection of God is prior to our imperfection, since our imperfection is a defect and negation of the perfection of God. And every defect and negation presupposes that of which it falls short and which it negates" (AT V 153: CSMK 338). It is thus the innate idea in us of the infinite mind of God that makes possible the clear and distinct conception of the self; for, as Descartes remarks to Gassendi in the Fifth Replies, "it is false that the infinite is understood through the negation of a boundary or limit; on the contrary, all limitation implies a negation of the infinite" (AT VII 365: CSM II 252).

Thus, while the infinite distance between the divine and the human intellect may not allow for a completely univocal sense of 'thinking,' the fact that the reflexive grasp of my own nature as a finite thinking thing depends upon the prior conception of God's infinite intellect suggests at least some sort of parallel between the two. It is this that is to be worked out in an elaboration of the preliminary interpretation sketched above. There is admittedly something very odd here. For an existing, thinking substance with a free will to understand through reflexion on its own nature what existence and thinking, what a substance, and what freedom are is one thing; for it to know by the same means the nature of God, that is, a being infinitely greater than itself, is another. The exact extension of Descartes's 'reflexive-dispositional concept of innateness' and its precise intensional meaning will be considered in Part Three (cf. chapters 18ff. below), where we shall have to pay particular attention to the innate idea of God. Though it serves as the paradigm of innateness, it is just not clear how 'God' can be an innate idea in the sense of the new theory pioneered by Descartes. So the idea of myself as a finite thinking thing somehow depends upon the *prior* possession of the idea of God who created me in his image. What light, if any, does this shed on the idea of my own thinking?

9.2 Consciousness, reflexion, mind, and reason

Reason, the *Regulae* suggest, is the faculty of immediate self-awareness and reflexion on all that I am pre-reflexively conscious of. Through such reflexion I become aware of myself as possessing reason and even of God as possessing actually and perfectly all that I possess only to a limited degree or potentially. For all its novelty, this chimes harmoniously enough with the traditional philosophico-theological dogma that intellect or reason is that in virtue of which mankind resembles the Godhead (cf. Genesis 1:27). But according to the time-hallowed definition, rationality is that which distinguishes man from the lower animals as well.[5] Whatever his reservations about the Scholastic definition of man as an *animal rationale*, Descartes at bottom concurs: "as regards reason or sense (*la raison, ou le [bon] sens*), ... it is the only thing that makes us men and distinguishes us from the beasts" (AT VI 2: CSM I 112).[6] For Descartes, there can be no question of distinguishing men and beasts as possessing differing degrees of rationality, as both Gassendi and the authors of the Sixth Set of Objections suggest (cf. AT VII 271: CSM II 189 and AT VII 414: CSM II 279, respectively). Nor can there be any thought of distinguishing some form of simple 'animal awareness' of external objects from rational thought in human beings by characterising the former as simple object-awareness without self-awareness, the latter as 'self-aware-object-awareness.' In regarding animals as material automata devoid of thought or intelligence Descartes was only drawing the obvious consequence of his analysis of the structure of thinking. Since thought necessarily involves self-consciousness, and since the latter is a function of the intellect or rationality, animals are incapable, not just of reasoning, but even of thinking. They can be said to sense or feel in a certain way, but *their* sensation is a function of the body, not the mind. In a letter to More on the subject (5 February 1649), Descartes writes: "I do not deny life to animals ...; and I do not even deny sensation, in so far as it depends on a bodily organ" (AT V 278: CSMK 366). And in a letter to Plempius (for Fromondus) of 3 October 1637, he adds:

He [Fromondus] supposes that I think that animals see just as we do, i.e. being aware or thinking they see (*sentiendo sive cogitando se videre*) ... But ... I explain quite explicitly that my view is that animals do not see as we do when we are aware that we see (*dum sentimus nos videre*), but only as we do when our mind is elsewhere [i.e., when we are almost oblivious of the fact that we are thinking]. In such a case the images of external objects are depicted on our retinas, and perhaps the impressions they make in the optic nerve cause our limbs to make various movements, although we are quite unaware of them (*nihil tamen prorsus eorum sentimus*). (AT I 413f.: CSMK 61f.)[7]

It is the impossibility of ascribing to animals mental object-awareness without self-awareness, as Leibniz was later to do (cf. Miles 1994a) and as Bourdin had done already in the Seventh Objections (cf. AT VII 533f.: CSM II 364, and Descartes's reply at AT VII 559f.: CSM II 382), that explains why, in the Second Meditation, thinking, mind, soul, intellect, and reason are simply identified by Descartes: "I am, then, in the strict sense only a thing that thinks; that is, I am a mind, or intelligence, or intellect or reason" (*mens, sive animus, sive intellectus, sive ratio*) (AT VII 27: CSM II 18). All thought, even simple sense-perception, being essentially *self*-aware object-awareness, necessarily involves an 'element' of reason or intellection: *intellectio nonnulla*, as Descartes writes in a passage of the Sixth Meditation (AT VII 78: CSM II 54) to be considered later. This is so even for voluntary movements of the limbs, included along with sense-perception in this passage of the Fifth Set of Replies: "as for movement and sensation, I refer them to the body *for the most part*, and attribute nothing belonging to them to the soul, *apart from the element of thought alone*" (AT VII 351: CSM II 243 e.a.). What that "element of thought" consists in is made clear later in the same set of Replies: "I was not ... dealing with sight and touch, which occur by means of bodily organs, but was concerned solely with *the thought of seeing and touching* [or moving a body part], which, as we experience every day in our dreams, does not require these organs [or body parts]" (AT VII 360: CSM II 249 e.a.). The *mental* act of thinking one is seeing or touching or moving one's limbs is that which is "within us in such a way that we are immediately conscious (*immediate conscii simus*)" of it (AT VII 160: CSM II 113). And this consciousness of our thought or mental acts is a function of that intellect or reason in which animals have no share.[8]

It may be the same point Descartes is making when he writes in the Second Replies: "As for your calling the idea of God which is in us an *ens rationis*, this is not a compelling objection. If by *ens rationis* is meant something which does not exist, it is not true that the idea of God is an *ens rationis* in this sense. It is true only in the sense in which *every operation of the intellect is an* ens rationis, that is, an entity that has its origin in reason" (AT VII 134: CSM II 96, with *ens rationis* left untranslated). Cottingham et al. translate the concluding phrase *a ratione profectum* as 'originating in thought' rather than 'in reason,' thus obscuring the point – if indeed it is Descartes's point here – that thinking as such, that is, every operation of the mind, springs from the faculty of reason. It may be, of course, that *operatio intellectus* is used in a narrow sense here to denote only the operations of the 'higher' cognitive faculty, the intellect or reason, in which case this passage does not support the present interpretation. As has been seen, however, *operatio intellectus* is frequently a synonym for *cogitatio*, figuring in the key definitions of 'thought' cited in chapter 6. Thus, Descartes can simply equate thought or mind and intellect (or reason) without implying thereby that the thought of which he is speaking is 'pure' rather than empirical thought, that is, that it is akin to what Kant understood by 'transcendental' as opposed to simple psychological consciousness.[9]

9.3 Transcendental realism

This, at any rate, is the conclusion to which the link between reason and self-consciousness points. It has been contested by Gueroult, though it is endorsed in one form or another by many of the older French commentators with whom he takes issue in the chapter of his *Descartes* devoted to the *cogito*.[10] It is also the view taken by Husserl within the "Digression" in his *Cartesian Meditations* entitled "Descartes' failure to make the transcendental turn" (Husserl 1960, 23ff.). By this Husserl means the turn toward transcendental subjectivity. This is not quite the same as the turn toward the pure *ego*, for in Husserl's sense of 'pure' this much at least was accomplished by Descartes (ibid., 4):

[G]reat weight must be given to the consideration that, in philosophy, the *Meditations* were epoch-making in a quite unique sense, and precisely because of their going back to the pure *ego cogito*. Descartes, in fact, inaugurates an entirely new kind of philosophy. Changing its total style, philosophy takes a radical turn: from naive objectivism to transcendental subjectivism.

Yet the turn to transcendental subjectivity, Husserl claims, was only properly executed by Kant; Descartes failed to make it "in the right manner" (ibid., 18). The regimen of doubt within the First Meditation carried out the 'phenomenological reduction' or transcendental *epoché*, suspending belief in a realm of material objects hitherto naively posited as existing independently of consciousness; yet Descartes "introduced the apparently insignificant but actually fateful change whereby the *ego* becomes a *substantia cogitans*, a separate human *mens sive animus*, and the point of departure for inferences according to the principle of causality – in short, the change by which Descartes became the father of transcendental realism, an absurd position" (ibid., 24).

The absurdity of transcendental realism has nothing to do with logical inconsistency. Assuming *res* to be synonymous with *substantia* (cf. above chapter 7, n. 18), the goal of philosophy, as Husserl might describe it, is to clarify what it means to say of any *res* whatever that it 'is' or 'exists'; to clarify, in other words, the meaning of substantial 'being' or 'substantiality.' In transcendental realism this is attempted for that specific domain of substance designated by the expression 'world.' The clarification is carried out in terms of the actually occurring modes or accidents of a different *res* or substance, the human mind. But whether it proceeds by means of inferences from the existence of ideas in the mind to their presumed causes, as in Descartes, or in terms of the order and coherence among the ideas themselves, as in Berkeley, nothing is accomplished. For the real existence of one kind of *res* has been 'explained' in terms of the *as yet unclarified* real existence of another. A meaningful philosophical clarification of the sense of 'reality' can only be achieved by recourse to that which is not itself real, not an actually existing entity, substance, or *res* at all, whether physical or psychical. This condition is fulfilled by the pure or non-entitative transcendental *ego* of Husserl, as by the 'I' of pure apperception, the pure '*Ich denke*' of Kant. It is not fulfilled by Descartes's *mens sive animus sive intellectus*, which, even if not identifiable with the individual man, René Descartes, nor with his mind, still stands for a *res*: any human mind whatever. Such 'transcendental realism,' as Husserl calls it, is accordingly nonsensical.

Descartes would certainly have baulked at any suggestion that he attempted to clarify the sense of the reality of one sort of being in terms of the as yet *unclarified* sense of the reality of another. Nothing can be more self-evidently clear than the existence of the mind and its states; to attempt to make it clearer by reference to anything else (say, a pure *ego*) would be to obscure it. Unless this is accepted as the maximally clear and self-evident starting point, the outcome, Descartes believed, must be complete scepticism. Yet while it is not clear that Descartes would have lost any sleep over it, the significance of arguments *like* that which Husserl employs here, their long and distinguished lineage going right back to Aristotle's (and Plato's own) criticisms of the theory of Forms, should be lost on no one.[11]

9.4 *Conscience intellectuelle* or *conscience psychologique*?

Gueroult mentions Husserl both in the chapter on the *cogito* (cf. 1968, I, 81) and in the short appendix on *ergo sum* published in the second volume of his *Descartes* (ibid., II, 316). In the appendix he distinguishes three senses of 'idea' in Descartes, conceding that in the 'phenomenological,' as distinct from the 'psychological' and 'metaphysical,' senses "la thèse du monde est suspendue: C'est ici et non dans le doute métaphysique, que se manifeste une *epoché* identique à celle de

Husserl." Gueroult's demurrer is instructive, if only because '*conscience intellectuelle* ou *conscience psychologique*' proves to be a false dichotomy in the end: neither the common acceptation of 'empirical consciousness' nor the Kantian notion of a pure consciousness captures what Descartes understands by the process of reflexive attention to that of which I am pre-reflexively aware; yet this is the distinctive thing about Descartes's founding principle.

If by 'empirical consciousness' is meant something akin to what Kant called 'inner sense,' what Locke and Hume understood as the sensuous awareness (perception) of one's inner states or acts, and what is nowadays designated by the word 'introspection,' Gueroult's criticism provides a valuable corrective to a serious misapprehension. Self-awareness is a function of the human intellect or reason for Descartes; and reason is the very essence of the mind. *Mens, intellectus*, and *ratio* are identical because the faculty in virtue of which the mind is pre-reflexively aware of its acts makes reflexion possible; and through reflexion the mind acquires clear and distinct perceptions of its thinking and existence, of substance, truth, freedom, and other innate concepts and principles, logical, mathematical, and metaphysical. Gueroult has little difficulty in showing that the act or process by which the mind grasps its own thinking and existence is an intellectual intuition rather than a sensuous perception.[12] But his interpretation of Descartes's identification of *mens, intellectus*, and *ratio* places Descartes in misleading proximity to Kant.

Gueroult attempts to dispose of the interpretation of Husserl and those French commentators mentioned earlier by setting up a direct parallel between the *cogito* of Descartes and Kant's *Ich denke*. At one place (ibid., I, 53 n. 5), he cites the passage from the letter to Mersenne of July 1641 quoted in section 7.3:

[T]he soul is nothing but a thing which thinks, and so it is impossible for us ever to think of anything without at the same time having the idea *of our soul as a thing* capable of thinking of whatever we think of. It is true that a thing of such a nature cannot be imagined, that is, cannot be represented by a corporeal image ... But that does not make it any less *conceivable*. (AT III 394: CSMK 186 e.a.)

Gueroult comments: "Le rapprochement s'impose ... avec le *Ich denke* kantien : Le « je pense » doit pouvoir accompagner toutes mes représentations, car autrement il y aurait en moi quelque chose de représenté qui ne pourrait pas être pensé, ce qui revient à dire qu'elle ne serait rien pour moi" (cf. 1968, I, 53 n. 5). Of course, what Kant is quoted as saying here is thoroughly Cartesian: a thought of which I am not conscious is a contradiction in terms; for an act of thinking to be 'in the mind' at all is for it to be immediately present to consciousness. For Kant, too, all empirical consciousness has the essential structure on which Descartes insists: 'I think that I am thinking something.' This self-reflexive structure of empirical consciousness, in virtue of which all my acts are acts of one and the same 'I,' Kant terms 'pure consciousness.' Since it forms the essence of empirical consciousness as a single unified whole, it can (so Kant) be called 'consciousness' with even greater justification than that which is ordinarily so called. 'Pure consciousness' is the 'condition of the possibility' of ordinary empirical consciousness. And it is this pure form of all thinking, furnished by the understanding's synthetic unifying acts, that Kant designates by the phrase '*Ich denke.*'

The intent of the passage from Descartes's letter to Mersenne is, however, quite different. The sphere of certainty of the *cogito,* Descartes points out, includes the 'I,' self, or *ego* that thinks, not indeed as something imaginable, but as something conceivable by the intellect and actually conceived whenever I think at all. Neither this nor any other passage in Descartes parallels Kant's distinction between empirical consciousness and its pure form; and there is certainly none that makes of this pure form the product of an act of synthesis on the part of the understanding. True, for Descartes as for Kant, it is a function of the intellect. But there the similarity ends. Descartes's *cogito (me cogitare cogitatum)* stands for the phenomenologically reduced structure of thinking as such, regardless of whether it is pure (intellectual) or empirical (sensory) in character; it is a variable the values of which may be cognitive, emotive, or volitional, and if cognitive, perceptual, imaginative, or purely intellectual. By the phrase '*Ich denke,*' on the other hand, Kant designates the pure form of empirical consciousness, the synthetic unity of apperception as the condition of the possibility of any empirical consciousness whatever.

The mind grasped in pure intellection, then, is not itself the pure intellect or reason in anything resembling the Kantian sense of a *facultas cognoscitiva superior*; it is the mind with all its faculties, cognitive, emotive, and volitional, with its adventitious and factitious no less than its innate ideas. Still, the mind so understood is not the object of empirical introspection but of a *non*-sensuous self-awareness that Descartes calls *conscientia* at times, but also *experientia, simplex mentis intuitus,* and *cognitio interna quae reflexam semper antecedit* (see section 15.1 below). This faculty Descartes regularly links both with self-consciousness and with clear and distinct perception in a broad sense that includes all the purely intellectual ideas and principles of logic, mathematics, and metaphysics. The most characteristic designation is perhaps *experientia* in phrases like *experior in me* and *in semetipsis experiuntur,* and so on. On that which is 'experienced inwardly' in this sense there *may* supervene what Descartes terms 'reflexion,' that is, that process of analysis by which what was formerly only pre-reflexively present to consciousness is explicitly grasped *in concreto.* What is thus seized concretely may then, through further reflexion, be grasped explicitly *in abstracto,* as a universal principle, though this represents a more advanced stage in the process of philosophical reflexion. It can even undergo further clarification through discursive reasoning, that is, logical analysis, both inter- and intra-propositional. But prior to this final stage of philosophical reflexion, the process is essentially intuitive rather than discursive.

A full account of this 'progress of the mind,' to be labelled 'intuitive induction,' is undertaken in Part Three (chapters 15 and 17). The point just now is only this. If we wish to avoid being misled about the precise import of 'the *cogito*' (in the restricted sense of this part), we must distinguish not two but three things. (1) Simple sensuous awareness of our own inner states, or what is ordinarily termed 'empirical self-consciousness,' the object of which is the empirical or psychological *ego* or self. This is what Gueroult designates by the expression "*conscience (moi) psychologique.*" It is without analogue in Descartes. For though the object of introspection is in fact the object of *conscientia*, that is, our actually occurring thoughts or mental states, *conscientia*, for Descartes, is a function of the pure intellect, the 'natural light,' rather than any sensuous faculty of introspection. From this we must distinguish (2) the Kantian 'I think' that accompanies all our acts of thinking as the pure form of thought in virtue of which all modes of thinking of objects outside us, cognitive, emotive, or volitional, are modes of one and the same self-consciousness. This is what Gueroult understands by "*conscience intellectuelle.*" It too lacks an exact counterpart in Descartes, although it is prefigured in some respects in Descartes's analysis of the innate concepts and eternal truths making up the basic furniture of the mind. Different again is (3), what Descartes designates by the term *experientia* and the other technical terms just mentioned, which will receive fuller consideration in Part Three. The merely negative answer to the question, whether the *cogito* refers to pure or empirical consciousness, is this: it combines aspects of (1) and (2) in a conception of thinking that coincides with neither. The positive answer will have to await Part Three.

PART TWO:
CERTAINTY AND TRUTH

So after considering everything very thoroughly, I must finally conclude that this proposition, *I am, I exist*, is necessarily true whenever it is put forward by me or conceived by my mind. (AT VII 25: CSM II 17)

Part One distinguished thought from consciousness, clarifying the relation of each to the *cogito* in that narrowly restricted sense that corresponds to the first word of Descartes's founding principle. Four separate items were identified as included within the sphere of certainty of the *cogito*.[1] It remains still to examine the precise sense in which any judgment of the reduced form 'I am conscious that I am thinking x'[2] is certain and "necessarily true" (AT VII 25: CSM II 17) for given values of 'thinking x.' This is attempted in Part Two.

Since the restricted sense of the *cogito* is only one of three to be distinguished here, we shall have to consider the certainty and necessity of the *cogito* in the other senses as well. The second is that familiar sense in which 'the *cogito*' stands, not for the first word, but for the whole principle as expressly conceived in reflecting upon one's actually occurring thinking and on the existence of the self that thinks. In the third sense, 'the *cogito*' refers again to the entire principle, but this time as the first *truth* within the deductively ordered system of scientific propositions called *vera & certa scientia* by Descartes.[3] To the extent that the first truth of metaphysics must assert the actual existence of something, and the existence of a substance or thing rather than an accident or mode, the latter two senses stress the final word of the formula, *sum*, much as the former stressed the first. The necessity of the *sum* is the main theme of this part as a whole.

The certainty of both *cogito* and *sum* is to be clarified with the help of a pair of meanings of 'perfect certainty': *persuasio* and *scientia*. What Descartes calls 'absolute' or 'metaphysical' certainty differs from what we would call 'reasonable' (and what Descartes calls 'moral') certainty only in degree, not in kind. These two degrees of certainty will be discussed in chapter 10. There are, moreover, two kinds of rational or absolute certainty. They differ from one another, not intensively or in degree, as they differ from moral certainty, but extensively, in respect of the time interval during which it is impossible to deny or even doubt something. Both kinds of certainty are perfect; but, with the notable exception of theological knowledge (about which more will be said presently), perfect certainty now (*persuasio*) does not entail perfect certainty at all times (*scientia*) except under two conditions: (1) the truths in question must be capable of being clearly remembered now to have been intuited or demonstrated with perfect certainty in the past; and (2) it must now be possible to recall the proof that God exists and can be no deceiver. These two kinds of perfect certainty will be discussed in chapter 11.

For Descartes, 'certainty' is in the first instance neither a normative term of epistemic appraisal nor a descriptive term for the logical distinctiveness of a certain class of self-referential statements ('I think,' 'I exist,' and so on); nor is it merely a descriptive psychological designation for what the human mind finds itself unable to doubt or deny given its own nature. 'Certainty' is simply synonymous with 'truth' in that primary sense of the term that Descartes took to be a primitive concept innate in the human mind. 'Truth' is an innate idea in the same sense as 'thought' was shown to be innate in Part One: what truth is is immediately present to consciousness in such a manner that the mind cannot help but become aware of it as soon as it begins to reflect on its thinking and existence and on the fact that it is true that it thinks and exists. 'Certainty' accordingly entails 'truth' in the only sense relevant to the establishment of the first principle of human knowledge, *cogito, ergo sum*. Only on this basis can something like 'the agreement of thought with its object,' which is the correct nominal definition of 'truth,' be established for all other knowledge. It is important to recognize that in the Second Meditation the sense in which the *cogito* principle is 'true' is not that of the nominal definition of truth, nor even *scientia*, but simply *persuasio*; the status of *scientia* can only be secured for it (and all other knowledge) *after* the proof of God's existence and veracity in the Third and the validation of the truth rule in the Fourth Meditation.[4] Until these items of *persuasio* have become *scientia*, the *cogito* principle cannot. Descartes's understanding of truth – to speak of a 'theory' would be to ignore his frequent admonitions that such simple ideas are only made more obscure by definitions – is the subject of chapters 12 and 13.

What we have termed the 'primary' conception of truth, and the only one that concerned Descartes in his search for a metaphysical first principle, has gone all but unnoticed in the vast literature on certainty and circularity. As a result, Descartes has been successfully acquitted of logical blunders and bootstrapping operations

only at the cost of underestimating the degree to which he was above all a speculative metaphysician concerned with the discovery of truth. He would hardly
have been content to have established, however irrefutably, conclusions, however innovative, about existential or other forms of logical inconsistency; about
stability, firmness, or other psychological features of beliefs; about irrevisability,
unmistakability, maximal warrant, or other evidential features of knowledge claims
generally. He undoubtedly addressed a variety of issues like these, but only incidentally; as a metaphysician he could not have accepted any of the surrogates for
truth that have been proposed in order to acquit him of the charges of psychologism,
circular reasoning, and outright contradiction.[5]

The distinction between *persuasio* and *scientia* gives rise to another among
three senses of 'clear and distinct perception': (1) *persuasio*, (2) that which is no
longer *persuasio* but not yet *scientia*, and (3) *scientia* itself. Only (2) is open to
doubt from the deceiving God hypothesis; (1) is not yet and (3) is no longer so.
These three senses of 'reason' are vital in exonerating Descartes of the charge of
attempting to validate reason by reason in a manner that is circular. Only that
which is recollected as having been intuited or demonstrated in the past, but is at
present no longer clearly and distinctly perceived, requires validation by the clear
and distinct perception of God's existence and veracity. Required is, of course,
scientia; otherwise everything lapses into uncertainty the instant I cease to attend
to the proofs of God's existence and veracity. However, *scientia* concerning the
existence of a veracious God is immediately attainable if *persuasio* can be got, as
the proofs in the Third and Fifth Meditations show Descartes believed it could;
for in the unique case of theological knowledge (the exception mentioned earlier)
that which is now clearly and distinctly perceived to be certain beyond the possibility of a 'metaphysical' doubt remains so ever after, unconditionally. This is
because even God cannot alter his own Nature at such times as we no longer
attend to it, although he can alter anything else of which we do not have current
clear and distinct perception. Thus, one aspect of the curious doctrine of the divine creation of the eternal truths comes to the aid of another; God's absolute
immutability is called in to dispel a doubt about recollected clear and distinct
perception engendered by the deceiving God hypothesis, a doubt to which the
clearly and distinctly perceived only becomes subject because of the doctrine of
divinely created eternal truths. For the Cartesian doctrine of truth by divine fiat
renders the eternal truths, if not contingent and mutable, then at least only relatively immutable, since they are alterable by God, or would be so alterable, unbeknownst to us, if God could be a deceiver. The Cartesian circle is the subject of
chapter 14.

10

The Degrees of Certainty

According to the "Synopsis" prefixed to the *Meditations*, the usefulness of the "extensive doubt" of the First Meditation

lies [1] in freeing us from all our preconceived opinions, and [2] providing the easiest route by which the mind may be led away from the senses. The eventual result of this doubt is [3] to make it impossible for us to have any further doubts about what we subsequently discover to be true. (AT VII 12: CSM II 9)

Thus, beyond furnishing a corrective for (1) the *failure to use one's reason* at all due to uncritical reliance on the judgment of others (prejudice), the systematic doubt of the First Meditation is expressly designed to achieve two further ends: to combat (2) the *misuse of reason* due to excessive reliance on the senses (precipitancy) and to overcome (3) the *mistrust of reason* due to excessive doubt (scepticism). Precipitancy in taking the testimony of the senses or the probable conjectures to which it gives rise as reliable guides to truth is common to ordinary pre-philosophical experience and to the philosophy of 'the Schools' (see section 6.1). Hence (2) supports (1) directly, where it might be thought to work against it, while (3), scepticism or the mistrust of reason, provides an added inducement to acquiesce in the teachings of some authority rather than exercise one's own native powers. Indeed (2) supports (3) directly, thereby further strengthening (1).

   This, at least, is the way the three uses of doubt are distinguished in the "Synopsis." Alternatively, the first two aims might be taken as targeting different kinds of prejudice: prejudices of authority and prejudices of precipitancy; for in a couple of places Descartes expressly refers to the misuse of reason due to an habitual attachment to the senses as falling victim to the "prejudices of the senses (*praejudica sensuum*)" (cf. AT VII 157 and 158: CSM II 111 and 112).[1]

10.1 Three uses of doubt

A detailed description of the "prejudices of the senses" is found in the Sixth Replies:

From infancy I had made a variety of judgments about physical things in so far as they contributed to preserving the life which I was embarking on, and subsequently I retained the same opinions I had originally formed (*praeconceperam*) of these things. But at that age the mind employed the bodily organs less correctly than it now does, and was more firmly attached to them; hence it had no thoughts apart from them and perceived things only in a confused manner. Although it was aware (*conscia*) of its own nature and had within itself an idea of thought as well as an idea of extension, it never exercised its intellect on anything without at the same time picturing something in the imagination. (AT VII 441: CSM II 297)[2]

The *praejudicia sensuum* are perceptual judgments based largely on habit. The underlying ideas are rendered obscure and confused when *hastily* assumed to be sources of knowledge of the natures of things outside us. That is why the misuse of reason due to *precipitancy* is much the same as habitual reliance on the prejudices of the senses: "I see that I have been in the *habit of misusing the order of nature*. For the proper purpose of sensory perceptions given me by nature is simply to inform the mind of what is beneficial or harmful for the composite of which the mind is a part; and to this extent they are sufficiently clear and distinct. But I *misuse* them by treating them as reliable touchstones for immediate judgements about the essential nature of bodies located outside us" (AT VII 83: CSM II 57 e.a.; cf. also *Principles*, II, 3 at AT VIII-1 41f.: CSM I 224).[3]

   The same three points mentioned in the "Synopsis" occur in the "Dedicatory Letter to the Sorbonne":

[A]lthough the proofs I employ here are in my view as certain and evident as the proofs of geometry ... it will be impossible for many people to achieve an adequate perception of them ... because they require a mind which is [1] completely free from preconceived opinions and which can [2] easily detach itself from involvement with the senses. What is more ... in geometry everyone has been taught to accept that as a rule no proposition is put forward in a book without there being a conclusive demonstration available; so inexperienced students make the mistake of accepting what is false ... more often than ... rejecting what is true. In philosophy, by contrast, the belief is that [3] everything can be argued either way; so few people pursue the truth, while the great majority build up their reputation for ingenuity by boldly attacking what is most sound. (AT VII 4: CSM II 5).

This provides a new perspective on (3). The third purpose of doubt is "to make it impossible to have any further doubts," this being what distinguished Descartes's manner of rooting out his former errors from the "sceptics, who doubt only for the sake of doubting and pretend to be always undecided; on the contrary, *my whole aim was to reach certainty*" (AT VI 29: CSM I 125 e.a.; cf. also AT V 147: CSMK 333). This is from the *Discourse*. But the passage from the "Letter to the Sorbonne" suggests that a generalized sceptical *relativism* popular in his own day, especially in regard to *philosophical* matters, may bulk just as large as the well-worn jibes at sense-experience and mathematical knowledge of the classical "Academics and Sceptics" (AT VII 130: CSM II 94). The "Preface to the Reader" confirms this. One passage begins indeed much like those cited already: "I would not urge anyone to read this book except those who are able and willing to meditate seriously with me, and to [2] withdraw their minds from the senses and [1] from all preconceived opinions" (AT VII 9: CSM II 8). But in the place of (3) there follows the famous reference to *l'ordre des raisons*, of which Gueroult (1968, 12f.) has made so much: "Those who do not bother to grasp the proper *order of my arguments* and the connection between them, but merely try to carp at individual sentences, *as is the fashion*, will not get much benefit from reading this book" (ibid., e.a.). Coming as it does after two points that mirror closely (1) and (2) of the "Synopsis," this may be more than a reminder that (as Descartes remarks to Gassendi) "what I wrote all fits together ... such that, for any given point, all the preceding remarks and most of those that follow contribute to the proof of what is asserted" (AT VII 379: CSM II 261; cf. also AT I 562: CSMK 87); it may be a veiled allusion to the prevalence of a generalized sceptical relativism that lifts philosophical conclusions out of their systematic context precisely in order to pick them apart more easily.

So much for scepticism or, as it is tempting to say in the light of the last few passages cited, 'misology.'[4] As for (2), a number of passages in the *Meditations* and Replies shed valuable light on the process of leading the mind "away from the senses." The first is from the Replies to Caterus: "For such a procedure made it much easier for me [1] to free myself from my preconceived opinions, [2] to attend to the light of nature" (AT VII 107: CSM II 77). This suggests that leading the mind away from the senses *just is* attending to the natural light of reason that the senses occlude. Thus, in the Second Replies Descartes writes: "if he [the reader] attends carefully to what I have written he should be able [1] to free himself from the preconceived opinions *which may be eclipsing his natural light, and to accustom himself to believing in the primary notions*, which are as evident and true as anything can be, in preference to opinions which are obscure and false, albeit fixed in the mind by long habit" (AT VII 135: CSM II 97 e.a.). An effort of attention is required in order to prevent these "primary notions" revealed by the natural light from being concealed by the habit of reliance on the senses.[5] Later in the Second Replies Descartes appeals to the judgment of "those who follow the road which I have indicated and who lay aside for a time whatever they have acquired from the senses, so as to attend to the dictates of *pure and uncorrupted* reason (*quid pura & incorrupta ratio dictet*) (AT VII 154: CSM II 109 e.a.). Somewhat later still he remarks that "they will be exercising the intellectual vision (*perspicuitatem intellectus*) which nature gave them, in the *pure* form which it attains when freed from the senses; for sensory appearances generally interfere with it and darken it to a very great extent" (AT VII 163: CSM II 115).[6] And in the Third Meditation, speaking of the truth of the axioms employed in the proof of God's existence, he notes: "There is nothing in all this that is not quite evident by the natural light to anyone who attends carefully (*quod diligenter attendenti non sit lumine naturali manifestum*). But when I relax my concentration, and my mental vision (*mentis aciem*) is blinded by the images of things perceived by the senses ..." (AT VII 47: CSM II 32). These passages are typical of many. *Acies mentis* (literally, the 'cutting edge' of the mind; cf. *acumen ingenij* at AT X 384: CSM I 23) harks back to Rule Five of the *Regulae*: "The whole method (*Tota methodus*) consists entirely in the ordering and arranging of the objects on which we must concentrate our mind's eye (*ad quae acies mentis est convertenda*)" (AT X 379: CSM I 20); and indeed, as Descartes writes in the very first Rule, "if someone seriously wishes to investigate the truth of things ... he should consider simply how to increase the natural light of his reason ... (*cogitet tantum de naturali rationis lumine augendo*)" (AT X 361: CSM I 10).

This should suffice on (3) scepticism and (2) detaching the mind from the senses. Something more should be said of (1), the prejudices due to authority, before considering a fourth use of systematic doubt not mentioned in the "Synopsis": providing an *operational definition and criterion of certainty* for the subsequent Meditations.

10.2 Precipitancy and authority

Gadamer (1960, 256 n. 1) has pointed out that the first to develop a detailed theory of prejudice, distinguishing clearly between *praejudicia auctoritatis et praecipitantiae*, was the Enlightenment figure Christian Thomasius.[7] However, the Enlightenment doctrine is strikingly prefigured in Descartes (as Gadamer notes, ibid., 261), who distinguished (1) the natural light of universal human reason not just from (2) the natural inclinations of the person or human being, but also from (3) the habit or custom of "misusing the order of nature" (AT VII 83: CSM II 57) and from (4) prejudices artificially acquired through subjection to the authority of others. If use of this fourfold division points forward both to Thomasius and to Schleiermacher's distinction between *Vorurteile aus Befangenheit* (failure to use reason) and *Fehlurteile aus Übereilung* (misuse of reason), it also harks back in an interesting way to the Greek distinction between *physis* and *nomos*. Interesting, too, are the differences between Descartes's and Hume's estimates of the respective roles of reason and custom or habit *within* human nature. Unfortunately, these historical questions cannot be pursued at any length here.[8] But it may be worth pausing a moment to document Descartes's schema somewhat more fully.

In an abortive effort within the Third Meditation to establish the extra-mental existence of something resembling the mind's sensory ideas of body, Descartes puts the question, "[W]hat is my reason for thinking that they [the ideas which I take to be derived from things existing outside the mind] resemble these things?" (AT VII 38: CSM II 26). His immediate response is, "Nature has apparently taught me to think this" (ibid.). He then goes on to draw a simple binary distinction between this natural or "spontaneous impulse" (ibid.) and the "natural light" (ibid.) of reason, the latter alone being a reliable guide to truth.

In the Sixth Meditation he returns to the question (AT VII 82: CSM II 56f.). Here, however, his aim is to establish "that everything that I am taught by nature contains *some* truth" (AT VII 80: CSM II 56 e.a.),[9] and so he introduces a further distinction between having "a real or positive inclination" (AT VII 83: CSM II 57) to believe something and having "simply made this judgment from childhood onwards without any rational basis" (ibid.). The former alone is a *natural* inclination, that is, is due to what "God has bestowed on me as a combination of mind and body" (AT VII 82: CSM II 57), while the latter is due largely to custom or habit. For 'nature,' in this context, means 'my own nature,' and this is defined as "nothing other than the totality of things bestowed upon me by God" (AT VII 80: CSM II 56). This God-given real inclination to believe certain things is distinct both from habit and from that positive propensity to believe certain things that God has given me *as a mind* or reason: the *lumen naturale*. The latter, however, is my 'nature' too in a restricted sense: "In this context I am taking nature to be something more limited than the totality of things bestowed on me by God" (AT VII 82: CSM II 57), namely those "things that belong *to the mind alone*" (ibid., e.a.). As the natural inclination to assent to certain things must be distinguished from the natural light, so too from those judgments that are due, not to anything positive received from God, but to the misuse of one's natural gifts owing to the habit of "treating them [sensory perceptions] as reliable touchstones for immediate judgements about the essential nature of the bodies located outside us" rather than in accordance with their "proper purpose," which is "simply to inform the mind of what is beneficial or harmful for the composite of which the mind is a part" (ibid.). Thus, as was suggested above, precipitancy in judgment is closely allied to habit or custom and set over against 'nature' both as natural light and as natural inclination. From here it is only a small step to the talk of *praejudicia sensuum* and another to *praejudicia praecipitantiae* – although, unlike the former, the latter was left, as Gadamer informs us, to Thomasius.

Just before composing the *Meditations*, Descartes comments in a letter to Mersenne on Herbert of Cherbury's *De Veritate*:

> He [Lord Herbert] recommends that one should above all follow natural instinct especially, from which he derives all his common notions. For my part, I distinguish two kinds of instinct. One is the natural light or mental vision (la lumiere naturelle ou *intuitus mentis*). This is the only instinct which I think one should trust. The other belongs to us *qua* animals, and is a certain impulse of nature towards the preservation of our body, towards the enjoyment of bodily pleasures, and so on. This should not always be followed. (AT II 599: CSMK 140)

Nominally, the distinction here is between two kinds of "instinct"; in truth, it is the same binary distinction drawn in the *Meditations* between reason ("natural light") and "spontaneous" (AT VII 38: CSM II 38) or "blind" (AT VII 40: CSM II 27) impulse. It can also be construed as a distinction between two kinds of 'common sense.' For the famous *bon sens* described at the outset of the *Discourse* as "the best-distributed thing in the world" (AT VI 1f.: CSM I 111), the *bona mens* (AT X 359: CSM II 9; also AT X 395: CSM I 30) and *mens pura* (AT X 368: CSM I 14) of the *Regulae*, and the *sanus sensus* and *sensus communis* ('common sense') of *The Search for Truth* (AT X 521: CSM II 415 and AT X 518: CSM II 412, respectively) simply coincide with the "natural light of reason" (the *lumen rationis naturale* of AT X 361: CSM I 10, called *lux rationis* at AT X 368: CSM I 14), described as *la lumière naturelle* or *intuitus mentis* in this passage. Here, admittedly, this (1) *philosophical* 'common sense,' universal human reason, is treated (in the manner of Lord Herbert) as a variety of instinct, the only trustworthy guide to truth and goodness; yet this is quite in keeping with a key feature of reason (or clear and distinct perception) to be discussed later (cf. section 12.4): its power to command assent. Reason, so understood, is opposed to (2) instinct as Lord Herbert understands it, the inclination of intellect and will that arises naturally from the mind's subjection to the bodily senses and desires. This is akin to *pre-philosophical* 'common sense,' *der gesunde Menschenverstand*. The convictions about the true and good that arise in this way are untrustworthy. Born of the mind's union with the body they are 'natural' in a sense different from convictions born of the mind's reflexion on itself, that is, natural human reason; yet like the latter they are in-born and so differ not just from (3) habit but also from

(4) those beliefs *artificially* induced by formal instruction and the reading of (authoritative) books.[10]

There is nothing canonical about a four-part scheme. In *The Search for Truth*, Descartes distinguishes (a) natural light, reason, or *bon sens*, that is, philosophical common sense from (b) natural inclination, or instinct *reinforced by habit*, that is, pre-philosophical common sense (*praejudicia sensuum*), and (c) philosophical teaching or prejudice due to authority. Thus Eudoxus, Descartes's spokesman, is "a man of moderate intellect but possessing a judgment which is not corrupted by any false beliefs and a reason which retains all the purity of its nature" (AT X 498: CSM II 401). He describes his method as one "which enables someone of average intelligence to discover for himself everything that the most subtle minds can devise" (AT X 506: CSM II 405). This clearly echoes Descartes's description of *his* method in the *Regulae*: "anyone who has mastered the whole method, however mediocre his intelligence, may see that there are no paths closed to him that are open to others" (AT X 399: CSM I 32). Of Eudoxus's interlocutors, Polyander ('many men') "has never studied at all," while Epistemon ('knowledgeable') "has a detailed knowledge of everything that can be learned in the Schools" (AT X 499: CSM II 401). They embody our two types of prejudice: *sensuum*, that is, natural inclination reinforced by habit, and *auctoritatis*. Accordingly, when Eudoxus describes Polyander as "unprejudiced" and "neutral" (AT X 502: CSM II 403), he means: free of the prejudices of learning and authority to which Epistemon is subject, but *not* free from the *praejudicia sensuum* (cf. the description of the *homo sensualis* in section 15.2 below). Polyander later describes himself as "a man who has never engaged in study *or accustomed himself to turning his mind so far away from things that are perceivable by the senses*" (AT X 512: CSM II 408 e.a.). At a still later point in the dialogue Eudoxus commends Polyander on his philosophical progress, remarking: "Provided we have proper direction, all we need for the discovery of the truth on the most difficult issues is, I think, common sense (*sensum communem*), to give it its ordinary name" (AT X 518: CSM II 412). This is a reference to philosophical *bon sens*, Polyander having been successfully led "by the hand along the path on which" Epistemon set him, that is, "away from the senses" (AT X 520: CSM II 414).

We shall return to the distinction between pre-philosophical and philosophical 'common sense' in the discussion of Descartes's subjectivism in the Conclusion (section 21.4). Regarding the *praejudicia auctoritatis*, it is interesting to note, in conclusion, how methodic doubt can be pressed into service to thwart appeals to authority without contesting their admissibility in principle or impugning any authority in particular. A good example is this mischievous passage in the Replies to the Fifth Set of Objections: "Your argument from authority is, I admit, sound enough," remarks Descartes to Gassendi, who has appealed to the authority of "many great thinkers" (AT VII 277: CSM II 193), "but, O Flesh, you certainly should not have presented it to a mind so withdrawn from corporeal things that it does not even know whether any people existed before it, and hence is not influenced by their authority" (AT VII 361: CSM II 249).[11]

10.3 A fourth use: Operational definition of 'certainty'

So much for the distinction of natural human reason from human nature, custom or habit, and authority. It bears on the three uses of doubt explicitly mentioned in the "Synopsis." It must be admitted that not all of Descartes's pronouncements on the usefulness of doubt are as instructive as the passage from the "Synopsis" with which we began; but neither are they all confined to the three uses considered so far.

In the letter to Clerselier written in reply to a compilation of Gassendi's most serious counter-objections Descartes states that "to prepare the mind in order to establish the truth at a later date ... was the *sole* aim" of the method of doubt employed in the First Meditation (cf. AT IX-1 205: CSM II 270 e.a.). This would appear to correspond to (3) alone, making it "impossible for us to have any further doubts about what we subsequently discover to be true," although it is possible to take 'preparing the mind' in a very broad sense that encompasses all three objectives. In the Second Replies Descartes writes that "the best way of achieving a firm knowledge of all things is first to accustom ourselves to doubting all things, especially corporeal things. Although I had seen many Ancient writings by the Academics and Sceptics on this subject, and was reluctant to reheat and serve this precooked material, I could not avoid devoting one whole Meditation to it" (AT VII 130: CSM II 94). This provides no clue at all as to the benefits to be derived from devoting, as Descartes here recommends, "several months, or at least weeks, to considering the topics dealt with, before going on to the rest of the book" (ibid.). In his reply to the first of Hobbes's objections, Descartes again speaks of "a threefold aim" of the *dubitandi rationes*, though the list differs slightly from that of the "Synopsis":

Partly [1] I wanted to prepare my readers' minds for the study of the things which are related to the intellect, and help them to distinguish these from corporeal things ... Partly [2] I introduced the arguments [*scil.* for doubting] so that I could reply to them in the subsequent Meditations. And partly [3] I wanted to show the firmness [i.e., certainty] of the truths (*quam firmae sint veritates*) which I propound later on, in the light of the fact that they cannot be shaken by these metaphysical doubts. (AT VII 171: CSM II 121)

The first aim here would appear to correspond to the second of the "Synopsis," detaching the mind from the senses, while the second and third are reminiscent of the third objective mentioned there, overcoming a misguided scepticism that ends in the distrust of reason itself.[12] However, the mention of 'firmness' points to a fourth objective, which must be considered more fully now. For in addition to those already mentioned – overcoming prejudice due to the mind's subjection to authority, prejudice due to its habitual reliance on the senses, and the mistrust of reason itself due to excessive scepticism – the regimen of doubt in the First Meditation has as its principal aim to provide an operational definition of perfect 'certainty.'[13]

According to the operational definition progressively elaborated in the course of the First Meditation, the term 'certainty' designates a property of all and only such beliefs as are able to withstand efforts to render them doubtful employing a succession of three increasingly radical grounds of doubt: (1) our proneness to be deceived by our senses; (2) our inability to distinguish reliably between waking experience and dreams; and (3) the hypothesis that we are deceived by an omnipotent but wicked God, or perhaps only by a demon less powerful than He, but very cunning. Such beliefs as withstand these grounds of doubt are presumed impossible to conceive or even imagine to be false. Emphasizing the impossibility of so much as feigning their falsity, Descartes writes in the *Discourse* that "while I could pretend (*feindre*) that I had no body and that there was no world and no place for me to be in, I could not for all that pretend that I did not exist" (AT VI 32: CSM I 127). Similarly, in the *Principles* he remarks that "it is easy for us to suppose that there is no God and no heaven, and that there are no bodies, and even that we ourselves have no hands or feet, or indeed any body at all. But we cannot for all that suppose (*supponere, supposer*) that we, who are having such thoughts, are nothing" (AT VIII-1 7: CSM I 194f.). What it means to be unable to 'feign' or 'suppose' the falsity of such things is spelled out *operationally* by the regimen of doubt within the *Meditations*: only if one doubts in the manner described there and nevertheless comes up against something that cannot be doubted or supposed false may one speak of perfect 'certainty.' The precise nature of the impossibility so defined will be considered in sections 12.2ff.

10.4 Metaphysical and moral certainty

This, then, at a first rough approximation, is the sense of 'certain' that characterizes the *sum* or *cogito, ergo sum*: imperviousness to doubt from each of three sources: (1) illusion, (2) dreams, and (3) the deceiving God hypothesis. Descartes, however, distinguished two degrees of certainty, corresponding in a rough general way to what might nowadays be termed 'rational' and 'reasonable certainty' respectively. The latter he himself terms 'moral certainty,' the former 'metaphysical' or 'absolute' certainty. In the First Meditation he speaks in one place of those "habitual opinions" that keep coming back "as a result of long occupation and the law of custom" as being "much more *reasonable* to believe than deny" (AT VII 22: CSM II 15 e.a.; cf. also AT VI 38: CSM I 130). On the face of it, his notion of reasonable certainty would seem to correspond pretty well to our own; and it does, extensionally at least, though the intensional meaning of 'reasonable certainty' is again defined in an idiosyncratic manner reminiscent of the operational definition of perfect certainty in Meditation One.[14]

Would Descartes give the name 'certainty' to anything less than perfect certainty? Surely not before the Sixth Meditation. But there the strict standard of certainty of the First Meditation is relaxed as even those things the truth of which is attested only by the senses are acknowledged to be immune from "the slightest doubt ... if, after calling upon all the senses as well as my memory and my intellect in order to check them, I receive no conflicting reports from any of these sources" (AT VII 90: CSM II 62). Such matters, though 'certain,' are clear without being distinct, and true without being necessarily so. The will has a natural propensity to assent to that the truth of which is uniformly attested by one or some of the senses, unless and until another of the senses or of the mind's cognitive faculties turns up contrary evidence. The fact that the other bodily senses are specifically mentioned is a faint but audible echo of the earlier argument from deception or illusion, from which, in the Sixth Meditation, even knowledge based on sense-perception is presumed exempt. The dreaming argument, too, is evoked as now no longer efficacious against the univocal testimony of the senses, as Descartes suddenly notices that there is a "vast difference" between being asleep and being awake, dreams being "never linked by memory with all the other actions of life as waking experiences are" (AT VII 89: CSM II 61). Although these vestiges of the conception of certainty operationally defined in the First Meditation remain, there is no mistaking the fact that Descartes has slackened his initial standard of evidence in order to widen the domain of certainty to correspond to that assigned it in Scholastic-Aristotelian philosophy and by sound common sense. The standard of certainty and truth invoked at the end of the Sixth Meditation is clearly that of reasonable rather than rational certainty.

It should be borne in mind that, as with the rational certainty of some matters clearly and distinctly perceived, matters perceived clearly but not distinctly are reasonably certain only once God's existence and veracity are metaphysically certain, that is, only once the deceiving God hypothesis has lost its force. It is from "the fact that God is not a deceiver [that] it follows that in cases like these [sense-perception under specified conditions] I am completely free from error" (AT VII 90: CSM II 62). Hobbes elicits an express clarification of this point by remarking that if "the certainty and truth of all knowledge depends solely on our knowledge of the true God," then "an atheist cannot infer that he is awake on the basis of memory of his past life" (AT VII 196: CSM II 137). To this Descartes replies: "An atheist can infer that he is awake on the basis of memory of his past life. But he cannot know that this criterion is sufficient to give him the certainty that he is not mistaken, if he does not know that he was created by a non-deceiving God" (ibid.). Descartes does not mean merely that the memory of his past life does not give the atheist perfect certainty; he means that without the knowledge of God one lacks even reasonable certainty that one is awake rather than asleep. From this it appears that however well Descartes's conception of reasonable certainty may accord extensionally with our own, intensionally it in fact differs sharply. For, as the Sixth Meditation and the reply to Hobbes make clear, the metaphysical knowledge of God is required not just for the founding of the sciences, but even for the reliability of pre-scientific experience of the world around us; and this is a very far cry from the ordinary understanding of 'reasonable certainty.'

'Metaphysical certainty' yields knowledge that is certain beyond the *logical* possibility of a doubt, moral certainty knowledge that is beyond a *reasonable*, not a logically possible, doubt. A related distinction is that between the certainty that is indispensable for action and that which is requisite for theoretical knowledge. Thus, in the First Meditation, Descartes remarks that he "cannot possibly go too far in [his] distrustful attitude ... because the task now in hand does not involve action but merely the acquisition of knowledge" (AT VII 22: CSM II 15). In this there is more than a faint echo of the famous "maxims" of the "provisional moral code" (AT VI 22: CSM I 122) adopted in Part Three of the *Discourse*: "Once I had established these maxims and set them on one side together with the truths of faith, which have always been foremost among my beliefs, I judged that I could freely undertake to rid myself of all the rest of my opinions" (AT VI 28: CSM I 125). The distinction between "matters pertaining to faith or the conduct of life" and "speculative truth" (AT VII 15: CSM II 11) was inserted into the "Synopsis" at the suggestion of Arnauld (AT VII 216: CSM II 151f.). In his reply to Arnauld, Descartes notes (AT VII 248: CSM II 172) that he had already adverted to the distinction between "the conduct of life and the contemplation of truth" in the Replies to the Second Set of Objections:

As far as the conduct of life is concerned, I am very far from thinking that we should assent only to what is clearly [and distinctly] perceived. On the contrary, I do not think that we should always wait even for probable truths; from time to time we will have to choose one of many alternatives about which we have no knowledge, and once we have made our choice, so long as no reason against it can be produced, we must stick to it as firmly as if it had been chosen for transparently clear reasons. I explained this on p. 26 of the *Discourse on the Method.* (AT VII 149: CSM II 106)

In the Fifth Replies he again points to "the distinction which I have insisted on in several passages between the actions of life and the investigation of the truth. For when it is a question of organizing our life, it would, of course, be foolish not to trust the senses" (AT VII 350f.: CSM II 243). Finally, in the Replies to the Seventh Set of Objections he contrasts "the kind of extreme doubt which ... is metaphysical and exaggerated" with that which is may be doubted "in practical life" (AT VII 460: CSM II 308). Later in the same set of Replies (AT VII 475: CSM 320) "metaphysical knowledge" is contrasted with "'knowing' in the practical sense which suffices for the conduct of life." These correspond in a rough general way to "metaphysical certainty" (AT VII 477: CSM II 321) and moral certainty, respectively. The parallel may even account in part for the designation of 'reasonable' as 'moral' certainty.

10.5 Naive realism

So much for 'certainty' in the strict sense of the First and the relaxed sense of the Sixth Meditation. According to the operational definition of Meditation One, 'certainty,' that is, rational, metaphysical, or absolute certainty, may be predicated only of those things that are utterly impervious to all three grounds of doubt. In order to distinguish both degrees of certainty more sharply, it will be useful to examine the precise extent of each of the three grounds of doubt involved in the operational definition of perfect 'certainty.'

First, however, it may be worth pausing to consider just how Descartes's argument from illusion differs from the argument now customarily so designated (classically formulated by Hume and partially cited already n. 2 of chapter 4) as well as from what Flew calls the "second kind of Argument from Illusion" (1971, 352ff.). The latter are both designed to provide support for representationalism (see sections 4.1 and 21.1ff.), though their starting points differ. One proceeds from cases in which we are mistaken about *what we are perceiving* to the conclusion that all we ever perceive are ideas in the mind. Examples are the bent stick (dutifully trotted out by Gassendi at AT VII 333: CSM II 231), the square tower, Berkeley's bucket of water (cf. Berkeley 1965, 116f.), and Hume's table (cf. Hume 1990, 183) – though these cases are by no means identical among themselves in all relevant respects. The second kind of argument from illusion reaches the same conclusion from examples like dreams. Here the starting point is the mistaken belief *that we are perceiving anything at all.*

Neither Descartes's argument from illusion nor his dreaming argument is intended to provide support for representationalism, any more than are the doubts about "natural inclination" or what "my own nature teaches me" (AT VII 80: CSM II 56) expressed in the Third and Sixth Meditations. From similar starting points – lucid dreams in the First Meditation (AT VII 19: CSM II 13; cf. AT X 511: CSM II 408), the tower example in the Sixth (AT VII 76: CSM II 53) – Descartes argues instead to a conclusion about the *certainty* of our knowledge of (1) the existence, (2) the essence or nature, and (3) the causal efficacy of the sensible things represented in ordinary sense-perception. The upshot is a doubt, "not flippant or ill-considered" (AT VII 21: CSM II 15), about their mind-independent existence as well as about the causal and representative realism implicit in everyday pre-philosophical experience. The naive convictions targeted by these arguments are best described in the Third Meditation as the beliefs "that there were things outside me [mind-independent existence] which were the sources of my ideas [causal realism] and which resembled them in all respects [unqualified representative realism]" (AT VII 35: CSM II 25). All three conclusions are probably implicit in the talk of the "truth of the things perceived by the senses" in the Sixth Meditation, though the focus is on *causal* realism:

> As for the reasons for my previous confident belief in the truth of the things perceived by the senses, I had no trouble in refuting them. For since I apparently had natural impulses towards many things which reason told me to avoid, I reckoned that a great deal of confidence should not be placed in what I was taught by nature [natural inclination]. And despite the fact that the perceptions of the senses were not dependent on my will, I did not think that I should on that account infer that they proceeded from things distinct from myself [causal realism]. (AT VII 77: CSM II 53 e.a.)

Under discussion here is the *truth or certainty* of causal realism: *not* whether we really perceive extra-mental objects rather than just ideas in the mind, but the degree of "confidence" to be placed in the natural assumption that such objects *cause* the sensory ideas in our minds. At issue is therefore – although neither question is explicitly mentioned here – whether such objects actually exist outside the mind as well as intentionally in it, and whether they resemble those ideas, at least in part.[15] Later in the Sixth Meditation Descartes remarks of "colours, sounds, smells and tastes, as well as differences in heat, hardness and the like": "I am correct in inferring that the bodies which are the source of these various sensory perceptions possess differences *corresponding to them, though perhaps not resembling them*" (AT VII 81: CSM II 56 e.a.). The reservation about the certainty of *representative* realism apparently does not hold to quite the same extent for causal realism. This much is apparent already at the conclusion of the explicitly *causal* proof of the existence of corporeal things: "They may not all exist in a way that exactly corresponds with my sensory grasp of them, for in many cases the grasp of the senses is very obscure and confused. But at least they possess all the properties which I clearly and distinctly understand, that is, all those which, *viewed in general terms*, are comprised within the subject-matter of pure mathematics" (AT VII 80: CSM II 55 e.a.). This is no more than a *qualified* representative realism, confined to general truths regarding "shape, number, motion and so on" (AT VII 63: CSM II 44). Like causal realism, however, it depends on the knowledge of God's existence and veracity. So does the knowledge of "other aspects of corporeal things which are either particular (for example that the sun is of such and such a size or shape), or less clearly understood, such as light or sound or pain and so on" (AT VII 80: CSM II 55). In fact, it is these that give rise to the whole "teachings of nature" doctrine with which the *Meditations* conclude, the doctrine that finally dispels the "exaggerated doubts" (AT VII 89: CSM II 61) occasioned by the illusion and dreaming arguments of the First Meditation.

So it is not just the existence of corporeal things that has been established with absolute or metaphysical certainty by the end of the Sixth Meditation; both causal and a qualified representational realism regarding ordinary sensible things have been established as at least morally certain as well. Causal and representative realism involving the extra-mental existence of material things make up 'naive realism' as Descartes might have used that expression. Nowadays the same expression is frequently applied to the denial of representationalism, that is, to the view allegedly subverted by the other two arguments from illusion distinguished by Flew. For Descartes, however, it is certain beyond the possibility of a doubt that ordinary sensible things exist *intentionally* in the mind as the *immediate* objects of thinking; this much is directly present to consciousness and therefore absolutely or metaphysically certain. As for the certainty with which such objects are naively supposed to exist actually outside the mind, to cause the corresponding ideas in the mind, and to resemble those ideas, all this is relatively uncertain and can never be rendered even morally certain *without the knowledge of God*. This is again just the 'epistemic difference' in a new guise (cf. section 4.2). But since *with* the knowledge of God, all this *can* be rendered perfectly certain, to ascribe to Descartes the theory of perception known as representationalism on the strength of *this* argument from illusion is surely misguided.

Similarly, in the Third and Sixth Meditations, where "natural inclination" and the "teachings of nature" are declared untrustworthy, the suggestion is in no wise that all we ever think about are our own ideas. The 'natural,' though philosophically 'naive,' tendency shown to be doubtful by this means has to do with the certainty commonly ascribed the knowledge of sensible things vis-à-vis knowledge of the mind, that is, with the relative uncertainty of knowledge of the objects of thought vis-à-vis the objects of consciousness. Here it is neither the illusion nor the dreaming argument, but the third main ground of doubt that is at work: "the possibility that my natural constitution made me prone to error even in matters which seemed to me most true" (AT VII 77: CSM II 53). As the use of the past tense ("seemed") indicates, it is the testimony of the senses, not clear and distinct ideas, that the meditator formerly took to be "most true." Thus, the possibility in question is that I have received from God a nature that deceives me about ordinary sensible things. The proof of the non-deceptiveness of everything that comes from God does not establish that what we perceive in ordinary sense-perception are things rather than just the ideas of things; that was never in question. It establishes rather that our belief in the existence of extra-mental corporeal causes of our ideas with natures that correspond to (without actually resembling) our sensory ideas is perfectly certain, however derivative such certainty may be in relation to the rational certainty attainable about the mind.

Whatever may have been the target of the stock arguments constituting the arsenal of 'the sceptics,' the illusion, dreaming, and deceiving God arguments of Descartes's First Meditation are intended to establish once and for all a new *order*, not a new *object*, of cognition. That is a very material difference, and one that has been consistently overlooked.

10.6 The illusion and the dreaming arguments

We now begin consideration of the precise extent of each of the three grounds of doubt. The first, the argument from illusion or the deceptiveness of the senses, is designed to call into question perceptual judgments regarding bodies observed under less than ideal circumstances, for example, "objects which are very small or in the distance" (AT VII 17: CSM II 12).[16] On the other hand, the same argument is acknowledged to have little or no force against observation statements about, say, middle-sized material objects perceived at an ideal distance from the observer under something like optimal conditions, and perhaps confirmed by various other sensory faculties: "for example, that I am here, sitting by the fire, wearing a winter dressing-gown, holding this piece of paper in my hands, and so on. Again, how could it be denied that these hands or this whole body are mine [or exist]? (*Manus vero has ipsas, totumque hoc corpus meum esse, qua ratione posset negari?*)" (AT VII 18: CSM II 13).[17] Observation statements like these correct others that prove delusive, hallucinatory, or in some other sense non-veridical; but it is unclear how they themselves could both be correctly described as performed under optimal conditions and yet require or admit of correction in the course of further observation. Of course, they might be corrected by some other faculty of the mind, by the intellect, for example; but that possibility is not raised here, even though Descartes suggests something of the kind later, in the

Third Meditation, where he speaks of exact "astronomical reasoning" (AT VII 39: CSM II 27) correcting one's perception of the diameter of the sun, and again in the Sixth, where he describes both memory and intellect as capable of confirming or infirming beliefs uniformly attested by "all the senses" (AT VII 90: CSM II 62). Here Descartes only observes that for him to doubt such things as these is to liken himself "to madmen, whose brains are so damaged by the persistent vapours of melancholia that they firmly maintain they are kings when they are paupers, or say they are dressed in purple when they are naked, or that their heads are made of earthenware, or that they are pumpkins, or made of glass. But such people are insane, and I would be thought equally mad if I took anything from them as a model for myself" (AT VII 19: CSM II 13). In the next breath, however, he dismisses this charge with derision ("A brilliant piece of reasoning!"), introducing the dreaming argument in order show that one would not have to be mad at all to doubt such things as these. The fact that "there never are sure signs by means of which being awake can be distinguished from being asleep" (ibid.) suffices to infix in the mind a doubt even about the existence of the objects of the clearest, multiply corroborated sense-perceptions.[18] For if nothing existed outside the mind corresponding to the ideas or images in it, then not only would *this* head and *these* hands not exist; neither would things *like* heads and hands, nor the sensory qualities of such things, for instance, the colours, which even the productive imagination is thought incapable of inventing rather than merely recombining in new ways, having borrowed the originals of all its reproductions from antecedent sense-perception of qualities actually existing in objects outside the mind. Moreover, if no extended things exist, then beliefs about "even simpler and more universal things" like "extension; the shape of extended things; the quantity, or size and number of these things; the place in which they may exist, the time through which they may endure, and so on" (AT VII 20: CSM II 14) are doubtful. For such quantitatively describable features of things are ordinarily believed to exist actually outside the mind as well as intentionally in it. This may be seen from the example of place. In the *Discourse*, Descartes remarks on having noticed that he could "pretend that [he] had no body and that *there was* no world and *no place* for [him] to be in" (AT VI 32: CSM I 127 e.a.), but not that he did not exist. From this he concludes that he knew he "was a substance whose whole essence or nature is simply to think, and which *does not require any place*, or depend on any material thing, in order to exist" (AT VI 33: CSM I 127 e.a.). If it is conceivable that "even simpler and more universal things" like size, shape, number, place, and so on exist nowhere but in the mind, then all our beliefs regarding them are at least doubtful.[19]

As to the precise extent of the dreaming argument of the First Meditation, it takes over where the argument from the deceptiveness of the senses leaves off, after (1) perceptual judgments regarding bodies observed under less than ideal circumstances. It provides collateral evidence for doubting these, but its real work begins with (2) ordinary pre-scientific sense-perceptions carried out under good conditions. From these it could be extended to (3) exact scientific observation conducted under ideal, perhaps controlled experimental, conditions – though Descartes does not spell this out. He does, however, mention (4) statements asserting the existence of objects of the same general kind as the objects of ordinary pre-scientific experience – not *this* head, *my* hands, and so on, but heads, hands, in general; for even if the particular objects that I think I see are only dream images and do not really exist outside the mind, at least the originals of our dreams and phantasies, *some* heads and hands, must exist somewhere outside the mind. It must be some such argument as this that is implicitly rejected in the sequel, presumably because it is not certain that the imagination is merely a reproductive rather than a productive faculty of the mind. Descartes next extends the doubt introduced by the dreaming argument to (5) statements about the sensory qualities that belong to these "general kinds of things" (AT VII 20: CSM II 13), their colours, odours, sounds, tastes, tactile qualities. Even if such things as hands and heads do not really exist outside the mind exactly as I picture them to myself, even if the imagination *is* productive after all in the sense that it can form ideas of objects that have never been seen and do not actually exist anywhere, at least the ideas of the qualities that we imagine such objects to possess must have been derived from qualities actually existing in things outside the mind rather than from the imagination. However, the assumption that the simple ideas of sensory qualities cannot be fictitious is implicitly rejected too as the dreaming argument passes directly to a consideration of (6): scientific theorizing about "simpler and more universal things" like body or "corporeal nature in general, and its extension; the shape of extended things; the quantity, or size and number of these things; the place in which they may exist, the time through which they may endure, and so on" (AT VII 20: CSM II 14). And it ends with (7) the sciences of "physics, astronomy, medicine" themselves, "and all other disciplines which depend on the study of *composite* things" (AT VII 20: CSM II 14 e.a.).

So all of the above are rejected on the strength of the dreaming argument, (1) having been rejected already on the basis of the argument from illusion. But it is equally important to note what the dreaming argument does *not* extend to. It does not extend beyond those "simpler and more universal things" mentioned under (6) to include (8): the "simplest and most general things" (ibid.) that are the objects of pure mathematics, propositions like "two and three added together are five, and a square has no more than four sides" (AT VII 20: CSM II 14), the denials of which are self-contradictory.[20] In other words, the dreaming argument suffices to show that empirically proceeding science as a whole is doubtful, since the truth of its theories concerning the mathematically describable features of the world depends upon the *existence* of physical objects outside the mind. Accordingly, the branches of knowledge included under (7) are regarded as uncertain even before the introduction of the deceiving God hypothesis. But (8) the truths of pure arithmetic and geometry are utterly resistant to the dreaming argument since they do not depend upon the existence of anything outside the mind *in rerum natura*, as Descartes says (AT VII 20: CSM II 14):

I find within me countless ideas of things which even though they may not exist anywhere outside me still cannot be called nothing ... When, for example, I imagine a triangle, even if perhaps no such figure exists, or has ever existed, anywhere outside my thought, there is still a determinate nature, or essence, or form of the triangle which is immutable and eternal, and not invented by me or dependent on my mind. (AT VII 64: CSM II 44f.)

The Latin text of the Fifth Meditation from which this passage is taken concludes with the words, "And now it is possible for me to achieve full and certain knowledge of countless matters, both concerning God himself and other things whose nature is intellectual, and also concerning the whole of that corporeal nature which is the subject-matter of pure mathematics." Instead of the final phrase, the French version has "... as the object of geometrical demonstrations which have no concern with whether that object exists" (AT IX-1 56: CSM II 49n). Similarly in the *Discourse*: "I noted also that there was nothing at all in these [mathematical] demonstrations which assured me of the existence of their object. For example, I saw clearly that the three angles of any given triangle must equal two right angles; yet for all that, I saw nothing which assured me that there existed any triangle in the world" (AT VI 36: CSM I 129). Since the conclusions of mathematical demonstrations, like the premises from which they are derived, do not depend for their truth upon the actual existence of material things, Descartes can indeed say: "whether I am awake or asleep, two and three added together are five, and a square has no more than four sides" (AT VII 20: CSM II 14). The truths of pure mathematics are secure against the dreaming argument.[21]

10.7 Ideas of *vera et realia entia* and other ideas

Prescind from Descartes's doctrine of divine creation of the eternal truths and it might be tempting to interpret the immunity of mathematics to the dreaming argument anachronistically, as though calling mathematical definitions and axioms 'true' meant that their denials were self-contradictory, while calling theorems 'true' implied only that they follow in logic from some set of conventional definitions, together with certain axioms, and postulates. This is one way of con-

struing truth in mathematics without bestowing existential import on its definitions, axioms, and theorems;[22] it has the added advantage of explaining how a
theorem demonstrably true within one formal axiomatized system might be demonstrably false in another. However, Descartes is so far from holding anything
like this general theory of truth or definition that he would not even countenance
it in the domains of logic and mathematics where, if anywhere, it belongs.[23] Though
immune from doubt occasioned by the dreaming argument (because independent
of anything actually existing *in rerum natura*), mathematical definitions and truths
have extra-mental objects for Descartes. Yet such objects are determinate natures
or essences rather than anything actually existing in bodies in space. In the conversation with Burman they are called *vera et realia entia*:

Thus, all the demonstrations of mathematicians deal with true entities and objects (*vera
entia et obiecta*), and the complete and entire object of mathematics and everything it
deals with is a true and real entity (*verum et reale ens*). This object has a true and real
nature (*habet veram et realem naturam*), just as much as the object of physics itself. The
only difference is that physics considers its object not just as a true and real entity, but
also as something actually existing with such a nature (*actu et qua tale existens*). Mathematics, on the other hand, considers its object merely as possible, i.e. as something
which does not actually exist in space but is capable of doing so. (AT V 160: CSMK 343)

The *more geometrico* proofs of the Second Replies list among the *axiomata
sive communes notiones*: "Existence is contained in the idea or concept of every
single thing, since we cannot conceive of anything except as existing. Possible or
contingent existence is contained in the concept of a limited thing, whereas necessary and perfect existence is contained in the concept of a supremely perfect
being" (AT VII 166: CSM II 117). The expression "possible or contingent existence" is puzzling, but appears to mean that possible rather than actual contingent
existence of an object *in rerum natura* is involved in any concept that is free of
contradiction, while actual and necessary existence of its object belongs to the
concept of God alone. If this is correct, then the first part of the axiom asserts that
anything that cannot be conceived without contradiction and hence as at least
capable of existing *in rerum natura* cannot be properly said to be conceived at
all; of such a thing we have no conception or idea whatsoever, the corresponding
word being just a *flatus vocis*, a sound to which no idea corresponds (cf. above
section 8.2 and n. 24 below).

However, Descartes has expressed himself elliptically here. The axiom is meant
to apply only to those things that are *clearly and distinctly* conceived, whether
they be objects (a) of simple ideas like 'knowledge,' 'doubt,' 'ignorance,' 'volition,' 'extension,' 'shape,' 'motion,' 'line,' 'three,' and so on, (b) of composite

ideas like 'a triangle' or 'a square,' 'mind,' 'body,' 'God,' or even (c) of still more complex ideas such as 'a triangle inscribed in a square.' It does not apply, however, to the objects of (d) simple sensory ideas of colours, odours, tastes, and so on, nor to those of (e) ideas designating so-called natural kinds like 'lion', 'horse,' and 'man.' Nor, finally, does it apply to the objects of (f) the fictions of the imagination such as 'hippogriff,' 'a winged horse,' 'an existing lion,' 'a supremely perfect body.' For (d) through (f) are obscure and confused ideas; they may contain a latent contradiction, just as the objects of (g) purported ideas like 'a round square' or 'a mountain without a valley' involve a contradiction that is perfectly apparent. Descartes's axiom, in short, does not mark the divide between the *ens necessarium* and all those contingent things that *may exist for all we know*; the divide is rather between God and all those objects *which we know may exist* if God so wills, since we clearly and distinctly perceive that their ideas are free of contradiction and that God can make actual anything we conceive as possible. The ellipsis is all the more unaccountable as Descartes expresses himself more fully elsewhere, for example in the First Replies: "It must be noted that possible existence is contained in the concept or idea of everything *that we clearly and distinctly understand*; but in no case is necessary existence so contained, except in the case of the idea of God" (AT VII 116: CSM II 83 e.a.). The addition permits a sharp demarcation between the *vera et realia entia* listed under (a), (b), and (c), and the objects that fall under (f) and (g). But while necessary, clarity and distinctness are not sufficient: in addition to being clear and distinct, the idea whose object is a *verum et reale ens* must be complete as well, though it cannot be demanded that it be adequate.[24]

10.8 Incomplete, complete, and adequate ideas

It is worth dwelling a moment longer on the distinction between the innate ideas under (a), (b), and (c), whose objects are clearly and distinctly perceived "true and immutable natures," and (e), those multivocal universals like 'man, 'horse,' and other 'natural kinds,' whose objects are neither distinctly conceived nor therefore *vera et realia entia*. Behind this portion of the classification lies a division of ideas into the incomplete, complete, and adequate. Of composite "true and immutable natures" like God, the mind, or a triangle we possess complete, if not adequate, concepts; the difference is explained to Arnauld in the Fourth Replies: "if a piece of knowledge is to be adequate it must contain absolutely all the properties which are in the thing which is the object of knowledge. Hence only God can know that he has adequate knowledge of all things" (AT VII 220: CSM II 155). A created intellect, "even though perhaps it may in fact possess adequate knowledge of many things (*etsi forte revera habeat [cognitiones adaequatas] rerum multarum*), can never know it has such knowledge unless God grants it a special revelation. In order to have adequate knowledge of a thing all that is required is that the power of knowing possessed by the intellect is adequate for the thing in question, *and this can easily occur*" (ibid., e.a.). Thus, anyone who reflects sufficiently will discover himself to have a complete idea of the "true and immutable nature" of a triangle, while a geometer who grasps many more of the *propria* belonging to its nature will possess a much more (though presumably still not completely) adequate idea of a triangle; and even were he to obtain a completely adequate idea of it, he could never know that he had done so except by "a special revelation."[25] By contrast, those 'natures' under (e), which are the products of mental abstraction, for example, the 'natural kinds' of Scholastic metaphysics, are neither adequate nor complete, since what they include and exclude depends upon the operation of the will in the process of mental abstraction. They are accordingly not ideas of *vera et realia entia* at all.[26]

In the cited passages there is also an implicit distinction between, on the one hand, (b) and (c), that is, composite ideas of "true and immutable natures" like those of a triangle, the mind (finite thinking substance) or God (infinite thinking substance), and, on the other, (a), simple ideas like those of volition or extension: of the latter we have not just complete but adequate knowledge, though we cannot know (by unassisted reason alone) that we know them adequately. At times, it is true, Descartes appears to deny that the human mind can possess fully adequate knowledge of anything, not excepting simple natures. To Gassendi he writes: "you fail to distinguish between, on the one hand, an understanding which is suited to the scale of our intellect (and each of us knows by his own experience quite well that he has this sort of [complete] understanding of the infinite) and, on the other hand, *a fully adequate conception of things (and no one has this sort of conception either of the infinite or of anything else, however small it may be)*" (AT VII 365: CSM II 252 e.a.). While this seems quite categorical, Descartes may not be speaking of simple natures at all here but only of smaller and smaller parts of the created universe. Alternatively, he may not be distinguishing between knowing and knowing that one knows: "Surely, no one's knowledge *of anything* has ever reached the point (*ita novit*) where he knows (*ut sciret*) that there is absolutely nothing further in the thing beyond what he is already aware of (*cognoscebat*)" (AT VII 129: CSM II 93 e.a.). Only some such interpretation would render this consistent with the position outlined in the *Regulae*:

For it can happen that we think we are ignorant of the things we really know, as for example when we suspect that they contain something else which is hidden from us, something beyond that which we intuit or reach in our thinking, even though we are mistaken in thinking this. For this reason, it is evident that we are mistaken if we ever judge that we lack complete knowledge of any one of these simple natures (*si quando aliquam ex naturis istis simplicibus a nobis totam non cognosci judicemus*). For if we have even the slightest grasp of it in our mind – which we must surely have, on the assumption that we are making a judgement about it – it must follow that we have complete knowledge of it (*nos totam illam [naturam simplicem] cognoscere*). Otherwise it could not be said to be simple, but a composite made up of that which we perceive in it and that of which we judge we are ignorant. (AT X 420f.: CSM I 45)

Thus, on what seems the most plausible interpretation, (1) we, who do not yet know it, can judge correctly that there is more to be known in our idea of a composite nature than we already know explicitly; and (2) an expert, who already knows what we do not, may even know this for certain. On the other hand, (3) we may mistakenly believe there to be more in our idea of any object than we already know, when in fact nothing more is contained in it than we already know explicitly. And another can make the same error. But (4) neither we nor anybody else can ever know for certain that we already know all that is contained in our idea of any nature, simple or composite, even though that is sometimes the case, except with the aid of divine illumination.

Out of the distinction between complete and incomplete ideas a further important category of ideas looms up in addition to those distinguished already: (h) ideas like 'substance,' 'existence,' 'duration,' 'magnitude,' 'number,' and 'order.' Like the innate ideas under (a) to (c), they are "very distinct" and therefore clear; and like those under (a), they are simple.[27] But like the factitious ideas of natural kinds they are not ideas of complete *res* or natures like 'thought,' 'extension,' or 'God.' For this reason, "the universals" (as Descartes calls them) are not *vera et realia entia*. This needs to be elaborated briefly, not only for its bearing on the question under consideration, the scope of the dreaming argument, but because it sheds fresh light on an interesting controversy concerning the place of mathematical entities in Descartes's ontology.

10.9 Universals, modes of thinking, and modes of things

The universals are treated as attributes in *Principles*, I, 62, where Descartes defines a conceptual distinction (*distinctio rationis*) as "a distinction between a substance and some *attribute* of that substance without which the substance is unintelligible; alternatively," he continues, "it is a distinction between two such attributes of a single substance ... For example, since a substance cannot cease to endure (*durare*) without also ceasing to be (*esse*), the distinction between the substance and its duration is merely a conceptual one" (e.a.). The universals 'duration' and 'existence' are called 'attributes' here; yet unlike the attributes 'thought' and 'extension,' "which can be regarded as constituting the *natures* of intelligent substance and corporeal substance" (I, 63 e.a.), they (and all other universals) "extend to all classes of things" (I, 48), mental or material, without constituting the *nature* of anything.[28] So there are two quite distinct kinds of attributes in Descartes: the "principal attributes" (I, 53) and the "universals" (I, 58).

In a hastily penned note of 1645 or 1646 (AT IV 349f.: CSMK 279f.) Descartes expressly describes attributes of the second type as *modi cogitandi duntaxat,* or *attributa sive modi cogitandi,* distinguishing them from *modi rerum ipsarum* or *modi proprie dicti.* By the "modes of things themselves," however, he does not mean the "principal attributes" of extended and thinking substance respectively, but rather the changing 'modifications' (cf. I, 56) *of* those (permanent) attributes: "shape and motion are modes, in the strict sense, of corporeal substance; because the same body can exist at one time with one shape and at another with another, now in motion and now at rest; whereas, conversely, neither this shape nor this motion can exist without this body" (AT IV 349: CSMK 280). By the same token, "love, hatred, affirmation, doubt and so on are true modes (*veri modi*) in the mind" (ibid.); and so, of course, are "all the modes both of perceiving and willing" (I, 48). Since "existence, duration, size, number and all universals are not ... modes in the strict sense ..., [t]hey are referred to by a broader term and called *attributes, or modes of thinking,* because we do indeed understand the essence of a thing in one way (*alio modo*) when we consider it in abstraction from whether it exists or not, and in a different way (*alio* [scil. *modo*]) when we consider it as existing; but the thing itself cannot be outside our thought without its existence, or without its duration or size, and so on" (AT IV 349: CSMK 280 e.a.).[29]

So unlike the changing modifications of the principal attributes of mind and body, the universals are "modes of thought" rather than "modes of things themselves": "some attributes ... are in the very things of which they are said to be attributes or modes, while others are only in our thought" (I, 57). "Number and all universals are simply modes of thinking" (I, 58); "we should regard the duration of a thing simply as a mode under which we conceive the thing in so far as it continues to exist. And similarly we should not regard order or number as anything separate from the things which are ordered and numbered, but should think of them simply as modes under which we consider the things in question" (I, 55). The same may be said of the five universals which are "commonly listed" in the Schools: *genus, species, differentia, proprium,* and *accidens* (I, 58).

Since certain of these "common universals" (ibid.) figure crucially in the Scholastic theory of definition, 'essence,' like 'existence,' must be counted among the universals.[30] In fact, the subject of the quick note cited earlier is "the distinction between essence and existence" (AT IV 348: CSMK 278), a distinction there said to be merely "conceptual," although Descartes hastens to add (as already in *Prin-*

ciples, I, 62, *in fine*) that this type of distinction was inaccurately termed "modal" in a passage at the end of the First Replies (cf. AT VII 120f.: CSM II 85f.).

To sum up: concepts of a yet higher order than either of the *duo summa genera rerum* (I, 48), 'thought' and 'extension,' the universals are like essential attributes in that they are distinguishable from the minds and bodies whose attributes they are only in thought (conceptually), not in fact (really); yet unlike the principal attributes these further attributes do not constitute the *nature* of anything: they are not ideas of natures conceptually distinguishable from the things whose essences they are, that is, not *complete* ideas, *genera rerum*, but *only* modes of thinking. While not merely *conventional* products of the will like the ideas of natural kinds, but rather innate, clear and distinct, and simple, they are nevertheless not ideas of complete things and hence cannot be considered *vera et realia entia*, on all fours with mathematical entities, that is, the objects of the truths of mathematics declared immune from any doubt arising from the dreaming argument.[31]

10.10 *Vera et realia entia*, universals, and simple natures

So much for universals. We are now in a position to bring out the precise sense of the expression *vera et realia entia*, distinguishing the ideas of them from universals and natural kinds on the one hand and from simple natures on the other.

In a well-known passage of the *Regulae* Descartes characterizes simple natures as either (1) "purely intellectual," (2) "purely material," or (3) "common" to both intellectual and material things. (1) and (2) include the principal attributes of mind and body, respectively, as well as all the modes of such attributes, for instance, shape and motion in the case of bodies. To (3) belong "existence, unity, duration and the like" (AT X 419: CSM I 44f.) as well as "common notions" like "'[t]hings that are the same as a third thing are the same as each other'" (ibid.), and the like. Included under (2) and (3) are also "the corresponding privations and negations, in so far as we understand these. For when I intuit what nothing (*nihil*) is, or an instant, or rest, my apprehension is as much genuine knowledge as my understanding of what existence is, or duration, or motion" (AT X 420: CSM I 45).[32] Thus, the expression *vera et realia entia* is deliberately so coined as to stress three important features of the class of entities or objects to which 'the mathematicals' belong: (a) their being *true* rather than either fictions of the imagination or generic concepts of natural kinds whose content is fixed by a voluntary (conventional or arbitrary) abstraction of the intellect (*vera*); (b) their being *positive* rather than mere privations or negations (*realia*); and (c) their being *entia per se ab omni alio diversa*, that is, ideas of complete *res*, entities, or natures at least *capable* (unlike the universals) of existing in their own right *in rerum natura* (*entia*).

With respect to the dreaming argument, then, Descartes's point regarding the objects of pure mathematics is not just (i) that such objects are *distinct* from particular acts or modes of thinking of them. He does insist that since, for instance, triangularity involves *propria* (like 'having internal angles equal to two right angles') not part of the complete idea or definition of a triangle, the idea actually occurring in this or that finite mind is only a transitory and more or less inadequate glimpse of the "true and immutable nature" of triangles. But beyond this, he wishes to assert (ii) that ideal objects having such natures *are* or *exist* whether or not any finite mind exists and thinks of them: "we should not suppose that eternal truths 'depend on the human intellect or on other existing things'; they depend on God alone, who, as the supreme legislator, has ordained them from eternity" (AT VII 436: CSM II 294). Of course, dependence on God is uncontroversially true of the real existence of corporeal substances as well (should there in fact be any such objects). The crux, therefore, is the final phrase, "or on other existing things," that is, (iii) that the objects of pure mathematics exist whether or not there exist any corporeal substances outside the mind for them to exist in. That is why pure mathematics is impervious to doubt from the dreaming argument. As for their existing only *possibly* rather than actually (cf. the *axioma sive notio communis* cited earlier), this is clarified in the conversation with Burman (AT V 160: CSMK 343) as referring to possible existence "in space," that is, in sensible material things. "True and immutable natures" exist 'actually' but in an ideal sense: their 'possible existence' *in rerum natura* just *is* their 'actual existence' in this ideal sense.[33]

Now that the exact scope of the dreaming argument has been cleared up (by a somewhat roundabout route), two final points lead into the controversy concerning the ontological status of mathematical objects. It would be wrong to infer from the foregoing that mathematical entities do not exist actually *in rerum natura*. Descartes is quite explicit about not having denied the real existence of geometrical figures as opposed to their existence *at the macroscopic level*: "although the world could undoubtedly contain figures such as those the geometers study, I nonetheless maintain that there are no such figures in our environment except perhaps ones so small that they cannot in any way impinge on our senses. Geometrical figures are composed for the most part of straight lines; yet no part of a line that was really straight could ever affect our senses, since when we examine through a magnifying glass those lines which appear most straight we find that they are quite irregular and always form wavy curves" (AT VII 381f.: CSM II 262). The point, clearly, is not that such natures do not exist "in space," but that their actual existence *in rerum natura* is irrelevant to the truth of pure mathematics, which is therefore perfectly secure against the dreaming argument.[34]

Beyond noting that the actual existence of true and immutable natures *in rerum natura* is strictly irrelevant to the truth of pure mathematics, and that they cannot exist at the macroscopic level, it is worth remarking that once the dreaming argument is overcome it turns out that they can and do exist as modes of corporeal substances. The relation of pure and applied mathematics is a bone of contention between Descartes and Gassendi. The latter objects to the opening statement of the Sixth Meditation that corporeal things are at least "capable of existing, in so far as they are the subject-matter of pure mathematics," urging that "material things are the subject-matter of applied, not pure, mathematics," and that "the subject-matter of pure mathematics – including the point, the line, the surface, and the indivisible figures which are composed of these elements and yet remain indivisible – cannot exist in reality" (AT VII 329: CSM II 228). Descartes dismisses this objection (AT VII 384: CSM II 264) as having been dealt with earlier on (AT VII 381: CSM II 261f.) where he had already traced it to Gassendi's dogmatic adherence to "the atomic conception of reality invented by Democritus and Epicurus." Although plainly inconsistent with the conception of matter as consisting of indivisible parts, the "true and immutable natures" that form the subject matter of pure mathematics "undoubtedly conform to the true nature of [material] things established by God," he claims. "Not that there are in the world substances which have length but no breadth [i.e., lines], or breadth but no depth [surfaces]; it is rather that the geometrical figures are considered not as substances but as boundaries within which a substance is contained" (ibid.). These boundaries are modes, not parts, of substances (since parts of material substances would themselves be substances, not modes): "the surface which is merely a mode and hence cannot be a part of a body. For a body is a substance, and a mode cannot be a part of a substance" (AT VII 433: CSM II 292). Thus, although it so happens that the objects of pure mathematics exist *in rerum natura* as modes of actually existing corporeal substances, the truth of mathematics does not depend on this fact. It is sufficient that they exist in the mind of God.

10.11 The ontological status of mathematical objects

This notion of *vera et realia entia* as "true and immutable natures" existing independently of both material things and human thought is profoundly puzzling; in the precise form in which Descartes held it, it may be unprecedented. It is the subject of an interesting controversy between Gewirth and Kenny. We conclude our discussion of the dreaming argument with a quick glance at this debate.

Point of departure for both interpreters is the "essential" as opposed to the "existential" version of the "ontological interpretation" of pure mathematics. It was Gewirth (1987b, 87ff.) who introduced the distinction between "operational," "conceptual," and "ontological" interpretations of Descartes's metaphysical doubt about the eternal truths of mathematics. The first type assigns the source of doubt to operations *other* than clear and distinct perception (for example, memory; cf. the 'memory solution' to the problem of the Cartesian circle, to be discussed in section 14.2 below). Conceptual interpretations, on the other hand, restrict the doubt to complex intuitions of conceptual relations as opposed to simple intuitions of concepts, the latter remaining strictly immune from doubt (for instance, Miller 1965). Both approaches are now pretty well discredited. Within the third or ontological category, Gewirth further distinguishes existential and essential versions. According to the former, "the truth of mathematical propositions requires that material objects of some sort exist, at least the 'simple' objects of which Descartes assumes all complex objects to be composed. Hence when he [has] doubts about '2 + 3 = 5' and the like, this is because he does not yet know whether any material things exist at all" (Gewirth 1987b, 89). Gilson, Keeling, Stout, and Kemp Smith are all identified as proponents of this view (ibid., n. 15).[35] On the 'essential' version of the ontological interpretation favoured by Gewirth, Descartes's metaphysical doubt concerns the conformity of the simple among the clear and distinct ideas in the mind to a class of separately existing "true and immutable natures" or essences. Given Descartes's staunch refusal to accord the eternal truths independence of God's intellect or will, the 'separateness' of such objects entails their independence (1) of the existence of material things and (2) of the existence and nature of the human mind, but not (3) of the divine Mind.[36]

While endorsing the essential version of the ontological interpretation, Kenny takes issue with Gewirth's claim that Descartes's position is somewhere "between Platonic and Aristotelian interpretations of mathematical essences," the Aristotelian feature being that "there cannot be essences of things that do not exist" (cf. Kenny 1970, 699). He regards it instead as "thoroughly Platonic." The salient point for Kenny is that Descartes's theory is not one of "nonexistent essences" so much as of "nonexistent objects that have essences" (692): "Descartes held that a geometrical figure was a mode of physical or corporeal substance; it could not exist, unless there existed a physical substance for it to exist in" (699); yet physical substance ('body') is itself no more than a "true and immutable nature" that exists only ideally. So there is no need for anything actually existing *in rerum natura*: the 'mathematicals' are not only conceivable, they can actually exist, apart from sensible matter. This flies in the face of the Aristotelian teaching handed down via Boethius to the Middle Ages (see section 2.3) and amounts (so Kenny) to pure Platonism.

That it is Gewirth who is on the right track here can be seen if we take as the joint Platonic tenets regarding mathematical essences, (P1) the mathematicals exist prior to and independently of the existence of particular sensible things, and (P2) such mathematicals are substances (Forms) capable of existing in their own right. Taking, next, as the joint Scholastic-Aristotelian tenets the denials of these propositions, we have: (SA1) the mathematicals cannot exist actually except as inhering in sensible matter (though the mathematician treats them as abstracted forms knowable, without being capable of actually existing, apart from sensible material things); and (SA2) such mathematicals are not substances or things in their own right but exist *in* the material things whose forms or modes they are.[37] From the evidence adduced by Gewirth and Kenny it appears that Descartes combines (P1) and (SA2), substituting 'mode' for the reviled 'form' and carving out a new position in the history of metaphysics on the ideal existence of mathematical non-substances. Whether it is a coherent position is another matter. (It is certainly not coherent on either Platonic or Aristotelian principles.) In the Conclusion (section 22.1) we shall see that Descartes hammered out a new position on the question of mind-body union by combining Platonic and Scholastic-Aristotelian elements in a similar way (cf. Miles 1983).[38]

10.12 The deceiving God

Since they do not assert the actual existence of anything *in rerum natura*, the truths of mathematics are perfectly immune from all doubt arising from the dreaming argument. The deceiving God hypothesis must therefore be introduced in order to render mathematical axioms and theorems doubtful. Though this is its distinctive role within the regimen of doubt, it nevertheless provides collateral support for the preceding stage:

[Y]et firmly rooted in my mind is the long-standing belief that there is an omnipotent God who made me the kind of creature that I am. How do I know that he has not brought it about that there is no earth, no heavens, no extended thing, no shape, no size, no place, while at the same time ensuring that all these things appear to me to exist just as they do now? (AT VII 21: CSM II 14)

If none of these things exists, then the supposed truths of the physical sciences are all falsehoods.

The deceiving God is one among a number of distinct but related hypotheses envisaged in the First Meditation, any of which might entail that one's faculty of clear and distinct perception is subject to error even in matters perceived (and not just mistakenly thought to be perceived) with the utmost clarity and distinctness. Thus, it is all one whether I sometimes err about matters that I perceive with perfect clarity and distinctness (a) because I was created by an all-powerful but deceptive God who could have given me a faculty of clear and distinct perception utterly immune from error but deliberately chose not to do so; or (b) because I was created by a being who bestowed on me a faculty of clear and distinct perception immune from error but who, as the omnipotent creator and sustainer even of the essences of things, loves to deceive me by altering the truths I formerly clearly and distinctly perceived once I no longer attend to them; or (c) because I was created by some "malicious demon" perhaps less powerful but still "of very great power and cunning (*summe potentem et calidum*)" (AT VII 22: CSM II 15); or (d) because I owe my being to some, perhaps benevolent and veracious, but less than omnipotent being who could not have given me an infallible faculty of clear and distinct perception, even though he may have wished to do so;[39] or, finally, (e) because I came into being "by fate, or chance, or a continuous chain of events" (AT VII 21: CSM II 14) rather than as a consequence of any plan or intention whatever. Though the "deceiving God" of Descartes refers only to (a) or (b), should *any* of these eventualities turn out to be the true account of how "I have arrived at my present state" (AT VII 21: CSM II 14), I may possess "a natural disposition to go wrong from time to time (*interdum*) in matters which I think I perceive as evidently as can be" (AT VII 70: CSM II 48 e.a.).

There are two contentious points in all this. The first arises from (a) and concerns the question whether the threat posed by a deceiving God extends to the possibility that the faculty of clear and distinct perception or reason itself might be inherently flawed and hence always liable to error, whenever and however it is employed.[40] It has frequently been urged that such doubt must prove, in Hume's words (1990, 181), "entirely incurable," since having once doubted one's reason it is impossible ever to reason one's way out of doubt.[41] Where Descartes first introduces the deceiving God hypothesis, he asks: "may I not ... go wrong every time (*quoties*) I add two and three or count the sides of a square, or even in some even simpler matter, if that be imaginable?" (AT VII 21: CSM II 14). This is innocuous enough, and might be taken to refer only to "a natural disposition to go wrong *from time to time* (*interdum*) in matters which I think I perceive as evidently as can be" (e.a.). That would leave the reliability of reason inviolate, provided such errors are detectable and correctable by reason. But still within the First Meditation Descartes remarks:

But perhaps God would not have wished me to be deceived in this way, since he is said to be supremely good. But if it were inconsistent with his goodness to have created me such that I am deceived all the time (*semper*), it would seem equally foreign to his goodness to allow me to be deceived even occasionally (*interdum*). (AT VII 21: CSM II 14)

And slightly further on he notes: "the less powerful ... my original cause, the more likely it is that I am so imperfect as to be deceived all the time (*semper*) (ibid.)

Faced with the shift from *interdum* to *semper*, there would seem to be no alternative but to portray the deceiving God in the manner in which Gibson describes the "malicious demon": as the marauding "enemy of the principle of reason in the universe" (Gibson 1932, 310). Short of this, it may be possible to press a distinction between the "deceiving God" and the "malicious demon," taking the latter to be finite and only "very powerful" rather than omnipotent (cf. Kennington 1971). The distinction itself seems correct. But nothing turns on it since, if the malicious demon, though finite, is yet powerful enough to deceive us all the time in matters that we perceive clearly and distinctly, reason itself is in jeopardy. After all, even a less-than-omnipotent being could still be capable of bringing it about both that false things seem utterly certain and that all those things which seem utterly certain are false. If so, it makes little difference whether 'malicious demon' is just another expression for 'deceiving God,' or whether Descartes in fact shifted his ground in the last paragraph of the First Meditation, replacing his omnipotent by a finite deceiver. Give that finite deceiver sufficient power to control human reason, and the prospect of delivery from doubt is as remote as that of a reasoned escape from the spectre of madness.[42]

Fortunately, the situation is not quite so desperate. For Descartes, *some* clear and distinct perception is strictly immune from doubt, so that if we employ our reason correctly and attend carefully to the clearly and distinctly perceived, reason is an utterly reliable source of truth and knowledge, regardless of whether we are the creatures of the "true God" (AT VII 53: CSM II 37; also AT VII 71: CSM II 49) or of a deceiver. The range of such clear and distinct perception cannot be determined along what might be called 'disciplinary' lines, as though the simple notions and axioms of, say, logic (principle of non-contradiction) or metaphysics (the *cogito-* and the causality-principle) were immune from even the most radical doubt, while the simple truths of mathematics are not. Nor can it be fixed in terms of Descartes's faculty psychology, as though axioms, immediate inferences, and perhaps short deductive chains of reasoning were strictly exempt from doubt at all times, while anything not encompassable within a single intuition requires the use of memory and so succumbs to doubt. On the contrary, even axioms and inferences that can be grasped within a single intuition may be doubtful, Descartes holds, when not actually the immediate object of attention; and although it is true that the conclusions of arguments too long to be embraced in a single intellectual gaze are inherently doubtful, the key distinction is not so much between intuition and deduction as between those clear and distinct perceptions – whether logical, mathematical, or metaphysical, whether immediate intuitions or short chains of inferences – that are *now actually occurring or immediately before the mind's eye* and those that are occurring no longer.

This view of the matter is perfectly in accord with Gibson's opinion that the doubt arising from the deceiving God hypothesis is *introduced* as an assault upon reason itself, wherever and however it is employed. The omnivorous intent of Cartesian doubt seems incontestable; it embraces, in the language of the Third Meditation, every modality of "clear and distinct perception," that is, the truth of the clearly and distinctly perceived as such. The repeated use of *semper* in the First Meditation, together with the doubt about the truth rule itself in the Third, make lost labour of efforts to limit the *intended* scope of Cartesian doubt. It is true, of course, that, were it possible to take the citadel of reason in this way, the enemy could never be dislodged. But the point is this: the attempt to doubt everything shatters against that current clear and distinct perception of one's own thought and existence that reveals *what truth itself is* as it discloses the first truth about the existence of a substance, *existo*.[43] Henceforward the force of the deceiving God hypothesis is confined to the certainty or truth of that which is no longer clearly and distinctly perceived. Exempt from doubt from this point on are, along with the *cogito* and *sum*, the axioms of logic, the simple truths and demonstrations of mathematics, and metaphysical demonstrations and principles of the natural light; for these, as long as one actually attends to them or the reasons for their truth, are certain and undeniably true. The deceiving God hypothesis continues to hold sway over these and all other items of knowledge when no longer clearly and distinctly perceived, until, in the Third Meditation, the existence and veracity of the "true God" are demonstrated employing actually intuited axioms and principles of logic and metaphysics. The proof of God's existence and veracity, in turn, establishes once and for all the reliability of the truth rule that "*whatever* I perceive clearly and distinctly is true" (e.a.). Thus, at the close of the Fourth Meditation Descartes is already in a position to remark:

[*E*]*very* clear and distinct perception is undoubtedly something, and hence cannot come from nothing, but must necessarily have God for its author. Its author, I say, is God, who is supremely perfect and who cannot be a deceiver on pain of contradiction (*repugnat*); hence the perception is undoubtedly *true*. (AT VII 62: CSM II 43 e.a.)

But the definitive endorsement of the truth rule comes only at the end of the Fifth Meditation, where it is formulated in terms of the distinction between current and recollected clear and distinct perceptions:

Now, however, I have perceived that God exists, and at the same time I have understood that everything else depends on him, and that he is no deceiver; and I have drawn the conclusion that *everything which I clearly and distinctly perceive is of necessity true.* Accordingly, *even if I am no longer attending to the arguments* which led me to judge that this is true, as long as I remember that I clearly and distinctly perceived it, there are no counter-arguments which can be adduced to make me doubt it, but on the contrary I have true and certain knowledge of it (*veram & certam de hoc habeo scientiam*). And I have knowledge not just of this, but of all matters which I remember ever having demonstrated, in geometry and so on. (AT VII 70: CSM II 48 e.a.)

It is at this point that a distinction drawn along what we earlier termed 'disciplinary' lines becomes important. The proof of God's existence and veracity is not itself subject to the slightest doubt, even when the argument is no longer actually under the direct scrutiny of reason. This is because theological knowledge now clearly and distinctly perceived is perceived as having to be true still at any subsequent time at which I may again turn my mental gaze upon it; for to know God is to understand that even he cannot alter his own nature as he can all else that I have ever perceived clearly and distinctly to be true. Here it suffices simply to be able to remember having clearly and distinctly perceived God's nature once in order to have *vera & certa scientia* of him, of the truth rule, and of everything else remembered to have been clearly and distinctly perceived. By contrast, in logic, in mathematics, and in metaphysical matters outside of natural theology, *scientia* is attainable only through, never without, knowledge of "the true God."[44]

That the unlimited scope of the deceiving God hypothesis comes to be limited in the manner described is more controversial than anything alleged earlier concerning the scope of the dreaming argument. This is the first of the two contentious issues referred to above (see p. 139). There are in fact two questions here: (1) How does the *cogito* principle differ from simple mathematical truths such that the very hypothesis that undermined the latter in the First Meditation proves ineffectual against the former in the Second? (2) How do these and other created eternal truths differ from truths about God's own nature? The detailed response to (1) turns on a distinction between two *kinds* of perfect certainty, to be elaborated in section 11.2, while (2) will be discussed in 12.6. The aim of the present chapter as a whole is to distinguish these various kinds of perfect certainty from that inferior *degree* of certainty introduced in order to reinstate the common-sense picture of the world in the Sixth Meditation.

The second contentious point referred to above concerns (b), the possibility that I was created by an omnipotent creator and sustainer of the essences of things who loves to deceive me by altering the truths I formerly clearly and distinctly perceived once I no longer attend to them. It is raised by Gueroult (1968, I, 42ff.), who rejects on general grounds of the "order of reasons" all interpretations that take the force of Descartes's third and most radical ground of doubt to reside in his peculiar notion of divine omnipotence, that is, in the conception of a being so powerful that he can create, not just the things themselves that exist *in rerum natura*, but even the natures or essences of things, the eternal truths. Since our interpretation is of this kind, Gueroult's objection should be faced now.

The question is whether it is in virtue of his omnipotence that God is capable of deception even in matters clearly and distinctly perceived, although he is prevented from using this power by his goodness. To the affirmative answer, versions of which are held by both Bréhier and Gouhier, Gueroult opposes his own view and that of Laporte (1950, 171): it is not the discovery of God's goodness that dispels the doubt to which the thought of divine omnipotence gives rise; it is rather the true ('véritable') idea of divine omnipotence that dispels the contradictory notion of a being both supremely perfect or omnipotent *and* deceptive, that is, imperfect. Thus, far from presupposing the true notion of divine omnipotence embodied in the doctrine of the creation of the eternal truths, the hypothesis of the deceiving God or malicious demon is dispelled by it.[45]

Of course, the means of deception are simply not spelled out in the formulation of the deceiving God hypothesis within the First Meditation. Nevertheless, it is not unreasonable to suppose that one possibility envisaged there was an omnipotent being capable of altering, unbeknownst to us, truths now only remembered as having formerly been clearly and distinctly perceived. If the deception is of this kind, then the underlying notion of divine omnipotence, though self-contradictory, still incorporates an important aspect of Descartes's definitive notion: that of the creator/sustainer of the eternal truths. Thus, both parties to the dispute are right: a partial notion of an omnipotent being gives rise to the deceiving God hypothesis, much as Bréhier and Gouhier maintain; what dispels it is, as Gueroult rightly insists, not so much the notion of divine goodness as a fuller and consistent understanding of divine omnipotence.[46]

However, it would be wrong to restrict the third reason for doubt to this one possibility. The point of the third of Descartes's *dubitandi rationes* is to evoke a whole range of possibilities, all of which are dispelled by the discovery of what truth is through the immediate experience of the truth that I think and therefore exist, coupled with the proof of the existence of an omnipotent and omnibenevolent creator God. There is (*pace* Gueroult) no better reason to confine the third of Descartes's grounds of doubt to (b) than to exclude (b) outright.

10.13 The malicious demon

To round out the discussion of the regimen of doubt in the First Meditation, we look briefly at the shift within the last paragraph from a "deceiving God" to a "malicious demon."

Apart from trying to forestall charges of "'horrible and impious blasphemy'" (AT V 8: CSMK 316), such as were in fact to come despite Descartes's best efforts, at least two reasons suggest themselves as to why Descartes switches from a "deceiving God" to a "malicious demon." First, while the deceiving God hypothesis was directed specifically against the truths of pure mathematics, the "malicious demon" is something of an 'all-purpose doubt-maker': it suffices to think of this one possibility in order to infix in the mind a doubt about all the various types of statements rendered doubtful by the three main *dubitandi rationes*. Thus, Descartes suggests that the malicious demon himself *uses* dreams and illusions to deceive him: "I shall think that the sky, the air, the earth, colours, shapes, sounds, and all external things are merely the delusions of dreams *which he has devised to ensnare my judgement* ... etc." (AT VII 22–3: CSM II 15 e.a.). The introduction of this single doubt-maker, then, rolls all three grounds of doubt into one, as a matter of convenience.[47]

Of course, there is no obvious reason why a deceiving God could not have performed this function.[48] The same cannot be said, however, of the purpose that Descartes himself assigns the final phase of doubt: counteracting the influence of habit and preconceived opinion on one's judgment. Leading up to the shift from a deceiving God to a malicious demon, he writes:

My habitual opinions keep coming back, and despite my wishes, they capture my belief, which is as it were bound over to them as a result of long occupation and the law of custom. I shall never get out of the habit of confidently assenting to these opinions, so long as I suppose them to be what in fact they are, namely highly probable opinions – opinions which, despite the fact that they are in a sense doubtful, as has just been shown, it is still much more reasonable to believe than to deny. In view of this, I think it will be a good plan to turn my will in completely the opposite direction and deceive myself, by pretending for a time that these former opinions are utterly false and imaginary. I shall do this until the weight of *preconceived opinion* is counter-balanced and the distorting influence of *habit* no longer prevents my judgement from perceiving things correctly. (AT VII 22: CSM II 15 e.a.)

In the Fifth Replies Descartes uses the illustration of a curved stick that has to be "bent ... round in the opposite direction" (AT VII 349: CSM II 242) in order to be straightened. And in the Seventh Replies he adds: "When in the First Meditation I said that I wanted for a time to try to convince myself of the opposite of the views which I had rashly held before, I immediately added that my reason for wanting to do this was as it were to counter-balance the weight of preconceived opinions so that I should not incline to one side more than the other" (AT VII 465: CSM II 312f.). Commentators have accordingly pointed to the "psychological" benefit derived from misusing one's freedom and counteracting the force of habit by taking that which is only doubtful on the deceiving God hypothesis to be the work of a malicious demon, that is, not just doubtful but false (cf. Gueroult 1938, 122f. and 1968, 39; Cottingham 1976, 260). The real point, however, is more metaphysical than psychological, since it has to do with the freedom of the will as exercised in judgment. This second reason for the shift from deceiving God to malicious demon is more speculative than the first but also philosophically more interesting.

Assuming that the malicious demon is not omnipotent but may yet have powers sufficient to deceive me even about the axioms and demonstrations of mathematics, logic, and metaphysics, the difference between an infinite God and a finite demon can be put this way. Both could, *ex hypothesi*, bring it about that false things seem utterly certain to me and that all those things which seem utterly certain are false; but the deceiving God would, in addition, have the power to make it impossible for me to withhold assent even from such things as are *not* clearly and distinctly perceived. For if the deceiver were truly omnipotent, he could control not only what seems certain to me but also what I assert or deny. There is, after all, no obvious reason why sheer omnipotence should be capable of manipulating human reason to such an extent but unable to control the will. Thus, on the supposition of an omnipotent deceiver it would seem that I cannot prevent myself from assenting to any falsehood, whether or not it appears certain; while if the deceiver is only very powerful, I am at least free to suspend judgment about matters that are open to the slightest doubt, thereby ensuring that I am not deceived. For 'to be deceived' is either to affirm something false or to deny something true, so that as long as I neither affirm nor deny anything I cannot be deceived. As Descartes notes elsewhere, "a distrustful person, as long as he remains in a state of distrust, cannot be led into error even by an evil demon" (AT VII 476: CSM II 320).[49]

If the deceiving God hypothesis were true, not only could reason itself be fallacious all the time, but there would be no freedom to affirm, deny, doubt, or suspend judgment regarding any matter whatever. Thus, in the final paragraph of the First Meditation Descartes writes: "I shall stubbornly and firmly persist in this meditation; and even if it is not in my power to know any truth, I shall at least do *what is in my power*, that is, resolutely guard against assenting to any falsehoods, so that the deceiver, however powerful and cunning he may be, will be *unable to impose on me in the slightest degree*" (AT VII 23: CSM II 15 e.a.). It is hard to see how the ability to withhold assent could resist the force of sheer omnipotence; but even assuming that the words "however powerful and cunning he may be" are intended to refer only to a finite deceiver, this passage unfortunately suggests that it is within one's power to withhold assent on any matter whatever. Of course, for all we know at this stage in the First Meditation, our freedom might be thus unrestricted; only later does it become apparent that the freedom in question does not extend to anything that is at the moment clearly and distinctly perceived (see section 12.2).

So I am *by nature* utterly defenceless against the threat to reason posed by either deceiver, should either be powerful enough to make that which is in fact false seem perfectly true at the precise moment I examine its truth or falsehood.

(This turns out to be beyond the powers even of an omnipotent deceiver.) There is a great difference between the deceivers, however, in respect of matters not thus clearly and distinctly grasped by the intellect. For though it is true of an omnipotent deceiving God that he can control not only the intellect but the will, so that I am always deceived even about matters that are doubtful, Descartes is quite explicit about the fact that the malicious demon is "unable to impose on [him] in the slightest degree." It remains to suggest why this difference may have seemed significant.

As pointed out earlier, the threat to the reliability of reason is removed by placing first the *cogito* and then all actually occurring clear and distinct perception beyond the reach even of an omnipotent deceiver; as for remembered clear and distinct perception, all doubt in this regard is dispelled by the proof of God's existence and veracity. The threat that hangs over all that is less than perfectly clear and distinct is removed by the same proof. Yet until its removal it is necessary to furnish some defence against what, according to the "Synopsis," are among the principal impediments to the unhampered use of reason and the chief sources of human error: precipitancy of judgment owing to prejudice and habit. The Fourth Meditation testifies to the great importance Descartes attached to the suspension of judgment as a means of avoiding error, a precaution that might have seemed futile without the shift from an omnipotent deceiver to a malicious demon. It may have been for this reason that it occurred to Descartes to retreat from the hypothesis of a deceiving God to that of a malicious demon in the last paragraph of the First Meditation.

If so, then the First Meditation ends with the task with which it began: the emancipation of reason through systematic doubt. The regimen of doubt whose purpose it is to free human reason from the bonds of authority, habit, and scepticism, while providing a standard of perfect certainty, ends with a puzzling shift that not only counteracts the force of habit, but safeguards the mind's freedom to reserve judgment until the reliability of human reason can be established and the extent and nature of human freedom precisely ascertained. Nevertheless, Descartes concludes the First Meditation with the curious reflection that, for all he knows, this freedom or indifference may be illusory – as indeed it is in the case of clear and distinct perception:

I am like a prisoner who is enjoying an imaginary freedom while asleep; as he begins to suspect that he is asleep, he dreads being woken up, and goes along with the pleasant illusion as long as he can. In the same way, I happily slide back into my old opinions and dread being shaken out of them, for fear that my peaceful sleep may be followed by hard labour when I wake, and that I shall have to toil not in the light, but amid the inextricable darkness of the problems I have now raised. (AT VII 23: CSM II 15)

The exact significance of this strange conclusion is hard to gauge. Its purpose may be to underscore the point that, as with the reliability of reason, so with the freedom of the will, nothing may simply be taken for granted until reflexion on the experience of the first metaphysical truth and on the nature of "the true God" gives the meditator complete assurance of the reliability of reason and of what he is and is not free to doubt or deny.

10.14 Concluding summary

We conclude this chapter with a brief schematic summary of the three main stages of doubt and the types of judgment that each is designed to render doubtful:[50]

I. The Argument from Illusion

(1) Perceptual judgments regarding bodies observed under less than ideal circumstances.

II. The Dreaming Argument

(2) Judgments based on ordinary pre-scientific sense-perception carried out under good conditions.
(3) Judgments based on exact scientific observation conducted under ideal, perhaps controlled experimental, conditions. (These are not mentioned by Descartes.)
(4) Judgments asserting the existence of objects of the same general kind as the objects of ordinary pre-scientific experience (not this head, my hands, but heads, hands, and so on, in general).
(5) Judgments about the sensory qualities belonging to the sorts of things mentioned under (4) (their colours, odours, tastes, sounds, tactile qualities).
(6) Judgments expressing scientific hypotheses about "simpler and more universal things" or regarding quantitative properties of things like space, time, place, extension and its modes.
(7) The sciences of physics, astronomy, and medicine themselves, "and all other disciplines which depend on the study of composite things."

III. The Deceiving God

(8) Judgments about the "simplest and most general things" that are the objects of pure mathematics, that is, propositions like two and three added together equal five, and a square has no more than four sides, the denials of which are self-contradictory.

11

The Kinds of Certainty

Something having all the earmarks of outright contradiction leaps to the eye in the transition from the Second to the Third Meditation. If the testimony of the famous passage in the Second may be taken as authoritative, only the statement *sum, existo* is able to withstand the third and most radical of the grounds of doubt adduced in Meditation One:

> But there is a deceiver of supreme power and cunning who is deliberately and constantly deceiving me. In that case I too undoubtedly exist, if he is deceiving me; and let him deceive me as much as he can, he will never bring it about that I am nothing so long as I think that I am something. So after considering everything thoroughly, I must finally conclude that this proposition, *I am, I exist*, is necessarily true whenever it is put forward by me or conceived by my mind. (AT VII 25: CSM II 17)

However, in the Third Meditation Descartes insists that *everything*, not excepting his own thinking and existence, is subject to the metaphysical doubt arising from the deceiving God hypothesis. Here there is no appreciable difference between the treatment of the *sum* and of principles of the natural light like 'Whatever thinks, is,' 'What is done cannot be undone' (cf. AT VIII-1 24: CSM I 209) or simple mathematical truths like '2 + 3 = 5.' The passage is worth citing in full:

> [Initial section:] [W]henever my preconceived belief in the supreme power of God comes to mind, I cannot but admit that it would be easy for him, if he so desired, to bring it about that I go wrong even in those matters which I think I see utterly clearly with my mind's eye. [Middle section:] Yet when I turn to the things themselves which I think I perceive very clearly, I am so convinced by them (*tam plane ab illis persuadeor*) that I spontaneously declare: let whoever can do so deceive me, he will never bring it about that I am nothing so long as I continue to think I am something; or make it true at some future time that I have never existed, since it is now true that I exist; or bring it about that two and

three added together are more or less than five, or anything of this kind in which I see a manifest contradiction. [Final section:] And since I have no cause to think that there is a deceiving God, and I do not yet know for sure whether there is a God at all, any reason for doubt that depends on this opinion is a very slight and, so to speak, metaphysical one. But in order to remove even this slight reason for doubt, as soon as the opportunity arises I must examine whether there is a God, and, if there is, whether he can be a deceiver. For if I do not know this, it seems that I can never be quite certain about *anything* else (*hac enim re* [scil. *Dei existentia et veracitas*] *ignorata, non videor de ulla alia plane certus esse unquam posse*). (AT VII 36: CSM II 25 e.a.)

The utter contradictoriness of Descartes's position would appear to be fittingly enshrined in this passage. Of the *cogito* principle, the "common notions,"[1] and the simple truths of mathematics alike it states, first, that they are (initial section), then that they are not (middle section), and finally, once again, that they are subject to doubt (final section). The only point on which Descartes does not waver is the sameness of treatment of the *cogito* principle and the other two classes of truths; and that, as already noted, is glaringly inconsistent with his differential treatment of the truths of mathematics and the *cogito* principle in the First and Second Meditations.

11.1 Two sets of problems

This notorious passage poses two sets of problems. Suppose, as the middle section suggests, that *all* clear and distinct perception is on the same evidential footing and the *sum* is perfectly certain without its certainty depending upon the proof of God's existence and veracity. It follows that the principles of the natural light and the simple truths of mathematics do not depend on the knowledge of God either and that it was inconsistent and indeed false for Descartes to maintain in the Second Meditation that, while the *cogito* principle is sheerly beyond doubt, the simple mathematical truths considered in the First Meditation are rendered doubtful by the deceiving God hypothesis.

To this it might be replied that the words "of anything else (*de ulla alia*)" in the final section can safely be discounted as a slip of the pen. Or that their sense is: everything "autre que l'existence de Dieu et ... le *cogito*" (cf. Gouhier 1969, 315 and the reply of M. Beyssade 1993, n. 39). However, Descartes's remarks here are typical of others in the *Meditations* and elsewhere (notably in *Principles*, I, 13; for further references, see J.-M. Beyssade 1993, 85f.). For example, following the ontological argument, he writes:

Although it needed close attention for me to perceive this [that God exists necessarily], I am now just as certain of it as I am of everything else which appears most certain. And what is more, I see that the certainty of *all* other things depends on this, so that without it *nothing* can ever be perfectly known (*absque eo nihil unquam perfecte sciri possit*). (AT VII 69: CSM II 48 e.a.)

'All other things' includes the nature and existence of the mind no less than corporeal nature; and Descartes says so:

[T]he certainty and truth of *all* knowledge (*omnis scientiae certitudinem & veritatem*) depends uniquely on my knowledge of the true God (*ab una veri Dei cognitione pendere*), so that I was incapable of perfect knowledge of *anything* in regard to *any other thing* (*nihil de ulla alia re perfecte scire potuerim*) until I came to know him. But now [that I know him] countless matters, both concerning God himself and other things whose nature is intellectual [i.e., minds], and also concerning the whole of that corporeal nature which is the subject-matter of pure mathematics, are plainly known to me and certain. (AT VII 71: CSM II 49 e.a.)

So the difficulties of the first set are not so easily disposed of. Simply alter one of the assumptions by supposing all three kinds of truth mentioned in the long Third Meditation passage alike *un*certain without the knowledge of "the true God," and a second group of problems arises. Assume the doubtfulness of *all* clear and distinct perception, as in the final section of the passage, and there is no prospect of removing the doubt by any clear and distinct perception or argument without contradicting oneself or arguing circularly.[2] Blithely heedless of these obvious difficulties, Descartes apparently *both* contradicts himself and resorts to a blatant *petitio principii* when he disposes of this "slight reason for doubt" by a proof of God's existence and veracity involving axioms clearly and distinctly perceived to be true. To make matters worse, he never concedes that he has argued circularly, even when reproached by his contemporaries; he is unable or unwilling to see or acknowledge the force of so obvious an objection.[3]

Both sets of difficulties can be overcome with the help of the distinction between two kinds of certainty and three different senses of 'clear and distinct perception.' For if what Descartes means is that all *now actually occurring* clear and distinct perception is perfectly indubitable, while that which is only *remembered* as having been clearly and distinctly perceived in the past is subject to a "metaphysical" doubt, the main difficulty vanishes. It would still have to be explained why the *cogito* principle was singled out with such fanfare in the Second Meditation as *the* first principle of knowledge, when in the Third it is again treated as practically on all fours with a number of other principles or "common notions," even with simple mathematical truths; but that explanation is in fact not difficult, given Descartes's insistence on the difference between "simple notions

... which on their own provide us with no knowledge of anything that exists" (AT VIII-A, 8: CSM I 196) and the knowledge of the existence of a substance that he is seeking as the foundation of his metaphysics. Much more intractable is the problem of how, on the proposed solution, Descartes is to be acquitted of the charge of psychologism. For clarity and distinctness are subjective features of perceptions; and the necessity or felt inability to withhold assent from the clearly and distinctly perceived is likewise a merely 'subjective,' introspectible feature of one's private mental states; that is why clear and distinct perceptions are deemed sheerly unmistakable whenever in fact present. But psychological certainty is one thing, and objective truth another; the former is reliably, even infallibly, ascertainable by simply attending to one's own mental states; not so, however, objective truth. Either Descartes bridges the gap psychologistically, by collapsing the latter into the former,[4] or it is not objective truth that he is after at all, but something else that follows (or that he at least took to follow) from the psychological feeling certainty. Among the truth-surrogates most frequently proposed are firmness, stability, unshakeability, by those who advocate versions of the psychological interpretation of Cartesian certainty; and irrevisability, maximal warrant, unmistakability, and incorrigibility among those who favour a normative or epistemic rather than descriptive psychological interpretation. Unlike proponents of the normative or epistemic view, advocates of the psychological interpretation are not usually intent on absolving Descartes of the charge of psychologism when they deny that what he was really after was truth rather than stability or unshakeability; for this reason, it was suggested earlier that most versions of the latter interpretation might be termed 'psychologistic.'

There is no need to review the entire range of solutions that scholars have proposed to this pair of difficulties. Instead, we shall set about trying to remove them with the aid of certain distinctions, beginning, in the present chapter, with that between two kinds of perfect certainty, *persuasio* and *scientia*. The charge of psychologism will be dealt with in chapters 12 and 13, employing a distinction between two senses of 'truth.' The second set of problems, concerning circularity, will be discussed in chapter 14, where the distinction between uncreated (theological) and created eternal truths will be combined with a number of more familiar distinctions to provide a solution to this vexed question.

11.2 *Persuasio* and *scientia*

A good place to start is the question of whether there are indeed conditions under which even the *sum* can be rendered doubtful by the deceiving God hypothesis. Mersenne, in the Second Set of Objections, took this to be the clear implication of the long Third Meditation passage:

Thirdly, you are not yet certain of the existence of God, and you say that you are not certain of anything, and cannot know anything clearly and distinctly until you have achieved clear and certain knowledge of the existence of God. It follows from this that you do not yet clearly and distinctly know that you are a thinking thing, since, on your own admission, that knowledge depends on the clear knowledge of an existing God, and this you have not yet proved in the passage where you draw the conclusion that you clearly know what you are. (AT VII 125: CSM II 89)

The solution to Mersenne's difficulty has to do with the fact that perfect certainty is of two kinds, either *persuasio* or *scientia.* According as the *sum* or *cogito, ergo sum* is taken to be certain in one or the other of these ways it is unconditionally, that is, perfectly certain only as long as I actually attend to it, or it is certain at all times, even when I *no longer* attend to it yet remember having done so at some time in the past. Unlike the distinction between metaphysical and moral certainty, that between *persuasio* and *scientia* as two kinds of metaphysical or perfect certainty is nowhere drawn in exactly these terms within the *Meditations* themselves. Even Descartes's reply to Mersenne's objection introduces only one term of a distinction that was much more fully elaborated in a letter to Regius of 24 May 1640. The key passage reads:

[Y]ou say: 'the truth of axioms which are clearly and distinctly understood is self-evident.' This too, I agree, is true, *during the time they are clearly and distinctly understood;* for our mind is of such a nature that it cannot help assenting to what it clearly understands. But because we often *remember* conclusions that we have deduced from such premisses without actually attending to the premisses themselves, I say that on such occasions, if we lack the knowledge of God (*si Deum ignoremus*), we can imagine that the conclusions are uncertain even though we remember that they were deduced from clear principles: because perhaps our nature is such that we go wrong even in the most evident matters. Consequently, even at the moment when we deduced them from those principles, we did not have knowledge (*scientia*) of them, but only a conviction (*persuasio*) of them. I distinguish the two as follows: there is conviction when there remains some reason which might lead us to doubt [at some subsequent time], but knowledge is conviction based on a reason so strong that it can never be shaken by an stronger reason [at any subsequent time]. Nobody can have the latter unless he also has knowledge of God (*qualem* [scil. *persuasionem*] *nullam habent qui Deum ignorant*). But a man who has once clearly understood the reasons which convince us that God exists and is not a deceiver, provided he remembers the conclusion 'God is no deceiver,' whether or not he still attends to the reasons, will continue to possess not only the conviction (*persuasio*), but real knowledge (*scientia*) of this and all other conclusions the reasons for which he remembers he once clearly perceived. (AT III 64f.: CSMK 147)

In the *later* reply to Mersenne's query within the Second Set of Objections, however, Descartes has only this to say:

When I said that we can know nothing for certain (*nihil nos certo posse scire*) until we know that God exists (*nisi prius Deum existere cognoscamus*), I expressly declared that I was speaking only of knowledge (*scientia*) of those conclusions which can be recalled when we are no longer attending to the arguments by means of which we deduced them [the reference is to the Fifth Meditation]. Now awareness (*notitia*) of first principles is not normally called 'knowledge' (*scientia*) by dialecticians. And when we become aware that we are thinking things, this is a primary notion which is not derived by means of any syllogism. (AT VII 140: CSM II 100)

The other term of the distinction, *persuasio*, is not even mentioned here, though without it the peculiar force of the talk of *scientia* remains obscure. However, even the express juxtaposition of *persuasio* and *scientia* in the letter to Regius invites misunderstanding in a number of respects. Admittedly, the key temporal axis of the distinction is clearly marked at the outset ("during the *time* they are clearly and distinctly understood ..." e.a.); that is important.[5] But there are two potential sources of confusion in that letter nonetheless.

11.3 Two sources of confusion

First, the word *persuasio* ('conviction') almost inevitably suggests a lesser degree rather than a different kind of certainty having the highest degree. This is misleading. In a passage to be interpreted more fully later (AT VII 145: CSM II 103), Descartes expressly states that *persuasio* "so firm that it is quite incapable of being destroyed ... is clearly the same as the *most perfect certainty*" (e.a.). *Persuasio* and *scientia* differ extensively and in kind rather than intensively and in degree, as this excerpt from the letter to Regius, quoted already, makes quite clear: "I distinguish the two as follows: there is *persuasio* when there remains some reason which might lead us to doubt, but *scientia* is *persuasio* based on an argument so strong that it can *never* be shaken by any stronger argument" (AT III 65: CSMK 147 e.a.).

This distinction reflects the very nature of Descartes's philosophical enterprise. In the First Meditation he recalls the considerations that led him "to demolish everything completely and start again right from the foundations if [he] wanted to establish anything at all in the sciences that was stable and likely to last" (AT VII 17: CSM II 12); and at the outset of the Second he cites the famous dictum of Archimedes in characterizing his own quest for "just one thing, however slight, that is certain and unshakeable" (AT VII 24: CSM II 16). The twofold aim of

finding "a fixed and immovable point" (AT X 515: CSM II 409) and establishing
"a body of knowledge firm and certain enough to deserve the name 'science'"
(AT X 513: CSM II 408) gives rise to two distinct senses of 'certainty': *persuasio*
and *scientia*. Although the use of the word *persuasio* is apt to obscure the fact
that what Descartes intends is by no means a lesser degree of certainty than
scientia or "perfect knowledge" (AT VII 144f.: CSM II 103), the impression is
at least mitigated by the express statement in the letter to Regius that, "*at the
moment*" when the conclusion of some proof is deduced from clear principles,
that conclusion is *persuasio*; for it is unmistakable that Descartes holds that at
that precise moment the conclusion is perfectly certain. This goes some way
toward rectifying matters; but it is easy to mistake the import of the distinction
nonetheless.

A second potential source of confusion are the successive references to 'our
nature.' This is where the earlier distinction (cf. section 10.2) between the natural
light and natural inclination proves helpful. The first reference is unmistakably to
the natural light of reason, to our native inability to withhold assent in matters
clearly and distinctly perceived. Propositions thus assented to are acknowledged
to be "true" in the letter to Regius, but only "during the time they are clearly and
distinctly perceived." The second reference to 'our nature,' on the other hand, is
not to the natural light of reason, but to the natural inclination to assent to matters
remembered to have been (but now no longer) clearly and distinctly perceived.
Here 'our nature' can lead us into error should what was once clearly and distinctly perceived no longer be true – a strange thought in itself, though not in the
light of Descartes's doctrine of divine creation, preservation, and mutability of
the eternal truths (see chapter 14). Nevertheless, following as it does hard upon
the first reference to 'our nature,' this looks confusingly like the expression of a
residual doubt concerning matters *now* clearly and distinctly perceived by the
natural light of reason – as though such matters might be false after all, even at
the very moment we assent to them. This cannot, without gross inconsistency, be
what Descartes means. The scruple can only concern that which is remembered
but now is *no longer* actually clearly and distinctly perceived. And so understood
it makes perfect sense. Nevertheless, the back-to-back references to 'our nature'
in different senses is apt to spawn confusion.

The potential for misunderstanding is enhanced by a passage of the Fifth Meditation to be considered more fully in a moment:

Admittedly, my nature is such that so long as I perceive something very clearly and
distinctly I cannot but believe it to be true. But my nature is also such that *I cannot fix my
mental vision continually on the same thing*, so as to keep perceiving it clearly; and often

the memory of a previously made judgement may come back, when I am no longer attending to the arguments which led me to make it. (AT VII 69: CSM II 48)

Here again back-to-back references to 'my nature,' the first, as in the letter to Regius, to the natural light of reason. This time, however, the second reference is fully spelled out, whereby no mention is made of anything beyond the mind's inability to keep constantly beneath its gaze all those truths it has perceived clearly and distinctly. Yet the passage concludes: "For I can convince myself that I have a natural disposition to go wrong from time to time in matters which I think I perceive as evidently as can be" (AT VII 70: CSM II 48 e.a.). If this is a reference to the natural tendency to believe what one only *recalls* having clearly and distinctly perceived, then all is well; the point is precisely that of the letter to Regius. The trouble is that this too appears to be the expression of a residual doubt about the light of reason at the very moment it is exercised in clear and distinct perception. The danger is that these references to 'my nature' as a potential source of error may cloud the initial expression of unqualified confidence in the deliverances of reason so long as they are actually clearly and distinctly perceived.

11.4 *Persuasio* and *notitia*

As already noted, in the reply to Mersenne, *persuasio* is not mentioned at all. Descartes does, however, juxtapose *notitia* to *scientia*. Yet he does so in a manner that is apt to give rise to new misunderstandings. By *principiorum notitia* he means precisely what he meant by the "clear principles" mentioned in the letter to Regius: now actually occurring intuition of self-evident truths. This the dialecticians do not call *scientia*.[6] Nor does Descartes. In the letter to Regius, in fact, he terms it *persuasio*, distinguishing it sharply from *scientia*. If he calls it *notitia* in the reply to Mersenne, this is an improvement in one respect at least: *principiorum notitia* does not suggest anything like a lesser degree of certainty. On the contrary, coupled with *principiorum*, the word *notitia* suggests certainty of the highest degree. Moreover, it captures something of the flavour of immediacy belonging to direct intuitive apprehension.[7] But coupled with *principiorum* it still tends to suggest that the contrast here is between the knowledge of *principles* or primitive truths and knowledge of *conclusions* deductively derived from such principles by a short chain of inference (so, for instance, Curley 1978, 78). In the letter to Regius, however, it was expressly stated that even the conclusions of arguments are *persuasio*, not *scientia*, so long as the deductions remain immediately before the mind's eye. Thus, knowledge of the conclusions could have been designated *conclusionum notitia*, since the arguments are, *ex hypothesi*, actually contained within the compass of a single actual intuition. Descartes's point, in short, is neither that only the knowledge *of principles* is *notitia*, nor that the knowledge of principles is *only notitia* and not *scientia*. Once I begin to reflect on my knowledge of God those first principles that were hitherto only *persuasio* or *notitia* take their place as first truths within the system of human knowledge (*scientia*). So the point is rather that clear and distinct perception *now* of first principles is not eo ipso *scientia*, any more than is clear and distinct perception now of the conclusions of sound deductive arguments. Despite the clear advantages of the word *notitia* over *persuasio*, it is far clearer in the letter to Regius than in the reply to Mersenne that the operative distinction is the temporal one between what is now and what is now no longer clearly and distinctly perceived by the natural light of reason. Whether what is in question be principles or conclusions derived from principles is irrelevant. So it is puzzling, to say the least, that Descartes expresses himself so elliptically in the Replies, a work destined for publication, on a crucial point about which he had been much more forthcoming in private correspondence.

11.5 The alleged change of position

It has recently again been suggested that Descartes modified his position in the Replies in order to meet Mersenne's objection.[8] This, however, would seem to be an unnecessarily historical way round a philosophical difficulty that can be resolved on its own terms. Nor is it correct to say, as does the same commentator, that Descartes's reply to Mersenne seriously misrepresents what he had in fact "expressly declared" in the Fifth Meditation passage to which he refers his friend – though, in the absence of any explicit working out of the distinction between *scientia* and *persuasio*, this may be a question of charity towards a great dead author. What Descartes in fact wrote in that Fifth Meditation passage is this:

Admittedly, my nature is such that *so long as* I perceive something very clearly and distinctly I cannot but believe it to be true. But my nature is also such that *I cannot fix my mental vision continually on the same thing*, so as to keep perceiving it clearly; and often the memory of a previously made judgement may come back, when I am *no longer attending to the arguments* which led me to make it. And so other arguments can now occur to me which might easily undermine my opinion, if I were unaware of God (*si Deum ignorarem*); and I should thus never have true and certain knowledge (*veram & certam scientiam*) *about anything*, but only shifting and changeable opinions (*vagae & mutabiles opiniones*). For example, when I consider the nature of a triangle, it appears most evident to me, steeped as I am in the principles of geometry, that its three angles are equal to two right angles; and *so long as I attend to the proof*, I cannot but believe this to be true. But *as soon as I turn my mind's eye away from the proof*, then in spite of still remembering that I perceived it very clearly, I can easily fall into doubt about its truth, if I am unaware of God (*si quidem Deum ignorem*). For I can convince myself that I have a natural disposition to go wrong from time to time in matters which I think I perceive as evidently as can be. (AT VII 69f.: CSM II 48 e.a.)

Of course, the subject of this passage is not specifically the *sum* or *cogito* principle, which was Mersenne's worry; only mathematical truths are cited as examples. And although Descartes's earlier letter to Regius leaves absolutely no doubt that he was already fully seized of the key distinction between *persuasio* and *scientia* well before publication of the *Meditations* – he seems to have received the Second Set of Objections in January 1641 (AT III 282) and to have completed his Replies to them around March of that year – he does not juxtapose them here or anywhere else in that work. Nevertheless, the heart of the matter is here. To forestall Mersenne's objection, Descartes had only to put his point in some such terms as these.

Taken as an item within a system of true propositions, which is what the dialecticians call *scientia*, the *sum* or *cogito, ergo sum* depends upon the proofs of God's existence and veracity. But matters stand differently when the *cogito* principle is taken as an item of *persuasio*. Such immediate and actual *notitia principiorum* those same dialecticians do not call *scientia*. So understood, the *cogito* principle does not depend for its certainty on God's existence and veracity. Nor does any other actually occurring clear and distinct perception, be it a *prima notio* or only inferred therefrom. At such times as the mind no longer attends to *primae notiones* or principles, however, even they become uncertain; moreover, the conclusions of demonstrations based on such principles are similarly uncertain the moment the mind no longer attends to the proofs. At such times a mind lacking knowledge of God would have neither *persuasio* nor *scientia* but only *vagae & mutabiles opiniones*; for this is what becomes even of *principiorum notitia* when those principles are not yet *scientia* but no longer *persuasio*. Without the knowledge of God, in short, nothing can become *scientia*. This holds for the conclusions of demonstrations not now actually before the mind's eye no less than for the premises of those demonstrations, that is, first principles. *With* the knowledge of God, however, such clear and distinct *persuasio*, be it intuitive or deductive, mathematical, logical, or metaphysical, becomes *vera & certa scientia*; from then on it is certain at all times, as long as I can remember having once clearly and distinctly perceived the truth of this *and* the truth that God exists and can be no deceiver.[9]

Thus, there is no inconsistency in Descartes's both affirming and denying dependence of the *cogito* principle on God's existence and veracity, for he is speaking of perfect certainty in two quite different senses: as *persuasio* or *notitia*, on the one hand, and as *scientia*, on the other. As the now actually occurring clear and distinct perception of my own thinking and existence and of the truth that if I think then I exist, the *cogito* principle is entirely independent of the knowledge of God. However, as the first item of metaphysical knowledge of the existence of a substance and as the foundation of all other truths within the ordered system of true propositions that the dialecticians call *scientia*, the certainty of the *cogito* and indeed of all knowledge, depends, without exception, upon the knowledge of God.

11.6 Three senses of 'clear and distinct perception'

There is no need, then, to posit a change in Descartes's position. All that is required is a distinction between two kinds of perfect certainty. Corresponding to these, three different senses of 'clear and distinct perception' can be distinguished. The first is (1) now actually occurring clear and distinct perception or *persuasio*. It is exemplified by the *cogito* or *existo* of the Second Meditation: the same certainty as is involved in the statements *cogito* and *existo* applies also to axioms or principles of the natural light and necessary truths concerning 'natures' outside the mind, provided we attend closely to the grounds of their truth as we assert them. Stressing the fulfilment of the attention condition, Descartes begins the middle section of the long Third Meditation passage with the words: "Yet *when I turn to* (*me converto ad*) the things themselves which I think I perceive very clearly, I am so convinced by them that I spontaneously declare: let whoever can do so deceive me ... etc."[10] He ends the passage, however, by reiterating the "metaphysical" doubt that remains. When propositions expressing the fact that I think and exist, mathematical truths, and principles of the natural light are intimated to be uncertain at such times as I am not expressly attending to them or their grounds, they are understood as (2) clear and distinct perception or *persuasio* that is no longer actual but only remembered, and remembered without an awareness of God; but when Descartes goes on to say of those same truths that they may be certain even when only remembered, provided one also remembers having clearly and distinctly perceived the existence and veracity of God at some time in the past, he is speaking of (3) clear and distinct perception as *scientia*.

These three senses of 'clear and distinct perception' are at least faintly in evidence in the famous Third Meditation truth rule:

I am certain that I am a thinking thing. Do I not therefore also know what is required for my being certain about anything? In this first item of knowledge there is nothing other (*nihil aliud*) than a clear and distinct perception of that which I am asserting; this would not be enough to make me certain of the truth of the matter if it could at any time be the case (*si posset unquam contingere*) that something which I perceived with such clarity and distinctness was false. So I now seem to be able to lay it down as a general rule that whatever I perceive clearly and distinctly is true. (AT VII 35: CSM II 24)[11]

The contrary-to-fact construction (*non sufficeret*) indicates that clear and distinct perception *is* in fact sufficient to render judgments certain when asserted, since it is impossible that what is now clearly and distinctly perceived be false at the very moment it is assented to; it "would not be enough," however, if "at any [other] time" I wished to assent to the same proposition, even though the grounds of its truth were no longer immediately present to my mind but only remembered as having been so formerly; for at such times my belief could indeed be false, unless I can recall having clearly and distinctly perceived that God necessarily exists and can be no deceiver. Though doubt is impossible, even on the deceiving God hypothesis, while I attend to what I clearly and distinctly perceive, given the mere possibility that God may be a deceiver, it can recur at any subsequent time. However, once

I have perceived that God exists ..., and that he is no deceiver ... and I have drawn the conclusion that everything which I clearly and distinctly perceive is of necessity true ..., [then] *even if I am no longer attending to the arguments which led me to judge that this is true*, as long as I remember that I clearly and distinctly perceived it, there are no counter-arguments which can be adduced to make me doubt it, but on the contrary I have true and certain knowledge of it. And I have knowledge not just of this matter, but of all matters which I remember ever having demonstrated, in geometry and so on. (AT VII 70: CSM II 48 e.a.)

Thus, once I know that God exists and is no deceiver, this and all other *persuasio* becomes *scientia* or "perfect knowledge" and is no longer subject even to the slightest doubt at any subsequent time.

That takes care of the main problem: the *sum* both is and is not open to a "metaphysical" doubt. At the outset of the Second Meditation *sum* is considered as an item of *persuasio* or *notitia*; so too in the middle section of the long Third Meditation passage cited above. But in the final section that same proposition is considered as no longer *persuasio* and not yet *scientia*. All this is perfectly consistent. It remains now to deal with a few related matters included in the first set of difficulties.

11.7 The temporal proviso on the *sum*

First, however, it may be worthwhile to reflect briefly on the different ways in which the condition explicitly attached to the certainty or truth of the *cogito* principle is expressed. In the *Discourse* (AT VI 32f.: CSM I 127), as late in the Second Meditation (AT VII 27: CSM II 18), the temporal condition is expressed: "as long as I think."[12] However, it is the formulation at the outset of the Second Meditation, *quoties a me profertur vel mente concipitur*, that highlights the crucial factor in Cartesian certainty: immediate inner experience of one's own thinking, coupled with a degree of attention to it. *Proferre* has the force of 'bringing forth,' 'making public,' 'making known,' even (though not usually) to oneself, while *vel mente concipere* adds that only a private thought-act (as opposed to a public speech-act) need be involved. After all, at this point in the *Meditations* nothing and no one apart from my own mind is known to exist, not even my body with its organs of speech-production. The wording of the *Discourse*, therefore, is elliptical. For while I am necessarily conscious of my thinking as long as I think, I do not necessarily attend to or reflect upon what I am thus conscious of at all times; indeed, for the most part, my own thought processes are the last thing I attend to. Deeply rooted in my nature "as a combination of mind and body" (AT VII 82: CSM II 57) is a powerful and salutary propensity to direct my attention to the objects of sense-perception, to really existing material things, including my own body, and to the beneficial or harmful effects upon it of other bodies around it (cf. AT VII 83: VIII-1 41f.). If the rider "whenever it is put forward by me," and so on, is indeed intended to restrict the perfect certainty of *cogito* or *existo* to those philosophical interludes during which my attention is turned from the objects of sense and of thought generally to thinking itself as what I am immediately conscious of, then at all other times my existence as a thinking thing is subject to a "metaphysical" doubt and perfect certainty will at such times depend upon a knowledge of God's existence and veracity.

It would be pointless to enquire whether the proviso states a necessary as well as sufficient condition of perfect certainty without taking into account the various senses of 'the *cogito*' distinguished above (Part Two, *in initio*). As long as I do not know "the author of my being" (AT VII 77: CSM II 53f.; cf. also AT VII 226: CSM II 159), the proviso states a necessary and sufficient condition of 'the *cogito*' in the first two senses, though for the truth of the *cogito* principle in the third sense, as the first truth of science, it is neither necessary nor sufficient. Once I know God, however, it is sufficient in all three cases though still not necessary in the last.

That non-fulfilment of the condition stated in the proviso is sufficient for uncertainty (possible falsehood) in the first two senses of 'the *cogito*' is explicit in the restatement in the context of the question "what this 'I' is, that now necessarily exists" (AT VII 25: CSM II 17): "I am, I exist – that is certain. But for how long? For as long as I am thinking. For it *could* be that were I totally to cease from thinking, I should totally cease to exist. At present I am not admitting anything except what is necessarily true" (AT VII 27: CSM II 18 e.a.). Fulfilment of the condition is accordingly both necessary and sufficient for the perfect certainty of 'the *cogito*' in the first two senses. As for the third, once God's existence and veracity have been established it is both necessary *and sufficient* merely to remember once having perceived clearly and distinctly both the *cogito* principle and that a veracious God exists in order to be absolutely certain of 'the *cogito*' as the first item within the newly erected system of *scientia*; it is not necessary that it be actually "put forward by me or conceived in my mind."[13]

11.8 The remaining difficulties in the first set

No more doubtful than the *cogito* principle itself are the axioms of arithmetic and geometry considered as *persuasio*. The same may be said of the metaphysical principles of the natural light. Thus, the truths of mathematics and the axioms of metaphysics are absolutely certain as long as I attend to them, but open to a "metaphysical" doubt at all other times, so long as I am unaware of God, that is, so long as they have not yet become *scientia*. The problem of the rejection of the simple truths of mathematics as doubtful in the First Meditation resolves itself exactly as did the main problem: as *persuasio*, they are perfectly certain, even without the knowledge of God; if they were rejected in the First Meditation, then it is because in that context they were not considered as *persuasio*. There is even some direct textual support for this. In the Replies to the Seventh Set of Objections, speaking of the truths of mathematics, Descartes refers to "the First Meditation, in which I was supposing that *I was not attending to* anything that I clearly perceived" (AT 460: CSM II 309 e.a.). In the First Meditation the truths of mathematics were *not* regarded as propositions the truth of which is immediately intuited either as self-evident or as following in logic from premises so intuited; they were taken rather as items within a previously established body of mathematical doctrine formerly learned and now remembered – for example, as theorems entertained without actually attending either to their derivation or to the definitions, axioms, and other theorems from which they may be deductively derived. The certainty of these truths at such times depends upon the knowledge of the existence and veracity of God.[14]

It is worth noting that Descartes's rejection in the First Meditation of his former belief in a "supremely good" (AT VII 21: CSM II 14) "omnipotent God" (ibid.) rests on exactly the same consideration as the rejection of the mathematical truths. In that particular context, the belief in an "omnipotent God" is taken in isolation from any grounds that might be adduced for his existence and goodness, simply as a "long-standing belief" (ibid.) acquired (as Descartes explains to Burman at AT V 146: CSMK 332) *per sensus*, that is, through hearsay (*per auditum*). Gouhier does not hesitate to designate the idea of "le bon Dieu" in the First Meditation "celle du catéchisme" (cf. 1969, 219; cf. also 253). While on the right track, this may go *too* far. From the *Discourse* on, Descartes is always careful to make "an exception of all matters concerning faith and morals in general" (AT VII 476: CSM II 321) before undertaking the general overthrow of his former opinions.[15]

The statement in the Seventh Replies is confirmed by Descartes's response to Mersenne's objection that "an atheist is clearly and distinctly aware that the three angles of a triangle are equal to two right angles," while being "so far ... from supposing the existence of God that he completely denies it" (AT VII 125: CSM II 89). He begins by noting that the conclusions of the atheistic geometer are in fact clearly and distinctly perceived, contrary to what Mersenne supposed; and that as long as they are so perceived, they are absolutely certain. But since it is humanly impossible to keep the grounds of their truth before the mind's eye indefinitely, they must become doubtful again the instant the atheist no longer attends to them. Not only are they not yet *vera scientia*; they can never become such as long as the atheist remains an atheist, that is, until he acknowledges God:

The fact that an atheist can be 'clearly aware (*cognoscere possit*) that the three angles of a triangle are equal to two right angles' is something I do not dispute. But I maintain that this awareness (*cognitio*) of his is not true knowledge (*vera scientia*), since no act of awareness (*cognitio*) that can be rendered doubtful seems fit to be called knowledge (*scientia*). Now since we are supposing that this individual is an atheist, he cannot be certain that he is not being deceived on matters which seem to him to be very evident (as I fully explained). And although this doubt may not occur to him, it can still crop up if someone else raises that point or if he looks into the matter himself. So he will never be free of this doubt until he acknowledges that God exists. (AT VII 141: CSM II 101)

Although simple mathematical truths may be just as certain as the *cogito* principle, the latter retains the title of first and founding principle for the reason mentioned already (chapter 7 *in initio*): the Archimedean point must not only be absolutely certain, it must also be a truth about the actual existence of something, and about the existence of a substance rather than a mere mode or accident. For along with the sameness of their evidential footing Descartes insists upon the importance, from a metaphysical perspective, of the difference between existential propositions like *sum* and logical truisms the denials of which are self-contradictory, but which do not assert the existence of anything. In a passage of the *Principles* to be interpreted at greater length in Part Three, he writes:

[W]hen I said that the proposition *I am thinking, therefore I exist* is the first and most certain of all to occur to anyone who philosophises in an orderly way, I did not in saying that deny that one must first know what thought, existence and certainty are, and that it is impossible that that which thinks should not exist, and so forth. But because these are very simple notions, *and ones which on their own provide us with no knowledge of anything that exists*, I did not think that they needed to be listed. (AT VIII-A 8: CSM I 196 e.a.)

Like these and other "simple notions" of metaphysics, the truth of simple mathematical propositions does not depend upon the existence of anything outside the mind:

I find within me countless ideas of things which *even though they may not exist anywhere outside me* still cannot be called nothing; for although in a sense they can be thought of at will, they are not my invention but have their own true and immutable natures. (AT VII 64: CSM II 44 e.a.)

The example given is that of a triangle and the truths "that its three angles equal two right angles, that its greatest side subtends its greatest angle, and the like" (ibid.). The difference between such truths as these and the *sum* is of the greatest significance for Descartes: apparently not troubled by its contingency or particularity, he was intent upon an assertion of the existence of a substance as the first principle of his philosophy. Hence, no insoluble problem arises regarding the primacy of the *cogito* principle within Descartes's metaphysical system.[16]

11.9 Conclusion

This concludes the treatment of the first set of difficulties. It is a historical curiosity of some note that the precise sense of that certainty operationally defined in the First Meditation is wide open to misunderstanding in the absence of a distinction that Descartes had drawn clearly enough in the letter to Regius (24 May 1640), but that is nowhere explicitly drawn in the *Meditations* themselves (completed April 1640) and at best only sketched in the Replies (published with the *Meditations* in 1641).[17] Without the distinction between *persuasio* and *scientia*, all that Descartes has to say about the certainty of the *cogito* principle is liable to serious charges of gross inconsistency or question-begging. First made by Descartes's contemporaries, these charges have been the stock-in-trade of commentators on Descartes's metaphysics ever since. Though he never acknowledged the justice of the charges, and had ample opportunity to rebut them adequately, Descartes never saw fit to resort to a distinction that he had already employed in his private correspondence and that, properly handled, might have forestalled further objections indefinitely. Similarly puzzling is his reticence on the subject of the divine creation of the eternal truths. To the latter doctrine he at least adverted, if not in the *Meditations* themselves, then in the very public Replies (AT VII 380: CSM II 261; and AT VII 431ff.: CSM II 291f.); so the concern "to prevent anything at all being found in my writings which could justifiably give offence to the theologians" (AT VII 245: CSM II 171; cf. also AT VII 252: CSM II 175), though never far from Descartes's mind, cannot (*pace* Bréhier) be the whole story of his diffidence. It probably cannot account for his apparent suppression of the distinction between *persuasio* and *scientia* either.[18]

12

The Modalities of Truth

The next task is to determine the precise sense in which truths perfectly certain are necessary or "necessarily true" (AT VII 25: CSM II 17). *Sum* being a logically contingent proposition, one might take it to be in quite different senses that Descartes speaks of (a) *sum* or *existo*, (b) the axioms of metaphysics and mathematics, (c) simple mathematical truths, and (d) propositions concerning God's nature or that of body as "clearly and distinctly perceived," as "perfectly certain," and as "necessarily true." And indeed, the sense of 'truth' that pertains to the *cogito* principle and metaphysical axioms differs from that in which, for example, the necessarily true propositions of arithmetic and geometry or the knowledge of God's existence and nature are 'true' or 'correspond' to their object. Nevertheless, all the varieties of proposition just mentioned are necessary in the same root sense: as that from which it is impossible to withhold assent, either as long as I actually attend to the grounds of its truth, or as long as I can remember having done so in the past while recalling the proof of God's existence.

From this it would appear that the necessity is psychological rather than what we ordinarily call 'logical' necessity. The logical peculiarity of propositions the denials of which are self-contradictory, though already the key thing for the Scholastics, as in the sequel for Leibniz, Hume, and Kant, figures in a relatively minor way in Descartes's account of the modalities of truth. More important than the distinction between logically necessary and contingent truth are two others. One is the distinction between two kinds of logically necessary or 'eternal' truths, the theological and the non-theological. This is elaborated in sections 10.12 and 14.4. The other is the distinction between two kinds of logically contingent truths, about the mind and about extra-mental things.[1] We shall return to it in section 14.8. The matter to be pursued now is the distinction of metaphysical (or psychological) from logical necessity and contingency (taking up again the theme begun in section 5.2). Since the discussion of the modalities of truth in the present chapter aims at clarifying the necessity and truth of the *sum*, metaphysical necessity will be considered first.

12.1 Psychologism: Subjective and objective truth

Since metaphysical necessity clearly has to do with the psychological inability to withhold assent from the clearly and distinctly perceived, and since objective truth as the 'agreement of thought with its object' does not follow from the psychological inability to doubt or deny, Descartes has been accused of a form of the fallacy known as 'psychologism': mistaking a subjective feature of the psychological act of judging for a reliable criterion of objective truth. If clear and distinct perception accompanied by "a great inclination in the will" (AT VII 58f.: CSM II 41) are psychological states whose presence is sheerly unmistakable, then they are insufficient to guarantee objective truth; while if they are sufficient to guarantee objective truth, the possibility of their presence depends on extramental states of affairs themselves not infallibly introspectible. In the first case, the 'mark' falls short of a criterion; it fails to specify a necessary, let alone a sufficient, condition of truth. In the second, the immediate identifiability of the very thing for which a reliable criterion is sought – objective truth – is taken for granted; 'psychologism' is avoided at the price of begging the question.

What this criticism[2] misses is not so much the nature of the necessity involved, which is indeed psychological, as the notion of truth relevant to the *cogito* and other first principles. This much is suggested by Descartes's own treatment of a similar query in his Replies to the Second Set of Objections. There the possibility that what we conceive as necessarily true might "appear false to God or an angel, so that it is, absolutely speaking, false" (AT VII 145: CSM II 103) is dismissed, not as logically impossible, but as psychologically incredible once one understands the nature of the truth sought for the metaphysical foundations of human knowledge. This controversial passage will be examined later (cf. section 12.5). The point just now is that any other version of the correspondence theory must be similarly irrelevant when it comes to the kind of truth belonging to Descartes's founding principle. Of course, from Descartes's perspective it makes perfect sense to speak of truth as the 'agreement of thought with its object,' even though this is only a nominal definition rather than the primary *phenomenological* sense of 'truth' (cf. section 12.4 below). The latter, however, is alone relevant to first principles. But as soon as we advance beyond the knowledge of the mind and the metaphysical principles employed in the proof of God's existence, a new type of truth-question arises. The point at issue in the central metaphysical doctrine of the real distinction of body and soul, for example, is indeed whether the order of ideas, the conceptual independence of 'body' and 'soul,' *corresponds* to the order of things, their real separateness or separability; and when it comes to the nature of extended substance the question is similar (see below section 13.1): do such things exist in a way (*tales* ...) that exactly corresponds with my ideas of them (*quales* ...). This secondary notion of truth will be elaborated in chapter 13. To repeat: where foundations or first principles are concerned (as in the case of the *sum*), it is not this nominal but the phenomenological sense of truth that is relevant. Before explaining this primary sense of 'truth,' more needs to be said about the necessity involved in Descartes's founding principle (section 12.2) and about the history of its interpretation (section 12.3).

12.2 Psychological or metaphysical necessity

The main question concerns the sense in which *sum, existo* is said to be "necessarily true" in the Second Meditation (AT VII 25: CSM II 17). Since 'certainty,' according to the operational definition examined earlier (section 10.3), means 'immunity from all three grounds of doubt,' the sense of "necessarily true" obviously depends upon the precise nature of the impossibility involved in indubitability. About this there is a great diversity of scholarly opinion. On the view to be taken here the impossibility in question is primarily of a psychological or metaphysical kind, according as one construes questions about determinism and free will in either or both of these ways. Thus, in the Fourth Meditation, Descartes writes: "from the very fact of my raising this question [whether anything exists] it follows quite evidently that I exist. I *could not but judge* (*non potui quidem non judicare*) that something which I understood so clearly was true; ... a great light in the intellect was followed by a great inclination in the will" (AT VII 58f.: CSM II 41 e.a.). This inability to prevent oneself from – or necessity of – assenting to what one clearly and distinctly perceives is a recurring theme in Descartes's discussions of certainty. At one place in the *Meditations* he writes: "And even if I had not demonstrated this, the nature of my mind is such that I *cannot but assent* to these things (*non possem iis non assentiri*), at least so long as I clearly perceive them" (AT VII 65: CSM II 45 e.a.). Or again: "Admittedly my *nature* is such that so long as I perceive something clearly and distinctly I *cannot but* believe it to be true (*non possim non credere verum esse*) (AT VII 69: CSM II 48 e.a.). Similar passages are found throughout the Objections and Replies. For example, in the Letter to Clerselier that in the French version of the *Meditations* forms an appendix to the Fifth Set of Replies, Descartes writes: "For when we examine it [the *cogito, ergo sum*] it appears so evident to the understanding that we cannot but believe it (*qu'il ne se sçauroit empescher de la croire*)" (AT IX-1 205: CSM II 271). Likewise in the Second Replies:

The fact that I exist so long as I am thinking, or that what is done cannot be undone, are examples of truths in respect of which we manifestly possess this kind of certainty ["perceptions so transparently clear and at the same time so simple that we cannot ever think of them without believing them to be true"]. For we cannot doubt them unless we think of them; but we cannot think of them without at the same time believing they are true, as was supposed. Hence we cannot doubt them without at the same time believing they are true; that is, we can never [as a matter of psychological fact] doubt them. (AT VII 145f.: CSM II 104)

Essentially the same point is made at several places in the *Principles*: "even if there were no way of proving this [i.e., that we 'never go wrong when we assent only to what we clearly and distinctly perceive'], the minds of all of us have been so moulded by nature that whenever we perceive something clearly [meant are the clear perceptions of the *intellect* alone: cf. AT VII 145: CSM II 104], we spontaneously give our assent to it and are quite unable to doubt its truth (*nullo modo possimus dubitare quin sit verum*)" (AT VIII-1 21: CSM I 207 e.a.).

The range of examples could easily be extended. The metaphysical force of the impossibility in question is perhaps least obscured where Descartes remarks (speaking of the ontological argument): "*I am not free* to think of God without existence" (AT VII 67: CSM II 46 e.a.), though even here the sequel – "as I am free to imagine a horse with or without wings" (ibid.) – is apt to suggest that no more than a logical impossibility is at issue. But even allowing for the fact that Descartes recognized no such sharp divisions between the logical, metaphysical, and psychological as would be insisted upon in discussions of necessity nowadays, the metaphysical question of free will is recognizably the dominant perspective in his account of necessary truth. Nevertheless, virtually all those readings that have stressed the psychological inability to withhold assent have divorced necessity from truth; in this they have followed the normative interpretations of the necessity of the *sum* that arose to contest those still earlier logical interpretations that merely perpetuated the misguided efforts of Descartes's contemporaries to see in the *cogito, ergo sum* a logical inference. It may be worth pausing to review these discussions of the necessity of the *sum*, starting with the logical, if only in order to establish just how much turns on discerning the relevant notion of truth.

12.3 Logical, normative, and psychological interpretations

Most writers on Descartes agree that the proposition *sum*, 'I am' or 'I exist,' is a logically contingent truth, and that there are a great many propositions of the form *cogito* – 'I see,' 'I will,' 'I doubt,' 'I deny,' 'I fear,' and so forth – that are necessarily true without being logically necessary. So at least some propositions, *cogito* and *sum* among them, may be absolutely certain without being logically necessary in the sense of that the denial of which involves contradiction.[3] Moreover, virtually all commentators acknowledge the converse as well: even logically necessary propositions may not be absolutely certain under all circumstances. This much seems to follow from the doubt expressed in the First Meditation concerning simple mathematical truths the denials of which are self-contradictory. Nevertheless, the impossibility of actually denying the *sum* is frequently taken to be 'logical' in some less customary sense of the term, and it is this view that must be confronted first, beginning with the closely related forms in which it was espoused by Hintikka and Ayer. We must then consider normative interpretations of indubitability that, while not 'logical' in the usual sense, nevertheless reflect preoccupations similar to those of the strictly logical interpretations. Along with the descriptive logical and normative 'epistemic' interpretations, the third chief way of understanding the necessity of the *sum* is again descriptive, but psychological rather than logical. The interpretation to be defended here is a variant of this view.

There is good reason to begin with Hintikka's classic article "*Cogito, Ergo Sum*: Inference or Performance?" (1962), for it was at the centre of the renewed scholarly controversy that began some thirty years ago and has continued until the present day. Hintikka notes that it would be logically inconsistent to deny the existential proposition *sum* while asserting the predicative *cogito*, since B(a) ⊃ (Ex) (x = a & B(x)) is "a provable formula of our lower functional calculi" (Hintikka 1962, 112). But, he acknowledges, if this were the whole story, the *cogito, ergo sum* would be of little philosophical interest; for the inference then turns on the existential presuppositions built into the common functional calculus, and it is perfectly possible to develop a system of logic free of these assumptions. This lays the *cogito, ergo sum* open to the charge of question-begging (cf. Curley 1978, 74). For Hintikka, accordingly, its real interest lies in the fact that the denial of *sum* is logically inconsistent in a sense having nothing to do with "the usual systems of functional calculus" (1962, 113). The statement 'I am' is "existentially self-verifying" (121) and its denial "existentially inconsistent" (ibid.) owing to the "*performatory* (performative) character" (118) of the act of making it.[4]

Hintikka was obviously drawing on Austin's and Searle's work on the logic of speech-acts, extending it to thought-acts and stressing the peculiar logical properties of acts, including statements, the performance of which actually *makes* that which is thought or asserted true. Ayer made a similar observation in more traditional logical terms, drawing attention to the fact that *cogito* and *sum* are among those propositions the truth of which is logically entailed by the fact they are asserted (Ayer 1956, 86).[5] It is presumably against Ayer that Frankfurt maintains that the *sum* is not to be classified among "statements which are rendered true by the mere act of making them" (1966, 347); but his main target is Hintikka's logically more sophisticated defence. Descartes's purpose is fundamentally misconceived, Frankfurt argues, if one supposes that the discussion of his existence in the Second Meditation is intended to establish that *sum* is true rather than merely 'certain' or 'indubitable.'[6] Certainty or indubitability is a *normative* concept for Frankfurt (ibid., 346); the indubitability of the proposition *sum* whenever it is pronounced or conceived entails, not that it is true (348), but only that one cannot (logically) have good grounds for doubting it at that very moment, even faced with the possibilities of dreaming and the evil demon. Thus, it is still the "unique logical status of *sum*" (339) that interests Frankfurt, but that status is now due to its being logically necessary that this contingently true existential proposition be indubitable in a normative sense on any occasion on which it might occur to anyone to doubt it. The logical peculiarity of the *sum* is therefore owing to its properties as an inference from *cogito* after all, not, as Hintikka maintained, to its character as a performance. Even the first part of Descartes's dictum, *cogito*, must not be taken as true rather than normatively indubitable. Its function is precisely to underscore the fact that "a premise from which *sum* can be elicited is an essential and inescapable element of every context in which the need for assurance concerning *sum* arises" (355). This dichotomy – inference or performance? – fixed the parameters of the renewed debate sparked by Hintikka, which were to remain more or less stable for decades to come.[7]

Responding in a second article to the critical remarks of Weinberg (1963), Hintikka (1963) reiterated his initial contention that inference and performance are not mutually exclusive. The *cogito* is "essentially" a performance, though it may be considered an inference "provided that the sole basis of this inference is the fact that the denial of the corresponding implication 'if I think then I exist' – namely, 'I think, but I do not exist' – is existentially inconsistent (self-defeating)" (Hintikka 1963, 489). This is to make the inference wholly dependent on features of the logic of performatory acts. Weinberg, however, understands 'inference' differently, though not in terms of the traditional syllogistic model. If any modern interpreter of Descartes takes the *sum* as the logically derived conclusion of a syllogism or indirect inference, the contingently true minor of which is *cogito* and whose suppressed major may be expressed as 'whatever thinks, is,' it is Hamelin (1921, 35).[8] Weinberg borrows his concept of inference from the doctrine in the *Regulae* regarding immediate intuition of simple natures and the immediately intuitable relations between them. As Hintikka puts it: "On Weinberg's view, the certainty of *sum* is derivative [from the *cogito*]; it depends (1) on the certainty of the fact that he is thinking as well as (2) on the certainty of a necessary connection between thinking and existence" (1963, 490). This is indeed the way Weinberg sets out the non-syllogistic immediate inference (cf. 1963, 488,

490), the nerve of which is the "grasp of simple notions and the concatenation of simple notions" (489). The "*sum* is not *syllogistically* deduced from *cogito*, but rather it is something known *per se*. But what is known *per se*, is ... not *sum* but *cogito, ergo sum*. What Descartes knows could be expressed in the following way: *I think, I cannot think and not be, ... I am*" (487).

There are, then, at least three distinct ways of interpreting the necessity of the *sum* descriptively as a logical insight: (1) that which takes 'logic' in the sense of traditional syllogistic logic and the *cogito* (notwithstanding Descartes's disclaimers) as a syllogism (Hamelin, according to most);[9] (2) that view which turns on the immediate inspection of logical relations, whether of an intra- or interpropositional nature (Weinberg et al.);[10] and (3) that which invokes a 'new' logic of a quite different kind (Hintikka).[11] On the first two, *ergo* marks a straightforwardly logical inference of a more or less conventional sort, while on the last it has no such force at all.[12] Add to these (4) the view that the *sum* is a direct intuition and (5) Frankfurt's normative account of the necessity involved, and we have, with one important omission, the main lines of the outer framework of the debate right down to the present day.[13]

Of the interpreters mentioned thus far, only Alexander construes the necessity of *sum* as logical in something like the ordinary sense of 'logically necessary truth' (cf. above, n. 3). Moreover, only Hamelin (1921, 235) apparently ignores Descartes's express admonition that the *cogito, ergo sum* is not to be construed as a piece of syllogistic reasoning. Nevertheless, Ayer, Hintikka, and Frankfurt all insist upon certain logical features of the attempt to doubt one's own existence or to persuade oneself that one does not exist. Can it seriously be denied that the *sum* embodies a logical insight?

Without much question, Descartes showed himself at times acutely aware of the logical peculiarities of the statements *cogito, sum*, and *cogito, ergo sum*.[14] Moreover, the normative force of this concept of certainty came frequently to his attention.[15] Yet both points can be conceded without granting that the sense of 'certain' or "necessarily true" is primarily logical or normative or that certainty and objective truth are in fact distinct and separated by a considerable gulf. Such evidence as there undeniably is for both logical and normative interpretations can be dealt with in the manner in which Tlumak (cf. n. 13 above) treats the evidence that certainty consists in the psychological impossibility of withholding assent: logical necessity, like normative irrevisability, may be frequent or constant concomitants of certainty in a sense simply synonymous with 'truth'; but 'certainty' and normative 'irrevisability' are no more to be identified with one another than are certainty and the logical impossibility of falsehood.

Advocates of the normative interpretation are concerned above all to drive a logical wedge between certainty and truth: though metaphysical is the highest degree of certainty attainable ("maximal warrant"), it nevertheless implies only "immunity to revision by epistemic possibilities (irrevisability)" (Tlumak 1978, 55); irrevisability "does not guarantee truth" (48) in all, but only in some cases. The concept of truth is obviously the crux here, as it is in those psychological interpretations of the necessity of the *sum* (cf. Rubin 1977; Larmore 1984; Bennett 1990; and Loeb 1992) that take psychological as a merely subjective certainty, either burdening Descartes with a form of 'psychologism' or crediting him with having found a way across the "chasm" (Bennett) separating psychological certainty from truth.[16]

Against all three interpretive tendencies (logical, normative, and psychological) it can be shown that 'truth,' in what for Descartes is the *primary* sense of the term, is actually entailed by 'perfect certainty.' For the experience of certainty, of a psychological impossibility or absolute limitation upon one's freedom to withhold assent, is nothing but the immediate inner experience of what truth itself is. Other accounts of truth, in particular the Scholastic definition *adaequatio intellectus et rei* or *ad rem*, amount to no more than nominal definitions of the *word* 'truth.' What truth is can only be adequately understood in and through immediate intuition or inner experience.[17]

That certainty as clear and distinct perception entails truth rather than some normative injunction for the rational believer to assent is clear from an amusing passage in the Replies to the Seventh Set of Objections. Speaking of a perceiver who may "be dreaming or mad," Descartes writes: "no matter who the perceiver is [i.e., even if he 'be dreaming or mad'] nothing can be clearly and distinctly perceived without its being just as we perceive it to be, i.e. *without being true*" (AT VII 461f.: CSM II 310 e.a.). In the light of this it will be difficult to maintain that what Descartes means by 'true' is in fact something akin to 'reasonable.'

Since normative and psychologistic interpretations obscure just how central the notion of truth is to Descartes's philosophical project, the main task in the remainder of this chapter is the elucidation of that concept. Only then can the various modalities of truth be set in a clear light. The next chapter will then examine certain contexts in which the traditional concept of truth features importantly after all.

12.4 A phenomenological approach to truth

Before the backcloth of this survey of scholarly opinion the argument to be advanced in support of the psychological character of the necessity of the *sum* will be seen to differ from the psychological interpretations just described in two respects. There is, to be sure, (1) the emphasis placed upon the metaphysical dimension of psychological necessity, that is, on the question of human freedom. But the main difference is that, rather than acknowledge a logical gap, this interpretation (2) identifies the psychological experience of the necessity of assenting with the experience of truth in the primary sense of the term and the only one relevant to the truth of the *cogito* principle. Since it gives no purchase to the charge of psychologism, the approach that takes psychological necessity in this way, simply equating it with truth, might be termed 'phenomenological' rather than 'psychological.' For in contrast to the prevailing 'realist' theory expressed in the nominal definition *adaequatio intellectus et rei*, Descartes's Third Meditation "rule that whatever I perceive very clearly and distinctly is true" (AT VII 35: CSM II 24) is remarkable for advancing a purely phenomenological theory of truth.

In the sense in which it is used here, 'phenomenological' refers neither to a specific theory of truth nor to a particular school or movement within philosophy, but to the philosophical device (antedating by far the school that lent it its name) of omitting all reference to the extra-mental objects of thought (*res*) and confining one's analyses to that which is immediately present to consciousness in the manner of acts and their immediately intuitable act-features and act-structures. For example, what clarity and distinctness are in general becomes evident in that very process of reflexive attention to one's perceptions through which the latter are first rendered clear and distinct.[18] It is by attending to my thinking that I become immediately aware of the difference between what I am thinking about (the mind-independent *res* that are the principal objects of my thinking) and the thought-acts themselves of which I am immediately conscious; this makes possible the restriction of attention to the latter, rendering my perceptions distinct as well as clear and furnishing, in the course of further reflexion, an understanding of what clarity and distinctness themselves are. This restriction to thought and its modes is the focus of the definition of 'clear' and 'distinct' within the *Principles* (I, 45; cited above, section 7.1), which, as it involves no reference to any *res*, to anything outside the mind, is purely phenomenological.[19]

However, clarity and distinctness form only one of a pair of strictly phenomenological criteria of necessary truth or certainty. This brings us to the other difference and the question of human freedom. The other criterion of truth, explicit in the Fourth Meditation, is volition or judgment that is unfree in the sense that one assents, not indeed against one's will, it being of the nature of human reason to assent willingly to all it clearly and distinctly perceives, but nevertheless involuntarily in that one has no choice or "cannot but assent" (AT VII 65: CSM II 45) so long as one attends strictly to what one is immediately conscious of. As with clarity and distinctness, the purely phenomenological character of the limits upon the mind's freedom to doubt and deny is more explicit in the *Principles* than in the *Meditations*:

That there is freedom in our will, and that we have power in many [though not all] cases to give or withhold our assent at will, is so evident that it must be counted among the *first and most common notions that are innate in us*. (AT VIII-1 19: CSM I 205f. e.a.)

The principle from which this is taken (I, 39) is entitled: "The freedom of the will is self-evident (*per se notam*)." Descartes continues:

This was obvious earlier on when, in our attempt to doubt everything, we went so far as to make the supposition of some supremely powerful author of our being (*aliquem potentissimum nostrae originis authorem*) who was attempting to deceive us in every possible way. For in spite of that supposition, the freedom which we experienced within us was nonetheless so great as to enable us to abstain from believing whatever was not quite certain or fully examined. (AT VIII-1 19f.: CSM I 206)

Being "innate," this "freedom to refrain from believing things which are not completely certain and thoroughly examined" (AT VIII-1 6: CSM I 194) is something we "experience in ourselves" immediately as we freely withhold assent from the doubtful (ibid.). However, "the indifference I feel when there is no reason pushing me in one direction rather than another is the lowest grade of freedom" in man (AT VII 58: CSM II 40). To the liberty of indifference Descartes opposes (adapting a distinction much discussed in his day) the liberty of spontaneity; for "in order to be free, there is no need for me to be capable of moving both ways; on the contrary, the more I incline in one direction ... the freer is my choice" (ibid.). Thus, to know what freedom is and to know that the will is free we need only direct our attention to our thinking and the difference between the objects of consciousness and of thought; for the same process of doubting by which we discover our ability not to assent to the existence of the doubtful (liberty of indifference) issues in the immediate awareness that we are not free to doubt the existence of what we are immediately conscious of so long as we attend to it (liberty of spontaneity). The necessity involved in this radical check upon our "freedom and indifference" (AT VIII-1 20: CSM I 206) is not only compatible with "spontaneity and freedom" (AT VII 59: CSM II 41); it is the very essence of freedom understood as something positive, as a "perfection" (AT VII 58: CSM II 40), liberty of indifference being a mere "defect in knowledge or a kind of negation" (ibid.). Although we are strictly determined to assent by the "great inclination of the will" that follows clear and distinct perception, we are not "determined by any external force" (AT VII 57: CSM II 40); and this, Descartes holds, warrants the designation of this necessity as freedom. As liberty of spontaneity is only the immediate inner experience of a limit on our indifference, it too is "something ... of which we have an intimate grasp and which we experience within ourselves" (AT VIII-1 20: CSM I 206). That is to say, it (like liberty of indifference) is an innate idea. Like clarity and distinctness, the experience of a limit upon our freedom to doubt and deny is a purely phenomenological criterion of perfect certainty and truth.

An important qualification must be added to the preceding remark that liberty of indifference is a defect. It is a defect in man but not in God. In the Fourth Meditation Descartes remarks that "it is only the will or freedom of choice which I experience within me to be so great that the idea of any greater faculty is beyond my grasp; so much so that it is above all in virtue of the will that I understand myself to bear in some way the image and likeness of God" (AT VII 57: CSM II 40). Thus, it is in his liberty of indifference that man resembles God; as God's will is perfectly indifferent at all times, so man's is somewhat indifferent at some times. However, "the indifference which belongs to human freedom is very different from that which belongs to divine freedom" (AT VII 432: CSM II 292) in this further respect: what is a negation or lack in man is a perfection in God: "the supreme indifference to be found in God is the supreme indication of his omnipotence" (ibid.). This is precisely what one would expect, since "no essence can belong univocally to both God and his creatures" (ibid.): "as for man, since he finds that the nature of all goodness and truth is already determined by God, and his will cannot tend towards anything else, it is evident that he will embrace the good and true all the more willingly, *and hence more freely*, in proportion as he sees it more clearly," that is, the more he is compelled to assent. "He is never indifferent except where he does not know which of the two alternatives is the better or truer, or at least when he does not see this clearly enough to rule out any possibility of doubt" (ibid., e.a.).

Thus, although the freedom of indifference is that in which man resembles God, it is neither a perfection in man, as it is in God, nor does it constitute the *essence* of *human* as of divine freedom; liberty of spontaneity does. Whatever belongs to the essence of anything, it cannot be without; yet man would still be free without the liberty of indifference: "not only are we free when ignorance of what is right [or true] makes us indifferent, but we are also free – indeed at our freest – when a clear perception impels us to pursue some object [or affirm some truth]" (AT VII 433: CSM II 292). The essence of *human* freedom consists, then, in the liberty of spontaneity that is something positive, a perfection in man, although one in which man does not resemble God at all.[20]

12.5 Phenomenological meaning *versus* nominal definition of 'truth'

If 'it is impossible to doubt p' has primarily the psychological or metaphysical sense of 'I am not free to believe not-p' (cf. AT VII 67: CSM II 46) rather than the logical force of 'I cannot think not-p without contradiction,' then *cogito* and *existo* are "necessarily true" (AT VII 25: CSM II 17) in a non-logical sense whenever they are asserted, whatever may be the peculiarities of their logical behaviour as self-referential statements, and whatever the nature of the inference from one to the other. It is no argument against assigning the necessary truth of such assertions the primarily metaphysical or psychological sense given it here that the psychological necessity of assenting does not entail truth on some of the most widely accepted theories of truth. As with 'thought,' Descartes would have dismissed any suggestion that there could be anything arbitrary about his employment of the concept of truth. The "true and immutable nature" of truth itself is an innate idea (AT VII 38: CSM II 26); "we have within us ideas of truth and falsehood" (AT VII 144: CSM II 103), for the explicit knowledge of what truth is is immediately given in reflexion upon our thinking anything. As Descartes explains to Mersenne in a letter concerning Herbert of Cherbury's *de Veritate*, it never occurred to him to examine what truth is "because it seems a notion so transcendentally clear that nobody can be ignorant of it" (AT II 597: CSMK 139). Of course, the *word* 'truth' may be defined as "conformity of thought with its object" (ibid.); this is merely a nominal definition, though as such perfectly correct. What truth itself is is perfectly clear to anyone who "wants to examine things for himself, and to base his judgements about them on his own conceptions" (AT X 523: CSM II 417) rather than relying on Scholastic definitions. For simple reflexion on one's thinking, even thinking about something not clearly and distinctly perceived, suffices to disclose the key phenomenological difference between what I am conscious of and what I am thinking, together with my sheer inability to doubt or prevent myself from assenting to the existence of my thoughts as modes of a thinking substance. This is to make clear to oneself what truth is in a manner that surpasses "logical definitions" (AT VIII-1 8: CSM I 195) in precisely the way in which "a man who walks across a room shows much better what movement is than a man who says [citing Aristotle's obscure formula] 'it is the act of being in potency, insofar as it is in potency' (*est actus entis in potentia prout in potentia*); and so for the others" (AT II 597: CSMK 139).[21]

Of course, the logical relationship between 'certainty' and 'truth' is in Descartes much as elsewhere: many things may be true without being certain, let alone known or even knowable, though everything that can be correctly said to be known with certainty is eo ipso true. Certainty is thus a sufficient condition of truth without being necessary. Of knowledge, however, it is both a necessary and a sufficient condition, while truth is only a necessary condition. So while 'certainty' and 'truth' are not *logically* equivalent, the immediate inner experience of perfect certainty in the clearly and distinctly conceived *cogito* principle reveals what truth itself is: not the nominal definition or meaning of the word 'truth' but the very nature of truth itself. This is not grasped through any process of logical analysis, but is immediately intuitable through reflexion on what one is implicitly conscious of in any act of thinking. Similarly, all truths expressing the immediate intuition of simple natures and axioms are true in a sense that can only be adequately grasped by reflecting on inner experience and that "logical definitions," even those purporting to be 'real' definitions, merely obscure. Such truths may be concerned with existence, as in the case of my own particular thinking and existence; or they may concern essence, as with the "true and immutable natures" ('thinking,' 'extension,' 'God'). While reflexive analysis reveals that clarity and distinctness are the infallible marks of the truth of such judgments, the inability to prevent oneself from assenting to what is clearly and distinctly perceived is that element in it which accounts for their necessity.

This is the phenomenological as distinct from the nominal meaning of 'truth' or 'certainty.'[22] That it is by such reflexion that one knows what truth is is implied in the brief preamble to Descartes's 'clear and distinct' rule, considered earlier: "I am certain that I am a thinking thing. Do I not therefore also know what is required for my being certain about anything?" (AT VII 35: CSM II 24 e.a.). This suggests that the only thing "required" for certainty "about anything" (in that primary sense in which the experience of certainty reveals the very meaning of 'truth') is known in and through simple reflexion upon one's thinking. There is no "derivation of the truth rule," no "argument" here, only simple inspection of what truth itself is, of the necessary and sufficient conditions of that truth which is alone required and adequate for Descartes's foundational enterprise.[23] What reflexion reveals is, along with clarity and distinctness, that absolute limitation upon my freedom, that sheer inability to deny or even withhold assent from that of which I am immediately conscious or anything I perceive in the manner in which I perceive that I think and therefore exist. It is by attending to what I am immediately conscious of when I attempt vainly to doubt my own thinking or existence that I grasp, with a clarity that is sheerly unsurpassable, what certainty is; and it is through the same process of reflexion that I grasp what truth is according to that idea of truth which Descartes regularly includes, along with 'thinking,' 'thing,' 'existence,' 'perfection,' and 'God,' among the innate ideas of the mind.[24] Having grasped this through reflexive attention to what I am immediately conscious of, I can no longer hanker after truth of any other kind for the first principles of my philosophy. To ask for more, to demand 'absolute truth,' remains, to be sure, a logical possibility; but having once perceived what truth is, to ask for more is not just unreasonable in the sense in which it is unreasonable to demand more when one already has all that is required; nor is it just unreasonable in the sense in which it is unreasonable to ask for more than one knows it to be possible to obtain. Rather, it is psychologically impossible to believe truth to be this 'more,' or anything but what simple reflexion on our thinking has revealed it to be. Accordingly, Descartes responds to a contemporary version of the objection that subjective necessity is no guarantee of objective truth (psychologism) in these terms:

What is it to us that someone may make out that the perception whose truth we are so firmly convinced of may appear false to God or an angel, so that it is, absolutely speaking, false? Why should this alleged 'absolute falsity' bother us, since we neither believe in it nor have even the smallest suspicion of it? For the supposition which we are making here is of a conviction (*persuasio*) so firm that it is quite incapable of being destroyed [as long as I attend to it]; and such a conviction is clearly the same as the most perfect certainty (*quae proinde persuasio idem plane est quod perfectissima certitudo*). (AT VII 145: CSM II 103 e.a.)[25]

As if to drive home the point that the impossibility in question is psychological, not normative, Descartes adds a few paragraphs later: "It is also no objection for someone to make out that such truths might appear false to God or to an angel. For the evident clarity of our perceptions *does not allow us to listen* to anyone who makes up this kind of story" (AT VII 146: CSM II 104 e.a.).

The chief obstacle to acknowledgment of the primarily psychological force of "certain" and "necessarily true" in Descartes is the failure to appreciate the extent to which the very meaning of 'truth' is grasped in reflexion on the experience of psychological certainty. The passages just cited, like the letter to Mersenne concerning Herbert of Cherbury's *De Veritate*, have frequently been quoted as straightforward endorsements of a correspondence theory.[26] What they in fact say, taken together, is, first of all, that 'correspondence with an object,' actual or possible, is no more than a nominal definition of truth, telling us nothing of the nature of truth in the sense that is alone relevant to first principles; and, second, that even were we to entertain some notion of 'absolute truth' different from what we have experienced truth to be in reflexion on the truths *cogito* and *sum*, we would be psychologically incapable of actually believing that anything of the kind is required for purposes of placing human knowledge on a sure foundation. For as long as we actually intuit the contingent fact of our own existence, there can be no question of giving the slightest credence to any other notion of truth than that which is accessible in the intuitive certainty we experience within ourselves as we attend to the grounds of this truth. And once we have grasped the logical necessity of God's existence and veracity in the same way, it must be forever impossible to countenance the notions of absolute truth and falsity at any subsequent time.

Here, then, is the answer to Frankfurt's searching question (1968, 226): "If what is perfectly certain may be absolutely false ... the notions of absolute truth and absolute falsity are irrelevant to the purposes of enquiry. Presumably [Descartes] would wish them to be replaced with other notions of truth and falsity. But what are these notions and how are they related to those which Descartes rejects?" That "other" notion which supplants 'absolute truth' is *persuasio*. Though not unintelligible in themselves, straightforwardly realist notions of absolute truth and falsity must be a matter of complete indifference to anyone in search of first principles who has experienced immediately within himself what truth is. The correct nominal definition of truth as *adaequatio intellectus et rei* is, to the inner experience of what truth itself is, much as the formal definition of thought is to the immediate inner experience of one's own thinking. The notions of 'absolute' truth or falsity are thus an extension of the nominal definition that, if adopted, leads straight to scepticism, since a first principle or "Archimedean point" that is true in this sense is simply unobtainable.[27]

Descartes might have said (with minor modifications) what Spinoza was later to say: "What can there be which is clearer and more certain than a true idea to serve as a standard of truth? As a light makes both itself and the darkness plain, so truth is the standard both of itself and of the false" (Spinoza 1994, 142f. [E II 43S]). In fact, Descartes says something very like this in a letter to Mersenne in which, speaking of Lord Herbert's *De Veritate*, he writes that the latter "takes universal consent as the criterion of his truths. I have no criterion for mine except the natural light" (AT II 597: CSMK 139). The same point is made more fully in the letter to Clerselier appended to the Fifth Objections and Replies: "Now we must be particularly careful to notice the ambiguity in the phrase 'my thought is not the standard which determines the truth of things.' If the claim is that my thought must not be the standard for others, ... then I entirely agree." Although *my* thought is never the standard of truth for others, *clear and distinct* thought *is* the standard of truth *for me*:

[I]f we take the word 'thought' to apply indifferently to any kind of operations of the soul, it is certain that we can have many [obscure and confused] thoughts which do not provide any basis for inferring the truth about things which are outside us. But this is irrelevant in the present [Second Meditation] context, where we are dealing only with the thoughts that are clear and distinct perceptions and the judgements which each of us must make within himself as a result of these perceptions. This is why I say that, in the sense in which the phrase should be understood here, the thought of each person – i.e. the perception or knowledge which he has of something – should be *for him* the 'standard which determines the truth of the thing'; in other words, all the judgements he makes about this thing must conform to his perception if they are to be correct. (AT IX-1 207f.: CSM II 272 e.a.)

This might have been expressed in Spinoza's words as "Truth is its own standard" (ibid.). That the notion of 'conformity' in the final sentence should not be construed as an oblique endorsement of any 'correspondence' theory of truth scarcely needs pointing out at this stage. On the contrary, it reflects the sense of 'clear and distinct' explained earlier (cf. section 7.1): attending explicitly to all that is immediately present to consciousness and prescinding in judgment from all that is not so present. It is in this primary sense of 'truth' that the true judgment conforms to its (mental) object. Whether Spinoza had any inkling of this cannot be explored here.

12.6 The truth of 'the *cogito*' and of the knowledge of God's existence

We must now consider (a) the special status of the truths concerning God's existence and veracity and (b) several different senses in which Descartes's founding principle may be said to be certain and "necessarily true."

To take the second question first: certainty can be ascribed to 'the *cogito*' in at least two different senses, according as it is taken in one or another of the three ways outlined earlier. 'The *cogito*' may be taken to stand for all statements of the *cogito* type, that is, statements that are strictly confined to that which is immediately present to consciousness in Descartes's technical sense of that term ('I see,' 'I imagine,' 'I understand, hope, fear, doubt, deny' and so on). Second, 'the *cogito*' may be understood to designate the abstract principle *cogito, ergo sum*, the truth of which the mind becomes immediately certain of as it attends to its own thinking (*cogito*), its existence (*sum*), and to the relation between them. Finally, 'the *cogito*' may be considered again as an abstract principle, but this time as the first principle within the reconstituted system of human knowledge, that is, within that body of systematically interrelated objective truths or propositions that Descartes, following the usage of "the dialecticians," calls *scientia*.

Taken in the first way, as the verbal expression of an actually occurring intuition of the existence of modes of thinking, the certainty of statements of the *cogito* type is not just truth-entailing, it is the immediate inner experience of truth itself – 'truth' understood in a sense corresponding to its "true and immutable nature" as an innate idea in the mind. As for the certainty of 'the *cogito*' in the second sense, this involves reflexion on that which is at first only pre-reflexively present to consciousness. Through reflexion upon one's actually occurring modes of thinking – even being in doubt (cf. AT X 514f.: CSM II 409f.) or being deceived will do – one can come to know, not only that the particular truths 'I am thinking,' 'I exist' are true, but also the truth of the abstract principle *cogito, ergo sum*. However, this is known to be true only as long as I attend to its truth. It is *persuasio* whose truth is entirely independent of the knowledge of God's existence. Taken in the third way, as the first truth (principle or proposition) within the stable, ordered totality of truths that is *scientia*, *cogito, existo*, and the principle *cogito, ergo sum* are certain and necessarily true only subject to the condition that God's existence and veracity are similarly known – as items of *scientia*. 'Certainty' in this sense is again not just truth-entailing; reflexion upon what I am thus certain of discloses the very meaning of 'truth' as scientifically established knowledge, as *vera & certa scientia* (AT VIII-1 10: CSM I 197). Like *persuasio*, *scientia* involves clarity and distinctness and the inability to withhold assent to the clearly and distinctly perceived; but unlike statements expressing immediately intuited natures, axioms, and demonstrations, *scientia* depends for its certainty and necessity on the proof that God exists and is no deceiver.

The sole exception is the knowledge of God's existence and veracity itself. This brings us to (a). Among all truths the grounds of which are merely recalled, the theological alone are certain and necessarily true at all times simply in virtue of having been clearly and distinctly perceived at one time. That is, in the unique case of knowledge of God *persuasio* is ipso facto *scientia*; and once we possess *scientia* in regard to God, all other *persuasio* becomes *scientia* too, the *cogito* principle as well as any other metaphysical truths of which we can attain *persuasio*. And with these, the "countless particular features regarding shape, number, motion, and so on, which I perceive when I give them my attention" (AT VII 63: CSM II 44), that is, the entire *corpus* of mathematical knowledge pronounced doubtful in the First Meditation becomes *vera & certa scientia*. As Descartes wrote in the letter to Regius:

[A] man who has once clearly understood the reasons which convince us that God exists and is not a deceiver, provided that he remembers the conclusion 'God is no deceiver,' whether or not he continues to attend to the arguments for it, will continue to possess not only the conviction (*persuasio*) but real knowledge (*vera scientia*) of this *and all other conclusions the reasons for which he remembers he once clearly and distinctly perceived*. (AT III 65: CSMK 147 e.a.)

The same point is clearly made at the conclusion of the ontological argument of the Fifth Meditation:

Now, however, I have perceived that God exists, and at the same time I have understood that everything else depends on him, and that he is no deceiver; and I have drawn the conclusion that everything which I clearly and distinctly perceive is of necessity true. Accordingly, even if I am no longer attending to the arguments which led me to judge that this is true, as long as I remember that I clearly and distinctly perceived it, there are no counter-arguments which can be adduced to make me doubt it, but on the contrary I have true and certain knowledge (*scientiam*) not just of this matter [i.e., God's existence], but of all matters which I remember ever having demonstrated, in geometry and so on. (AT VII 70: CSM II 48)

Should Descartes's treatment of theological knowledge appear to be at odds with his stated views on *persuasio* and *scientia* generally, one has only to consider the doctrine of the immutability of the divine nature. For unlike the remainder of the eternal and – in a qualified sense – 'immutable' truths that God, who created them, might alter at any time, God's own nature, which is uncreated, is not subject to change by anything whatever, not even himself. As Descartes remarks, the "natural light enables us to perceive that it is impossible for such a being to have the power and will to give itself something new; rather his essence is such that he possesses from eternity everything which we can now suppose he would bestow on himself if he did not yet possess it" (AT VII 241: CSM II 168). God's immutable nature, then, ensures that the conclusions of the proofs of his existence and veracity, and with them the conclusions of all other sound demonstrations, metaphysical and mathematical, are perfectly impervious to doubt "at any time," even when the grounds of their truth are no longer attended to. This theme will be developed further in chapter 14.

12.7 Concluding summary

This concludes the discussion of the necessary truth of the *sum*. It is now possible to take stock of all the modalities of truth met with up to this point. The necessity of the *sum* has been clarified without explicit attention to how such metaphysically necessary truth is related to metaphysically contingent truth, or how both are related to logically necessary and contingent truth. To rectify this all that is needed is a quick retrospective glance over the course of this part of the book.

We began our treatment of truth and certainty with a distinction between two degrees of certainty (cf. chapter 10). These Descartes called 'metaphysical' or 'absolute' and 'moral' certainty, respectively. The former is the highest degree of certainty to which unassisted human reason can attain. Descartes calls it 'metaphysical' because (cf. AT VII 352: CSM II 244) it is immune even from that "slight and so to speak metaphysical doubt" occasioned by the deceiving God hypothesis. This is not the sense in which we spoke of 'metaphysical necessity' in describing the psychological necessity of the *sum*. Nevertheless, that use of 'metaphysical' had its justification, since a key factor in certainty of this kind is the restriction of human freedom as immediately experienced in the sheer inability to doubt or withhold assent. All truths evident by the natural light of reason are 'metaphysically necessary' in this sense, though by no means are all such truths logically necessary; to take the obvious example, the *cogito* principle is not.

Next we distinguished two kinds of perfect certainty, *persuasio* and *scientia*, leading to a threefold division among clear and distinct perceptions: *persuasio*, *scientia*, and that which is no longer *persuasio* but not yet *scientia* (cf. section 11.6). The last of these is not metaphysically certain or necessary at all, so that one could speak of two types of *im*perfect certainty or metaphysically contingent truths: on the one hand, those that are no more than morally certain, being clearly but not distinctly perceived; on the other, those that are more than morally certain, being clearly *and* distinctly perceived, but that are no longer or not yet metaphysically certain. The former are logically as well as metaphysically contingent – for example, ordinary judgments concerning the objects of sense-perception. The latter may be logically necessary, like the simple truths of mathematics, or logically contingent, like the *cogito* principle; yet as soon as they are no longer *persuasio*, and as long as they are not yet *scientia*, they are metaphysically contingent.

Thus far we have considered two degrees of certainty, imperfect and perfect, and two kinds of the latter, *persuasio* and *scientia*. Truths known with perfect certainty, it was said, are all metaphysically necessary, though such truths (whether *persuasio* or *scientia*) may be either logically necessary or contingent. The final distinction to emerge in the foregoing was that between two species of logically *and* metaphysically necessary truths: the created and the uncreated. All truths that are both logically and metaphysically necessary are 'eternal truths' in Descartes's sense; but some are, though not subject to change by our will and hence 'eternal,' nevertheless mutable by the will of God who created, preserves, and can alter them, if he chooses. Into this category fall all the logically necessary truths of mathematics and the axioms of metaphysics. By contrast, the uncreated among the eternal truths are strictly immutable, even by God. This is where the metaphysical truths of natural theology belong.

We will return to this distinction in section 14.5. At this point, we have assembled all the pieces required to deal with the second set of problems (cf. section 11.1 above), pertaining to the 'Cartesian circle.' It may be useful, in conclusion, to present the contents of the last few paragraphs in tabular form.

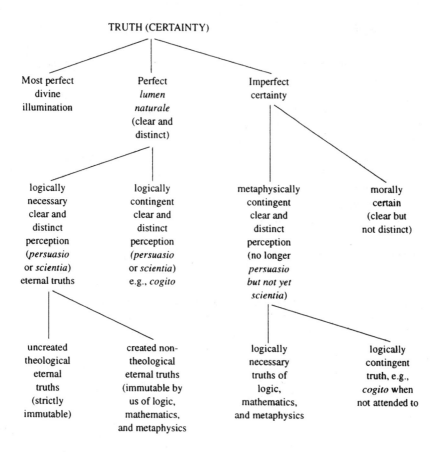

13

Truth and Correspondence

If the argument of the preceding chapter is sound, the not infrequent charge that Descartes confounded objective truth with a psychological feeling of certainty is entirely misplaced. That psychological inability to withhold assent that characterizes all clear and distinct perception (*persuasio*) is both unmistakable when present and the infallible mark of truth; for simple reflexion on first principles reveals that their truth consists in clarity and distinctness together with the felt inability to withhold assent from the clearly and distinctly perceived. Apart from this phenomenological sense, there is another meaning of 'objective truth' in Descartes, one more akin to the "absolute" truth discussed in section 12.5. This straightforwardly realist conception of truth as 'correspondence' or conformity of thought to its object deserves careful consideration, for what lends colour to the charge of psychologism is above all the mistaken assumption that it is the *only* conception of truth in Descartes.

Lying behind the interpretation of the truth of the *sum* as 'objective validity' or correspondence is once again the tendency to view Descartes's philosophical enterprise in a later, Kantian perspective. At times Gueroult verges on caricature of this tendency, imposing the Kantian notion of objective validity even on the *cogito* principle to which it is completely alien. Just how distortingly Kantian is his whole treatment of Descartes's philosophy is plain from the frequent use of blatant Kantianisms like "les conditions de la possibilité" (cf. *Bedingungen der Möglichkeit*) and "validité objective" (cf. *objektive Gültigkeit*), and so forth. This perspective even dominates the treatment of the *cogito*, in which "validité" or "valeur objective" and "vérité de la chose" are opposed to the "nécessité purement subjective" (1968, I, 87) of the "order of reasons" (cf. AT II 266: CSMK 266), "la vérité de la science." The central problem of Descartes's philosophy (so Gueroult) is whether what is true in the order of reasons, "les nécessités de notre esprit" (ibid., I, 70), is also objectively true; even in the case of the self or mind, the question at issue is, "ce qui vaut pour l'ordre des raisons doit-il être tenu pour vérité de la chose?" (I, 83). This is fair enough in the context of the metaphysical demonstration of the real distinction between soul and body in the Sixth Meditation; but it distorts the *cogito* principle of the Second rather badly. Of course, objective validity or the "truth of science" cannot be established before the proof of God's existence and veracity in the Third Meditation (I, 91); that is the role of God in Descartes's philosophy according to Gueroult.[1] Kant, by contrast, sought to accomplish the same task without recourse to a divine guarantor, by a 'Copernican revolution' (cf. Buchdahl 1969, 118). But if Gueroult acknowledges that the solutions differ widely, he remains firmly convinced that the problem is at bottom the same: "Dans les *Méditations* ... c'est de métaphysique qu'il s'agit; et *le problème primordial* est celui du fondement de la validité objective de nos connaissances" (I, 75 e.a.). This neo-Kantian use of 'metaphysics' could only have baffled Descartes.[2]

While this at least has the merit of acknowledging that it is truth (*scientia*) Descartes is after, not psychological certainty or normative indubitability, one should be wary of interpreting 'objective truth' in narrowly Kantian fashion. Taking the expression literally, the "problème primordial" of Descartes is not the step from subjective to objective certainty or knowledge but from simple *persuasio* to *vera & certa scientia*; that is, from perfect certainty or truth *now* to perfect certainty *at all times*. On (1) the metaphysical knowledge of the mind and certain metaphysical principles innate in it depends (2) the metaphysical knowledge of God, (3) the demonstration of the real distinction between mind and body, and (4) the epistemological project of establishing the objective validity of *all* those concepts and principles that are innate or 'inborn,' that is, 'born of the mind's reflexion upon its own thinking,' including the concepts and principles of pure mathematics and mathematical physics. This much is widely recognized. But while (2), (3), and especially (4) give some purchase to the Kantian notion of truth as objective validity, (1) provides none at all. Moreover, the extent of the similarity, even where it exists, should not be exaggerated. The present chapter examines Descartes's *other* conception of truth, that embodied in the nominal definition, and the contexts to which it is applicable.

13.1 The nature of body

The clearest analogue of the Kantian question concerning the objective validity of the mind's concepts and principles is to be found in the Sixth Meditation, where Descartes concludes by a causal inference from (1) the occurrence of sensory ideas in the mind and (2) the existence of a veracious God that (3) corporeal things exist. Analogous is not the proof of the existence of bodies – Kant's proof

of the existence of the external world is altogether different – but the nature ascribed to them here in the Sixth, as already in the Fifth, Meditation:

They may not all exist in a way that exactly corresponds to my sensory grasp of them
(*Non tamen forte omnes tales omnino existunt, quales illas sensu comprehendo*); for in
many cases the grasp of the senses is very obscure and confused. But at least they possess
all the properties which I clearly and distinctly understand, that is, all those which, viewed
in general terms, are comprised within the subject-matter of pure mathematics. (AT VII
80: CSM II 55)

This important qualification is more fully developed in other places, notably in
the wax example of the Second Meditation, though the question there concerns
the essence of body in general, that is, discerning the essential nature from the
accidental properties of body, not the distinction between real accidents actually
existing in bodies themselves and those that exist only in relation to the knowing
mind.[3] A distinction unambiguously of the latter sort is found, however, in the
Sixth Replies and at various points in Part I of the *Principles*:

I observed ... that nothing whatever belongs to the concept of body except the fact that it
is something which has length, breadth and depth and is capable of various shapes and
motions; moreover, these shapes and motions are merely modes which no power whatever can cause to exist apart from body. But colours, smells, tastes and so on are, I observed, merely certain sensations which exist in my thought, and are as different from
bodies as pain is different from the shape and motion of the weapon which produces it.
And lastly, I observed that heaviness and hardness and the power to heat or to attract, or
to purge, and all the other qualities which we experience in bodies, consist solely in the
motion of bodies, or its absence, and the configuration and situation of their parts. (AT
VII 440: CSM II 297)

There is perhaps no need to belabour the point. As this points in the direction of
the primary-secondary quality distinction found in the Greek atomists, Galileo,
Gassendi, Hobbes, Locke, and Boyle, so also (*mutatis mutandis*) toward Kant's
notion of truth as the objective validity of a priori principles and of the pure
concepts they employ.

13.2   Knowledge of the 'real distinction'

Yet once we turn from this context – in Kantian terms, the transcendental deduction of the categories or the metaphysical first principles of natural science, depending on how one takes it – to the mind-body relation, the parallel with Kant is

already greatly attenuated. For one thing, the question in Descartes is one of *order*. The full significance of this is by no means clear at first sight. In the Preface to the *Meditations* Descartes introduces what appears to be a distinction between the (as we should say) 'subjective' order of ideas (*in ordine ad meam perceptionem*) and the 'objective' order of things (*in ordine ad ipsam rei veritatem*):

In the *Discourse* I asked anyone who found anything worth criticizing ... to point it out to me. In the case of my remarks concerning God and the soul, only two objections worth mentioning were put to me ... The first objection is this. From the fact [1] that the human mind, when directed towards itself, does not perceive itself to be anything other than a thinking thing, it does not follow [2] that its nature or essence consists only in its being a thinking thing, where the word 'only' (*tantum*) excludes everything else that could be said to belong to the nature of the soul. My answer to this objection is that in that passage it was not my intention to make those exclusions *in an order corresponding to the actual truth of the matter* (which I was not dealing with at that stage) but merely *in an order corresponding to my own perception*. So the sense of the passage [in the *Discourse*] was that I was aware of nothing at all (*me nihil plane cognoscere*) that I knew belonged to my essence except that I was a thinking thing, or a thing possessing within itself the faculty of thinking. I shall, however, show below how it follows from the fact that [1] I am aware of nothing else belonging to my essence (*nihil aliud ... cognoscam*), that [2] nothing else does in fact (*revera*) belong to it. (AT VII 8: CSM II 7 e.a.)

The argument targeted in the objection to which this is the reply has been dubbed the "Argument from Doubt."[4] It will be examined presently (cf. 13.4). The last sentence quoted, however, refers to an argument not found in the *Discourse* or the Second Meditation but only in the Sixth. It is this argument (known as the 'argument from clear and distinct perception'), Descartes insists, that takes the step from (1) to (2). Where, in the Fourth Set of Objections, Arnauld presses a related form of the same objection (AT VII 198f.: CSM II 139f.) against *both* arguments,[5] Descartes resorts again to the very distinction drawn in the Preface:

[H]ad I not been looking for greater than ordinary certainty, I should have been content to have shown in the Second Meditation that the mind can be understood as a subsisting thing despite the fact that nothing belonging to the body is attributed to it, and that, conversely, the body can be understood as a subsisting thing despite the fact that nothing belonging to the mind is attributed to it. I should have added nothing more in order to demonstrate that there is a real distinction between the mind and the body, since we commonly judge that the order in which things are mutually related in our perception of them (*in ordine ad nostram perceptionem*) corresponds to the order in which they are related in actual reality (*in ordine ad ipsam veritatem*). But one of the exaggerated doubts which I put forward in the First Meditation went so far as to make it impossible for me to be certain of this very point (namely whether things do in reality correspond to our perception of them [*quod res juxta veritatem sint tales quales ipsas percipimus*]), so long as I was supposing myself to be ignorant of the author of my being. And this is why everything I wrote on the subject of God and truth in the Third, Fourth, and Fifth Meditations contributes to the conclusion that there is a real distinction between the mind and the body, which I finally established in the Sixth Meditation. (AT VII 226: CSM II 159 e.a.)

Here, then, is a second passage in which Descartes distinguishes between the 'order' of ideas and of things. In the light of this, it may be tempting to agree with Malcolm that what "is delayed until the *Sixth Meditation* is the resolution of the radical doubt as to whether our clear and distinct perceptions (ideas, conceptions) may not be mistaken." This, writes Malcolm, "is a doubt about whether there is any correspondence at all between reality and our clear and distinct perceptions" (1968, 324). But whether this doubt about 'correspondence' (*tales ... quales*) applies to *all* clear and distinct perception, including the *cogito, ergo sum*, is precisely the point at issue in this chapter. It applies, to be sure, to our clear and distinct conceptions of mind and body as distinct natures – things of which we have only complete, if not adequate, concepts, but at least not just abstract notions arbitrarily fashioned by the mind itself.[6] The question in this regard is whether the things thus perfectly distinct (logically unrelated) and separa*ble in thought* (without abstraction of any kind) can actually exist separately *in fact*. And the answer this passage suggests is that we cannot be certain of this without the knowledge of God, though once "the author of my being" is known it can be demonstrated with perfect certainty. Still, the certainty of the *cogito, ergo sum* may be a different matter.

Before considering the difference, it may be worth examining two further passages. Something resembling the distinction drawn in the last two is at least latent in the Second Meditation itself, though the idea of 'order' is not found there: "And yet may it not perhaps be the case that these very things which I am supposing to be nothing, because they are unknown to me ['a structure of limbs which is called a human body,' 'some thin vapour which permeates the limbs,' 'a wind, fire, air, breath'], are *in reality* (*in rei veritate*) identical with the 'I' of which I am aware (*non differant ab eo me quem novi*)?" (AT VII 27: CSM II 18 e.a.). Since he is here reflecting only on what he thus far knows himself to be with perfect certainty, this possibility cannot be ruled out right away: "I do not know, and for the moment I shall not argue the point, since I can make judgements *only about things which are known to me*" (ibid., e.a.). The way in which the objection is side-stepped here makes it clear that it will have to be faced later. When it is, in the Sixth Meditation, the body is shown to be numerically distinct from the 'I' *in rei veritate*. That is not the question in Meditation Two, where it is explicitly left open.[7]

A similar distinction is met with in a related context as early as the *Regulae*. Here the idea of order is again clearly expressed: "when we consider things in the order that corresponds to our knowledge of them (*in ordine ad cognitionem nostram*) our view of them must be different from what it would be if we were speaking of them in accordance with how they exist in reality (*prout revera existunt*)" (AT X 418: CSM I 44).

All four passages have been duly noticed and commented on, usually in impeccable Kantian phraseology.[8] The question is only how far any of them actually mirrors the familiar 'subjective-objective' dichotomy bequeathed to subsequent philosophy by Kant. On the face of it, the talk of contrasting *orders* (as characteristic for Descartes and his medieval predecessors as it is foreign to Kant) suggests a somewhat different distinction: between what is first, primitive, simple, independent, or separable in the order of knowing, thought, or perception ('for us,' *pros hēmas*) and what is first, and so on, in the order of being or reality ('in itself,' *kath' hauto*, 'by nature,' *tēi physei*, or 'absolutely,' *haplōs*). But this said, it has to be owned that this and the later Kantian distinction are related.

There are three things worth noting about the four cited passages: (1) Descartes's recognition of a logical divide, (2) his claim to be able to cross it, and (3) his claim not even to have attempted to do so in the Second Meditation. While (1) and (2) are straightforward enough, commentators have been understandably sceptical about (3). And indeed, whatever he may say in the Preface, in the Second Meditation Descartes could hardly have wished to be understood to suspend, however provisionally, all consideration of the ontological order, all claims about the existence and essence of things as they really are in themselves. In the third of the cited passages he only claims not to be addressing the ontological order *in so far as it is not yet known to him with perfect certainty*. The distinction implicit there is in fact different from that in the other passages: not between subjective necessities (necessities and impossibilities *of thought*) and objective reality, but between those primitive truths about existence and essence *thus far known* and the whole truth about the ontological order ultimately knowable. For purposes of providing an answer to the question 'What am I?,' only that which is already known to exist, *as* it is known to exist, comes in question. None of those things whose existence and essence the meditator is still uncertain of is definitively denied of it; instead, they are 'bracketed' at this stage of the enquiry. As Descartes was to remark to Gassendi:

I said in one place that while the soul is in doubt about the existence of all material things, it knows itself precisely, *praecise tantum*, as an immaterial substance; and seven or eight lines further down I showed that by the words *praecise tantum* I do not mean an entire *exclusion or negation* but only an *abstraction* from material things; for I said that in spite of this we are not sure that there is nothing corporeal in the soul, even though we do not recognise anything corporeal in it. (AT IX-1 215: CSM II 276 e.a.)

Were (3) intended to imply that the ontological order of things is not addressed at all in the Second Meditation, it would indeed be difficult to take at face value. However, it is equally clearly not just the 'subjective' relations among pure concepts that is under investigation there.[9] What Descartes is seeking in his *Meditations* is nothing less than perfectly certain knowledge of the whole order of being, including God, the mind, and material things. His very project is defined by the strictly probative advance from objective knowledge (*persuasio*) of the existence and essence of that which comes first in the order of knowing to that which comes afterwards; all other knowledge depends on that of the self, while the elevation of all *persuasio* to the status of *scientia* depends on the knowledge of an omnipotent creator God's veracity. In this way the whole order of being, that is, the strictly objective relations of ontological dependence, independence, and interdependence among all things (cf. section 22.1 of the Conclusion), are mapped out gradually, culminating, within the Sixth Meditation, in the demonstration of the reciprocal ontological independence of mind and body despite their common dependence on God. In the Second Meditation he knows only a part of that order with complete certainty, the existence and nature of the mind or 'I,' and even that certainty (*persuasio*), though perfect, is not yet the *kind* of certainty sought for the founding principles of human knowledge (*scientia*). Nevertheless, it has to be admitted that in the last stage of the project, the divide – suggested to Kant by Hume – between the 'subjective' necessities of thought and 'objective' relations of dependence and independence among things themselves comes to play a very prominent role as Descartes advances from the very first truths about existence and essence to the real distinction between body and mind, that is, that central thesis about the ontological order of things explicitly inserted into the revised title of the *Meditations*. But it is important not to overlook key differences between these and the first truths.

As regards (3), then, we may say that in the Second Meditation all Descartes can assert with complete assurance (*persuasio*) concerning the ontological order of things is that he exists and that nothing imaginable, that is, nothing bodily, is included in his nature *as he then knows it: sum igitur* precise tantum *res cogitans, id est, mens, sive animus, sive intellectus, sive ratio.* Earlier (section 9.2) we dwelt at some length on the sense of the expression *mens, sive animus*, etc. Below (cf. section 13.5) we shall have to examine the words *praecise tantum* as well, for it is in this regard that some commentators have suggested that (3) misrepresents the argument of the Second Meditation. But first it may be instructive to consider how the distinction between the two orders is employed in the *Regulae* passage cited above and how the idea of a strict proof or demonstration of the real distinction evolved gradually in the transition from the *Regulae* via the *Discourse* to the *Meditations*.

13.3 From the *Regulae* to the *Meditations*

In the context of the passage from the *Regulae* cited above, the immediate task is "to distinguish carefully the notions (*notiones*) of simple things from those which are composed of them" (AT X 417: CSM I 43). Descartes confines himself here to the question of which 'natures' are simple or first and which are compounded or dependent on the simple ones "with respect to our intellect," that is, *in ordine ad nostram perceptionem*. That the things *conceived* first and independently may not *be* simple, first, or independent "in reality" is freely granted:

If, for example, we consider some body which has extension and shape, we shall indeed admit that, with respect to the thing itself (*a parte re*), it is one single and simple entity (*quid unum & simplex*). For, viewed in that way, it cannot be said to be a composite made up of corporeal nature, extension and shape, since these constituents (*partes*) have never existed in isolation from each other. Yet with respect to our intellect (*respectu vero intellectus nostri*) we call it a composite made up of these three natures, because we understood each of them separately before we were in a position to judge that the three of them are encountered at the same time in one and the same subject. That is why, *since we are concerned here with things only in so far as they are perceived by the intellect*, we term 'simple' only those things which we know so clearly and distinctly (*tam perspicua ... & distincta*) that they cannot be divided by the mind into others which are more distinctly known. Shape, extension and motion etc. are of this sort; all the rest we conceive to be in a sense compounded out of these. (AT X 418: CSM I 44 e.a.)

Although the concept 'body' cannot be "clearly and perspicuously" grasped apart from 'shape,' 'motion,' and 'extension,' we must nevertheless consider any body existing *in rerum natura* as a simple nature (*quid unum & simplex*) rather than a composite entity made up of corporeality, extension, shape, and motion as its component parts. The latter do not exist separately "in reality"; nor therefore does any actual body come to be through their composition – as it clearly does through the composition of its till then separately existing bodily parts. When we consider what is to be called 'simple' *respectu intellectus nostri*, the only question is whether the 'natures' themselves ('corporeality,' 'extension,' 'shape,' and 'motion') can be divided by the mind into others clearer and more perspicuous. If not, they are simple natures. By this test, then, 'shape,' 'extension,' and 'motion' are simple, while 'body' is a composite notion 'made up' of these simpler ones. By the same criterion, as Descartes later points out, "the nature of a triangle" is composite, "composed of ... other natures" like 'line,' 'three,' 'angle,' 'shape,' 'extension' that are "better known than the triangle" (cf. AT X 422: CSM I 46) and themselves simple.

The term 'idea' is not found in its later technical use in the *Regulae*, any more than the Scholastic terms *distinctio rationis* and *distinctio realis* that Descartes was later to employ in his threefold 'distinction among distinctions': conceptual, modal, and real.[10] Yet the operative distinction in the passage just cited is (in the language of the mature philosophy) between the *order of ideas in the mind*, that is, the conceptual or logical dependence of the composite on the simple, and the *order obtaining among things themselves* – their 'real' or merely 'modal' distinctness. While the *modes* of both mind and body figure among the 'simple natures' of the *Regulae* (cf. AT X 419: CSM I 44f.), Descartes had apparently not yet thought of attempting a rigorous *demonstration* that mind and body themselves are substances capable of existing in their own right; allowing that the order of being need not correspond to the order of knowing, apparently without any thought of showing it to be otherwise for those natures conceivable apart from one another, he simply restricts himself to the order of knowing and to the consideration of what he later termed 'modes.'[11]

Of course, the metaphysical doctrine of the real distinction of body and soul is already present in the *Regulae*: "the power through which we know things in the strict sense is purely spiritual, and is no less distinct from the whole body than blood is distinct from bone, or the hand from the eye" (AT X 415: CSM I 42). But demonstration is far from Descartes's mind. This is partly (1) because he is ostensibly only setting out certain *suppositiones*: "Of course, you are not obliged to believe that things are as I suggest. But what is to prevent you from following these suppositions if it is obvious they detract not a jot from the truth of things, but simply make everything much clearer" (AT X 412: CSM I 40). It is partly also (2) because he still takes the matter to be self-evident rather than requiring demonstration. Later in the same rule (XII) he gives an example of a necessary conjunction between things that might nevertheless be thought contingent: "'I have a mind distinct from my body'" (AT X 421: CSM I 46). Yet here too he is ostensibly only setting out "certain assumptions ... which perhaps not everyone will accept (*hic loci, quemadmodum in superioribus, quaedam assumenda sunt quae fortasse non apud omnes sunt in confesso*" (AT X 417: CSM I 43). These two considerations, then, jointly rule out any thought of demonstration.[12]

Even in the *Discourse* there is as yet no such bridging operation between 'separate conceivability' or 'distinct in thought' and 'really distinct' or 'distinct in fact' as is attempted in the Sixth Meditation and later the *Principles*. At issue in Part IV are not just the modes of mental and material substance, as in the *Regulae*, but the independence of mind and body themselves: "From this I knew I was *a substance* whose whole essence or nature is solely to think, and which does not require any place, or depend on any material thing, in order to exist" (AT VI 33: CSM I 127 e.a.). But as we have seen, in the Preface to the *Meditations* Descartes acknowledges the logical gap he claimed not even to have tried to close in the *Discourse*, promising to bridge it "below" in the Sixth Meditation (AT VII 78: CSM II 54), where "everything I wrote on the subject of God and truth in the Third, Fourth, and Fifth Meditations contributes to the conclusion that there is a real distinction between the mind and the body" (AT VII 226: CSM II 159). It is God's omnipotence that makes possible the strictly demonstrative transition from the order of knowing to the order of being. This much is clear from the very beginning of the Sixth Meditation passage in question: "everything which I clearly and distinctly understand is *capable* of being created by God so as to correspond exactly with my understanding of it. The fact that I can clearly and distinctly understand one thing apart from another is enough to make me certain that the two things are distinct, *since they are capable of being separated, at least by God*" (AT VII 78: CSM II 54 e.a.; cf. also AT VII 71: CSM II 50, AT VII 227: CSM II 160, AT VII 425: CSM II 287, and AT VIII-1 28f.: CSM I 213). This principle is then applied to the conceptions of mind and body in order to *demonstrate* the real distinction between them in Sixth Meditation, as it had not been demonstrated (or even attempted) either in the Second or in the *Discourse*.

We are now in a position to consider the argument of the Second Meditation known as the argument 'from doubt' in relation to the Sixth Meditation argument 'from clear and distinct perception.'

13.4 A "glaring paralogism"?

First formulated in a letter to Silhon written just before publication of the *Discourse*, the Argument from Doubt takes a very similar form in both places. In the letter to Silhon: "a man who thus doubts everything material cannot for all that have any doubt about his own existence. From this it follows (*d'ou il suit*) that he, that is to say the soul, is *a being or substance* which is not at all corporeal, whose nature is solely to think, and that it is the first thing one can know with certainty" (AT I 353: CSMK 55 e.a.). And in the *Discourse*: "I saw on the contrary that from the mere fact that I thought of doubting the truth of other things, it followed (*il suivait*) quite evidently and certainly that I existed ... From this I knew (*ie connû de la*) *I was a substance* whose whole essence or nature is solely to think, and which does not require any place, or depend on any material thing, in order to exist. Accordingly, this 'I' – that is, the soul by which I am what I am – is entirely distinct from the body" (AT VI 32f.: CSM I 127 e.a.).[13] Arnauld, who takes it to be repeated in the Second Meditation, summarizes the argument thus: "I can doubt whether I have a body. Yet I cannot doubt that I am or exist. Therefore I who am doubting and thinking am not a body. For, in that case in having doubts about my body I should be having doubts about myself" (AT VII 198: CSM II 139; cf. also AT X 518: CSM II 412). To this he objects pointedly: "How does it follow, from the fact that he is aware of nothing else belonging to his essence (*nihil aliud ad essentiam suam pertinere cognoscat*), that nothing else does in fact (*revera*) belong to it?" (AT VII 199: CSM II 140). He is unable to locate any answer to this question at all in the Second Meditation, and finds only a very unsatisfactory one in the Sixth, to which Descartes's Preface referred him. Descartes, in reply, has to admit that "it may be that there is much within me of which I am not yet aware (*quae nondum adverto*) (for example, in this passage [of the Second Meditation] I was in fact supposing that I was not yet aware (*me nondum advertere*) that the mind possessed the power of moving the body, or that it was substantially united to it). Yet since that of which I am aware (*adverto*) is sufficient to enable me to subsist with it and it alone, I am certain that I could have been created by God without having these other attributes of which I am unaware (*quae non adverto*), and hence that these other attributes do not belong to the essence of the mind" (AT VII 219: CSM II 154f.). As the conclusion of this reply clearly refers to the argument 'from clear and distinct perception,' so the first part obviously bears on that 'from doubt.'

Cottingham, who quotes Arnauld's summary approvingly (1986, 112), brands the inference the "recurring fallacy," "one of the most notorious nonsequiturs in the history of philosophy" and a "glaring paralogism."[14] He describes Descartes as moving illicitly "from the proposition [1] that he can doubt the existence of his body to the conclusion [2] that he can exist without his body" (ibid.); or again, from "[1] 'I can doubt I have a body' to [2] 'the body is not essential to me'" (244). While Cottingham suggests that it was disingenuous of Descartes to refuse to acknowledge this step, Malcolm argues that Descartes, while perfectly sincere, was simply mistaken in describing himself as having asserted in the *Discourse* only (1) that he *knew* of nothing other than thinking that pertained to his essence, not (2) that nothing else did pertain to it.[15] Descartes in fact argued (so Malcolm) from the premise (1) "that he could doubt the existence of his body but could not doubt his own existence" to the conclusion (2) "that he was not his body, or that there was no essential connection between him and his body" (1968, 328). But to infer (2) from (1) is "obviously fallacious" (323).

If there is indeed an *argument* here (in anything like the usual sense of that term), then, given Descartes's choice of words in both the *Discourse* and letter to Silhon, a more faithful summary might be: 'I am not as yet certain of the existence of my body. Yet I *am* certain that I think and exist. Hence, the 'I' *whose thinking and existence I am certain of* can neither be nor include my body (or anything corporeal, any corporeal mode).' The conclusion, in other words, is *not*: 'I am or know myself to be *only a thinking thing*,' but rather 'I *only know myself* to be a thinking thing.' The question regarding the sense of 'only' (*tantum*) will occupy us more particularly in the next section.[16]

This reconstruction of the argument is at least valid (thanks to the restrictive relative clause). Moreover, it is consistent with the remark made later in the Fourth Meditation: "besides the knowledge that I exist, in so far as I am a thinking thing, an idea of corporeal nature comes to my mind; and *I happen to be in doubt* as to whether the thinking nature which is in me, or rather which I am, is distinct from this corporeal nature or identical with it. I am supposing that my intellect has *not yet come upon any persuasive reason in favour of one alternative rather than the other*. This obviously implies that I am indifferent as to whether I should assert or deny either alternative, or indeed refrain from making any judgement on the matter" (AT VII 59: CSM II 41 e.a.). The question is obviously what is *thus far known with certainty* and what is still subject to doubt; and thus far I *only* know myself to be a thinking thing. Moreover, the above reconstruction reflects Descartes's own wording more accurately in that it makes express and emphatic mention of the *thing or substance* that thinks. When I resolve to doubt the existence of the material objects I see, what is immediately present to consciousness as actually and indubitably existent are not just my doubting and various other modes of willing, perceiving, and so on; careful attention reveals all these as modes of (the essential attribute of) thought *belonging to a substance*. This and nothing more – in particular, nothing corporeal – is immediately present to consciousness and revealed as so present by attention to what is before the mind's eye when I doubt the existence of material things and discover that I cannot doubt my own existence. In the *Discourse,* Descartes actually highlights the role of attention: "Next I examined *attentively* (*examinant avec attention*) what I was" (AT VI 32: CSM I 127 e.a.). Citing this, Malcolm comments (1968, 314f.): "Descartes is trying to pick out, from various candidates, that which he is," using a complex "test" or "criterion." But examining *attentively* has in fact quite the opposite force: not singling something in particular out by the application of a test, but rather focusing attention on *all* that is immediately present to consciousness while warily *ex*cluding anything not so given. In other words, the meditator takes great pains to include in his answer to the question, 'What am I?' *all and only* that which he already – first implicitly, now explicitly – knows himself to be, all that is immediately present to the conscious mind and hence clearly and distinctly perceived as long as he thinks and attends to his thinking: "I must be on my guard against carelessly taking something *else* to be this 'I,' and so making a mistake in the very item of knowledge that I maintain is the most certain and evident of all" (AT VII 25: CSM II 17 e.a.).

It is only in the letter to Silhon that Descartes uses the expression, suggestive of inference, 'it follows' (*il suit*); in the *Discourse* he writes simply: "from this I knew," using "it followed" only of the existence of the substance 'I.' Yet in the former place he continues: "If you spend a sufficient time on this meditation, you acquire by degrees a very clear, dare I say intuitive, notion of intellectual nature in general (*une connoissance tres-claire, & si i'ose ainsi parler intuitive, de la nature intellectuelle en general*)" (AT I 353: CSMK 55). Is there any compelling reason in all this to speak of an *argument* or *inference* from a certain *premise* to the *conclusion* 'the body is not essential to me,' 'I can exist without my body,' 'I am not my body,' or 'there is no essential connection between me and my body'? Or is what is in question here, as Descartes himself suggests in the letter to Silhon, a meditative exercise designed to facilitate the process of forming a very clear, intuitive notion of intellectual nature *in general*, excluding from it everything that cannot belong to it, not because it is *logically* excluded from it, but because there is no immediate warrant for including it? Or better: because, as I attend to the immediately given, I find no such grounds for its inclusion as will withstand radical doubt.[17]

This process of meditative turning toward the immediately given, toward that which is intuitively grasped in inner experience, while at the same time turning away from all else, all that is not thus present to consciousness, obviously has a good deal to do with clear and distinct perception as interpreted above (cf. section 7.1). It will be suggested later that it is the key to understanding the 'inference' by which *sum, existo* is shown to 'follow' from *cogito*, the process to be called 'analytical reflexion,' 'reflexive analysis,' and 'intuitive induction' in Part Three. With a view to the topic of the next section, it can be termed *precisification*. Such precisification or 'prescinding from ...' is one aspect of a process of reflexion whose chief focus is *explicitation*: making explicit what is at first only implicit. The two go together (see below chapter 15, n. 28). In the light of this, it is by no means obvious that Descartes is either insincere or mistaken if, in the Second Meditation, he confines his attention to what he *thus far knows* to be "objectively" true with immediate, intuitive certainty, prescinding (cf. *praecise*) or abstracting, as he explains to Gassendi, from things not so known, yet not negating or excluding the latter. Of course, if, as Cottingham holds, Descartes really has advanced by the end of the paragraph from (1) 'this is the only thing I know myself to be when I abstract from everything that admits of the slightest doubt' to (2) 'I am in truth only this, strictly speaking' by "subtly insinuating that any attempt to identify the mind's nature with something material would be radically misconceived" (1992b, 244), then his remark about the force of *praecise tantum* is only a dodge and the move is indeed grossly fallacious. But nothing in the Second Meditation suggests that this step would be "radically misconceived" except in the sense of 'totally unwarranted,' namely, not "authorised" (Hamelin) by that which is immediately given as I attend carefully to all that I am immediately conscious of.[18]

In the Second Meditation Descartes is in fact at some pains to confine himself scrupulously to the initial proposition or "premise" of the so-called Argument from Doubt, to what he "knows" or is "aware of," elaborating it both positively and negatively without implying anything about what he in reality *is not* as opposed to what he *does not yet know himself to be*. By the same token, he is perfectly cognizant of the fact that the transition to the "conclusion" drawn in the Sixth Meditation requires a further, theological premise. To Mersenne (24 December 1640) he writes:

> You should not find it strange, either, that I do not prove in my Second Meditation that the soul is really distinct from the body, but merely show *how to conceive it without the body*. This is because I do not yet have, at that point, the premises needed for the conclusion. You find it later on, in the Sixth Meditation. (AT III 266: CSMK 163 e.a.)

The missing premise is that an omnipotent God exists who can cause all those things to exist separately from one another that the human mind is capable of conceiving in isolation from each other. This is the bridging mechanism of which Descartes was apparently not fully seized before writing the *Meditations*. By the time he penned the Preface to that work, he was keenly aware that nothing in the *Discourse* corresponded to this premise. However questionable the argument is for us owing to its key theological premise, Descartes must have been well pleased with it, reinforcing as it does the capital point for the sake of which he claims he wrote the *Meditations*: that all other knowledge depends for its reliability on the knowledge of God.

The doctrine of the real distinction between mind and body, then, is one context in which the role of the divine guarantor is indeed to convey the meditator across the epistemological gulf separating the 'subjective' order of knowing from the 'objective' order of being. The talk of two orders nevertheless points to a certain disanalogy between this and the familiar Kantian dichotomy. On the other hand, no such discontinuity was apparent in the context of the question of the 'objective validity' of the mind's innate concept of material things – though there it was not so much God's omnipotence as his veracity that Descartes appealed to (on this, see Curley 1978, 198). The main point at issue in this chapter is whether any analogy with Kant, however remote, is possible in the case of the truth of the *cogito* principle, or whether only Descartes's primary phenomenological notion of truth is applicable to these first principles of his metaphysics. From the foregoing, it appears that the concept of truth applicable to the *cogito* principle and to the knowledge of the *essence* of the mind is precisely the same. Before attempting to determine whether the role assigned the divine guarantor in these two contexts is the only or even the primary one, it will be useful (especially in view of the interpretation of the *Regulae* in chapter 20) to consider the force of the *praecise tantum* affixed to the famous *sum res cogitans* of the Second Meditation.

13.5 *Praecise tantum*

It has been suggested that the notion of proof implicit in the label '*Argument* from Doubt' is out of place. Gassendi is one who charges Descartes with not having proved, but simply assumed, all manner of things (cf. AT VII 262f.: CSM II 182f.; and again at AT VII 337: CSM II 233f.), for instance: "that you do not have a body which you inform," "that your nature is not such that you are nourished and move in conjunction with the body," "that the power of thought is something ... far beyond the nature of body," "that this solid body of yours contributes nothing whatever to your thoughts," "that you think independently of the body," and so forth. To this Descartes replies, not unreasonably, that the "onus of proof" is rather on Gassendi to establish the denials of these things. His opponent should realize that

in order to philosophise correctly there is no need for us to prove the falsity of everything which we do not admit because we do not know whether or not it is true. We simply have to take great care not to admit anything as true when we cannot prove it to be so. Hence when I discover that I am a thinking substance and form a clear and distinct concept of this thinking substance that contains none of the things that belong to the concept of corporeal substance, this is quite sufficient to enable me to assert that I, *in so far as I know myself*, am nothing other than a thinking thing. This is all that I asserted in the Second Meditation ... I did not have to admit that this thinking substance was some mobile, pure and rarefied body, since I had no convincing reason for believing this. If you have such a reason, it is your job to explain it; you should not demand that I prove the falsity of something which I refused to accept precisely because I had no knowledge of it. (AT VII 354f.: CSM II 245f. e.a.)

As for his having assumed certain things, Descartes replies that "it is false that I assumed anything I did not know. On the contrary, since I did not know whether the body was identical with the mind or not, I did not make any assumptions on this matter, but considered only the mind; it was only afterwards, in the Sixth Meditation, that I said there was a real distinction between the mind and the body, and here I did not assume it but demonstrated it" (AT VII 357: CSM II 247).

All this has a direct bearing on the sense of the words *praecise tantum* in the statement *sum igitur praecise tantum res cogitans*, etc. In the letter to Clerselier (for Gassendi) cited in section 13.2 Descartes claims not to have meant to say that he was "to speak precisely, only a thinking thing," but rather that he was indeed a thinking thing, but with this qualification (translating freely): "only (*tantum*) while I prescind (*praecise*) from all that of which I am not absolutely certain." As noted earlier, Cottingham finds the comment "at least partly disingenuous," since by the end of the paragraph Descartes seems to have ruled out any attempt to identify the mind's nature with something material: "none of the things that the imagination enables me to grasp is at all relevant to this knowledge of myself which I possess, and ... the mind must therefore be most carefully diverted from such things if it is to perceive its own nature as distinctly as possible" (AT VII 28: CSM II 19). And the comment would in fact be disingenuous were it indeed declared (as later in the Sixth Meditation) necessarily false rather than just not yet known to be either true or false on the basis of immediate inner experience.

At first sight the nuance perhaps seems over-subtle. The remark may in fact have been an after-thought on Descartes's part. Still, in the light of the letter to Silhon, the conclusion – that the mind must be "carefully diverted from all such things" if it is to form the conception of an "an intellectual nature in general," including its own – does seem to lend *praecise* something like the force Descartes claims for it. In the passage "seven or eight lines further down" to which he refers Gassendi, Descartes asks whether "these very things which I am supposing to be nothing, because they are unknown to me, are in reality (*in rei veritate*) identical with the 'I' of which I am aware." The answer is not 'no' (as Cottingham implies), but "I do not know, and for the moment I shall not argue the point, since I can make judgements only about things (*de iis tantum*) which are known to me ... I know that I exist ... If the 'I' is understood strictly (*praecise*) as we have been taking it, then it is quite certain that knowledge of it does not depend on things of whose existence I am as yet unaware (*nondum novi*)" (AT VII 27f.: CSM II 18f.). The Latin of the final sentence, *Certissimum est huius praecise sumpti notitiam non pendere*, etc., might be rendered more literally (if less elegantly): "It is very certain that the knowledge of it, as it is precisely understood, does not depend ... etc." What of this *praecise*? Does it go together with the *tantum* of the previous sentence to support the nuance of meaning on which Descartes insists?

With this occurrence of the two words in successive sentences compare again that statement which gave rise to the controversy in the first place: *sum igitur praecise tantum res cogitans* (AT VII 27: CSM II 18). Cottingham et al. translate:

"strictly speaking." However, for this Descartes is just as apt to use some such phrase as *proprie loquendo* (cf., for instance, AT VII 47: CSM II 32); for him *praecise* still has something of the literal force of our 'prescinding': *abstracting* from, turning one's attention away from one thing and focusing it upon another. Lost in the well-worn 'strictly' or 'precisely' of learned discourse, this literal meaning has to be spelled out for Gassendi: "I did not mean an entire exclusion or negation *but only an abstraction* from material things" (AT IX-1 215: CSM II 276). That this is the way the word *praecise* is used in certain key contexts in the *Regulae* will be seen in chapter 20. It is quite clearly so used in the following passage from the second version of the Third Meditation proof of God's existence: "For since I am nothing but a thinking thing – or at least since I am now concerned only and precisely with that part of me (*de ea tantum mei parte praecise*) which is a thinking thing – if there were such a power [of preserving myself in existence] in me, I should undoubtedly be aware of it (*ejus proculdubio conscius essem*)" (AT VII 49: CSM II 33f.). That *tantum* goes together with *praecise* here is clear enough; and that the two   go together in the other passages considered seems at the very least plausible.   If so, *sum igitur praecise tantum res cogitans* can be accurately paraphrased as follows: 'as long as I prescind from all that is not immediately present to consciousness in the manner of my acts, their act-characters, the "I" to which they all belong, and their intentional objects, I am (i.e., *know myself with certainty to be*) a thinking thing and nothing else.' If this is correct, then the 'ruling out' is to be understood quite differently than Cottingham supposes and there is nothing disingenuous about Descartes's disclaimer at all.

13.6 The role of the divine guarantor

From the foregoing it appears that the answer to the metaphysical question – can those things the conceptions of which are entirely independent of one another (different in nature, logically unrelated) actually exist separately (different in number, *two* substances) – depends on the knowledge of an omnipotent being; and the knowledge of the existence of such a being depends on the *cogito, ergo sum* as well as the axioms or principles of the natural light implicit in it. Still, the "problème primordial" for Descartes is neither the epistemological puzzle that exercised Kant nor the metaphysical mind-body problem, but the clear and distinct conception of the nature and existence of the mind. In the case of the mind, the relevant notion of 'objective truth' is not 'correspondence' or 'objective validity' at all. The question on which the possibility of *all* knowledge as *scientia* turns is rather, Is that which I *now* clearly and distinctly perceive still true when I no longer attend to it; in other words, can this first item of *persuasio*, the foundation of the entire edifice of human knowledge, be established as *vera & certa scientia*?

So the question regarding the *cogito* is not Gueroult's question, which is just

Kant's question transposed to a different plane: whether what I conceive and cannot but believe to exist in a certain way might in fact exist or be otherwise *in rei veritate* at the very moment I attend to my clear and distinct conception of it. For Descartes, this logical possibility is one we are psychologically incapable of taking seriously given adequate reflexion on the phenomenologically evident meaning of 'truth.' The question is rather: whether what is perfectly certain and objectively true now, as I attend to it and experience its truth inwardly, may be relied upon to be true still at such times as I am no longer attending to it. It is here that God's veracity comes into play in its primary role. True, a question of the other sort arises later with respect both to the metaphysical mind-body problem and the truths of mathematical physics. There the notion of 'truth' as "conformity of thought to its object" indeed has its place. So therefore does God's role as guarantor of 'objective validity.' And yet, the primary function of the knowledge of God's existence and veracity is in relation to the *cogito* principle; and here its role is different.

This leaves the question, Where do the truths of pure mathematics and natural theology fit in? As regards pure mathematics, *both* questions arise: considered as propositions about actually existing though merely ideal "true and immutable natures," the 'correspondence model' is surely applicable to mathematical truths.[19] Yet the main question in their regard is, How can I know that what is perfectly certain and objectively true now, as I experience and reflect upon its truth, may be relied upon to be true still at such times as I no longer attend to it? The same holds for the knowledge of God's existence and nature: both questions arise here too, though here, as we have seen, *persuasio* automatically converts to *scientia*, so that the second is easily answered. To the *cogito* principle, by contrast, the correspondence model and the Kantian question are utterly foreign. And so also to the questions regarding the essence of that which is known in the *cogito* principle, the *ego*, and the truth of the principles of the natural light or common notions.

One final problem concerning the role of the divine guarantor. At the outset of the Sixth Meditation, Descartes makes a theological statement that seems strangely inconsistent with the conception of divine omnipotence staunchly defended elsewhere (cf. sections 5.2 and 14.4):

For there is no doubt that God is capable of creating everything that I am capable of perceiving in this manner [i.e., clearly and distinctly]; and I have never judged that something could not be done by him except on the grounds that there would be a contradiction in my perceiving it distinctly (*nisi propter hoc quod illud a me distincte percipi repugnaret*). (AT VII 71: CSM II 50)

Is Descartes's doctrine not that God can in fact conceive and do even things that are self-contradictory and hence strictly inconceivable by the human intellect, the only exception being his inability to alter truths concerning his own nature? He goes even further than this in the letter to Arnauld, 29 July 1648:

I do not think that we should *ever* say of *anything* that it cannot be brought about by God. For since *every basis of truth and goodness* depends on his omnipotence, I would not dare to say that God cannot make a mountain without a valley, or bring it about that 1 and 2 are not 3. I merely say that he has given me such a mind that I cannot conceive a mountain without a valley, or a sum of 1 and 2 which is not 3; such things involve a contradiction in my conception. I think the same should be said of a space which is wholly empty, or of an extended piece of nothing, or of a limited universe. (AT V 224: CSMK 358f. e.a.)

Two different solutions to this apparent inconsistency suggest themselves. The first turns on the use of the past tense ("I have never judged," that is, never until embarking on these meditations). Descartes may be speaking here only of the ordinary, unclarified, not his own, philosophical, conception of God's omnipotence. Alternatively, the passage may mean: I understand God (even now) to be *in*capable only of those things which I conceive, not as *self*-contradictory, but as somehow *contradicting his nature*. After all, Descartes's word *repugnat* covers both logical absurdity, the denial of created eternal truths (the only examples in the letter to Arnauld), and metaphysical or theological absurdity, the denial of the uncreated among the eternal truths. In the Sixth Meditation passage it may be only the latter that are meant, so that God can indeed do what is contrary to the created among the eternal truths, that is, revoke his decrees, even though I cannot conceive how this is possible.

If the second solution is to be adopted, it must be admitted that it is hard to say exactly how each metaphysical absurdity contradicts God's own nature. The general response would appear to be: any action by which "the creator would have to tend toward non-being" (AT VII 370: CSM II 255) contradicts his nature and is therefore *absolutely* impossible. Thus, God cannot be a deceiver because "the form of deception is non-being, towards which the supreme being cannot tend" (AT VII 428: CSM II 289).[20] But it is difficult to establish a clear connection between each metaphysical absurdity and God's own nature in this way. For example, Descartes suggests it is impossible *even for God* to make shapes and motions exist apart from body: "moreover, these shapes and motions are merely modes which *no power whatever* [not even God's?] can cause to exist apart from body" (AT VII 440: CSM II 297 e.a.). This restriction on God's power in relation to modes does not apply to substances, which *can* be made to exist separately even if de facto intimately conjoined. Now it seems plausible enough that the impossibility of conceiving a mode clearly and distinctly without the substance whose mode it is depends on the principle *nihili nullae sunt proprietates* rather than the 'law of contradiction' alone. If so, this basic metaphysical principle presumably belongs among the *un*created eternal truths. In other words, for God to contravene this *metaphysical* axiom would again be for omnipotence to tend toward non-being (*nihil*) – though, admittedly, it is hard to see exactly why. By contrast, creating a mountain without a valley, or a round square, or a sum of two and three greater or less than five does not involve non-being and is therefore perfectly possible for God though inconceivable for us. However, earlier (AT VII 249: CSM II 173) Descartes apparently denies the very thing said about modes here: "my saying that modes are not intelligible apart from some substance for them to inhere in should not be taken to imply any denial that they can be separated from a substance by the power of God: for I firmly insist and believe that many things can be brought about by God which we are incapable of understanding." So the situation is unclear, to say the least. Apart from the textual problem, though, the second solution has much to recommend it and should perhaps be adopted as the most workable way out of the difficulty.

13.7 Conclusion

So much for the notion of truth as 'correspondence' and 'objective reality.' It constitutes a lesser strand alongside the primary, phenomenological conception of truth, which it nevertheless tends to overshadow in the accounts of most commentators. We conclude with a terminological observation and a brief summary.

It is a commonplace that the meanings of *subjectum* and *realitas objectiva* in Descartes and the medievals are just the opposite of 'the subject' and 'objective reality' in Kant and post-Kantian philosophy. As the meaning of *subjectum* changed from 'the object of knowledge' to 'the knower' (that is, 'das Subjekt' in Kant's sense, the self-conscious mind), so the meaning of *realitas objectiva* changed: instead of 'represented content in the mind' (as for Descartes and the medievals[21]), its German transliteration – one can hardly speak of translation – *objektive Realität* means 'the agreement between the represented content and the thing represented.' The profound significance of both changes, in which it is possible to discern a complete reorientation of philosophy toward the human subject, has been clearly recognized by some, grossly misunderstood by others.[22]

Despite these terminological differences, the Kantian question concerning the "objective validity" of metaphysical and mathematical concepts and principles that are a priori or 'subjective' in origin is easily formulated in Cartesio-Scholastic terms: What assurance have we that there actually exists anything, the formal reality of which corresponds to the objective reality of those ideas and principles that are innate in the mind? Descartes held that a sufficient warrant for this belief as *scientia* could be had only on the basis of the knowledge of God and only for the clearly and distinctly perceived among our ideas of material things. If the expression 'qualified representative realism' is used to designate this view, then Descartes is as much a representative realist as he is a causal realist on the question of the origins of sensory ideas of material things (see section 10.5).[23] Here the Kantian notion of truth as 'objective reality' fits well enough, even if the expression is strangely out of place. Still, the Kantian puzzle concerning the objective validity of the concepts and principles of pure mathematics and pure natural science, their correspondence with things, notwithstanding their subjective origin, is a relatively minor, though not unimportant, component of Descartes's project – much as the provision of a metaphysical foundation for physics is a relatively less important feature vis-à-vis the proofs that God exists and that the soul is a thinking substance capable of existing without the body (see above, section 3.3). More important by far is the metaphysical mind-body problem itself, while the "problème primordial" of Cartesian metaphysics is without much question the nature and existence of the mind and God. The tendency to emphasize the lesser strand both obscures the primary role of God in Descartes's philosophy and fosters charges that the Father of Modern Philosophy bizarrely confused subjective certainty with objective truth in laying the very foundations of human knowledge.

14

Certainty and Circularity

The analysis of the proposition *sum* began with the question of whether there are conditions under which even the *cogito* principle is made doubtful by the deceiving God hypothesis. The temporal restriction "whenever it is put forward by me or conceived by my mind" (cf. section 11.7) suggests that Descartes believed there were; that even my own thinking and existence are open to a "very slight and, so to speak, metaphysical doubt" whenever I do not attend to them expressly. In respect of certainty, then, the metaphysical principle *cogito, ergo sum* is no different than other clear and distinct perceptions, the simple truths and demonstrations of mathematics, for example, or metaphysical axioms and proofs: all such clear and distinct perceptions, whether intuitive or demonstrative, mathematical or metaphysical, are perfectly certain as now actually occurring *persuasio*; they are uncertain when no longer clearly and distinctly perceived but only remembered; and they are again perfectly certain once the knowledge of God's existence and veracity has transformed all *persuasio* into *vera & certa scientia*. Only theological knowledge forms an exception to the rule that *persuasio* only recollected is subject to doubt; for God's immutability entails that *persuasio* regarding his existence and nature is *vera & certa scientia*.

14.1 Three charges of circularity

From the first, the central argument of the *Meditations* has been thought to unfold in a manner that is viciously circular. Before considering the forms this charge has taken, it may be useful to reflect briefly on the general nature and main varieties of circular reasoning. The underlying principle is the same: 'you cannot use x to establish x'; but according as 'x' is either (1) a *faculty of the mind*, or (2) a particular *truth*, or (3) a *form of proof*, the specific charge of circularity differs. The fallacy is most obvious in (1) attempts to establish the reliability of some faculty of the mind using that very faculty. It need not be reason, or clear and distinct perception, that is in question, since it is obviously equally futile to attempt to establish the reliability of, say, sense-perception by means of observation. The most common form of the fallacy, however, is (2) the attempt to establish the truth of a conclusion employing a premise the knowledge of which presupposes the truth of the conclusion.[1] Less common, but obviously relevant here, is (3) the attempt to establish the validity of a certain form of proof or principle of argument by means of an argument or proof that itself has that form or employs that principle; for example, proving the validity of the syllogism by an argument that itself has the syllogistic form.

In the first place, then, Descartes has been charged with circularity for simply assuming what he sets out to prove when he infers God's existence and veracity from his nature, deriving therefrom the certainty of the truth rule and from the truth rule the certainty of all other clear and distinct perceptions. For the reliability of the ratiocinative faculty employed in the proof of God's existence is precisely the point at issue. This is the thrust of Hume's dismissal of "the Cartesian doubt."

Second, Descartes's causal proof that God exists and is no deceiver turns on the "common notion" that 'something cannot come from nothing.' Yet certain passages suggest that axioms or common notions can be known to be true only if God is known to exist and be no deceiver. Hence, by employing this principle of the natural light as a premise, Descartes takes for granted the conclusion of his proof. This is the form in which the objection was put by Burman (cf. AT V 148: CSMK 334).[2]

Lastly, Descartes's truth rule can be characterized as an 'inference licence' or principle of argument. It justifies the inference from 'p is clearly and distinctly perceived' to 'p is true.' To justify this type of inference, Descartes has to prove that God exists and is no deceiver. He does so by inferring 'God exists necessarily' from 'I clearly and distinctly perceive that God exists necessarily'; and by inferring 'God can be no deceiver' from 'I clearly and distinctly perceive that God can be no deceiver.' But one cannot justify a principle of argument by means of an argument that employs that principle. This is the version of the charge of circularity memorably formulated by Arnauld in the Fourth Set of Objections (cf. AT VII 214: CSM II 150).

14.2 The "bewildering variety of solutions"

Recently Loeb has attempted to bring the "bewildering variety of solutions" (1992, 201) to the problem of the Cartesian circle under two broad heads, the 'epistemic' and the 'psychological.' He alludes to a third main head, dubbed 'the memory answer' by Bennett (1990, 87 and 89), which would include the early interpretations of Gilson (1947a), Stout (1968), Gibson (1932), Keeling (1968) and Doney (1955). However, Loeb points out, interpretations "in which memory, not clear and distinct perception, is called into doubt have not been a live option in the aftermath of the critique of Frankfurt" (ibid., n. 2). Bennett concurs: "Nobody accepts this account now" (ibid., 88).[3] Yet Loeb quite ignores what Bennett (ibid., 90) calls "'the continuing truth answer'" defended by Smith (1952, 273ff.) and Etchemendy (1981). In any case, Bennett dismisses this option almost as lightly as he and Loeb both dismiss the memory account. In what follows, a modified version of the continuing truth answer will be defended.

The first of Loeb's categories corresponds in the essentials to what was called the 'normative' interpretation of metaphysical necessity in section 12.3; in this category Loeb places Frankfurt, Curley, Doney (*bis*), and Gewirth.[4] Gewirth's treatment of the problem (1987a) was seminal here. The hypothesis that God is a deceiver, he points out, rests on reasons whose criterion of validity is (and can only be, after Descartes has doubted the *truth* of clear and distinct perceptions), clarity and distinctness. In showing that the hypothesis is arbitrary or irrational *by its own criterion*, Descartes proceeds in a manner that is merely "negative" or "refutative," employing only the "internal" or "intra-rational" considerations still available to him. So the removal of *all* grounds for "metaphysical doubt" about clear and distinct perception establishes the "metaphysical certainty" or indubitability of God's veracity, while God's veracity guarantees the *truth* of clear and distinct perceptions in the sense of their "correspondence" with their extra-mental objects, actual or possible (ideal). Frankfurt merely picked up on Gewirth's suggestion that "the ground upon which the clear and distinct perception of God's existence and veracity is regarded by Descartes as overthrowing the metaphysical doubt ... is that the rationality of the former reveals the 'reasons' of the latter to be irrational'" (1987a, 23f.), developing it into the 'normative interpretation' (cf. Frankfurt 1970).

For his own part, Loeb proposes a psychological rather than normative interpretation, following in this Larmore, Rubin, and Bennett. It is unclear exactly how this schema, epistemic versus psychological, fits in with the older classificatory scheme proposed by Doney (1987, Introduction). Doney regarded advocates of the normative or epistemic approach as defending a "relaxation thesis," since for them the only thing required for certainty is to show that it would be unreasonable to doubt p, not that p is true. This is indeed to relax the strict requirement of truth in favour of a less stringent standard, at least until the existence of a veracious God has been established and the truth rule vindicated. But most advocates of the psychological interpretation of certainty belong in this category as well. To those, on the other hand, who argue that at least some clear and distinct perception is strictly immune to metaphysical doubt and therefore simply true (as on both the 'memory answer' and the 'continuing truth answer'), Doney ascribes what he calls the "limitation thesis." This tactic avoids circularity by allowing Descartes to establish God's existence and veracity as true without employing the truth rule, thus validating the rule without presupposing that *everything* perceived clearly and distinctly is true, but only that some things are.[5]

So far it seems that what we termed 'normative' and Loeb's 'epistemic' interpretations are one form of Doney's relaxation thesis, while the psychological interpretations are another. After all, notions like 'unshakeability,' 'solidity,' 'firmness,' and so on are expressly intended to vie with (normative) 'reasonableness' as explanations of that relaxed standard of certainty that falls short of truth. According to psychological interpretations, unshakeable belief in the existence of a veracious God cannot presuppose the truth rule that it validates, since unshakeability, not truth, is the goal; Loeb argues that even after establishing God's existence and the truth rule it is only unshakeability that Descartes is after.[6] Knowledge of the truth rule is, however, a necessary condition of the unshakeability, not of current, but only of recollected clear and distinct perception (cf. 205ff.). This is where something more like Doney's notion of limitation comes in after all.

As Bennett has observed, the distinction between now actually occurring and recollected clear and distinct perception is "common property" among those who attempt to exonerate Descartes of the charge of circular reasoning. But Loeb (1992, 214, 217) stresses what appears to be an important further distinction concerning "two kinds of recollected clear and distinct perceptions": the "unshakability [of everything else] depends upon retaining the ability to reproduce the demonstration of the truth rule" rather than a constant awareness of it; the truth rule itself is unshakeable as long as we retain this ability (whether we exercise it or not).[7]

This much seems correct; there is, however, one matter on which both Loeb and Bennett seem mistaken. Loeb rightly acknowledges an exception to the rule that recollected clear and distinct perception is open to doubt; but this "asymmetry between two kinds of recollected clear and distinct perceptions" (ibid., 214) does not in fact concern the truth rule, as he suggests. The exception is rather the knowledge of God's existence and veracity. In consequence of the strict immutability of the divine nature, theological knowledge is immune from doubt even when no longer immediately before the mind but only recollected or capable of being recalled. Bennett, for his part, recognizes the pivotal role assigned such theological knowledge by Descartes, yet fails to see how this or anything else can validate the truth rule and so propel Descartes across the "chasm" (1990, 100ff.) separating psychological "conviction" from truth.[8] No more can Loeb, who accordingly abandons the assumption that truth is the goal. Bennett tries instead to disengage two strands in Descartes's thought, a "truth project" that is the dominant but philosophically weaker strand, and a "stability project" which is largely recessive, though philosophically more promising – even if it too fails spectacularly in the end. Yet he at least acknowledges that Descartes, if asked to settle for stability or the "(factual) inability to doubt" (ibid., 85), "would probably recoil, protesting that nothing would satisfy him but the truth" (105). However, since this merely shows that Descartes was "not in touch with his own thinking" (ibid.), Bennett undertakes to reverse the roles of the two projects, bringing the psychological interpretation to the fore. So the "search for truth" gets rather short shrift after all.

Some canvassing of scholarly opinion is scarcely avoidable when broaching a subject like the Cartesian circle, though the literature is too vast for an exhaustive survey. Whatever the extent to which they correspond, the classification schemes of Loeb and Doney may help throw certain features of the following interpretation into higher relief. While clearly akin to other psychological interpretations in some respects, it nevertheless rejects both descriptive-psychological and normative surrogates for truth. Like most versions of the limitation thesis and especially the 'continuing truth answer,' it turns crucially on the doctrine of divine creation of the eternal truths; but unlike them, it assigns a key role to the doctrine of divine immutability.

14.3 Doctrines bearing on the Cartesian circle and its solution

The doctrine of divine immutability is only one of seven that bear significantly on the problem of the 'Cartesian circle' and its resolution.[9] Apart from (1) the epistemological distinction among different senses of 'reason' or 'clear and distinct perception' (*persuasio*, *scientia*, and that which is no longer *persuasio* but not yet *scientia*) and (2) the phenomenological conception of truth discussed in the previous chapter, five straightforwardly metaphysical doctrines are pertinent here. Central is (3) 'theological voluntarism' or the doctrine that eternal truths concerning ideal or possible essences are created and as dependent upon God's will as are creatures with their actual essences existing *in rerum natura*. The next three doctrines are closely affiliated with (3). The first is the teaching alluded to earlier (cf. section 10.11) in discussing the "existential version" of the ontological interpretation of pure mathematics: that (4) "we cannot conceive of anything except as existing," since "existence is contained in the idea or concept of every single thing" (AT VII 166: CSM II 117). Descartes lists this among his *axiomata sive communes notiones* in the *more geometrico* proofs of the Second Replies. What it asserts is that every object of clear and distinct perception exists in some sense, either (a) actually *in rerum natura*, (b) possibly, as an ideal 'essence' or 'nature,' or (c) necessarily – the last in the unique case of God (cf. AT VII 116: CSM II 83). Next, there is (5) the teaching that "every clear and distinct perception" in the human mind "is undoubtedly something, and hence cannot come from nothing, but must necessarily have God for its author" (AT VII 62: CSM II 43; cf. AT VII 54: CSM II 38, AT VII 144: CSM II 103, and AT VI 38: CSM I 130). According to this, truths concerning ideal natures exist at least potentially in the human mind, having been "implanted" there by God, who created us in his own image. In one of his last formulations of the doctrine of the eternal truths, Descartes stresses the fact that the denials of certain truths are unintelligible because God so fashioned the human mind that it cannot conceive them: "I would not dare to say that God cannot make a mountain without a valley, or bring it about that 1 and 2 are not 3. I merely say that he has given me such a mind [i.e., such a *nature*] that I cannot conceive a mountain without a valley, or a sum of 1 and 2 which is not 3; such things involve a contradiction in my conception" (AT V 224: CSMK 358f.). How (5) bears on the problem of the circle and its solution will become clearer presently. In addition, there is (6) Descartes's atomistic theory of time: "There is no relation of dependence between the present time and the immediately preceding time, and hence no less a cause is required to preserve something than is required to create it in the first place" (AT VII 165: CSM II 116). A corollary of this is employed in the second version of the causal proof of God's existence in the Third Meditation: "For a lifespan can be divided into countless parts, each completely independent of the others, so that it does not follow from the fact that I existed a little while ago that I must exist now, unless there is some cause which as it were creates me afresh at this moment – that is, which preserves me" (AT VII 49: CSM II 33). Coupled with theological voluntarism, the "independence of the divisions of time" (AT VII 369: CSM II 255) entails that everything created by God must be conserved by an act of his will from each moment to the next; and that everything created as necessarily thus and so must be conserved as necessary through each successive instant of time. From the conjunction of (3) through (6) arises the possibility that even what is clearly and distinctly perceived as necessarily true at one moment in time may not be so the next or at any other instant at which we are not expressly attending to it, unless we know the creator of these truths and our clear and distinct ideas of them to be no malicious demon but the wise and benevolent being whom we call 'God.' Of course, the consideration that now actually occurring clear and distinct perception is perfectly immune from doubt, even from the deceiving God hypothesis, already goes a long way toward allaying worries about circularity; but it is only by (7) the doctrine of the absolute immutability of God's own nature, and the consequent anomalousness of theological clear and distinct perception, that

Descartes is prevented from running into a new circle or an infinite regress.

These are the elements of the solution to be set out in the remainder of this chapter.

14.4 Theological voluntarism and related doctrines

Since the expression 'theological voluntarism' has potentially misleading connotations when used to describe Descartes's doctrine of divine creation of the eternal truths, it is important to be clear about what it can and cannot mean when so employed.

A question not unlike that by which the Platonic Socrates exposed the pretensions of the religious zealot Euthyphro in the dialogue of that name can be put to Descartes, not just regarding 'the pious' (or 'good'), but even concerning 'the true.' Since knowledge is a function both of intellect and will, these being distinct in us but sheerly indistinguishable in God,[10] one can ask: 'Are true propositions true because God knows them, or does God know them because they are true?' In the latter event, truths about the natures of things might be thought to exist independently of God; he knows them for the simple reason that they are true and that he is omniscient. The first horn of the dilemma, however, entails that no truth is independent of God's will; whatever is true is made so by his willing-knowing it. And since he creates the natures or possible essences of things as well as the things that actually exist *in rerum natura* together with their actual essences, he is the author of all conceptual as well as factual truths. Consequently, his willing-knowing such truths must be in some sense arbitrary: he could have no reason for affirming them before doing so. On the face of it, this makes nonsense of the doctrine of divine omniscience for precisely the same reasons as theological voluntarism in ethics makes nonsense of the notion of divine goodness: as we call someone 'good' for deliberately choosing good over evil (or the lesser among evils), so we call someone 'wise' or 'knowing' for affirming (after investigation and deliberation) the true rather than the false; neither goodness nor wisdom in this sense can be predicated of Descartes's God, however, who makes the good good and makes the true true by willing or affirming it. God's goodness and wisdom therefore must have a sense altogether different from this.[11]

This will do as a first, very rough sketch of the positive content of the doctrine. Kenny (1970, 693) has observed that both Scotus and Ockham defended forms of voluntarism regarding moral truth, but that neither extended it to metaphysical or mathematical truths, let alone to the most basic laws of nature.[12] If Descartes's extension of the doctrine along such lines is to be called 'voluntarism,' there are at least three things this *cannot* mean.

First, it should not be taken to entail any thesis about the modality of *all* propositions (see section 5.2). A key distinction is preserved by Descartes between the contingent and necessary truths willed by God. The latter are indeed only contingently necessary since God, who both decreed them true and implanted them in our minds, making it impossible for us even to conceive the truth of their denials, could have made other truths necessary instead; though all truths are *contingently* created, some are created *as necessary*, some *as contingent*, even if the boundary between them runs rather differently than one might expect.

Nor, secondly, should 'voluntarism' be understood to entail the priority of God's will to his intellect. In the third of the three letters to Mersenne of 1630 dealing with the eternal truths, Descartes writes: "In God, willing, understanding and creating are all the same thing without one being prior to the other even conceptually" (AT I 152f.: CSMK 25f.). And in the preceding letter: "In God willing and knowing are a single thing in such a way that by the very fact of willing something he knows it and it is only for this reason that such a thing is true" (AT I 149: CSMK 24). As late as 1644 he admonishes Mesland not to "conceive any precedence or priority between his intellect and his will; for the idea which we have of God teaches us that there is in him only a single activity, entirely simple and entirely pure. This is well expressed by the words of St. Augustine: 'They are so because thou see'est them to be so'; because in God *seeing* and *willing* are one and the same thing" (AT IV 119: CSMK 235).[13]

Third, and finally, 'theological voluntarism' should not be taken as implying the utter arbitrariness or irrationality of the Divine Will – though they must be arbitrary in some sense for reasons to be outlined in a moment. Of course, to say that the concepts of divine goodness and omniscience become vacuous is still relatively mild compared to Frankfurt's charge (1987b, 228) that if God "is to be compared to a king who lays down laws for his kingdom, he might be compared to a king who is utterly capricious and quite mad."[14] From Descartes's perspective, a certain kind of arbitrariness (having no *reason* to affirm or choose something), far from emptying the notions of divine wisdom and goodness of all meaning, constitutes one of God's principal perfections, his absolute liberty of indifference: "I wrote that indifference in our case is rather a defect than a perfection of freedom; but it does not follow that the same is the case with God" (AT III 360: CSMK 179). Not only does it not follow, it is in fact "self-contradictory (*repugnat*) to suppose that the will of God was not indifferent from eternity with respect to everything which has happened or will ever happen; for it is impossible to imagine that anything is thought of in the divine intellect as good or true, or worthy of belief or action or omission, prior to the decision of the divine will to make it so" (AT VII 432: CSM, II, 291). To Burman's query (cf. AT V 160: CSMK 343), "what then of God's ideas of possible things? Surely these are prior to his will," Descartes responds, unperturbed: "These too depend on God, like everything else. His will is the cause not only of what is actual and to come, but also of what is possible and of the simple natures. There is nothing we can think of or ought to think of that should not be said to depend on God" (ibid.). It is rather those who hold that God's knowledge or choice is constrained either by essences or laws existing independently of him who are the blasphemers according to Descartes:

As for the eternal truths, I say once more that they are true or possible only because God knows them as true or possible. They are not known as true by God in any way which would imply that they are true independently of him. If men really understood the sense of their words they could never say without blasphemy that the truth of anything is prior to the knowledge which God has of it. In God willing and knowing are a single thing in such a way that by the very fact of willing something he knows it and it is only for this reason that such a thing is true. (cf. AT I 149: CSMK 24)

Whoever denies this, accordingly, restricts God's omnipotence:

If anyone attends to the immeasurable greatness of God he will find it manifestly clear that there can be nothing whatsoever which does not depend on him. This applies not just to everything that subsists, but to all order, every law, and every reason for anything's being *true or* good. If this were not so, then ... God would not have been completely indifferent with respect to the creation of what he did in fact create. If some reason for something's being good had existed prior to his preordination, this would have determined God to prefer those things which it was best to do. But on the contrary, just because he resolved to prefer those things which are now to be done, for this very reason, in the words of Genesis, 'they are very good'; in other words, the reason for their goodness depends on the fact that he exercised his will to make them so ... I also understand that it would have been easy for God to ordain certain things such that we men cannot understand the possibility of their being otherwise than they are [e.g., that 2 and 3 added together *not* equal 5 or the radii of a circle not be equal]. And therefore it would be irrational for us to doubt what we do understand correctly just because there is something which we do not understand and which ... there is no reason why we should understand. Hence we should not suppose that eternal truths 'depend on the human intellect or on other existing things'; they depend on God alone, who, as the supreme legislator, has ordained them from eternity. (AT VII 435: CSM II 293f. e.a.)

Thus, the problem of the eternal truths poses itself as a simple alternative for Descartes: either (1) they are *created and dependent* on God or (2) they are *uncreated and independent* of God (cf. Frankfurt 1987b, sect. III). Since (2) leads straight to the anthropomorphic, pagan Greek notion of divinities themselves subject to a higher law, Descartes embraced the hardly less heretical (1) – without even considering what was in fact the standard teaching of Christian philosophers throughout the Middle Ages. For St Thomas, God creates the actual essences of things in bestowing existence upon them; yet *possible* essences, considered apart from every mode of being actual in individuated natures or in human cognition, are (3) *uncreated and dependent* upon God. They are not creatures but belong to God's creative essence itself.[15] They *depend*, therefore, not on God's efficient, but on his exemplar causality; for he understands them in contemplating his own eternal essence, his nature, in which they are included as in the perfectly simple unity of all reality or perfection.[16]

This is as much of the positive content of the doctrine as is strictly relevant to our immediate purpose here. The question that concerns us is why even the clear and distinct perception of eternal truths becomes subject to doubt the moment they are no longer actual but only remembered. The answer suggested by the foregoing is: because the omnipotent author of all being and truth[17] created not only me, the heavens, the earth, and all existing things, but even the natures or essences of those as well as of other possible things. To some of these natures, both mental and material, he gave actual existence *in rerum natura*; to others, like the true and immutable natures of mathematical entities, he gave only possible, not actual existence. And what he made, he can alter, even if I am unable to conceive how this is possible. Even for such eternal truths to remain necessarily true he must preserve them so continually by the same act of creation by which he brought them into being in the first place. So at the precise moment that I am actually intuiting mathematical and metaphysical natures, not even an omnipotent deceiver could mislead me. But the instant I no longer actually attend to them, I lack perfect assurance that they are still what I formerly perceived them to be, since an omnipotent deceiver (or a malicious demon of sufficient power) could have changed them unbeknownst to me. Although the true God's immutability implies that he cannot alter his own nature, he can (for all I know) alter his decrees regarding created things, be they contingent and actual existents or true and immutable natures. For he can conceive the latter otherwise than they are, though we are utterly unable to do so; and he could actually make them other than they are, were it not for the fact that to do so would be deception on his part.

Of course, the mere alteration of an eternal truth once it has become known does not obviously constitute deception. All I may be sure of, as Descartes remarks in the Fourth Meditation, is that "since God does not wish to deceive me, he surely did not give me the kind of faculty which would ever enable me to go wrong *while using it correctly*" (AT VII 54: CSM II 37f. e.a.; cf. *Principles*, I, 30 and IV, 206). So as long as I am capable of again turning my mental gaze on the natures of things, I am in a position to discover that they have been changed and so to avoid error. If I fail to do so, believing something true simply because I remember having perceived it clearly and distinctly in the past, the fault is mine. After all, though I am sheerly incapable of withholding assent in matters now clearly and distinctly perceived, nothing prevents me from doing so in matters only remembered to have been so perceived in the past. And if nothing prevents my confirming my former clear and distinct perceptions now, or suspending judgment until I have done so, it is not clear why altering his decrees would make God a deceiver.

Enter the doctrine that "every clear and distinct perception is undoubtedly something, and hence cannot come from nothing, but must necessarily have God for its author" (AT VII 62: CSM II 43). This entails that when God fixes the eternal truths by arbitrary fiat he determines the human mind to conceive them in a certain way, even though he himself can conceive them otherwise. In the very first formulation of the doctrine in the letter to Mersenne of 16 April 1630, Descartes states that "God ... has laid down these laws [the eternal truths of mathematics] *in nature* just as a king lays down laws in a kingdom" (AT I 145: CSMK 23 e.a.). Since the eternal truths of mathematics do not assert the actual existence of anything *in rerum natura*, it can only be *vera et realia entia* that are "laid down in nature" by God. Moreover, "in nature" refers to human nature as well as the nature of things as merely possible, that is, it refers to the human mind – as is in fact suggested by the remainder of the passage: "They are all inborn in our minds (*mentibus nostris ingenitae*) just as a king would imprint his laws on the hearts of all his subjects if he had enough power to do so" (AT I 145: CSMK 23). Therefore, simply to alter the eternal truths would be deceptive after all; for as long as human nature remains unchanged, I continue to be unable to conceive such matters otherwise than I formerly clearly and distinctly perceived them.

Could then God alter the eternal truths themselves *and* human nature? If so, my choosing to rely on memory rather than immediate intuition would not constitute deception on his part. Yet a God powerful enough to manipulate human reason in this way is just not countenanced in the *Meditations*. If it were, reason itself would become fluctuating and antinomical in its deliverances from one moment to the next. *Persuasio* would still be possible – or intervals of it – but not *scientia*. That way lies scepticism, and (as should be clear by now) it is precisely in order to safeguard the possibility of *vera & certa scientia* that Descartes confines the powers of an omnipotent being within limits, thus not only avoiding a doubt that must prove "incurable" (Hume), but also establishing the dependence of all *vera & certa scientia* on the knowledge of "the true God."

14.5 Divine immutability

So far we have considered the doctrines in (3) through (6). However, (1), the different senses of 'clear and distinct perception,' and (7), the doctrine of divine immutability, are enough to make it reasonably clear that there need be nothing viciously circular in Descartes's manner of validating clear and distinct perception by clear and distinct perception.

Descartes developed the distinction between *persuasio* and *scientia* in the letter to Regius some time before actually being confronted with the charge of circularity brought against the ontological argument by Arnauld. Faced with the objection that he had begged the question, justifying his truth rule through appeal to God's veracity and then proving God's existence and veracity by means of the truth rule (cf. AT VII 214: CSM II 150), he responded by drawing a distinction between arguments the conclusions of which are certain because we are immediately conscious of the grounds of their truth and those whose conclusions are certain even though the arguments themselves are no longer immediately before the mind's eye:

> we are sure that God exists because we *attend* to the arguments which prove this; but subsequently it is enough for us to remember that we perceived something clearly in order for us to be certain that it is true. This would not be sufficient [for certainty] if we did not know that God exists and is not a deceiver. (AT VII 246: CSM II 171 e.a.)

If the conclusions of valid inferences from axioms and principles of the natural light immediately present to the attentive mind are absolutely certain as long as we attend to them, then certainty in regard to God's existence and veracity depends on clear and distinct perception in one sense (*persuasio*) while guaranteeing the truth of the clearly and distinctly perceived in another (*scientia*).[18]

While there is nothing circular in this, it still does not remove the difficulty entirely. Unless the knowledge of God is an anomaly among clear and distinct perceptions of simple natures, of axioms or 'eternal truths,' and of valid demonstrations, including the proofs of God's existence, either nothing is gained or the circle comes back to haunt us. For if the clear and distinct demonstration that God exists and can be no deceiver is an item of *persuasio*, it too is open to doubt the moment the grounds for its truth are no longer immediately under my intellectual scrutiny; with it all those clear and distinct perceptions of simple natures, axioms, and demonstrations whose status as *scientia* it is supposed to guarantee become doubtful as well. So either nothing is won or we embark on an infinite regress. On the other hand, if the clear and distinct demonstration of God's existence is *scientia*, but its becoming *scientia* is subject to the same conditions as all other *persuasio*, the result is again either a new charge of circularity or an infinite regress. So some reason must be given why perfect certainty *now* that God exists and can be no deceiver (*persuasio*) entails perfect certainty *at all times* and hence *scientia*, rendering all other *persuasio scientia* as well. That reason is supplied by (7), the doctrine of divine immutability.[19]

In the proofs of God's existence and veracity, *persuasio* remembered, or capable of being remembered, is ipso facto *scientia*, since what is known now, as I attend to the axioms and proofs that render God's existence and veracity certain and necessarily true, cannot be believed false at any subsequent time, provided I am capable of recalling that I once perceived its truth clearly and distinctly. For God's perfections, which include his manner of existence, are immutable in a sense in which most other 'eternal truths' are not. The latter were created and remain alterable by him; God's own nature, by contrast, is immutable in an absolute sense. Alluding to this difference in the letter to Mersenne of 6 May 1630, Descartes calls the existence of God "the first and *most eternal* of all possible truths" (AT I 150, CSMK 24 e.a.). We have already cited the passage (cf. section 12.6) in which he remarks that the "natural light enables us to perceive that it is impossible for such a being to have the power and will to give itself something new; rather his essence is such that he possesses from eternity everything which we can now suppose he would bestow on himself if he did not yet possess it" (AT VII 241: CSM II 168).

Thus, Descartes is only too ready to concede Gassendi's point that "it seems very hard to propose that there is any 'immutable and eternal' nature apart from almighty God" (AT VII 319: CSM II 221; cf. also the quotation from St Thomas in n. 16 above as well as n. 24 below). If 'immutable' is understood to mean 'independent of God,' that is, uncreated and hence not subject to alteration even by the divine will, nothing is immutable apart from God's own nature. "You would be right to think this if I was talking about existing things [*in rerum natura*], or if I was proposing something as [absolutely] immutable in the sense that its immutability was independent of God" (AT VII 380: CSM II 261), writes Descartes. But he goes on to add that there is another sense of 'immutable':

[J]ust as the poets suppose that the Fates were originally established by Jupiter, but that after they were established he bound himself to abide by them (*ipsum se iis servandis obstrinxisse*), so I do not think that the essences of things, and the mathematical truths which we can know concerning them, are independent of God [who established them by his free decrees]. Nevertheless I do think that they are immutable and eternal [i.e., necessary], since the will and decree of God willed and decreed that they should be so. (ibid.)

If 'immutable' is taken in *this* sense, then, contrary to what Gassendi maintains, there are many, indeed "countless" truths (AT VII 63: CSM II 44; AT VII 71: CSM II 49) concerning the natures of things that cannot be altered by *our* wills, and are therefore necessary and immutable. We simply cannot conceive them otherwise, let alone abrogate them. For example, it is not up to us whether, this being a triangle, its internal angles are equal to two right angles or not. Having once understood the reasons for this, we are simply incapable of grasping how it could be otherwise. But such truths are nevertheless not 'immutable' in the strict or absolute sense, for dependence on God's will applies "not just to everything that subsists, but to all order, every law, and every reason for anything's being true and good" (AT VII 435: CSM II 293f.). It applies, in short, not just to every contingently existing thing, but to all the *created* among the eternal truths as well, moral, logical, mathematical, or metaphysical. It does not apply, however, to the uncreated, that is, to those eternal truths that belong to God's creative essence or nature. In order to become *scientia*, therefore, theological *persuasio* is by no means subject to the very conditions it is supposed to fulfil for all other clear and distinct perceptions, since theological knowledge alone among the "eternal truths" and demonstrations converts unconditionally from perfect certainty now to perfect certainty at all times owing to God's *absolute* immutability. Thus, the doubt about reason furnished by Descartes's strange doctrine of God's creation of the eternal truths is laid to rest by the no less eccentric doctrine of divine immutability.

A God who has not created and hence cannot alter his own nature cannot alter the eternal truths that belong to his creative essence either; this is fairly conventional theological wisdom. But a God whose decrees are immutable only in the sense that he has bound himself to abide by them once made, owing to his own goodness, is another matter. All this may be bizarre metaphysics; but as a piece of reasoning it is neither formally fallacious nor viciously circular.[20]

14.6 Rebuttal of the three charges

It is now an easy matter to acquit Descartes of all three charges of circularity. First, Descartes neither says nor implies that reason itself is inherently unreliable in all its intuitive, discursive, and ratiocinative operations, only then to use reason to show that it is reliable after all. Exempt from doubt are current clear and distinct perceptions of natures and axioms or "common notions." Exempt, moreover, is even the remembered clear and distinct perception of God's nature, and that not just during the actual act of remembering, but as long as I am capable of remembering having perceived God's existence and veracity clearly and distinctly. Not exempt from doubt, on the other hand, are remembered clear and distinct perceptions of natures other than God's, mathematical or metaphysical, or remembered axioms and "common notions." The latter are rendered certain by the former.

Second, although the proof that 'God exists and is no deceiver' employs the premise 'something cannot come from nothing,' the conclusion is only taken for granted by the use of this axiom if the axiom really presupposes it. But such is the case only for knowledge of the axiom that is *scientia*, not for *persuasio*; and all that Descartes requires at this point is *persuasio*. As long as we actually intuit its truth, this premise is knowable without knowledge of the conclusion. The same applies, *mutatis mutandis*, to the use of the truth rule within the ontological argument.

Finally, the truth rule 'whatever I perceive clearly and distinctly is true' is ambiguous. It can mean either 'whatever I perceive clearly and distinctly is true as long as I actually perceive it clearly and distinctly'; or 'whatever I perceive clearly and distinctly is true as long as I can remember having once perceived it clearly and distinctly.' The proof of God's existence and non-deceptiveness presupposes the truth of clear and distinct perception in the former of these two senses and justifies it in the latter. Thus, there is no attempt to establish a principle of inference by means of an inference that employs that very principle.

14.7 The mutability of God's decrees

At this point an objection must be faced. The doubt from which even clear and distinct perception is not immune was said to arise because the omnipotent creator of everything (including the essences of things and common notions) can abrogate his decrees, modifying unnoticed the truth-value even of some necessary propositions. Yet there is some evidence that the free decrees of "the true God," once made, are in fact immutable.

The force of this objection is not great. Even should *God's* decrees be immutable, as long as it remains doubtful whether the omnipotent author of all being and truth really is "the true God" rather than a Deceiver, necessary truth remains open to at least a "metaphysical" doubt; for if an omnipotent Deceiver could, nothing really turns on whether God can alter or revoke his decrees.

When pressed on this question, Descartes retreats to the position that we just cannot know whether or in what precise sense the decrees of "the true God" are immutable; we understand that nothing *external* to him can prevent him from changing them; but without a more perfect understanding of his nature than finite human reason can achieve, we simply cannot be sure that he cannot alter certain of the eternal truths, but only that he cannot do so unbeknownst to us, since that would make him a deceiver. In the end, Descartes takes refuge in the doctrine of the *incomprehensibilitas Dei*, though he says a variety of interesting and apparently conflicting things about the immutability of God's decrees along the way. So even if it raises no very telling objection against the preceding interpretation, the suggestion that God's decrees are simply immutable is worth examining for the light it sheds on Descartes's concept of God, divine incomprehensibility, and the doctrine of the creation of the eternal truths.

Against the immutability of God's free decrees stands Descartes's often repeated claim that God cannot divest himself of his power of revoking his decrees, for example, by separating what he has once joined together. Since to forfeit this power would be to alter his own nature, *mutability*, not immutability, of God's decrees appears to follow immediately from his immutable nature. The point about God's power is made clearly with reference to the union of the human mind and body and of the parts of matter: "Even if we imagine that God has chosen to bring it about that some particle of matter is incapable of being divided into smaller particles, it will still not be correct, strictly speaking, to call this particle indivisible. For, by making it indivisible by any of his creatures, God certainly could not thereby take away his own power of dividing it, since it is quite impossible for him to diminish his own power, as has been noted above" (AT VIII-1 51f.: CSM I 231f.).[21] The earlier passage to which Descartes adverts here is *Principles*, I, 61, where he had already noted: "And even if we suppose that God has joined some corporeal substance to such a thinking substance so closely that they cannot be more closely conjoined, thus compounding them into a unity, they nonetheless remain really distinct. For no matter how closely God may have united them, the power which he previously had of separating them, or keeping one in being without the other, is something he could not lay aside" (AT VIII-1 29: CSM I 213; cf. also AT III 567: CSMK 214). Similarly, by saying that the "pure" among created substances "cannot ever cease to exist unless they are reduced to nothingness by God's denying his concurrence to them" (AT VII 14: CSM II 10; cf. AT III 429f.: CSMK 193f.), Descartes implies that God, having decreed that a material universe exist, *can* still revoke his decree and annihilate the universe.[22]

The existence of a material universe, like that of certain derivative laws of nature freely instituted by God, is logically contingent. So is the union of some particular mind and body or of certain parts of matter. The real distinction of mind and body and the divisibility of matter, on the other hand, are logically necessary. Like the most basic laws of nature,[23] they are eternal truths, dependent on the divinely decreed "true and immutable nature" of mental and material substance respectively. When it comes to such eternal truths, the picture is considerably more complex than that just described. In the end, as we shall see, Descartes simply cuts the Gordian knot by appeal to the doctrine of the *incomprehensibilitas Dei*.

Recall Burman's query, "what then of God's ideas of possible things? Surely these are prior to his will" (AT V 160: CSMK 342). Descartes responds: "[T]hese too depend on God, like everything else. His will is the cause not only of what is actual and to come, but also of what is possible *and of the simple natures* [like mind, body, and the "common notions"]. There is nothing we can think of or ought to think of that should not be said to depend on God" (ibid., e.a.). This is quite general and applies to all eternal truths, those of logic and mathematics no less than of metaphysics and morals. Burman then instances a case of patent *moral* absurdity: "does it not follow from this that God could have commanded a creature to hate him, and thereby made this a good thing to do?" (ibid.). This is a fairly standard objection against theological voluntarism in ethics. Descartes replies: "God could not *now* do this: but we simply do not know what he could have done. In any case, why should he not have been able to give this command to one of his creatures?" (ibid., e.a.). From this it appears that what God could have done and what he can now do may differ; while he might have decreed anything "from eternity," he cannot change his eternal decrees once made. This suggests that God's decrees are neither simply mutable nor immutable; he chooses freely, but is thenceforth *bound* by his own choice. Though the eternal truths *could have been* otherwise *for all we know*, they are yet not *now* subject to change – this much we know with certainty, but only once we know God's nature and goodness.

Something like this is indeed suggested by the language of the Fifth Replies (partly cited earlier in 14.5), where Descartes employs this reflexive notion of binding oneself:

You say that you think it is 'very hard' to propose that there is anything immutable and eternal apart from God. You would be right to think this if I was talking about existing things, or if I was proposing something as immutable in the sense that its immutability was independent of God. But just as the poets suppose that the Fates were originally established by Jupiter, but that after they were established *he bound himself to abide by them*, so I do not think that the essences of things, and the mathematical truths which we can know concerning them, are independent of God. Nevertheless I do think that they are immutable and eternal, since the will and decree of God willed and decreed that they should be so. (AT VII 380: CSM II 261 e.a.)

In this passage Descartes acknowledges the appropriateness of the analogy between God's relation to the eternal truths and that of Jupiter to the Fates, despite having remarked in the letter to Mersenne of 15 April 1630, almost contemptuously, that "to say that these [mathematical] truths are independent of God is to talk of him as if he were Jupiter or Saturn and to subject him to the Styx and the Fates" (AT I 145: CSMK 23). The reason for this is probably that in the earlier context he conceived the Fates in something like the Greek manner, that is, as independent of Jupiter, while in the Fifth Replies he explicitly treats them as having been established by Jupiter himself (cf. Curley 1987, n. 15). Descartes's point, then, is that nothing *independent and outside* of God binds his will; his having "bound himself to abide by" his decrees implies no restriction on his power or freedom *ab extra*, since (on Descartes's idiosyncratic reading of "the poets" here) even the Fates are established by Jupiter.

As no Greek would have been able to make much sense of this notion of a Zeus not subject to a higher, moral law in the universe (*moira, tuchē, ananke, dikē*), so Descartes, for his part, can genuinely make none of "anything immutable and eternal apart from God." The counter-examples of the *Timaeus*, of Suarez, Vasquez, and others (see above chapter 5, n. 4), though perfectly intelligible in 1630, are no longer so from the perspective of the Fifth Replies. The result is at least in verbal accord with orthodox Scholasticism.[24] But Descartes clearly wants to have it both ways: truths that are both distinct from God's creative essence *and* eternal. That creat*ed* essences or natures are both is implied by the separation of the "most eternal" truths (pertaining to God's nature) from those that depend on his will. Since no orthodox Scholastic ever held both these things, the agreement is of course *merely* verbal.[25]

Before leaving the question of the mutability of God's decrees, it may be worth taking a closer look at the letter of 15 April 1630 to Mersenne itself. Descartes here faces an objection to his doctrine that the eternal truths are "all inborn in our minds just as a king would imprint his laws on the hearts of all his subjects if he had enough power to do so": "if God had established these truths," the objection runs, "he could change them as a king changes his laws." This obviously bears directly on the question that concerns us here. To this Descartes replies: "Yes he can, *if* his will can change" (e.a.). On the face of it, this suggests (so Gouhier 1969, 246) that God's will *cannot* change, that he cannot alter these truths. The imaginary objector, however, presses his point, taking the reply ("Yes he can ...") to mean that the eternal truths are indeed alterable, at least by God: "'But I understand them [the truths] to be eternal and unchangeable.'" Descartes replies: "I make the same judgement about God." The point of this may be that *only* God's nature, and what follows from the necessity of his nature, rather than his free decrees, really possesses that perfect or absolute immutability that the objector tacitly and wrongly assigns to the freely created among the eternal truths; the latter are in fact *not* strictly immutable (only God's nature, etc., is), since their being and remaining as they are depends on God's will. There remains, of course, a qualified sense in which the truths of mathematics may still be called 'eternal and immutable.' Willed from eternity as necessary, we cannot conceive the possibility of their denials being true; they are necessary for and immutable by *us*, given the nature of our intellect and will. Of course, once we understand God's existence and veracity, we understand them to be immutable even by God. But it is only the former sense of 'immutability' that Descartes appears to have in mind in this letter, not 'willed from eternity such that God binds himself not to make any change.' The latter comes to the fore only later, in the Fifth Replies.

The objector is left understandably perplexed by all this: "'But his will is free.'" The perplexity stems from the fact that to say of an action that it is 'free' (in anything like the ordinary sense of the word) entails that it is contingent, just as to say of a truth that it is necessary entails that it is immutable, that is, cannot be otherwise. This is precisely the conundrum with which Descartes is grappling, trying out different solutions: truths freely established by God as necessary and immutable and yet alterable by the divine will. Instead of spelling out relative and absolute senses of 'necessity' and 'immutability' or pressing into service the distinction between willing that necessarily p and willing it necessarily (cf. the letter to Mesland of 2 May 1644; AT III 118f.: CSMK 235), the exchange concludes abruptly with an allusion to the incomprehensibity of God: "Yes, but his power is beyond our grasp. In general we can assert that God can do everything that is within our grasp but not that he cannot do what is beyond our grasp. It would be rash to think that our imagination reaches as far as his power."

This is not very satisfactory. The solution reached later, in the Replies to the *Meditations*, is not very satisfying either. It is worth noting, however, that the resort to protestations that certain matters are simply beyond our comprehension is an integral feature of Descartes's philosophy, early and late, and not just where God or the infinite is concerned.[26]

Again, there is no need to ask how God could have brought it about from eternity that it was not true that twice four make eight and so on; for I admit this is unintelligible to us. Yet on the other hand I do understand, quite correctly, that there cannot be any class of entity [actual or merely possible] that does not depend on God; I also understand that it would have been easy for God to ordain certain things such that we men cannot understand the possibility of their being otherwise than they are. And therefore it would be irrational for us to doubt what we do understand correctly just because there is something which we do not understand and which, so far as we can see, there is no reason why we should understand. Hence we should not suppose that eternal truths 'depend on the human intellect or on other existing things' [as the Sixth Objections had suggested]; they depend on God alone, who, as the supreme legislator, has ordained them from eternity. (AT VII 436: CSM II 294)

According to this, the fact that we cannot understand how "true and immutable natures" can be alterable by God should not deter us from holding them to be so, provided we understand perfectly that it is not impossible for him to alter them while yet withholding from us the capacity to understand how he can do so. In a similar vein, Descartes assures the Princess Elizabeth that the difficulties she is experiencing conceiving the possibility of mind-body interaction are no obstacle to rational acceptance of the doctrine, provided she has once clearly and distinctly conceived that the mind is a thinking unextended thing and the body an extended unthinking thing; for the fact that the remoter implications of a doctrine are inconceivable is no good reason for rejecting them, especially when every sensation and every voluntary motion assures us of their truth. How much more so, then, when the clear and distinct conception of God's nature assures us that what we cannot comprehend must yet be possible for him, especially when there is no reason we can see why we should comprehend it and his revelation informs us that it is true?[27]

14.8 Conclusion

To conclude this chapter, a rapid summary of its findings in respect of the central question, the necessity of the *sum*.

Although commentators have proposed various ways of construing the certainty of the *cogito, ergo sum* as a purely logical insight, the only truth regarding existence that Descartes recognized as both logically and metaphysically necessary pertains to the One Necessary Being, God.[28] Although they are certain and metaphysically necessary in the same way as the necessary truths of mathematics, logically speaking, statements of the form *cogito* and *existo* are contingent. The logical point concerning the "existential inconsistency" (Hintikka) of actually denying either proposition, like the more straightforward inconsistency of affirming the first while denying the second, was not entirely lost on Descartes, as a variety of formulations of his point attest; but the significance of the key insights embodied in the *cogito, ergo sum* cannot be adequately explained in terms of the distinction between logically necessary and contingent truth alone.

Historically, Descartes's doctrine of the creation of the eternal truths achieved something of a *succès de scandale* by blurring the distinction between logically contingent and necessary truth. Even logically necessary truths are contingent in a certain sense, since the impossibility of our denying such truths without contradiction depends upon the arbitrary decree of God. Moreover, that decree must be constantly renewed from moment to moment if the eternal truths are to continue to exist unaltered. Only truths concerning God's own nature are unconditionally or absolutely immutable and hence strictly necessary in the way in which strict logical necessity is usually thought of today, since even God cannot conceive his own nature as other than it is.

This no doubt has its bearing on the certainty of the *cogito, ergo sum* as an item of *scientia*. But the profound significance of Descartes's founding principle lies in a different, epistemological or phenomenological, distinction between two types of logically contingent propositions. Reflecting on the existence of thinking itself and attempting to place it in doubt, Descartes made clear to himself the difference between the objects of thought and of consciousness. By directing attention to the one or the other of these, while at the same time reflecting on his freedom to withhold assent to their existence, he became immediately aware of what existence, what perception is, what clarity and distinctness, what volition, doubt, and freedom are, what truth or certainty is. Reflexive attention to his own thinking revealed an *epistemic difference* between existential statements regarding extra-mental objects and existential statements of the form *cogito*. For while the former are obscure and confused for the most part, only occasionally attaining to clarity, the latter are both clear and distinct; while both are logically contingent, the latter are metaphysically necessary. Given the immediately evident nature of truth itself, the epistemological gulf separating truths of these two kinds must have seemed to Descartes as wide as that customarily believed to obtain between contingent truths about the objects of the senses and logically necessary truths of the kind met with in the axioms of logic and mathematics. Moreover, even logically necessary truths and the conclusions of valid inferences from true premises owe whatever certainty they possess, not to logical necessity as clearly and distinctly grasped by the intellect, but to the metaphysical or psychological necessity they possess through their power to coerce the will. This they do whenever the mind attends to them, or recalls having attended to them in the past, while it is able to recall having clearly and distinctly perceived the logical impossibility that God not exist or be a deceiver.

Such is the certainty or truth on which Descartes founds his science. Truth, in the sense of *vera & certa scientia*, is not obtainable without the knowledge of God. Nor is such *scientia* required in the first phase of the foundation of human knowledge, since, having attained "perfect knowledge" (AT VII 71: CSM II 49) or *persuasio* of my own existence as a thinking being, I have found an 'Archimedean point.' That nothing more is required Descartes affirms not just as a normative matter of what it is reasonable to ask for, but also as a matter of psychological fact: it is sheerly impossible for anyone who has reflected sufficiently upon the self-evident nature of truth to believe that absolute truth (in a sense corresponding to Descartes's locution "absolute falsity") is really required for the establishment of the sciences. If, through not having attended to the nature of truth, we are so unreasonable as to demand more than *persuasio* for the foundations, the result can only be scepticism. However, having once grasped what truth is and attained to the knowledge of "the true God," even truth as *scientia* (and, where appropriate, as *adaequatio* or *convenientia*) is perfectly within our reach.

14.9 Epilogue: The autonomy of reason

The wider significance of the distinction between *persuasio* and *scientia* is apparent from its implications for the autonomy of human reason.

Rational certainty (indubitability *now*) does not entail truth at all times except in the unique case of the knowledge of God's existence and veracity; in all other cases, prior knowledge of God is required if assertions based on immediate intuition are to take their place within the ordered system of true propositions that is science. But though *persuasio* does not entail *scientia*, the inference can be secured by the knowledge of God's veracity, so that even the science of nature, that is, knowledge of "the essential nature of bodies" as actually existing "outside us" (AT VII 83: CSM II 58) belongs to the sphere of *vera & certa scientia*. Even without knowledge of God, however, *persuasio* entails truth in the primary sense of the term; for what truth is is immediately evident through reflexion upon the *experience* of certainty implicit in the structure of every act of thinking as such. Over against the heteronomy of reason in *scientia* must be set the complete autonomy of reason in *persuasio*. Depending upon how it is taken, the *sum* may be said to be certain and necessarily true only in the latter or in both senses of 'perfect certainty.'

Inattention to the autonomy of reason in its principal, intuitive role, coupled with a tendency to overlook the primary sense of 'truth,' leads to the 'epistemic' interpretation according to which the *Meditations* undertake the 'validation of reason.'[29] Against this stands the plain fact that human reason is self-validating in *persuasio*, its own law and authority, completely independent of the divine intellect and will. Nevertheless, the heteronomy of reason in *scientia* is at least as significant an aspect of Descartes's basic epistemological and metaphysical outlook as its autonomy in *persuasio*. For as long as certainty and truth now does not guarantee certainty and truth at all times, that is, as long as I do not know God, doubt can recur the moment I cease to attend to the grounds of that which was a moment ago intuitively certain.

In an interesting study of this whole question Miller has remarked on "a powerful undercurrent of irrationalism in Descartes, the first of the modern rationalists" (1965, 49). Beneath the surface texture of Cartesian rationalism (exemplified by the familiar doctrines of the 'natural light' and of simple natures infallibly known in intuition) lies a deep vein of irrationalism, Miller suggests, evident above all in those doctrines whose focus is that "the criterion of clear and distinct ideas requires metaphysical support" (ibid.) from the divine guarantor. We conclude Part Two with a few remarks prompted by Miller's reflections.

Where at least some of the deliverances of reason are accepted as providing an absolutely reliable guide to truth, the recognition that there are limits upon the autonomy of reason is not usually called 'irrationalism.' That term is better reserved for the outright rejection of the claims of reason in all its uses. 'Scepticism,' by contrast, is best suited to the view that such claims cannot be *shown* to be warranted ('mitigated' scepticism), or can be shown to be *un*warranted (radical scepticism). As opposed to both irrationalism and scepticism, the recognition that reason requires scrutiny *by* reason, that some rational warrant must be provided for some of the deliverances of reason itself, even though none is possible without a certain circularity, is commonly called 'critical rationalism' (cf. Popper 1945, chap. 24). If it must be labelled, Descartes's philosophy is perhaps more aptly described as 'critical rationalism' than either 'irrationalism' or 'scepticism.'

A further point: where such warrant as is required for the reliability of reason lies outside of reason itself, in a divine guarantor, critical rationalism involves the heteronomy of reason. This, however, is still a far cry from what is ordinarily termed 'irrationalism.' By contrast, the intuitionist's acceptance of the deliverances of reason as bearing on the face of them the unmistakable mark or standard of truth itself, so that reason in its primary employment is completely self-validating or autonomous, is rightly regarded as the mark rationalism par excellence. On this point, at least, Miller is perfectly correct about Descartes.

Though Descartes was no sceptic at the end of the day – or after his sixth day of meditation – few thinkers have faced as squarely as he what Gewirth has called "the dilemma of total skepticism":

Any skeptical doubt about some proposition or set of propositions, and *a fortiori* any attempt at a total skepticism, must rest on reason, for otherwise it is arbitrary and irrational and there is no ground or justification for accepting it. But if it rests on reasons, then to that extent the skepticism lapses (and of course is not 'total'), for the reasons themselves must be at least tentatively accepted, although, of course, they need not be regarded as certain or indubitable. (Gewirth 1987b, 93)

In other words: doubts about reason must either be based on reason itself or baseless; if baseless, then frivolous – or not doubts at all (assuming that by 'doubt' is meant something more than mere musings about logically possible falsity, without the slightest grounds for supposing anything false).[30] If based on reason, however, then the reliability of reason is presupposed: the attempt to validate reason by reason is circular, as the invalidation of reason by reason is self-contradictory. While Descartes perhaps never faced the dilemma in quite this form (nor skirted round it in the manner Gewirth goes on to suggest), he nevertheless pushed his questioning to the limits of both scepticism *and* rationalism, falling neither into arbitrariness nor into circularity nor into contradiction. What he accomplished involved setting in motion a metaphysical machinery that no philosopher today would think of employing; but as Bréhier once observed (1937, 208), "the creation of the eternal truths," and the rest of the elaborate machinery involved, is "the reverse side of the autonomy of reason" rather than the subversion of reason itself.

PART THREE:
REFLEXION AND INFERENCE

So many things are contained in the idea of a thinking thing that it would take whole days to unfold them. (AT X 527: CSM II 420)

Through the uses to which he put the terms 'thought,' 'consciousness,' 'reflexion,' 'idea,' and their cognates Descartes provided the essentials of a metaphysical analysis of mind and of the structure of the mental that was to be more fully exploited outside its original metaphysical context in the subsequent history of modern philosophy by a sequence of major thinkers, culminating in Husserl and his school. Part One began the elaboration of this thesis for 'thought' and 'consciousness,' distinguishing simple *conscientia* from reflexive attention to what one is conscious of and from second- and higher-order reflexive acts. The present part will complete the task by considering Descartes's use of the term 'idea,' attempting a detailed analysis of reflexion as a form of inference.

Although the items included within *conscientia* were only enumerated at first, a notational device adapted from Husserl and Heidegger (cf. section 8.1) set off the embracing formal structure of thought by means of four fundamental distinctions. The first was (1) between acts of thinking and the immediate awareness of such acts. The latter is not a second-order reflexive act, nor indeed an act at all, but an essential feature of all acts in virtue of which it is impossible to perform them without being to some degree aware that one is doing so. Then (2) reflexive attention to one's acts, which is again not an act, was distinguished from second- and higher-order acts of reflexion. Next a distinction was introduced (3) between acts as the immediate objects of consciousness (perhaps also of reflexive attention) and the intentional objects of such acts. Finally, (4) the intentional object, *cogitatum*, or 'thing in so far as it is thought about' was distinguished from the same entity in so far as it exists independently of the mind in the 'external world' (*res*). Once these distinctions have been drawn in terms other than Descartes's own, it is a relatively easy matter to locate them in the form in which Descartes himself drew them using the outmoded and sometimes confusing Scholastic vocabulary of his day.

Chapter 15 traces the first two distinctions as drawn by Descartes, chapter 16 the remaining pair. In chapter 17 the answer to the main question of this part, the nature of the transition of the mind from *cogito* to *sum*, is elaborated on the basis of the distinction of discursive and ratiocinative processes from that strictly intuitive mental process that we term 'reflexive attention,' 'analytical reflexion,' or 'reflexive analysis.' In the light of Descartes's concept of reflexion it is possible to discern various stages within what he calls 'intuition,' so that it makes at least some sense to speak of an 'inference' of the mind to denote the *movement* of thought within intuition itself from implicit to explicit insight. However, the term 'inference' is usually reserved for those rule-governed discursive and ratiocinative processes of the mind that are opposed to the intuitive or non-inferential. In the end, not much hangs on whether reflexion is opposed to inference or treated as itself a variety of inference characterizable as *intuitive induction*; the important thing is to understand what is distinctive about this progress of the mind and what sets it apart from the Aristotelian notion of intuitive induction to which it has often been likened. The key (though by no means only) difference lies in the concept of the experience – sense-perception for Aristotle, inner, reflexive experience for Descartes – from which intuitive induction takes its rise. Following a detailed examination of Descartes's theory of innateness in chapter 18, it will be shown that Descartes's concept of experience presupposes a theory of the mind as remote from Aristotle and Leibniz as it is from empiricist philosophies like those of Hobbes, Locke, and Gassendi (chapters 19 and 20).

15

Consciousness, Thought, and Reflexion

As for the first pair of distinctions, Descartes elaborates the inherently self-reflexive structure of thinking, distinguishing consciousness from thought and both of these from reflexive attention and second-order reflexive acts in responding to the two principal objections brought against the primitiveness of the *cogito, ergo sum.* In addition to those passages containing the four main responses (Sixth Replies, *The Search for Truth*, Second Replies, *Principles*, I,10), we must consider Descartes's reply to Burman's objection that the response within the Second Replies is inconsistent with *Principles*, I, 10. Discussion of two further objections, one from Burman, the other from Bourdin, will complete the treatment of the first pair of distinctions in the present chapter. The chapter concludes with a set of related considerations bearing on analytic and synthetic method and on the mathematical sciences.

15.1 Objections and the four main responses

What Descartes understands by a 'principle' was discussed earlier (chapter 7 *in initio*). A primitive or first principle is one of which it is true to say that "there is no other on which it depends and none which is easier to discover" (AT IV 444f.: CSMK 290). This is the focus of the first of the two main objections to the primitiveness of the *cogito, ergo sum* heading the compilation prepared by Mersenne and published as the Sixth Set of Objections. In order to know that one thinks and exists, it is objected, one must first know what 'thinking' and 'existence' mean. As for 'thinking,' one cannot possibly know that this means anything at all, for this would require an infinite series of acts directed upon other acts (cf. AT VII 413: CSM II 278).

To this Descartes replies that one's certainty that one is thinking indeed presupposes knowledge of "what thought is and what existence is. But," he continues, this does not require reflexive knowledge (*scientia reflexa*), nor knowledge acquired by demonstration, much less knowledge of reflexive knowledge, i.e. knowing that we know and knowing that we know that we know and so on *ad infinitum*. This kind of knowledge cannot possibly be obtained about anything. It is quite sufficient that we should know it by that internal awareness which always precedes reflexive knowledge (*cognitio illa interna, quae reflexam semper antecedit*). This inner awareness of one's thought and existence is so innate in all men that although we may pretend that we do not have it if we are overwhelmed by preconceived opinions and pay more attention to words than to their meanings, we cannot in fact fail to have it. (AT VII 422: CSM II 285)[1]

The same objection occurs in *The Search for Truth*. Here the "inner awareness of one's thought and existence" is specifically termed *conscientia*. Eudoxus, Descartes's spokesman in the dialogue, concedes Epistemon's point "that we must know what doubt is, what thought is, what existence is" (AT X 523: CSM II 417) in order to be certain of *cogito, ergo sum*. "But do not imagine," he warns, "that in order to know what these are, we have to rack our brains trying to find the 'proximate genus' and the 'essential differentia' which go to make up their true definition" (ibid.). Such would be a "logical definition" (AT VIII-1 8: CSM I 195) of 'thought' and 'existence.' Eudoxus continues:

I would never have believed that there ever existed anyone so dull that he had to be told what existence is before being able to conclude and assert that he exists. The same applies to doubt and thought. Furthermore, no one can learn such things or be persuaded of them otherwise than through his own experience and that *consciousness or internal testimony* (*eaque conscientia, vel interno testimonio*) which everyone experiences within himself (*in seipso experitur*) ... [I]n order to know what doubt and thought are, all one need do is to doubt or to think. That tells us all it is possible to know about them, and explains more about them than even the most precise definitions. (AT X 524: CSM II 417f. e.a.)[2]

It appears that what Descartes terms (1) 'consciousness' or 'internal cognition' ('testimony') is being contrasted with two different mental processes in this pair of passages. In the Replies to the Sixth Set of Objections he distinguishes consciousness primarily from (2) second- and especially (& *multo minus*) higher-order acts of thinking about thinking (about thinking ... etc.). In *The Search for Truth*, on the other hand, he contrasts it principally with (3) that discursive form of reflexion in which the logical relations among genera and species are discerned and embodied in formal definitions. In Descartes's reply to the other of the two principal objections brought against the primitiveness of the *cogito, ergo sum* consciousness is distinguished from a mental process different from both these two. According to this second objection, which was explicitly raised by Gassendi (AT IX-1 205: CSM II 271), the *sum* is the conclusion of a syllogism, the premises of which are 'whatever thinks, exists' (major) and *cogito* (minor). Hence, the certainty of one's own existence depends on the prior knowledge of the major.

Now for Descartes (4) syllogistic reasoning is a discursive, indeed ratiocinative process, while the *cogito, ergo sum* is intuitive.[3] He conveys this point graphically in a much-cited letter (to Silhon or the Marquis of Newcastle) of March or April 1648:

Will you not grant me that you are less assured of the presence of the objects that you see than of the truth of this proposition: I think, therefore I am. Now this knowledge is by no means the work of your reasoning nor something which your masters taught you; your mind *sees* it, *feels* it, *handles* it. (AT V 138: CSMK 331 e.a.)

Descartes stresses the intuitive character of such knowledge also in his Replies to the Second Set of Objections, the authors of which fail to distinguish the intuitive certainty of the *cogito, ergo sum* from deductive inference, charging that the *cogito, ergo sum* cannot be relied upon without prior knowledge of God (cf. AT VII 127: CSM II 91). The reply is that, while this is true of the conclusions of deductive arguments recalled in isolation from their premises, *cogito, ergo sum* is no such argument:

[W]hen I said that we can know nothing for certain until we are aware that God exists, I expressly declared that I was speaking only of knowledge (*scientia*) of those conclusions which can be recalled when we are no longer attending to the arguments by means of which we deduced them. Now the awareness (*notitia*) of first principles is not normally called 'knowledge' (*scientia*) by dialecticians. And when we become aware (*advertimus*) that we are thinking things, this is a primary notion, as it were (*prima quaedam notio*), which is not derived by means of any syllogism (*ex nullo syllogismo*). When someone says 'I am thinking, therefore I am, or I exist,' he does not deduce existence from thought by means of a syllogism (*per syllogismum*), but recognizes it as something self-evident by a simple intuition of the mind (*simplici mentis intuitu*). This is clear from the fact that if he were deducing it by means of a syllogism, he would have to have had previous knowledge of the major premise 'Everything which thinks is, or exists'; yet in fact he learns it from experiencing in his own case (*apud se experiatur*) that it is impossible that he should think without existing. It is in the nature of our mind to form general propositions out of knowledge of particulars. (AT VII 140f.: CSM II 100)

The operative distinction in this passage is obviously between knowledge that is pre-discursive, that is, intuitive and acquired through immediate inner experience of a particular instance, and deduction as a ratiocinative process. However, in the final sentence a more encompassing distinction is adumbrated between knowledge that begins from particulars, proceeding thence to the general, and knowledge that proceeds from the general to the particular in the manner of deductive reasoning. The capital point is the precise nature of the process whereby the mind 'forms' general notions and principles on the basis of prior knowledge of particulars, a process that Descartes regards as revealing the very nature of the human mind. Does this progress of the mind take place *within* pre-discursive knowledge itself, such that the general is *intuited* in the particular? Or is it rather a process of transition *from* intuition proper to discursive knowledge, the universal being graspable only in and through the discursive operations of the mind? We shall see that the former is the correct alternative and that this sheds an interesting light, not just on Descartes's attitude toward formal logic and the synthetic method, but above all on the analytic method of discovery described as "the truest method of instruction," it having been this method "alone" that Descartes employed in the *Meditations* (AT VII 156: CSM II 11).

15.2 Implict and explicit knowledge

That the first is indeed the correct alternative is apparent from Descartes's reply to Burman's charge of inconsistency between the remark in the Second Replies that our awareness of ourselves as thinking things is not derived from any syllogism (*ex nullo syllogismo*) and *Principles*, I, 10. In the *Principles* Descartes anticipates both objections to the primitiveness of the *cogito, ergo sum* that we have been considering:

And when I said that the proposition 'I am thinking, therefore I exist' is the first and most certain of all to occur to anyone who philosophizes in an orderly way, I did not, in saying that, deny that one must first know what thought, existence and certainty are, and that it is impossible that that which thinks should not exist (*quod fieri non possit, ut id quod cogitet non existat*), and so forth. But because these are very simple notions (*simplicissimae notiones*) which on their own provide us with no knowledge of anything that exists, I did not think they needed to be listed. (AT VIII-1 8: CSM I 196)

Though the proposition 'it is impossible that that which thinks should not exist' is universal, and though it is here allowed to be prior to the *cogito, ergo sum* in some sense, nowhere is the priority said or implied to be the logical priority of a universal major to a particular conclusion within a syllogistic inference. That is why one can legitimately wonder whether this passage is indeed inconsistent with the Second Replies, as Burman thought it was.[4] If we consider the phrase *ex nullo syllogismo* alone, which is all Burman cites from the Second Replies, it is not; whereas if we take the whole passage into consideration, there does seem to be a fundamental inconsistency. For the passage from the Second Replies not only denies that *cogito, ergo sum* is derived from a previously known universal proposition by means of a syllogism, but also, in its final sentence, that knowledge of particulars, of which the *cogito, ergo sum* is an instance, depends upon prior knowledge of the general in any sense whatever, our mind being "so constituted by nature that general propositions are formed out of the knowledge of particulars." The *Principles*, on the other hand, clearly assert that the *cogito, ergo sum* depends upon the "simple" or universal notions 'thought,' 'existence,' and 'it is impossible that that which thinks should not exist.'

Though the evidence of the conversation with Burman is insufficient to determine exactly where the latter thought the contradiction lay, there is a certain way of construing the difficulty that seems to accord best with Descartes's response. Suppose Burman found this passage inconsistent with the phrase *ex nullo syllogismo* in the Second Replies because he was at a loss to conceive the priority of the general 'it is impossible that that which thinks should not be' to 'I think, therefore I am' otherwise than on the syllogistic model. To remove this difficulty, it would be sufficient to draw attention to an altogether different sense of derivativeness and dependence among items within the order of knowledge. This is the course that Descartes in fact adopts.

His reply falls into three distinct parts. That he takes Burman to understand *Principles*, I, 10 as asserting a logical dependence of the *cogito, ergo sum* on certain general notions and principles is clear from the first part, in which the point is restated using the logical terms 'major' and 'conclusion':

Before this inference (*conclusio*), 'I am thinking, therefore I exist,' the major 'whatever thinks, exists' can be known; for it is in reality prior to my inference, and my inference depends on it. That is why the author says in the *Principles* that the major premise comes first, namely because implicitly it is always presupposed and prior. (AT V 147: CSMK 333)

The obvious force of this is to allow that the *Principles* assert, as Burman correctly supposes, the dependence of the *cogito, ergo sum* on the principle 'whatever thinks is,' and to endorse that assertion. The further assumption that the dependence is logical in nature is evoked by the use of the terms 'conclusion' and 'major,' though not endorsed, since the second part of the reply is devoted to elaborating a quite different sense in which knowledge of the *cogito, ergo sum* derives from certain universal notions and principles:

But it does not follow that I am always expressly and explicitly aware (*expresse et explicite cognosco*) of its priority [*scil.* that of the 'major' 'whatever thinks, is'], or that I know it before my inference. This is because I am attending only to *what I experience within myself* (*in me experior*), for example, 'I am thinking, therefore I exist.' I do not pay attention in the same way to the general notion 'whatever thinks, exists.' As I have explained before, we do not separate out these propositions from the particular instances; rather it is in particular instances that we think of them. This then is the sense in which the words cited here [*ex nullo syllogismo*] should be taken. (AT V 147: CSMK 333 e.a.)

The phrase translated 'as I have explained before' refers to a distinction drawn just before this, a distinction between "common principles and axioms" considered "in the abstract, or apart from material things and particular instances" (AT V 146: CSMK 332), and those same principles and axioms as they are known in and through particulars. The 'principles' etc. cited as examples are the law of (non-)contradiction and the innate "ideas of God and of ourselves" (ibid.). It is important to consider this third part of Descartes's reply to Burman in interpreting the second. Speaking of the First Meditation Descartes is reported as saying that

the author is considering at this point a man who is only just beginning to philosophize and who is paying attention only to what he knows himself to know (*quae scit se nosse*). As regards the common principles and axioms (*principia communia et axiomata*), for example, 'It is impossible that one and the same thing should both be and not be,' men who are creatures of the senses (*homines sensuales*), as we all are at a pre-philosophical level, do not consider these or pay attention to them. On the contrary, since they are at present in us from birth [*innata*] with such clarity, and since we experience them within ourselves (*in semetipsis experiuntur*), we neglect them (*omittunt*) and think about them only in a confused manner and never in the abstract and apart from material things and particular instances (*in abstracto et separata a materia et singularibus*). Indeed, if people were to think about these principles in this way, no one would have any doubt about them; and if the sceptics had done so, no one would ever have been a sceptic; for they cannot be denied by anyone who carefully focuses his attention on them. (AT V 146: CSMK 332)

The chief distinction put to work in the second part of the reply to Burman is that between implicit and explicit knowledge. There the contrast is between explicit knowledge of my own particular thought and existence, including the principle *cogito, ergo sum*, and the implicit knowledge of certain general principles having no existential import, for instance, 'whatever thinks, exists.' However, in the third part a similar distinction is drawn between two kinds of knowledge of general propositions: between implicit knowledge of universal principles *in concreto*, that is, *in singularibus*, and explicit knowledge of those same principles *in abstracto et separata a materia et singularibus*. This is plain from the reference to *homines sensuales* who do not attend to these general principles (*non considerant nec attendunt*), though, as long as they are conscious of their thinking, even if only in the diverse modes of sense-perception, they cannot fail to "experience them in themselves," that is, to know them implicitly, since they are inborn (*innata*). Not having attended to these principles, the *homo sensualis* is apt to deny them when first confronted with them; not so, however, the man who applies his mind to them attentively (*attente ad illa animadvertit*). Even the "man who is only just beginning to philosophize" is at bottom just a *homo sensualis*. He expressly attends only to "what he knows himself to know" (*scit se nosse*) and hence overlooks the simple notions and principles of the natural light that he knows without knowing that he knows them, that is, without attending to them. Even when, no longer a pure beginner, he comes to know the principle *cogito, ergo sum* explicitly, that is, both to experience it in himself and attend to or know that which he experiences, he still does not attend to the general principle 'whatever thinks, exists' or the simple notions of thought, existence, certainty, freedom, and so on, that he experiences, as he does the *cogito, ergo sum*, but without knowing them explicitly and "in separation" from the latter. That comes later in an order of philosophizing of which the *cogito, ergo sum* is the starting point.

From the third part of the reply to Burman it is plain that the distinction between the implicit and the explicit does not coincide with that between the universal and the particular since common notions and universal principles may be known explicitly as well as implicitly. As for the principle *cogito, ergo sum*, it presumably remains knowledge of the particular even though explicitly grasped *in abstracto* (cf. chapter 17 below). The distinction between the implicit and the explicit also cuts across that between intuition and discursive reasoning. For whether implicit or explicit, the knowledge of common notions and principles remains intuitive, a form of insight rather than discursive analysis or ratiocinative inference. Three things are distinguished in the reply to Burman, all of which belong to the order of intuition itself: (1) implicit knowledge of certain simple and universal notions and principles; (2) explicit knowledge of the *cogito, ergo sum*; and (3) explicit knowledge of those same universal notions and principles referred to under (1). All three are stages in what was earlier termed *persuasio*, that is, within intuition itself.

Burman's difficulty thus resolves itself in the following manner. The *Principles* assert that (1) is prior to (2), and in the first part of his reply to Burman Descartes confirms that (2) really is dependent upon (1), which precedes it. The Second Replies, however, state that no syllogism, no discursive reasoning is involved, since it is in the nature of the mind to proceed from the particular to the universal, that is, as the second part of the reply to Burman makes clear, from (2) to (3), from the explicit knowledge of the *cogito, ergo sum* to the explicit knowledge of the logical, mathematical, and metaphysical principles of the natural light, the eternal truths implicitly contained in it, including 'whatever thinks, is.' (1), (2), and (3), however, all belong to the domain of pre-discursive knowledge. In question is, in each case, intuition, direct insight, inner experience, accompanied by varying degrees of attention to the intuited; not, however, (4) discursive or ratiocinative processes of the kinds mentioned previously.[5]

It appears from the foregoing that the task of reconciling the Second Replies and the *Principles*, while showing that the *cogito, ergo sum* cannot be part of a syllogism with a suppressed major premise, falls, not to the implicit-explicit distinction alone, but to three different distinctions, two of which (particular-general, intuitive-discursive) figured already in the previous replies to challenges to the primitiveness of the *cogito, ergo sum*. Still, the implicit-explicit distinction deserves pride of place.[6] By contrast with these three, the further distinction between "simple notions" having no existential import and existential propositions like 'I exist,' of which much appears to be made in the *Principles*, features in a relatively minor way.[7]

In interpreting the passages cited earlier from the Sixth Replies, *The Search for Truth*, and the Second Replies, three quite different forms of cognition were considered: second- and higher-order reflexive acts directed upon acts; definitions by genus and specific difference; and syllogistic reasoning. Set over against such reflexive, discursive, and ratiocinative knowledge is that which, in the same sequence of passages, Descartes variously designates *conscientia, testimonium internum, experientia, simplex mentis intuitus,* and *cognitio interna quae reflexam semper antecedit.* However, the reply to Burman brings to light a characteristic 'movement' or 'inference' of the mind *within* pre-discursive knowledge: the mind's progress from the implicit understanding of certain simple notions and universal principles *in concreto* to the explicit philosophical (though still intuitive) grasp of those very notions and principles *in abstracto*. The essence of this process consists in attending explicitly to what is only implicit in the mind's intuitive certainty that it thinks and therefore exists. Thus, *reflexive attention* begins *after* (1) the merely implicit knowledge of innate universal notions and principles. It makes possible (2) the *explicit* knowledge of one's own *particular* thinking and existence, *cogito, ergo sum*. Further reflexion leads to (3) the explicit grasp of the *abstract* principle *cogito, ergo sum*, along with all the other abstract or universal notions and principles mentioned already. All this is prior to (4) the discursive employment of those same principles *in abstracto* in definitions and deductive reasoning. In view of its role within the analytic method of discovery (of which more below), this reflexive attention might be called 'analytical reflexion' or 'reflexive analysis' in order to distinguish it from *scientia reflexa* and from logical reflexion, both of which belong to a later and derivative stage of philosophical enquiry. In terms of the schema just introduced, its place is before discursive reasoning, (4). To the extent that (3), the explicit knowledge of "common principles," "axioms," and 'general notions" *in abstracto*, is the starting point of logical definition and deductive reasoning, the latter can only succeed, never precede, intuition and reflexive attention to the intuited.

15.3 Consciousness and reflexion

What has been termed 'analytical reflexion' or 'reflexive analysis' might also be called 'reflexive consciousness' in view of a rather special use of the term *conscius* in another passage from the conversations with Burman.

What Descartes understands by *conscientia* resembles *scientia reflexa* in that it too is reflexive; but unlike *scientia reflexa*, *conscientia* designates that constitutive reflexive structure that belongs to every act of thinking as such. "I claim that we have ideas not only of all that is in our intellect," writes Descartes to Mersenne in a letter of 28 January 1641, "but also of all that is in the will. For we cannot will anything without knowing that we will it, nor could we know this except by means of an idea" (AT III 295: CSMK 172). That *conscientia* refers to an act-structure rather than an act is well brought out by the emphatic denial that the idea of the act (in this case, the perception of volition) "is different from" the act (volition) itself: "but I do not claim that the idea is different from the act itself" (ibid.).

This passage calls for a brief terminological digression before broaching the main philosophical point as brought out by two further objections of Burman. The term rendered 'act' in the above quotation is the French *action*. There are at least three senses of 'action,' in Descartes, as there are two quite distinct senses of 'passion' (cf. AT XI 342f.: CSM I 335f.). The latter are well known: 'passions' are either (1) 'perceptions' in general ('passions' in the loose sense) or (2) that particular species of perception that we today call 'emotion' ('passions' in the strict sense). The senses of 'action' are usually less sharply distinguished. In the first sense, only (1) those mental acts that originate in the will are actions, all other mental acts being species of perception and thus passions in the loose rather than actions in this strict sense. It is in this narrow sense that *action* is used in the passage just quoted, for the act in question is a volition. In a second sense, however, both perceptions and volitions, indeed (2) all mental acts whatsoever may be termed 'actions' or 'operations' of the mind. Thus, in this passage *action* has this second sense as well. Finally, (3) certain ways of performing acts, namely with reflexive attention to that of which we are conscious rather than that of which we are thinking, are called 'actions' by Descartes.

Now it seems that, in the passage cited above, Descartes is using the term 'idea' to refer to the immediate reflexive awareness of one's actually occurring acts of thinking, that is, for an act-structure rather than an act of thinking. We have already seen *percipere* used in this way (cf. section 8.4). Discussion of Descartes's use of the term 'idea' must be left for the next chapter (cf. 16.3 for this particular use). Regardless of exactly how 'idea' is used here, what Descartes is saying is something like this: I do not claim that the 'consciousness of volition' or 'volition of which one is immediately conscious' means anything different than 'volition' *tout court*. That this is so is clear from the parallel passages within the Third Replies and the *Passions of the Soul*:

I am taking the word 'idea' to refer to whatever is immediately perceived by the mind [same use of 'idea']. For example, when I want something, or am afraid of something, I *simultaneously* perceive that I want, or am afraid; and this is why I count volition and fear among my ideas. (AT VII 181: CSM II 127 e.a.)

For it is certain that we cannot will anything without thereby perceiving that we are willing it. And although willing something is an action with respect to our soul, the perception of such willing may be said to be a passion in the soul. But because this perception is really one and the same thing as the volition (*ne sont en effet qu'une mesme chose*), and names are always determined by whatever is most noble, we do not normally call it a 'passion,' but solely an 'action.' (AT XI 343: CSM I 335f.)

In light of these passages it seems reasonably clear that when Descartes writes "but I do not claim that the idea is different from the act (*action*) itself," he means by *action* the volition itself as involving consciousness, that is, as an act. In other words, it is the first and second senses of 'action' that are in question. We shall consider a use of the same term in the third sense presently.

So much for terminological preliminaries. The chief philosophical point arising from Burman's further objections is this. *Conscientia* or awareness of my act (of volition, say) is not itself a discrete act "different" from the act of which I am conscious (the volition). Rather, it designates the reflexive structure inherent in all acts. It follows that attending to, or analytical reflexion upon, that which is implicit in *conscientia* cannot be a discrete act of thinking in its own right either. Still, the intuitive process whereby the implicit contents of thinking are rendered explicit is undeniably an *action* of sorts. It is in response to the further objection brought by Burman against the doctrine "there can be nothing in the mind ... of which we are not conscious (*cuius [res cogitans] non sit conscia*)" (AT VII 246:

CSM II 171) that Descartes makes it clear that reflexive attention to what is implicitly contained within an act is not itself a further act. Here he specifically terms reflexive attention *reflectere*, sharply distinguishing it from reflexion understood as a second-order act of thinking directed upon another act.

Burman urges a somewhat confusing but obviously very radical objection designed to render the very notion of reflexive awareness of one's own thought incoherent. If the sense in which it takes 'to be conscious' were admissible, the objection would show, not just that there can in fact be some thoughts of which we are not conscious, but that there can be no thought of which we are strictly speaking conscious. In what way, Burman asks,

could you be conscious, since to be conscious is to think [i.e., an act]? To think that you are conscious you go on to another thought (*ad aliam cogitationem*) [i.e., you pass on to a different act having as its object a no longer actual act], and thus you are no longer thinking of what you were thinking previously, and thus you are not conscious of thinking (*non es conscius te cogitare*) but of having thought (*te cogitasse*). (AT V 149: CSMK 335)

In short, one cannot be conscious of the act of thinking something at the very moment one is thinking it; one can at best be conscious now of the act of having thought something a moment ago.[8]

To this Descartes replies:

To be conscious (*conscium esse*) is certainly to think (*cogitare*) and to reflect (*reflectere*) on one's thought; but that this cannot occur so long as the previous thought remains (*manente priori cogitatione*) is false, because, as we have already seen, the soul can think several things at the same time, persevere in its thought, and whenever it pleases reflect on its thought, and thus be conscious of its thought. (ibid.)

The word *reflectere* is here used to designate what we have called 'reflexive attention' to what one is thinking; and *conscium esse* is used, *for once*, synonymously with *reflectere*. That is, in this context 'being conscious' does not designate that necessary structural feature of every act that Descartes has in mind when he insists that "there can be no thought in us of which, at that moment in which it is in us, we are not conscious" (AT VII 246: CSM II 171), or, as he puts it in the First Set of Replies, "there can be nothing within me of which I am not in some way aware (*conscius*) (AT VII 107: CSM II 77). 'Being conscious' is here something that the mind can do "as often as it pleases" rather than something it does always and necessarily in virtue of the inherent structure of its acts.[9] Perhaps it is only because Burman mistakenly takes *conscius* to imply the occurrence of a further act at a subsequent moment in time that Descartes, wishing to oppose to this the simultaneous *action* of reflecting, takes *conscium esse* in the sense of reflexive attention, contrary to his customary use of *conscientia* and *conscius*.[10] At any rate, if, on the strength of this passage, we designate reflexive attention or analytical reflexion 'reflexive *consciousness*' as well, it is important to distinguish it from *conscientia simpliciter*. The latter is pre-reflexive in a special, heightened sense, namely: prior to second- and higher-order reflexive acts (*scientia reflexa*); prior to discursive and ratiocinative reflexion; and prior to reflexive attention as well.

The words "as we have already seen" again refer Burman to a still earlier objection and reply. Burman was among those who took the Third Meditation proof of God's existence to be circular (see section 14.1). The proof, he noted, proceeds *per axiomata* (AT V 148: CSMK 334). In regard to these axioms the author of the *Meditations* cannot be certain that he is not deceived, claims Burman, as he does not yet know that there is a God who is no deceiver, this being the very thing those axioms are employed to prove. To this Descartes responds that the author can very well be certain of these axioms "since he attends to them (*ad ea attendit*); but as long as he does this, he is certain that he is not deceived, and is compelled to assent to them" (ibid.). Burman retorts that many axioms are employed in the proof; since an act of thinking takes place in an instant, he argues, the mind, confronted with many axioms, many thoughts at the same time, cannot attend to them all at once. On this follows the point that Descartes afterwards recalls:

First, it is not true that the mind can only conceive one thing at a time. It cannot indeed conceive many things at the same time (*simul*), but it can conceive more than one ... Secondly, that thought also takes place in an instant is false, since my every action (*actio*) takes place in time and I can be said to continue and persevere in the same thought (*in eadem cogitatione*) during a certain time. (ibid.)

Recalling in the passage cited before that, according to this, it is possible to think more than one thing at the same time, Descartes points out that it is therefore perfectly possible to reflect upon or be conscious of our thinking and to think 'at the same time.' But the force of the earlier passage was not just *simul*, 'at the same time,' but more particularly 'in the same thought,' *in eadem cogitatione*. To be conscious of or to reflect upon one's thinking is not to pass *ad aliam cogitationem*, as Burman supposes, but precisely "to continue and persevere in the same thought" while engaging in a further *actio* (in the third sense distinguished above). Thus, in the *Discourse*, Descartes writes that "since the action of thinking (*l'action de la pensée*) by which one believes something is different from that by which one knows that one believes it, the one is often without the other" (AT VI 23: CSM I 122). Juxtaposed here are not two *pensées*, two *cogitationes*, but two *actions*, thinking and reflexive attention to one's thinking. Though every *cogitatio* is an *actio*, the converse is not true: reflexive attention to our acts of thinking is a further action or process of the mind that, if it occurs at all, belongs to one and the same act of thinking in so far as it is performed with attention. Thus, when Descartes remarks, at the outset of his reply, that "to be conscious is certainly to think and to reflect on one's thought," he asserts neither that *conscientia* nor that reflexive attention is an act of thinking; for *conscientia*, as a necessary structure of thinking, is not in question here at all; and that reflexive attention, as a contingent action of the mind, is another rather than the same *cogitatio* is the very thing insistently denied in the remainder of the passage.[11]

15.4 Thought and reflexion

If there remains any doubt about the meaning of the passage from the *Discourse* just cited or about the relation of consciousness and reflexion to thinking, it can be dispelled by a passage in Descartes's comments on the Seventh Set of Objections by Bourdin. Responding to the latter's charge that "to enable a substance to be superior to matter and wholly spiritual ... it is not sufficient for it to think; it is further required that it should think that it is thinking, by means of a reflexive act (*actu reflexo*)," Descartes remarks:

This is as deluded as ... saying that a person who is skilled in architecture must employ a reflexive act to ponder on the fact that he has this skill before he can be an architect. It may in fact be that all architects frequently reflect on the fact that they have this skill, or at least are capable of so reflecting. But it is obvious that an architect does not need to perform this reflexive act in order to be an architect. And equally, this kind of pondering or reflecting (*consideratio sive reflexio*) is not required for a thinking substance to be superior to matter. The initial thought by means of which we become aware of something (*prima quaevis cogitatio per quam aliquid advertimus*) *does not differ from* the second [i.e., *conscientia*] by which we become aware that we were aware of it (*per quam advertimus nos advertisse*), any more than this second differs from a third [i.e., that *consideratio sive reflexio*] by which we become aware that we were aware that we were aware. (AT VII 559: CSM II 382 e.a.)

As reflecting upon the fact that one possesses a skill is to exercising it, so reflecting upon one's consciousness of one's thoughts is to thinking: just as possessing the requisite skill is essential rather than accidental to building correctly, so simple consciousness that one is thinking is essential to thinking itself; but reflecting upon one's awareness of one's thinking, like reflecting on one's possession of a skill, is a separate matter, a separate action, that need not be performed at all.

For Descartes, then, (1) neither consciousness nor reflexive attention is an *act* of thinking, though reflexion is undeniably an *action*. Moreover, (2) consciousness is simultaneous with the act *within* which it occurs, as is reflexive attention; the latter is only a heightened degree of awareness of what we are already conscious of.[12]

If we wish to make clear to ourselves just how innovative is Descartes's analysis of the structure of the mental we have only to contrast it with the dominant tradition stemming from St Thomas and followed in key respects by such leading seventeenth-century figures as Hobbes and Leibniz. Both (1) and (2) are explicitly rejected by Leibniz, who follows Aquinas and Hobbes in holding that consciousness is the product of second-order reflexive acts: "To think ... and to consider that one thinks ... are two very different thoughts" (Leibniz 1989, 188). Upon these still further reflexive acts of a yet higher order may be directed. Like Thomas and Hobbes, moreover, Leibniz was acutely sensible of the danger of an infinite regress as a result of saying that all acts are conscious in virtue of higher-order conscious acts.[13] So, of course, was Descartes, who averted this danger by making consciousness a formal act-structure rather than a higher-order act directed upon a first-order act. Leibniz avoided the difficulty by simply stopping the chain, that is, abandoning the claim that we must be conscious of all mental acts: "It is not possible that we always reflect expressly on all our thoughts," he writes,

otherwise the spirit would reflect on each reflection to infinity without ever being able to pass to a new thought. For example, in apperceiving some present sentiment, I would have to think that I have thought it, and then think that I think of thinking of it, and so on to infinity. But it is necessary that I cease to reflect on all these reflections and that there be in the end some thought which one allows to pass without thinking about it; otherwise one would dwell always on the same thing. (Leibniz 1875–90, V, 108)

On the other hand, Leibniz followed Hobbes in taking consciousness or reflection to be a form of memory. In the Third Set of Objections Hobbes writes that "although someone may think that he *was* thinking (for this thought is simply an act of remembering), it is quite impossible for him to think that he *is* thinking, or to know that he is knowing. For then an infinite chain of questions would arise: How do you know that you know that you know ...?" (AT VII 173: CSM II 122f.). So too for Leibniz: the act of thinking and the second-order act of consciousness of the original act succeed one another in time; the act of thinking of an act occurs immediately after the original act. Consciousness or reflection is just the immediate intellectual memory of having thought a moment ago. "The present or immediate memory, or the memory of that which took place immediately before, that is, the consciousness or reflection which accompanies an internal action cannot naturally deceive; otherwise one would not even be certain that one is thinking of this or that, for it is likewise only of the past action that one says that it is in one, not of the very action of saying so" (ibid., 220f.).[14]

15.5 Logic and synthetic method

The preceding account of the progress of the mind in analytical reflexion explains in large measure Descartes's attitude toward formal logic (or 'dialectics,' as he called it) and toward the synthetic method. Though typically scornful of the syllogisms of the 'dialecticians' and of logical formalism generally,[15] Descartes's discussions of the synthetic method are tinged with an element of genuine recognition. He consented, after all, to set out certain of his doctrines in synthetic order (the obvious example being the *more geometrico* proofs of God's existence and the real distinction between body and soul appended to the Second Replies); and the *Principles* as a whole are cast in a form that is broadly synthetic (as Descartes acknowledges to Burman at AT V 153: CSMK 338). Though the synthetic order of discursive reasoning, proceeding from the general to the particular, differs from the analytic order of discovery followed in the *Meditations*, it is not without utility to reflect discursively upon that which was first intuited and then made explicit through careful attention to the intuited; for discursive and ratiocinative logical analysis can serve to explicate still further those concepts and principles first grasped implicitly in intuition and then made explicit through reflexion, articulating the logical relations obtaining among them, whether in definitions and axioms or in a train of deductive reasoning.[16] This is a far cry from the often empty definitions and barren 'proofs' based on probable premises to which Descartes refers contemptuously as 'the logic of the Schools' (for instance, AT IX-2, 13). It is worth noting the more balanced tone of his criticism of Gassendi's objection to the primitiveness of the *cogito, ergo sum*:

But the most important mistake our critic makes here is the supposition that knowledge of particular propositions must always be deduced from universal ones, following the same order as that of a syllogism in dialectics. Here he shows how little he knows of the way in which we should search for truth. It is certain that if we are to discover the truth we must always begin with particular notions in order to arrive at general ones later on (though we may also reverse the order and deduce other particular truths once we have discovered general ones). (AT IX-1 205f.: CSM II 271)

This is not to say that those whom Descartes calls 'dialecticians' do not employ the method of analysis at all. On the contrary, wherever their use of syllogisms and synthetic order does in fact lead to conclusions that are certain, it is due to the circumstance that their premises were such as already contained the conclusion in the manner of that which is *already known* implicitly:

> to make it even clearer that the aforementioned art of argumentation (*illam disserendi artem*) [i.e., dialectics] contributes nothing to our knowledge of the truth, we should realize that, on the basis of their method, dialecticians are unable to formulate a syllogism with a true conclusion *unless they are already in possession of the matter of the conclusion*, i.e. *unless they have previous knowledge of the very truth deduced* in the syllogism (*nisi prius ejusdem materiam habuerint, id est, nisi eamdem veritatem, quae in illo deducitur, jam ante cognoverint*). (AT X 406: CSM I 36f. e.a.)

The point here is not that made later by John Stuart Mill and no doubt already well known to Descartes from Sextus Empiricus and the Renaissance sceptics, that syllogistic reasoning is inherently circular since knowledge of the truth of the particular conclusion is a necessary condition of knowing the truth of the universal major (cf. Curley 1978, 26f.). The criticism of Gassendi quoted above suggests that Descartes's anti-formalism rests, not on formalistic considerations of this kind, but on his peculiar conception of the nature of the human mind. If so, then the point of the unless-clause is rather that, qua *dialectician*, the practitioner of the art of argumentation is incapable of discovering any particular truth not already implicit in his premises (though yet to be explicitly discovered). By starting from probable premises and proceeding syllogistically, from the universal to the particular, the dialectician "contributes nothing to our knowledge of truth"; while if he starts from natures and axioms immediately intuited through reflexion on his own thinking, explicating in his universal major and in his particular conclusion (in part by logical analysis) only what is already implicitly contained in the minor premise regarding simple natures and the relations between them, then, even though he may present his arguments in what is outwardly the synthetic order, he will contribute positively to the growth of human knowledge – although not through his knowledge of syllogistic patterns, that is, not qua dialectician.[17]

The merely negative part of the *Regulae* passage cited last – that syllogistic reasoning contributes nothing to the growth of knowledge – is reiterated in Rule XIV where, however, instead of suggesting that the synthetic order may foster the analytic method of discovery (at least *per accidens*), Descartes treats it as a positive hindrance:

> the syllogistic forms are of no help in grasping the truth of things (*ad rerum veritatem percipiendam*). So it will be to the reader's advantage to reject them altogether and to

think of all knowledge whatever – save knowledge obtained through simple and pure intuition of a single, solitary thing – as resulting from a comparison between two or more things. In fact the business of human reason consists almost entirely (*tota fera rationis humanae industria*) in preparing for this operation [whereas dialectics makes it less, not more fit for it]. For when the operation is straightforward and simple, we have no need of a technique to help us intuit the truth which the comparison yields; all we need is *the light of nature*. (AT X 439f.: CSM I 57 e.a.)

Formal logic may indeed at times aid and complete, but at times it also threatens to distract us from, the "business of reason." Hence, Descartes is constantly vacillating in his estimate of logic, though on the whole his anti-formalism is fairly pronounced.[18]

The talk of the "business of reason" calls to mind Descartes's picturesque metaphor for the Scholastic as distinct from the analytic method of demonstration: reason "taking a holiday."

Some will perhaps be surprised that in this context, where we are searching for ways of making ourselves more skilful at deducing some truths on the basis of others, we make no mention of any of the precepts with which the dialecticians suppose they govern human reason. They prescribe certain forms of argumentation (*formas disserendi*) in which the conclusions follow with such irresistible necessity that if our reason relies on them, even though it takes, as it were, a holiday (*ferietur*) from *considering a particular inference clearly and attentively*, it can nevertheless draw a conclusion that is certain *merely in virtue of the form*. (AT X 405f.: CSM I 36 e.a.)

By contrast with this, "discernment in the methodical deduction of one thing from another" (AT X 400: CSM I 33) as described elsewhere in the *Regulae* might be called 'reason at work,' busily elaborating through careful attention to that of which one is already implicitly aware the whole network of interconnections among simple or primitive ideas and truths as well as those that follow from them.[19] And just as it sometimes falls to the dialectician's lot (though only *per accidens*) to put his reason to work, so it is the mathematician's fate at times to lapse into sterility though failure to exercise his reason:

For there is really nothing more futile than so busying ourselves with bare numbers and imaginary figures that we seem to rest content in the knowledge of such trifles. And there is nothing more futile than devoting our energies to those superficial proofs which are discovered more through chance than method and which have more to do with our eyes and imagination than our intellect; for the outcome is that, in a way, *we get out of the habit of using our reason*. (AT X 375: CSM I 18 e.a.; cf. also AT VI 17f.: CSM I 119f.)

This lax practice (Descartes is describing his own early forays into the field of mathematics) is immediately contrasted with cultivating "certain primary seeds of truth naturally implanted in human minds" (AT X 376: CSM I 18), that is, with "the light of the mind" (*mentis lumen*) itself. That this refers to the analytic method of reflexion seems obvious enough in the context; that it is the method employed by the 'true' mathematician is to be argued in what follows.[20]

15.6 Analysis and synthesis

So much for Descartes's ambivalent attitude toward logic or 'dialectics' and the synthetic method. We turn next to the 'logic of discovery' and the range of its applicability. It remains to be shown (1) that the analytic method of discovery described in the *Regulae* and employed in the *Meditations* coincides in the essentials with the process of analytical reflexion described above; and (2) that the scope of this method extends to both pure and applied mathematics (the special physical sciences) and to metaphysics itself. (1) will be attempted in this, (2) in the next section. First, a brief terminological disgression on 'analysis' in its Cartesian and Kantian uses.

Exactly how the method of analytical reflexion differs from logical procedures of deductive derivation based on "the form" (AT X 405f.: CSM I 36 e.a.) of propositions (logical operators) and on definitions of non-logical terms can perhaps be best clarified by contrasting Descartes's with Kant's analytic-synthetic distinction in a couple of key respects. For the process of *analytical*, as distinct from both discursive and ratiocinative *logical*, reflexion furnishes what, from Kant's perspective, would be 'synthetic' rather than merely analytic a priori truth or knowledge – though Descartes's own use of 'synthetic' and 'synthesis' is just the reverse of Kant's, as the following considerations should make clear.

The purely logical analysis of concepts and truths can itself be correctly described as rendering explicit what is initially only implicit. It does so, however, in a manner different from the method of analytical reflexion. For that which is implicit in the manner of an implicit *logical* consequence of the known need not itself be known, even implicitly. Thus, given the logic of the word 'knows,' 'x knows p' implies 'p'; and if 'p' entails 'q' *logically*, then 'x knows p' also implies 'q.' But it does *not* imply 'x *knows* q' or that x has ever had any idea of 'q,' *even an implicit or vague one*.[21] This, however, is precisely what is entailed when 'p' (some thought) contains 'q' (a certain idea or principle) implicitly *as capable of being made explicit through analytical reflection*. By such non-logical reflexion the mind does not first come to know something of which it was formerly completely unaware; it becomes aware of what it already *knows*, though only implicitly, that is, without having ever *attended* to the fact that it knows it. By merely logical reflexion, on the other hand, the mind becomes explicitly aware of something of which it may not have been previously aware at all.[22]

Put this way, it appears that discursive and ratiocinative logical reflexion must be called – quite literally – 'syn-thetic,' since by their means the mind actually acquires something new, augments its existing stock of knowledge by adding something it had not formerly grasped at all, not even implicitly. Although implicitly *contained* in the concepts or premises from which it is derived, prior to its derivation such knowledge was not known or grasped at all, not even vaguely or implicitly. Conversely, attending reflexively to what is already implicit in one's thinking, what one knew without knowing that one knew it, should be called 'analytic' rather than 'synthetic'; for through such reflexion no new knowledge is acquired except the knowledge that one already knew ... x. This is precisely Descartes's use of 'analysis' and its cognates. It reverses Kant's more familiar usage – or rather, Kant reversed the meaning both terms had for Descartes, which is in important respects continuous with the older tradition.

Certainly, 'analytic' and 'synthetic' are for Descartes, as for "the ancient geometers" (AT VII 156: CSM II 111; cf. also AT X 376f.: CSM I 18f. and AT VI 17: CSM I 119), the names of two fundamentally opposed *methods* or *modes of demonstration*, while for Kant they designate different types of judgments, propositions, or truths. However, to the extent that Kant is a 'justification rationalist' (cf. Miles 1986, 175), concerned, not with the origins, but the manner of justification or demonstration, of certain truths, this difference is perhaps not as fundamental as it might seem at first sight. After all, analytic judgments are those that can be *demonstrated* or *shown* to be true by the process of analysis.[23] The distance separating Descartes from Kant appears even less when one considers how closely allied are the question of *method* and the search for a first *truth* in the Cartesian project. Indeed, the problem of method must be regarded in the same light as questions of epistemology and the philosophy of mind discussed in the Introduction: as the existence and nature of the mental (as one of the two branches of the supersensible) belong unproblematically to first philosophy or metaphysics, so too the classification of the varieties of the mental and the elaboration of the correct method of discovering truth; for the method follows directly from the examination of the cognitive faculty. This overarching metaphysical framework of the problem of method is admittedly not yet in place in the *Regulae*; here it makes sense to speak of the method as the fruit of epistemological reflexion (cf. McRae 1961, 64). Even in the *Discourse*, metaphysics is one field of application of the method rather than the science of the soul dealing (among other things) with the method of discovering truth. In the *Meditations*, however, the universal method is fully integrated into the metaphysical enterprise itself. Like the *cogito* principle and other first truths, the analytic method of discovery is itself just the fruit of another 'method': *metaphysical* doubt.[24]

The apparent gap between the analytic and the synthetic as two methods and two types of truth is narrowed further by the consideration that Descartes's analytic *ratio demonstrandi* is not just a procedure for advancing or ascending from one truth to others derivative from it; it is above all a reductive procedure for reverting to a certain kind of truth as starting point (see also Kemp Smith 1952, 20 and Buchdahl 1969, 130; cf. Rule V of the *Regulae*). At bottom, the analytic method combines *both* elements: (a) selection of the correct *order* (which presupposes a *measure* by which to determine what is first), that is, choosing the proper starting point of knowledge, the simple, including simple or primitive *truths*; and (b) choice of the right path to the discovery of *all further knowledge* about the object domain circumscribed by the starting points, that is, of *all* complex objects knowable in terms of these same simples. Thus, Descartes introduces the analytic/synthetic distinction in the Second Replies in the following way:

I make a distinction between two things which are involved in the *modo scribendi geometrico*, the order, and the manner of demonstration (*ratio demonstrandi*):
    The order consists simply in this. The items which are put forward first must be known entirely without the aid of what comes later; and the remaining items must be arranged in such a way that their demonstration depends solely on what has gone before. I did try to follow this order very carefully in my *Meditations* ... As for the manner of demonstration, this divides into two varieties: the first proceeds by analysis and the second by synthesis. (AT VII 155f.: CSM II 110f.)

At first glance it appears from this that the *rationes demonstrandi*, analysis and synthesis, fall under (b), the path, which can be traversed in different directions. However, (a), the selection of the starting point, determines the way the path is traversed. And since the manner of advancing from first to other truths is an essential part of each method, it can be said that *a certain kind* of synthesis is integral even to the analytic method. In the French version, the last sentence is expanded to read: "l'une par l'analyse *ou resolution*, & l'autre par la synthese *ou composition*" (AT IX-1 121 e.a.). Given the dual aspect of the analytic method, it is not surprising that Röd (1971, 12) draws a distinction between resolution and composition on the one hand and analysis and synthesis on the other; for analysis *includes* a certain progression or 'composition' – one hesitates to say 'synthesis' – of its own. The 'way up' is the ascent from that which is first in the order of cognition *for us*, the knowledge of the particular, the concrete, to that which is first in the order of knowing itself, the abstract universal principles implicit in, and really presupposed by, the starting point of knowledge, though explicitly known only later; the 'way down' is the advance from the first truth *and* these abstract principles to other truths derivable from them.[25]

Synthesis, Descartes goes on to explain, involves "a long series of definitions, postulates, axioms, theorems and problems, so that if anyone denies one of the conclusions it can be shown at once that it is contained in what has gone before" (AT VII 156: CSM 110f.). Analysis, by contrast, "contains nothing to compel belief in an argumentative or inattentive reader" who "fails to attend to even the smallest point," there being "many truths which, although they must be attended to, are scarcely touched upon, since they are clear to anyone who pays attention" (ibid.). In the synthetic 'mode,' one lays out *first* those things that *are* first in themselves, making them explicit at the outset in definitions, axioms, and postulates before deducing theorems and problems from them. One thus proceeds "a posteriori," working back from 'effect' to 'cause,' that is, from the conclusions (theorems) to be proved to the 'grounds' for them (premises). Analysis, by contrast, starts from what is first *for us*, namely particular truths intuitively grasped in inner experience, proceeding thence to the universal concepts and axioms that careful attention reveals as already implicit in them. Though cognitively prior in themselves, the latter are disclosed through analytical reflexion only later in the order of cognition, whence synthesis, which sets them out explicitly first, is *in a way* "more a priori" than analysis. Analysis is, however, also a priori in so far as it starts from truths first *for us* and proceeds via others discovered later (yet first in themselves) to an intuitive grasp of still further items of knowledge likewise implicit in these first truths and capable of being made explicit through a sustained process of reflexive attention to inner experience along with logical analysis.

Doctrinally, these remarks from the Second Replies represents virtually no change from the *Regulae*, where the term 'analysis' is used only sparingly.[26] In Rule II Descartes notes "that there are two ways of arriving at a knowledge of things – through experience and through deduction (*per experientiam vel deductionem*)."

Moreover, we must note that while our experiences of things are often deceptive (*experientias rerum saepe esse fallaces*), the deduction or pure inference (*deductionem vero, sive illationem puram*) of one thing from another can never be performed faultily by an intellect which is in the least degree rational, though it may be omitted if not seen [i.e., through "inadvertence," as Descartes puts it a few lines later]. Furthermore, those chains with which dialecticians suppose they regulate human reason seem to me to be of little use here, though I do not deny that they are very useful for other purposes. In fact none of the errors to which men ... are liable is ever due to faulty inference; they are due only to the fact that men take for granted certain poorly understood experiences (*experimenta quaedam parum intellecta supponantur*), or lay down rash and unfounded judgements. (AT X 365: CSM I 12)

Surprising is the air of sheer obviousness with which commentators are disposed to take *experimenta* in this passage to mean 'observation' and *deductio* to refer to logical derivation as the procedure of the mathematical sciences (cf., for example, Buchdahl 1969, 83). As far as *deductio* is concerned, the syllogistic inferences of the "dialecticians," whose premises are not certain, are expressly *excluded* from the extension of the term in the above passage; for such indirect logical inferences from *merely probable* premises fail to meet the condition stated in the earlier definition of 'deduction' as "all that is necessarily inferred from other things *known with certainty*" (*illud omne quod ex quibusdam alijs cognitis certis necessario concluditur*) (AT X 369: CSM I 15 e.a.). The "deduction or pure inference of one thing from another" is another matter, however. This refers to immediate logical inferences of a very simple kind. Otherwise it would be difficult to see why they "can never be performed faultily by an intellect which is in the least degree rational," since logical errors occur quite frequently, as do errors in mathematical reckoning, once we advance beyond the simplest operations.[27] However, direct inferences of one proposition from another are nowhere sharply distinguished from the process of analytical reflexion in the *Regulae*. That is why Descartes goes on to suggest that error occurs not just through failure to notice the inferences to be drawn but especially through choosing as starting points or premises *experimenta* (things immediately experienced inwardly) which are *parum intellecta*, that is, not clearly and distinctly perceived. The point is not just that such *experimenta* are not certain, so that nothing directly inferred from them by logical means can be certain either; what makes such experiences downright "deceptive" (*fallaces*) rather than just unreliable is the fact that men either (1) suppose more to be contained in them than is actually immediately present to consciousness; or (2) fail to attend carefully to all that is actually contained in them.[28] In the former case, in particular, it is further analytical reflexion on experience that produces a doubt, not the subsequent discovery of an immediate logical inference (or link in a chain of inferences) that had initially escaped one's notice. This is implied in the reason why arithmetic and geometry "prove to be much more certain than other disciplines: they alone are concerned with an object so pure and simple that they *make no assumptions* that experience might render uncertain (*nihil plane supponant, quod experientia reddiderit incertum*)" (AT X 365: CSM I 12 e.a.). In this connection it is worth quoting the oft-cited definition of *intuitus* in Rule III: "the conception of a clear and attentive mind, which is so easy and distinct that there can be *no room for doubt about what we are understanding*" (*mentis purae et attentae tam facilem distinctumque conceptum vt de eo, quod intelligimus, nulla prorsus dubitatio relinquatur*) (AT X 368: CSM I 14 e.a.). For such "easy and distinct" conceptions are *experimenta perfecte intellecta* as opposed to the *experimenta parum intellecta* of the passage cited above.

If this is correct, then the word *experimenta* refers to *inner* experience of con-

cepts and truths immediately present to consciousness, the starting points of knowledge, while *deductio* covers immediate logical inferences as well as the fruits of
analytical reflexion on those innate ideas and axioms. The further conclusion
Descartes draws from the certainty of arithmetic and geometry is not that only
pure mathematics deserves to be called 'science,' but "that in seeking the right
path of truth we ought to concern ourselves only with objects which admit of as
much certainty as the demonstrations of arithmetic and geometry" (AT X 366:
CSM I 12f.) For as with the truths of arithmetic and geometry, so in the sciences
generally,

all truths are interconnected (*se invicem consequuntur*) and are mutually held together by
a bond (& *mutuo inter se vinculo continentur*). The whole secret is [a] to *begin* with the
first and simplest truths, and then [b] to *proceed* gradually and as it were step by step to
the most remote and most complex truths (*a primis et simplicissimis incipiamus, & deinde
sensim & quasi per gradus usque ad remotissimas & maxime compositas progrediamur*).
(AT X 526f.: CSM II 420 e.a.)

This passage from *The Search for Truth* should be understood in the light of the
doctrine of the Second Replies and the *Regulae*. To translate the initial sentence
in the manner of Cottingham et al. (cf. CSM II 419f.), "all truths follow *logically*
from one another" (e.a.), is simply to ignore all that is distinctive about the analytic method of discovery and therefore all that is new and innovative in Descartes's
reflexions on method. It is likewise Descartes's conception of the analytic method
of discovery that lies behind the often cited but frequently misunderstood passage in Rule I: "It must be acknowledged that all the sciences are so closely
interconnected (*inter se connexas*) that it is much easier to learn them all together
than to separate one from the other" (AT X 361: CSM I 10; cf. the even more
famous passage from the *Discourse* at AT VI 19: CSM I 12). Any translation that
highlights *logical* deduction and thereby *synthetic* method and a *deductivist* model
of science exaggerates the importance of what is surely a minor and, relatively
speaking, barren intellectual operation in Descartes's eyes. Of key importance is
the method of analytic reflexion on the clearly and distinctly perceived data of
inner experience by which the mind advances from the "seeds" of knowledge to
the explicit understanding of all that is implicit in them.[29]

15.7 The mathematical model

In the preceding section it was argued that the analytic method of discovery refers principally, though not exclusively, to the process of analytical reflection. It
remains to be shown that the scope of this method extends both to pure and applied mathematics as well as to the metaphysical treatment of mind, matter, and

God. That the method described in the *Regulae* is that employed in the mathematical sciences, and that Descartes there advocates its extension to the special physical sciences, is quite uncontroversial; contentious are the joint claims that the method is that of metaphysics and that its essence (and hence that of mathematics) consists in analytical reflection. The word *mathēsis* provides a useful starting point.

The preceding account of the progress of the mind in analytical reflection sheds an interesting light on Heidegger's claim (1962, 53ff., esp. 57 and 80) that the measure of the influence of the 'mathematical' ideal of knowledge on seventeenth-century thought is not so much its preoccupation with calculation and quantitative methods as its appreciation of the original Greek sense of *mathēsis*: "Zur-Kenntnis-nehmen dessen, was wir schon haben" ('taking cognizance of what we already know'). As early as the *Regulae*, in which there is as yet no explicit terminological distinction between *conscientia* and *reflexio* (see section 20.3), Descartes notes that

since it is not easy to review all the connections together [i.e., the individual series of interconnected truths], and moreover, since our task is not so much to retain them in our memory as to distinguish them with, as it were, the sharp edge of our minds (*acumen ingenij*), we must seek a means of developing our intelligence in such a way (*aliquid ad ingenia ita formanda*) that we can notice them immediately whenever the need arises. In my experience, there is no better way of doing this than *by accustoming ourselves to reflecting with some discernment on the minute details of the things we have already perceived*. (AT X 384: CSM I 22f.)

There is no better way, in short, than reflexive attention (*cum sagacitate reflectere*) to the minute details (*ad minima*) of what we *already* know, that is, what we are pre-reflexively conscious of (*quae jam ante percepimus*). For the latter, Descartes also uses the term *perspicacitas* in the *Regulae*, so that *perspicacitas* and *sagacitas* correspond in the essentials to the later *conscientia* and *reflexio*. Although "discernment (*sagacitas*) in the methodical deduction of one thing from another" is directly opposed to "perspicacity (*perspicacitas*) in the distinct intuition of particular things" (AT X 400: CSM I 33), the two are nevertheless continuous, discrete stages in a progressively unfolding process of intuition. They "seem to coalesce into a single operation," Descartes remarks, "through a single movement of thought, as it were, which involves carefully intuiting one thing and passing on at once to the others" (AT X 408: CSM I 38). Whether they are called 'insight' and 'inference,' or, as Descartes prefers to say in the *Regulae*, *intuitus* and *deductio*, matters little; at issue is the correct understanding of Descartes's theory of the mind. The vital point is therefore that deduction cannot be equated with (though it does not exclude) logical inference, being primarily a matter of focusing one's attention selectively on all that is contained implicitly within a single intuition, thus rendering explicit what is first known only implicitly. Instead of *deductio* he also uses the terms *enumeratio* and *inductio*. The reasons for the substitution, along with the fluid and fixed boundaries between *deductio* and mental intuition, will be considered in section 20.1 below.

The bearing of this distinction on the 'heuristic paradox' of the *Meno* (80 D–E) and on Aristotle's notion of *epagōgē* should be lost on no one.[30] Of course, in the *Regulae* Descartes appears to attach no such significance as Heidegger to the Greek *word* for learning. Simply equating *mathēsis* and the Latin *disciplina*, he notes that applied sciences such as "astronomy, music, optics, mechanics, among others" have as much right to be called 'mathematics' as the 'pure' mathematical sciences, arithmetic, geometry, and algebra (AT X 378: CSM I 19). But on closer inspection he observes that "the exclusive concern of mathematics is with questions of *order or measure*" (ibid., e.a.). The abstract *mathesis universalis* he then goes on to describe, a more general science even than pure arithmetic and geometry (*mathesis vulgaris*), abstracts from the subject matters of all particular disciplines, confining itself to the *principles of order and measure*. By distinguishing the simple from the complex by reference to "some third term" (cf. AT X 451: CSM I 65), to a "common *measure*" (ibid., e.a.), the "true mathematics" (AT X 377: CSM I 19) reduces the complex to the simpler and the simpler to the simplest, beginning every enquiry from the simplest and proceeding thence to the more complex in accordance with the correct *order*.

It is tempting to interpret "order and measure" so narrowly that "the conception of a *mathesis universalis* in Descartes is restricted to the realm of measurable quantities and proportions in their usual mathematical sense" (Mittelstraß 1979, 603, cf. also 1978, 192; Kemp Smith 1952, 90ff.). Yet the matter is by no means straightforward.[31] True, Descartes describes his method as having been successfully applied only to pure mathematics *thus far* (Rule II); and the whole point of the regress from (1) mixed or applied to (2) "pure" (AT X 385: CSM I 23) and thence to (3) the "true" (AT X 376: CSM I 18f.) or universal mathematics is ostensibly to demonstrate the possibility and necessity of extending the method to *all* physical subjects in so far as they admit of mathematical treatment. Rule XII shows how this might be accomplished in the physical explanation of colours (AT X 413: CSM I 40f.), while Rule XIII uses sound to illustrate how "imperfect [physical] problems can all be reduced to perfect [mathematical] ones" (AT X 431: CSM I 52) – a task Descartes was to come to regard (not without a certain ambiguity) as "beyond the reach of the human mind" (cf. AT I 250f.: CSMK 38; and AT II 142: CSMK 103), abandoning it and leaving the *Regulae* a literary torso.

However, Descartes's predilection for using purely numerical ratios, ratios of extensions, and other pure and applied mathematical examples provides only scant support for this interpretation, especially in the Rules after XII, where the treatment of 'simple propositions' ends and that of the perfectly understood mathematical problems begins.[32] In Rule IV Descartes states unequivocally: "This discipline should contain the primary rudiments of human reason and extend to the discovery of truths *in any field whatever* (*ad veritates ex quovis subjecto eliciendas se extendere debet*)" (AT X 374: CSM I 17).[33] The universal science of order and measure described more fully in the headings of Rules V and VI is illustrated in the sequel by examples drawn predominantly, it is true, though not exclusively, from mathematics and physics. The wording of both Rules suggests that *order* is best understood very broadly in terms of the *relations of prior and posterior*, while *measure* is to be interpreted in the light of the general distinction between *the varieties of the simple and the complex* (or "absolute" and "relative" as Descartes designates them, still more generally, in Rule VI).[34] Thus, when Descartes writes in Rule VI that "we should attend to what is most simple in each series of things ... and should observe how all the rest are more, or less, or equally, removed from the simplest," he understands the simplest" as the "common measure" of the more complex, that is, the simple as "common natures" (AT X 440: CSM I 57) and the common natures as common measures of the complex. If so, it is mistaken to suggest that the method cannot be applied outside pure and applied mathematics to simple and complex propositions bearing on metaphysical subjects like God and the soul.[35]

This not only seems contrary to the plain sense of Rules V and VI; it runs counter to the quite parallel treatment of mathematical and metaphysical illustrations in one important context. Distinguishing in Rule XII between necessary and merely contingent "conjunctions" of simple natures, Descartes provides examples of the former from both mathematics and metaphysics. The plain fact that his philosophical example conforms to the pattern of analytical reflexion described earlier rather than to the 'synthetic' method of logical derivation strongly suggests that mathematics, too, is in important respects the product of one and the same operation – if indeed reason itself, as Descartes remarks of human wisdom in Rule I, "remains one and the same, however different the subjects to which it is applied, it being no more altered by them than sunlight is by the variety of the things it shines on" (AT X 360: CSM I 9). The passage reads:

[I]f I say that 4 and 3 make 7, the composition is a necessary one, for we do not have a distinct conception of the number 7 *unless in a confused sort of way we include 3 and 4 in it.* In the same way, whatever we demonstrate concerning figures or numbers necessarily links up with that of which it is affirmed. This necessity applies not just to things which are perceivable by the senses [i.e., *res corporeae*, including pure mathematical objects] but to others as well. If, for example, Socrates says that he doubts everything, it necessarily follows that he understands at least that he is doubting, and hence that he knows that something can be true or false, etc.; for there is a necessary connection between these facts and the nature of doubt. (AT X 421: CSM I 46 e.a.; on Socrates cf. also AT X 433: CSM I 53)

In this there is not the slightest indication that Descartes sees any difference between the arithmetical example considered first and the process of analytical reflexion on one's thinking (or doubting) described afterwards; nor was any such difference noted earlier in Rule III: "Thus everyone can mentally intuit that he exists, that he is thinking, that a triangle is bounded by just three lines, and a sphere by a single surface, and the like" (AT X 368: CSM I 14).[36]

If not, then those (like J.-M. Beyssade 1979, 237ff. and Röd 1971, 51f.) who stress the affinity between the later *cogito* principle and *mathematical* procedure are correct – without perhaps appreciating the extent to which it is above all the process of analytical reflexion that Descartes has in mind when he writes that "arithmetic and geometry ... consist entirely in deducing conclusions by means of rational arguments (*in consequentiis rationabiliter deducendis*)" (AT X 365: CSM I 12). There is perhaps no particular temptation, in a Cartesian context, to read *consequentia rationaliter deducenda* as referring to straightforward *logical* derivation of analytic truths from statements based on conventional definitions. But statements based on immediate intuition of simple natures may be another matter. Thus, Buchdahl (cf. 1969, 158) cites the mathematical example quoted above ("we do not have a distinct conception of the number 7 unless in a confused sort of way we include 3 and 4 in it"), remarking that it "would be tempting to interpret this as implying that Descartes thought the proposition to be 'analytic'" in Kant's sense. But, he adds, "we have seen that such sharp distinctions do not yet obtain at this stage of philosophical history." It is certainly true that the *terminology* is not fixed at this stage; yet the distinction itself between intuition (including its natural 'extension,' the process of analytical reflexion) and discursive and ratiocinative processes is both philosophically evident in itself (see previous section) and perfectly clear to Descartes, who calls the former the 'method of analysis' even though it yields what are, from Kant's perspective, synthetic a priori propositions (ibid.). Buchdahl himself goes on to suggest as much: "It is at any rate just possible that Descartes's view is more suitably explained by tightening it to give something like Kant's 'synthetic *a priori*' account of the propositions of arithmetic ... Such a view implies that the propositions in question are neither merely 'empirical' (since they are capable of acting as necessary 'norms'), nor simply the product of arbitrarily chosen definitions or axioms" (1969, 159). This seems indeed the correct view of the matter.[37]

Turning now from mathematical to physical subjects, the bearing of analytical reflexion on *mathesis universalis* appears in a fresh light. It is a commonplace that Descartes recognizes the existence of a boundary between things knowable a priori like the principles or foundations of the philosophy of nature, and the explanations of particular physical phenomena such as heat, light, sound, refraction, gravitation, magnetism, and the circulation of the blood. As interpreters eager to rescue Descartes from the shallow 'rationalist' stereotype rightly insist, the latter sort of explanation can only be successfully achieved by recourse to experiment or observation (cf. Gewirth 1941, 183 and n. 1 for references to the earliest French commentators to insist on this point; further, Kemp Smith 1952, 92ff., McRae, 1961, 64ff.; Buchdahl, 1969, 87, 96, 119ff. etc.; also Clarke, chap. 4, and a host of others). As regards these latter subjects, Descartes had no wish to be lumped together with "philosophers who take no account of experience and think that truth will spring from their brains like Minerva from the head of Jupiter" (AT X 380: CSM I 21). Of course, Descartes's reason for insisting on the need for sensory experience is characteristically metaphysical: "the supreme craftsman of the real world could have produced all that we see in several different ways" (cf. *Principles*, IV, 204), all of them compatible with the immediately intuited structure of matter and the general mechanical principles known a priori to be necessarily true in any world we are capable of conceiving clearly and distinctly (see chapter 5 n. 10). Observation, then, is required to determine which one he in fact chose. But if certainly not all, it is relatively less clear just *how much* of the science of nature Descartes actually thought capable of presentation as something resembling a formal deductive system.

It seems reasonable to assume that the situation here parallels that of logically necessary and contingent truth quite closely. Descartes retains such a distinction, it was seen, though the line of demarcation between necessary and merely contingent truths runs rather differently than we might draw it today. He includes, for example, within the realm of the logically necessary all the basic concepts and most universal laws of physics. This suggests that the method of *ordo et mensura*, too, is applicable to portions of the applied mathematical sciences that we today regard as requiring a different sort of treatment. True, Descartes himself saw these sciences as unable to progress very far without recourse to "suppositions" or subsidiary hypotheses about which no more than moral certainty is attainable, no matter how well confirmed the hypotheses are by the phenomena. But beyond the most general principles common to them all, he certainly regarded the first principles proper to each science as amenable to discovery by an a priori method. If the parallel with logically necessary and contingent truth holds, it is certain that much (though uncertain *how* much) that would nowadays be regarded as 'hypothetical' is regarded by Descartes as necessarily true and knowable a priori by the process of analytical reflexion.

If the bounds of the method are thus "fluid" or "epistemically opaque" (Buchdahl 1969, 121f.), and if Descartes is generally quite sanguine about what falls unproblematically within the scope of his purely formal 'deductive' science, it may prove difficult to confine *mathesis universalis* to "a general theory of quantities and proportions" (Mittelstraß 1979, 597) in any sense that excludes from the sphere of rigorous *mathesis universalis* metaphysical subjects beyond those Descartes describes as "the principles of my physics" (AT III 233: CSMK 157; cf. also AT VII 602: CSM II 397). It will similarly be hard to maintain a sharp distinction between *mathesis universalis* and *scientia* or *sapientia universalis*, that is, between logically 'unified science' ("Programm einer Einheitswissenshaft") and a universal scientific method based on a common 'logic' or *structural* unity of the sciences (Mittelstraß 1969, 177f.; cf. also McRae 1961, 62). Mittelstraß acknowledges that the distinction is not sharply drawn in the seventeenth century and is particularly blurry in Descartes's case (1969, 177f.; also 1979, 597). The safest conclusion to draw is that, when applied to Descartes, the talk of a "logische Einheit der Wissenschaften" (1969, 179) remains ambiguous as between (1) a thoroughgoing interconnection of all particular sciences, that is, "inhaltliche Einheit in einem System der Wissenschaft" (182f.) and (2) a "methodische Einheit in einer Theorie der Größen and Größenverhältnisse" or "Organon" of the sciences (ibid.).[38] Descartes would appear to mean both these things by *scientia*, *sapientia*, or (synonymously) *mathesis universalis*. More helpful than this distinction is Mittelstraß's observation: "Die Einheit der Wissenschaften liegt ... für Descartes in der Einheit der Vernunft (bona mens bzw. bon sens) begriffen" (178). For this points to an application of the method of analysis well beyond the *principia et proprietates magnitudinum et numerorum* mentioned in the entries in seventeenth-century lexica (cf. ibid.); it points to a method coextensive with the sphere – however imprecisely defined – of 'pure' reason itself.[39]

To conclude this section, a couple of brief observations on the "ancient geometers" alleged by Descartes to have kept their method of analysis from posterity "like a sacred mystery" (AT VII 156: CSM II 111; cf. AT X 376: CSM I 19). Given Descartes's own reticence on the subject, there is surely a wry piquancy to Leibniz's suggestion that Descartes himself left his method of analysis unexplained (Leibniz, 1875–90, IV, 331). The other observation has to do with whether Descartes might indeed have understood "reflecting with some discernment (*sagacitate*) on the minute details of the things we have already perceived" to be the *peculiarly Greek* sense of *mathēsis*, rejecting only the idea that this is appar-

ent from the etymology of the word *mathēsis*. (Heidegger, of course, is not talking about etymologies either when he interprets *mathēsis* as "taking cognizance
of what we already know" implicitly, though he is not speaking about the Greek
mathematicians in particular). In this regard, it is perhaps worth citing a good
brief account of the method of Pappus and Diophantus (third century A.D.), to
whom Descartes refers in the *Regulae* (AT X 376: CSM I 18):

> Both are said to be methods enabling mathematicians to *prove* theorems. 'Synthesis' is
> more or less equivalent to what is now called the 'axiomatic method' of proof, the most
> ancient model for which is Euclid's *Elements*. In this a theorem is proved by deriving it
> from axioms already known or assumed to be true; Pappus calls them 'first principles,'
> and the Greek assumption was presumably that the truth of these should be 'self-evident.'
> The converse, analysis, starts by assuming the truth of the theorem to be proved, and
> deduces from the latter some other proposition, theorem or axiom, *already* known or
> assumed to be true. In other words, here we move from the 'unknown' to the 'known,'
> though it will be realised that this is not actually a method for *discovering*, but only for
> proving a proposition. The analytical proof is complete, if subsequently the theorem can
> also be proved 'synthetically.' (Buchdahl 1969, 126f. e.a.)

For Descartes, by contrast, analysis is precisely a method of discovery proceeding from the "relative" to the "absolute," that is, from effect to cause, from the
composite to simple, from the more difficult to the easier. This much conforms in
a rough general way to most senses of 'analysis' or 'resolution' in the past or to
come. Yet unlike any but the Greek sense of *mathēsis* enshrined in the heuristic
paradox – and even here, the parallel is only formal – Descartes's analytical method
of discovery proceeds *from the explicitly known particular to implicitly known
universal truths, rendering the latter explicit* through analytical reflexion and
explicating with their aid (as well as deducing in the opposite direction) further
items of knowledge. Still, it would have been easy for Descartes to overlook
substantive differences between this and earlier conceptions of analysis, assimi-
lating the method of the "ancient geometers" to his own. Further discussion of
deductio in *Regulae* will be postponed till section 20.1.[40]

15.8 Conclusion

While it is no doubt correct to say that Descartes was deeply imbued with the
mathematical ideal of science, this implies neither that he embraced a 'deductivist'
model of science (in the now customary sense) nor that the only objects knowable with strict rigour are "quantity and number" (Hume). On the contrary, if the

view of the matter taken in the two preceding sections is correct, Descartes's model of scientific knowledge is the analytic method of discovery. It was no doubt the unquestioned certainty of pure mathematics that first led him to it, and it was in this field that he first applied and became adept at it (cf. AT VI 19ff.: CSM I 120ff.); but the consummate illustration of the power of this new method was to be found only later in the process of analytical reflexion on the first principle, *cogito, ergo sum*.

If Descartes's early vision of a unified science having the structure of a universal mathematics – dating perhaps from his dream of 1619 – served as a clue to the discovery of the nature of the mind, it was the theory of the mind as developed in the context of metaphysics that ultimately determined the universality of *mathēsis*. Henceforth *mathēsis* includes not just the metaphysical portion of physics but metaphysics proper, knowledge of God and the soul; however, the paradigm of method is no longer the seeds of truth as developed in mathematical analysis, but the process of analytical reflexion on the principle *cogito, ergo sum*. Accordingly, the early vision of an overarching *mathēsis universalis* with metaphysics, pure mathematics, and 'pure physics' ranged under it gives way to a new image of the unity of the sciences: "the whole of philosophy is like a tree. The roots are metaphysics, the trunk is physics, and the branches emerging from the trunk are all the other sciences" (AT IX-1 14: CSM I 186). At this point it is still possible to speak of 'Descartes's mathematical ideal of science,' but not without serious fore-shortening.[41]

As the process of analytical reflexion leading from implicit to explicit insight or intuition is the key to Descartes's doctrine of analytic method, so also to his theory of innateness, the natural light of reason, and the nature of the intellect in general. It also has a direct bearing on whether and in what sense an inference is involved in the *cogito, ergo sum*. Only the fuller elaboration of these themes can render the order of intuition outlined above less schematic, showing how the ideas and principles of Descartes's metaphysics, as well as those of mathematics and of mathematical physics, are grasped through reflexive attention to what is implicitly contained *in concreto* in the *cogito, ergo sum*. This will be attempted in chapters 18 through 20, which complete the account of Descartes's theory of the mind begun in chapter 6.

Our dominant concern throughout the present chapter has been the formal structure of thought as Descartes understood it. The sharp separation of *conscientia* (act-structure) from *cogitatio* (act), *scientia reflexa* (second- or higher-order acts), and reflexion (action) takes care of the first two distinctions employed in articulating the structure of thought in Part One. After outlining Descartes's manner of drawing the two remaining distinctions (chapter 16), we must consider the bearing of the findings of the present chapter on the precise nature of the transition of the mind from the *cogito* to the *sum*. For it is as an 'inference' (in the widest possible sense) that we have characterized the progress of the mind from implicit to explicit knowledge of certain notions and principles through reflexive attention to what it is conscious of. This issue will be pursued in chapter 17.

16

Idea and Object

Of the distinctions sketched briefly at the outset of Part Three, two remain to be discussed. Those between consciousness and thought and between reflexive attention and second-order reflexive acts have already set the primitiveness of the *cogito, ergo sum* in a clearer light (chapter 15); the two remaining distinctions are to clarify what is and is not included within this first item of knowledge. Encompassed within the consciousness of acts are (cf. section 7.2) their act-characters, the self or *ego* to which they belong, and their *intentional* though not their real objects. Acts, their act-characters, and the *ego* have been discussed already. How does Descartes draw the two remaining distinctions: (1) intentional and real object and (2) act and intentional object?

The first will be traced in the last section of this chapter. We begin with (2). Since Descartes draws this distinction in terms of the material and objective senses of 'idea' (or, equivalently, the formal and objective reality of ideas), (2) will involve a detailed discussion of Descartes's use of the term 'idea.' Formal and objective reality, however, must be distinguished in the case of extra-mental objects as well as ideas, so that the discussion of (1), the distinction between the merely mind-immanent *cogitatum* and the *cogitatum* as transcendent thing or *res*, follows quite naturally upon that of 'idea.'

The interpretive and philosophical issues involved in (1) and (2) were vigorously debated in the seventeenth century by Malebranche and Arnauld. Invoking the authority of Descartes, Arnauld defends a theory of ideas as *acts* that coincides in the essentials with that ascribed to Descartes here. McRae (1965, 179f.) acknowledges that a theory not unlike Arnauld's is to be found in Descartes's writings, while tracing to sources in Descartes two other theories as well: (a) that ideas are the immediate *objects* of acts, that is, a form of 'representationalism' not unlike that frequently ascribed to Malebranche and Locke; and (b) that ideas are *dispositions*, that is, a theory like that later elaborated by Leibniz. In an interesting appendix on "The Arnauld-Malebranche Debate," Nadler (1992) distinguishes two phases of scholarly commentary on this seventeenth-century debate. In the first, it was taken to be a debate between two representationalists (cf. also Yolton 1975a, 157f.); in the second, between a representationalist (Malebranche) and a direct realist (Arnauld). McRae belongs to this second phase, as does Yolton, while Lovejoy (1923) inaugurated the first. Nadler himself argues that both Malebranche and Arnauld were direct realists. Given the state of the scholarly controversy as it enters its third phase, the Arnauld-Malebranche debate had better be left aside here. Still, familiarity with it and with attempts to sort out the use of the term 'idea' in seventeenth-century thought going right back to Thomas Reid's *Essays on the Intellectual Powers of Man* (1785) should dispel any lingering suspicions of anachronism that our Husserlian notation may have occasioned (cf. sections 8.1–3).

16.1 Formal and objective reality

Replying in the Preface to the *Meditations* to an objection brought against the earlier *Discourse* version of the Third Meditation proof of God's existence, Descartes distinguishes two senses of 'idea':

'Idea' can be taken materially, as an operation of the intellect (*pro operatione intellectus*) ... Alternatively, it can be taken objectively (*objective*) as the thing represented (*re repraesentata*) by that operation. (AT VII 8: CSM II 7)

Here is a first version of the distinction between act and intentional object. When, in the Third Meditation proof itself, Descartes comes to make explicit the distinction left vague in the *Discourse*, he notes that in so far as ideas

are only certain modes of thought (*modi cogitandi*), there is no inequality recognizable among them ... But in so far as one represents one thing, another another, it is clear that they differ widely. Undoubtedly, the ideas which represent substances to me amount to something more and, so to speak, contain within them more objective reality than the ideas which merely represent modes or accidents. (AT VII 40: CSM II 27f.)

Descartes really has two things in mind here. The idea 'roundness' and the idea 'apple' are both ideas, perfectly alike when taken simply as modes of thought; but in so far as one represents an apple, the other the apple's shape, they differ. And they differ not just in regard to what is represented, their representational content, but also with respect to the amount or degree of reality of that which is represented: an apple is a substantial being, roundness a mere mode of a substance. If we consider the apple's redness, the idea itself is again a mode of thought, like 'roundness' and 'apple,' though it differs from the latter ideas both in respect of (a) *what* it represents and in respect of (b) *how much*, colour being 'less real' than shape, which is in turn less real than substance. (This talk of more and less reality will become clearer presently.)

The distinction in the Third Meditation passage just cited corresponds to that drawn in the Preface between the material and objective senses of 'idea.' Yet within the Third Meditation Descartes speaks of the "actual or formal reality" (AT VII 41: CSM II 28) of ideas, meaning that which, in the Preface, he called an 'idea' in the material sense of the word: the idea as act, operation of the soul, mode of thought. The substitution is puzzling, since the formal and the material are customarily opposed to one another, whereas here the 'idea' in the material sense is precisely the idea considered with respect to its formal reality.[1] As for 'ideas' in the objective sense, there is no such mismatch of vocabulary here: the objective sense of 'idea' coincides with the 'objective reality' of ideas. But on further examination it turns out that Descartes applies the term 'formal' to the objective reality of ideas as well, distinguishing the objective reality of ideas taken formally from the formal reality of ideas taken materially. This occurs in the Replies to the Fourth Set of Objections by Arnauld, where what is unmistakably the same distinction serves as the basis for the contrast between material and formal falsity:

Since ideas are *forms of a kind* (*formae quaedam*), and are not composed of any matter, when we think of them as representing something we are taking them not *materially* but *formally*. If, however, we were considering them not as representing this or that but simply as operations of the intellect, then it could be said that we were taking them materially. (AT VII 232: CSM II 163 e.a.)

Descartes again uses 'form' (Latin *species, forma*, Greek *eidos*) in the sense of 'ideas taken formally,' that is, with a view to their *objective*, not their formal reality, when he writes in the Replies to the Third Set of Objections by Hobbes: "by an 'idea' I mean whatever is the *form* of a given perception" (AT VII 188: CSM II 132 e.a.). One can make at least some sense of this use of *form* and *formaliter* since the *idea formaliter sumpta* is just the idea insofar as it represents what exists *formally* in its extra-mental object, that is, insofar as what exists actually in the object exists objectively in the idea (see section 16.5 below). But initially, at least, Descartes's employment of the form/matter dichotomy seems ideally suited to foster total confusion about a relatively simple matter, for after carefully distinguishing two senses of 'idea,' he applies both 'form' and 'matter' (or their cognates) to each sense in turn.

Once the impression of terminological chaos wears off, the basic distinction will be found to be clear enough. The question is, Are the material and objective aspects of ideas, that is, their formal and objective reality, simply equatable with thinking and the intentional object of thought? In the treatment of thought and consciousness so far a good deal has been made of the differences between acts, their structures, and their intentional objects; but little has been said of ideas – obviously a powerful weapon in the Cartesian arsenal and one frequently turned against Descartes by his critics. In order to determine whether the distinction between two senses of 'idea' coincides in fact with that between what Husserl calls 'acts' and their 'intentional objects' we must clarify the exact logical relations obtaining among 'thought,' 'consciousness,' 'idea,' and 'judgment' in the technical senses given these terms by Descartes.

16.2 'Thought' and 'idea'

It was long ago noted by Gilson among others that Descartes was the first to employ the term 'idea' with reference to human thinking; the Scholastic tradition, remarks Gilson, "réservait habituellement ce terme pour désigner les archétypes éternels dans lesquels Dieu pense les choses."[2] To this observation Gilson appends a series of interpretive remarks, two of which are particularly deserving of attention. When God knows things through thinking his own essence as imitable by them,[3] he has knowledge of them that is both a representation and purely intellectual, that is, devoid of any admixture of the sensible. Descartes's adoption of the term 'idea,' Gilson suggests, was motivated by the purely intellectual representations of God, the human soul, and the nature of body toward which he wished to guide his readers (Gilson 1947a, 319f.). Moreover – and this is the second point – 'idea' is "pratiquement équivalent" to 'thought' (318): the two terms are for all intents and purposes synonymous.

As to Gilson's first point, it must be acknowledged that thinking, for Descartes, always represents something, an object, and that the need to conceive thought and the soul in a manner untainted either by sense or imagination is frequently stressed in Descartes's writings (for references, see section 10.1) – more, certainly, than the crucial importance of experience and observation in science, though this too is a key feature of Descartes's theory of knowledge (cf. section 15.7). Yet to conceive thinking purely intellectually means, for Descartes, to construe its occurrence in a manner that entails the actual existence or formal reality of a mental act along with the intentional existence or objective reality of its object *though not the actual existence of any extra-mental thing*. So the key distinction underlying Descartes's appropriation of the Scholastic term *idea* is arguably not so much the general epistemological one between sense and intellect suggested by Gilson as the specifically phenomenological distinction between two analyses of 'I think x.' On the first, certain values of 'I think x,' for example, 'I perceive x (by means of the senses)' entail the real existence of a sensible object outside the mind no less than the actual occurrence of thinking in it. The other analysis is that adopted provisionally by Descartes in the first five Meditations. It reduces *all* values of 'I think x,' including 'I perceive x,' to exclusively phenomenological, that is mental, terms. And this is what it is to conceive thinking or the mind 'intellectually' in Descartes's sense, consciousness of the mind's operations, with all that is implicitly contained in them, being the essence of the pure intellect (cf. section 9.1f.). 'Idea,' then, is Descartes's term for that purely intellectual conception of thinking that, like the activity that characterizes the divine intellect, does not presuppose the actual existence of an extra-mental reality.[4]

This, of course, does not yet take fully into account the all-important representational force of the word 'idea' mentioned by Gilson and brought out particularly in Descartes's definition of 'idea' in the Second Replies and by their description as *tanquam rerum imagines* in the Third Meditation. Both texts will be discussed presently (section 16.4). As for Gilson's second main point, the alleged equivalence of 'thought' and 'idea,' there are not just two but four separate senses of 'idea' to be considered. To these four senses, other, relatively less important uses will be added in the course of the first three sections.

(1) In the first and broadest sense 'idea' is indeed used synonymously with 'thought' to cover all varieties of mental acts or operations, not only the perceptions or later so-called passions (sensation, imagination, and intellection), but also actions (volitions and judgments) and even emotions. The material and objective aspects of the idea so understood just spell out in detail what is entailed by the phenomenologically reduced statement 'I have an idea (in this loose sense) of x': the occurrence in me of an act of a certain kind having a certain objective reference or reality.

(2) 'Idea' is frequently used also in a second sense to designate the objective reality of the idea in the first sense. The intentional object of thinking (whatever the act-character of the act) is termed an 'idea' in this sense in the First Replies, that is, an *idea formaliter spectata*: the "idea [of a thing] is the thing which is thought of in so far as it has objective being in the intellect" (*rem cogitatam, quatenus est objective in intellectu*) (AT VII 102: CSM II 74). One of the *marginalia* of the Latin translation of the *Discourse* (possibly from Descartes's own pen, though this is uncertain) reads: "here and throughout the following the word 'idea' is taken generally for everything that is thought of (*pro omni re cogitata*) in so far only as it has a certain objective being in the intellect" (AT VI 559). This corresponds to the objective aspect of ideas alone.

(3) In addition to this use of 'idea' to designate an *abstract moment* of ideas in

the first sense, there is a third important use of the same term to designate found-ing as opposed to complex founded modes or acts of thinking, that is, not an *aspect* but a *subclass* of ideas in the first sense. In the Third Meditation (AT VII 37: CSM II 26) Descartes distinguishes this strict from the loose sense of 'idea' under (1), the former comprising all and only ideas whose primary function is to represent objects, whether real or merely imagined. As we shall see, the same strict sense of 'idea' is in question in the puzzling formal definition of the *more geometrico* proofs of the Second Replies, where 'idea' and 'thought' differ as species and genus. Had Descartes there meant 'idea' in the loose sense, he could hardly have given a separate definition of 'idea' after having defined 'thought' in the preceding definition. It is in this narrow sense of the term that Descartes writes to Mersenne (July 1641), "[B]y the term 'idea' I mean in general every-thing which is in our mind when we conceive something, no matter how we conceive it" (AT III 392f.: CSMK 185); for as defined here 'idea' coincides with 'act of perception' in the broadest acceptation ("no matter how we conceive it") and excludes volition, emotion, and judgment.

(4) Finally, there is another sense of 'idea' that focuses exclusively upon the formal reality of mental acts in abstraction from their intentional or 'ideational' content; but this is not a particularly characteristic use of the term outside the context in which it is distinguished from the second sense of 'idea' within the "Preface to the Reader" (AT VII 8: CSM II 7).

The logical relations between 'thought' and 'idea' may now be summed up this way. While 'thought' and 'idea' in the first sense are used synonymously for any intentionally structured mental act whatever, in the second sense no idea is a thought, that is, an act of thinking rather than an abstract moment of such acts, the intentional object. Some thoughts may indeed be termed 'ideas' in this second sense, but only those that happen to be the intentional objects of second- or higher-order reflexive acts. In the third or (as Descartes calls it) "strict" sense of 'idea,' all ideas are thoughts but some thoughts – for instance, volitions, judgments, and emotions – are not ideas. In the fourth sense, 'idea' again designates an abstract moment of a thought rather than a thought.

More important than Gilson's vague claim that "les deux termes [*idée* and *pensée*] sont pratiquement équivalents, toute idée étant une pensée, et nulle pensée n'étant consciente de son contenu que sous forme d'idée" (1947a, 318) is what lies behind it. The phrase 'sous forme d'idée' is ambiguous. It could mean that thought involves awareness of a content (of an object, say, a material thing) only insofar as *thinking itself* 'takes the form' of an idea. If so, all is well. But since, grammatically, *contenu* rather than *pensée* may be the referent of 'sous forme d'idée,' the point could be that thought involves consciousness of a content only insofar as that *content or object* is an idea in the mind rather than an extra-mental reality. If so – and this seems the better reading – we are in the presence of the totally misguided notion of an act of thinking whose immediate object is an idea and whose indirect object is that extra-mental thing which is the immediate object of the idea. Together with the assumption that only the former can be known with certainty, the bizarre doctrine that we cannot think of or perceive extra-mental reality directly but only through the intermediary of our ideas leads inescapably to the sceptical conclusion that we cannot obtain certain knowledge of it at all.

Epistemologically, taking the object of thought for an idea, so that things outside the mind are only indirectly knowable, via interposed ideas, is a dead end. Since Descartes employs the term 'idea' both for thought itself and for the object of thinking, the responsibility for the confusion is partly his, though *he himself never fell into it*. On the contrary, Descartes's distinction between formal and objective reality closely mirrors that carefully drawn later between acts and their intentional objects. The temptation to misconstrue the relation of act and object by interposing a 'veil-of-perception' between thoughts and things is due, however, not only to the ambiguities of 'idea' just examined, but also to the tendency of the commentators to read the later views of Malebranche, Locke, or Hume back into the Father of Modern Philosophy. The best antidote is the sort of examination of the different senses of 'idea' and their logical relations to other technical terms in Descartes's vocabulary in which we are now engaged.[5]

16.3 'Idea,' 'consciousness,' and 'judgment'

We turn next to the logical relations of 'thought' and the other senses of 'idea' just distinguished to *conscientia*. The latter refers neither to a thought nor to an idea in any of the senses distinguished thus far, but to the necessarily self-reflexive character of all thought as such. There is, however (cf. chapter 6 *in initio* and section 8.4), a *pars pro toto* use of 'perception' in Descartes, who sometimes refers to the immediate consciousness of one's thoughts as 'perception'; and there is a corresponding (though relatively rare) use of 'idea' as well (ibid.). Volitions and emotions count as ideas, Descartes suggests, precisely because they necessarily involve *conscientia* or 'perception.' In an oft-cited passage from the Replies to the Third Set of Objections (quoted already in section 15.3) Descartes remarks that he takes the word 'idea' "to refer to whatever is immediately perceived by the mind. For example, when I want something, or am afraid of something, I simultaneously perceive that I want, or am afraid; *and this is why I count volition and fear among my ideas*" (AT VII 181: CSM II 127f. e.a.). The simultaneous 'perceiving' in question here is *conscientia*, being conscious of willing or fearing. A letter to Mersenne of 28 January 1641 expressly designates it an 'idea':

"I claim that we *have ideas* not only of all that is in our intellect, but also of all that is in the will. For we cannot will anything without knowing that we will it (*sans sçauoir que nous le voulons*), nor could we know this except by means of an idea; but I do not claim that the idea is different from the act itself" (AT III 295: CSMK 172 e.a.). This is the very point made in terms of perception rather than knowing or ideas in the passage from the *Passions* cited earlier: "For it is certain that we cannot will anything without thereby perceiving that we are will-ing it. And although willing something is an action with respect to our soul, the perception of such willing may be said to be a passion in the soul. But because this perception is really one and the same thing as the volition ... etc." (AT XI 343: CSM I 335f.). The perception is not "different from the act itself," that is, it is not *another* act, but a necessary structural feature of "one and the same" act. It is this which Descartes designates a 'perception' here and in the Third Replies and an 'idea' in the letter to Mersenne. This, then, is a further use of 'idea' (5) in addition to those distinguished already.

As for the relation of ideas to judgments, it will be recalled that judgments are thoughts for Descartes and hence 'ideas' in the broad sense. This fact is some-times regarded as symptomatic of a serious confusion. Yet the fact that Descartes takes 'having an idea of x' or 'thinking x' to include such mental states as 'having an idea that x is p' does not entail that he rashly confused judgments or proposi-tions with concepts or ideas.[6] Though 'having ideas' is not restricted to such *pre-predicative* acts of thinking as intuiting simple natures or forming sensory images in the imagination, Descartes nevertheless distinguishes rather carefully between ideas and judgments, notably in the well-known Third Meditation passage (AT VII 37: CSM II 25f.) cited several times already. Here it is not so much the logi-cal distinctness of concepts and the propositions in which they occur that detains him – though, from the *Regulae* on, the differences between grasping a concept and intuiting the relations between concepts in judgments are perfectly clear to him. In the Third Meditation the important thing is the distinction between the merely passive mental state of perceiving (ideas in the strict sense, whether pre-predicative or propositional) and the action involved in affirming, denying, or suspending judgment as to the propositional states of affairs perceived, that is, represented. This difference, according to which perceptions are one and all pas-sions, while volitions, including judgments, are actions of the soul, is not yet explicitly worked out in the *Regulae*. It entails that 'having the idea of x' is by no means equivalent to the judgment 'it seems to me that I am perceiving x,' any more than 'having an idea that x is p' is equivalent to the judgment 'it seems to me that x is p.' The reason is not that the judgments are assertions about x, an extra-mental object; even taken as assertions about my own actually occurring mental states (for instance, 'I am in a mental state which, to me, is indistinguishable from actually seeing x as having the property p'), 'it seems to me that x is p' is still an action of the will and as such it is a judgment distinct from the passive operation of the intellect on which it supervenes. In fact, understood in the former way, 'it seems to me that x is p' is a multiple volition since a deliberate suspension of judgment (*epochē*) about the extra-mental object goes together with the forthright assertion about my own actually occurring mental state. Even taken in the other way, however, as a cautious assertion about x, 'it seems to me that x' is still a simple volition and as such quite distinct from perception of the corresponding propositional state of affairs.[7]

Two further distinctions are relevant to Descartes's use of the term 'idea,' bringing the total number of different senses of the term to seven. The first is that between (6) corporeal ideas in the brain and ideas in the mind (cf., for example, AT VI 55: CSM I 139; AT VII 181: CSM II 127; AT VII 366: CSM II 253). The other is the distinction between ideas as actually occurring "operations" (AT VII 232: CSM II 162) of the mind and (7) ideas as mental capacities or dispositions to perform such acts. The former is relevant to what follows mainly in that *ideae corporeae* (as Descartes calls them) are mentioned in the context of the formal definition of 'idea' within the Replies to the Second Set of Objections.[8] It is also alluded to later in the passage from the Third Replies quoted above, where Descartes explains why he has applied this Scholastic term to the human mind. We shall consider both passages in the next section. The second distinction is pertinent chiefly to the division between innate and other classes of idea, and hence to Descartes's use of 'innate' rather than of 'idea' generally. It thus plays a key role in Descartes's theory of innateness, to be examined in chapter 18, but is not directly relevant here.[9]

16.4 'Idea' in the Second Replies and Third Meditation

However motivated philosophically, whatever the exact nature of the assimilation of the human to the divine Mind, Descartes's choice of the Scholastic term 'idea' was, he tells us, dictated at least in part by want of a better term. The passage from the Replies to the Third Set of Objections partially quoted above continues: "I used the word 'idea' because it was the standard philosophical term used to refer to the forms of perception belonging to the divine mind, even though we recognise that God does not possess any corporeal imagination [i.e., corporeal ideas]. And besides, *there was not any more appropriate term at my disposal*" (AT VII 181: CSM II 127f. e.a.). As the examples of volition and fear in the immediately preceding sentence make plain, 'idea' is used here in the first or loose sense. In the explicitly so-called 'definition' of the *more geometrico* proofs, by contrast, 'idea' is taken in the third or strict sense: idea as a subclass of *cogitatio*, as a species of thought comprising only simple, founding acts. These are present in all complex, founded acts of thinking as that element which gives them their representational character as thought *of* an object. It will be suggested that this is indeed the best interpretation, partly because it squares well with the much clearer definition of 'idea' in the Third Meditation, though the definition in the Second Replies is too obscure to warrant much confidence.

Within the *more geometrico* proofs the formal definition of 'idea' comes second in the initial list of definitions, after the definition of 'thought':

[First section:] By the word 'idea' I understand that form of any thought (*cuiuslibet cogitationis formam illam*) by the immediate perception of which (*per cujus immediatam perceptionem*) I am conscious of that same thought (*ipsius ejusdem conscius sum*). [Second section:] Thus I cannot express anything in words and understand that which I say without its being certain thereby (*quin ex hoc ipso certum sit*) that the idea of what the words signify is in me. [Third section:] Thus it is not only the images depicted in the imagination which I call 'ideas.' Indeed, in so far as these images are in the corporeal imagination, that is, are depicted in some part of the brain, I do not call them 'ideas' at all. I call them 'ideas' only in so far as they give form to (*informant*) the mind itself, when it is directed towards that part of the brain. (AT VII 160f.: CSM II 113)

Of the three sections into which the definition falls the latter two are intended to clarify, first positively, then negatively, the sense in which ideas are representations or images: not at all in the way in which actual pictures "depicted in the corporeal imagination" (AT VII 181: CSM II 127) or in the matter of the brain are images; nor yet only as purely mental pictures painted by the mind's faculty of imagination are images (third section); but rather as 'images' in that extended sense in which the mind is commonly said to 'have an idea' of an object when it understands the ideal sense of the linguistic expressions in which the concept of that object is correctly employed (second section). Thus, to the objection brought against the Third Meditation proof of God's existence by friends of Clerselier, namely, "not everyone is aware of the idea of God within himself," Descartes responds:

[I]f we take the word 'idea' in the way in which I quite explicitly stated I was taking it [i.e., ideas as *tanquam rerum imagines* (AT VII 37: CSM II 25)], and do not take refuge in ambiguity, like those who restrict this term to the images of material things formed in the imagination, then we will be unable to deny that we have some idea of God. The only way of denying this would be to say that we do not understand the meaning of the phrase 'the most perfect thing which we can conceive of'; for this is what everyone calls *God*. It is indeed going to extraordinary lengths in the desire to raise objections to say that one does not understand the meaning of one of the most ordinary phrases in common use. (AT IX-1 209: CSM II 273)

If 'having the idea of an object' has to be sharply separated from the occurrence of mental imagery that may sometimes accompany the understanding of certain expressions, it is not just a matter of understanding the syntactico-semantical rules that govern the use of word either. Rather, to have the idea of an object is to be intentionally related to that object *immediately* through understanding the ideal content of the concept that designates it; or, better, through understanding the ideal meaning of at least some propositions in which the concept is correctly employed. It is in this sense that ideas in the strict sense are forms or images (*tanquam rerum imagines*) and yet, as modes of thinking, altogether unlike what we usually called images, namely pictures, imprints, or material representations of something.[10]

This leaves the first section of the definition still to be interpreted. It was necessary to deal with the other two first, since they help clarify the sense in which 'form' is used. The wording *forma ... per cujus immediatam perceptionem ...* etc. is anything but clear. Kemp Smith (1952, 149 n. 2.) interprets the 'form' to refer to a corporeal idea in the brain. He is followed in this by Hatfield (1992, 335f. and n. 49). But given Descartes's remarks to Clerselier concerning corporeal ideas, not to mention the clear statement in the third section of the definition, this seems untenable.

On what appears a more promising interpretation, the "form" Descartes speaks of here refers to *conscientia* in the technical sense. After all, it is said to be met with in "any and every thought" (*cuiuslibet cogitationis*), as is *conscientia*. Through it (*formam per cujus perceptionem*), moreover, I am immediately "conscious" of that very thought, *ipsius ejusdem* [*cogitationis*] *conscius sum*. Furthermore, the expression "the form by the immediate perception of which I am conscious of that same thought" is reminiscent of Descartes's' technical use of *conscientia* in the immediately preceding definition of *cogitatio*: "everything that is within us in such a way that we are immediately conscious (*immediate conscii simus*) of it." And since Descartes on occasion applies the terms *percipere* and *idea* to *conscientia* (cf. above and sections 8.4 and 16.3), the use of *perceptio* in the phrase *formam per cujus immediatam perceptionem* would not be surprising.

Unfortunately, this interpretation of *forma* is not very satsifactory either. Both Leibniz (cf. Gewirth 1968, 256) and Arnauld (cf. McRae 1965, 182) take the word 'form' in this definition to refer to the *act* of thinking. This seems indeed the best interpretation, though Descartes probably does not mean any and all acts of thinking but a particular subclass. If, as Gilson rightly stresses,[11] forms are traditionally image-like, similitudes, and if this is still so for Descartes, then the term 'idea' here defined as *forma per cuius perceptionem* etc. will likely designate a particular species of acts of thinking, the specific nature of which consists in being object-representing (though not pictorial) and which are found in all other acts of thinking as their basic form. The second and third sections of the definition, interpreted above, clearly highlight this particular connotation of the word 'idea': 'image,' 'representation' (though only *tanquam*, 'as it were'). This is the idea in the strict sense ([3] in the earlier enumeration): thought as representational act. Since the emphasis lies on the representative character of the act, the *idea formaliter sumpta*, Descartes speaks (confusingly, but not without at least some justification) of a *form*.

In defining ideas as 'forms,' then, Descartes's intent is to distinguish the *basic* form that is the idea in the strict sense, the non-pictorial representation of an object, from other forms that may be contained along with it in a particular act of thinking but that are not image-like.[12] That it is this representative character of certain basic acts or 'forms' that Descartes has in mind can perhaps be gathered from the words *ipsius ejusdem* in the definition. An act of thinking is not one and same act in virtue of its taking place in a single instant. The mind, as Descartes explained to Burman (AT V 148: CSMK 335), cannot indeed think many things, *multa*, at one and the same time, but it can think more than one thing, *plura*, within the temporal duration of a single act. Moreover, it can attend selectively to this or that among simultaneously performed acts, or to this or that structural moment within individual acts; for example, to what it is immediately conscious of rather than to what it thinks in some particular act of thinking; and within what it is conscious of, to its own existence as an enduring substance rather than that of its passing thoughts, and so on. *What* an act represents, its intentional object, no less than the particular *way* in which it represents that object, is a key part of what makes it *eadem cogitatio*, numerically the same act. Since, however, the same object may be represented in the same way by acts that are numerically distinct and that, moreover, differ in respect of their act-character, intending the same object in the same way is a necessary rather than sufficient condition of numerical identity in acts. Depending on whether it is a simple act that merely represents a certain object in a certain way, or a complex one that both represents an object in a certain way *and* affirms or denies, approves or disapproves, desires or shuns what is thus represented, the perception is an idea in the strict sense defined here, a simple representation of something, or it is more than this, namely a representation, form, or idea *together with* another, supervenient form, which is itself not a simple representation nor a representation at all and which alters the act-character of the perception so as to render it a volition, a judgment, or an emotion. Even to such complex acts, however, the *form* that is the idea proper remains basic.

Thus, an act or idea in the loose sense may be simple or complex. It may represent the same object in the same way by means of a single form, in which case it is a simple act of thinking or an idea in the strict sense. Or it may represent one and the same object in the same way through a multiplicity of simultaneously occurring forms, the 'idea' in the strict sense being the basic form in virtue of which one and the same thought represents something as something. Upon the basic form other forms supervene, modifying the act-character of the act so as to make it, for example, an act of affirming, desiring, loving, or the like, instead of a simple act of perceiving, whether sensory, imaginative, or intellectual. These other forms are, of course, not acts; only the basic form is an act in its own right. They are, however, present along with it in one and the same complex act whenever the mind affirms or denies, loves or hates that which is represented by the simple, underlying idea. So, for example, the supervenient form involved in my fearing the wolf I suddenly catch sight of is not strictly the act of fearing but the form that renders the whole act a complex one of fearing *something*, a wolf, rather than a simple one of seeing the wolf. The emotion of fear (on this theory of emotion) is a complex act that includes an element of perception or cognition – the 'idea' in the strict sense – as the basic act on which it is founded and that gives it its intentional reference to an object, its 'ideational content,' as we might say. And so too with acts of judging and willing.[13]

If this is correct, then we can perhaps paraphrase the first part of Descartes's obscure definition as follows: By the word 'idea' I understand that basic underlying form to be found in any thought, through the immediate perception (*perceptio*) of which I am conscious (*conscius*) of the thought as that very (and not another) thought (*ipsius ejusdem*).

If this is indeed the concept 'idea' as defined within the *more geometrico* proofs of the Second Replies, then the definition only repeats the much more straightforward statement on the subject found in the Third Meditation (so too Kenny 1968, 111). There Descartes provides the following well-known classification of his thoughts:

Some of my thoughts are as it were the images of things (*tanquam rerum imagines*), and it is only in these cases that the term 'idea' is strictly appropriate – for example, when I think of a man, or a chimera, or the sky, or an angel, or God. Other thoughts have various *additional forms*: thus when I will, or am afraid, or affirm, or deny, there is always a particular thing which I take as the object of my thought, but my thought includes something more than the likeness (*similitudinem*) of that thing. Some thoughts in this category are called volitions or affects (*voluntates sive affectus*), while others are called judgments. (AT VII 37: CSM II 25f. e.a.)

It hardly needs pointing out that despite the use of the words *imago* and *simili-*

tudo this is no imagist account of the relation between thought and its intentional object.[14] The illustrations show this clearly enough. It is not the presence in the mind of an image of God, of a chiliagon (cf. AT VII 72: CSM II 50f.), or of any other true and immutable nature that is the idea of that object. Though having an idea *may* involve the occurrence of mental imagery, it does not presuppose it, being rather a matter of possessing certain concepts, that is, understanding expressions in which those concepts are correctly employed. This much was clear from the definition considered previously. Of particular interest in the Third Meditation passage is the explicit distinction Descartes draws between simple and complex acts, that is, those involving a single and those involving multiple forms. Since the latter always presuppose ideas or simple forms, the distinction can also be regarded as that between simple founding and complex founded acts. As containing within themselves a simple founding act or idea in virtue of which they represent, that is, are intentionally related to an object, even complex founded acts may be called 'ideas,' though only in the broad, loose sense of the term. Elsewhere, of course, Descartes suggests that the loose sense of 'idea' is justified by the inherently reflexive or self-conscious character of all acts of thinking (cf. above, 16.3), so that it is difficult to be sure which of the two is the underlying reason for the broad use of the term. It may be that in the definition of 'idea' in the Second Replies, he merges form as founding act and form as structure. That would explain the difficulty of the passage and the need for extreme caution in interpreting it.

16.5 Intentional and real object

So much for the terms in which Descartes distinguishes between an act and its intentional object (the first distinction) and for the logical relations among 'idea,' 'thought,' 'consciousness,' and 'judgment.' The other distinction, between the intentional object, *cogitatum*, or 'thing in so far as it is in the mind,' and the same entity in so far as it exists outside the mind, is crucial for purposes of confining the sphere of thought to that which exists "in such a way that we are immediately conscious of it" (AT VII 160: CSM II 113). And this, as we have seen (section 7.2), is to delimit, at least in a preliminary way, the sphere of absolute certainty. Descartes is as explicit on this point as his outmoded Scholastic vocabulary will permit. For here again he deploys the Scholastic distinction between formal and objective reality or being, extending it now to entities other than ideas, that is, to things (*res*).

Mind-immanent ideas like (to take Descartes's example) 'the sun' are in the mind formally or actually as acts of representing; mind-transcendent things like the sun itself are 'in' the mind only objectively, not formally. Formally, the sun is in the heavens, not in the mind. To say that the sun is 'in' the mind objectively or intentionally is simply equivalent to saying that the idea of the sun is in the mind formally or actually (cf. also Yolton 1975a, 150 on Kenny 1968, 116). While being objectively in the mind is no doubt a purely 'extrinsic denomination' of the sun as it really exists outside the mind, and being in the heavens an intrinsic one, a mode of the sun as a mind-transcendent material thing, being in the mind is an intrinsic denomination of the *idea* 'sun,' which is really there and nowhere else. Since the real being in the mind of the idea of the sun is simply equivalent to the objective being in the mind of the sun, the latter too is an intrinsic denomination (though not of the sun), a reality of sorts.

That 'existing in the mind' is not only an extrinsic but also an intrinsic denomination requiring some sort of causal explanation is crucial to the Third Meditation proof of God's existence based on that of the idea of God in the mind. For the proof turns on the causal principle that there must exist formally in the cause of an idea at least as much reality as there is objectively in its effect (cf. AT VII 41: CSM II 28); the effect, accordingly, must have at least some reality for the proof to work.

In the First Set of Objections Caterus urged that objective being in the mind is only an extrinsic denomination that adds nothing to the thing itself. "Just as 'being seen' is nothing other than an act of seeing attributable to myself," he argues,

so 'being thought of' or having objective being in the intellect, is simply a thought of the mind which stops and terminates in the mind. And this can occur without any movement or change in the thing itself, and indeed without the thing in question existing at all. So why should I look for the cause of something which is not actual, and which is simply a bare denomination and nothing? (AT VII 92: CSM II 67)

To this Descartes replies that he had expressly noted the identity of the real being of the idea and the objective being of the thing of which it is the idea: "But I wrote that 'an idea is the thing which is thought of in so far as it has objective being in the intellect'" (AT VII 102: CSM II 74). When his objector speaks of 'being objectively in the intellect,' he notes, he refers to "the thing itself as something really situated outside the intellect" (ibid.). In respect of the thing and its formal reality, being objectively in the intellect is indeed a purely extrinsic denomination.[15] By contrast, Descartes himself, in speaking of 'objective being in the intellect,' refers not to the thing as it really exists outside the mind but to the idea of the thing that is "never outside the intellect and in respect of which the 'objective being' *of things* means 'being in the intellect' in the manner in which objects are usually in it" (ibid., e.a.), as the intentional objects of ideas. Descartes gives an example:

[I]f anyone asks what accident [or reality] of the [actually existing] sun its being objectively [i.e., intentionally] in my intellect is, the best answer is that it is nothing but an extrinsic denomination, namely that it 'terminates' an operation of the intellect in the manner in which a [really existing] object does so. But if the question is about what the *idea* of the sun is, and we answer that it (*illam*) [*scil. ideam*] is the thing which is thought of in so far as it has objective being in the intellect, no one will take it [this idea] to be the [really existing] sun itself in so far as this extrinsic denomination ['objective being in the intellect'] is in it. (AT VII 102: CSM II 74)

Given the starting point of the Third Meditation proof of God's existence, what is to be accounted for in terms of the causal principle can only be a certain idea in the mind of which God is the intentional object (the idea 'God'), not some obviously extrinsic denomination of God himself as he really exists outside the mind. Descartes proceeds with his example:

'Objective being in the intellect' will not here [when the question is about the *idea* of the sun] mean 'terminating its operation in the manner in which a [really existing] object does so,' but 'being in the intellect in the way in which its objects are usually there' [i.e., as the intentional object of an actually occurring act or idea]. (ibid.)

Next Descartes recalls again that the objective being or intentional existence of the thing in the mind is simply identical with the real being of the idea of that thing in the mind: "Thus the idea of the sun *is* [e.a.] the sun itself existing in the mind; not, however," he continues,

formally, as it exists in the heavens, but objectively, i.e. in the way objects are usually in the mind. Now this mode of being [the objective being of the sun] is of course much less perfect than that [real being] possessed by things which exist outside the mind; but as I did explain, it is not therefore simply nothing. (AT VII 102f.: CSM II 75)[16]

As the sun's 'being in the mind' is not "simply nothing," a purely extrinsic denomination of the sun as it exists outside the mind, so the existence in the intellect of the idea 'God' is not simply an extrinsic denomination of God himself and nothing more, but something real for which there must be an adequate cause. If that cause can be no other than God himself as actually existing outside the intellect, then the Third Meditation proof stands, or at least does not topple before Caterus's objection. In the present context the main thing to note is not the rebuttal itself (which is indeed rather subtle) so much as the distinction on which it hinges between the intentional object considered as mind-immanent and that same object regarded as a mind-transcendent thing.

This concludes the attempt to show that the various distinctions introduced earlier correspond to distinctions actually drawn by Descartes himself, and that Descartes therefore expressly recognized the constitutive elements and the embracing formal structure of thought later elaborated by Husserl and others.

17

The Inferential Import of the *Ergo*

We return now to the first of the outstanding questions raised in section 15.8: whether and in what sense an inference is involved in the *cogito, ergo sum*. As we do so it may be useful to recall very briefly the gist of Descartes's reply to Burman's objection concerning *Principles*, I, 10 as set out in section 15.2.

It is a necessary condition of that intuitive certainty which assures the mind of its own existence as soon it reflects upon its thinking and attempts to call its existence into question that there be in the thinking mind an immediate though only implicit intuition of certain "simple notions which on their own provide us with no knowledge of anything that exists" (VIII-A 8: CSM I 196). As for explicit knowledge of the meaning of 'existence,' 'thinking,' 'certainty,' and that 'whatever thinks, exists,' this is so little necessary for immediate intuitive certainty of the principle *cogito, ergo sum* that, if we do ever acquire such knowledge – those who never philosophize never do – it is only through further reflexion upon what is implicit in the *cogito, ergo sum* itself.

What bearing has this on the question of whether *cogito, ergo sum* is an inference?

17.1 The principle *nihili nullae sunt proprietates*

Among the "very simple notions, and ones which on their own provide us with no knowledge of anything that exists," the *Principles* cite (I, 11) the principle of the natural light: *nihili nullas esse affectiones sive qualitates* ("that nothing has no attributes or qualities"). Descartes glosses it as follows: "wherever we find some attributes or qualities, there is necessarily some thing or substance to be found for them to belong to" (AT VIII-1 8: CSM I 196). In another place this principle of the natural light is formulated as follows: "a real attribute cannot belong to nothing" (AT VII 161: CSM II 114). Later in the same work (I, 52), Descartes calls it a "common notion" (VIII-1 25: CSM I 210), which is synonymous with 'simple notion':

[W]e cannot initially become aware of substance (*non potest substantia primum animadverti*) merely through its being an existing thing since this alone does not of itself have any effect on us. We can, however, easily come to know a substance by one of its attributes, in virtue of the common notion that nothing possesses no attributes, that is, no properties (*proprietates*) or qualities. Thus, if we perceive the presence of some attribute, we infer (*concludimus*) that there must also be present an existing thing or substance to which it may be attributed. (VIII-1 25: CSM I 210)[1]

A passage from the Replies to the Third Objections brings out the direct bearing of this doctrine on the transition of the mind from *cogito* to *sum*:

He [Hobbes] is quite right in saying that 'we cannot conceive of an act without its sub-ject.' We cannot conceive of thinking without a thinking thing, since that which thinks is not nothing. It is certain that thinking cannot exist without a thing that is thinking; and in general no act or accident can exist without a substance for it to belong to. But we do not come to know a substance immediately through being aware of the substance itself (*ipsam substantiam non immediate per ipsam cognoscamus*); we come to know it only through its being the subject (*subjectum*) of certain acts (*quorumdam actuum*) [i.e. that which underlies them, in which they inhere, or to which they belong]. (AT VII 175f.: CSM II 123f.)

Since I cannot come to know a substance immediately but only through its acci-dents, I do not come to know that I exist as a thinking thing (*sum*) immediately but only through my actually existing modes or, as Descartes says here, "acts" of thinking (*cogito*).

Interpreting this in the light of the reply to Burman, the 'inference' involved (*concludimus*) may be described in the following way. Although explicit knowl-edge of the abstract principle "no act or accident can exist without a substance for it to belong to" follows upon rather than precedes explicit knowledge of the *cogito, ergo sum*, the former is nevertheless prior to the latter in a certain sense: the transition of the mind from the explicit knowledge of the existence of particular modes of thinking to the existence of a thinking substance really depends upon that universal principle's being implicitly understood *in concreto* in the process of analytical reflexion on the *cogito*. Of course, the supposed 'major' does not "on its own" assert the existence of anything, but only the absurdity of asserting the existence of an attribute or quality while denying that any substance exists to which it may be attributed. Moreover, the *sum* is no more the conclusion of a syllogistic inference from 'nothing has no properties' and an existential *cogito* ('certain thoughts exist as properties') than it is deduced from *cogito* and the major 'everything which thinks is.' For the *express* knowledge of both principles comes *after* the *cogito, ergo sum*. So although the *ego sum, ego existo* (AT VII 25: CSM II 17) *can* be 'inferred' from the *cogito* employing this common notion of the natural light, the progress of the mind in the discovery of the first principle of human knowledge is not correctly represented as a piece of deductive or syllogistic reasoning. Distinctive of the movement of thought in the transition from *cogito* to *sum* is rather the temporal sequence of what we specifically *attend* to in reflecting upon our thinking: first to the occurrence of certain modes of thinking, then to the existence of that substance in which they inhere. When reflection begins, our attention is naturally focused upon the former, though even then the latter is implicitly understood. This is the point made in the letter for Pollot, cited earlier: the consciousness of our thinking, for instance, "the thought of breathing [i.e., 'I think, feel, believe that I am breathing'] is present to our mind *before* the thought of our existing ..." (AT II 38: CSMK 98 e.a.). That is, we attend to the former before actually attending to the latter. Behind Descartes's use of the particle *ergo* lies the temporal order of attending signified by this "before" rather than any logical order of precedence. To say that what guarantees the transition from *cogito* to *sum* is the principle 'nothing has no properties' is to construe the principle as an inference licence; if we say instead that the mind exhibits a natural tendency to pass from *cogito* to *sum* and thence to the knowledge of the principle *nihili nullae sunt proprietates* in virtue of its reflexive structure and implicit understanding of this innate principle of the natural light, we present the 'inference' as Descartes seems to have understood it: as a gradually unfolding intuition or process of analytical reflexion. Nevertheless, Descartes, as we have seen, is not disinclined to talk about it in the former way too.

It can legitimately be wondered whether the intuitive progress of the mind described in the reply to Burman can be used in this way to interpret the transition of the mind from the existence of some act or mode of thinking immediately present to consciousness to that of a substance that thinks. After all, the *terminus a quo* of the reflexive process described to Burman is an implicit, and the *terminus ad quem* an explicit, understanding of certain universal notions and principles having no existential import. In pointing out that such notions and principles as are implicitly contained in the *cogito, ergo sum* become explicitly known through analytical reflexion, Descartes is relatively chary of details concerning the process leading up to the express knowledge of the *cogito, ergo sum* itself. He does say that the latter is expressly or explicitly known. Is such knowledge the outcome of a reflexive process of attending to what one is implicitly conscious of whenever one thinks? Can what Descartes says of universal notions and principles "which provide us with no knowledge of anything that exists" be extended in this way to the *cogito, ergo sum*, so that the latter too, while remaining knowledge of the existence of a particular, comes to be grasped in the abstract, as a principle, through a process of analytical reflexion? It may be conflating two different 'stories' to employ the reply to Burman to interpret what is said in the Third Replies and the *Principles* concerning the impossibility of knowing the existence of a substance otherwise than through its modes and the principle 'nothing has no properties.'

Given the meagre and equivocal textual support for any interpretation of the *cogito, ergo sum* that goes beyond saying what it is not, extrapolating from the reply to Burman in this way may be warranted, especially if what is found there is indeed, as Descartes suggests elsewhere, a theory of "the nature of our mind" (AT VII 141: CSM II 100); for such a theory will be applicable to cognitive processes other than those to which Descartes specifically applies it in trying to satisfy Burman on a particular point.

What we have to go on is, first, Descartes's consistent denial that any syllogistic inference is implied by his use of the particle *ergo*. This simply rules out construing the role of the principle 'nothing has no properties' on the syllogistic model. In addition, consideration of the certainty of the *cogito* in section 12.3 made it clear that no specifically logical insight of any other kind is involved either: though Descartes undoubtedly had some inkling of the peculiar logical features of asserting *cogito* and *existo*, as of denying *existo* while affirming *cogito*, his decisive insights are of a different, phenomenological and epistemological order (cf. section 14.8). A further important point was established in section 7.2: along with the actual occurrence of my acts of thinking, their specific act-character, and their intentional objects, I am immediately (though only implicitly) conscious of the existence of an 'I' to which all such acts belong as modes to a substance. It now appears that there is more that I am thus immediately but only implicitly aware of, including the axioms 'nothing has no properties' and 'whatever thinks, exists.' Unlike the notion that *sum* is the conclusion of a deductive inference, the process described to Burman as an intuitive progress of the mind through reflexive attention to what is immediately present to consciousness accords well with the idea of that which, while an inference of sorts, is yet non-deductive, indeed not really logical in nature at all, though it can be cast in a logical form. Furthermore, the only detailed account (as opposed to examples) that Descartes furnishes of the nature of the intuition involved in the knowledge of metaphysically necessary truths like 'nothing has no properties' is that found in the conversation with Burman, where it is employed in connection with the first such truth, *cogito, ergo sum*, even if the implicit-explicit distinction is not specifically applied to the latter. Moreover, the account of the matter given Burman yields a different interpretation of the relation between intuition and deduction from the familiar but unsatisfactory 'immediate intuition / direct inference' account (cf. sections 15.6–8). Finally, this story accords well with still other key doctrines of Descartes. This will be shown for the doctrine of innateness later. Another doctrine, however, is particularly relevant here.

17.2 Intellection and consciousness

That doctrine has been outlined already (cf. section 9.2). It is met with in the Sixth Meditation and concerns the very nature of the mind. It states that intellection alone belongs to the mind's nature or essence; neither sensation nor imagination is "a necessary constituent of my own essence, that is, of the essence of my mind" (AT VII 73: CSM II 51; cf. AT VII 78: CSM II 54). And yet "some intellection (*intellectionem nonnullam*) is included in their essential definition" (AT VII 78: CSM II 54).

This puzzling teaching that intellection is somehow contained in every act of thinking, even sense-perception and imagination, makes excellent sense in the light of the link established earlier (see section 9.2) between the intellect (or rationality) and the consciousness that accompanies all modes of thinking, not as an act, but as the internal reflexive structure of thought acts as such. Descartes hints broadly at this link in the Replies to the Fifth Set of Objections, where he writes that when we "are asleep and are aware (*advertimus*) that we are dreaming, we need imagination in order to dream, but to be aware that we are dreaming (*quod nos somniare advertamus*) *we need only the intellect*" (AT VII 359f.: CSM II 248 e.a.). He does more than just hint at it in a letter to Arnauld of 29 July 1648. Distinguishing the "first and simple thoughts" of infants, which are "*direct* and not reflexive – for instance the pain they feel when some wind distends their intestines, or the pleasure they feel when nourished by sweet blood" from the "reflexive thoughts" of adults, Descartes writes: "when an adult feels something, and simultaneously perceives that he has not felt it before, I call this second perception *reflexion, and attribute it to the intellect alone*, in spite of its being so linked to sensation that the two occur together and appear to be indistinguishable from each other" (AT V 221: CSMK 357 e.a.). Of course, Descartes is not speaking of simple consciousness without reflexive attention here, but it is a safe inference that, as with the latter, so the former too depends on the intellect alone.[2]

Further hints at the same doctrine are provided by the juxtaposition of two related passages, the first from the *Passions of the Soul* and the second from the letter to Regius of May 1641. The former has been cited twice already, first where it was noted that 'action' like 'passion' is ambiguous in Descartes. To repeat:

'passion' can mean either (a) 'perception' as opposed to volition or (b) a specific type of perception that we today term 'emotion.' 'Action' can denote either (i) a volition as opposed to a perception, or (ii) any act of thinking whatever, that is, volitions and perceptions of all kinds, or (iii) a certain way of performing such acts, namely with reflexive attention to the act itself rather than its object. Now for the two passages themselves:

[I]t is certain that we cannot will anything without thereby perceiving that we will it. And although willing something is an action [in sense (i)] with respect to our soul, the perception of such willing may be said to be a passion [in sense (a)] in the soul. But because this perception is really one and the same thing as the volition [i.e., part of one and the same act rather than a separate act], and names are always determined by whatever is most noble, we do not normally call it a 'passion,' but solely an 'action.' (AT XI 343: CSM I 335f.)

What is not said here is that the perception in question is a function of the pure intellect. That is supplied by the other passage:

Finally, where you say 'Willing and understanding differ only as different ways of acting in regard to different objects,' I would prefer 'They differ only as the activity [=action in sense (i)] and passivity [=passion in sense (a)] of one and the same substance.' For strictly speaking, understanding (*intellectio*) is the mind's passivity and willing is its activity; but because we never will anything without at the same time understanding (*quin simul intelligamus*) [that we will it], and because we scarcely ever understand something, without at the same time willing [i.e., passing judgment, assenting or denying] something, we do not easily distinguish in this manner passivity from activity." (AT III 372: CSMK 182)

The doctrine faintly adumbrated in the Sixth Meditation and in the passages just cited becomes much more comprehensible in the light of the reply to Burman interpreted earlier. For as Descartes explains to Burman, a number of intellectual notions and principles is contained implicitly in every (reflexively structured) act of thinking, not just in willing but even in sensing, for example. Of these we are necessarily conscious whenever we think, though only implicitly. When we begin to reflect upon our thinking, that is, attend to what we are immediately conscious of whenever we think anything, we make use of those innate notions and principles (for example, 'thinking,' 'existence,' 'whatever thinks, exists') even before attending to them fully, arriving by their means at the express knowledge of the *cogito, ergo sum*. The faculty in virtue of which we are necessarily conscious of all our acts of thinking is thus the very faculty by which the mind furnishes itself with innate ideas and principles through reflexion on that of which it is *pre*-reflexively conscious. The same operation of the mind that, when performed with attention, is called *intellectio* or *ratio*, is, as *conscientia*, a necessary structural feature of all modes of thinking as such. It is for this reason that it belongs to the "essential definition" of thought.[3]

All this, while somewhat conjectural, seems plausible enough. The question is whether Descartes would say that the thinking that implicitly contains these notions and principles pre-reflexively therefore contains an implicit or pre-reflexive understanding of the *cogito, ergo sum* that can be made explicit through reflexion. If so, the stages in the whole cognitive process look something like this.

By reflecting upon my thinking and making explicit that which is initially only implicit in it I attain first (1) an express knowledge that I exist as a particular thinking thing or substance. This is due to the innate principle 'nothing has no properties' as 'experienced' (immediately intuited) in all individual acts of thinking even before it is attended to. Other notions and principles are involved as well, notably the concepts 'thinking' and 'existence' and the principle 'whatever thinks, is,' which is presumably derivative from 'nothing has no properties.' By the same process of reflexive analysis I attain next (2) an explicit grasp of the *cogito, ergo sum* as an abstract principle or axiom regarding the actual existence of a particular thing. Through still further reflexion on this first principle asserting the existence of a substance I arrive finally at (3) an express awareness of the non-existential principle 'nothing has no properties,' and of all other notions and principles presupposed by the *cogito, ergo sum*: of 'thinking,' 'existence,' 'whatever thinks, exists,' 'freedom,' 'volition,' 'certainty,' or 'truth' – in short, everything of which Descartes says that it is implicit in our thinking and made explicit by reflexion. Thus, the further I carry this process of reflexion, the more adequately is my mind stocked with those concepts and principles necessary for the derivation of still other truths not immediately intuitable in this way. This, at least, is what extrapolation from the reply to Burman would suggest regarding the nature of the inference from *cogito* to *sum*.[4]

17.3 Intuitive induction

How might such a cognitive process be labelled? In light of the fact that it merely explicates what one is already implicitly aware of in the *cogito*, it may be tempting to describe it as an immediate inference rather than an intuition. Certainly, it employs a universal principle ('nothing has no properties') that, being intuited *in concreto* in the *cogito* itself, is co-constitutive of the sole premise of the inference (*cogito*) and not a further premise. But even then the immediate inference would not be from a predicative to an existential proposition, but rather from the immediate apprehension of the existence of a mode or accident to the existence of the substance it inheres in, that is, from one insight expressible in an *existential* statement (*cogito*) to another (*sum*).[5]

While 'immediate inference' is sometimes used loosely to designate any deductive inference from a single premise, the term is closely associated with Aristotle's compilation of canonical logical forms of such inference in the 'traditional square of opposition.' Moreover, the inference as interpreted here involves the tacit use of a metaphysical rather than formal logical principle to explicate the peculiar relation of what may be called (literally, but not in the logical sense) 'implication' between *cogito* and *sum*. Thus, this 'progress of the mind' resists assimilation to immediate logical inference in a crucial respect. If we must assign it a label, perhaps 'intuitive induction' fits best – provided, of course, that what is distinctive of this unique inference regarding the existence of a particular (*sum*) is borne in mind along with what it has in common with the cognitive processes described in general terms to Burman and elsewhere.

Since the deliberate contrast with *de*ductive inference suggests that intuitive induction too is an inference of sorts, the question naturally arises as to whether the progress of the mind so designated can legitimately be characterized as inferential. Perhaps not, if 'inference' is given that restricted sense proposed by Cohen and Nagel in stipulating that what W.E. Johnson labelled 'intuitive induction' in Aristotle cannot be called an inference "by *any* stretch of the term" since it "is not a *type of argument* analyzable into a premise and a conclusion." Being only "a perception of relations ... not subject to any rules of validity," it "represents the gropings and tentative guessings of a mind aiming at knowledge. Intuitive induction is therefore not antithetical to deduction," they conclude, "because it is not a type of inference at all ... *There can be no logic or method of intuitive induction*" (Cohen and Nagel 1934, 274 e.a.).

This may be a fair comment on the relevant concept of *epagōgē* in the *Posterior Analytics*.[6] Still, even in Aristotle 'induction' and 'deduction' can be usefully opposed as different types of inference. At the very least, this may help to bring out what is after all a significant, if merely formal, point of contrast: while the latter proceeds from the universal to the particular, the former reverses the order, 'grasping the universal in the particular,' sometimes on the basis of a single instance (cf. for instance, Aristotle 1949a, 47 [*An. Post.*, 71a 8]). In Descartes we encounter a similar, quite deliberate reversal (cf. AT VII 140: CSM II 100). Given his careful delineation of the movement of thought or progress of the mind in analytical refexion in the conversation with Burman, "not by *any* stretch of the term" is surely too strong in Descartes's case – as perhaps it is also in Aristotle's. If Cohen and Nagel have a point it is that the analytic progress of the mind is not one that can be checked by the application of a set of well-defined rules of inference – though this realization may have been hard to come by for Descartes himself, as the much criticized Rules of the *Regulae* and Part Two of the *Discourse* attest. If there is no stronger objection than this to extending the customary sense of 'inference' to include Descartes's analytical reflexion and Aristotle's *epagōgē*, one's reluctance may be less on considering all Descartes has to say, directly and indirectly, about the analytic method of discovery. The process of analytical reflexion was shown to be largely synonymous with the 'Cartesian method' that was to find its most adequate expression in the elaborate structure of argument that is the *Meditations* (cf. above, sections 15.6f.). At bottom, there is exactly the same justification for regarding *cogito* as the premise of an inference as there is for treating the principle 'nothingness has no attributes' as an inference licence. While perhaps not ideal, in the absence of a more fitting designation the name 'intuitive induction' will have to do – provided, of course, that the relevant difference in starting point between Descartes and Aristotle is carefully borne in mind.

The experience of the particular through reflexion on which the basic concepts and universal principles of human knowledge are acquired is, for Descartes, not so much ordinary connected experience of extra-mental objects – which is what Aristotle understands by *empeiria* – as the concomitant *inner* experience of one's own thinking about such objects. For it is through reflexive attention to my actually occurring acts of thinking that I acquire the basic concepts, not just of thinking, but of existence, duration, truth, God, and freedom. In the next chapter, it will be shown that the same is true of *all* those ideas and principles that Descartes terms 'innate,' the basic concepts and principles of logic and mathematics no less than the basic metaphysical *and physical* concepts, principles, or laws. For the express understanding of some of these, ordinary outer experience may be indispensable; but it is the reflexion on the concomitant inner experience that actually gives rise to the basic concepts and principles of mathematics and physico-mathematical natural science in the mind.

This fundamental difference between Descartes's starting point and that of Aristotelian science is consistently overlooked by Clarke and Hoenen, with the distorting result that, for Clarke, Descartes is little more than "an innovative Aristotelian" (1982, chap. 8) in his conception of scientific method, while for Hoenen he merely elevated a principle found already in Aristotle and frequently enunciated by St Thomas to the status of *the* first principle of philosophy. McRae, on the other hand, sees the relevant sense of 'experience' in Descartes clearly, though he too stresses the affinity with Aristotle rather than the differences. McRae's and Clarke's interpretations of innateness will be discussed in chapter 18. We conclude this treatment of the inferential import of the *ergo* with a discussion of Hoenen's interpretation of the "mouvement de la pensée" signalled by the presence of the logical particle *ergo*.

17.4 The 'movement of thought' in a historical perspective

Starting from Hamelin's question of whether the *cogito, ergo sum* is a *jugement* or a *raisonnement* – or rather, from Descartes's apparently contradictory pronouncements on the subject – Hoenen reaches the conclusion that Descartes's founding principle is akin to a distinctive type of a hypothetical judgment called a "causal proposition" by the Scholastics and known to Stoic logicians under the name *axioma aitiodēs*. This type of proposition is supposed to fuse elements of two others, the purely logical relation *(liaison nécessaire)* of material implication ('if I am abc, then I am a') and a merely accidental conjunction of contingent propositions having existential import (for instance, 'I am thinking and I am hearing a melody'). "Le *cogito, ergo sum* est donc vraiment ... une proposition causale, qui est le fruit d'une seule intuition ... virtuellement multiple, parcequ'elle s'exprime par une formule qui contient trois affirmations" (Hoenen, 1937, 464). The three affirmations are: "[1] affirmation de l'existence (accidentelle) de ma pensée, [2] affirmation de l'existence (substantielle) du moi, de mon âme, [3] affirmation de la liaison *nécessaire* entre les deux existences, ma pensée actuelle *supposant nécessairement* l'existence de mon ame [*sic*] et me révélant celle-ci; c'est cette dernière affirmation qui est exprimée par l'ergo" (462). Hamelin's question, 'process of reasoning *or* simple affirmation?' thus exaggerates "la différence entre les deux opérations de l'esprit humain (468)," according to Hoenen, by opposing affirmation to inference roughly as rest to motion; whereas the Scholastic causal proposition is an immediate intuition which, being multiple, is also a necessary "mouvement de la pensée."

   The first and second affirmations embody Hoenen's interpretation of the *cogito* and *sum*. There is little to quarrel with here. The third, he says, conveys the sense of the *ergo*, which expresses a logically necessary connection, though one grasped in the course of a single (though multiple) intuition rather than through any discursive or ratiocinative process. The notion of an intuition that is "multiple" seems entirely apposite here. Yet Hoenen's interpretation of the *ergo* fails to capture the temporal sequence in which all that of which one is implicitly conscious becomes, by stages, explicit through the selective focusing of reflexive attention now on one, now on another aspect of that which is immediately present to consciousness: on the *cogito*, on the *sum*, on the abstract principle, and finally on the innate universal notions and principles, especially *nihili nullae sunt proprietates*, the implicit understanding of which makes the *cogito*, the *sum*, and the transition of the mind from one to the other possible.

   Having interpreted the *ergo* as described, Hoenen turns next to the conversation with Burman and the universal proposition '*quicquid cogitat, est*': "une première expérience me donne le *cogito* tout seul, un retour sur cette intuition me révèle l'*ego sum* et la connexion nécessaire, connexion qui s'exprime par l'*ergo*; un second retour m'apprend la vérité universelle: « pour penser il faut être », ou plutôt m'apprend l'universalité de cette vérité" (1937, 467). It is this "second retour," involving "l'intuition de l'universelle" (ibid.) in the particular, that suggests the parallel with Aristotle's concept of induction, not the initial progress of the mind from *cogito* to *sum*, which is simply a causal proposition.

Apart from the failure to recognize the difference between what Descartes and Aristotle understand by 'experience,' there is a further serious shortcoming to note. According to Hoenen, the relation of the particular to the universal is not a sequence within the order of cognition itself. Rather, Descartes's use of *reipsa* in the remark to Burman that the universal proposition *quicquid cogitat, est* is "in reality (*reipsa*) prior" (AT V 147: CSMK 333) is taken to signify a distinction between what is first 'in itself,' in "l'ordre ontologique" (ibid.), and what is first "pour notre connaissance" (ibid.) or in "l'ordre de la connaissance" (ibid., 466). The universal proposition is also prior in what Descartes himself refers to as the synthetic order of proof or demonstration, while in the order of discovery or knowing the particular truth, *cogito, ergo sum*, is first: "La proposition universelle ne semble être énoncée ... que pour couper court à toute dispute, pour clore le débat, en indiquant le fondement ontologique, *in re ipsa*, de la proposition causale" (467). This simply overlooks the fact that those universal principles that only come to be known *explicitly* after the particular truth *cogito, ergo sum* are nevertheless known *implicitly* even prior to the latter and must be so known if it is to be explicitly known at all. It is thus the order of cognition, that is, the order of discovery that is *alone* in question, whereby the distinction between the implicit and explicit has the decisive role to play. Not every earlier use of the implicit-explicit distinction is relevant to the sense of the *ergo* in Descartes's founding principle. This is plain enough for the transition from implicit to explicit knowledge in syllogistic reasoning, since Descartes himself points out the difference between these two stages of the process of 'making explicit' (see sections 15.2 and 15.6).[7] Likewise in the case of "causal propositions": St Thomas's theory of the "transition de la puissance à l'acte" in judgment (ibid., 468) is simply not the same as the transition of the mind from the implicit to the explicit in passing from *cogito* to *sum* or from *sum* to the universal truth *quicquid cogitat, est*. Although Descartes was willing to describe the latter in the language of potentiality and actuality, and did in fact so describe it in the *Comments on a Certain Broadsheet* (for example, VIII-2 361: CSM I 361) and elsewhere (cf. AT XI 65), the underlying theory of the mind is *toto coelo* different from both Aquinas's and Aristotle's. What it means for Descartes for an idea to be in the mind only 'potentially,' that is, to be in the faculty of thinking rather than actually present to consciousness, will be discussed in section 18.5.[8]

What is most distinctive about Descartes's concept of reflexion as a process of selectively attending to what is immediately present to consciousness is thus largely obscured by Hoenen's preoccupation with antecedents. It is to St Thomas, not Aristotle, that he turns in the end to find a concept of *inner* experience resembling Descartes's. However, Descartes's notion of immediate self-awareness in fact bears little resemblance to Aquinas's doctrine of "la connaissance de l'âme par l'âme" (1937, 471) in second-order reflexive acts. This in itself suffices to show that it is quite wrong to suggest that the only thing radically new here is the rather arbitrary elevation of the very principle already recognized by Aquinas as one among others to the status of *the* first principle of philosophy (cf. ibid., 465n., 470). For Hoenen, there is almost nothing of philosophical significance in the *cogito, ergo sum* that cannot be traced to some ancient or medieval source; in this he resembles the Bourdin of the remark cited as the epigram of this study. But if the interpretation developed here is at all plausible, Hoenen's painstaking and erudite analysis serves only to show that there is in fact very little that is not in large measure strikingly new and boldly innovative. This must be shown more fully in chapters 19 and 20.

18

Reflexion and Innateness

At the close of chapter 15 it was observed that the process of analytical reflexion leading from implicit to explicit insight has much to do with (1) the inferential import of the *ergo*, with (2) the Cartesian doctrine of innateness, and with (3) Descartes's conception of the intellect or the natural light of reason. It obviously has an important bearing on the Cartesian notion of analytic method as well (see sections 15.6 and 15.7). The first subject has now been dealt with. The second will be discussed here and the third in chapters 19 and 20.

18.1 McRae on innate ideas

McRae has provided an instructive account of how the metaphysical concepts of substance, truth, freedom, and so forth are derived from the *cogito, ergo sum*, that is, rendered explicit in the manner dictated by what he terms Descartes's 'reflective theory' of innateness:

When Descartes maintains the primitive character of the *cogito, ergo sum* ... he is not asserting the logical priority of the knowledge of the particular; rather he is concerned with the transition from the implicit to the explicit within 'experience' or 'consciousness.' Descartes' entire activity in the first four *Meditations* of extracting the concepts of 'thing,' 'thought,' 'truth,' 'substance,' 'God,' 'freedom' is that of directing attention to, or reflecting upon, what I am pre-reflectively conscious of in the *cogito*. (McRae 1972a, 40)

This captures precisely the root sense of 'innate' in Descartes. That McRae confines this process to the first four Meditations has to do with the fact that the Fifth and Sixth are concerned largely with material things. As he shows (ibid., 34), Descartes can legitimately extend this reflective theory to the concepts of duration, number, and order as "common" or "simple notions" that apply to all things as such, including the mind;[1] but it seems that any reflective theory must be limited to those concepts directly or indirectly involved in the self's knowledge of its own thinking and existence. Given that the 'I,' mind, or self exists as a thinking thing having neither size nor shape, it is difficult to grasp how, for example, simple geometrical ideas of particular shapes and sizes could intelligibly be said to be acquired through reflexion upon thinking. This is more striking still in the case of the idea of extension in general: since the mind is not extended, it is hard to see how the idea of extension could be acquired through reflection on the *cogito, ergo sum.*

The latter difficulty was raised already by Gassendi in his objections to the Third Meditation proof of God's existence: "There is a considerable difficulty about how you can derive these ['ideas of corporeal things'] from yourself or simply from the idea of yourself, when you claim to be incorporeal and consider yourself as such. For if you have knowledge only of an incorporeal substance, how can it be that you also have some grasp of corporeal substance (AT VII 293: CSM II 204)? Brushing aside the genuine perplexity behind the question, Descartes conveniently takes Gassendi to be waggishly burdening him with the view that all, even sensible, ideas of corporeal things are derived from the *cogito, ergo sum*:

I did not assert that the ideas of material things are derived from the mind, as you some-what disingenuously make out. Later on I explicitly showed that these ideas *often* come to us from bodies, and that it is this that enables us to prove the existence of bodies. (AT VII 367: CSM II 253 e.a.)

Gassendi's quite legitimate query is thus left unanswered: how can the clear and distinct idea of corporeal substance be derived from the mind's reflexive atten-tion to its own thinking, when the mind itself is incorporeal? And a similar ques-tion might have been put, with equal justice, regarding simple geometrical ideas.[2]

Two ways around both difficulties suggest themselves. Either the ideas in ques-tion are not innate but adventitious; or they are innate in some sense other than that presupposed by the reflective theory. McRae exploits both strategies. The idea of extension in length, breadth, and depth is an adventitious idea (1972a, 45f.; cf. also McRae 1976, 99f.); as for ideas of particular shapes and simple mathematical truths, these are innate in a sense different from the metaphysical ideas and common notions, a sense that McRae dubs 'the *anamnesis* theory': "If Descartes regards the ideas and truths of geometry as innate in the mind they are so in the sense that they are *logically* entailed by an idea which is in the mind, namely extension, without reference, however, to whether the idea of extension itself originates in sense experience or not" (1972a, 47). From the reflective and *anamnesis* theories of Descartes McRae then distinguishes Leibniz's conception of innate ideas as "dispositions or tendencies" in the mind, ruling out the ascription of any dispositional theory to Descartes.

There appear to be three difficulties with this account. First, with regard to the idea of extension, it rests at bottom on an argument that the adventitious character of the idea is indispensable to Descartes's causal proof of the existence of the external world in the Sixth Meditation. Whatever the merits of McRae's argument here, the fact remains that express denials of his conclusion are to be found at several places in Descartes's works and letters. So there are serious textual obstacles to be overcome.³ As for the *anamnesis* version of innateness, McRae's account, notably his emphatic use of '*logically*,' evokes what have been termed 'discursive' and 'ratiocinative' processes above. Yet there is no evidence that the simple mathematical ideas of shapes or the axioms employed by the geometer are arrived at by any discursive or ratiocinative process; on the contrary, all the evidence points to an immediate intuitive grasp of such concepts as 'square,' 'triangle,' and 'circle,' or the axioms that 'the whole is greater than its parts' or 'if equals are taken from equals the remainders are equal' (cf. AT I 476: CSMK 77). So there is a certain difficulty with the way McRae handles the mathematical concepts of geometrical shapes as well. Finally, the rejection of the dispositional theory seems to run counter to the plain sense of certain passages of the *Comments on a Certain Broadsheet* to be considered later.

18.2 Clarke on innateness

A second influential treatment of the theme of innate ideas is found in Clarke (1982, chap. 3). His strategy is complex, involving the amalgamation of McRae's reflective and dispositional senses into a single theory that he distinguishes from the rather misleading conception of innateness in the following passage from the *Broadsheet*:

[W]e must admit that in no case are the ideas of things presented to us by the senses just as we form them in our thinking. So much so that there is nothing in our ideas which is not innate to the mind or the faculty of thinking, with the sole exception of those circumstances which relate to experience (*solis iis circumstantiis exceptis, quae ad experientiam spectant*), such as the fact that we judge that this or that idea which we now have immediately before the mind refers to a certain thing situated outside us. We make such a judgment not because these things transmit the ideas to our minds through the sense organs, but because they transmit something which, at exactly that moment, gives the mind occasion to form these ideas by means of the faculty innate to it. Nothing reaches our mind from external objects through the sense organs except certain corporeal motions ... But neither the motions themselves nor the figures arising from them are conceived by us exactly as they occur in the sense organs, as I have explained at length in my *Optics*. (AT VIII-2 358f.: CSM I 304)

According to McRae, this passage shows that the dispositional analysis of the *Broadsheet* applies to Descartes's theory of perceptual *judgments* as expounded in the *Optics*, not to innate ideas as such.[4] Clarke, by contrast, takes Descartes to be calling attention to "the special status of ... ideas vis-à-vis their causes"; in order to do so, "he calls all ideas in the mind innate" (Clarke 1982, 50). This peculiar sense in which all ideas are 'innate' is distinct from the reflective theory employed to clarify the concept of a "native disposition or propensity of the human mind to conceive of a particular class of ideas among the many which are possible, and to realise this capacity independently of any extra-mental agency" (52).

For Clarke, then, there are these two senses of 'innate,' which he distinguishes as innate$_1$ and innate$_2$: "Descartes uses the word 'innate' to characterise two rather different features of ideas. All ideas are innate$_1$, and this is a metaphysical thesis about the irreducibility of (intellectual) ideas to the physical stimulations and brain-states which often cause their occurrence in the mind. Among innate$_1$ ideas some are even more independent of experience in so far as the mind can come to have these ideas by reflection on its own intellectual activities or by inferences from these reflections. [These are the innate$_2$ ideas, as Clarke goes on to say.] It is in this sense that the idea of truth, of doubt or of thought is acquired, as is the idea of the soul. Even the idea of God is innate$_2$ only in the sense that I can come to have the idea of a perfect being by reflection on my own imperfection" (Clarke 1982, 53). Obviously, this latter sense of 'innateness' is the crucial one for the understanding of Descartes's model of the mind; like McRae, Clarke has well understood the root sense of 'innateness' in Descartes ('born of the mind's reflexion on its own operations'), though, unlike McRae, he correctly regards it as a dispositional theory (see below). As for the precise extension of the second concept, Clarke's conclusion is again very like McRae's:

This dispositional analysis of innateness involves more than the simple possibility of having certain ideas. It implies something actually present in the human mind which tends to give rise to innate$_2$ ideas once certain conditions are fulfilled ... For example, a person who has exercised his intellectual faculties for some time has had experience of making judgments, of denying propositions, of pondering decisions, etc., and therefore can be said to have innate ideas of truth, doubt, and certainty. This amounts to implying that *the exercise of one's cognitive faculties is alone sufficient to produce in the reflective mind the concepts of truth, doubt, etc.* These ideas are innate$_2$ in the sense that they are not derived from any sensory experience; at the same time, *the mind is not necessarily aware of them at all times in an explicit manner.* The propensity to generate these ideas spontaneously in the mind by reflecting on our intellectual activities is what Descartes means by claiming that we have innate$_2$ ideas. (ibid., 52 e.a.)

This restriction of the concept 'innate$_2$' to the ideas of "intellectual things" like truth, doubt, and so on Clarke finds confirmed by the *Regulae*:

Precisely those ideas which are elsewhere said to be innate$_2$, such as the ideas of doubt or ignorance, are also recognised in the *Regulae* as innate$_2$, or as being purely intellectual ... On the other hand those ideas which are elsewhere thought to result from our sensory experience are likewise classified as material simple natures in the *Regulae, and are acquired as usual through sensory experience.* What *seems* troublesome here is the suggestion that all simple natures are acquired by the operation of the 'pure *intuitus*,' despite their [sensory] origins. However this is nothing more than the familiar Cartesian thesis that all ideas are innate$_1$, i.e. that it is only in the understanding [i.e., mind] and not in the senses that one has ideas of any kind and that these ideas are irreducible to their sensory causes. (57f. e.a.)

Thus, quite independently of McRae, whose work he does not appear to know, Clarke asserts that the idea of extension is adventitious; where Descartes suggests otherwise, he means innate$_1$. Even the notorious *inspectio mentis* of the wax example is "consistent with Descartes' innateness$_1$ theory," according to Clarke, *inspectio mentis* or *sola mente percipere* being "a usefully vague way of referring to this thesis" (58) about the irreducibility of ideas to their causes. Similarly, the axioms or common notions of logic, mathematics, and metaphysics are only innate$_1$ (cf. 62).

18.3 Problems with both interpretations

Clarke's analysis represents no significant advance on McRae's in respect of the first difficulty, unless Descartes's repeated claim that extension is an innate idea perceived not "by the senses or the faculty of imagination but by the intellect alone" (AT VII 34: CSM II 22) is indeed a reference to innateness$_1$ rather than innateness$_2$. This seems, at the very least, highly unlikely. In the letter to Mersenne cited by McRae (see note 3 above) the ideas of body and a triangle are ranged alongside those of the mind and God as innate in a sense clearly opposed to both 'factitious' and 'adventitious.' And from the prior rejection first of the senses and then of imagination as possible sources of the idea of an *extensum quid, flexibile et mutabile* (the wax), it seems that innateness$_2$ is in question in the Second Meditation as well. So the textual obstacles mentioned earlier remain.

As for the second difficulty, Clarke provides no such detailed analysis as

McRae's (cf. 1972a, 45) of the operations performed upon the alleged datum of sensory experience in arriving at simple geometrical ideas and axioms. Innate in the sense of the *anamnesis* theory for McRae, they are no more than innate₁ for Clarke. Without making mathematical concepts and axioms questionably dependent on discursive operations, as does McRae, Clarke nevertheless assigns the senses and imagination a significant supporting role in the intellect's pure intuition. Like McRae, he holds that the "innateness of ideas does not preclude a relevant empirical input in appropriate cases; *intuitus* does not preclude reflexion on ordinary experience" (1982, 70). This is what "the Cartesian theory of our cognitive faculties" suggests to him (72). More than the term *intuitus* itself, the modifier *purus* is to blame for obscuring the role of "ordinary experience" in the functioning of the intellect: "Descartes' use of expressions such as '*intuitus purus*' ... admittedly has unfortunate connotations for the contemporary reader, connotations of a kind of direct, non-empirical inspection of the essence of rather suspect ontological simples" (60).

It was suggested earlier (cf. section 5.1) that Descartes's use of 'pure' is ambiguous as between Husserl's and Kant's senses: 'purged' of (1) extra-mental, that is, material or of (2) sensory elements. They by no means coincide, since 'purged of sensory content' entails 'purged of material elements,' but not vice versa.⁵ According to Clarke, in designating an intuition 'pure' Descartes is not "denying the relevance of sense and imagination to *intuitus*"; he is denying "that one can *define* the term by reference to the characteristic functions or normal operation of the senses and the imagination" (ibid., 59 e.a.). The interpretation of 'pure' in terms of 'indefinability' or 'unanalysability' seems far-fetched in a way that the appeal to the more conventional senses of 'pure' in Husserl and Kant does not. In any case, Clarke's thesis is apt to suggest that *intuitus purus* is sheerly unanalysable in terms of *anything* else. This simply overlooks the detailed analysis given Burman of the stages or phases of intuition as a process of analytical reflexion on the pre-reflexively conscious. If *that* is "the Cartesian theory of our cognitive faculties" (Clarke), the role of "ordinary experience" in the purely intellectual knowledge of material things is very different from that described by either McRae or Clarke and there is absolutely nothing "unfortunate" about the Kantian overtones of the word *purus*. Quite the contrary (cf. chapter 19).

Nor do matters stand any better in regard to the third difficulty. Clarke's innateness₂ integrates the reflective and dispositional theories, whereas McRae discounted the latter as inconsistent with Descartes's *tabula rasa* or 'wax tablet' model of the mind (1972b, 51). Yet Clarke too ascribes just this model to Descartes; he simply interprets the active disposition or "propensity to generate" certain ideas "spontaneously ... by reflecting on our intellectual activities" (1982, 53) in a manner consistent with it. And, in point of fact, if confined to ideas like "the innate ideas of truth, doubt, and certainty," the dispositional theory does seem to go little beyond Locke's "ideas of reflection." For his part, McRae dismissed the blanket application of the dispositional theory in the *Broadsheet* precisely because it involves a model of the mind of the type championed by Leibniz against Locke, one that subverts empiricist theories of the mind, from Aristotle and Locke to Hobbes and Gassendi (cf. 1973a, 52f.). The fundamental issue, then, is the model of the mind, and here both commentators are perfectly at one.[6]

18.4 The extent of the reflexive-dispositional theory of innateness

The last-mentioned point will be taken up in the next two chapters. The immediate task is to exploit the results of chapters 15 and 17 in order to show that there is a single theory of innateness in Descartes, having an extension much wider than that assigned it by either McRae or Clarke. It can conveniently (if inelegantly) be labelled the 'reflexive-dispositional theory.' 'Reflexion,' 'attention,' 'faculty,' 'power,' 'tendency' (*dispositio*) are, however, not the explanatory ultimates of this theory – at least not if we may extrapolate further from the detailed explanation given Burman. The aim here is to revise McRae's reflective theory in a manner consistent with Descartes's model of the mind as possessing a *passive* tendency or disposition to form certain ideas and principles by reflecting upon its own thinking (cf. section 19.3); for the model applies not just to intellectual or metaphysical "things" and a few "common notions," but to everything to which Descartes applies the term 'innate' (cf. section 20.3 below).

Descartes's published works frequently address this reflexive-dispositional theory in language that is misleading. Consequently, the theory retains just enough in the way of vestigial remains of the old Platonic-Stoic-Ciceronian 'imprint theory' to give at least some point to Locke's polemic against innate ideas and principles even in regard to Descartes.[7] Of course, the "seeds of truth" doctrine in the *Regulae* and *Discourse*, like the talk of ideas and axioms "implanted" in or "imprinted" on the mind, tends to mask the real theory, while suggesting rightly nonetheless that Descartes embraced a theory or model of the mind fundamentally opposed to that of all 'empiricisms,' ancient or modern. The reflexive-dispositional theory differs also from Leibniz's account of the mind as possessing *active* dispositions to produce certain ideas. While Clarke uses the language of Leibniz, the theory he in fact ascribes to Descartes does not obviously go beyond what Locke might have held. And McRae argues insistently against reading a theory of active dispositions such as Leibniz's back into Descartes. The scope of Descartes's reflexive-dispositional theory of innateness will be dealt with in this, the underlying model of the mind in the next, chapter.

The former question may be put this way. Is it, as McRae and Clarke hold,

merely (1) the abstract metaphysical notions of thinking, of existence, of freedom, truth, and God, together with (2) certain "common notions" like 'duration'
and 'number,' which are derived from the *cogito, ergo sum* by the mind's reflection on its own thinking? Or is it likewise (3) the idea of extension in length,
breadth, and depth and (4) of all such particular shapes as are "true and immutable natures"? Can, moreover, (5) the eternal truths of logic (*impossibile est idem
simul esse & non esse*) and (6) the axioms of mathematics ('the whole is greater
than the part,' 'if equals are taken away from equals the remainders are equal') be
understood as innate in the same sense as (1) and (2)? Can even (7) the metaphysical principles of the natural light (*ex nihilo nihil fit, nihili nullae sunt
proprietates, quod factum est, infectum esse nequit*) and (8) the most basic laws
of physics (inertia, rectilinearity, conservation of motion) be assigned the very
origin in reflexion upon the *cogito, ergo sum* that was assigned *is qui cogitat, non
potest non existere dum cogitat* in the conversation with Burman?[8]

Another, perhaps tendentious, way of putting the same question is to ask, What
may and may not plausibly be included among the *principia communia et axiomata*
that Descartes ranges alongside the "idea of God and ourselves, which never
were in the senses" in the conversation with Burman? Apart from these concepts,
which are only examples of ideas that are innate, the sole propositional 'nature'
that Descartes actually instances is the principle *impossible est idem esse et non
esse* (AT V 147: CSMK 333). If the argument of the previous chapter was at all
persuasive, *nihili nullae sunt proprietates* and *quicquid cogitat, est* must be included among the *principia communia et axiomata* as well. This furnishes an
answer to the question regarding (5) and (7). But it still leaves us in the dark
about the mathematical concepts, axioms, and laws mentioned in (3), (4), (6),
and (8) as well as the specific sense of the innateness invoked in each.

So put, the question is tendentious because it assumes that the relevant sense
of innateness is that of the theory of reflexion explained to Burman, when that is
the very thing to be established. To avoid prejudicing the issue unnecessarily, it
will be well to begin with the idea of God. Not only is it treated rather fully in
both the *Meditations* and the *Broadsheet*; it is in many ways the paradigm of an
innate idea for Descartes. Next, (3), (4), (6), and (8) will be treated separately.
The point is to establish that, for Descartes, the ideas of extension, of simple
geometrical natures, of mathematical axioms, and the most universal laws of
nature are all innate in the manner described in the reflexive-dispositional theory.
Exactly what that theory involves will be spelled out gradually through contrasts
with Leibniz and Aristotle in chapters 19 and 20.

18.5 The idea of God

In a famous passage of the Third Meditation, Descartes speaks of the idea of God as "placed ... in me to be, as it were, the mark of the craftsman stamped on his work" (VII 51: CSM II 35).[9] Precisely this idea of God was seen (cf. section 9.1, and Clarke's testimony above) to be *acquired* through reflexion upon the self as an imperfect thinking thing. It is thus acquired *after* the *cogito, ergo sum* and *sum res cogitans* are explicitly known. But it must *already* have been in the mind and implicitly understood prior to reflexion upon them; for, "how could I understand that I doubted or desired – that is, lacked something – and that I was not wholly perfect unless there were in me some idea of a more perfect being which enabled me to recognise my own defects by comparison?" (AT VII 46: CSM II 31). When Burman found this inconsistent with something in the *Discourse*, Descartes replied:

In that part of the *Discourse* ... the author recognised his own imperfection by recognising the perfection of God. He did this implicitly if not explicitly. Explicitly, we are able to recognise our own imperfection before we recognise the perfection of God. This is because we are able to direct our attention to ourselves before we direct our attention to God. Thus we can infer (*concludere*) our own finiteness before we arrive at his infiniteness. Despite this, however, the knowledge of God and his perfection must implicitly always come before the knowledge of ourselves and our imperfections, since our imperfection is a defect and negation of the perfection of God. And every defect and negation presupposes that of which it falls short and which it negates. (AT V 153: CSMK 338)

What is essentially the same observation is found also in a letter to Clerselier of 23 April 1649: "in order to be able to conceive a finite being, I must take away something from this general notion of [infinite] being, which therefore precedes it" (AT V 356: CSMK 377). The point is of great importance to Descartes. If the idea of the true and immutable nature of the Perfect Being were derived from the idea I have of myself as a finite thinking thing – say, by negating my own imperfections – then the idea of God would be factitious. This would vitiate the causal inference to God's existence outside the mind from the presence of the idea of God within. To Gassendi's suggestion (AT VII 287: CSM II 200; also AT VII 295f.: CSM 205f., AT VII 299: CSM 208, AT VII 303f.: CSM II 211f.), likewise fatal to the causal proof, that we fashion the idea of God by amplifying those perfections which we notice in ourselves rather than negating our imperfections, Descartes replies: "You yourself admit that these perfections must be amplified by our intellect if they are to be attributed to God ... [H]ow could we have a faculty for amplifying all created perfections (i.e. conceiving of something greater or more ample than they are) were it not for the fact that there is in us an idea of something greater, namely God?" (AT VII 365: CSM II 252). In the light of this Descartes seems to be courting trouble when he explains "the idea I have of God's understanding" to Hobbes in these terms: "Now everyone surely perceives that there are things he understands. Hence everyone has the form or idea of understanding, and by indefinitely extending this he can form the idea of God's understanding. And a similar procedure applies to the other attributes of God" (AT VII 188: CSM II 132). On the face of it, this suggests an idea of God produced by extending indefinitely the compass of one's own understanding, goodness, and so on.[10] But as the reply to Burman made clear, "extending indefinitely" is not a process of amplification but of gradually *making explicit* the compass of an unlimited understanding, the idea of which already exists implicitly in the mind. This is in fact the language Descartes uses in replying to Gassendi:

[O]nce the idea of the true God has been conceived, although we may detect additional perfections in him which we had not yet noticed, this does not mean that we have augmented the idea of God; *we have simply made it more distinct and explicit*, since, so long as we suppose that our original idea was a true one, it must have contained all these perfections [implicitly] ... [T]he idea of God is not gradually formed by us when we amplify the perfections of his creatures; it is formed all at once and in its entirety as soon as our mind reaches an infinite being which is incapable of any amplification. (AT VII 371: CSM II 256 e.a.)[11]

These are arguments out of the same stable as the notorious Platonic sophism that in order to recognize x as greater than y in some respect (say, beauty) one must possess the idea of perfect Beauty as a standard or paradigm against which to measure both, thus discovering that one "falls" further "short" (Descartes's expression, as it is Plato's) of absolute perfection.[12] Although the pure exemplar is, for Descartes, an innate idea rather than an item situated outside the mind in a world of transcendent universals, a peculiar Platonizing tendency is apparent nonetheless in Descartes's insistence that an implicit notion of the perfect being, God, is presupposed by the explicit grasp of our own imperfections in the *cogito, ergo sum* and *sum res cogitans*: "And when I consider the fact that I have doubts, or that I am a thing that is incomplete and dependent, *then* there arises in me (*mihi occurrit*) a clear and distinct idea of a being who is independent and complete, that is, an idea of God" (AT VII 53: CSM II 37 e.a.). As will be seen presently, this chimes in well with many other passages in which Descartes suggests that the idea of God is in the mind only *potentially* until it becomes actual through reflexive attention to thinking itself. The salient point is that the idea of God must be there *first, if only implicitly*, in order for the human mind to grasp its own imperfection, even though it is only through reflexion on the *cogito, ergo sum* and the *sum res cogitans* that the idea of God is made explicit. The hold that such arguments 'from degrees of perfection' have exercised on some of the greatest minds in the Western tradition may surprise us; but given Descartes's repeated statements of adherence to the doctrine, in conversation with Burman, in the letter to Clerselier, and in the Replies to the Fifth Set of Objections, the fact that he held it can scarcely be disputed.[13]

This argument from the awareness of our own imperfection to the prior though only implicit awareness of an infinite or Perfect Being is as straightforward an illustration of the process of analytical reflexion described to Burman as one could wish for. The starting point is an implicit understanding of certain concepts and principles: 'existence,' 'thinking,' 'truth,' and the principles 'nothing has no properties' and 'whatever thinks, is.' They are implicit in the *cogito, ergo sum*. To these concepts and principles must be added 'perfection,' that is, the concept of a perfect thinking thing or God. The next stage is the explicit understanding of the *cogito, ergo sum*, not as an abstract philosophical principle – that requires further reflexion – but as a particular truth regarding the existence of a substance, a finite thinking thing or mind – my own. Then comes the *explicit* grasp of those notions and principles, the idea of perfection or God among them, which were hitherto only implicitly understood, but without which the *cogito, ergo sum res cogitans finita* could not have been expressly grasped in the first place. As the final stage come such logical inferences, direct or indirect, and such further fruits of analytical reflexion as can be drawn from the stock of explicit concepts and principles (logical, mathematical, or metaphysical) with which the mind has thus furnished itself.

To this point, nothing has been said of the account of the idea of God in *Comments on a Certain Broadsheet*, a work central to the interpretations of both McRae and Clarke, or of Descartes's employment of the (otherwise reviled) potentiality-actuality distinction to explain his meaning both there and in the Replies to the Fourth Set of Objections by Arnauld.

In the *Broadsheet* the theme of innateness is first introduced in the much-cited comment on article twelve of Regius's tract:

I have never written or taken the view that the mind requires innate ideas which are something distinct from its own faculty of thinking. I did, however, observe that there were certain thoughts within me which neither came to me from external objects nor were determined by my will, but which *came solely from the power of thinking within me*; so I applied the term 'innate' to the ideas or notions which are the forms of these thoughts in order to distinguish them from others which I called 'adventitious' or 'factitious.' This is *the same sense* as that in which we say that generosity is 'innate' in certain families, or that certain diseases ... are innate in others; it is not so much that the babies of such families suffer from these diseases in their mother's womb, but simply that they are born with a certain 'faculty' or tendency (*dispositione*) to contract them. (AT VIII-2 357f.: CSM I 303 e.a.)

This is quite general, without specific reference to the idea of God. So too the comments on Regius's thirteenth article:

In article *thirteen* he draws an extraordinary conclusion from the preceding article. Because the mind has no need of innate ideas, its powers of thinking being sufficient, he says, 'all common notions which are engraved in the mind have their origin in observation of things or in verbal instruction' – as if the power of thinking could achieve nothing on its own, could never perceive or think anything except what it receives through observation of things or through verbal instruction, i.e. from the senses. (AT VIII-2 358: CSM I 304)

Descartes is simply incredulous at Regius's suggestion. Next, with reference to article fourteen, he explains that certain ideas "come to us from no other source than our own faculty of thinking" and are therefore "innate in us, i.e. they always exist in us *potentially*, for to exist in some faculty is not to exist actually but *merely potentially*, since the term 'faculty' denotes nothing but a potentiality" (AT VIII-2 361: CSM I 305 e.a.). His comments here concern the idea of God specifically, as does the response to Jacques de Rives's *Gemina Disputatio Metaphysica de Deo* (1647) which concludes the *Broadsheet*:

[B]y 'innate ideas' I have never meant anything other than what the author himself ... explicitly asserts to be true, *viz.*, that 'there is present in us a natural power which enables us to know God.' But I have never written or even thought that such ideas are *actual*, or that they are ... distinct from our faculty of thinking. (AT VIII-2 366: CSM I 309)[14]

This squares well with what was written by the author of the *Annotations to the Principles*, whom Leibniz at least took to be Descartes:

I do not understand the idea of God to be in us in any other way than that in which the ideas of all self-evident truths are in us. That is, I do not understand them to be always actually depicted in some part of our mind as many verses are contained in a book by Vergil, but *only potentially*, as various figures are depicted in wax. That is to say, in such a way that just as wax takes on this or that figure, according as it meets with other bodies this way or that, so the mind, according as it is applied to the consideration of this or that, whether by itself or by other causes, notices in itself this or that idea of what it is considering. Innate ideas differ nevertheless from adventitious and constructed or factitious in that an action of the will contributes to the factitious and that of the senses to the adventitious, while to the innate the perception of the intellect alone does. (AT XI 655 e.a.)

From this sequence of passages it appears that the real crux is the nature of the potentiality in question here. On this hinges the correct interpretation of the wax model of the *Annotations* in particular. If the point were simply that the mind is 'in potency' with regard to all ideas alike, that is, capable of possessing them actually given the appropriate sensory stimuli or other occasion to do so, 'potentiality' would be no more than a "bare faculty" (*faculté nue* in Leibniz's language) and all ideas would be innate. Although Descartes speaks of 'innateness' in a sense akin to this in his comments on article thirteen, it is plainly not that of the other passages cited. The potentiality in question is rather a disposition or propensity of the mind to *acquire* certain ideas by reflecting on its own mental processes. The question is only whether 'acquires' means 'generates,' as Clarke claims (1982, 53), or whether it is a matter of 'discovering' what one already knows or has, of explicitly attending to what is already present to consciousness, though only implicitly. On this depends whether the disposition in question is primarily active or passive, a spontaneous activity of producing, or a 'leading forth' of what is already present. Clark interprets it in the former way, thus drawing Descartes into close proximity to Leibniz (if not Kant). Moreover, his interpretation of the dispositional theory as an active disposition restricts it to a subset of those ideas and principles that Descartes terms 'innate' – the ideas of *res intellectuales* and a few common notions. Yet it provides very few clues as to the precise 'movement of thought' involved as the mind produces – or pro-duces – its innate ideas. Extrapolation from the conversation with Burman suggests a much wider extension for the reflexive-dispositional theory and a philosophically richer account, not only of the *passive* potentiality in question, but of the exact process of aquisition.

This passive potentiality will be set in a clearer light in section 19.4. Confining ourselves for the moment to the idea of God, the first point to note is that when Descartes denies that the innate idea of God is actual, or actually in the mind, at or before birth (in the womb), he uses the expressions 'being in the mind' and 'having an idea' just as he always uses them: for 'being present to consciousness.' By 'being actually in the mind,' he means 'being the object of consciousness in a particular way,' namely explicitly, while by 'being potentially in the mind' he means 'being implicitly present to consciousness and *apt* to become explicit if nothing hinders.' He explains this clearly in a letter to Hyperaspistes of August 1641: "I do not doubt that everyone has within himself an implicit idea of God, that is to say, an aptitude to perceive it explicitly (*ideam Dei, saltem implicitam, hoc est aptitudinem ad ipsam explicite percipiendam*); but I am not surprised that not everyone is aware that he has it [i.e., of this implicit idea together with the aptitude to make it explicit] or notices that he has it. Some people will perhaps not notice it even after reading my *Meditations* a thousand times" (AT III 430: CSMK 194). Thus, Descartes cannot deny that the innate idea of God is present

to the consciousness of the infant or foetus *at all*, since that would be tantamount to saying that it is not 'in the mind' in any sense whatever; it is rather
pre-reflexively present to the consciousness of the infant who, at that stage of
life, is in fact incapable of becoming explicitly conscious of it at all. Thus, to
Burman's query, "[S]ince we have an innate idea of God and of ourselves, would
not the mind of an infant ... have an actual idea of God?" Descartes responds
cautiously that it would be "rash to maintain that, since we have no evidence
relevant to the point. It does not, however, seem probable that this is so. For in
infancy the mind is so swamped (*immersa*) inside the body that the only thoughts
it has are those which result from the way the body is affected" (AT V 149: CSMK
336). By 'the only thoughts it has' Descartes here means, of course, 'the only
thoughts apt to be explicit,' 'the only thoughts it *attends to* at all.' Thus, the letter
to Hyperaspistes continues:

So if one may conjecture on such an unexplored topic, it seems most reasonable to think
that a mind newly united to an infant's body is wholly occupied in perceiving in a confused way or feeling the ideas of pain, pleasure, heat, cold and other similar ideas which
arise from its union and, as it were, intermingling with the body. None the less, it has in
itself the ideas of God, of itself and of all such truths as are called self-evident, in the
same way as adult human beings have these ideas *when they are not attending to them*;
for it does not acquire these ideas later on, as it grows older. I have no doubt that if it were
released from the prison of the body, it would find them within itself. (AT III 424: CSMK
190 e.a.)[15]

Unlike adventitious and factitious ideas, the innate idea 'God' is implicitly,
that is, pre-reflexively present to consciousness *always*, that is, whenever the
mind thinks at all. While only implicitly or potentially so in the foetus or infant,
in the adult mind it is always present to consciousness *either* potentially and
implicitly *or* actually and explicitly. Of course, it *need* never become explicit
through reflexion on what one was until then only pre-reflexively conscious of
(not even after reading the *Meditations* "a thousand times"). This much Descartes
had already conceded (without hyperbole) in his defence of the ontological argument within the *Meditations*: "admittedly it is not necessary that I ever light upon
any thought of God; but whenever I do choose to think of the first and supreme
being, and *bring forth the idea of God from the treasure house of my mind*, as it
were ... etc." (AT VII 67: CSM II 46 e.a.). Nevertheless, there is a natural tendency, disposition, or aptitude of the mind to reflect upon its thinking, which is
impeded only by the body with which it is conjoined. As Descartes explained to
Burman: "The body has an obstructive effect on the soul ... The body is *always* a
hindrance to the mind in its thinking, and this was especially true in youth" (AT V

150: CSMK 336 e.a.). Even should this idea of God be made explicit through
reflexion, it cannot remain so constantly. When Hobbes urges that no ideas are
innate since "what is innate is always present (*semper adest*)," Descartes concedes the validity of the inference: "when we say that an idea is innate in us, we
do not mean that it is always there before us (*nos semper obversari*). This would
mean that no idea was innate" (AT VII 189: CSM II 132). No idea can be constantly present to consciousness in the sense envisaged by Hobbes, that is, explicitly, as the express focus of attention. Nevertheless, the innate idea of God is
always immediately present to consciousness to some degree, and there is a natural tendency for it to become so explicitly when the occasion arises, a tendency
that grows stronger as the mind, through maturation and training, detaches itself
from the body and the senses. Thus, if not in Hobbes's, there is still a perfectly
legitimate sense in which one can say that even the *express* idea of God is *always*
before the mind; for, notes Descartes, "when we say we *always* do something,"
we usually mean "that we do it whenever the occasion presents itself" (AT III
431: CSMK 195). (Consider: "I *always* spend my holidays at the seaside.")

This account of what it is for innate ideas to be always in the mind potentially
accords well with that given Arnauld in the Fourth Replies concerning "faculties
or powers." Arnauld considered it false to assert that there is nothing in the mind
of which it is not conscious since the "mind of an infant in its mother's womb has
the power of thought but is not conscious of it" (AT VII 214: CSM II 150). In
reply, Descartes distinguishes between thoughts as "the acts or operations of our
minds" and the mind's faculties or powers. We "cannot have any thought of which
we are not conscious at the very moment when it is in us. In view of this, I do not
doubt that the mind begins to think as soon as it is implanted in the body of an
infant, and that it is immediately conscious (*conscia*) of its thoughts, even though
it does not remember this afterwards because the impressions of these thoughts
do not remain in the memory" (AT VII 246: CSM II 171f.). On the other hand,
"we are not always conscious of the mind's faculties or powers, except potentially (*potentiâ*). By this I mean that when we concentrate on employing one of
our faculties (*ad utendum aliqua facultate accingimus*), then immediately, if the
faculty in question resides in our mind, we become actually conscious of it
(*fiamus ejus actu conscii*)" (ibid.).

According to this, actual consciousness of a faculty is explicit consciousness
achieved through exercising that faculty and attending to one's capacity to do so.
In the case of some non-mental faculty that one possessed but had never exercised, to be only 'potentially' conscious of it would indeed mean: to be altogether
*un*conscious of it. But this cannot be the case for the faculty of thinking. As
remarked in section 6.2, two claims are advanced in the reply to Arnauld: (1) that
the mind always thinks, and (2) that there is nothing in the mind of which it is not

(at least implicitly) conscious. According to (1), the faculty or power of thinking is always exercised, even in the womb. To be only potentially conscious of this faculty must therefore mean: to be conscious of it implicitly, without attending to what one is conscious of, perhaps without even – as seems at least probable in the case of the infant – having so much as the possibility of doing so.[16]

We are now in a position to interpret Descartes's puzzling remarks that the idea of God exists only "potentially, for to exist in some faculty is not to exist actually but only potentially, since the term 'faculty' denotes nothing but a potentiality" (AT VIII-2 361: CSM I 305); that the mind has no need of such an idea "as something distinct from its own faculty of thinking" (AT VIII-2 358: CSM I 303; cf. 363: 307); and, finally, that the idea of God comes "to us from no other source than our own faculty of thinking" (AT VIII-2 360f.: CSM I 305).[17]

The faculty of thinking cannot be said to be innate as a "bare faculty," an unactualized potentiality to think, since from the instant of its infusion into the body the mind always thinks. Hereby the faculty of thinking is always at least implicitly present to consciousness. It would be explicitly so, were it not for the fact that the mind's attention is distracted by the body to which it is conjoined. That is what it means for the faculty of thinking to exist only potentially in the mind. Since the idea of God is said to be innate in no other sense than the faculty of thinking, it too must always be present to consciousness, at least implicitly.

All three points are elucidated further by the relevant exchange with Burman. A potential consciousness of the idea of God is implicit in that of one's own thinking and existence. The latter becomes explicit first, since "explicitly we are able to recognise our own imperfection before we recognise the perfection of God. This is because we are able to direct our attention to ourselves before we direct our attention to God" (AT V 153: CSMK 338). Nevertheless, "the knowledge of God and his perfection must implicitly always come before the knowledge of ourselves and our imperfections" (ibid.). Through reflexion it is possible to become explicitly aware of the *faculty* of thinking. That faculty, being finite, cannot be explicitly grasped as such apart from an implicit idea of the infinite thinking thing, God. The idea of God, then, comes from "no other source than our own faculty of thinking" in this sense: it is by reflection on my thinking that I grasp explicitly my faculty of thinking and the degree of perfection it possesses; and it is by further reflexion that I become explicitly aware of the idea of God, that is, "the wholly perfect *power* of thought which he possesses" (AT VII 373: CSM II 257 e.a.). However, without a prior implicit consciousness of God, we could not become explicitly conscious of "that less perfect faculty which we possess" (ibid.) in the first place.

This interpretation is borne out by Descartes's response to Regius's statement in article fourteen that the idea of God derives "'from divine revelation, or verbal instruction, or observation of things'" (AT VIII-2 360: CSM I 305). He invokes the distinction between "the proximate and primary cause, without which [something] cannot exist" and the "remote and merely accidental cause, which gives the primary cause the occasion to produce its effect at one moment rather than another. Thus the workers are the primary and proximate causes of their work, whereas those who give them orders to do the work, or promise to pay for it, are accidental and remote causes, for the workers might not do the work without instructions" (ibid.). Having introduced this distinction, Descartes notes that "verbal instruction or observation of things is often a [remote and accidental] cause which induces us to give some attention to the idea which we can have of God, and to bring it directly before the mind" (ibid.). As for the proximate cause, it is the faculty of thinking itself in so far as it contains within itself the idea of God upon which verbal instruction and observation only serve, as Descartes explains, to focus attention.

As was seen earlier (section 9.1f.), pre-reflexive consciousness or self-consciousness, like reflexion itself, is a function of the pure intellect; and both are stages in what Descartes terms *intuitus* or the exercise of the 'natural light.' That is why all innate ideas and principles have their "source" in the pure intellect, the "perception of the intellect alone." It is not, as with adventitious ideas, sensory stimulation, or, as with factitious ideas, some specific action of the will that is the "efficient or proximate cause." It is rather the very act of thinking that, owing to these accidental causes, becomes the object of reflexive attention and proximate cause of the idea. If Descartes nevertheless assigns sensory experience of various kinds, and even imagination, a distinctive role in the acquisition of innate ideas and principles other than those of intellectual things and a few common notions, it is still an open question whether they are more than "remote causes," removing the impediment to the process of analytical reflexion on what one is pre-reflexively conscious of (see chapter 20).

One final point about the idea of God will serve as a transition from the innate ideas of "intellectual" to "material things." That we can acquire the concepts 'existence,' 'thing,' and 'thinking' through reflexion on and hence *after* the *cogito, ergo sum* seems straightforward enough: we *are* thinking things. But what of the ideas 'infinite' and 'perfection'? These too are supposed to be acquired through simple reflexion upon the *cogito, ergo sum*, for the idea of God figures alongside the other 'metaphysical' and 'common notions' acquired in the manner described by the 'reflective theory.' So say both McRae and Clarke. However, I am only a finite, imperfect thinking thing. It is therefore no more obvious how I could acquire the idea of an infinite or perfect being simply by reflecting on my nature than how I could acquire the idea of a finite corporeal thing, given that I am a finite incorporeal being. In fact, quite the contrary: the former is much less clear.[18] And yet, by all accounts, I do so acquire the idea of God. Why not then the idea of body as extension in length, breadth, and depth, of particular geometrical figures, and of mathematical axioms like 'things equal to the same thing are equal to each other'?

18.6 The idea of extension

If those mathematical ideas and principles mentioned earlier are implicit in the *cogito, ergo sum* in much the same way as the notion of God, then they too are 'inborn' or 'innate,' not indeed as something that is 'in me' prior to thinking, since prior to thinking I, or my mind, did not exist, but as implicitly present to consciousness whenever the mind thinks and capable of being made explicit, given the appropriate occasions for reflexion.

As for 'extension,' in two letters to the Princess Elizabeth of May and June 1643 Descartes explains that the idea of body is, like that of the soul, a "primitive notion" conceivable by the pure intellect. Its characterization as a "primitive notion" does not entail that the idea of body is innate, since Descartes goes on to describe a third such primitive notion, the union of the mind with the body, as deriving from the senses. On the other hand, its designation as a primitive notion *conceivable by the intellect alone* does seem to carry the implication of innateness. We have, however, a second idea of body, Descartes explains, which stems from the intellect "aided by the [corporeal] imagination" (cf. AT III 663ff. and 690ff.: CSMK 217ff. and 226ff.). Indeed, as the Sixth Meditation makes clear, we even have a third idea of body ("colours, sounds, tastes, pain, and so on"), which is derived from the senses (AT VII 75: CSM II 52). It is this sensory idea of body on which the second or certain proof of the external world in the Sixth Meditation turns (ibid.), as was pointed out to Gassendi in a passage considered earlier. Since this idea of body is adventitious, and since the proof turns entirely on its being so, McRae concludes that the idea of extension is adventitious. But it is just one of three ideas of body, only the first of which may be described as the idea of extension in length, breadth, and depth. And that first idea, which is a "primitive notion" and "purely intellectual," would certainly appear to be innate.[19]

This still leaves open the precise sense in which it is innate. The first proof of the existence of a body in the Sixth Meditation is probable rather than certain; it turns on what is advanced as a likely account of the difference between imagining and pure intellection.[20] The initial proof contrasts the first and second of the three ideas of body just distinguished, the purely intellectual idea with that of the intellect "aided by the imagination," while the second or "certain" proof employs only the third or adventitious idea of body.

From the first or probable proof it is reasonably clear that Descartes understands the innateness of the idea of body or extension in terms of his reflexive-dispositional theory. The conclusion underscores the point:

[W]hen the mind understands, it in some way *turns toward itself* and inspects one of the ideas which are within it; but when it imagines, it turns toward the body and looks at something in the body which conforms to an idea understood by the mind [i.e., the innate idea of the intellect] or perceived by the senses. (AT VII 73: CSM II 51 e.a.)

This talk of the mind 'turning toward itself' highlights its reflexive acts of attention to something purely mental, something implicit in its own acts of thinking. What is in question here are of course ideas of "material," not of what Descartes elsewhere calls "intellectual things." 'Turns toward the body,' on the other hand, refers to the brain, though here too – for example, in imagining a triangle – a purely intellectual idea "understood by the mind" underlies the process of representation and variation of extended magnitude involved in imagining particular geometrical shapes. Elsewhere Descartes expresses this by saying that the mind, in imagining, "applies itself" to a corporeal semblance (*species*) which it forms rather than "receives" from without:

[T]he pure understanding both of corporeal and incorporeal things occurs without any corporeal semblance. In the case of imagination ... we do indeed require a semblance which is a real body [i.e., corporeal]: the mind applies itself to this semblance but does not receive it. (AT VII 387: CSM II 265)

This applies to the ideas of particular geometrical shapes as well as extension. Later Descartes makes the point explicitly for the latter: "Nor does it [the mind] understand extension by means of an extended semblance which is present within it (although it does *imagine* extension by turning toward a corporeal semblance which is extended)" (AT VII 389: CSM II 266). The indispensable role of imagination in forming the concrete images of discrete spatial quantities used in elaborating the particular theorems of the science of geometry does not alter the fact that the underlying ideas of both continuous spatial magnitude (extension) and a discrete geometrical shape are themselves "understood by the mind" rather than factitious. On the other hand, when what is in question is conjuring up or recalling an image of an object no longer present to the senses, or the recombining of such images to form that of a chimera, for example, the image in the brain conforms to something "perceived by the senses."[21]

    This way of interpreting the conclusion of the probable proof gives a certain point to the contrast between representing body by the intellect *alone* and by the intellect *aided by the imagination*. Descartes is opposing (1) the purely intellectual ideas of extensive magnitude or continuous quantity and of discrete geometrical shape to (2) the imaginative representation and variation of these ideas by the mathematician in elaborating the proofs of theorems. (On this difference, see AT X 440f.: CSM I 58.) The operations performed upon the ideas of discrete quantities having determinate shapes are only possible *on the basis* of (1) *with the aid* of the imagination.

The probable proof for the existence of body in the Sixth Meditation thus provides the strongest support available for the claim that the idea of extension in length, breadth, and depth is innate in the sense of the reflexive-dispositional theory. By contrast, the well-known passage at the beginning of the Fifth Meditation dealing with the innateness of both 'extension' and particular geometrical shapes is inconclusive. The theme, as indicated in the title of the Meditation, is "the essence of material things." The passage reads:

Quantity, for example, or 'continuous' quantity as the philosophers commonly call it, is something I distinctly imagine. That is, I distinctly imagine the extension of the quantity (or rather of the thing which is quantified) in length, breadth and depth. I also enumerate various parts of the thing, and to these parts I assign various sizes, shapes, positions and local motions; and to the motions I assign various durations.

Not only are all these things very well known and transparent to me when regarded in this general way, but in addition there are countless particular features regarding shape, number, motion and so on, which I perceive when I give them my attention. And the truth of these matters is so open and so much in harmony with my nature, that on first discovering them it seems that I am not so much learning something new as remembering what I knew before; or it seems like noticing for the first time things which were long present within me although I never had turned my mental gaze on them before. (AT VII 63f.: CSM II 44)[22]

McRae is surely right to insist that Descartes's use of the word 'imagine' in the first two sentences is deliberate; the continuous quantity that he is considering here is not extension as conceived by the pure intellect but "as visualised or imaged" (McRae 1972a, 44f.). Nevertheless, since Descartes goes on to juxtapose pure intellection and imagination in the next Meditation, it cannot be made out from this passage alone whether or not innate ideas of continuous quantity and particular geometrical shapes acquired in reflexion on one's thinking underlie the ideas described here as represented by the imagination. That this is indeed the case for particular geometrical shapes is at least indicated by the immediately following passages leading up to the ontological argument, to be considered next.

18.7 The ideas of particular geometrical shapes

In examining, on the threshold of the ontological argument, the "true and immutable natures" of geometrical figures, Descartes's purpose is plainly to compare and contrast mathematical ideas and truths with the metaphysical idea of God and the knowledge of his existence.[23] Thus, he begins (AT VII 64f.: CSM II 44f.) by noting (a) that ideas of geometrical figures "cannot be called nothing," that is, represent (are ideas of) something *positive* rather than negations or privations. In other words, being clear and distinct, they are materially "true." Moreover, (b) such ideas are *not derived from the senses*: "It would be beside the point for me to say that since I have from time to time seen bodies of triangular shape, the idea of the triangle may have come to me from external things by means of the sense organs. For I can think up countless other shapes which there can be no suspicion of my ever having encountered through the senses" (ibid.). Neither are they (c) "dependent on my mind," by which Descartes means that *what* they represent, their positive representational content, is not 'dependent upon my will'; for he goes on to explain that "various properties can be demonstrated of a triangle, for example that its three angles equal two right angles ... and since these properties are ones which I now clearly recognise *whether I want to or not* ... it follows that they cannot have been invented by me" (ibid., e.a.).

These are the severally necessary and jointly sufficient conditions of an idea's being that of a "true and immutable nature": it must be (a) positive, (b) non-adventitious, and (c) non-factitious, that is, innate, clear and distinct, and complete (cf. section 10.8 above). The idea of God possesses these characteristics. But while the *vera et realia entia* represented by the ideas of geometrical shapes (d) "may not exist anywhere outside me" (AT VII 64: CSM II 44), that is, have no actual or formal existence *in rerum natura*, actual existence belongs to the true and immutable nature of God in precisely the same way as having internal angles equal to two right angles belongs to the true and immutable nature of a triangle.

This point of contrast between the idea of God and all other ideas of "true and immutable natures" provides the axis on which Descartes's ontological argument turns. He initiates the argument, however, by stressing, not this difference in respect to (d), but the sameness of origin between this metaphysical and those geometrical ideas: "But if the mere fact that *I can produce from my thought* the idea of something entails that everything which I clearly and distinctly perceive to belong to that thing really does belong to it, is not this a possible basis for another argument to prove the existence of God? ... etc." (AT VII 65: CSM II 45 e.a.). Of course, what is meant by 'producing an idea from my thought' is not explained here, though in the present context this, and not the ontological argument itself, is the matter of immediate concern.

That the ideas of those geometrical figures 'produced from my thought' are *innate* is at best implied rather than stated in the run-up to the ontological argument – though 'not derived from the senses' is arguably a near equivalent of 'innate.'[24] Responding to Gassendi's objections to this passage, Descartes notes that even before perceiving a triangle as infants the *idea veri trianguli* was already "in us" (cf. AT VII 382: CSM II 262). The triangle is again only an example; what holds of it holds equally, not only for the ideas of other geometrical shapes such as a square, circle, or straight line, but for "true and immutable natures" generally. And although the word 'innate' is not used, 'in us' is again a reasonable facsimile. The vital question remains: 'innate' in what sense? Gassendi's objection deserves careful consideration, for Descartes's reply, when read in conjunction with the conversation with Burman and the Fourth Replies, suggests that 'in us' means exactly what it was found to mean in the case of the idea of God: 'in us *potentially*,' that is, implicitly present to consciousness whenever the mind thinks at all, and apt to become distinctly or explicitly so unless the mind is impeded by the body. This answer may be puzzling, given that the mind is incorporeal and the idea of the triangle a corporeal idea; but it is at least *no more* puzzling than the case of the idea of God. The latter is universally agreed to be innate; yet the mind which produces it through reflexion on its thinking is finite while the idea so produced is that of an infinite being. If the idea of God is acknowledged to be innate, why not that of a triangle?

Behind Gassendi's objection lies a view of mathematical 'natures' or 'essences' that is perhaps best taken as a form of 'conceptualism' *avant la lettre*: universals, even mathematical 'natures,' are no more than abstractions first deliberately, then habitually formed by the intellect or imagination upon observing a number of "individual natures" that agree in certain respects.[25] It receives a much fuller treatment than Hobbes's nominalistic objection to the preamble to the ontological argument, which Descartes simply dismisses as having been refuted earlier. According to Gassendi's theory, it cannot be maintained that these natures existed before the particulars, or that, even after the "intellect performed the abstraction" (cf. AT VII 320: CSM II 222), they "exist anywhere outside the intellect" (ibid.). He illustrates his point using the concept 'man,' concluding that

we should not therefore say that ... a triangle is something real, or that it is a true nature distinct from the intellect. For it is the intellect alone which, after seeing material triangles, has formed this nature and made it a common nature, as we have explained in the case of the nature of man. It follows that we should not suppose that the properties demonstrated of material triangles belong to them because they derive them from the ideal triangle ... And yet, O Mind, you claim that you have the idea of a triangle *and would have it even if you had never seen bodies with triangular shape*, just as you have the idea of many other figures which have never impinged on your senses. (AT VII 321: CSM II 223 e.a.)

This is not intended to imply that the concepts 'man' and 'triangle' are alike in all respects, and Gassendi closes with the remark that he "should also have said something here about the false [i.e., fictitious] nature of a triangle," to which nothing *in rerum natura* corresponds (AT VII 322: CSM II 223f.).[26]

Descartes responds to this in tones of confident superiority: "as for the essences we know clearly and distinctly, such as the essence of a triangle or of any other geometrical figure, I can easily make you admit that the ideas of them which we have are not taken from particular instances" (AT VII 380: CSM II 261). The initial argument is brief and *ad hominem*: on Gassendi's own showing, "'the subject-matter of pure mathematics ... cannot exist in reality.' It follows that no triangle ... has ever existed, and hence that these essences have not been derived from any existing things" (AT VII 380f.: CSM II 261). Thereupon Descartes endorses the premise on grounds entirely different from the "atomic [i.e., 'atomistic'] conception of reality" (AT VII 381: CSM II 262), which he takes to be Gassendi's reason for denying that these essences can be instantiated *in rerum natura*, arguing to the same conclusion as follows (partially quoted and interpreted already in section 10.10):

I do not, incidentally, concede that the ideas of these figures ever came into our mind via the senses, as everyone commonly believes. For although the world could undoubtedly contain figures such as those the geometers study, I nonetheless maintain that there are no such figures in our environment except perhaps ones so small that they cannot in any way impinge on our senses. Geometrical figures are composed for the most part of straight lines; yet no part of a line that was really straight could ever affect our senses, since when we examine through a magnifying glass those lines which appear most straight we find they are quite irregular and always form wavy curves. Hence, when in our childhood we first happened to see a triangular figure drawn on paper, it cannot have been this figure that showed us how we should conceive of the true triangle studied by geometers, since the true triangle is contained in the figure only in the way in which a statue of Mercury is contained in a rough block of wood. But since the idea of a true triangle was already in us, and could be conceived by our mind more easily than the more composite figure of the triangle drawn on paper, when we saw the composite figure we did not apprehend the [composite] figure we saw, but rather the true triangle. (ibid.)

Gassendi having begun from the concept 'man,' Descartes illustrates his point with a related example:

It is just the same as when we look at a piece of paper on which some lines have been drawn in ink to represent a man's face: the idea that this produces in us is not so much the idea of these lines as the idea of a man. Yet this would certainly not happen unless the human face were already known to us from some other source ... Thus we could not recognise the geometrical triangle from the diagram on the paper unless our mind already possessed the idea of it from some other source. (AT VII 382: CSM II 262)[27]

It would be mistaken to conclude from this that the idea of the triangle is no more innate than that of a human face. True, the parallel concerns (in the language of the conversation with Burman) the *particular* grasped *in concreto* and the *universal* understood *in abstracto et separata a materia et singularibus*. In Gassendi's terms, it concerns the *material* versus the *ideal* triangle – although Descartes differs from Gassendi in regarding the ideal triangle of the geometer, not the material triangle, as the "true triangle." It is also the case that what Descartes wishes to bring out by means of the analogy is the difference in origin between the universal and the particular ideas of the triangle. The point, however, is neither that the universal 'triangle' has, nor that all universal concepts have, the same origin as the concept 'human face.' The theory of universals is not much help here.[28] More to the present point is Descartes's remark in the Second Replies that it "is in the nature of our mind to construct general propositions on the basis of the knowledge of particular ones (*generales propositiones ex particularium cognitione efformet*)" (AT VII 141: CSM II 100). As *Principles,* I, 10 and the conversation with Burman make clear, even the non-propositional, conceptual natures 'thought' and 'existence' are prior to the explicit grasp of the existence of one's own thinking, *cogito*, much as in the case of the universal proposition *illud omne, quod cogitat, est sive existit*. Seen in the light of this definitive pronouncement on "the nature of our mind," what the reply to Gassendi suggests is the following.

If one is to recognize in the diagram (that is, in the particular sensible image drawn on paper) the "true" triangle of the geometer and to perform on it in imagination those operations by which the geometer gradually unfolds its *propria* in the elaboration of his science, then the mind must already possess at least an implicit understanding of the true and immutable nature 'triangle.' That is, the 'true' triangle must be immediately present to consciousness *beforehand* in order for the material triangle to be represented by the senses and imagination as that which it is: not an individual material thing, the isosceles, scalene, or equilateral figure depicted on the sheet, but the true and immutable *nature* 'triangularity.' The lines drawn on paper are only the "remote cause which induces us to give some attention to the idea ... and bring it directly before the mind," as the *Broadsheet* remarks of the innate idea of God. In order to become explicit on the occasion of actually seeing the diagram, the universal concept must be "in us" already; it cannot have its "proximate and primary" or "efficient" cause in this sensory experience, therefore, but derives "from some other source." That source may be earlier sensory experience, as in the case of the concept 'human face'; or it may be "other causes," as Descartes frequently puts it when he wishes to designate the faculty of thinking itself as the proximate cause of its own ideas – "an idea understood by the mind," as he says in the conclusion of the probable proof of the existence of body. This is the case with 'triangle.'[29]

The much-discussed illustration of the statue of Mercury contained *potentially* (as Descartes hardly needs to add) in the block of wood is misleading unless one understands the distinctive sense in which the faculty of thinking and its innate ideas are potentially in the mind. Invoked already in the *Broadsheet*, the relevant notion of potentiality is elaborated only in the Fourth Replies. Nevertheless, from saying that the "true triangle is contained in the figure only in the way the statue of Mercury is contained in a rough block of wood," Descartes passes rapidly to a much apter formulation: "the idea of the true triangle was already in us [*scil.* potentially] and could be conceived by our mind more easily than the more composite figure of the triangle drawn on paper." This is at least to situate the potential being where it belongs, in the mind or intellect, not in the image drawn on paper. There, 'to be *potentiâ*' means, as Descartes explained to Arnauld, 'to be present to consciousness always but only implicitly.' The example of Mercury in the block of wood is admittedly ambiguous and possibly misleading; but it at least admits of an interpretation consistent with what Descartes explains more fully elsewhere.

Nowhere in the passages examined thus far is it stated or even suggested that the ideas of extension and particular geometrical shapes are innate in a sense different from that in which the idea of God is innate. And just the opposite is expressly maintained elsewhere. For example, in the *Annotations to the Principles*, cited earlier:

I do not understand the idea of God to be in us *in any other way than that in which the ideas of all self-evident truths are in us*. That is, I do not understand them to be always actually depicted in some part of our mind as many verses are contained in a book by Vergil, but only potentially, as various figures are depicted in wax. (AT XI 655 e.a.)

At this point it seems we cannot postpone much longer the consideration of the model of the mind suggested by Descartes's use of the wax analogy (section 19.1ff.). We conclude the discussion of the extent of Descartes's reflexive-dispositional theory of innateness with a consideration of the mathematical axioms and the basic laws of nature.

18.8 Mathematical axioms

In a letter to Plempius of 20 December 1637 Descartes writes:

The principles or premises from which I derive these conclusions [in the *Discourse*] are only the axioms on which the geometers base their demonstrations: for instance 'the whole is greater than the part,' 'if equals are taken from equals the remainders are equal'; but they are not abstracted from all sensible matter as in geometry (*non autem ab omni sensibili materia abstracta, ut apud Geometras*) but applied to various observational data which are known by the senses and indubitable (*sed varijs experimentis sensu cognitis atque indubitatis applicata*). (AT I 476: CSMK 77)

While this has suggested to some (e.g., Clarke; cf. 1982, 62) that mathematical axioms are derived or 'abstracted' from sensory experience, Descartes is clearly speaking here, not of the *origin* of the axioms in question, but of their *employment*, their application. Even the untutored *homo sensualis* has an implicit understanding of these axioms, which, however, he never considers *in abstracto et separata a materia et singularibus* as the geometer does. There is nothing here or elsewhere in Descartes's writings to suggest that such axioms have any other origin than the metaphysical axioms, or that they are innate in anything but the same sense. On the contrary, the first mention of axioms in the *Principles* (I, 13) is of mathematical axioms. The wording leaves no room for doubt about their origin. The mind, writes Descartes, "finds certain common notions [in itself] ... For example, the mind *has within itself* ideas of numbers and shapes, and it also has such common notions as: *If you add equals to equals the results will be equal*" (AT VIII-1 9: CSM I 197 e.a.). At I, 18 the metaphysical axiom *ex nihilo nihil fit* is termed "evident by the natural light" rather than a "common notion." But at I, 49 the same metaphysical axiom is designated "an eternal truth which resides within our mind (*quae in mente nostra sedem habet*)." I, 52 pronounces the metaphysical principle *nihili nulla sunt attributa* a "common notion." At I, 49, speaking of *ex nihilo nihil fit*, Descartes remarks:

Such [eternal] truths are termed common notions or axioms (*communis notio, sive axioma*). The following are examples of this class: *It is impossible for the same thing to be and not to be at the same time; What is done cannot be undone; He who thinks cannot but exist while he thinks*; and countless others. It would not be easy to draw up a list of all of them; but nonetheless we cannot fail to know them *when the occasion for thinking about them arises, provided we are not blinded by preconceived opinions* (*cum occurrit occasio ut de iis cogitemus, & nullis praejudiciis excaecamur*). (AT VIII-1 23: CSM I 209 e.a.)

Taken together, the passages in this sequence very strongly suggest that Descartes regarded the logical and mathematical axioms as entirely on all fours with the metaphysical. Moreover, the idiom of *Principles*, I, 49 is unmistakably that of the reflexive-dispositional theory, so much so that the translation of *praejudicia* by "preconceived opinions" may be misleading. That the impediments here described as inhibiting an express grasp of the axioms, even when the occasion arises, are in fact the *praejudicia sensuum* (AT VII 157 and 158: CSM II 111 and 112) rather than *auctoritatis* is made clear at I, 71, where we find Descartes's fullest description of the mental condition and development of the infant – the *homo sensualis* par excellence. It concludes with the remark that "from infancy our mind was swamped with a thousand ... prejudices" (*praejudiciis ... imbuta est*) (AT VIII-1 36: CSM I 219). Thus, all the salient features of the reflexive-dispositional theory are found in the *Principles* and applied without distinction to the logical, mathematical, and metaphysical principles of the natural light. This is a very significant advance on the first metaphorical formulation of the doctrine of innateness in the letter to Mersenne of 15 April 1630:

> Please do not hesitate to assert and proclaim everywhere that it is God who has laid down these laws ["the mathematical truths which you call 'eternal'"] in nature just as a king lays down laws in his kingdom. There is no single one that we cannot grasp *if our mind turns to consider it*. They are all inborn in our minds (*mentibus nostris ingenitae*) just as a king would imprint his laws on the hearts of his subjects if he had enough power to do so. (AT I 145: CSMK 23 e.a.)

But even here the phrase "si notre esprit se porte a la consyderer" points forward to the later elaboration of the reflexive-dispositional theory of innateness.

18.9 The basic laws of nature

It remains, finally, to consider the innateness of the most fundamental laws of Cartesian physics. Something has been said of this already in the Introduction (section 5.2). Rather than attempt a full treatment of the subject, we shall confine ourselves to an aspect of the question that does not generally receive much attention: the 'seeds of truth' doctrine.

The doctrine is first encountered in the *Regulae*:

> So useful is this method that without it the pursuit of learning would, I think, be more harmful than profitable. Hence I can readily believe that the great minds of the past were to some extent aware of it (*aliquo modo perspectam*), guided to it even by nature alone. For the human mind has within it a sort of spark of the divine (*nescio quid divini*), in which the first *seeds* of useful ways of thinking are sown, seeds which, however neglected and stifled by studies which impede them, often bear fruit of their own accord. (AT X 373: CSM I 17 e.a.)

If in the *Principles* it was primarily the *praejudicia sensuum* that Descartes had in mind as impeding the natural light of reason, that is, preventing the seeds from germinating, here in the *Regulae* it is just as clearly the *praejudicia auctoritatis*. Just a few short pages later, speaking of the Greeks' infatuation with mathematics, Descartes writes:

But I am convinced that *certain primary seeds of truth naturally implanted in human minds* thrived in that unsophisticated and innocent age [i.e., in Classical Greece!] – seeds which have been stifled in us through our constantly reading and hearing all sorts of errors. So the same light of the mind which enabled them to see (albeit without knowing why) that virtue is preferable to pleasure, the good preferable to the useful, also enabled them to grasp true ideas in philosophy and mathematics, although they were not yet able fully to master such sciences. (AT X 376: CSM I 18 e.a.)

Notice that in the first of these passages Descartes speaks only of certain "innate principles of ... *method*" (AT X 373: CSM I 17 e.a.) as 'seeds,' while in that just cited he speaks of certain mathematical and philosophical seeds *of truth*, that is, "ideas" or concepts from which propositions or principles may be derived. That the most basic laws of nature are among the truths discovered by cultivating these seeds in accordance with the method is suggested by the *Discourse*, where the same doctrine crops up again. In Part Five there is a reference to "certain laws which God has so established in nature, and of which he has *implanted* such *notions in our minds*, that *after adequate reflexion* we cannot doubt that they are exactly observed in everything which exists or occurs in the world" (AT VI 41: CSM I 131 e.a.). And in Part Six he speaks in a similar vein of having derived the *principles* "of everything that exists or can exist in the world ... only from certain *seeds of truth* which are naturally in our souls" (AT VI 64: CSM I 143f. e.a.). In question in the *Discourse* is neither a method nor simple mathematical or metaphysical axioms; the phrase "exists or can exist" indicates that such reflexion extends to more than the "common notions," though probably not further than those most basic laws of the actual physical universe that form the general conceptual framework of Cartesian science: the laws of inertia, rectilinearity, and the conservation of motion (cf. *Principles*, III, 46). This is borne out by *Principles,* IV, 203, which contains at least an oblique reference to the 'seeds of truth' doctrine. Among "the simplest and best known principles, knowledge of which is naturally implanted in our minds" (AT VIII-1 326: CSM I 288) are not just "shapes, sizes and motions," but also "the rules in accordance with which these three things can be modified by each other – rules which are the principles of geometry *and mechanics*" (AT IX-2 321: CSM I 288 e.a.).

Can this talk of seeds implanted in our nature be dismissed as the primitive ancestor of the later theory of innateness? The attempt may meet with some sympathy in the context of the early *Regulae* or the letter to Mersenne of 15 April 1630, where Descartes speaks of the king who would "imprint his laws on the hearts of all his subjects" (AT I 145: CSMK 23). As for the *Discourse*, Clarke has suggested that 'reflexion' here must not be understood in the way in which the later (reflexive-dispositional) theory of innateness has been interpreted here.[30] It is admittedly harder to decide whether to include Descartes' three laws of nature within the extension of the reflexive-dispositional theory – although Gilson, for one, did not hesitate to call them innate.[31] We must therefore consider this question briefly.

The language of the *Discourse* is unquestionably much more strongly reminiscent of the familiar imprint than the reflexive-dispositional theory of innateness. Yet to insist on this point may be to press for a sharp distinction where none existed in Descartes's mind. Granted, the talk of 'seeds' of truth 'implanted' in the mind looks a crude metaphor alongside the sophisticated reflexive-dispositional theory; still, its occurrence *together* with the latter in the first of the two *Discourse* passages cited above suggests that Descartes himself did not so regard it. Naturally, when it comes to the question of how the laws governing natural phenomena can be 'contained' in the mind's acts of thinking such that by reflecting on its thinking the mind becomes expressly aware of these laws, any reflexive theory faces a real problem: what is readily comprehensible for the metaphysical concepts of substance, thinking, truth, and freedom, since the mind itself is a thinking substance with clear and distinct perceptions, a freedom of spontaneity and indifference, and so on, is hard to fathom when extended to the basic concepts and principles of mathematical physics. Rather than attempt to paper them over, it should be acknowledged that such difficulties actually begin even with the paradigmatic metaphysical concept of God. Accordingly, even in the *Meditations* Descartes resorts to metaphors no less crude and primitive than those found in the *Discourse* in an effort to extend his reflexive-dispositional theory to the idea of the Perfect Being. God is the divine 'workman' who puts his 'stamp' upon his creatures, and so forth. In the light of passages like this, it is very difficult simply to discount the 'seeds of truth' or imprint theory as somehow negligible. That Descartes constantly reverted to one or the other of them may indicate some vague inkling of the difficulties of extending his theory of innateness beyond the concepts clearly derivable from the mental; but that he shrank from including among the innate concepts and principles the most universal laws of the material universe seems unlikely.

If consideration of the concept 'God' makes one thing clear, it is that any very sharp division between imprint, dispositional, and reflexive theories of innateness may prove hard to sustain. The reflexive theory may even *call for* one of the others once extended beyond the narrow confines of the mental. Descartes no doubt distanced himself from the particular imprint theory pilloried by Locke, since no idea is in the mind prior to its thinking and experiencing *inwardly* all that is implicitly contained in its thinking.[32] Moreover, such principles or "common notions" as are contained in its thinking are by no means universally assented to, neither by all men, nor by all who have attained the use of reason, nor even by all reasonable men upon first being confronted with them (these being among the senses of 'innate' considered and rejected by Locke in Book I of the *Essay*). On the contrary, careful reflexion and focusing of attention is required. This much Descartes had occasion to note explicitly in the letter to Mersenne of 16 October 1639, since Lord Herbert, as he observes,

> takes universal consent as the criterion of his truths. I have no criterion for mine except the natural light. The two criteria agree in part: for since all men have the same natural light, it seems that they should have the same notions; but there is also a great difference between them, because hardly anyone makes good use of that light, so that many people – perhaps all those we know – may share the same mistaken opinion. Also there are many things which can be known by the natural light, but which no one has yet reflected on. (AT II 597: CSMK 139)

But if not in Herbert's (which is at bottom Locke's) nor in Hobbes's sense, how then might the ideas of God and body and the most fundamental laws of nature be implicitly 'contained' in every mode of thinking before being explicitly acquired through reflexion when the appropriate occasions arise? Since the reflexive-dispositional theory alone provides no satisfactory answer to this question, and yet some sense must be given the notion of implicit containment, Descartes resorted again and again to evocations of the familiar imprint theory.

19

The Model of the Mind

Arguably, a *theory* of innateness is only that when it elaborates a conception of the mind markedly different from the *tabula rasa* model rather than gratuitously applying the term 'innate' to features of that very model. Locke provides well-known examples of such misuses of 'innate' in Book I of the *Essay* (cf. the last paragraph of the previous chapter), as does Hume in Section II of the *Enquiry* (1990, 67f.) By this criterion, the reflective account elaborated by McRae is not really a theory of innateness at all; for even Locke might have endorsed this theory of "the *perception of the operations of our own minds* within us."[1] McRae's *anamnesis* theory provides an instructive account of the workings of the mind in geometrical knowledge, while Clarke's innate$_1$ conveys a fundamental and important tenet of Cartesian mind-body interaction; yet these special uses of 'innate' are clearly intended to shore up that empiricist or *tabula rasa* model of the mind seriously undermined by certain of Descartes's other uses, so that to apply the term 'innateness' to precisely these aspects of his thought is to invite needless verbal controversy. By the same token, Clarke's innate$_2$ is not properly a theory of innateness either; for it too scarcely ventures beyond Locke.[2]

By contrast, the reflexive-dispositional theory elaborated in the previous chapter sets out a model of the mind strikingly at odds with that found in broadly empiricist philosophies like those of Hobbes, Locke, or Gassendi. It differs also from the models employed by the old Platonic-Stoic-Ciceronian imprint theory and in Aristotle's account of *epagōgē*. It even differs in vital respects from the model of the mind introduced by Leibniz, with which it is regularly lumped together in accounts of "the rationalist doctrine of innate ideas" (cf. Edgley 1970, passim). Since the tag 'intuitive induction' has been applied to the transition of the mind from implicit to explicit understanding, the contrast with Aristotle's notion of *epagōgē* will be of particular interest. It will be the focus of chapter 20. In the present chapter, we undertake the examination of the other theories mentioned, especially that of Leibniz and the imprint theory.

Whatever the merits of the queries, fashionable for decades now, concerning the well-worn empiricist-rationalist dichotomy of the philosophy curriculum, it is surely helpful to distinguish broadly between what can, without gross inaccuracy, be called 'archetypal' and 'ectypal' theories or models of the mind. The latter treat the mind as predominantly passive, receptive, and dependent on the non-mental in the process of cognition; the former stress its spontaneity, creativity, and power of drawing on its own resources, now only for the form, now even for the materials of knowledge. True, there is some overlap, so that, for example, Locke's manner of distinguishing primary from secondary sensible qualities is largely prefigured in Descartes's qualified representative realism (cf. AT VII 440: CSM II 297); and to the extent that both viewpoints recognize an active, spontaneous as well as a passive, receptive factor in cognition, the difference is to some extent one of emphasis.[3] But it makes a considerable difference whether the elements of knowledge revealed as the mind's gaze turns inward upon its ideas are only simple sense impressions, variously combined, compounded, or rendered univeral by the mind in accordance, say, with associationist principles; or whether what is revealed are primitive concepts and principles or axioms (truths), necessary and universal (at least within some specified domain of sensory experience), yet not borrowed from the experience (of that domain). And it likewise makes a very great difference whether the possession of such knowledge is a matter of having a "bare faculty" to frame certain ideas and truths on the basis of stimuli received from external causes acting on the bodily sense organs, or whether it is a spontaneous activity by which certain concepts and principles are discovered by a process of non-sensory reflexion on thinking itself, the occasions only being provided by external stimuli.

Given some such division as this, can it seriously be doubted that Descartes's theory is of the one and Locke's of the other type? What might seem to tell against rejection of the *tabula rasa* model on Descartes's part is chiefly his repeated use of the wax analogy to illustrate his theory of the mind (cf. McRae 1972a, 50). Apart from the possibly spurious *Annotations*, there are three contexts in which Descartes employs the wax-and-seal model: Rule XII of the *Regulae*, the letter to Mersenne of 16 October 1639 concerning Herbert of Cherbury's *De Veritate*, and a letter to Mesland of 2 May 1644. Examining each in turn, we must consider the extent to which Descartes's theory of innateness points forward to that of Leibniz and Kant as well as back to the imprint theory of antiquity. In this way the highly schematic contrast between ectypal and archetypal theories of the mind can be fleshed out into a reasonable approximation to two basic historical tendencies of thought about the mind. They are both still very much with us today – amidst a great deal of apparent confusion about the exact historical antecedents of each.

19.1 The wax analogy in the *Regulae*

Rule XII provides no support whatever for the *tabula rasa* model, being inter-pretable in a manner perfectly consistent with the reflexive-dispositional theory of innateness. The illustration of a malleable bit of wax is first introduced as part of an exact or literal account of *sense-perception*, the latter expressly understood as a *bodily* function common to man and the lower animals or what was earlier termed 'organic sensation' (cf. chapter 9, nn. 7 and 8; chapter 10, n. 2):

[I]n so far as our external senses are all parts of the body, sense-perception, strictly speak-ing, is merely passive ... sense-perception occurs in the same way in which wax takes on an impression from a seal. It should not be thought that I have a mere analogy in mind here: we must think of the external shape of the sentient body as being really changed by the object in exactly the same way as the shape of the surface of the wax is altered by the seal. (AT X 412: CSM I 40)

Here the wax is certainly not intended to be illustrative of anything mental. The 'common sense' or imagination likewise functions like a seal "fashioning ..., as if in wax, the same figures or ideas which come, pure and without body, from the external senses" (AT X 414: CSM I 41). But the imagination is expressly said to be "part of the body" (AT X 414: CSM I 41), as is the "phantasy" or the "purely corporeal imagination" that we ascribe even to animals, "even though we refuse to allow that they have any knowledge of things (*rerum cognitio*)" (AT X 415: CSM I 42). It is even termed a "true" or "genuine part of the body" (*veram partem corporis*). So far, then, Descartes has not applied the wax-and-seal model to that "power through which we know things in the strict sense" and which is "purely spiritual, and is no less distinct from the whole body than blood is distinct from bone, or the hand from the eye" (ibid.), since he has yet to speak of anything but the body. Turning next to the "cognitive power" or mind, the wax is appealed to again, though here it is expressly said to be "a mere analogy," the very thing earlier denied:

[T]he cognitive power is sometimes passive, sometimes active; *sometimes resembling the seal* [NB!], sometimes the wax. But this should be understood merely as an analogy, for nothing quite like this power is to be found in corporeal things. It is one and the same power: when applying itself along with imagination to the common sense, it is said to see, touch, etc.; when addressing itself to the imagination alone, in so far as the latter is invested with various figures, it is said to remember; when applying itself to the imagina-tion in order to form new figures, it is said *to imagine or conceive*; and lastly, when it *acts on its own*, it is said to understand. (AT X 415: CSM I 42 e.a.)

No very clear explanation is provided here of the difference between imagining and conceiving body; nor does Descartes explain straightaway how the *pure* intellect functions "on its own (*sola*)" when it is said to "understand." Consequently, a very material question is left unanswered, namely, whether the pure intellect is the source of an intellectual idea of body, or whether it is only the mental or, as Descartes often says, "intellectual things" that are grasped through its operations. Postponing further discussion of understanding, and noting that the "intellect can either be stimulated by the imagination (*moveri possit*) or act upon it (*in illam agere*)" (AT X 416: CSM I 43), Descartes proceeds almost immediately to draw the following moral:

[W]hen the intellect is concerned with *matters in which there is nothing corporeal* or similar to the corporeal, it cannot receive any help from those faculties [sense and imagination]; on the contrary, if it is not to be *hampered* by them, the senses must be kept back and the imagination must, as far as possible, be divested of every distinct impression. If, however, the intellect proposes to examine *something which can be referred to body*, the idea of that thing must be formed as distinctly as possible in the imagination. In order to do this properly, the thing itself which this idea is to represent should be displayed to the external senses. (ibid., e.a.)

Holding the senses and imagination in check is of great importance in conceiving of anything mental, while, when it comes to "something which can be referred to body," it is vital to exhibit one's purely intellectual ideas to the external senses. This refers not just to the use of diagrams in geometry, but to conceptual problems of the foundations of physics as well. In Rule IX Descartes illustrated the point being made here, employing the example of the physical concept of a "natural power":

If ... I wish to enquire whether a natural power can travel instantaneously to a distant place ... I shall not immediately turn my attention to the magnetic force or the influence of the stars, or even the speed of light to see whether actions such as these might occur instantaneously ... I shall, rather, reflect upon the local motions of bodies, since there can be nothing in this whole area that is more readily perceivable by the senses ... For instance, if I move one end of a stick, however long it may be, I can easily conceive that the power which moves that part of the stick necessarily moves every other part of it instantaneously. (AT X 402: CSM I 34)[4]

On reading this, one can scarcely help being reminded of the explanation Descartes gave Mersenne as to why he made no attempt to define 'truth': "a man who walks across a room shows much better what motion is than a man who says 'it is the act of being in potency, insofar as it is in potency' etc." (AT II 597: CSMK 139).[5] To grasp clearly and distinctly what is meant by 'body, 'figure,' 'motion,' 'natural power,' and so on, the innate ideas in the mind must be 'exhibited' as simply as possible in external sensation; whereas in order to know what truth is, all that is required is careful attention to what we experience within ourselves when we grasp that it is true that we think, that we therefore exist, and that whatever thinks exists. This difference between (a) that reflexion through which the mind grasps "intellectual things" and (b) that through which it attains to a clear and distinct conception of "material things" is not a distinction between innate ideas and others derived from reflexion upon sense-perceptions or ordinary experience; in both cases it is simple reflexion *on what is immediately present to consciousness* or *inner experience* that issues in clear and distinct ideas of the intellectual or material objects in question. Reflexion is a matter of *attending* to what is *already* before the mind *implicitly*, and what is *always* so, as long as we think at all. Still, the aid of the senses or imagination is required in order to focus the mind's attention on innate ideas "pertaining to body." That is why Descartes speaks of "the thing itself which this idea is to represent" as "displayed to the *external* senses." As will be shown in detail later (cf. section 20.3) it is the concomitant *inner* experience that is the source of the clear and distinct conception of these material as of those intellectual things.

This is intimated already in Rule IX. The example of the motion transmitted instantaneously from one end of the stick to the other merely illustrates "how to cultivate ... perspicacity in the distinct intuition of particular things (*perspicacitatem scilicet, res singulas distincte intuendo*)" (AT X 400: CSM I 33). The role of *sensory* intuition or *outer* experience is to focus attention on something that is "understood by the mind" rather than "perceived by the senses." Perspicacity in the use of the natural light of reason is here clarified *by analogy* with perspicacity in ordinary sense-perception; however, the intuitive process of rendering an implicit insight of the intellect explicit is only roughly illustrated by reference to the ordinary sense of 'perspicacity': "If one tries to look at many objects at one glance, one sees none of them distinctly. Likewise, if one is inclined to *attend* to many things at the same time in a single act of thought, one does so with a confused mind" (ibid., e.a.). Just as craftsmen who become perspicacious in the performance of "delicate operations ... never let their thinking be distracted by many different objects at the same time, but always devote their whole attention to the simplest and easiest of matters" (ibid.), so we who seek to attain certainty must "concentrate our mind's eye totally on the most insignificant and easiest matters (*ingenii aciem ad res ... faciles convertere*), and dwell on them long enough to acquire the habit of intuiting the truth distinctly and clearly (*distincte & perspicue*)" (AT X 400: CSM I 33). Accordingly, exhibiting one's ideas to the external senses is no more than the "accidental and remote" cause of the clear and distinct ideas of body, figure, motion, and a natural power; the "proximate and primary" causes are those innate ideas that exist *potentially* in the faculty of thinking itself.

That this is so may not be fully apparent yet. But *if* it is so (as will be shown below), then the account of the *Regulae* conforms by and large to the conception of innateness sketched in the Sixth Meditation and clarified in the Fourth Replies and the *Broadsheet*. The most plausible interpretation of the words "the cognitive power is sometimes passive, sometimes active; sometimes resembling the seal, sometimes the wax" is that the mind is wax-like when it senses and remembers, but like a seal when it "imagines or conceives" and understands. If so, this particular use of the wax analogy provides no support at all for the *tabula rasa* model – quite the contrary.

19.2 The wax analogy in the letter to Mersenne

The letter to Mersenne of 16 October 1639, in which the wax analogy is employed a second time, is that concerning the *De Veritate* of Lord Herbert. This author, writes Descartes, "would have it that we have as many faculties as there are different objects of knowledge. This seems to me like saying that because some wax can take on an infinite number of shapes, it has an infinite number of faculties for taking them on" (AT II 598: CSMK 139f.). This is risky from Descartes's perspective since it suggests to the ignorant "a similar diversity of little entities in our soul" (ibid.). For his own part, Descartes wishes to posit no more than certain potentialities or dispositions as innate in the mind: "I prefer to think that the wax, simply by its flexibility, takes on all sorts of shapes, and that the soul acquires all its knowledge by the reflexion which it makes either on itself (in the case of intellectual matters) or (in the case of corporeal matters) on the various dispositions of the brain to which it is joined, which may result from the action of the senses *or from other causes*" (ibid., e.a.). Just as all the shapes of wax stem from a single faculty or potentiality, flexibility, so all the perceptions the mind is capable of may be ascribed to a single faculty or power, which however functions in different ways.

McRae takes "other causes" to refer to the source of factitious ideas. Thus, the mind's reflection on itself produces the ideas of "intellectual things," which are alone innate; its reflection on the dispositions in the brain produced by "the senses" and by "other causes" gives rise to adventitious and factitious ideas, respectively. "In the case of the fictitious or imaginary ideas the images have been imprinted on the brain by the mind itself, that is, the mind gives the images to itself. But in all cases the mind acquires its ideas by attending to something present to it" (McRae 1972a, 50).

This seems a plausible reading. Before accepting it, however, it must be asked: in what sense does the mind give itself images? Is Descartes here alluding to the manner in which the intellect acts upon the imagination to form images of discrete quantities or particular geometrical shapes in accordance with ideas understood or conceived by the intellect itself? If so, then "other causes" refers not so much to factitious ideas of the imagination as to the innate ideas of the pure understanding that underlie even our ideas of corporeal things. Admittedly, if this is what is meant, then we must emend slightly the remark that "the soul acquires *all* its knowledge by the reflexion which it makes either on itself (in the case of intellectual matters) or (in the case of corporeal matters) on the various dispositions of the brain to which it is joined, which may result from the action of the senses or from other causes." Descartes means: "either on itself *alone* or on the various dispositions of the brain ... etc. *as well*." But to emend in this way is only to bring this letter into line with that to the Princess Elizabeth, cited earlier, and with the conclusion of the probable proof of the existence of body in the Sixth Meditation. So the use of the wax analogy here is not incontrovertible evidence for the empiricist model of the mind either.

19.3 The wax analogy in the letter to Mesland

We come, finally, to the letter to Mesland of 2 May 1644, much more famous for its pronouncements on the eternal truths than for the following passage:

I regard the difference between the soul and its ideas as the same as that between a piece of wax and the various shapes it can take. Just as it is not an activity but a passivity in the wax to take various shapes, so it seems to me, it is a passivity in the soul to receive one or other idea, and only its volitions are activities. It receives its ideas partly [1] from objects which come into contact with the senses, partly [2] from impressions in the brain, and partly [3] from prior dispositions in the soul and [4] from movements of the will. Similarly, the wax owes its shapes partly to the pressure of other bodies, partly to the shapes or other qualities which it already possesses, such as heaviness or softness, and partly also to its own movement, in so far as it has in itself the power to continue moving when it has once been set in motion. (AT IV 113f.: CSMK 232f.)

Assuming, as seems clear enough, that the two forms of *passivity* and *receptivity* described first ([1] and [2]) correspond to sense and corporeal imagination, it appears plausible to take the third and fourth, "prior dispositions in the soul" and "movements of the will," to refer to the pure intellect's pre-reflexive and reflexive awareness of thinking, respectively. For reflexive awareness of that of which I am pre-reflexively conscious requires a focusing of attention on thinking itself; and this, while a different way of performing the same act of perception rather than a discrete act of volition, is nevertheless an "action" of the mind or, as Descartes says here, a "movement" of the will.

It is surely significant that [3] the "prior disposition" or "power" is not an active but a *passive* potentiality of the mind. Descartes conceived its physical analogue, "the power to continue moving when ... once set in motion," as a *passive* force in bodies by which they *resist* any change in their current state owing to "God's preserving each thing by a continuous action" (AT XI 44: CSM I 96; cf. AT VIII-1 62: CSM I 240f.). Although the effect of an *action* in God, in bodies themselves the tendency to retain the same "size, shape, rest and numerous other things ... so long as collision with others does not force it to change that state" (ibid.) is merely a passive power, a *vis resistendi*, as Newton was to say of his *vis inertiae*.[6] Admittedly, Descartes is not as explicit as Newton on this point. Yet that the power to continue or remain in a certain state is a force of resistance is reasonably clear from *Principles*, II, 43:

> [W]hat is joined to another thing has some *power of resisting* separation from it; and what is separated has some *power of remaining* separate. Again, what is at rest has some *power of remaining* at rest and consequently of *resisting* anything that may alter the state of rest; and what is in motion has some power of persisting in its motion, i.e. of continuing to move with the same speed and in the same direction. (VIII-1 66f.: CSM I 244 e.a.)

Thus, the point of the wax analogy, at least as far as the intellect is concerned, can be put this way. Just as a body has a natural though only passive power or tendency to continue in its current state unless prevented from doing so by impressed forces, so the soul, which always thinks and is conscious of its thinking, has a natural tendency or disposition to persevere in this state of self-consciousness unless impeded by the body. And just as there is nowhere *in rerum natura* a material body on which no external forces act, so the soul is (in this life) always impeded by its body to a greater or lesser extent, whether the impediment be the habit formed in infancy of attending to bodily sensations or other prejudices acquired later. As for that "movement" of the will by which what is only recessively present to consciousness becomes dominant, this involves *action*. But the whole point of the analogy resides in the fact that the immediate *pre-reflexive* consciousness of one's acts is not an act or even an action but a condition or state of the soul in which it persists *quantum in se est* (AT VIII-1 62: CSM I 240), that is, qua mind as opposed to embodied mind.

This gives depth and dimension to the image of reason as the 'natural light' of the mind enkindled and kept alight by the creator. The *lumen naturale* is closely allied to the immediate but only implicit consciousness (*conscientia*) of one's thinking and to those fundamental ideas or concepts and truths or axioms contained implicitly in all thought. Natural reason, for Descartes, is like a light kindled within us; already burning, it simply shines forth, illuminating everything on which it falls, unless its power be diminished or its rays misdirected owing to interference from the body or preconceived opinions. Philosophical reflexion, accordingly, is not so much a matter of kindling the light as preserving it by counteracting the ever-present sources of occultation.[7]

19.4 Active *versus* passive disposition

While the letter to Mesland thus fails to provide any support for the *tabula rasa* model of the mind, it is helpful in distinguishing the Cartesian from the Leibnizian model of the mind, a distinction seldom sharply drawn in the literature.

In a well-known passage of the preface to his *New Essays*,[8] Leibniz, who reintroduced primitive *active* force into the metaphysics of nature, proposes a model of the mind apparently in sharp contrast with the Mercury-in-a-block-of-wood and wax models of Descartes. Descartes's analogies Leibniz wrongly takes to be rough equivalents of the older 'wax tablet' or *tabula rasa* model to which the Scholastics gave expression in the dictum: *nihil est in intellectu quod non antea in sensu fuerit*. This, Leibniz holds, is to suppose there to be by nature nothing more in the mind than a *faculté nue*. Descartes, of course, invests both models with a sense quite different from this, expressly rejecting the doctrine of the dictum *nihil est in intellectu ... etc.* in various places (cf. AT VI 37: CSM I 129 and AT VII 75f.: CSM II 52). Nevertheless, Leibniz goes further than Descartes, linking innate ideas to a spontaneous *active* disposition or power in the mind. Accordingly, he substitutes for Mercury in a block of wood the model of Hercules in a block of *veined* marble. It seems unlikely that the decisive differences between his and Descartes's model were entirely clear to Leibniz, since he even minimizes the extent to which his is a departure from Locke's perspective. With characteristic optimism, he suggests that since Locke recognized reflection as a source of ideas distinct from sensation, he perhaps "will not entirely disagree with my opinions":

[R]eflection is nothing other than attention to what is within us, and the senses do not give us what we already bring with us. Given this, can anyone deny that there is a great deal innate in our mind, since we are innate to ourselves, so to speak, and since we have within ourselves being, unity, substance, duration, change, action, perception, pleasure, and a thousand other objects of our intellectual ideas? And since these objects are immediate and always present to our understanding (though they may not always be perceived consciously [*apperçus*] on account of our distractions and our needs), why should it be surprising that we say that these ideas, and everything that depends upon them, are innate in us? I have also used the comparison of a block of veined marble, rather than a completely uniform block of marble, or an empty tablet, that is, what the philosophers call a *tabula rasa*. For if the soul were like these empty tablets, truths would be in us as the shape of Hercules is in a block of marble, when the marble is completely indifferent to receiving this shape or another. But if the stone had veins which marked out the shape of Hercules rather than other shapes, then that block would be more determined with respect to that shape and Hercules would be as though innate in it in some sense, even though some labour would be required for these veins to be exposed and polished into clarity by the removal of everything that prevents them from appearing. This is how ideas and truths are innate in us, as natural inclinations, dispositions, habits, or potentialities (*vitualités*) are always accompanied by some corresponding, though often insensible, actions. (Leibniz 1989, 294)

That this has nothing whatever to do with Locke goes without saying.[9] Striking, on the other hand, is the resemblance it bears to the theory of Descartes. The resemblance is such that it would be easy to overlook key differences regarding (1) the nature of reflexion itself, (2) that on which reflexion supervenes, and (3) the relation of reflexion to the discursive and ratiocinative operations of the mind. Regarding the *active* character of the disposition in question, (2) is decisive. This is not the place for a detailed development of these themes. A few brief and necessarily allusive comments may suffice, however, to throw certain features of Descartes's theory of the natural light into higher relief.[10]

Leibniz distinguished three grades of substances or 'monads': bare entelechies characterized by perception, animal souls capable both of perception and of sensation, and rational souls, minds, or spirits endowed not only with capacities for perception and sensation but also with consciousness of self. As in Descartes, self-consciousness includes consciousness of one's own acts, the 'I' or self that performs them, and of innate ideas and eternal truths. Chief among the eternal truths are Leibniz's "two great principles," of contradiction and sufficient reason, on which all our reasonings depend.

For self-consciousness Leibniz employed a variety of designations, among them his new technical term 'apperception.' Nevertheless, he continued to use that term in a non-technical manner corresponding to its everyday signification in standard French.[11] The terms 'consciousness,' 'reflexion,' 'attention,' and 'intellectual memory' he employs in senses closely akin to the *technical* use of 'apperception,' although these terms do not appear to be exactly equivalent in all instances of their use.[12] The last of them, intellectual memory, reflects the circumstance, noted earlier (section 15.4), that Leibniz followed Hobbes and St Thomas in holding that self-consciousness is the product of an act that supervenes upon an immediately *preceding* act, not, as in Descartes, an act-structure inherent in and hence simultaneous with the act of which one is conscious. This reflexive act of attention transforms perceptions, raising them to the level of what Leibniz termed 'thought.'[13] From this it is plain why Leibniz rejected the Cartesian dogma that the mind always thinks. The mind, he held, does not always think, though it always *perceives* and sometimes *reflects upon* or *apperceives* its perceptions, thus becoming conscious that it is perceiving; only then does it 'think' or 'understand' in Leibniz's sense, discovering the innate metaphysical ideas and eternal truths inherent in its thought.[14]

The precise relationship among the various terms Leibniz employed to designate self-consciousness is a matter of dispute. By all accounts, however, Leibniz distinguished various degrees of self-consciousness in rational souls. On what seems the best account of his usage, he speaks of 'reflexion' rather than 'apperception' in regard to those simple acts of attention to what is in us through which the mind is conscious of its acts, reserving the term 'apperception' for the process whereby attention is directed primarily to the self that acts and the innate ideas of 'being,' 'unity,' 'substance,' 'duration,' 'change,' 'activity,' and so on. Although for Leibniz, as for Descartes, consciousness of one's acts, of the self, and of an object are necessarily co-present in every act, it is nonetheless possible to direct one's attention *primarily* to the one or the other. The mind, accordingly, *apperceives* rather than merely *reflecting* by shifting the focus of its attention from the acts to the 'I' that thinks and to the innate ideas contained it. Moreover, Leibniz distinguishes between (a) that immediate apperception which picks out the primitive innate ideas and truths and (b) ratiocinative and other processes of the mind through which it is possible to form further, derivative innate ideas and eternal truths on the basis of the primitive ones.

Contrasting Leibniz's view with Descartes's, the first thing to note is that the former regards the varying degrees of self-consciousness in minds as the product of distinct *acts*, not as actions in Descartes's sense. That is, self-consciousness is the product of higher-order acts of attention or apperception directed upon perceptive acts, not, as in Descartes, a different manner of performing one and the same act.

Second, what *precedes* self-consciousness through reflexive acts is, for Leibniz, the sequence of *un*conscious acts of perception. For Descartes, thinking is always already 'lit up' from within; the natural light of *conscientia* (=*ratio*) illumines each act of thinking even prior to the occurrence of reflexion. Reason, as the faculty of innate ideas and eternal truths, is thus like a lamp that shines; its effects may be diminished by the influence of the body or augmented by focusing the mind's attention on that which it illumines; but we do not *make* it shine. For Leibniz, by contrast, the natural light of reason is *enkindled* by certain higher-order acts of the intellect that cast a ray of light onto that which till then lay in utter darkness. Reflexion, so understood, is not a passive power of persevering in the same act while focusing one's attention differently; it is rather the performance of a new act that actually transforms the act or state on which it supervenes (cf. McRae 1972b, 69f.).

Third and finally, Leibniz did not distinguish sharply between reflection and the discursive or ratiocinative processes of the mind. That is why he showed no reluctance to characterize the manner in which the eternal truths are innate in our thinking by analogy with enthymemes and to appeal to the *anamnesis* theory of the *Meno* to illustrate his point.[15] Descartes, of course, steadfastly resisted suggestions that confounded this intuitive progress of the mind from implicit to explicit insight with the very different process involved in logical analysis and enthymematic inference.

19.5 The *tabula rasa* model and the furniture of the mind

The insight that thinking necessarily involves a concomitant awareness that one is thinking finds clear expression at least as early as Aristotle and was never entirely lost sight of in the subsequent philosophical tradition. It was Descartes, however, who emphasized the difference in evidence between the knowledge of the existence of thinking and of extra-mental objects. Apart from making knowledge of the first kind the foundation of his metaphysics, Descartes also emphasized that the mind thereby increases its stock of ideas, furnishing itself not just with ideas of its own mental acts, processes, and faculties, but with certain key metaphysical ideas as well. The point was reiterated, with modifications, down through the modern era by thinkers as disparate in epistemological outlook as Locke and Leibniz. At issue was only the appropriateness of the term 'innate' in this regard. The tendency of Locke, and even more of Hume, was to enforce strict limits on the ideas and principles so derived, refusing to call them 'innate.' In this way they hoped to restrict the scope of metaphysical speculation based on innate ideas and principles. In their case, as in Aristotle's, it makes perfect sense to speak of a *tabula rasa* model of the mind, even though neither employed this particular image.

The tendency of Descartes, by contrast, was to extend the furniture of the mind beyond the knowledge of its own operations and faculties, not just to universal notions and principles applicable to everything that is, but even to the idea of God and the structure and laws of the physical universe. All of these he took to be innate. But this created a puzzle. How could ideas and principles not derived from any experience of the external world reveal its structure? From Leibniz's perspective, the problem lay in the assumption of a fundamentally *different* structure in mental and material reality; accordingly, the difficulty could be solved either by attributing to material things too a metaphysical structure read off from the mental, or by adopting a form of phenomenalism; and at different phases in his philosophical career, Leibniz at least toyed with both solutions (see chapter 1, n. 18 and chapter 21, n. 5). As for Descartes, radical dualism, coupled with a fundamentally realist tendency, left no means whatever of solving this problem – save by recourse to a God who created both the human mind and the material universe, giving the former certain innate dispositions to think the latter in specific ways. Part of the appeal of this solution must have lain in the fact that it helped solve a related problem: how can ideas and principles having their necessity in the nature of the human mind reflect the true natures of mere possibles, that is, the eternal truths? God can conceive these matters otherwise and actually make them so, however inconceivable that may be to us. To posit a God whose immutable goodness guaranteed that he would not alter the true and immutable nature of things existing *in rerum natura*, or of mere possibles (without simultaneously altering the nature or dispositions of the mind), is to solve both problems at once.

What to later thinkers may have seemed an unacceptable *deus ex machina* must have seemed to Descartes a powerful inducement to accept his theory of the mind, since it drove home the point he described as "the one thing that I set myself to prove in these Meditations" (AT VII 16: CSM II 11). However unsatisfactory Descartes's solution to the difficulties involved in extending the reflexive-dispositional theory beyond the "intellectual things" and common notions, even the imprint theory to which he resorted at times must have seemed very congenial to him. For it bears directly on the central purpose for which Descartes says he undertook the writing of his *Meditations* in the first place: to show that the knowledge of God is more certain even than mathematical knowledge, and that all other knowledge depends on it. It is misleading, therefore, to read back into Descartes the restrictive tendencies of the ectypal model of the mind fashioned by his empiricist predecessors and successors.

19.6 Conclusion

The evidence examined in this and the previous chapter suggests that Descartes was perfectly at ease *astride* the imprint, dispositional, and reflexive theories of innateness, which were perhaps not so distinct in his mind as McRae would have one keep them. If so, then Descartes's reflexive-dispositional theory is different from, though prospective of, those of Leibniz and Kant, both of whom employed notions of apperception that fused elements of a dispositional with what is at bottom a reflexive account of a priori knowledge.

Discovery of the basic characteristics of the mental requires only the exercise of the capacities to think and reflexion on one's thought; but for a finite thinking thing to discover the ideas of the infinite and the extended more is required. It need not be an imprint theory in the Lockean sense. But it is clear that the structure of thought in virtue of which to think is to be aware that one is thinking, that one exists, that in order to think one must exist, and so forth, cannot account for the ideas of an infinite God and extended body in the same way as those of thought, existence, substance, freedom, truth, and so on. Since the mind cannot furnish itself with these ideas through reflexion without having already been furnished with a pre-reflexive consciousness of them, they must have been implanted or enkindled in it in some other way. Is it surprising, then, that in the paradigmatic case of a metaphysical idea, 'God,' Descartes resorts openly to theories of innateness other than the basic reflexive theory, both cruder ones like the "trademark" theory and the "seeds of truth" doctrine, and sophisticated theories like the dispositional account of innateness in the *Broadsheet*? Once the significance of this exception among metaphysical ideas is grasped, McRae's general point about the difference between the metaphysical concepts and others of the ideas termed 'innate' by Descartes retains its force. What might be proposed as a possible improvement on his view is the following.

The reflexive-dispositional theory of innateness is *strictly* applicable only to certain metaphysical notions like 'substance' or 'thing,' 'thinking,' 'existence,' 'truth,' and 'freedom,' as well as to a number of "common notions." Nevertheless, having once made sense of innateness in these terms, Descartes sought to extend the theory – unwisely, perhaps, but understandably – to *all* innate ideas and eternal truths without exception. He extended it to the idea of body no less than the concepts of geometrical shapes, the idea of God, and the logical, mathematical, and metaphysical principles or truths of the natural light. He even extended it to the most fundamental laws of physics. In doing so, he had to shore up his new theory by resorting to the language, if not the content, of another conception of innateness: the old Platonic-Stoic-Ciceronian notion of "impressions which the souls of men receive in their first beings, and which they bring into the world with them, as necessarily and really as they do any of their inherent faculties."[16] Although Descartes never held this precise theory, the related notion of a native *disposition* implanted in the mind by the creator was so congenial to him that he incorporated it into his argument for the dependence of all other knowledge on the knowledge of God without so much as highlighting its role. It is worth quoting one last time the concluding passage of the "Synopsis" that Descartes prefixed, in all humility and sincerity, to his *Meditations*:

The great benefit of these arguments ["namely that there really is a world, and that human beings have bodies and so on"] ... is that in considering ... [them] we come to realise that they are not as solid or as transparent as the arguments which lead us to knowledge of our own minds and of God, so that the latter are the most certain and evident of all possible objects of knowledge for the human intellect. Indeed, this is the one thing that I set myself to prove in these Meditations. (AT VII 15f.: CSM II 11)

20

Experience and Induction

According to Clarke, "Descartes consistently proposed the theory that the observation of common natural phenomena, accompanied by critical reflection, could provide both the basic concepts and the fundamental laws that would explain all natural phenomena" (Clarke 1982, 200). To the question *what* exactly the mind reflects upon, Clarke's answer is clear: "By analogy with Aristotelian *epagōgē*, Descartes established the first principles of physical science by reflection *on ordinary experience*" (ibid., 201 and passim, e.a.). Ordinary experience of sensible things provides the data from which the fundamental concepts and laws of corporeal things are derived. As for "intellectual things," the non-sensory or "intellectual awareness" of such objects is likewise subsumable "under the rubric of Cartesian experience" (19f.). 'Experience' thus includes "acts of awareness or consciousness of our own mental activity," perceptions as well as volitions, and "naturally extends to the experience of innate ideas" such as "the infinite ..., or the idea of doubt, thought, etc." (ibid.). Although experience in this latter sense is said to be "an activity of the natural light of reason" (ibid.), it is nevertheless identified with "*introspection* of the contents or operations of one's own mind" (ibid., e.a.). This in effect reduces the natural light of reason to what Locke proposed might be "properly enough called internal sense" (1977, 34). Since the other uses distinguished by Clarke (ibid., chap. 2) refer to outer experience of one kind or another, Descartes's chief uses of the term 'experience' come down to 'introspection' on the one hand and 'sense-perception' or 'observation' of various kinds on the other.[1]

Without contesting the fact that the *word* 'experience' and its cognates are used in various ways (cf. also Röd 1971, 80ff. and Marion 1975, §6), it will be argued in this chapter that the starting point of reflexion is one and the same whether "corporeal" or "intellectual things" are in question: *inner experience*. Though we must certainly have recourse to ordinary experience, or "the observation of common natural phenomena" (Clarke), it is not the "proximate and primary" but only the "remote and accidental cause" or "origin" (AT X 396: CSM I 30) of the discovery of the concepts and principles of corporeal things. However, even in the case of intellectual things, 'inner experience' cannot be identified with 'inner sense,' 'introspection,' or 'empirical self-consciousness.'[2] In question is a uniquely Cartesian sense of 'experience,' as remote from Aristotle's notion of *empeiria* as it is from the distinctions drawn later between internal and external sense (Locke), inward and outward sentiment (Hume), and inner and outer sense (Kant).[3] As a result, Descartes's conception of the 'progress of the mind' in analytical reflexion differs in a decisive respect from Aristotle's *epagōgē*: whatever may be the similarity of their conceptions of intuitive induction itself, there is a decisive difference concerning the datum on which it is performed. From this at least one other significant difference follows (see section 20.5 below). Despite these differences, however, there are striking similarities, and these too are worth noting with some care.

Our starting point is Descartes's concept of *intuitus* in the *Regulae*. The boundary between intuition and deduction is notoriously fluid in the *Regulae* – almost to the point of vanishing completely on some accounts. It is a commonplace that *deductio* is employed with extreme latitude in that work; the substitution of *inductio* in one particular context (cf. AT IX 368: CSM I 14) strikes one as perfectly natural, *deductio* being used at times to designate inferential processes more akin to inductive and/or hypothetico-deductive strategies than to strictly logical inferences. Quite unnoticed in the literature, by contrast, is the use of *deductio* for intuitive induction, the process termed 'reflexive consciousness' or 'analytical reflexion' in the foregoing, though the same process is also included under *intuitus mentis* in a broad sense. Even those, like Clarke, who assign 'deduction' a very broad range of meanings (1982, §8) fail to take account of this key use. It may be worth while, therefore, to consider this intuitive form of *deductio* and the different senses of *intuitus mentis* before proceeding to Descartes's concept of experience and to the contrast of his with Aristotle's notion of intuitive induction.[4]

20.1 The boundary between *intuitus* and *deductio* in the *Regulae*

As defined in Rule III, the term *deductio* can be applied to the knowledge of "propositions which are *immediately inferred* (*immediate concluduntur*) from first principles" (AT X 370: CSM I 15 e.a.), as "when we deduce (*deducamus*) that nothing which lacks extension can have shape, on the grounds that there is a necessary connection between shape and extension" (AT X 425: CSM I 48). Though "deduced" from first principles, propositions so inferred "can be said to be known *in one respect* through intuition, and *in another respect* through deduction" (AT X 370: CSM I 15 e.a.): through deduction insofar as we "conjoin" (*conjungamus*) things, *deductio* being among the ways in which the mind forms ideas of composite natures through elementary reflexion on first principles;[5] through *intuition*, however, insofar as we "intuit that the conjunction of one with the other is wholly necessary" (AT X 425: CSM I 48).[6] Accordingly, *mentis intuitus* and *deductio certa* differ *only* to the extent that "we are aware of a movement or a sort of sequence (*motus sive successio quaedam concipiatur*) in the latter but not in the former" (AT X 370: CSM I 15). It is one and the same truth the knowledge of which is describable in these two ways.[7]

In Rule XI (AT X 407: CSM I 37) Descartes remarks that while intuition is contrasted with *deductio* in Rule III, later, in Rule VII (AT X 387: CSM I 25), the contrast is between *intuitus* and *enumeratio* (or *inductio* as he now terms it), "which we defined as an inference (*illatio*) drawn from many disconnected facts. But in the same passage we said that a simple deduction of one fact from another is performed by means of intuition." The disparity is explained by the difference in the way the "movement of our mind" (AT X 407: CSM I 37) is regarded in Rule III and Rule VII. A constant in both contexts is the fact that

two things are required for mental intuition: first, the proposition intuited must be clear and distinct; second, the *whole* proposition must be understood *all at once*, and not bit by bit. But when we think of deduction as a *process to be carried out* (*si de illa facienda cogitemus*), as we did in Rule III, it does not seem to take place all at once: inferring one thing from another involves a kind of movement of our mind. In that passage, then, we were justified in distinguishing intuition from deduction [as a movement of thought or progress of the mind]. But if we look on deduction *as a completed process* (*si vero ad eandem, vt jam facta est, attendamus*), as we did in Rule VII, then it no longer signifies a movement but the completion of a movement. That is why we are supposing that the deduction is made through intuition when it is simple and transparent, but not when it is complex and involved. When the latter is the case, we call it 'enumeration' or 'induction,' since the intellect *cannot simultaneously grasp it as a whole*, and its certainty in a sense *depends on memory*, which must retain the judgments we have made on individual parts of the enumeration if we are to derive a single conclusion from them taken as a whole. (AT X 407f.: CSM I 37 e.a.)

Distinguished are here (1) that which can only be called 'intuition'; (2) that which may be called either 'intuition' or 'deduction,' depending on whether the process of thought is so "simple and transparent" as to be regarded as finished or complete (so in Rule VII) or so "complex and involved" as to be viewed as proceeding toward completion (as in Rule III); and (3) that which does not even seem to take place "all at once" in the manner of intuition, but includes an ineliminable element of (reproductive) imagination or memory. For (3), which can only be called 'deduction,' the term *enumeratio* or *inductio* is introduced.[8] From this latter the other sense of *deductio* is distinguished as the finished product in which "memory is left with practically no role to play, and I seem to be intuiting the whole thing at once" (AT X 409: CSM I 38). That is (interpreting the "movement" involved to include that described in the preceding chapters as 'analytical reflexion'): I seem to have brought all that was formerly *only implicitly known in* my judgments within the compass of a single intuition so as to grasp everything, if not strictly "all at once," at least in one continuous movement of thought.

For this interpretation of enumeration there is no unambiguous support in the *Regulae*. There is, however, this passage from Rule VII, which *seems* to be an example of induction in the modern sense: "say I wish to show by enumeration that the area of a circle is greater than the area of any other geometrical figure whose perimeter is the same length as the circle's. I need not review every geometrical figure. If I can demonstrate that this fact holds for some particular figures, I shall be entitled to conclude *by induction* that the same holds true in all the other cases as well" (AT X 390: CSM I 27 e.a.). Cottingham et al. annotate their translation as follows: "'Induction' here seems to have its standard sense of 'inference from particular instances of something to all instances,'" that is, the first of the three Aristotelian senses of *epagōgē* distinguished above (see section 5, n. 3) and the dominant one ever since Hume and Mill. However, what Descartes has in mind here is arguably not this at all but an instance of 'grasping the universal in the particular' on the basis of a few examples. If so, it is more akin to intuitive induction, that is, *epagōgē* in the third sense. True, the mention of 'enumeration' at the beginning of the passage naturally conjures up the idea of 'induction by complete enumeration,' that is, the second sense of *epagōgē* in Aristotle. But the fact that Descartes makes a point of requiring only "sufficient," not "complete," enumeration (AT X 389f.: CSM 26f.) may be a deliberate attempt on his part to differentiate both this mathematical example of *inductio* based on a few relevant cases and the immediately preceding metaphysical example based on a single case of *distinct* perception (cf. ibid.) from 'induction based on *complete* enumeration.'[9]

If it is relevant to quote from the later writings, two passages may serve to document Descartes's use the verb *deducere* to describe what is clearly the process of analytical reflection, whereby what is implicit in all thought is made explicit as something universal and necessary. The first is from the letter to Father Dinet (to be quoted more extensively later; cf. chapter 22, n. 1): "as far as principles are concerned, I only accept those which in the past have always been common ground among all philosophers without exception, and which are therefore the most ancient of all. Moreover, the conclusions I deduce (*deduco*) are *already contained and implicit in these principles*" (AT VII 580: CSM II 392 e.a.). The other example occurs in the (Latin portion of) *The Search for Truth*. At one point Eudoxus urges Polyander to draw out the consequences (*consequentias deducere*) that follow from the *cogito, ergo sum* (AT X 518: CSM II 413), commending him when he has done so (the consequences in question concern what he is *not*) in these terms:

I cannot but stop you here ... to make you consider what good sense (*sanus sensus*) can achieve if given proper direction. For is there anything in what you have said which is not exact, which is not validly argued, which is not correctly deduced (*recte deductum*) from what has gone before (*ex antecedentibus*)? All these points have been stated and worked out not by means of logic, or a rule or pattern of argument, but simply by the light of reason and good sense (*sine Logica, sine regula, sine argumentandi formula, solo lumine rationis & sani sensus*). When this light operates on its own, it is less liable to go wrong than when it anxiously strives to follow numerous different rules, the inventions of human ingenuity and idleness, which serve more to corrupt it than render it more perfect. (AT X 521: CSM II 415)

Here there can be no question but that 'deduction' differs from merely logical derivation, since Descartes says so expressly.

If this is correct, then, to take Descartes's example, the proposition 'nothing which lacks extension can have shape' is one that is already intuited pre-reflexively; through reflexion it comes to be grasped explicitly, that is, deduced. In this *deductio* a certain movement is discernible, a process of the mind not involving memory; whereas in the immediate intuition of the necessary connection between shape and extension there is no movement of any sort at all. Enumeration, which "consists in a thorough investigation of all the points relating to the problem at hand, an investigation which is so careful and accurate that we may conclude with manifest certainty that *we have not inadvertently overlooked anything*" (AT X 388: CSM I 25f. e.a.) is just the operation of running over repeatedly in imagination or memory a series of related concepts or truths. While "required for the completion of our knowledge" (*ad scientiae complementum*) (ibid.), it neither makes everything that pertains to a certain subject or problem clear nor renders all that which is already clear (but only implicitly present to consciousness) distinct or explicit. These are the work of logical (discursive or ratiocinative) and of reflexive analysis, respectively. But enumeration ensures that *all* relevant concepts and truths are considered and their logical interrelations clarified so that we may be sure of obtaining *all* knowledge we are capable of concerning any particular object; and this includes 'filling out' (*complere*) our knowledge by rendering explicit what is *already* known.

It must be admitted that the correspondence between the "movement of the mind" described in the *Regulae* and the process of analytical reflexion from the particular proposition *cogito, ergo sum* to explicit knowledge of the universal *id quod cogitat, est* is not perfect. The exact analogue of *nihil* [*potest*] *esse figuratum quod non sit extensum* would be *nihil potest percipere quod non cogitet*. Still, the existential proposition *id quod cogitat, est* is an analogue of sorts. Both universal truths issue from reflexive attention to "simple natures" like extension and shape, thinking and existence, the ideas of which are implicit in all thinking; both are 'deduced' through reflexion on thinking, in which they are implicit. Like the "common notions" and "simple natures," the universal truths *id quod cogitat, est* and *id quod figuratum, extensum est* are only implicitly present to consciousness even once the reflexive awareness of one's thinking, the particular truth *cogito, ergo sum*, has been made explicit; further reflexion is required to render them explicit. But unlike the simple natures, they require a definite progress of the mind and can therefore be regarded as *deductio* even though the process is intuitive, that is, non-discursive in nature.

So the term *deductio* is applied not just to (a) mediate *logical* inferences from first principles, that is, from the universal to the particular, and especially to (b) chains of logical inferences too long to be encompassed within a single continuous intuition; it is applied also to (c) the acquisition of concepts and knowledge of propositions through the process of analytical reflexion on first principles, proceeding from the particular to the universal. It is due to (b), however, that a distinction between *intuitus* and *deductio* "had to be made" in the first place,

since very many things (*res*) which are not self-evident are known with certainty, provided they are inferred from true and known principles through a continuous and uninterrupted movement of thought (*cogitationis motus*) in which each individual proposition is clearly intuited. This is similar to the way in which we know that the last link in a long chain is connected to the first: even if we *cannot take in at one glance* all the intermediate links on which the connection depends, we can have knowledge of the connection provided we survey the links one after the other (*modo illos perlustraverimus successive*), and keep in mind (*recordemur*) that each link from first to last is attached to its neighbour. (AT X 369f.: CSM I 15 e.a.; cf. also CSM X 389: CSM I 26)

Nevertheless, the distinction is extended to (c) as well, since it too involves a *motus (cogitationis)* or *successio quaedam* not found in direct intuition of "simple natures" and "common notions." True, it is the "remote conclusions" of (b) that can *only* be described as 'deduction': as "first principles themselves are known only through intuition" and not through deduction, so "remote conclusions are known only through deduction" and not through intuition. That is why "immediate *self*-evidence is not required for deduction, as it is for intuition; deduction in a sense gets its certainty from memory" (ibid., e.a.). But not all deduction depends on memory, only that which is irreducible to intuition or a sequence of intuitions. Here, then, runs the rigid boundary between intuition and discursive or ratiocinative thinking: intuitive *self*-evidence reaches the end of its tether the moment *memory* of principles and inferences no longer immediately intuited must be relied on. At that precise instant the understanding is no longer intuitive in any respect at all: it is strictly discursive or ratiocinative.[10] Between *intuitus* and the remoter conclusions of logical deduction, however, lies a different kind of *motus* or *successio quaedam*, likewise irreducibly different from that awareness of "simple natures" and "common notions" that can *only* be called *intuitus*, but distinct as well from the 'movement' involved in syllogistic reasoning from the universal to the particular, especially where memory is involved. So along with the sharply drawn boundaries between analytical reflexion (from the particular to the universal) and logical inference (from the universal to the particular), the other salient point in the *Regulae* is the striking continuity between *intuitus* of first principles and *deductio* understood as analytical reflexion.

20.2 Experience of intellectual things

Of the range of expressions that Descartes was seen (section 15.2) to use to indicate the pre-reflexive nature of the insight and the non-discursive character of the inference embodied in the *cogito, ergo sum – conscientia, testimonium internum, simplex mentis intuitus, cognitio interna quae reflexam semper antecedit* – those most consistently employed are *intuitus, experior*, and their cognates. Forms of the latter are found in the *Meditations* and Replies, in the *Principles, The Search for Truth*, and in the conversation with Burman. In the last-mentioned place (AT V 147: CSMK 333), the expression *in semetipsis experiuntur* is applied, not to the *cogito, ergo sum*, but to "the common principles and axioms" (*principia communia et axiomata*), for instance, 'it is impossible that one and the same thing should both be and not be.' Since the passage refers to "the common principles *and the ideas of God and ourselves*, which never were in the senses" (AT V 146: CSMK 332 e.a.), it seems natural to take what is said of the common principles to apply equally to the ideas of God and ourselves: all are *experienced* within; all are acquired through attention to what is contained in our thinking, what we are immediately but only implicitly conscious of.

That is once again the sense of 'innateness' in Descartes. It is nowhere clearer than where Descartes reflects on the innate idea of freedom: "I cannot complain that the will or freedom of choice which I received from God is not sufficiently extensive or perfect, since I know *by experience* (*experior*) that it is not restricted in any way" (AT VII 56: CSM II 39 e.a.). To what experience does Descartes refer here? That it is *inner* experience becomes clear a few lines later: "It is only the will, or freedom of choice, *which I experience within me* (*quam in me experior*) to be so great that the idea of any greater faculty is beyond my grasp" (AT VII 57: CSM II 40). Similarly, in the *Principles*: "But whoever turns out to have created us, and however powerful and however deceitful he may be, in the meantime we nonetheless *experience within us* (*in nobis ... experimur*) the kind of freedom which enables us always to refrain from believing things which are not completely certain" (AT VIII-1 6: CSM I 194). Or again, in the Replies to the Third Set of Objections, where the link with the *lumen naturale* is particularly clear: "On the question of freedom, I made no assumptions beyond what we all experience within ourselves (*experimur in nobis*). Our freedom is very evident by the natural light" (AT VII 191: CSM II 134). When Gassendi denies "certain propositions about the indifference of the will," Descartes responds that they are "self-evident" (*per se manifesta*): "These are the sorts of things that each of us ought to *know by experience in his own case* (*apud se debeat experiri*) rather than having to be convinced of them by rational argument ... You may be unfree, if you wish; but I am certainly very pleased with my freedom since I experience it within myself (*cum illam apud me experiar*)" (AT VII 377: CSM II 259).

Although Descartes does not use *experior* of the innate idea 'thinking' with anything like the same frequency, he does so use it at least thrice, first in the Fifth Replies: "the mind, when engaged in private meditation (*meditabunda apud se ipsam*), can *experience* its own thinking (*experiri se cogitare*)" (AT VII 358: CSM II 247 e.a.). And in the Sixth Replies:

[S]ome people have such a confused conception of everything and cling so tenaciously to their preconceived opinions ... that rather than change them they will deny of themselves what they cannot fail to experience within themselves all the time (*quod non possunt non semper apud se experiri*). We cannot fail constantly to experience in ourselves that we are thinking (*non potest quin semper apud nosmetipsos experiamus nos cogitare*). It may be shown that animate brutes can perform all their operations without any thought, but this does not entitle anyone to infer that he does not himself think. Such an inference would be made only by someone who has previously been convinced that he operates in exactly the same way as the brutes, simply because he has attributed thought to them; he then remains so stubbornly attached to the sentence 'Men and the brutes operate in the same way' that when it is pointed out to him that the brutes do not think, he actually prefers to deny his own thought, of which he cannot fail to be aware (*illa sua, cuius non potest non esse sibi conscius, cogitatione*), rather than change his opinion. (AT VII 427: CSM II 288)

A similar expression occurs in *The Search for Truth*, where Polyander explains what he meant in replying "a man" to Eudoxus's question "What are you – you who ... cannot doubt that you yourself exist?":

I was thinking, rather, about the things we see, touch, perceive with our senses, and experience within ourselves (*in nobismetipsis experimur*) – in a word, about things which even the most simple-minded of men (*omnium simplicissimus hominum*) know just as well as the greatest philosopher in the world. Undoubtedly I am a certain whole made up of two arms, two legs, one head, and all the other parts which make up what we call the human body, and which besides is nourished, walks, perceives by the senses and thinks. (AT X 517: CSM II 412)

What we "experience within ourselves" is, of course, only the last-mentioned item: thinking.

So much for 'thinking.' While the word 'experience' may not occur in connection with the idea 'mind,' Descartes nevertheless remarks in a similar vein: "I did not doubt that 'I had a clear idea of my mind,' since I had a close inner consciousness of it (*mihi intime conscius eram*)" (AT VII 443: CSM II 298). As for the idea of truth, there is no explicit mention of 'experience,' much less of *inner* experience, in the letter to Mersenne dealing with truth (cited several times already). Yet at the end of that letter there is a clear reference to the role of *outer* experience in exhibiting the idea of motion, and the suggestion at least that the idea of truth originates in a corresponding way in *inner* experience.

Another pertinent use of *experior* occurs where, in the Third Meditation, Descartes considers his grounds for believing that adventitious ideas are caused by and resemble things outside the mind. He cites three grounds for this belief. After noting that "Nature has apparently taught me to think this" (AT VII 38: CSM II 26), he gives as his second reason: "But in addition I know by experience (*experior*) that these ideas do not depend on my will, and hence that they do not depend simply on me. Frequently they are met with (*obversantur*) even when I do not want to" (ibid.). What Descartes here claims to experience inwardly (and apparently infallibly) is that sensations occur mostly without a concurrent act of willing, and sometimes even preceded or accompanied by inner experience of an act of willing that they not occur. Examining the cogency of this argument in the next paragraph, he points out that "it does not follow" from this that his adventitious ideas "must come from things located outside me," since "there may be some other faculty not yet fully known to me which produces these ideas without any assistance from external things" (AT VII 39: CSM II 27). From this it appears that (1) the mind can possess faculties or powers of which it has no experience, though (2) it cannot perform acts of thinking (sensing and willing) without at the same time "experiencing" inwardly that it is doing so, that is, without being conscious of the occurrence of its simultaneous or successive acts, or of the occurrence of one without the other, for instance, of sensations without volitions.

The first of these two points is immediately rendered doubtful by the second proof of the existence of God in the same Meditation and later by the certain proof of the existence of body in the Sixth. In the proof of God's existence Descartes asks "whether I possess some power enabling me to bring it about that I who now exist will still exist a little while from now." The reply is that he cannot possess such a power or faculty: "For since I am nothing but a thinking thing – or at least since I am now concerned only and precisely with that part of me (*de ea tantum mei parte praecise*) which is a thinking thing – if there were such a power (*vis*) in me, I should undoubtedly be aware of it (*eius proculdubio conscius essem*). But I experience no such power (*nullam esse experior*), and this very fact makes me recognise most clearly that I depend on some being distinct from myself" (AT VII 49: CSM II 33f.).

Inner experience can only possess this authority given some such principle as the denial of (1): the mind cannot possess a power or faculty of which it is completely unaware. The thrust of the Sixth Meditation proof of the existence of body is similar. Here the cause of my sensory ideas of body is sought; and once again the matter is settled by appeal – this time tacit appeal – to *experience* and the principle that where there exists a power or faculty of producing ideas there is also an immediate inner awareness of it:

Now there is in me a passive faculty of sensory perception, that is, a faculty for receiving and recognizing the ideas of sensible objects; but I could not make use of it unless there was also an active faculty, either in me or in something else, which produced or brought about those ideas. But this [active] faculty cannot be in me, since clearly it presupposes no intellectual act on my part and the ideas in question are produced without my cooperation and often even against my will (*me non cooperante sed saepe etiam invito*). So the only alternative is that it is in another substance distinct from me. (AT VII 79: CSM II 55)[11]

More than one commentator has found one or both these passages grossly inconsistent with the assumption made earier in the Third Meditation that I might well possess a faculty or power of producing certain ideas without being conscious of it (cf. Norton 1968 and McRae 1972b, n. 18). Is there a way around this difficulty? It was suggested earlier (cf. section 18.5) that I might be in possession of some faculty without being aware that I possessed it provided I had never exercised it; in that case to be merely 'potentially' conscious of it would mean, to be altogether *un*conscious of it. But this schema does not fit either case at hand, since the effect (the 'advent' of certain ideas or my continued existence from one moment to the next) is taken as given; if that cause were some power in me, it would have to have been exercised already. Still, the other notion of potential consciousness of something, namely actual but only implicit awareness, may furnish a solution to the apparent contradiction.

In the Replies to the Fourth Set of Objections Descartes wrote that "although we are always actually aware (*conscios*) of the acts or operations of our minds, we are not always conscious of the mind's faculties or powers, except potentially (*potentiâ*). By this I mean that when we concentrate on employing one of our faculties (*ad utendum aliqua facultate accingimus*), then immediately, if the faculty in question resides in our mind, we become actually conscious of it (*fiamus ejus actu conscii*)" (AT VII 246: CSM II 171f.). So actual as opposed to merely potential consciousness of a faculty is explicit consciousness achieved through exercising that faculty and attending to one's capacity to do so. Simply exercising it (consciously, but without attention) is not enough. There is no "essential inconsistency" (Norton 1968) in suggesting both that I cannot possess a faculty without being (at least potentially or implicitly) aware of it, that is, without *experiencing inwardly* that I possess it, and also that it is entirely possible to possess a faculty without (actual or explicit) awareness of it, since the latter requires, in addition to inner experience, reflexion on that of which I am conscious. This still leaves a puzzle as to why the question whether I am the cause of my adventitious ideas was not settled immediately in the Third as it apparently is later in the Sixth Meditation by focusing attention on the relevant mental processes; but that is a different question, to which plausible answers are not hard to find, even if it cannot be answered definitively.

So much for the sense of 'experience' in the context of the knowledge of the ideas and faculties or powers belonging to "intellectual things." It is to the less straightforward question of the sense of 'experience' in the knowledge of the first principles of *material* things that we turn next.

20.3 Experience of corporeal things

Just as the pertinent sense of 'experience' in the case of 'freedom,' 'thinking,' or 'truth' is not 'introspection' or 'empirical self-consciousness' (cf. section 9.4 and the previous section), so in the case of ideas of "corporeal things" the experience on which the mind reflects is not ordinary sensory experience of extra-mental objects. There is certainly no denying that it is ordinary sensory experience, specifically seeing, to which Descartes refers in stressing the requirement of "displaying" (AT X 417: CSM I 43) the ideas of corporeal things. Nor is this requirement confined to the idea of 'natural power,' as in the *Regulae* (cf. above, section 19.1): essentially the same point is made in regard to the idea of 'motion,' not just in the letter to Mersenne concerning truth, but also in *Le Monde* (cf. AT XI 40: CSM I 94). It is safe to say that it applies to all attributes and modes of corporeal substance. And yet the ideas of "corporeal things" are not acquired or made explicit through reflexion upon ordinary experience as their "proximate and primary cause"; that primary cause is rather attention to *the concomitant inner experience of what is immediately present to consciousness while* I 'exhibit' these ideas to the external senses. They are acquired, in other words, through the very experience in which the ideas of "intellectual things" originate. If so, then the relevant sense of 'experience' coincides neither with sense-perception, nor with everyday connected sensory experience (which is Aristotle's notion of *empeiria*), nor with that 'introspection' customarily opposed to 'outer sense' in post-Cartesian modern philosophy.

That is the thesis of this and the next section. That no distinction in Descartes corresponds to those drawn later between inner and outer sense appears to be belied by the very 'definition' of 'experience' given in Rule XII of the *Regulae*, and it is on this that our re-examination of the role of experience in the knowledge of corporeal things must focus. The 'definition' is to be interpreted in the light of another key passage from Rule XII in which Descartes draws a distinction between two senses of *intuitus*, one broader, the other the strict or narrow sense of the term. This passage will be examined in the present section, the definition of experience in the next, where it will be shown to corroborate rather than tell against our thesis regarding the knowledge of corporeal things.

According to Rule VIII, the task of Rule XII is to distinguish the (1) simple natures that are "spiritual or corporeal or belong to each of these categories" from the "complex or composite natures" (AT X 399: CSM I 32). The latter the intellect either (2) "experiences as composite before it decides to determine anything about them," or else they (3) "are put together by the intellect itself " (ibid.). This, at least, is the first task of Rule XII. The second is to show "that there can be no falsity save in composite natures which are put together by the intellect" (ibid.). In accordance with this plan, the investigations of Rule XII are divided as follows: (1) *intuition* of simple natures, (2) *experience* of complex natures, and (3) *composition* of complex natures, the last comprising (3a) composition "through impulse," (3b) composition "by way of conjecture," and (3c) deduction (AT X 424: CSM I 47). (3a) and (3b) are shown to be the sources of falsity or error, while (3c), like (1) and (2), is error-free. Our immediate task is, more exactly, to show that 'intuition' is used both in a narrow sense for (1) and in a broad sense that includes (1), (2), and part of (3c).

Before distinguishing the intuition of simple natures from experience and composition, Descartes divides the simple natures into three classes: (a) "purely intellectual," (b) "purely material, and (c) "common to both" (AT X 419f.: CSM I 44f.). Simple natures are known either by the pure intellect alone or "by the intellect as it intuits the images of material things" (ibid.). "Those simple natures which the intellect recognises by means of a sort of innate light, without the aid of any corporeal image, are purely intellectual" (or "spiritual," as Rule VIII has it). Those that are "common to both" are known either by the pure intellect or "by the intellect as it intuits the images of material things" (ibid.). Descartes does not say how the third class is known, that is, those simple natures "which are recognised to be present in bodies – such as shape, extension and motion etc." – the very class that interests us here. Clarke takes it that they too are known *only* "by the intellect as it intuits the images of material things," remarking that it "seems almost redundant for Descartes to have to add that the material simples can be known in the way in which acquired ideas of any physical object or event are known – namely, through the joint co-operation of sensory experience and understanding" (Clarke 1982, 56). Yet in the second of the two letters to the Princess Elizabeth written some fifteen years later Descartes states that while body can be known "by the intellect aided by the imagination," it "(i.e. extension, shapes and motions) can likewise be known *by the intellect alone*" (AT III 691: CSMK 227 e.a.). So unless Descartes changed his views in the intervening period, it seems prima facie unlikely that the simple natures of corporeal things are knowable *only* by reflexion on ordinary experience. They are known in this way, to be sure, and, as Descartes assures Elizabeth, this is the way in which they are *best known* (ibid.). But they are known also by the intellect alone.[12]

So much for (1) the intuition of simple natures. Coming now to (2) experience, we note that Descartes offers what looks very much like a general 'definition' of *experientia* in Rule XII, focusing on the extension of the concept:

[T]hose natures which we call 'composite' are known by us either [A] because we learn from experience (*experimur*) what sort they are, or [B] because we ourselves put them together (*nos ipsi componimus*). Our experience (*Experimur*) consists of [A1] whatever we perceive by means of the senses, [A2] whatever we learn from others, and in general whatever reaches our intellect either from external sources (*aliunde*) [i.e., from A1 and A2] or [A3] from its own reflexive self-contemplation (*quidquid sensu percipimus, quidquid ex aliis audimus, & generaliter quaecumque ad intellectum nostrum, vel aliunde perveniunt, vel ex sui ipsius contemplatione reflexa*). (AT X 422: CSM I 46f.)

So, in addition to (1), the ideas of simple natures with which it furnishes itself in mental intuition, the mind supplies itself also with ideas of composite natures from each of two sources: on the one hand (2) *experitur*, it experiences such ideas as composite, on the other (3) *componit*, it puts such ideas together itself.[13] As for the two kinds of (2) experience distinguished here, the difference between A1 and A2 on the one hand and A3 on the other certainly suggests an inner-outer distinction of the kind just said *not* to be found in Descartes. In order to interpret the 'definition' correctly we must examine attentively the two senses of 'intuition' distinguished by Descartes elsewhere in Rule XII, for they provide a solution to the problem.

The second task of Rule XII noted earlier is to pinpoint the sources of falsity and error. There is obviously no falsity in (1) mental intuition of simple natures: "these simple natures are all self-evident and never contain any falsity" (AT X 420: CSM I 45). However, "the intellect can never be deceived by any experience" (AT X 423: CSM I 47); so (2) cannot be the source of error either. Nor, finally, is there falsity in "deductions," that is, in the third kind of composition (3c): deduction is "our sole means of compounding things in a way that enables us to be certain of their truth" (AT IX 424: CSM I 48). This includes both logical inferences from self-evident intuitions and truths discovered through the process of analytical reflexion on the immediately evident (section 20.1). Error occurs rather in composition of the other two kinds, (3a) "through impulse" and (3b) "by way of conjecture." There follows the famous moral drawn by Descartes as the first of four "conclusions" based on the seven "assumptions" set out to this point in Rule XII. Here we encounter the two senses of 'intuition':

> [T]here are no paths to certain knowledge of the truth accessible to men, save manifest intuition and necessary deduction (*praeter evidentem intuitum, & necessariam deductionem*) ... It is clear that mental intuition (*intuitus mentis*) extends (*extendi*) both to [i] all these simple natures and [ii] to our knowledge of the necessary connections between them [i.e., those composite natures known by deduction], and in short [iii] to *everything else* which the intellect experiences exactly within itself or in the corporeal imagination (*ad reliqua omnia quae intellectus praecise, vel in se ipso, vel in phantasia esse experitur*). (AT X 425: CSM I 48 e.a.)

This echoes the descriptions of the "actions of the intellect" in Rule III (intuition and deduction) rather than the "two ways of arriving at a knowledge of things" (experience and deduction) of Rule II.[14] While Descartes here again speaks of *two* paths to certain knowledge, it is striking that the first, *intuitus mentis*, "extends" to the knowledge of complex no less than of simple natures, whether the complex be [ii] compounded by the mind in *deductio* or [iii] grasped as already composite in *experientia* (cf. AT X 399: CSM I 32). The first section above pointed out the fluid boundary between *intuitus* and *deductio* in the *Regulae*. On the basis of this passage, it is tempting to go a step further. Instead of saying that *deductio* includes, in addition to the shorter and longer discursive or ratiocinative processes sometimes so designated by Descartes, the intuitive process of analytical reflexion as well, we may now distinguish a broader and a narrower sense of 'pure intuition.' The narrow is confined to [i] in the above passage, the intuition of simple natures, while *intuitus mentis* in the broad sense includes [i], [ii], and [iii]. That is, it covers [ii] *deductio* as the knowledge of immediately intuited necessary connections between such simple natures, including both analytical reflexion upon thinking itself and short chains of logical inference from first principles not involving memory; but it does not include longer chains of reasoning that rely on memory. Moreover, it includes "everything else which the intellect experiences," as Descartes says, that is, immediate [iii] *experientia* of complex natures insofar as the mind attends *praecise* to what it actually experiences "within itself or in the corporeal imagination." What exactly Descartes means by *experientia* in this context is suggested by his use of *praecise*.

What the mind *prescinds from* in [iii] is not said explicitly, but given the context (determining the sources of error) it seems reasonable to suppose that a version of the distinction drawn later between the objects of *conscientia* and of *cogitatio* is in play here (see above, chapter 15, n. 30). If so, then when the intellect experiences anything *praecise*, that from which it prescinds is the extra-mental object of thought, so that only the complex object of consciousness remains as the immediate object of *intuitus* in this broad sense. Not obviously present here or in the 'definition' of *experientia*, however, is the later distinction of *conscientia* from *reflexio* – even though Descartes draws a primitive form of the same distinction already in the *Regulae*, opposing *perspicacitas* to *sagacitas* (cf. section 15.7). However, it is the disjunctive "within itself *or* in the corporeal imagination" (e.a.) that indicates that both kinds of experienced complex nature are included under [iii] *experientia*, the intellectual and the material. If this is correct, then the *contemplatio sui ipsius* described as *reflexa* in the earlier 'definition' of *experientia* involves a double conflation: (1) of simple *conscientia* and analytical reflexion (*perspicacitas* and *sagacitas*) under the heading 'reflexive contemplation' of complex natures and (2) of complex natures of the intellectual with those of the material kind.

The first conflation is perfectly understandable. As shown earlier (section 15.4) *conscientia/perspicacitas*, too, is reflexive in the literal sense of *reflectere*. Only after the *Regulae*, perhaps as early as the *Discourse*, was Descartes to distinguish 'reflexion' proper as an action from (pre-reflexive) consciousness as an act-structure (see section 15.3). As for the second conflation, the inclusion of complex *corporeal* natures under the objects of *contemplatio sui ipsius*, there remains an obstacle standing in the way of our thesis that the ideas of corporeal natures originate in inner experience as their primary and proximate cause. For the 'definition' of *experientia* seems to suggest an inner-outer distinction of the sort said not to be found in Descartes. We turn now to the 'definition' and the resolution of the problem it poses.

20.4 Descartes's 'definition' of *experientia*

If the preceding interpretation of the famous moral drawn in Rule XII is correct, then the words *ex sui ipsius contemplatione reflexa* (A3) in the 'definition' of *experientia* refer to the movement of thought whereby ideas whose objects are complex *a parte re* are rendered explicit. Starting from what is immediately yet only implicitly present to consciousness in every act of thinking, the complex idea is rendered explicit through attention or reflexion, without in any way 'going beyond' or adding to it through the two illicit forms of composition. This reading gains some support from Descartes's account of that with which *experientia* is contrasted, *compositio*. We shall consider it in a moment. First we must examine the term *aliunde* (i.e., A1 and A2 in the 'definition') for the light it sheds on Descartes's conception of that 'ordinary experience' which he contrasts with 'inner experience' or the ideas that reach the mind *ex sui ipsius contemplatione reflexa*. For the contentious point is whether the ideas of complex *corporeal* natures are acquired through the mind's "reflexive self-contemplation" rather than from any operations performed on the deliverances of the external senses.

For ease of reference, we cite the 'definition' again:

Our experience (*Experimur*) consists of [A1] whatever we perceive by means of the senses, [A2] whatever we learn from others, and in general whatever reaches our intellect either from external sources (*aliunde*) [i.e., A1 and A2] or [A3] from its own reflexive self-contemplation (*quidquid sensu percipimus, quidquid ex aljis audimus, & generaliter quaecumque ad intellectum nostrum, vel aliunde perveniunt, vel ex sui ipsius contemplatione reflexa*). (AT X 422: CSM I 46f.)

However elusive the meaning of *contemplatio reflexa* here, that of *aliunde* is made clear on the spot: *quidquid sensu percipimus, quidquid ex alijs audimus*. The reference to hearing and hearsay harks back to the explanation given Burman of the expression *a sensibus, vel per sensus* used in the First Meditation (AT VII 18: CSM II 12). *Per sensus* is glossed as, "Through the senses, i.e. through hearing (*auditum*); for this is how I acquired and gleaned what I know, from my parents, teachers, and others" (AT V 146: CSMK 332). This calls to mind the *degrez de Sagesse* distinguished in the preface to the *Principles* (AT IX-2 5: CSM I 181). The first degree consists only of "notions which are so clear in themselves that they can be acquired without meditation (*sans meditation*)," that is, in the language of the *Regulae*, the intuition of simple natures. The second consists of "everything we are acquainted with through sensory experience (*experience des sens*)." Meant is, of course, ordinary non-reflexive (outer) experience. "The third comprises what we learn by conversing with other people (*la conversation des autres hommes*)," that is, knowledge acquired *per sensus sive auditum*.

And one may add a fourth category, namely what is learned by reading books – not all books, but those which have been written by people who are capable of instructing us well. For in such cases we hold a kind of conversation with the authors. I think that all the wisdom (*Sagesse*) which is generally possessed is acquired in these four ways. I am not including divine revelation in the list, because it does not lead us on by degrees but raises us at a stroke to infallible faith. (ibid.)

These "degrees of wisdom" or knowledge in turn call to mind Descartes's comments on the thirteenth and fourteenth articles discussed in the *Broadsheet*. In article thirteen Regius had written that "all common notions which are engraved in the mind have their origin in observation of things or in verbal instruction (*ex rerum observatione, vel traditione*)" (AT VIII-2 358: CSM I 304). In fourteen he had added that even "the idea of God which is within us derives its being not from our faculty of thinking, in which the idea is innate, 'but from divine revelation (*revelatione*), or verbal instruction (*traditione*), or observation of things (*rerum observatione*)'" (AT VIII-2 360: CSM I 305). To this Descartes replied, incredulous: "as if the power of thinking could achieve nothing on its own, could never perceive or think anything except what it receives through observation of things or through verbal instruction, *i.e. from the senses (a sensibus)*" (AT VIII-2 358: CSM I 304). Taken together, these passages render the sense of *aliunde* quite precise: it means 'from or through the senses,' including the second, third, and fourth degrees of wisdom. It thus includes outer or ordinary sensory experience of composite sensible things.

Ex sui ipsius contemplatione reflexa is harder to interpret. What we have to go on is only that such "reflexive self-contemplation" is (1) *experientia* and (2) one of several sources of ideas of *composite* natures. *Experientia* in the sense of "whatever reaches our intellect ... *ex sui ipsius contemplatione*" is thus opposed not only to (a) "whatever reaches our intellect *aliunde*," but also to (b) the ideas of *simple* natures which derive either from the "pure intellect," or "the intellect as it intuits the images of material things" (AT X 420: CSM I 45). Although Descartes gives no examples of such *purely intellectual* ideas of *composite* natures, examples are 'God' or 'a triangle.' These are complex ideas, though they derive from the same source as intellectual ideas of simple natures like 'thinking' or 'extension.' Thus, the intellectual idea of a composite spiritual nature, of God as an infinite thinking substance, derives from the "pure intellect" alone, while that of composite corporeal nature, a triangle or any other geometrical figure, derives from "the intellect as it intuits the images of material things" (ibid.).[15]

If this is correct, then unlike ordinary sensory experience, but like the ideas of simple natures, the ideas that stem from the mind's "own reflexive self-contemplation" are non-sensory or innate ideas. Moreover, unlike the ideas of thinking and extension acquired through *intuitus* in the narrow sense, but like the ideas of ordinary sensory experience, they are ideas of *composite* natures.

Furthermore, unlike the ideas of such simple natures as thinking and extension, but again like ordinary sensory experience, they are not actually 'put together' or 'formed' by the mind's own acts of composition but simply grasped, *experienced as composite* in reality, *a parte rei*. That is what distinguishes *experientia* generally from *compositio*. Finally (and the chief thing to be established), like the ideas of simple natures, the ideas that the mind derives from "its own reflexive self-contemplation" are ideas of "corporeal" ('a triangle') no less than "intellectual things" ('God').

At least indirect support for this reading of *ex sui ipsius contemplatione* is provided by Descartes's handling of the three forms of composition that he goes on to distinguish from both forms of *experientia* – direct and indirect sensory experience and *contemplatio sui ipsius reflexa* – as well as from *intuitus* of simple natures. The forms of composition are different ways of "determining" something, that is, passing judgment on the simple and composite natures, ideas of which are already immediately present to consciousness either through pure intuition or through sensory experience or through experience in the sense of the mind's intellectual self-contemplation. As already noted, only here does the possibility of error arise, intuition and experience being such as never to deceive. This anticipates the later teaching that formal falsity and error (cf. section 7.1) are to be found not in ideas but only in the judgments by which the mind assents to something that goes beyond what is immediately present to consciousness (AT VII 37: CSM II 26). In the *Regulae* what is at bottom the same doctrine is expressed this way:

We should note here that the intellect can never be deceived by any experience (*a nullo unquam experimento decipi posse*), provided that when the object is presented to it, it intuits it in a fashion exactly corresponding to the way in which it possesses the object, either within itself or in the imagination (*si praecise tantum intueatur rem sibi objectam, prout illam habet vel in se ipso vel in phantasmate*). (AT X 423: CSM I 47)

If we again ask, what does the mind *prescind from* when it intuits the object in this way, a plausible answer is, all that is not experienced as immediately present to consciousness. Thus, in *some* forms of composition the mind *goes beyond* what it immediately "experiences exactly within itself or in the corporeal imagination" (AT IX 425: CSM I 48). Upon the passage just quoted follows an example of composition through impulse that illustrates just this point:

Furthermore, it must not judge that the imagination faithfully represents the objects of the senses, or that the senses take on the true shapes of things, or in short that external things always are just as they appear to be. In all such cases we are liable to go wrong ...

But the understanding of the wise man will not be deceived in such cases ... But whenever we believe that an object of our understanding contains something *of which the mind has no immediate experience*, then it is we ourselves who are responsible for its composition. (*Componimus autem quoties in illis* [*scil. rebus quas intelligimus*] *aliquid inesse credimus, quod nullo experimento a mente nostra immediate perceptum est*). (AT IX 423: CSM I 47 e.a.)

The question broached here is what is and is not immediately present to consciousness, what is and is not *experienced inwardly* at the very moment external objects are perceived by means of the bodily senses. In composition by impulse we believe or judge something "not because good reasons convince us of it, but simply because we are caused to believe it, either by some superior power, or by our free will, or by a disposition of the corporeal imagination" (AT X 424: CSM I 47). Thus, either divine revelation ("some superior power") or our own judgment ("our free will") or habit ("the disposition of the corporeal imagination") may cause us to pass judgment concerning something *quod nullo experimento a mente nostra immediate perceptum est* without "good reasons" for doing so. The first, of course, is never a cause of error, the second occasionally, and the third "almost always" (ibid.).

The judgments of the intellect go beyond what is immediately present to consciousness in composition by conjecture (3b) as well. It never "really deceives us, so long as we judge it to be merely probable, and never assert it to be true; nor for that matter does it make us any the wiser" (AT IX 424: CSM I 48). This way of putting it suggests that to make a conjecture while taking it to be no more than probable is not really to go beyond the immediately experienced at all – as though asserting the conclusion of an inductive generalization with extreme caution were tantamount to not going beyond the evidence contained in the premises. However mistaken this may be as an interpretation of probable inference, it at least explains why Descartes regards composition by conjecture as making us no wiser than before: if made thus cautiously, he suggests, our judgment does not really extend beyond what is *immediately present to consciousness* and hence known already. But, of course, men are sometimes not so cautious and fall into error.

As for the last form of composition, deduction (3c), this indeed makes us wiser, being the "sole means of compounding things in a way that enables us to be certain of their truth" (ibid.). Yet even here we must be sure we actually intuit the conjunction of one concept with another – or risk falling into error. Not only ideas (whether concepts and propositions) themselves, but also the relations between them can either be or fail to be actually intuited, immediately present to consciousness. Only either discursive logical analysis or analytical reflexion will decide the question. So even deductive logical inferences from universal to particular and analytical reflexion proceeding from the particular to the universal rest on the immediate actual intuition of necessary connections. As long as memory is not brought into play, there is not the slightest risk of error. Otherwise, there is very great danger precisely because the relations about which we judge are no longer immediately before the mind's eye.

To conclude, then, the examination of Rule XII in this and the previous section suggests that even in composition, where the experiential datum is typically *outer* experience, the focus of Descartes's attention is upon *that which is immediately present to consciousness as we reflect on the deliverances of our external senses* as distinct from *judgments that 'go beyond' the immediately experienced*. Thus, as with the knowledge of intellectual things, so with the knowledge of corporeal things: the key to the discovery of truth and avoidance of error is the concomitant *inner* experience, *intuitus mentis* in the broad sense outlined above. Such inner experience is the source of certain ideas that "never were in the senses," both ideas of intellectual natures, like the mind and God, which require for their elaboration the aid neither of the senses nor of the imagination, and ideas of corporeal natures, either simple or complex, where the senses and imagination must come to the aid of the intellect. Where the ideas are of complex natures and already "composite in reality" (AT X 399: CSM I 32) rather than compounded by the mind, the source is *experientia, contemplatio sui ipsius reflexa*, not introspection and not ordinary sensory experience. This is what our earlier conclusions regarding the progress of the mind in intuition suggest, and it is now borne out by the text of the *Regulae*. It remains now only to comment on the significance of this in relation to Aristotle's conception of intuitive induction.

20.5 Cartesian and Aristotelian 'induction'

In Rule XII, then, Descartes distinguishes the intuition of simple natures from experience as the source of ideas of composite things, sensory or intellectual, and from those operations of the mind through which other ideas of composite natures are formed by the intellect itself. Mental intuition of simples, 'experience' of composites, and deduction – these are the "paths to certain knowledge of the truth" that Descartes speaks of in that first of his four "conclusions." There mental intuition (*intuitus mentis*) is said to extend "to *all* these simple natures *and* to our knowledge of the necessary connections between them, *and* in short to *everything else* which the intellect *experiences precisely* within itself or in the corporeal imagination" (AT X 425: CSM I 48 e.a.). What the verb 'experiences' means here – the word is glossed rather translated in the standard English translation – is not ordinary sensory experience of composite things (as in Aristotle); nor is it inner experience in the sense of introspective self-awareness. Meant is rather the acquisition of ideas of composite natures, intellectual *and* material, by the intellect that first grasps them intuitively and then makes them explicit through analytical reflexion, whether with (so in the case of material natures) or without (intellectual natures) the aid of the corporeal imagination.

Scholars have remarked on the similarity of this mental process to one of Aristotle's uses of *epagōgē* in the *Posterior Analytics* (cf. i, 18 and ii, 19). As noted earlier (cf. above, section 5.1 n. 3), *epagōgē* has at least three senses in Aristotle, and we must now very briefly examine two of them if we are to establish the main point to which we have been leading up throughout this chapter: that the chief difference between Descartes's and Aristotle's conceptions of intuitive induction lies in their respective concepts of experience. There is, however, a second key difference deserving of attention. For Aristotle, the universal that is 'grasped in the particular' exists in the things themselves; for Descartes it is implicit in thought as the object of consciousness and made explicit through attention to what we are conscious of. Both differences will be elaborated presently. We begin with two senses of 'induction' in Aristotle.

Aristotle, Ross notes (Aristotle 1949a, 37), only "speaks as though there were other forms of inference than syllogism – induction, example, and enthymeme"; his "predominant view" is that "if inference is to be valid it must take the syllogistic form." To put the same point differently, whether or not induction is a (valid) form of inference depends, for Aristotle, on the specific sense of 'induction' in question. There is a famous passage of the *Prior Analytics* (ii, 23) in which inductive inference is reduced to syllogistic form. "But," notes Ross, "the induction which is so reduced is the least important kind of induction – the perfect induction in which, having noted that membership of any of the species of a genus involves possession of a certain attribute, we infer that membership of the genus involves it" (ibid.). Perfect induction by complete enumeration, then, is indeed a "valid argument by which we pass from seeing that certain species of a genus have a certain attribute, and that these are all the species of the genus, to seeing that the whole genus has it" (ibid., 50) – though Ross perhaps downplays Aristotle's misgivings about the completeness of any enumeration involving natural kinds (cf. von Fritz 1964, passim).

So much for perfect induction or induction by complete enumeration. In his most frequent use of the term, Aristotle means by 'induction' (in Ross's words again) "the process by which, from seeing for instance that in the triangle we have drawn (or rather in the perfect triangle to which this is an approximation) equality of two sides involves equality of two angles, we pass to seeing that any isosceles triangle must have two angles equal" (ibid., 37). Unlike perfect induction, this "cannot be regarded as an inference," notes Ross; "if you regard the first proposition as a premiss you find that the second does not follow from it; the 'induction' is *a fresh act of insight*" (ibid., e.a.). Elsewhere (50) Ross describes it graphically as "the flash of insight by which we pass from knowledge of a particular fact to direct knowledge of the corresponding general principle" or universal truth, the general distinction between induction and demonstration (*syllogismos*) being "that demonstration proceeds from universals to particulars, induction from particulars to universals" (47). The induction in question here is "not proof of the principle, but the psychological preparation upon which the knowledge of the principle supervenes. The knowledge of the principle is not produced by reasoning but achieved by direct insight ... This is in fact what modern logicians call intuitive induction. And this is far the most important of the types of induction which Aristotle considers" (49).

From this account we glean some understanding of why Ross would not wish to call Aristotle's intuitive induction a (valid) form of 'inference' at all: the conclusion does not 'follow' (in logic); the knowledge of it is 'direct'; it is a matter of 'psychological preparation' rather than 'proof' or demonstration. It was suggested earlier that these reasons are not compelling, and that they are even less so in the case of Descartes (cf. section 17.3). As for the starting point of intuitive induction, Ross is absolutely clear about the fact that "induction starts from sense-perception" (ibid., 48).[16] 'Sense-perception,' of course, translates Aristotle's *aisthēsis*, which is used to designate ordinary (non-reflexive) perception, 'outer experience,' that is, what we normally understand as experience *tout court*. Von Fritz makes the point nicely when he writes of the two chapters (i, 18 and ii, 19) of the *Posterior Analytics* in which Aristotle discusses intuitive induction explicitly: "In beiden Fällen handelt es sich um das Verhältnis einer aus allgemeinen Prinzipien beweisenden Wissenschaft zur Wahrnehmung bzw. *um die Unentbehrlichkeit der Wahrnehmung für die beweisende Wissenschaft*" (1964, 33 e.a.). '*Wahrnehmung*' is again *aisthēsis* which, as Aristotle expressly notes, is "of particular things (*tōn kath' hekaston*)," that is, ordinary sense-perception, not, as in Descartes's analytical reflexion, inner experience, reflexive attention to what is immediately present to consciousness *inwardly* whenever one thinks.

Despite this important difference, the mental process described by Descartes to Burman still bears more than a passing resemblance to the notion of *epagōgē* in the *Posterior Analytics*. But it would be wrong to suppose the two have much more in common than has been noticed already. Kneale (1949, 31) is surely right to insist on another key difference. Aristotle's intellectual intuition (*nous*), he writes, "is not, like Plato's reminiscence or Descartes's intuition, the uncovering of something innate in the mind, but a kind of induction which 'exhibits the universal as implicit in the clearly known particular.'" The "clearly known particular" is the individual thing given in non-reflexive sensory experience. Again, it is von Fritz who goes right to the heart of the matter (cf. 1964, 38). For Aristotle, the universal *is actually in* the particulars given in sense-perception; it does not spring from the mind's reflexion on its own thinking – which is the sense of 'innateness' in Descartes – nor need it involve memory, least of all in Plato's sense. True, some forms of intuitive induction require memory: understanding *why* something is so, the discovery of necessary and universal causal relations, is constitutive of genuine *epistēmē* for Aristotle; and this is not always possible without *connected* experience (*empeiria*) involving memory. But since a single instance *may* suffice at times, memory and connected experience, while requisite for some, are not essentially involved in all, *epagōgai*. And as the grasping of the universal in the particular need not involve memory, it *never* involves focusing attention upon what is in the mind and accessible in inner experience rather than present in the things themselves as given in ordinary sensory experience.[17]

By contrast, Descartes's analytical reflexion does not even require outer experience except (in certain cases) as the remote cause of the mind's awareness of certain concepts and principles implicit in its consciousness of its own thinking. As for memory, reliance on it was seen to mark the rigid boundary between *intuitus* and *deductio* (see above, section 20.1); so empirical memory is actually excluded from the process of analytical reflexion as Descartes understands it. Intellectual memory, on the other hand, figures in Descartes's theory, as we have seen, only vestigially, in varied traces of the old Platonic-Stoic-Ciceronian imprint theory; it is much more in keeping with the Thomistic-Hobbesian-Leibnizian notion of an act following upon another act – which may account in part for Leibniz's receptiveness to the recollection theory of the *Meno*. In sum, then, Descartes's theory of intuitive induction, while significantly different than Aristotle's, probably owes much less to Platonic influences than Kneale suggests by lumping Descartes and Plato together. Nevertheless, to the extent that the contrast is between a conception of (1) knowledge as direct access to something in the things themselves, mediated by the senses; and (2) knowledge as immediate, reflexive, and non-sensory access to something in the mind itself that only *happens* to exist outside as well, it is clear that Descartes and Plato both subscribe, although for different reasons, to the conception described under (2).

At bottom, then, there is scarcely more than a purely formal parallel between Aristotle's and Descartes's conceptions of intuitive induction. Still, Aristotle, too, might have written that it is "of the nature of our mind to construct general propositions on the basis of our knowledge of particular ones" (AT VII 141: CSM II 100), that is, to proceed from the particular to the universal in the knowledge of those first principles or truths that form the basis of demonstrative science. While this formal symmetry leaps to the eye, the differences in their respective concepts of experience have gone largely unnoticed. Not surprisingly, since at first sight the wording of Descartes's 'definition' of *experientia*, "reaches our intellect from external sources (*aliunde*) or from its own reflexive self-contemplation," strongly suggests a distinction between the deliverances of the external senses and of introspective self-awareness. From this it would follow that only *some* of those first truths arise from the mind's reflexive attention to its own thinking. Yet on closer inspection *contemplatio reflexa* turns out to be the source of intellectual ideas of all simple as well as composite natures, material as well as spiritual. It is this inner experience, then, that provides the experiential datum required for the progress of the mind in intuitive induction in Descartes's sense; and it is this that Descartes has primarily in view when he defines 'experience,' distinguishing it from *intuitus* in the narrow sense and from *compositio*. This concept of experience is not significantly altered in the later works. Nothing could be further from Aristotle's concept of experience than this, or point to a philosophical starting point more fundamentally at odds with that of the unbroken tradition stemming from the Stagirite. This point will be elaborated further as we confront the old with the new metaphysics from a variety of different perspectives in the course of the Conclusion.

CONCLUSION

[T]here remains always a purely philosophical attitude towards previous philosophers – an attitude in which ... we seek simply to discover what are the great types of possible philosophies. (Bertrand Russell)[1]

The principle *cogito, ergo sum* owes its founding character to the epistemic difference between knowledge of the existence of the thinking self and knowledge of the existence of all other things. The truth of *sum* is an intuitively evident insight gained through simple reflexion on what I am immediately conscious of whenever I think; by contrast, the existence of both God and sensible things can only be demonstrated by logical inference from this first truth, employing principles of the natural light intuitively evident in reflexion on the *cogito, ergo sum* itself. Hence, the *cogito* principle is the first item of metaphysical knowledge and the foundation of all knowledge whatsoever.

The formula *ego cogitans existo* (cf. AT VII 481: CSM II 324) embodies the same fundamental insight regarding the order of knowing.[2] It may even be preferable to what has become the signature piece of Cartesianism, *cogito, ergo sum*, partly as forestalling the misunderstandings to which the *ergo* has given rise, partly as underscoring the primarily *metaphysical* thrust of this first item of knowledge as that of the *existence* (*existo*) of an immaterial *substance* (*ego*).

What deserves closer attention now, in conclusion, is the *order and idea of being or existence in Descartes's metaphysics*. This is the subject first broached in the Introduction (sections 3.2 and 5.1) and there postponed until the Conclusion. If establishing a new order of knowing is Descartes's chief epistemological concern, his most conspicuous ontological or metaphysical achievement is the establishment of a new order of being. Together these shape the distinctive methodological approach inherent in Descartes's founding principle. More fundamental than either the order of knowing or of being, however, is the guiding idea of being or existence underlying Descartes's system as a whole and much subsequent modern philosophy as well. This can be called the 'meta-ontological' or 'fundamental ontological' dimension.

Taken up successively or by turns, the epistemological, metaphysical, methodological, and fundamental ontological perspectives cast a fresh and interesting light on Descartes's place within the philosophical tradition and on his basic posture as one of the perennial possibilities of philosophy.

21

Realism, Subjectivism, and Transcendence

The starting point is the new order of knowing described in the preceding parts. It is confusion about this, after all, that has given rise to much misleading talk of the 'subjective turn' and the 'idealist standpoint' of modern philosophy. In this epistemological perspective, several forms of realism can be distinguished from metaphysical or ontological realism and from each other. A second source of confusion is the talk of realism and idealism in the order of being. Accordingly, different types of ontological or metaphysical idealism must be distinguished as well. In most senses of the term, Descartes is a realist, both epistemologically and metaphysically. The exception is that one sense of 'epistemological realism' that has to do with the order of knowing; in this regard, Descartes is indeed an anti-realist or 'subjectivist' – though not in the odd sense in which that term is frequently applied to his philosophy today.

The attempt to situate Descartes's philosophy in the context of what Russell, in the epigraph to this Conclusion, terms the "great types of possible philosophies," is not confined to the epistemological and metaphysical perspectives, however. Though it starts from Gilson's older classification of philosophies into two broad categories, the 'Platonic' and the 'Aristotelian,' this schema is modified in a predominantly methodological perspective. The upshot is a new classification to replace the well-worn empiricist-rationalist, idealist-realist, materialist-idealist, and Platonic-Aristotelian dichotomies: *philosophies of immanence and philosophies of transcendence*. Of each there are both 'pure' and 'mixed' varieties to consider.

21.1 Epistemological and ontological realism

From the vantage point of most commentators whose fundamental epistemological convictions are those of Scholastic-Aristotelian realism, the salient fact about

Descartes's founding principle is that it ushered in the disastrous dogma that has since come to be known as 'representationalism': that (1) we do not perceive or know extra-mental reality immediately but only indirectly, by inference from ideas in the mind. Since that from which something is inferred is epistemologically prior to what is inferred from it, it follows from the fact that sensible things cannot be known directly or non-inferentially that (2) they cannot be the starting point of knowledge. It does *not* follow from (1), however, that (3) sensible things cannot be known with complete or perfect certainty. Still, (3) follows from (1) together with (1'): only that which is grasped immediately and non-inferentially is known with perfect certainty. What does not follow in logic from (1) *even with* (1') is (4): that sensible things cannot strictly be said to exist as entities in their own right, distinct from and independent of the mind and its ideas, or to be knowable as they are in themselves apart from the mind and its ideas.

Logically, then, (2) follows from (1); and historically, Descartes clearly held (2). But he cannot have derived it from (1), having never held the latter. As for (3), it too has been read back into Descartes by the commentators, whether through mistaking it for the consequence of (1), or on the basis of a correct inference from (1) and (1'). Along with (3) goes much else that is dubious about modern scepticism and idealism, including, in extreme cases, (4) (see section 21.4 on 'encephalic subjectivism'). But historically, Descartes clearly never held (4), nor even (3); and even had he held the latter, he could not have inferred it wrongly from (1) or correctly from (1) and (1'), since he accepted neither.

Getting down to cases now, (3) is ascribed to Descartes by Kant (see section 21.3), possibly under Hume's malign influence (see chapter 15, n. 8). Kant accordingly labels Descartes's epistemological outlook 'problematic,' that is, *sceptical* idealism, distinguishing it from the 'dogmatic' idealism of Berkeley that includes, as a metaphysical component, (4). This may be Gilson's Descartes as well, though his position on (3) is somewhat uncertain (see section 16.2). (1) and (2), however, figure very prominently in Gilson's picture of Descartes as the founder of modern philosophy, which is that of most of those, though not *only* those, who share his basic epistemological outlook. Kant, after all, who can hardly be accused of Scholastic-Aristotelian sympathies, offered much the same estimate of Descartes's epistemological orientation a century and a half earlier. It has since become canonical. Yet if the conclusion reached in the preceding chapters is even roughly correct, Descartes did not hold (2) as a consequence of the 'veil-of-perception' doctrine at all, but on the basis of the epistemic difference between statements about ideas and about extra-mental things.[1]

However intractable the problems it bequeathed to subsequent philosophy, the Cartesian outlook is in fact much less obviously the abandonment of realism and sound common sense than is frequently supposed. To identify as the starting point

of cognition the indubitable givenness of thinking itself while doubting the existence of the things thought of; to postpone all knowledge claims until after the
analysis of the structure and varieties of the mental and of the conditions of knowledge or certainty in general – this is by no means the only or even an obvious way
to begin philosophizing. But neither does it presuppose or entail the denial of
such obvious truths as that ordinary material things exist independently of their
being thought of; that they are as they are quite apart from the way the mind
conceives them or whether there exist any minds at all; that we can perceive such
things directly and know them as they really are in themselves; and that we do in
fact so know them, at least in part. Descartes wished to deny none of these things,
though he maintained with insistence that it was necessary to doubt them at least
"once in a lifetime" to achieve something firm and lasting in the sciences.[2] The
first sceptical, then reductivist, approach adopted provisionally at the outset of
the *Meditations*, as a methodological device for establishing the correct order of
knowing, is apt to obscure the basic realism of the epistemological and metaphysical outlook firmly established at their conclusion through overcoming such
"hyperbolic" doubts (AT VII 89: CSM II 61).[3]

Once we rid ourselves of the misguided notion that Descartes's conception of
the order of cognition derives from the crude 'veil-of-perception' doctrine, the
larger epistemological, metaphysical, and methodological questions at issue between Descartes and his Scholastic predecessors appear in a different light. If
Descartes really denied none of the things just mentioned, holding indeed (2), but
neither (1), (3) or (4), then his world is in important respects closer to Aristotle's
than to Plato's or to the 'inverted world' of later idealisms. True, as has been
noted repeatedly, the traditional order of knowing is radically reversed in (2),
even if not quite in the manner frequently supposed; for unlike the knowledge of
existence, the order of cognition of the essences of things opposes an earlier to a
later stage of intuition, not insight to inference.[4] The order of being, on the other
hand, is only altered, not reversed in Descartes's thought. Yet this ontological
shift away from Scholastic-Aristotelian hylomorphism to the new ontological
realism later dubbed 'dualism' was momentous enough to confront the then contemporary world with a metaphysical dilemma profounder and more enduring
than the scientific dilemma of the two chief world systems of Galileo. It is this
dilemma that comes clearly into view as we broaden our outlook now to take in
the new order of being underlying Descartes's methodological outlook. It is a
dilemma that is still very much in the background of philosophical debate today.

21.2 Immanence and transcendence

It is no doubt possible, without gross distortion of the historical record, to see in

the Platonic and Aristotelian traditions the two great metaphysical and epistemological world-views that the Western philosophical tradition has brought forth
thus far. To the extent that this is so, one can agree with Gilson:

> Il n'y a guère que deux grandes voies ouvertes à la spéculation métaphysique: celle du
> Platon et celle d'Aristote. On peut avoir une métaphysique de l'intelligible, méfiante à
> l'égard du sensible, de méthode mathématique et se prolongeant par une science qui
> mesure; ou une métaphysique du concret, méfiante de l'intelligible, de méthode biologique
> et se prolongeant par une science qui classe. Le mécanisme est au bout de l'une comme
> l'animisme est au bout de l'autre. Puisqu'il venait de sortir de l'aristotélisme où ses maîtres
> avaient essayé de l'engager, Descartes ne pouvait que rentrer dans le platonisme. (Gilson
> 1951, 199)

    Gilson here distinguishes two main types of philosophies on the basis of
(a) the principal object of knowledge (sensible and concrete versus intelligible
and abstract), (b) the sources and method of knowing (empirical, biological, and
classificatory versus a priori, mathematical, and deductive), and (c) the paradigm
of rational explanation (animistic versus mechanistic). To this it need only be
added that much that is pretty clearly neither one nor the other can be usefully
understood as combining elements of both. Thus, Leibniz deliberately pursues a
"middle way," combining both approaches by carefully separating the physical
and metaphysical levels of explanation. A strict mechanist and proponent of mathematical methods in physics, he seeks to rehabilitate something at least remotely
resembling the substantial forms of Scholastic-Aristotelian natural philosophy at
the metaphysical level. His 'biologism' in regard to composite material substances
or 'natural machines' (living organisms) is much less pronounced, however, than
the 'animistic' traits exhibited by his general doctrine of substance. The latter is
nonetheless unlike most forms of 'animism' in that it draws heavily on the revolutionary Cartesian analysis of *anima* or mind.[5]
    However serviceable this schema is for most purposes, some revisions are
required if we are to chart at all accurately the intersection of Descartes's path
with these two broad speculative avenues. Apart from (i) the principal object and
(ii) the sources of knowledge, which Gilson treats partly under (a), partly under
(b), it is instructive to consider as well (iii) the foundation or starting point of
knowledge. In addition to all these primarily epistemological considerations, there
is the metaphysical question of (iv) the kinds of entities there are as well as the
order of being, that is, the relations of independence, dependence, interdependence, or inter-independence obtaining among them. Closely connected with the
first part of (iv), that is, the question of ontological monism versus pluralism, is
the question of (v) methodological monism versus pluralism, that is, whether a

single paradigm of knowing is invoked, as in Gilson's (c), or whether different principles of explanation are employed in different spheres, and whether those principles conform to or conflict with the assumptions of ordinary pre-philosophical experience.[6] In this final question the order of knowing [(iii)], of being [(iv)], and the sources and objects of knowledge [(i) and (ii)] merge into a single encompassing methodological perspective. However comprehensive, it is still not the *ultimate* or most basic perspective from which to consider the "great types of possible philosophies." That distinction belongs to the meta-ontological perspective, which will occupy us in the next chapter.

These further questions yield a much more detailed matrix with which to plot Descartes's historical position as a perennial possibility of philosophy. Of (i) and (ii) a good deal has been said already. For instance, that the intuition of first principles requires an initial stimulus from sense-experience, yet proceeds largely independently of experience, has been shown at length (cf. the treatment of innateness in chapters 18 and 19). So too that the existence of material things is known with perfect certainty, if only indirectly, while the essence of such things is known directly by intuition rather than by inference from ideas (cf. section 4.2 and passim). To this there is little to add regarding either the sources or the objects of knowledge. (iii), the question of the starting point of knowledge, was touched on in the previous section. Unlike those manifestations of epistemological and metaphysical 'anti-realism' itemized under (1), (3), and (4), (2) was acknowledged a genuinely Cartesian doctrine; for in his selection of the starting point of knowledge Descartes is *not* an epistemological realist at all but rather a 'subjectivist.' Given the frequent misapplication of this term to Descartes, however, something more needs to be said about the subjectivism Descartes actually introduced into modern philosophy as distinct from certain later, quite different, forms with which it is often confused. As for (iv), the order of being, this was first raised in the Introduction, where detailed consideration was postponed until later. Discussion of this point (in section 22.1) will allow us to situate Cartesian metaphysical dualism in respect of the other principal forms of ontological realism, particularly reductive and non-reductive materialism, that is, Scholastic-Aristotelian hylomorphism.

The question of (v), methodological monism versus pluralism, overlaps, as already noted, with (i) to (iv), providing a complex but particularly interesting point of view from which to classify "the great types of possible philosophies": philosophies of immanence, that is, broadly naturalistic, 'this-worldly' philosophies like Aristotle's, Hume's, Heidegger's, and Quine's, versus philosophies of transcendence like those of Plato, Descartes, and Leibniz.[7] One distinguishing feature of 'pure' philosophies of immanence and transcendence is that (disregarding purely formal sciences, whose objects do not exist) there is one and only one method, a single universally valid pattern of scientific explanation of all things, one 'unified science' capable in principle at least of encompassing everything that is and is knowable. By this criterion, Plato's is a pure philosophy of transcendence, the only objects of genuine knowledge being for him the supersensible Forms, which alone truly exist. For Descartes, by contrast, sensible as well as supersensible things both are and are knowable, though by altogether different paths; his, therefore, is a 'mixed' philosophy of transcendence. By the same criterion, Hume's is a pure, Aristotle's a 'mixed,' philosophy of immanence. For though, in Aristotle, the same form-matter schema of interpretation is applicable, in whole or in part, to the analysis of all things, the supersensible and the sensible, there are nevertheless these *two* realms, both susceptible of knowledge; while for Hume there is only one type of entity, sensible things, and one path of genuine knowledge based on inner or outer sensory experience.

Characteristic of Descartes's system of thought as a mixed philosophy of transcendence are at bottom three things. To begin with, there is (a) a deep *ontological* rift within the totality of what is, and (b) a corresponding *methodological* dualism: one set of principles for the knowledge of corporeal nature, sensible things, and another, completely different set for the understanding of the 'transcendent' or (literally) 'super-natural' realm of mind (and Mind). Such a vertical rift *within* what is, a 'duality' of realms of being, one sensible, natural, immanent, the other supersensible, supernatural, or transcendent, is obviously a very different matter from a horizontal rift *between* the transcendent realm of being, the realm of permanence and oneness, on the one hand, and the immanence sphere of becoming, of manyness and change, on the other. Accordingly, the talk of 'dualism' and 'transcendence' has an altogether different sense when applied to Plato and Descartes.

Even to speak of a vertical rift within being is apt to be confusing, however, since God and the mind are supersensible or transcendent in different senses for Descartes. God transcends the whole realm of created, dependent being, while the mind transcends only the part of created being that is sensible in nature. So on one side of the vertical line we have a further horizontal division. Thinking of it as a dyptich with a single panel on the left and twin panels, one above another, on the right, the left, lower-right, and upper-right panels can be labelled 'sensible-immanent,' 'supersensible-immanent,' and 'supersensible-transcendent,' respectively. Alternatively, they can be labelled 'sensible-immanent,' 'finite transcendent,' 'infinite transcendent.' The latter may reflect Descartes's way of looking at the sciences of the sensible (physics) and the supersensible (metaphysics) best, so that it may be preferable after all to speak of vertical *and* horizontal divisions within the totality of what is. Neither Cartesian schema bears any resemblance to the Platonic notion of the transcendent, though the former of the two shows an obvious affinity with the sensible-supersensible split in the Aristotlelian tradition.

So much for (a). (b) sets Descartes still further apart from Plato's pure philosophy of transcendence, in which there is no more room for genuine knowledge than there is for real being of immanent changing particulars. For Descartes, by contrast, as for Aristotle, there is indeed genuine knowledge of sensible things. The key thing encapsulated in (b) is the disparity of the first principles employed in obtaining knowledge of the sensible (*res extensa*) and the supersensible (*res cogitans* and God), respectively, despite a few genuinely "common" notions applicable to both. As regards their source, the principles are one and all intelligible or non-sensible; but in respect of content, they are not only different, but contradictorily opposed. We shall return to this point in section 22.1 below, where the differing methodological outlooks of Scholastic-Aristotelian hylomorphism and Cartesian dualism will be discussed along with their shared features as different forms of ontological realism.

As far as (a) and (b) go, then, Descartes appears to have somewhat less in common with Plato and more with Aristotle than Gilson's simple schema would suggest. For Aristotle, after all, the sensible and supersensible are set apart *within* the totality of what is, as in Descartes; moreover, both are perfectly knowable, as they are for Descartes. True, the rift separating sensible from supersensible beings does not, for Aristotle, divide minds from material bodies but rather Mind and Intelligences from the totality of sensible things, including living and intelligent corporeal beings like ourselves. Moreover, the ontological rift is horizontal, as in Plato, rather than vertical *and* horizontal, as in Descartes. But what sets Descartes decisively apart from Aristotelian naturalism, aligning him with Plato after all, is the fact that in addition to (a) the vertical and horizontal ontological divisions separating mind from matter and from Mind and (b) the methodological divide between the principles appropriate to each sphere, there is also (c) a methodological cleavage of a different kind: the metaphysical first principles of each of the two great domains of knowledge, the physical and the metaphysical or supersensible, are not continuous, but profoundly at variance with the testimony of ordinary pre-philosophical experience regarding the nature of self, of world, and Deity. That is, knowledge of the causes and first principles of the things of each domain is not obtainable by reasoning from the data of ordinary experience, but rather by correcting the defective ideas of experience and plain common sense by the exercise of reason alone. True, unlike Plato, Descartes stops short of demoting *all* knowledge of changing particulars to something of the order of opinion about images or appearances of the real, confining his strictures to pre-philosophical 'naive' judgments about the self, world, and divinity based on ordinary sensory experience; and yet the sharp discontinuity between the *levels* of ordinary experience and rational contemplation is undeniably a Platonic feature of Descartes's thought, setting him over against Aristotle and all subsequent 'naturalisms' or philosophies of immanence. In a 'pure' philosophy of immanence like Hume's (if we attend more to the basic thrust than the deliberately sceptical tenor of his writings), not only is there a single, universally applicable paradigm of knowledge, there is likewise a continuous progression from the pre-philosophical to the scientific and ultimately to the metaphysical understanding of self and world, so that ordinary connected experience is made transparent in its underpinnings rather than overthrown by the principles of scientific and philosophical thinking. From this perspective, Aristotle's, too, is a philosophy of immanence, though the other aspects discussed already make it a 'mixed' rather than a 'pure' exemplar. In sum, then, the similarity between Descartes and Aristotle does not extend significantly beyond the fact that each introduces a (very different) immanence-transcendence division *within* the totality of what is, regarding each of the domains so sundered as a sphere of genuine knowledge.[8] For the rest, Descartes sides with Plato. The result is a distinctively new type of philosophy of transcendence.

21.3 Epistemological and ontological idealism

The results of the two preceding sections can be put this way: what from both the epistemological and the ontological points of view is undeniably a form of realism about sensible things, is, from a methodological perspective, a qualified or 'mixed' philosophy of transcendence. It has long been customary to classify philosophies as either materialist or idealist, empiricist or rationalist, intuitionist or formalist, associationist or foundationalist, monist, dualist, or pluralist, realist or anti-realist, and so forth; and though increasingly unfashionable nowadays, it is arguably still useful to do so – provided these terms can be made sufficiently precise for the particular purpose in view. What has been suggested in the foregoing is that the much less common distinction between philosophies of immanence and transcendence provides a more instructive viewpoint from which to classify the "great types of possible philosophies." This may in fact be what Gilson is really after in his staunchly conservative classification of philosophies as either Platonic or Aristotelian.[9] Just how remote Cartesian dualism at bottom remains from the metaphysical realism of Scholastic-Aristotelian hylomorphism (as one type of non-reductive materialism) will be considered more fully in a moment. First, we must return briefly to the different strains of anti-realism considered in the initial section. For the failure to distinguish sharply among these gives rise to a perplexing ambiguity in the persistent and often misleading talk of Cartesian 'idealism' and 'subjectivism.'

As we have seen (n. 1 above), the talk of 'epistemological idealism' may refer to (1), representationalism or the 'veil-of-perception' doctrine. Sometimes, however, it refers to the combination of (1), a certain theory of perception, and (2), a general thesis about the order of cognition: that the starting point of knowledge is the mind and its ideas rather than sensible things. An example of this use will be cited presently. Kant, for his part, speaks of epistemological 'idealism' in a sense that combines the first *and third* forms of anti-realism: given (1) that the objects immediately perceived and known to exist are only ideas in the mind, (3) no knowledge or certainty is possible regarding the existence (in Kant's vocabulary 'reality') of anything else. "The term *'idealist,'*" he writes, "is not ... to be understood as applying to those who deny the existence of external objects of the senses [cf. (4)], but only to those who [according to (1)] do not admit that their existence is known through immediate perception, and who [according to (3)] therefore conclude that we can never, by way of any possible experience, be completely certain as to their reality" (Kant 1929, A 368f.). Such idealism Kant immediately goes on to describe as 'empirical.' In the "Refutation of Idealism" he distinguishes two forms of empirical (also called 'material') idealism: the problematic idealism of Descartes and the dogmatic idealism of Berkeley. Both differ from Kant's own transcendental idealism (cf. A 370), which is formal and non- or anti-dogmatic: formal in that it assigns only the universal and necessary spatio-temporal categorial *form* of things a subjective origin in the intuitions and concepts of the human mind; and non-dogmatic in that it takes those things as appearances, not as things in themselves.

What distinguishes problematic from dogmatic empirical idealism, according to Kant, is the answer given by each to the question of whether certainty regarding something correctly describable as existing outside the mind is ultimately attainable at all, even if only by inference. For Descartes the answer is plainly 'yes'; his 'problematic' idealism is at bottom a means of showing that secure knowledge of sensible things can be had only via the knowledge of the mind and of a veracious creator God – a method, in short, for clarifying the correct *order of knowing*. For Berkeley, the answer is just as clearly 'no.' But though impossible of attainment, certain knowledge of mind-independent objects is not *necessary* either, in Berkeley's view, in order for one to go right on speaking intelligibly of genuine knowledge of things and of their real existence outside the mind. This is where (4), a new reductivist *order of being*, renders Berkeley's epistemological idealism 'dogmatic,' that is, metaphysical. Of course, when posed in anything like either the ordinary pre-philosophical or the dominant philosophical way of speaking about the knowledge of mind-independent things, the question itself is unintelligible from Berkeley's point of view: at best merely unclear or confused, it is at worst flatly self-contradictory or nonsensical.[10]

On the now customary interpretation of what Kant calls 'dogmatic' material or empirical idealism, the existence of material things is reducible without remainder to actual and possible representations of some mind; as representations or ideas exist only in minds, so too the things represented: *esse est percipi*. When we today speak of 'Berkeleian' or 'subjective' idealism, what is meant is usually (4), the paradoxical thesis about the *order of being* elaborated by Berkeley as a means of avoiding the sceptical consequences of the philosophical doctrine of material substance or "real essence" in Locke (see n. 10). Though it may not be common to invoke the 'order of being' in this regard, nothing else is meant at bottom by the familiar claim that the existence of what are commonly regarded as material substances *depends upon* the existence of the mind and the vivacity, coherence, and so on of its ideas.[11]

When Kant himself applies the 'idealist' label to Berkeley in the passage quoted above, however, he has in mind not so much the new order of being implicit in (4) as (1), representationalism, and (3), the impossibility of ever achieving genuine cognition (certainty) of anything extra-mental. When he adds the qualifier 'dogmatic,' on the other hand, it is arguably (4) that he has in view, Berkeley's metaphysical idealism, though what is today the dominant feature of Berkeleian idealism only comes fully into play later, in Kant's "Refutation of Idealism."

There is a similar disparity between Kant's and certain contemporary uses of 'idealism' in the case of Descartes. It is often (2), or the combination of (1), representationalism, and (2), the new order of knowing, that is meant by Cartesian 'idealism' today. Consider (to furnish the example promised earlier) Gueroult's comment (quoted already in chapter 1, n. 10) that the principle "le *Cogito* est la première des connaissances, l'esprit est plus aisé à connaître que le corps ... ouvre l'ère de l'idéalisme moderne et renverse le point de vue scolastique." Here 'idealism' refers not so much to representationalism itself (this is only implicit) as to the Cartesian *method* of starting from the mind and its ideas as the non-inferentially given and perfectly certain. Such *epistemological* idealism or 'subjectivism' flows directly from the epistemic difference between statements about ideas and about extra-mental objects, that is, the difference in evidence between statements about the mind and those about extra-mental things; for reasons discussed already, it cannot be based, as it was to be later, on the 'veil-of-perception' doctrine. Yet for Gueroult and others, including Kant, the new order of knowing inaugurated by Descartes is the direct consequence of that representationalism mistakenly and stubbornly thought to constitute Descartes's distinctive legacy to modern philosophy. If Kant adds the qualifier 'problematic,' it is because in the order of knowing the initial restriction of knowledge to the mind and its ideas is only temporary; it is to be transcended later through inferential knowledge of the extra-mental. As for the order of *being* in Descartes, it is of course as remote as possible from Berkeleian *as from Kantian* metaphysical idealism due to the fundamentally realist assumption that the existence of things – not appearances, but the things themselves – is irreducibly 'more' than all actual and possible perceptions of one or all possible perceivers. Of course, that has not prevented some interpreters from drawing misleading parallels between Descartes's *cogito* principle and the *'Ich denke'* of transcendental apperception (cf. sections 1.1 and 9.4).

So much for 'idealism' in Kant's and contemporary philosophical usage. Kant also uses the term 'realism' in a variety of ways that (not surprisingly) do not conform exactly to contemporary usage either. Thus, he designates the empirical idealist a 'transcendental realist' who takes space and time, which are only the forms of inner and outer appearances, for real entities existing in themselves "independently of our sensibility" (Kant 1929, A 369). As noted earlier (cf. section 9.3), Husserl too applies the term 'transcendental realism' to Descartes and Berkeley – though in a sense quite different from Kant's (on Kant see Allison 1983, chap. 2). However, it is fairly common nowadays to designate the denial of representationalism as 'realism,' either 'naive' or 'epistemological direct' realism; and sometimes, as we have seen, the term 'epistemological realism' is applied, not to the denial of the 'veil-of-perception' doctrine, but to the assertion of a certain order of knowing associated with the Scholastic-Aristotelian mainstream of philosophy before Descartes, an order that begins with things rather than the mind and its ideas. Lovejoy (see chapter 4, n. 4) further muddies the waters by referring to representationalism as 'epistemological dualism,' distinguishing it from 'metaphysical dualism,' that is, the new order of being inaugurated by Descartes. Little wonder if interpreters of the history of philosophy are tempted to renounce the idealist-realist dichotomy altogether.

Of course, the ambiguities and overlap among 'realism,' 'idealism,' and 'dualism' do not end there. Even ignoring the time-honoured application of 'realism,' 'idealism,' *and* 'dualism' to Plato's two-world metaphysics (see chapter 22, n. 2), there are still the realist-nominalist and realist-instrumentalist (or operationalist) dichotomies to consider. Earlier (section 10.5) we spoke of representational and causal realism as jointly comprising what Descartes might have called 'naive' realism – as opposed to the now customary meaning. While it is thus not difficult to see why the 'realist-idealist' dichotomy is such a potent source of confusion, it is enough if some of the pitfalls can be avoided by distinguishing (1) to (4) and employing the term 'subjectivism' rather than 'idealism' for (2).

21.4 Subjectivism and objectivism

From the preceding section it is clear that representationalism is not the only type of epistemological idealism nor of idealism *tout court*; another concerns itself with the question, not of whether things themselves (as opposed to the ideas of those things) can be known immediately (or at all), but of what sorts of things are most reliably known and hence 'first' in the order of cognition, sensible or non-sensible beings. This is the question of the starting point of knowledge. It opposes 'subjectivism' and 'objectivism,' as we may say, substituting these terms (to avoid confusion) for the corresponding senses of 'idealism' and 'realism.'

For most thinkers outside the Platonic tradition, as for everyday pre-philosophical common sense, the sensible things around us are known first and most reliably; such knowledge as there is of non-sensible being – of God who causes and of the mind that experiences the world – is either obtained by reasoning from the immediately known existence and nature of the sensible things around us (so in the case of God), or in some other secondary way (e.g., when the mind knows itself through reflexion). Even where it is 'earlier' in the order of being ('in itself'), as in the case of the creator of all things, immaterial or supersensible being is still 'later' in the order of knowing ('in relation to us') than the objects of ordinary sense-experience.[12]

The view that ordinary sensory experience of material objects is the perfectly reliable and indispensable starting point of all other knowledge contrasts starkly with the subjectivism exemplified by Descartes's founding principle. For Descartes, what the mind knows first and most reliably are its own modes of thinking and itself as a thinking substance; such clear and distinct perception, moreover, provides the standard and basis of all other knowledge, whether acquired through reflexion or by inference. This radical reversal of the traditional order of knowing gave modern philosophy a new subject-oriented 'slant.' Henceforth the starting point is not the physical cosmos around us, accessible in ordinary non-reflexive sense-experience, but the contents and nature of the human soul within us, the human subject as accessible in special reflexive acts of self-knowledge. Whether or not they are prior to material things 'in themselves' – only God is in fact thus prior – both the soul and God are at least prior 'for us'; moreover, without prior knowledge of them there can be no reliable knowledge whatsoever of anything else, even in mathematics and the physical sciences, since the pure and empirical sciences depend for their certainty on metaphysical knowledge of the soul's ideas and of God's veracity.

If, as in the first section, for example, 'epistemological realism' is applied (*inter alia*) to that straightforward objectivism that puts material or sensible things first in the order of knowing, then Descartes is no realist. Yet in designating the Cartesian reversal of the order of knowing 'subjectivism' rather than 'idealism' care must be taken not to confuse this with the popular use of the term for the position that truth itself is 'subjective,' or 'merely subjective'; that it is without objective certainty or 'relative' to the individual knower or group; or that truth is somehow 'made' rather than discovered. As used here, the term 'subjective' and the talk of a 'subjectivist turn' in modern philosophy mean simply this: henceforth the first object (Latin: *subjectum*) of perfectly certain ('objective') knowledge is the mind, self, or soul. As noted in section 13.7, within a short time after Descartes made the mind or self the object of knowledge par excellence, the word 'subject' underwent a change in meaning from what we now call 'the object,' that is, the thing or things known, to 'the subject' in the sense of 'the knowing mind.'[13]

Talk of Cartesian 'subjectivism' is beset by *two* main sources of confusion. It invites, first of all, the psychologistic misunderstanding of Descartes's project as an attempt to overcome doubt by replacing 'objective' with 'subjective' (psychological) certainty. Of course, the same preoccupation with "subjectivistic doubt" (Heidegger) that is reflected in the titles of the well-known works of Frankfurt (1970), Curley (1978), and Popkin (1979) has led to other truth surrogates apart from psychological conviction. Of these normative certainty is perhaps the most appealing. Yet none has much more to do with the subjectivism described in the preceding paragraph than has the second source of confusion: what one proponent calls "encephalic subjectivism" (Murchland 1974, 210). That is why psychological and normative certainty may be taken together with the other truth surrogates as instances of a single type of misunderstanding.

As for the other source of confusion, encephalic subjectivism, it has been described in this way: "we detect in Descartes a conspicuous instance of the tendency to exchange the world we have been given for one *of our own making.* This is the modernist dilemma in a nutshell and goes by the name of subjectivism, a belief that order and meaning are *fabrications of an autonomous mind* rather than features of objective reality" (Murchland 1974, 207ff. e.a.).[14] If this is "the modernist dilemma," then, historically at least, the tendency here described owes nothing at all to Descartes, who would have recoiled from it in horror. On the other hand, it will be hard to absolve Kant and certain latter-day interpreters of modern philosophy of all responsibility for this monstrosity – including perhaps those behind the first type of confusion.

What is in truth "detectable" in Descartes is not this at all but rather a "conspicuous instance of the tendency to exchange the world" *and the self* "we have been given" for those of Cartesian dualistic metaphysics. Of course, what is arguably the primary way of understanding ourselves and our environment, the understanding in which we actually *live* day to day, is simply bypassed. From the perspective of Descartes's *homo sensualis,* what is "given" is, presumably, the self as 'man' or 'human being' (cf. chapter 6, n. 6) along with the motley, noisy, redolent world of sensible things. It is supplanted in Cartesian metaphysics by the abstract, worldless, solipsistic *ego cogitans* accessible in reflexive contemplation as existing alongside a realm of *substantia extensa*, that is, extended, flexible, mobile, divisible matter. These two are distinct both in number and in nature, though intimately conjoined in the human person. Since the pre-philosophical outlook of the *homo sensualis* also underlies the philosophical anthropology and natural science of Scholastic-Aristotelian philosophy – or so Descartes firmly believed (cf. section 6.1) – the task of philosophy is to replace *both* with a purely rational account of the true nature of ourselves and the material universe. What is revealed in that account, far from being a 'fabrication' of anyone's or everyone's devising, is *objective truth* certified by the unimpeachable authority of universal human reason. Nothing could be further from the "encephalic subjectivism" just described.

That philosophical 'reason' is thus at odds with ordinary experience has not seemed obvious to philosophers of immanence before Descartes or since. Whether it is or not will depend as much on what is understood by 'experience' as by 'reason.' What assurance have we that detached theoretical observation or sense-experience is really the primary way of understanding ourselves and our human and non-human surroundings? Or, for that matter, that speculative, reflexive reason furnishes a deeper and altogether different insight into our own natures or that of other persons and things? These are questions one can reasonably ask. We shall return to them briefly later. The main point just now is that, for Descartes, there can be no question of there being anything 'subjective' about the deliverances of reason – though something of the kind must indeed be said of ordinary pre-philosophical sense-experience.

The key to the question of Cartesian 'subjectivism' is the passage from the letter to Clerselier (AT IX-1 208: CSM II 272), quoted in section 12.5 above, in which Descartes affirms that "my thought is the standard of the truth." Rightly understood, the 'universal human reason' designated by 'my thought' in this passage is just identical with *le bon sens, bona mens, sensus communis, sanus sensus* (cf. above, section 10.2). Once one distinguishes this philosophical from ordinary pre-philosophical 'common sense,'[15] the two will be found to differ, from Descartes's perspective, as reason emancipated from habit and prejudice differs from reason labouring under the prejudices of authority and the senses. Thus, Descartes tacitly reads his own dualistic metaphysics back into man's 'natural' understanding of himself and his world, claiming that it is implicit in the latter though overlaid with distorting *praejudicia* of various kinds. However dubious, this convenient move is just the antithesis of "encephalic subjectivism."

What has been asserted of self and world applies equally to the knowledge of the Deity: a single innate idea, the deliverance of universal human reason, underlies the various historical representations of divinity in different cultures, each of which contains a distorting admixture of elements acquired through sense-experience and teaching – *a sensibus vel per sensus*, as Descartes writes in the First Meditation (AT VII 18: CSM II 12).[16] It is true that Descartes nowhere confronts the standard objection of the moral sceptic that the idea of the supreme being cannot be the dictate of universal human reason since it is found to be very different in diverse cultures and epochs. But given his conception of innateness, he would have had no difficulty in doing so (cf. above, section 18.5). The closest he comes is in the Replies to the Second Set of Objections, the authors of which suggest that certain peoples possess no such idea of God as Descartes describes: "You derived this idea [of God] from earlier preconceptions," these theologians write, "or from books or from discussions with friends and so on, and not simply from your mind or from an existing supreme being ... [T]he fact that the natives of Canada, the Hurons, and other primitive peoples, have no awareness of any idea of his sort seems to establish that the idea does come from previously held notions" (AT VII 124: CSM II 88f.). Behind this lies something like the 'universal consent' criterion of innateness familiar from Locke's *Essay*. In his reply, Descartes remarks that "there is no force in this suggestion. If I ask these other people (from whom I have allegedly got this idea) whether they derive it from themselves or from someone else, the argument proceeds in the same way as it does if I ask the same question of myself: my conclusion will always be that the original source of the idea is God" who implanted it in my mind (AT VII 136: CSM II 98). This seems a rather formal way round the objection; Descartes presumably resorted to it because there simply was not space to elaborate the relevant concept of innateness. But then, he never saw fit to elaborate it fully elsewhere in his published works either.

22

The Old and the New Metaphysics

The mention of immanence at the close of the preceding chapter recalls the methodological perspective. Integral to the latter are various ontological considerations. These now become the focus of attention in their own right as detailed consideration begins, first, of the new ontological order, then of the new guiding idea of being in Descartes's philosophy.

The key thing to be examined afresh is the nature of the contrast between the old and the new metaphysics.[1] Against the standard view, Scholastic-Aristotelian hylomorphism and Cartesian dualism are contrasted here as *two types of metaphysical realism*. They differ not just in the order of knowing and in a key facet of the order of being; they part ways above all through their differing methodological outlooks as philosophies of immanence and transcendence, respectively. The final pages of this study are devoted to the meta-ontological or fundamental ontological perspective: first, by way of preparation, to the different concepts of experience in each of the "great types of possible philosophies" (section 22.2); then, finally, to the guiding idea of being in each (section 22.3). Here again, as earlier in the case of Gilson, point of departure is another's scheme for classifying the "great types of possible philosophies" – in this case, the illuminating schema proposed by Owens.

22.1 Dualism and hylomorphism

In addition to the three types of epistemological realism distinguished earlier (section 21.1) there are various kinds of metaphysical realism having to do with being rather than knowing. Ontological realism is at bottom a thesis about the kinds of beings there are and the order obtaining among them. As such it is opposed to metaphysical or ontological idealism. It was remarked earlier that Cartesian metaphysical dualism is just another form of ontological realism alongside traditional Scholastic-Aristotelian hylomorphism.

As a thesis about what sorts of things there are, ontological idealism recognizes, in the final analysis, only minds and their ideas;[2] all else is either reducible without remainder to thinking and its modes, as in Berkeley, or must at least conform to the necessary structure that thought imposes on its objects, as in Kant. What does not so conform is strictly unintelligible; its existence and nature are simply unknowable by us. Ontological realism, by contrast, posits spatio-temporal material things, *res,* as existing and known to exist in their own right as they are in themselves, irrespective of whether or how they may be conceived by the human mind. For reductive materialists such corporeal things are ultimately the *only* such existents, while for dualists a realm of immaterial entities or minds exists as well. For those dualists who are non-reductive materialists, minds, though irreducibly different from, nevertheless depend upon, material things like the brain for their existence, and on both the brain and external bodies for all or most of the specific content of their thinking, though the converse is not true: the material depends neither for its existence nor for its nature on the mind.

This, at a very rough approximation, is what is widely understood by 'dualism' today.[3] From this, nowadays the standard orthodoxy of common sense and non-behaviourist empirical psychology, Cartesian dualism differs in two main respects.[4] The first has to do with the infinite Mind, God, the second with the dependence of mind on body.

The great synthesis of faith and reason, of Greek (Aristotelian) science and the Judaeo-Christian Bible, carried out in the philosophy and theology of the Middle Ages was to come undone gradually in the course of modern philosophy from the seventeenth century onward. Like most thinkers before the Enlightenment, Descartes's chief quarrel was with the 'reason' of the ancients, that is, Aristotelian science; it was for Hume, Kant, and the eighteenth-century to launch the attack on that other component of the great medieval synthesis, the creator God of the Hebrew Bible.[5] For his own part, Descartes accepted a certain philosophical version of the creation story, about whose theological orthodoxy he seems to have been very uneasy.[6] Thus, while there are exactly two kinds of substances in the universe, the material and the immaterial, immaterial substance, for Descartes, comprises both the one infinite spiritual substance (God) and a finite number of finite human minds or souls.

That is the first difference. It concerns the *order of being* no less than *what there is*, since Descartes also retained the ontological primacy of God: on God, as the Infinite Mind, the uncreated being or 'first cause,' all else depends for its existence, while he depends on no other thing, since existence belongs to his nature. Pursuing the order of being further within the created realm we come upon the second difference. Descartes rejected the assumption that the mind or soul depends upon the body or brain for its existence, positing instead *two separate and independent realms of created beings*, neither of which enjoys ontological priority over the other. Bodies exist and are as they are irrespective of whether or what any finite mind thinks about them; similarly, minds can exist and think regardless of whether they are united with material bodies or whether the material things they think about actually exist outside their thoughts.[7]

So Cartesian dualism comes down to a thesis about the *order* of being obtaining among mental and material as the only *kinds* of substances there are, everything else being either an attribute or a mode of an attribute of one of these two types of substance. It asserts at bottom that infinite thinking substance is absolutely first and independent of anything else, while finite mental and material substances are alike dependent on infinite thinking substance and independent of each other. While the absolute primacy of uncreated being in Scholastic-Aristotelian realism remains unchanged, within the created realm the asymmetrical dependence of mind on body is not reversed but replaced by symmetrical independence or inter-independence. Descartes's dualistic conception of what there is thus displays none of the reductive tendencies of either 'Gods' or 'Giants.' Moreover, his conception of the order of being involves nothing like that dependence of matter on mind that is characteristic of later idealism. Still, it is the mind's alleged independence of matter, not the reverse, that sets Cartesian apart from other dualisms. The 'scandal of Cartesianism'[8] was no doubt fuelled by the Platonic-Augustinian tradition, though the upshot is a distinctively new metaphysical outlook whose affinities with ontological realism are at least as important as its debt to Platonism.

If so, then the choice between Descartes's and the earlier epistemological and metaphysical world-view of the Scholastics is hardly one between traditional realism and an incipient empirical, transcendental, or quasi-Platonic idealism. It is a choice between two realisms. Of course, the term 'dualism' is frequently employed in a more restricted manner to refer to Descartes's theory of the mind-body relation in human beings.[9] This, however, is a corollary of the dualism just described, a notoriously ill-starred attempt to apply it to the understanding of human nature. Platonizing tendencies are unmistakable here too. Nevertheless, Descartes stopped short of outright Platonism. The joint Platonic tenets that (1) *the union with the body is accidental to the soul* and (2) *the soul is the man, person, or human being* are flatly contradicted by the Scholastic-Aristotelian doctrines that (1) *the union with the body is essential to the human soul* (this being what distinguishes it from Higher Intelligences according to St Thomas) and (2) *the union of soul and body is the human person*. Descartes's considered opinion is an amalgam of these two; it coincides with Platonism on (1) and with Aristotelianism on (2). Consequently, having a body is accidental to the soul, but not to the human being. Unfortunately, Descartes gives this *tertium quid* the Scholastic label 'substantial union,' claiming that man, for him too, is an *ens per se*. In view of the important difference between his and the Scholastic-Aristotelian teaching regarding man this is surely misleading. But neither is his position the unadulterated Platonism for which it is sometimes mistaken.[10]

From the methodological perspective, Gilson's basic intuition regarding Descartes's affinity with Plato is confirmed to this extent: Cartesianism is *the* philosophy of transcendence and prime target of all subsequent 'naturalisms,' beginning with Hobbes and Hume, and culminating in the positivists' push toward 'unified science,' in behaviourism, and most recently in the proposed 'naturalization' of epistemology.[11] Yet the fact remains that it laid much of the philosophical groundwork for the scientific revolution of the seventeenth century as well. So this is no pure philosophy of transcendence in the Platonic vein. The real crux is the radical discontinuity between the realms of immanence and transcendence in Descartes, both of which are realms of being and genuine knowledge.

Aristotle's world, like St Thomas's, is strikingly continuous with the world of ordinary experience.[12] Its cognitional, valuational, and emotional dimensions are not yet separated into distinct strata; nor is any dimension assigned a factitious origin in the activity of the human mind. Philosophy or science and ordinary experience are all of a piece: the structure of the world as analysed by the intellect is continuous with the testimony of the senses. Here there can be no question of thinking with the learned and speaking with the vulgar.[13] Moreover, that structure as a whole is intelligible, from the highest to the lowest point, in terms of the same form-matter schema of rational explanation. For all these reasons, Aristotle's is not the world of modern science.

By contrast, Descartes's *substantia extensa* is just that. His is not a universe divided horizontally into the *ici bas* of changing particulars, which men opine about, and a transcendent realm of eternal, changeless, perfect universals, the only objects of true knowledge. The objects of true knowledge are the same changing individual minds and bodies that men opine about. Yet Descartes's is a universe riven vertically into two autonomous and disparate domains, each with a structure peculiarly its own, each analysable in conceptual terms not only different from, but contradictorily opposed both to those of the other domain and to ordinary experience of oneself and the world. The mind is "a thing that thinks and is not extended," while body is "a thing that is extended and does not think" (AT VII 44: CSM II 30); "body is by its nature always divisible, while the mind is utterly indivisible ... This one argument would be enough to show me that the mind is completely different (*omnino diversa*) from the body" (AT VII 86: CSM II 59). And as the mental is itself layered, with the "additional forms" (AT VII 37: CSM II 26) of volitional and emotional acts supervening upon simple ideas or perceptions, so too the material world. Its sensible or "manifest image" (to use

Sellars's apt phrase) is superimposed on the intelligible or "scientific image" of those properties "comprised within the subject-matter of pure mathematics" (AT VII 80: CSM II 55). Thus, even prior to the operation of the desires and the will the world of sensible cognition is already, in a certain sense, a figment of the human mind. However, the scientific image of the world is still nothing like the pure product of thought to which it was reduced by some later idealisms, which may therefore be called 'subjectivist' in a sense quite different from that in which the term was earlier applied to Descartes. For Descartes, the ideas innate in the mind reflect the structure of reality as it is in itself, since the veracious God who created the human mind also made the material world and even the essences of things. Of course, neither their conformity to the structure of the actual world, nor that there is such a world, is immediately evident as *vera & certa scientia*; nor can these things ever become *scientia* without the knowledge of God. Once God's existence and veracity are known, however, the correspondence between the scientific image and the structure of reality can be known in a manner that leaves no room for even the slightest doubt. That world is yet no less sharply discontinuous with the human world of pre-scientific experience than is the world of Platonic Forms. Whether, in a universe like this, any understanding of man is possible, except as an utterly mysterious entity poised awkwardly astride two thoroughly disparate realms, partly in the one, partly in the other, is still a matter of dispute.[14]

In short, each of these two great metaphysical world-views has its intractable side; while it is not easy to turn one's back on three centuries of philosophy and science, closing "the door of reason" (AT IX-1 212: CSM II 275), as Descartes calls it, it is no simple matter to dismiss the immediate testimony of ordinary experience either. A similar dilemma is found in ancient philosophy, where the fundamental tendency of Platonic Idealism clashes with Aristotle's striving to achieve philosophic understanding through deepening rather than overturning our everyday conception of the world. To the extent that these fundamentally opposed tendencies are perennial possibilities of philosophy, there seems to be very good reason to suppose that variants of these two world-views will continue to find adherents in the future as they have in the past.[15]

22.2 Metaphysics and experience

If Descartes's radical reversal in the order of knowing at least does not involve the denial of any of our normal assumptions about the mind-independent existence and direct knowability of the things around us, then the choice between Descartes's and Aristotle's worlds is at the very least not one that can be decided by any straightforward appeal to experience. Here the parallel with the dilemma posed by Galileo's *Two Chief World Systems* breaks down. For while there are decisive empirical reasons for choosing the Copernican over the Ptolemaic system,[16] it is difficult to see how this could be the case with the two leading world-views of metaphysics. This may be only to say that the scientific notion of experience and paradigm of rationality have no particular authority in metaphysics. It may be tempting to conclude from this (with the later Russell, for example) that metaphysics therefore lies outside the pale of human knowledge.[17] However, this is to assume the sphere of human knowledge to be coterminous with the field of applicability of the investigative techniques of science. Admittedly, an accepted canon of rational choice among competing metaphysical theories may prove more elusive than the corresponding criteria in science. But the question of other possible patterns of rationality, apart from those of logic and the mathematical sciences, on the one hand, and the natural, social, and biological sciences on the other, is one that philosophers may usefully ask. If it can be answered at all, then presumably it is not by looking to other branches of learning and their methods (except perhaps as providing a foil), but through reflexion on the activity of philosophy itself and on the perennial types of possible philosophies.

Such reflexion has already drawn attention to one reason why metaphysical disputes are unlikely to be settled in any final way: scientific observation and experience play no decisive role outside science, undecidability by ordinary empirical criteria being part of what makes an issue speculative or metaphysical rather than scientific. Yet if the speculative metaphysician, while certainly no scientist in the contemporary sense, is no mere phantast either, experience will be the final arbiter here too, as in most other fields of human endeavour. The question is perhaps not whether, but what order of experience is to provide the standard and touchstone of metaphysical theorizing.

The earlier discussion of Cartesian intuitionism brought out two senses of 'experience': sense-perception of external objects for Aristotle and inner experience of one's own thinking for Descartes. The latter forms the basis of that meditative reflexion through which immediate intuitive certainty is attainable, not just about one's own nature and existence, but about natures other than the mind's as well. Descartes's procedure thus reverses the direction of Aristotelian experience, turning inward upon the mind and its ideas. This surely is not the ordinary concept of experience. Is Aristotle's?

Without much doubt, Aristotle's concept of experience is *closer* to what we call 'ordinary' experience than Descartes's. But is perception of sensible things, perhaps coupled with inner awareness of our own experiencing, our primary mode of relatedness to ourselves and the world? Whether any predominantly cognitive attitude, even sensible intuition, can lay claim to this title is open to question from a variety of standpoints, notably that of the early Heidegger. The quasi-practical or, as it is called in *Being and Time*, "circumspective" attitude of "average every-dayness" is, among other things, an attempt to identify within pre-cognitive experience the standard-setting mode of access to the being of the entities within the immediate environment and the beings we ourselves are. In a variety of respects, this seems much closer to what might be called 'ordinary' experience than simple sense-perception. Thus, Heidegger goes back beyond Descartes, but not to Aristotle, who highlights one, the cognitive, dimension of such experience; he goes back beyond Aristotle to a new philosophical starting point with potentially stronger claims than Aristotle's to be the most basic notion of experience.

In the light of this it is tempting to revise the thought-provoking analysis of Owens, who portrays the philosophies of the ancient/medieval, modern, and postmodern eras in terms of three different starting points of cognition: in the things themselves, in thought or ideas, and in words or language.[18] A different way of making the same point might be this. Aristotle, Descartes, and philosophies of language all start from *experience*: Aristotle from experience as "the ordinary way of knowing with which we are immediately acquainted" (Owens 1993a, 113); Descartes from experience in the Pickwickian sense of 'inner experience,' that is, reflexive awareness of one's own mental states; and philosophies of language from experience understood as a relation of thought to reality that is neither unmediated, as in Aristotle, nor mediated by ideas, as (so Owens) in Descartes, but mediated by language. This last is perhaps the most implausible sense of 'experience' and that least suited to provide a reliable standard for metaphysical thinking. For once a signifier is interposed between thought and reality, the likely next step is to interpose an endless series of signifiers. The final step is then to dispense with reality (the *hors-texte*) altogether, much as idealisms dispense with mind-independent things. Heidegger, of course, would accept none of these starting points. Though regarded by some, including, one suspects, Owens, as a 'hermeneuticist,' his point of departure is not primarily language at all but *Seinsverständnis* (which, of course, has a linguistic dimension). This can be called 'experience' too, but in a fourth sense, distinct from the other three, yet far closer in tendency to Aristotle and Aquinas than to the different senses of 'experience' in Descartes and the postmoderns.

That is the first revision. Though at bottom only a different way of putting the same point, it may recommend itself for two reasons. First, it highlights the deeper-lying agreement among these diverse philosophical postures, their common starting point in 'experience' variously understood. At the same time, it stresses that philosophy, like other spheres of enquiry, has its regulative principle in experience, this being what distinguishes philosophical analysis from 'speculation' in the pejorative sense.

Two further revisions may perhaps be suggested. One involves broadening

Owens's concept of philosophies of language in such a way as to include among proponents of a starting point in experience as mediated by language not just hermeneuticists and linguistic analysts, including ordinary-language philosophers, but all those for whom the analysis of the logical structure of 'the language of science' supplants metaphysics as the fundamental discipline of philosophy. Here belong above all those modern empiricists whose goal it has been to replace the categorial frameworks of traditional ontology with linguistic frameworks analysable in terms of their semantic and syntactical rules, thus reducing metaphysical (pseudo-)problems about what there is and the structure of reality to theoretical problems of the logic of the language of science, ultimately, however, to pragmatic questions of choosing among alternative linguistic frameworks.[19]

The third and final revision is an elaboration of a viewpoint developed in the other of Owens's two studies, that devoted to the concept of being in Aristotle and Aquinas (1993b). Owens shows in concrete detail how the guiding idea of being under which each philosopher stands produces widely divergent philosophical results, even where the starting point of philosophical enquiry and the metaphysical terminology employed are largely the same. For both Aristotle and Aquinas that starting point is the world of material things experienced directly in sense-perception rather than reflexively in inner experience. Yet Aquinas, the product of the medieval Christian monastic tradition and of the theological faculties of thirteenth-century Paris and Cologne, could only look upon being as "the proper name and nature of a creative and provident God" (ibid., 54). Owens cites the verse (Exodus 3:14) in which God reveals his own name in terms of being: *Ego sum qui sum* (I am who am) in the Vulgate. "That was for Aquinas the 'sublime truth' that the Christian knew about being. It was the very name and nature of God" (ibid.). Thus, while in sensible things, being is grasped immediately as an existential act received from without yet limited in each case by the thing's own nature, *in its own notion*, being is a substance whose nature is 'to be': the first cause of all created being, pure actuality, infinite existence. Accordingly, Aquinas saw in external material things *sensible existents* in which an act of existence-bestowing efficient causality *ab extra* (creation *ex nihilo*) was immediately discernible as antecedent even to (Aristotelian) form.[20]

How otherwise for Aristotle! A product of Plato's academy and the high tide of Athenian culture in the fifth and fourth centuries BC, Aristotle was similarly deeply imbued with the pagan Greek view of life. He stood under the direct influence of "the notion of finite form that had been cultivated with admirable success through Greek art and intellectual contemplation" (Owens 1993b 42).[21] Thus, Aristotle glimpsed in those same beings, not sensible existents, but *sensible natures* or finite forms, their mode of existence indistinguishable from *what* they are, even in thought. Embraced within a cosmic order that is eternal, they require a separate and immobile substance only as final, not as efficient, cause. Thus, from different ideas of being momentous differences result at almost every nodal point in the two systems of thought; and that despite a starting point and an arsenal of philosophical concepts that are deceptively similar.

This final revision provides a further perspective in which to characterize the great historical epochs and types of possible philosophies. Apart from differences in starting point and conception of experience, the guiding idea of being under which each great type of philosophy stands distinguishes it from the others. This was earlier termed the 'meta-ontological' or 'fundamental ontological' perspective. From it springs a last, perhaps the strongest, reason for thinking the issue between the two great metaphysical world-views unlikely to be settled in any definitive way: behind every large-scale metaphysical system of thought lies a complex, cultural *ethos* embodying a distinctive, at times complex, idea of being. The latter finds immediate expression in philosophy but pervades indirectly every other domain of science and culture as well.[22] As the example of Aquinas illustrates so well, even where, under one limited description, the conception of experience and the starting point of knowledge are the same, the dominant idea of being may have changed. Whenever this occurs we may speak of a new era in the history of thought. When supplanted in the transition from the thought of one period to the next, the underlying conceptions of being, knowledge, and experience are never merely discarded as the errors of the past; they remain, as the early Russell seems to have understood, the hallmarks of the "great types of possible philosophies," a living philosophical tradition that continues to inform in a variety of ways the philosophical no less than the historical conversation of the present.

Unfortunately, this third revision also casts doubt on the talk of *two* great metaphysical world-views rather than three or even four. The guiding idea of being in Aristotle and Aquinas is so vastly different that the designation "ancient/medieval" must appear highly questionable despite the agreement on the starting point of knowledge and the nature of experience. (Cf. Owens's reservations about the label "Aristotelico-Thomistic" in 1993b, 38ff.) If we classify on the basis of starting point, then the result may indeed be some such schema as 'ancient/medieval, modern, postmodern' – though this fails to take account of the unique starting point of Heidegger. If, on the other hand, we classify from the meta-ontological perspective, the outcome is neither the simple binary opposition from which we began (ancient/medieval hylomorphism *versus* Cartesian dualism), nor Owens's preferred schema, nor yet a typology corresponding to the customary periodization of philosophy (ancient, medieval, and modern), but a fourfold division. We conclude this study with a brief examination of the question of the "great types of possible philosophies" from this meta-ontological perspective.

22.3 The guiding idea of being

Though preserved by medieval thinkers in the ubiquitous "substantial principles," matter and form, the Aristotelian form-concept is already assigned a secondary place vis-à-vis the "entitative principles," essence and existence.[23] While itself a composite of (finite, substantial) form and (prime) matter, essence is understood, not just as distinct from existence, but as matter or potentiality for a proportionate *act* of existence or *form.* However, the ubiquity of form-matter talk at these two levels cannot disguise the fact that the original Aristotelian matrix of metaphysical analysis is already in the throes of dissolution. Once the act of existence has supplanted finite form as the guiding idea of being, as in the mainstream of medieval thought, the stage is set for an entirely new concept of essence to replace substantial form on the other side of the newly forged essence-existence couplet of the medievals. This step is taken by Descartes.

In Scholastic-Aristotelian philosophy, the substantial nature or form of a substance cannot be "clearly and distinctly" perceived in isolation from its correlative matter; that is precisely the point of its functioning as a *co*-principle along with matter. Not so, however, the Cartesian "principal attributes" of mind and body. Thought and extension are distinguished from their modes or accidents precisely by their ability to be clearly and distinctly conceived without the latter (*Principles*, I, 61). Along with the substantial forms, moreover, the associated concepts of formal and final causality are banished from philosophico-scientific thought by Descartes. At best sterile, explaining nothing, the forms are at worst confused and obscure ideas of body, reflections of a naive animism that posits 'little souls' in lifeless matter.[24] Once the clearly and distinctly perceived principal attribute supplants the notion of substantial nature or form, the accidental forms or real qualities can be eliminated too, that is, reduced to the quantitatively describable modes of extension, that is, shape (figurability), divisibility, and mobility. With this, all varieties of change in the erstwhile 'real accidents' or 'real qualities' of corporeal substance are reduced to a single type, local motion, change of shape being no more than the rearrangement or change of place of the extended, mobile, and divisible parts of matter.[25]

This radically new substance-essence-accident ontology lends itself admirably to the task of laying 'metaphysical foundations' (in the later, Kantian sense of the expression) for the new mathematico-mechanistic science of nature. But the manner in which it arose has at least as much to do with strictly metaphysical, that is, meta-ontological, considerations as with the rise of modern science. In other words, although the changes just described are not completely intelligible outside the context of the new science, it is equally impossible to understand them adequately apart from the continuing *metaphysical and theological* critique of the Aristotelian form-concept. Already begun in the Middle Ages, the critique took a decisive step forward with Descartes, who, despite thinly disguised contempt for the philosophy of "the Schools," elaborated his new notions of essence, accidents, and change by building on the radical critique already carried out by his medieval predecessors. That he himself did not understand his project in these terms is irrelevant; at the end of the day the distance separating the new dominant idea of being from the Aristotelean conception of finite form emerges as far greater than at any time in the past. And this is due in very large part to the gap already opened by the preceding metaphysico-theological critique of the medievals. Yet in destroying, root and branch, the vestiges of Aristotelian finite form still present in the Christian metaphysics of the Middle Ages Descartes did not as yet carry through to completion the destruction of the Scholastic-Aristotelian framework of metaphysics as a whole. That was to be left to Kant.

Turning our attention briefly to this final stage in the process, we run up against a further deterrent to overestimating the impact of the scientific revolution on the formation of Descartes's metaphysics. The historical developments sketched thus far take place under the undiminished sway of the metaphysico-theological idea of creation *ex nihilo*. In fact, the guiding idea of the being of sensible things as efficiently caused *existentia* is preserved not only in Descartes but throughout much of the remainder of the seventeenth century.[26] Just how radical a challenge it was to face in the following century can be best gauged by considering briefly Kant's famous refutation of the ontological arguments of St Anselm and Descartes: "Being is obviously not a real predicate ... It is merely the positing of the thing, or of certain determinations, as existing in themselves" (1929 B626).

The first and merely negative part of this acknowledges the distinctness of the two ontological or entitative principles, existence and essence. While essence is here understood in broadly Cartesian terms rather than as substantial form, existence (*Sein* or *Dasein*), for Kant, as for Aquinas, is really distinct from essence in finite sensible things – though, for Kant, unlike Aquinas, existence is not prior to essence (see n. 20 above). The cause of existence must therefore be sought outside the thing's own nature. But whereas St Thomas located that cause immediately in another existing thing and ultimately in the First Cause of all dependent beings, the *summum ens* or God, the second or positive part of Kant's dictum assigns as the 'cause' of existence something that is not a being at all and hence not a transcendent being: a synthetic act of positing (*Setzen*), an existence-bestowing faculty, formal principle, or structure of the human mind. With this remarkable incursion into the sphere of what was later to be called 'transcendental subjectivity,' the old Aristotelian matrix of the science of being qua being, already radically transformed by the Scholastics and by the Cartesian revolution, is definitively dismantled and expelled from the new philosophical mainstream of thought. Here, if anywhere, it is tempting to speak (with Marion; cf. section 3.2) of the elevation of the *ego cogitans* or knowing mind to the rank and dignity of *summum ens*; or of the science of *ens qua ens* as supplanted by the study of the order of knowing, of the *ens qua cognitum*. To the objection that talk of an "*étant par excellence*" is misleading, since the transcendental I, self, or subject is not an entity at all, the reply can be made that something similar holds true of the *ipsum esse* of St Thomas. But as should be obvious by now, Descartes would have recoiled from the new science of being inaugurated by Kant. Although the road to the *Ich denke* and the Copernican Revolution of Kant leads unmistakably through Descartes's *cogito, ergo sum* and the rejection of the whole complex order of formal causality (cf. Menn 1995), the Cartesian idea of the cause of existence is much closer to Aquinas and the medievals than to Kant and modern idealisms, of which pragmatism and postmodernism are but the latest – and by no means the most compelling – manifestations.

The upshot of these considerations may be put this way. While starkly opposed to Scholastic-Aristotelian thought on the question of 'experience,' the guiding idea of being in Descartes's metaphysics and theology remains in important respects continuous with that of medieval Christendom. Both stand unmistakably under the sign of the biblical creation story. In both, accordingly, there is a sharp separation of existence and essence, with a clear primacy accorded existence and efficient causality. On the other hand, Descartes stands also under the sign of the scientific revolution of the seventeenth century. The Greek idea of science that was for the medievals the paradigm of natural knowledge was supplanted in Descartes's thought by the mathematico-mechanistic ideal of the new science of his age. That is of far-reaching significance for the new idea of being – of substance, essence, accidents, and change – in Descartes; but so is the strictly metaphysical critique of the Aristotelian form-concept already begun by his medieval predecessors and brought to a conclusion by Descartes.

Thus, as has been observed repeatedly throughout this study, Descartes's radical reversal of the order of knowing is accompanied by what is only a modification, not the complete overthrow, of the old order and idea of being. From a new starting point, alien to the ancients and medievals alike, he radicalized a critique of the Greek-Aristotelian concept of being. Begun already in medieval thought, the critique of finite form was carried through to the point of complete eradication by Descartes. So began a new, the modern, era of philosophy. Yet key features of the Scholastic order and idea of being remained in place well into the following century. By the end of the century they too were largely eliminated – as Kant's dictum attests. In the light of this, should one not speak of *four* "great types of possible philosophies," subdividing 'modern' and 'ancient/medieval' alike? This too has a lot to recommend it. But as long as the inner complexity of what is included within each designation is clearly understood, there is perhaps no harm in employing simple binary oppositions – the old and new metaphysics, hylomorphism and dualism, philosophies of immanence and of transcendence – as has been done throughout this Conclusion.[27]

22.4 Coda

To situate within the rich cultural *ethos* of the period that spawned it the guiding idea of being lying behind each of "the great types of possible philosophies" is arguably the critical stage in any sustained reflexion on our intellectual heritage. To the suggestion that it is the ultimate goal, the later Heidegger would no doubt respond that it is not the *ethos* that determines the dominant idea of being; Being itself determines the *ethos* of each successive epoch through a new ontological dispensation (*Seinsgeschick*). Exploration in this direction is obviously beyond the scope of scholarly research. From the limited perspective adopted in this Conclusion, the sum of its findings may perhaps be put this way.

As one looks back over the great historical epochs of philosophy, two fundamental tendencies of thought appear, the one continuous, the other at odds with ordinary experience. Though each can be further analysed into various strands, at the outset, at least, there appear to be these two basic alternatives: philosophies of immanence like the very different 'hylomorphisms' of Aristotle and the medievals, and philosophies of transcendence like those of Plato and Descartes. Over the choice between them science and the scientific paradigm of rationality have no jurisdiction at all. The attempt to decide the issue by selecting a reliable starting point in immediate human experience is frustrated by the ambiguities of the concept of experience itself. Even where the same beings are selected as starting point, that is, even where the same concept of experience is operative, different guiding ideas of being beget diverging approaches within the same general 'type' of philosophy – as in Aristotle and Aquinas, for example. As a consequence, the prospect of a final resolution of the issue is poor – which is perhaps only to say that the prospects for fruitful philosophical debate are excellent.

For the foreseeable future, as for the past three and a half centuries, the debate will no doubt centre on the transcendent dualistic metaphysics of Descartes, with all its puzzles and perplexities, including the sceptical and idealistic paradoxes developed a century or more later but mistakenly laid to the blame of the Father of Modern Philosophy. Out of these difficulties there may be no such simple way back to Aristotle or St Thomas as has sometimes been supposed; but neither, it should be admitted, is there any reason to assume the superiority of the later, or that genuine progress in philosophy cannot consist in a return to beginnings.

Notes

INTRODUCTION

1: The "Twin Pillars" of Cartesianism

1 This question was raised in Descartes's own time and transmitted to him by
   Clerselier. Cf. Descartes's response in the letter to Clerselier of June or July 1646
   (AT IV 443ff.: CSMK 290), to be discussed in chapter 7 (*in initio*).
2 This question too was raised in Descartes's own day, possibly as early as "dès le
   lendemain du *Discours*" (Hamelin 1921, 122f.), first by Mersenne, then by Colvius,
   and finally, in the Fourth Set of Objections, by Arnauld. Cf. Gilson 1947a, 295ff.
   for the exact references and a wealth of relevant material. Also the forthcoming
   work by Menn (in press), which was not available at the time of completion of the
   present work.
3 The first of Kant's charges, echoed by many writers since, is discussed in section
   7.3. The second is addressed in the discussion of Descartes's metaphysical realism
   within the Introduction and Conclusion.
4 The former question is discussed in chapters 7 (*in initio*) and 15 (esp. 15.1 and
   15.2), the latter is the subject of chapter 17 as a whole.
5 The shortcomings of Scholz's own interpretation have been rightly assessed by
   Hoenen (1937, 461).
6 Cf. the view of the matter summarized in the English abstract of Röd's 1979 paper
   on the twentieth-century debate concerning the *cogito, ergo sum*: "three hundred
   years after Descartes there is still no generally accepted interpretation of 'Cogito
   ergo sum.' *At present we are even further than ever from such an interpretation*"
   (e.a.). For this Röd gives reasons (cf. below, n. 12) quite different from those to be
   offered here (and at odds with the interpretation of the *ego* offered in chapter 9. Cf.
   n. 12 below).

Concerning "three little words," compare the motto from Kürnberger selected by Wittgenstein for the *Tractatus*: "and whatever a man knows, whatever is not mere rumbling and roaring that he has heard, can be said in three words." However exaggerated the statement itself, Descartes might have appreciated the sentiment behind it.

7 Gilson 1951, 198: "Il semble donc que l'on se trouve ici entre deux écueils à éviter: exagérer ou minimiser induement les ressemblances. On exagèrerait en oubliant cette longue suite de conséquences vers lesquelles se dirige le *Cogito* de Descartes; on minimiserait induement en parlant du *Je pense, donc je suis* comme d'une découverte cartésienne sans précédent, ou comme si son auteur avait été le premier à discerner la valeur de ce principe comme réfutation du scepticisme absolue et fondement de toute démonstration de la distinction réelle entre l'âme et le corps. Mais le parallélisme va plus loin, car il faut ajouter que, dans les deux doctrines, la certitude de la pensée est encore le fondement sur lequel s'appuie la preuve de l'existence de Dieu." In the end, Gilson too minimizes the differences. In this he follows Blanchet (1920). Marion (1986, §11) exaggerates them, defending Descartes's own estimate of the differences between himself and Augustine, much as Pascal had done (for the reference, cf. ibid., 141 n. 7).

For a listing of the relevant passages in St Augustine's writings and a short bibliography of the main discussions of the subject, see Marion 1986, 138 n. 1.

8 Cf. Aristotle 1962 (*EN* 1170a 29 – 1170b 1). Also 1924 (*Met.*, XII, 1074b 35–36), 1955 (*Parva Naturalia*, 448a 25f.), and 1961 (*de An.*, 425b 12f.). Bréhier (1943) and Schul (1948) pursue the question of a "source aristotélicienne" of the *cogito*. Heidegger comments: "*Aristoteles* sah bei Gelegenheit der Analyse des Vernehmens, daß wir z.B. ein Sehen selbst als Seiendes mitvernehmen. Er legt sich die Frage vor, welche Art des Vernehmens es denn ist, mit der wir das Sehen und dgl. wahrnehmen. Ebenso ist es bei der *noesis* und wiederum die Frage: Ist das Vermeinen, das das Vernehmen vermeint, vom selben Seinscharakter? Beide Fragen bleiben unentschieden" (1994, 48).

9 'Material' and 'sensible' are used interchangeably throughout this work, so that shadows, reflections, mirror images, and the like are every bit as much 'ordinary material things' as the things that produce them.

Descartes does not speak of the 'order of knowing' or 'order of cognition,' in the works of his maturity, though 'better known' (*notior*), 'prior in [the order of] knowing' (*cognitu prior*) are used interchangeably with 'more evident' (*evidentior*) and 'more certain' (*certior*) in most contexts. Cf. AT VII 384: CSM II 264: "it [the knowledge of God] is *prior in the order of knowledge* (*cognitu prior*) and more evident and more certain" (e.a.) than mathematical knowledge. In Rule VI of the *Regulae* he remarks that "all things can be arranged in various series, not insofar as they belong to some genus of beings (*genus entis*), as philosophers divide them into their categories, but in so far as some things can be known on the basis of others (*inquantum unae ex aliis cognosci possunt*)" (AT X 381: CSM I 21). Here the order of knowing is deliberately distinguished from the traditional order of being as treated in categorial theory. In Rule XII he writes: "[W]hen we consider things in the order that corresponds to our knowledge of them (*in ordine ad cognitionem nostram*), our view of them must be different from what it would be if we were speaking of them in accordance with how they exist in reality (*prout revera existunt*)" (AT X 418: CSM I 44).

Gueroult (1968, 26f.) sets these two orders in parallel with the analytic and synthetic *rationes demonstrandi*: the analytic method follows the order of knowing, the synthetic the order of being, i.e., the real relations of dependence, independence, and interdependence among things themselves. For details, see Garber and Cohen 1993, 137 and n. 4. That this is a misinterpretation of the analytic and synthetic methods is argued in section 15.6, esp. n. 29.

10 Cf. Gueroult (1968, I, 16): "La position de ce principe qui se formulera dans la *Seconde Méditation* de la façon suivant: le *Cogito* est la première des connaissances, l'esprit est plus aisé a connaître que le corps, mais le corps ne peut se connaître sans l'esprit, ouvre l'ère de l'idéalisme moderne et renverse le point de vue scolastique." Also Beck (1952, 21): "When Descartes argues ... that we can know nothing until we know what is mind itself, since the knowledge of all things depends on the knowledge of the mind itself and knowledge of mind itself does not depend on knowledge of things, he is laying down the principle of all idealist logics which are to follow." While Gueroult and Beck have in mind the epistemological priority of the mental, others – notably Hamelin – understand 'idealism' in terms of ontological priority. See below and Wolz's comment in the next note. On the forms of realism and idealism cf. also the Conclusion, sections 21.1. and 21.3

As for Descartes's having "reversed the Scholastic point of view," it is well to bear in mind that it is equally the point of view of ordinary pre-philosophical common sense that is reversed. Cf. below, sections 6.1 and 21.4

11 Cf. Wolz's comment (1950, 261): "Gifted as he [Hamelin] is with a great insight into Descartes's thought, he is also burdened with an idealistic outlook which he never tires of trying to impose on our philosopher." This is perhaps harsh, but fair.

12 This view is argued independently by Röd (1979, sect. 2 and 3). The appeal of the transcendental phenomenological interpretation (so Röd) lies in its recognition that Descartes's first principle is not itself a truth about an object of possible experience but a condition of the possibility of experience as such. The lack of consensus on the meaning of this principle is due to the wide variation in theories of experience (ibid., 142). The same broadly Kantian approach is developed at much greater

length in Röd 1971. Cf., for example, ibid., 54, where he claims that "Descartes's
Konzeption der Ersten Philosophie als einer analytischen Metaphysik der
Erfahrung" (!) anticipated "die Kantische Konzeption eine analytischen
Metaphysik, wenn auch in relativ primitiver Form."

Marion too holds that the *ego cogitans* is a transcendental subject, speaking "du
cogito, sum ou du sujet transcendental" (Marion 1975, 50 e.a.). He suggests (ibid.)
that "les conditions formelles de l'*experientia*" (i.e., Kant's "Bedingungen der
Möglichkeit der Erfahrung") are grasped in the *cogito*. This is very much in the
spirit of Röd.

On the transcendental philosophical interpretation of the *ego*, see below, section
9.4. On the concept of experience in Descartes and the tradition, see the Conclusion, section 22.2.

13 A number of different logical approaches will be discussed in section 12.3.

14 On the distinction between attributes and modes, see esp. *Principles*, I, 48, 53, and
56 and *Comments on a Certain Broadsheet*, AT VIII-2 348: CSM I 297. Some
different senses of 'attribute' and 'mode' are discussed in section 10.9.

15 There are two questions here: (a) the independence of thinking of material bodies
other than our own and (b) its independence of our own bodies.

Regarding (a), cf. Aristotle 1924 (*Met.*, 1010b 35ff.): "For sense-perception
(*aisthēsis*) is not of itself, but there is something else too besides sense-perception,
which must be prior to sense-perception; because that which moves is by nature
prior to that which is moved." As for "the thinking soul" (*hē dianoetikē psuchē*), it
"never thinks without the *phantasmata* derived from sensation (Aristotle 1961 [*de
An.*, 431a 16ff.]). The mind or soul, for Aristotle, is only potentially the forms of the
things known; it cannot provide them itself but depends upon external sensible
things to do so. Cf. Owens 1985, 36f. and 228 n. 12. Also Owens 1993a, 107:
Aristotle "showed that the human mind is entirely blank before it becomes sensible
things in the actuality of cognition ... Of itself the human mind has no original
content [i.e., objects] other than sensible things." In short: no innate ideas. On this,
see Heidegger 1994, 223. (The thorny question of the separability of the intellect
cannot be broached here.)

For Descartes, sense-perception is not "of itself" either. Nevertheless, *sensus*
does not depend for its existence purely as a mode of thought on the existence of
anything extra-mental. On this as the principal reason for Descartes's adoption (and
adaptation) of the word 'idea,' cf. chapter 16 below. And if sense-perception is not
thus dependent, how much less then 'pure' thought, free of all sensory elements?

Regarding (b), cf. the statement in the Sixth Meditation (AT VII 78: CSM II 54)
that "imagination and sensory perception" (which depend upon the body) are ines-
sential to my nature as a mind: for "I can clearly and distinctly understand myself

as a whole without these faculties." This will be discussed further in section 17.2.
    See also Wilson 1978b, 199: "Descartes ... believes there are corporeal correlates of mental acts only in certain cases ... Pure understanding is carried on independently of all physical processes." Also Cottingham 1986, 116: "Descartes insists that what he calls 'pure thought' (for example, a volition to contemplate some abstract object, or an abstract perception of the intellect) can occur without any physiological events taking place, in the brain or anywhere else" (cf. *Passions*, I 20: AT XI 344; CSM I 336). Apparently oblivious of this prominent feature of Descartes's theory, Curley remarks (1978, 193) that "Cartesian dualism is very much a live option in the philosophy of mind" today. Wilson's article sets out to combat this fairly common oversight.

16 The immediate (non-inferential) character of our knowledge of the essence of sensible things will be discussed in section 4.2. As for the reflexion on its own thinking by which the mind acquires the ideas of God and material bodies, a full account of this process will be undertaken only in Part Three (cf. chapter 18).
    Throughout the present work, the words 'immediate' and 'direct' are used synonymously to mean 'non-inferential.' It would be useful to observe a pair of distinctions here: (1) between 'immediate' and 'inferred' or 'inferential' knowledge; and (2) between 'direct' knowledge of things and 'reflexive' (or 'reflective') knowledge of the mind's own acts of thinking. Though distinguishing between 'immediate' and 'direct' in this way has obvious advantages, this usage is not well enough established to avoid confusion at all times. Hence the term 'non-reflexive' will be employed instead of 'direct' in (2).

17 Cf., e.g., Popkin 1979, 191. For a recent example, see Cottingham 1992b, 245. Cottingham does not pose the problem quite in the terms used here. His view is discussed in detail in sections 13.4 and 13.5.

18 According to an interpretation developed by Broad (1975, 67ff.), MacIntosh (1970–1), and Furth (1972), and taken up by Loeb (1981, sect. 32–3), and Woolhouse (1993, chap. 4; cf. also pp. 22 and 97), Leibniz too took the step to phenomenalism in his final period. Cf., however, McRae's demurrer (1976, 140) and the telling criticisms of Jolley (1986) and Wilson (1987). For a recent discussion, cf. Rutherford (1995, sect. III). My own view is indicated briefly in chapter 21 nn. 5 and 8.

2: Scholastic-Aristotelian Metaphysics

1 On the historical development of the concept of metaphysics as transmitted to the seventeenth century by figures like Fonseca, Göckel, Eustache of St Paul, Scipion Dupleix, C. d'Abra Raconis, Pereira, and Suarez, see Marion 1986, I, §4, and 1981a, 14–16, and Vollrath 1962. With the exception of Eustache (cf. AT III 232:

CSMK 157), Raconis (cf. AT III 234 and 251), and Suarez (see below), relatively little is known about Descartes's first-hand acquaintance with these authors. In the context in which Descartes cites Suarez's *Metaphysical Disputations* he notes explicitly that he has "never spent very much time reading philosophical texts." Cf. also the letter to Mersenne of 10 May 1632: "as you know, I have no books, and even if I had, I would begrudge the time spent in reading them" (AT I 251: CSMK, 38). Elsewhere (AT III 185: CSMK 154), however, he claims to recall the Coimbrans, Toletus, and Rubius, authors of Scholastic textbooks he would have studied as a student. Mersenne attributes to him a sound knowledge of Scholastic philosophy (AT II 287). It is unclear, therefore, just how much these near-contemporaries may have contributed to his understanding of metaphysics or first philosophy. On the whole question of "Descartes and Scholasticism," see Ariew 1992, particularly the balanced conclusion formulated on 76f.

The chief features of metaphysics as Descartes understood it appear to be traceable to the medieval interpreters of the Stoics and Aristotle. If the sharp distinction drawn by Marion between 'metaphysics' and 'first philosophy' seems questionable in Descartes's case (see chapter 3 below), it is equally so in that of the earlier thinkers he examines. Even St Thomas does not adhere consistently to a single usage, as will be seen in the present chapter.

2 This compressed account of Aristotelian metaphysics follows the main lines of that found in the introduction to Sir David Ross's edition of the Greek text of the *Metaphysics* (Aristotle 1924) and the "Historical Introduction" of Owens 1985.

The classic study of the history of the name 'metaphysics' is Reiner's 1954 article. Cf. Zimmermann's comment on the twentieth-century debate (1965, 89): "Sind uns doch, vor allem seit den Forschungen Werner Jaegers über die Erste Philosophie des Aristoteles, die innere Probematik dieser Schriften, ihre Uneinheitlichkeit und Vieldeutigkeit von neuem sehr deutlich zu Bewußtsein gekommen. Die Versuche, diese Uneinheitlichkeit verstehend und erklärend zu bewältigen, hören seitdem nicht mehr auf." Something like the concluding remark might be made of thirteenth- and fourteenth-century controversies on the same subject.

A few milestones in the recent debate since Jaeger: Owens (1978), Merlan (1960, chap. 7), A. Mansion (1958), Patzig (1960), Düring (1966), and Aubenque (1962). Marx (1972, 71–80) furnishes a useful summary of the positions (theology, ontology, or both), methodologies (*entwicklungsgeschichtlich*, *gedankengeschichtlich*, and *exegetisch*) and arguments of these and a few other works.

3 Though it still crops up, typically unsupported, in accounts of the name 'metaphysics.' Cf. Woolhouse 1993, 4ff.

4 Cf. Owens 1966, 131: "In Aristotle, the separate substances are reached in

metaphysics, in a process of reasoning that takes its starting point from the demonstrations of the eternity of the cosmic motion in natural philosophy." Cf. also Jaeger 1967, 380ff.

5 'Hive off' translates the Greek participle *apotemomenai* (ibid. [*Met.*, 1003a 25]).

6 Cf. Vollrath 1962, 270: "Dieser Versuch [die verschiedenen Bestimungen des Aristoteles vom Wesen und Gegenstand der Ersten Philosophie einheiltlich zu verstehen] ist im Grunde von jedem Kommentator und jedem Interpreten der aristotelischen Metaphysik gemacht worden, heiße er nun Albertus Magnus, Thomas von Aquin, Franciscus Suarez und wie auch immer."

7 For the full range of solutions to this problem during the twelfth and thirteenth centuries, cf. Zimmermann 1965. On the two basic solutions, see ibid., "Schluss." The following discussion draws heavily on the work of Zimmermann (1965) and Wippel (1983 and 1993), and for some points on Moreno (1966).

8 Cf. Zimmermann 1965, 185: "Siger nennt Gott zwar nicht ein Teil des Subjekts, aber diese Kennzeichnung seiner Lehre vom Verhältnis Gottes zum Seienden als Subjekt der Metaphysik ist wohl kaum falsch."

Wippel (1993, 86) suggests that this view goes back to Avicenna. As for Scotus and Suarez, see Owens 1985, chap. 8, n. 12, especially the quotation from Suarez: "the first and most essential division of being is into finite and infinite." Descartes too understands being as a common concept with two principal divisions *under* it, finite and infinite. About the 'commonality,' he says only that it is *not* univocal (see below). Phelan (1967, 121) therefore goes too far in stating baldly that univocity is "the realm of clear and distinct ideas." But he is right to suggest that the 'clear and distinct' rule is inimical to those types of equivocity that, from Aristotle to Aquinas, were so central to the metaphysical as distinct from the logical enterprise.

Marion (1981a, §§5–7) argues that Descartes turned against the Suarezian teaching that had perverted the Thomistic doctrine of the *analogia entis* so thoroughly as to warrant talk of a "dérive ... vers l'univocité" (133). However, three things should be distinguished here: (1) Descartes's tacit rejection of the *analogia entis* – and indeed of any doctrine of substance or being *in general* (for references, see below n. 25 and section 17.1); (2) his express denial of the univocity of 'being,' 'substance,' or any attribute predicated both of God and creatures (see below nn. 18, 25); and (3) his inclusion of God *under* the concept of being (as the infinite being). (1) and (2) do not, *pace* Marion, entail the denial of (3). Nor does (1) signify a break (*refus*) with *theological* tradition (cf. Marion, ibid., 141) so much as the rejection of what are arguably *the* fundamental *ontological* questions: the "community of being" among creatures and between God and creatures (cf. Owens 1985, 117) and the unity of the manifold meanings of 'being.' One need not subscribe to the detail of Heidegger's thesis regarding the 'forgottenness of Being' (*Seinsvergessenheit*) to acknowledge that Descartes displays a singular aversion to questions of this order. Of course, by *Seins-vergessenheit* Heidegger means something to which even the Aristotelian doctrine of 'focal' (*pros hen*) meaning and the Thomistic *analogia entis* are not really exceptions. Cf. Miles 1989 and 1994b.

9 Cf. Maurer (Aquinas 1986, vii), who follows Decker (Aquinas 1959, 44), and Wippel (1993, n. 9), who follows Weisheipl (1983, 359f.) in the dating of these works. For a list of other places in which Thomas deals with the nature of metaphysics, cf. Zimmermann 1965, 173 n. 2. References to Thomas's Boethius commentary are mainly to the passage soon to be quoted, otherwise by question and article. Quotations from the commentary on the Aristotelian *Metaphysics* follow, with some modifications, the translation of Rowan (Aquinas 1961). Since the whole Prooemium is slightly less than a page in the Marietti edition, no page references are given.

10 Aristotle treats of the division of the theoretical sciences chiefly in three places: *Met.*, VI, 1 (paraphrased in section 2.1 above), *Met.*, XI, 7 (a recapitulation of VI, 1), and *de Anima*, III, 4. Two distinctions intersect in the division of the *Metaphysics*: (1) separable and inseparable and (2) unchanging (immobile) and changing. The former is ambiguous as between two senses of *choriston*: (a) substantial as opposed to accidental being and (b) separability from sensible matter. Cf. Marx 1972, 29, n. 37: "Gegenüber diesem Gebrauch von choriston, abgetrennt, wonach es das Abgetrenntsein von der sinnlichen Materie meint, bleibt jener andere Gebrauch festzuhalten, nach dem dasjenige choriston ist, was als Einzelnes und Begrenztes ein eigenständiges Bestehen hat," i.e., substantial being. The medieval commentators routinely interpreted VI, 1 in terms of separability *from matter*. Matter being the principle of change, 'separability' in this sense simply entails 'immobility,' and vice versa. Cf. Zimmermann 1965, 99f.

On the reception of this division of the sciences (as modified by the old Stoic division into logic, physics, and ethics) in Fonseca, Suarez, Eustache of St Paul, and others, see Marion 1986, §2.

11 Cf. Aquinas 1986, 56 (*BDT*, 5.4 ad 5): "We say that being and substance are separate from matter and motion not because it is of their nature to be without them [as it is for God and angels], but because it is not of their nature to be in matter and motion, although sometimes they are in matter and motion, as animal abstracts from reason, though some animals are rational."

12 In a not dissimilar way Thomas brings the consideration of potency and act, unity and plurality, etc. under this one science: "These parts of being ['the science treating of potency, or that treating of act or unity or anything of this sort'] require the same manner of consideration as being-in-general (*ens commune*) because they

too are independent of matter. For this reason the science dealing with them is not distinct from the science of being-in-general" (Aquinas 1986, 22 [*BDT*, 5.1 ad 7]).

13 Phelan (1967, 74): "'Ens' is, as it were, a 'Habens Esse.' It is obviously not the same thing to *have* being and to *be* being." And Owens 1986, 112: "subsistent being is not included in the notion of common being. But it is the cause of everything directly included in the notion of common being, and so may be called the cause of common being." See Maurer's introduction to Aquinas 1986, n. 21 and Wippel 1993, n. 5 for the chief references to this doctrine in Thomas's writings. Also Zimmermann 1965, 175 n. 4 and 178 for some important qualifications.

14 "Accordingly, there are two kinds of theology. There is one that treats of divine things, not as the subjects of the science but as the principles of the subject. This is the kind of theology pursued by the philosophers and that is also called metaphysics. There is another theology, however, that investigates divine things for their own sakes *as the subject of the science*. This is the theology taught in Sacred Scripture" (Aquinas 1986, 52 [*BDT*, 5.2] e.a.).

15 In the middle of the following century Scotus could still begin his *Metaphysics* commentary with the question "Whether the subject of metaphysics is the *ens qua ens*, as Avicenna held, or God and the Intelligences, as the Commentator Averroës held" (quoted by Zimmermann 1965, 243).

16 Cf. Zimmermann 1965, 86: "Geht es an, daß man sich zufrieden gibt, wenn etwa [a prominent neo-Kantian like] Nicolai Hartmann sein Urteil über die Entwicklung der Metaphysik wie folgt zusammenfaßt: » die alte Metaphysik war eben eine inhaltlich abgegrenzte Disziplin: Gott, Seele, Ganzheit der Welt waren ihre Gegenstände. Von der Antike bis auf Kant hat sich ihr Begriff gehalten. Aber diese Metaphysik war es, die der Erkenntiskritik weichen mußte «?"

This concept of metaphysics barely goes back beyond the beginning of the seventeenth century. To read it into "antiquity" is almost perverse. So, however, is the suggestion that metaphysics simply gave way to "critque of knowledge" in the eighteenth century. For Kant, 'metaphysics' still denotes the science of 'first principles.' 'First principles' are neither particular contingent truths (as in Descartes) nor basic laws of human nature (as in Hume); they are neither purely formal (as on some interpretations of Aristotle's axiom), nor tentative hypotheses (as in the contemporary debate concerning metaphysics). As perfectly certain synthetic a priori knowledge and the condition of the possibility of all empirical knowledge they are both first principles of knowledge (*principia cognoscendi*) and of the things themselves (*principia essendi*) qua appearances. At least, this is Kant's conception of metaphysics *as a science*. Alongside it stands the other concept of metaphysics as "a natural disposition" (1929, B22), i.e., of 'transcendent' metaphysics, whose subject matter Kant summed up in the famous phrase "God, freedom, and immortality" (B7). Although its lineage scarcely extends back beyond the German *Schulmetaphysik* of the seventeenth century (cf. Vollrath 1962, 260), the phrase is still frequently regarded as circumscribing the whole subject matter of metaphysics.

The role of Descartes's *principia cognitionis humanae* (the title of Part I of the *Principles*) in the evolution of the concept of metaphysics just described will be discussed in the next chapter, as will Hume's concept of metaphysics (cf., n. 12). As for contemporary usage, cf. Feyerabend (1980, 185f.): "there are empiricists who demand that science start from observable facts and proceed by generalization, and who refuse the admittance of *metaphysical* ideas at any point of this procedure. For them, only a system of thought that has been built up in a purely inductive fashion can claim to be genuine knowledge. Theories which are partly *metaphysical* or '*hypothetical*' are suspect" (e.a.). Also ibid., 189: "the formulation of *assumptions* which are not yet directly connected with observations; this means ... the invention of new *metaphysics*" (e.a.). Faced with this, it is tempting to ask (taking a leaf from Zimmermann's book): Is it acceptable to characterize 'metaphysics' in terms of 'hypotheses' and 'theoretical assumptions,' when this understanding of 'first principles' cannot even be traced back as far as Kant?

17 Cf. Thomas's own argumentation in the 'Second Way' (Aquinas, 1947–8, vol. I, 13 [*ST*, Ia.2.3]).

18 Cf. *Principles*, I, 51: "Hence the term 'substance' does not apply *univocally*, as they say in the Schools, to God and to other things; that is, there is no distinctly intelligible meaning of the term that is common to God and his creatures" (AT VIII-1 24: CSM I 210). In denying any type of univocity of predicates applied to God and created beings (cf. AT VII 137: CSM II 98; AT VII 443: CSM II 292; AT V 347: CSMK 375) Descartes likewise diverges from Thomas, who defended a doctrine of analogical unity of the predication of perfections of God and his creatures. Cf. Wippel 1993, sect. X on Thomas; and Gueroult 1968, chap. 8 and Marion 1981a and 1986, on Descartes.

19 Commentary on *Met.*, VIII, 1 (*CM*, sect. 1682). Cf. also *Met.*, on III, 2 (*CM*, sect. 398): "it is the province of the first science, to which it belongs to examine being as being, to examine substance as substance; and thus it considers all substances according to the common aspect (*communem rationem*) of substance."

20 For this and the previous quotation, see Suarez 1965, 11. Marion 1986, 56f. shows that virtually all the *minores* who are Descartes's near contemporaries follow Suarez in this regard. Cf. also Marion 1981a, 135 on Suarez in particular. Conze (1928, 15) regards it as the *communis opinio* of the Scholastics. Cf., however, Zimmermann's warning regarding Conze's work (1965, 86 n. 3).

21 Cf. Zimmermann's comment (1965, 358f.) on Suarez's version of the history of the

debate: "Alle bedeutenden Philosophen des Mittelalters erscheinen als Vertreter der einen Position, nach welcher das Seiende als Gegenstand der einen Metaphysik auch das höchste Seiende, Gott, umfasse."

22 Cf. Marion, 1981a, 112: "Au contraire, même si de droit Dieu mérite le titre de substance, le concept de *substantia* fonctionne, en fait, dans le champ du créé." This is anticipated in neo-Scholastics like Scipion Dupleix (who, however, tends to vacillate on this point) and Eustache of St Paul (117ff.). A similar course of development is charted for the concept *ens*. For Suarez, "il s'agit, en fait, de marginaliser l'acceptation de l'*ens* en Dieu, afin que l'*ens* se dise d'abord et avant tout des créatures" (99). For Eustache, God cannot be comprehended under *any* of the categories, not even the first.

23 It is sometimes suggested that the term 'trialism' would be more appropriate in this context, since Descartes holds that the union of soul (a substance) and body (another substance) produces a *third* substance, the man or human being (cf., e.g., Cottingham 1986, 127–32 and Hoffman, 1986, passim).

24 So Woolhouse 1993, 23f. Exception is sometimes taken to this use of 'dualism' on the grounds that Descartes really has a *three*-substance ontology: God-mind-matter. On this sort of trialism, cf. Watson 1987, 47f. and Woolhouse's rejoinder (ibid.). But if the number rather than kinds of entities is the issue, it would have to be said that there are not two but many entities for Descartes: one God, a finite number of human minds or souls, and an indefinite number of bodies. For a more thorough discussion of dualism, see the Conclusion, section 22.1.

25 This is from *Principles*, I, 63. Cf. the other, related passages cited in section 17.1 below, notably VIII-1 25: CSM I 210; AT VII 222: CSM II 156; and AT IX-1 227: CSM II 277.

   Descartes's reluctance to proceed to the meta-metaphysical or meta-ontological level of reflection – the consideration of the idea or meaning of 'being' (or 'substance') in isolation from all attributes and modes – is tantamount to rejection of the doctrine of analogical unity, of its prototype in Aristotle, *pros hen* univocity, as of *any* univocal (*kath' hen*) concept of being, whether Scotist or Suarezian. For more on the meta-metaphysical or fundamental ontological dimension, see the Conclusion, especially section 22.3.

   In rejecting the *problem* of the sense in which 'being' and 'substance' are predicable both of God and creatures, Descartes appeals to the doctrine of the *incomprehensibilitas Dei*. This much, however, *can* be known: there is no distinctly intelligible *univocal* sense in which God and creatures are called 'substances' or 'beings.' See *Principles*, I, 51, cited in n. 18 above. Nevertheless, both *are* substances and beings for Descartes, i.e., God falls *under* both concepts. Thus, while providing a negative response, Descartes dispenses himself from the task of furnishing any positive answer to the meta-ontological question. Cf. Heidegger 1977, 124f.

That there is nonetheless an implicit guiding idea of being in Descartes's philosophy – as there is in any great metaphysical philosophy – will be argued in the Conclusion (section 22.3).

26 On this list, which includes but goes beyond 'the opposites' of Aristotle, cf. Moreno 1966, 129–34 and Wippel 1983, 56, n. 4.

27 The notion of a 'ruling science' is perhaps prefigured in Book I as well. Cf. Aristotle's description (1924 [*Met.*, 982b5]) of this science ('first philosophy') as *archikōtatē*.

3: Cartesian Metaphysics

1 Twentieth-century philosophy, according to Gewirth (1987b, 81), "consists in a series of reactions to Descartes's metaphysics." Examples are "Ryle's castigations of the Cartesian mind-body dualism, Sartre's and Hare's attacks on Cartesian intellectualism and intuitionism, Chomsky's support of Cartesian innatism, and the opposed views taken on Cartesian doubt by Russell and Husserl on the one hand and by Moore, Dewey, Austin and the later Wittgenstein on the other." The list could easily be expanded. (The omission of Heidegger is striking, though not surprising.)

Some of these "reactions" employ convenient caricatures of Descartes's thought. On Ryle, see Curley's critical discussion of Ryle's famous account of the "official theory" of the mind stemming from Descartes (1978, chap. 7). For his own part, Curley is convinced that Descartes contradicts himself "extensively" (ibid., 185) on the key points of interest to Ryle. Nor is the doctrine "very plausible" in itself, he finds (189). For an attempt to render it more so, while reconciling Descartes's apparently contradictory statements on consciousness, thought, and reflexion, see chapter 15 below.

2 Cf. Roth, 1937, 104f.: "Apart altogether from the work of Newton, the whole structure of Cartesian physics was open to attack on all sides and had ceased to have much meaning, and that within fifty years of its appearance." Also Mouy 1934 and Butterfield 1950, 142. J.-M. Beyssade speaks of "une physique ... dépassé à peine née, et dont le géométrisme sans nuance faisait dès l'époque de Leibniz l'archétype des erreurs mémorables" (1979, 130).

3 A similar occurrence of *res metaphysicae* is found at AT VII 162: CSM II 115. This very phrase crops up in an early (beginning of the thirteenth century) *Metaphysics* commentary by an anonymous English *magister* (cf. Zimmermann 1965, 125): *Utrum de rebus metaphysicis possit esse scientia.* Glossing the title Zimmermann notes: "Unter metaphysischen Dingen werden die Gegenstände verstanden, die

nicht im Bereich des sinnlichen Erkenntnisvermögens liegen." Gassendi appears to understand 'metaphysical' in much this way when he writes: "I acknowledge, of course, the existence of almighty God and the immortality of our souls; my hesitation simply relates to the force of the arguments that you employ to prove *these and other related metaphysical matters (alia Metaphysica cohaerentia)*" (AT VII 257: CSM II 179 e.a.). Descartes responds by characterizing Gassendi as one of those "whose minds are so immersed in the senses that they shrink from all *metaphysical* thoughts" (AT VII 348: CSM II 241 e.a.).

Citing both a medieval and a contemporary Scholastic source, Owens remarks that while the use of 'metaphysical' as a synonym for 'supersensible' "is not without some sanction in Scholastic tradition," it is "hardly to be recommended" (1985, 312, n. 2). This is because restricting the metaphysical to the supersensible leaves out those transcendental aspects that 'climb across' the divisions between the categories and between sensible and supersensible beings. Still, in respect of the *goal* as opposed to the subject matter of metaphysics, the restriction to the supersensible is not without justification, even for Aquinas. Cf. ibid., n. 3.

4 See Vollrath (1962, 267f.) on the work of the Spanish Jesuit Bruno Pereira. It had a decisive influence on German Protestant *Schulphilosophie* after 1595 (the date of first publication of his *De communibus omnium rerum naturalium principiis et affectionibus* in Cologne), giving rise to the 'bracketing' of theology and psychology in a single discipline, 'pneumatology' or the science of intelligible (immaterial) souls. Descartes could have been exposed to Pereira's views by his teachers at La Flèche.

5 Cf. Vollrath's comment on the title of Descartes's work (1962, 280): "Es kommt hier alles darauf an zu sehen, daß in diesem Titel alle Elemente der späteren Metaphysica specialis unter dem Namen einer Ersten Philosophie vereinigt sind." Not that Descartes is himself principally responsible for much more than the later inclusion of rational cosmology within *metaphysica specialis* (ibid., 281), according to Vollrath. Still, in giving his *Meditations* their full baroque title Descartes is no doubt reacting to some of the same pressures arising from the ambiguities in the Aristotelian concept of metaphysics that shaped the conception of metaphysics in German *Schulphilosophie* as well.

On Vollrath's contention that the inclusion of *cosmologia rationalis* within *metaphysica specialis* is a "Rest der cartesiansichen Mathesis universalis" (ibid.), cf. section 15.7 below.

6 'In the Aristotelian tradition' so as to avoid imputing a distinction between existence and essence to Aristotle. Cf. Owens 1993a, 118: "For Aristotle, quiddity and existence were melded together. One might distinguish the two logically, in one's mind or in definition. But for practical purposes it was better not to do even that." Cf. also Owens 1993b, 39, 45, 48 and nn. 2 and 3. Gilson (1952, 41–73)

traces the beginnings of the distinction to Avicenna and the origin of the celebrated controversy to Averroës's critique of the latter. Plenty of medievals (particularly Averroists like Siger of Brabant) had difficulty accepting the distinction precisely because of their staunch Aristotelianism. For Thomistic and neo-Thomistic metaphysics, however, it is central. Cf. Gilson, ibid., and Owens 1985, 140: "Metaphysics aims to investigate beings insofar as they are beings. To understand them from the viewpoint of being, it has to explain them in the light of their entitative principles. It isolates these principles as being [i.e., the act of existence] and essence."

7   On *ontologie grise* ('epistemo-ontology' or 'onto-epistemology,' as it may perhaps be glossed), see Marion 1975, §§30–2. On the history of the word 'ontology,' cf., n. 2 of the article "L'Ambivalence de la métaphysique cartésienne" added as an appendix to the second edition of the work. In the appendix, Marion speaks of a "transcription de l'ontologie en épistémologie" (1981b, 192).

8   Cf. Kant 1972, 195 (Kant to Markus Herz, 11 May 1781, cited by Marion 1986, 3, n. 4; cf. Vollrath 1962, 258).

9   Cf. also the works of Clarke, Hatfield, Buchdahl, and Menn mentioned in nn. 22 and 28 below. McRae (1961, 57f.) avoids some of the pitfalls of this type of interpretation by distinguishing two senses of 'metaphysics' in Descartes: "taken in one of these senses it is the science of 'immaterial or metaphysical things.' Metaphysics is also, however, the science of 'the principles of knowledge' ... Considered as the science of the principles of knowledge, metaphysics supplies the logical foundations of physics."

10   The 'underlabourer theory' was memorably formulated by Locke (cf. 1977, xlii f.); it was reformulated for twentieth-century philosophy by Wittgenstein (cf. 1971, 49): "The word 'philosophy' must mean something whose place is above or below the natural sciences, not beside them" (*Tractatus*, 4.111). Of course, this still leaves open *two* possibilities: above *or* below. The description of philosophy in the immediately following aphorism (ibid.) decides the matter, placing Wittgenstein squarely in Locke's camp. Opposed to the 'underlabourer' theory is what Ayer (1959, 16) aptly terms the 'overlord' theory, of which Aristotle, Descartes, and Kant are adherents. There is agreement, however, between the camps that the question of the order of the sciences is one that belongs, not to science, but to philosophy.

The 'underlabourer theory' reached its apogee in the programmatic writings of certain twentieth-century positivists. Cf., e.g., Carnap 1959a, 77: "But what, then, is left over for *philosophy*, if all statements whatever that assert something [cognitively meaningful] are of an empirical nature and belong to factual [i.e., positive] science? What remains is not statements, nor a theory, nor a system, but only a *method*: the method of logical analysis."

11   The gradual switch from 'first and therefore universal' to 'universal and therefore

first' explains in part why, from the seventeenth century onward, the question of the *unity* of the sciences looms as large as had the question of the *divisions* of the sciences in the Aristotelian tradition, sometimes even eclipsing the latter. There are valuable hints in Weisheipl (1965, 220ff., 237) that this general trend represents a return to an earlier Platonic conception of the hierarchical order and division of the sciences found, for instance, in the Oxford Platonists.

On the evolution of the ideal of the unity of the sciences in the seventeenth and eighteenth centuries, see McRae, who suggests that the divisions among the sciences suffer complete "obliteration" in the case of Descartes (1961, 15; cf. ibid., 7 and 14). This is no doubt true for divisions *based on differences of method*. There simply are none: "*method* knows no lines of division separating the different sciences according to their subject matters" (ibid., 56 e.a.). Still, in the *Regulae*, "Descartes introduces such diversities in the simple natures as would correspond to the differences of subject matter of the sciences" (ibid.). These form the basis of the hierarchical classification of the sciences on the basis of subject matter in the preface of the *Principles*.

It may be thought that the contrast drawn above carelessly compares metaphysics (Aristotle) and method, since in Descartes, at least, it is the method that is universal. Yet on Descartes's understanding of 'metaphysics,' method, like epistemology and philosophical psychology, is just a part of metaphysics itself. See below, section 15.6, on *mathesis universalis* and metaphysics.

12 The understanding of metaphysics as 'the science of the first principles of knowledge,' prevalent in Anglo-American philosophy today, stems from Hume, who simply jettisoned the first two connotations of the working definition of 'metaphysics' elaborated above, retaining the third alone. Cf. Hume 1967, Introduction and 1990, 30. If Descartes played any part in these developments, he did so unwittingly; with the exception of certain 'common notions,' the *principia cognitionis humanae* are clearly still largely *principia essendi*, principles of being (existence and essence).

13 Idiosyncratic, in my view, but in fact widespread among French commentators. Consider Maritain's comment: "Comme le notait très justement M. Émile Bréhier ... un renversement complet se produit chez Descartes du fait qu'il *substitue* la recherche de « l'ordre des raisons » [i.e., the order of knowing] à celle de l'ordre des choses" (Maritain 1937, 40 e.a.). Obviously, Gueroult figures in the same tradition.

14 Cf. Rule VI of the *Regulae* and Marion (1975, 52) on the sense of *prima principia* in that work ("termes premiers pour l'ordre de la connaissance" as opposed to the "principes ontologiques au sens où l'entendait Aristote").

15 Cf. AT VII 67: CSM II 46: "It is not that my thought ... imposes any necessity on any thing; on the contrary, it is the necessity of the thing itself ... which determines

my thought." Cf. Röd 1971, 55ff. and 141, where he corrects his own earlier 'subjectivist' interpretation on this point (Röd 1964). On 'subjectivism' and 'objectivism,' see also section 21.4.

16 Cited passim, almost as a mantra (cf. 1986, 35, 36, 39, 45, 50, 51, 52, etc.).

17 Marion 1986, 40. Cf. ibid., 38: "Celle-ci [first philosophy] recouvre le domaine de celle-là (Dieu et l'âme [the domain of metaphysics]) tout en l'outrepassant vers « toutes les premières choses en général »." Similarly, Menn 1993, n. 11. Röd also distinguishes the two, but only as a useful convention, since "Descartes zwischen beiden Ausdrücken nicht scharf unterschied" (1971, 3).

The terminological distinction between metaphysics and first philosophy is not well supported by the texts. This is not to contest the fact that such a distinction existed in a variety of forms in philosophy before Descartes. Vollrath shows (cf. 1962, 267ff.) that Pereira distinguished between metaphysics as theology and first philosophy as ontology. This constitutes "eine metaphysische Verlegen-heit," however, implying as it does that theology is *not* first philosophy. The embarassment was removed in the seventeenth century through the efforts of Johannes Micraelius (1579–1658). On Micraelius's solution, cf. Vollrath 1962, 269f.

18 Cf. also 1986, 39: "La primauté – qui assure d'ailleurs seule à la philosophie première sa priorité sur la métaphysique – resortit à l'ordre de la connaissance, telle qu'elle détermine la manière cartésienne de philosopher. Selon l'ordre de la connaissance, la connaissance a une priorité absolue, donc le premier étant que connaîtra la connaissance sera celui qui l'exerce, l'*ego*."

In his earlier work on the *Regulae*, Marion deliberately echoes the famous formula of the first book of Aristotle's *Metaphysics* to express the changed conception of metaphysics in Descartes (cf. 1975, 92): "ce qui se dit « le plus seigneurialement, premièrement et le plus », ce qui est recherché « jadis, maintenant et toujours » ne sera plus l'*ousia*, mais l'*ego*." The influence of Vollrath (cf. 1962, 283) may be at work here: "Dieser Wissenschaftsbegriff des Descartes legt aber jegliches Seiende so an, daß es hinsichtlich seiner Stellung zur menschlichen Mens erkannt werden kann ... Was Descartes dabei versäumt, ist die Prüfung, ob die Anordnung des Seienden hinsichtlich des menschlichen Erkennens dieses Seiende in seinem Sein betrifft." This surely means, not just that the question of the order of knowing takes on a new importance, but that it eclipses the order of being entirely – which is Marion's position exactly: "l'étant n'entre plus en jeu et subit une disqualification dès qu'entre en scène l'*ordo cognoscendi*" (1975, 40).

19 For an instructive look at Marion's recent thoughts on onto-theology, cf. Shaney 1996.

20 Cf. Locke 1977, xi: "Were it fit to trouble thee with the history of this *Essay*, I should tell thee that five or six friends, meeting at my chamber and discoursing on a subject very remote from this, found themselves quickly at a stand, by the difficul-

ties that rose on every side. After we had awhile puzzled ourselves, without coming any nearer a resolution of those doubts which perplexed us, it came into my thoughts that we took a wrong course; and that before we set ourselves upon inquiries of that nature, it was necessary to examine our own abilities and see what objects our understandings were, or were not, fitted to deal with."

21 Cf. AT X 396f.: CSM I 30: "to prevent our mental labours from being misguided and haphazard, we ought once in our life carefully to enquire as to what sort of knowledge human reason is capable of attaining before we set about acquiring knowledge of things in particular." See also AT X 397: CSM I 31: "But the most useful inquiry we can make at this ['preliminary'] stage is to ask: What is human knowledge and what is its scope?" Also AT X 398: CSM I 31: "There is, I think, nothing more foolish than presuming, as many do, to argue about the secrets of nature, the influence of the heavens on these lower regions, the prediction of future events, and so on, without ever enquiring whether human reason is adequate for discovering matters like these." With these passages compare Locke 1977, 1 [*Essay*, 1.1.2]: "This, therefore, being my *purpose*, to inquire into the original, certainty, and extent of human knowledge."

22 Compare, for example, the measured and reasonable tones in which Clarke (1982, §1) overstates the case "that Descartes's primary interest was in physical science," not metaphysics. As a critique of the practice of reading Descartes's methodological writings and interpreting his method in the light of the metaphysics rather than his own scientific work, Clarke's polemic may be justified; but by insisting that the metaphysics must be read in the light of the scientific work, he skews Descartes's philosophical outlook badly.

   In a similar spirit, Buchdahl attempts to show "how Descartes's philosophical and metaphysical position arises easily and naturally out of his scientific preoccupation" (1969, 80), i.e., how the technical detail of the latter "supplies the concrete 'paradigmatical' background for the direction of Descartes's metaphysics" (147). This too suggests a foundationalist enterprise focused primarily on science. Menn (1993, 537) speaks in a similar vein of "Descartes's project of turning an old metaphysics into the foundation of his new science." Röd (1971, 2) writes: "Descartes verstand nämlich unter 'Erster Philosophie' (hinsichtlich der in ihr angestrebten Resultate) die Lehre von den Prinzipien der Naturwissenschaften bzw. der Naturphilosophie." Cf. also ibid., 86ff. and 90f.

23 Section 10.12 and chapters 12 and 14 deal with the difference in evidence between the truths of (a) natural theology, (b) the rest of metaphysics, (c) logic, and (d) mathematics; also with the way (c), (d), and (b) – including the metaphysical underpinnings of natural science – depend on (a) for their certainty. In one place Röd (1971, 90f.) denies that natural theology belongs to first philosophy at all. But this is due to the artificial distinction he introduces between metaphysics and

first philosophy (see above, n. 17). Elsewhere in the work (ibid., 10) he points this out explicitly.

24 Unless, of course, Descartes is disingenuous after all, as Adam, Leroy, Caton, Dorter, and Loeb believe. For the exact references, see n. 1 of the paper by Loeb (1986). Kennington's distinction (1972, 89ff.) between a genuine 'rationalist' and a dissembling 'apologetic' strand is unconvincing. For the opposing viewpoint, cf. Cottingham (1992b, 237): "it would be wrong to dismiss as a mere specious afterthought his [Descartes's] professed religious motivation for writing on mind-body metaphysics." Apart from the early (25 November 1630) letter to Mersenne cited by Cottingham, cf. also the letters mentioned in n. 10 of that article (to which might be added the letter to Vatier of 22 February 1938 [AT I 564: CSMK 88]). Heidegger's comment on the dedicatory epistle seems perfectly just (cf. 1994, 266): "Deutlicher, als Descartes dies hier tut, kann man die Absicht der Meditationen nicht klarmachen." If testimony from Descartes's contemporaries is wanted, there is this from the Second Set of Objections: "You have embarked on your arguments for the greater glory of God and the immense benefit of mankind" (AT VII 122: CSM II 87). Of course, it is always possible that Descartes pulled the wool over the eyes of these "philosophers and theologians." But how credible is it that he either did or wished to?

25 This is not the whole story. On Descartes's attitude in his later career toward the persistent controversies of 'the Schools,' cf. also the letter to Father Dinet, especially AT VII 581f.: CSM II 392.

   His ambivalence about philosophy is no doubt to be explained by his belief that he had discovered the source of all the controversies and uncertainties of the Schools: "All the mistakes made in the sciences happen, in my view, simply because at the beginning we make judgements too hastily, and accept as our first principles matters which are obscure and of which we do not have a clear and distinct notion" (AT X 526: CSM II 419). So the problem is remediable rather than endemic to philosophy as such in virtue of its subject matter.

26 The terminological distinction drawn (and usually observed) by Descartes between *intelligere* or *entendre* on the one hand, and *concipere*, *concevoir* and *comprehendere*, *comprendre* on the other, has been much discussed in the literature since Alquié first remarked on the "étonnante formule" of the letter to Clerselier of 23 April 1649: "it is sufficient for me to understand *the fact that God is not grasped* (*non comprehendatur*) *by me* in order to understand (*ut intelligam*) God in very truth as he is, provided I judge also that there are in him all perfections which I clearly understand (*intelligo*), and also many more which I cannot grasp (*comprehendere*)." Cf. Gouhier's (1969, chap. 8) development of this theme, which inspired two studies by J.-M. Beyssade (1981, 1993). The earlier of the two is the definitive examination of Descartes's terminological usage in this regard, while the

later reconciles the doctrine that the idea of God is *maxime clara et distincta* with the teaching of the *incomprehensibilitas Dei.*

27 Cf. the opening sentence of the Fourth Meditation: "I have taken careful note of the fact that there is very little about corporeal things that is truly perceived, whereas much more is known about the human mind, and *still more* about God" (AT VII 52f.: CSM II 37 e.a.). Descartes is less than perfectly consistent on this. Compare: "our knowledge of a thinking thing is ... much more extensive than our knowledge of *anything else*" (AT VII 387: CSM II 266 e.a.) with this from the First Replies: "God provides much more ample and straightforward subject matter for clear and distinct knowledge than does *any* created thing" (AT VII 114: CSM II 82 e.a.).

28 As Hatfield writes (1992, 336): "judging from the attention that [Descartes] devoted to physiological and psychological topics, they, along with the rest of his physics, formed the raison d'être of his philosophical program." In a variety of relatively less important senses this is no doubt true: many more pages of the Cartesian *corpus* are devoted to physical science than to metaphysics; natural scientific, particularly physiological considerations are never far from his mind nor entirely absent even from his more strictly philosophical writings; such interests, moreover, antedate and may have spawned some of Descartes's most characteristic metaphysical and epistemological doctrines.

For a more balanced view (which nonetheless accords pride of place to the foundational project in regard to science), see Menn 1993, who recognizes the crucial importance of the concluding sentences of the "Synopsis" (cf. ibid., 549).

29 On the precise question (the letter of Mersenne is lost), cf. Marion 1981a, 162ff.

30 At AT III 505: CSMK 208 Descartes speaks of "metaphysical or theological" (*Metaphysica, sive Theologica*) arguments or reasons, again apparently treating the terms as convertible, much as in the case of 'metaphysical' and 'immaterial.'

For a brief listing of the works and letters in which the doctrine of the eternal truths is unfolded, see Gouhier 1969, 243. Gouhier rather surprisingly regards the doctrine as part of natural philosophy (ibid., 245), though he admits that it only ends up there after being expelled from the chapter of theology devoted to the divine attributes as a consequence of Descartes's refusal to acknowledge so much as a conceptual distinction between the divine intellect and will (ibid., 236).

4: The New Order of Knowing

1 Cf. Phelan (1967, 146f., n. 48): "our knowledge is not a knowledge of concepts but of things *by means of* concepts" (e.a.). That is precisely the sense of *par l'entremise.* 'Concept' is taken here in the Scholastic sense of 'objective concept,' i.e., "the thing or essence which is known and which, therefore, exercises ... an act of existence in the intentional mode of being" (149), i.e., the object as it exists

objectively or intentionally (cognitively) in the mind. To say of a thing that it exists
in the mind "in the intentional mode of being" is just to say that an actual act of
thinking of that thing exists there really, formally, or actually. In Descartes's
language this act of thinking is called an 'idea,' though the same term is used in
other senses as well. On the different uses of 'idea' in Descartes, cf. chapter 16.

2 On Aristotle, cf. Owens 1993a, 112: "What you see or know directly [for Aristotle]
is the desk or the table, and not the act of seeing or of knowing it. You are, of
course, concomitantly aware of your own cognitive acts, but only in the course of
attaining something else. What you see is something else, and not directly the act
of seeing. What you know directly is likewise something other than the act of
knowing, even though awareness of the act itself is always concomitant." This is
(*pace* Owens) Descartes's view as well.

    Whatever the words *par l'entremise* may suggest, the view expressed in the letter
to Gibieuf has nothing to do with Hume's fancy that the "most vulgar philosophy
informs us, that no external object can make itself known to the mind immediately,
and *without the interposition* of an image or perception" (1967, 239 e.a.). In the
first *Enquiry*, Hume presents the same notion as the conclusion of the notorious
'argument from illusion': "the slightest philosophy ... teaches us, that nothing can
ever be present to the mind but an image or perception, and that the senses are only
the inlets, through which these images are conveyed, without being able to produce
any immediate intercourse between the mind and the object. The table, which we
see, seems to diminish, as we remove farther from it: but the real table, which exists
independent of us, suffers no alteration: it was, therefore, nothing but its image
which was present to the mind ... and no man, who reflects, ever doubted, that the
existences, which we consider, when we say *this house* and *that tree*, are nothing
but perceptions in the mind" (1990, 183). For Hume, then, only an idea can "make
itself known to the mind immediately"; for Descartes (see previous note), things
make themselves known immediately "by means of" ideas.

3 Cf. Owens: "In Berkeley the denial of a material universe appears as a consequence
of the Cartesian doctrine that what the human mind directly knows are its own
ideas" (1985, 311, n. 1; cf. 267 n. 12). (This would be unexceptionable were it not
for the mention of Descartes. Cf. also Owens 1993b, 53 and Ashworth 1972, 89.)

4 Cf., e.g., O'Neil (1974), Van Cleve (1979, n. 17), and notably Yolton (1984, chap.
1). Yolton canvassed the whole issue in an earlier article (Yolton 1975a) and in his
1974 presidential address to the Canadian Philosophical Association, "On Being
Present to the Mind. A Sketch for the History of an Idea" (Yolton 1975b). Lurking
in the background of the latter (as the subtitle perhaps suggests) is Lovejoy's classic
study, *The Revolt Against Dualism*. By 'dualism' Lovejoy understands both
metaphysical dualism and "epistemological dualism," i.e., the "theory of representative perception." The latter he glosses as the "supposition, so long accepted as

unchallengeable, that all apprehension of objective reality is mediated through subjective existents, that 'ideas' forever interpose themselves between the knower and the objects which he would know" (Lovejoy 1960, 3).

Kemp Smith (1952, 51f.) rejects the ascription to Descartes of "a doctrine of representative perception," i.e., the "assumption that physical entities can be apprehended only by way of mental duplicates." For his own part, he finds in Descartes a hybrid form of representationalism very different from "the view currently held" by such commentators as Gilson, Keeling, and Laporte (ibid., 147 and n. 2). The immediate object of sensory awareness is a corporeal idea that is not "apprehended by any intermediaries, 'ideal' or otherwise, but directly in a face-to-face manner" (ibid., 150). This still leaves the apprehension of physical entities other than one's own body (or "brain-patterns") a form of mediate knowledge. Smith claims support for his view from Hamelin (1921, 282ff. and 352f.) as well.

5 Inconsistency "with the new mathematical science of nature" covers a multitude of sins. Descartes's precise reasons for rejecting the 'real qualities' and 'substantial forms' of the Schoolmen are too complex to be treated adequately here. See Gilson's classic study (1951, pt. II, chap. 1) and Menn's recent paper (1995) on real qualities. Menn claims that Descartes simply "abstained" (e.g., n. 24) from the use of 'real qualities' (and 'real accidents' or 'forms' in the other categories) in scientific explanation, regarding them as superfluous. But this, even when tied into a metaphysical account of how God actually created the world (cf. Menn, ibid.), is only part of the story, and not the most interesting part.

In the Replies to the Third Set of Objections (AT VII 185: CSM II 130) Descartes appears agnostic on the question of real qualities: "if there are real qualities ... they are things to a greater extent (*magis res*) than modes ... etc." But in the Sixth Replies he sets out to "demolish the doctrine of the reality of accidents" (AT VII 434: CSM II 293), employing three arguments. The first assumes a mechanical model of efficient causality on which only the surfaces of bodies can enter into causal transactions in sense-perception (cf. also AT VII 249ff.: CSM II 173ff. and AT VII 255: CSM II 177). It follows that real qualities (or real accidents in the other categories) must be imperceptible. And yet, Descartes concludes, "the only reason why people have thought that accidents exist is that they have supposed that they are perceived by the senses." The second argument urges that the very notion of something both an accident and real (i.e., a *res* or substance) is flatly self-contradictory (*omnino repugnat*), while the third merely shows that such entities are methodologically superfluous (much as Menn suggests). This should be compared with the *Meteors*, AT VI 239, and Rule XII (AT X 413: CSM 41), where, explaining the real quality of colour in terms of shape alone, Descartes speaks of the "useless assumption and pointless invention of some new entity" over and above extension, figure, and motion. Somewhat later in the same set of Replies (AT VII 441f.: CSM

297f.) a fourth argument is added. 'Gravity' is offered as an example of a 'real accident' or 'active quality' in bodies, this notion having arisen through the illicit mixing of the mental and the material.

As for substantial forms, they too are rejected as without explanatory value and illicitly confounding the notions of the body and the soul, i.e., as a form of 'animism' and hence – from the perspective of radical dualism – a 'category mistake' *avant la lettre* (e.g., AT III 667f.: CSMK 219; AT III 424: CSMK 190; AT V 222: CSMK 358; on this see Gilson 1951, pt. II, chap. 1). At times Descartes will suggest that the very talk of such forms is meaningless (e.g. AT III 649: CSMK 216), at others that the forms are fictions of our own making (AT VII 443: CSM II 298). Cf. Miles 1990, 92, n. 7. That the very notion is self-contradictory is suggested at AT III 502: CSMK 207: "when we deny substantial forms, we mean by the expression a certain substance joined to matter, making up with it a merely corporeal whole, and which, no less than matter and even more than matter – since it is called an actuality and matter only a potentiality – is a true substance or self-subsistent thing."

Gilson (ibid.) and Hoenen (1968) have long since dealt faithfully with Descartes's blatant misunderstandings (*pace* Menn, ibid., nn. 7 and 9) of the Scholastic doctrines of real qualities and substantial forms criticized in these ways.

This subject will be taken up again in the Conclusion, section 22.3.

6 Nor, on the other hand, did he commit himself to the thesis: "My knowledge of my own mental states is certain and infallible; my judgements about them cannot be erroneous" (cf. Wilson 1978a, 151). Provided one confines one's judgments accurately to one's own actually occurring mental states, there is indeed no possibility of error; but to do so is the exception, while to misdescribe one's mental states is the rule. Thus, the idea of an 'epistemic difference' in the degree of certainty proper to each of two kinds of judgments is intended as a corrective to this "incorrigibility thesis" (Radner 1988, 443) as well as to representationalism, though only the latter is to be discussed here. The former will be taken up in section 7.1, "Clear and distinct perception."

7 In traditional terms (see below) what is 'present' in the world may be said to be '*re*presented' in the mind. In the use to which the same terms are put here, that which is 'present' is in the mind in one sense (immediately present to consciousness), while that which is '*re*presented' is in the mind in a quite different sense (as the immediate object of thought and hence as only mediately present to consciousness), whether or not it is also present in the external world.

The *locus classicus* of the traditional contrast is, of course, Aristotle. Cf. Owens (1993a, 107): "In *Peri hermeneias* Aristotle described human thought as meant to represent things, while words and language express what is thought about those things ... The knowable content is what is *present* in the things, *represented* in thought, and *conveyed* in speech" (e.a.).

8 Cf. O'Neil (1974). The phrase 'veil-of-perception-doctrine,' used in the next two chapters, is adapted from Bennett (1965, 121ff.), who attributes the doctrine to Locke. About this he is probably mistakenly (cf. Yolton 1975a, n. 2). The theory so designated is generally referred to as 'representationalism' in the present work, though it can also be called the 'dual object' theory, 'proxy' theory (taking ideas in the mind as proxies of extra-mental objects), 'representationism,' 'representative theory' of perception or ideas, etc. Perhaps the only major philosopher who can be said with complete confidence to have held the theory is Hume (see n. 2 above), though Malebranche (like Locke) has been widely regarded as an exponent and Arnauld as an opponent of the theory. On the Arnauld-Malebranche debate, cf. chapter 16 *in initio*.

5: Synopsis

1 Cf. the letter to Reneri for Pollot of April or May 1638 (AT II 38: CSMK 98), to be cited in section 7.4. On the whole question of anachronism, see section 8.3.

2 Descartes uses the Latin verbs *inferre* and *colligere* in connection with the *cogito, ergo sum* at VII 352: CSM II 244; the noun *ratiocinium* at X 523: CSM II 417; the Latin noun *conclusio* (twice) at AT V 147: CSMK 333, and again in *Principles*, I, 9; both the French verb *inférer* and the French noun *conclusion* are used in speaking of *je pense, donc je suis* in the authorized French translation of *Principles*, I, 9 (IX-2, 28). The French verbs *inférer* and *raisonner* are used in the same context, the first in a letter to Colvius of November 1640 (AT III 248: CSMK 159), the latter in the preface to the *Principles* (IX-2, 10). The Latin verb *sequitur* is employed in the Third Meditation example of something known by the natural light: *ex eo quod dubitem sequatur me esse* (AT VII 38: CSM II 27), and again in the Fourth Meditation: *adverterem ex hoc ipso quod illud examinarem, evidenter sequi me existere* (AT VII 58: CSM II 41). Finally, in the Fifth Replies, responding to Gassendi's suggestion that any other action might do as well as *cogito*, Descartes uses the Latin term *illatio* (AT VII 352: CSM II 244). Many of these passages (the list is not intended to be exhaustive) were cited by Hintikka 1962, 11, who may have cobbled his list together out of Hamelin and Gueroult. Röd produces a similar compilation (1959–60, 180).

 Scholz noted long ago (1931, 131 n. 1) that *conclusio* and *conclusion*, in Descartes, are sometimes to be understood as *Schlußsatz* (i.e., 'conclusion' in our sense), sometimes as *Schlußprozeß* (what we would call 'inference'), and that neither meaning is sharply distinguished from the third, *Implikation* as a logical relation obtaining between or among two or more propositions. Cf. also J.-M. Beyssade (1979, 237, n. 4) and Kenny's musings (1968, 52) on the sense of *conclusio* at AT V 147: CSMK 333.

3 According to Ross (Aristotle 1949a, 37), Aristotle "means by induction, in different

places, quite different things." He settles (ibid., 50) on three basic uses of the term. The first and least important is (1) induction as "a mode of argument from particulars which merely tends to produce belief in a general principle without proving it" (ibid.). This is the sense that comes closest to what has been understood by 'induction' by philosophers and historians of science since Hume and Mill. It is, as Aristotle clearly recognized, incapable of yielding certainty. The other two correspond to what are called (2) 'intuitive' and (3) 'perfect induction,' respectively. Both yield certainty on Ross's interpretation of Aristotle.

Regarding (2), Cohen and Nagel 1934, 274 point out that the expression 'intuitive induction' was first coined by W.E. Johnson. Cf. also McRae 1972a, 38. For (3) Kneale (1949, 30) prefers to use the expression 'summative induction,' since 'perfect induction' suggests that the other varieties are merely imperfect approximations to induction by complete enumeration, whereas in fact (2) refers to an altogether different process of establishing universal principles with complete certainty.

Von Fritz (1964, 40 and 42ff.) distinguishes (2) and (3) as "die unmittelbare ἐπαγωγή" and "der epagagogischer Syllogismus" or "Schluß" (also "vollständige Induktion"), respectively. He agrees with Kneale that they are altogether distinct, while differing from both Kneale and Ross on the certainty of "complete induction," at least where (as in Aristotle) natural kinds, rather than arbitrarily devised classes about whose membership there can be no uncertainty, are in question (cf. ibid., 51). As for (1), von Fritz supplies the name "generalisierende Induktion" (ibid., 44) for this, perhaps borrowed from Bochenski 1963, 26, whom he cites in n. 84 as one who distinguishes 'complete' from 'generalizing induction.'

On intuitive induction in Descartes and Aristotle, see section 20.5 below.

4 On the long and tortuous history of the debate concerning whom Descartes thought he was attacking, cf. Cronin (1987), Wells (1987), and Kenny (1970). According to Marion (1981a, 57): "deux grands théologiens jésuites [Suarez and Vasquez], dont les oeuvres connaissaient une large diffusion et une renommée considérable, tenaient les vérités éternelles pour indépendantes de Dieu; ce qui renforce d'autant l'hypothèse que Descartes aurait visé ... des positions précises, identifiables, et connues de tous." Cf. also ibid., 62.

Did Suarez enunciate the position as his own doctrine, or only in the context of a criticism of Thomas's view as he understood it? For a defence of the latter position, see Curley 1987, sect. V.

Marion goes on to add Eustache of St Paul (63f.), Scipion Dupleix (64f.), Göckel (67f.), Mersenne (175ff.), Kepler (esp. 196), and Galileo (221ff., especially 226: "En Galilée Descartes éprouvera bien le plus proche adversaire des thèses de 1630") to the list of those who held some form of the thesis rejected by Descartes.

All the pertinent references to the early stages of the debate are to be found in Wells.

5 Prudence or insincerity are the usual explanations of Descartes's reticence on the subject of the creation of the eternal truths. Cf. Bréhier 1968, 192f., and Doney's rebuttal 1987, 110f. Gueroult (1968, I, 24, n. 32) had already rejected Bréhier's hypothesis (as expressed in an earlier work) some years before. As noted earlier, Gouhier assigns the doctrine of the eternal truths to the philosophy of nature rather than metaphysics, which explains its absence from the *Meditationes de prima philosophia*. None of these explanations is very satisfactory, though no better account is to be offered in the following.

6 The voluntarist reading is developed by Frankfurt 1987b, the 'iterated modalities' account (roughly: 'p is necessary' = 'it is contingent that p is necessary') by Curley 1987. Curley (ibid., n. 3) identifies Cronin (1966), Wells (1987), and (with some qualifications) Marion (1981a) as sharing Frankfurt's view, while his own (ibid., n. 23) was anticipated by Geach (1987). Marion (1981a, 283, n. 18) had earlier included Curley (1978) among the many "authorities" who have endorsed the voluntarist interpretation (along with Belaval, Lenoble, Brunschvicg, Koyré, Cottingham); he himself explicitly rejects it (ibid., 282ff.).

As for the third (or necessitarian) account, it turns largely on whether the most basic laws of nature are true, not just in this world, but in all possible worlds God might have created. If the latter, then the most basic laws of nature are, like the axioms of mathematics, metaphysics, and morals, necessary truths (cf. Osler 1985, 361). Even so, unless the initial state of the universe as a whole were likewise necessary, the result would still not be a thoroughgoing necessitarianism like Spinoza's. Curley takes the necessitarian account of the basic laws of physics as far as one can in a later work on Spinoza (see Curley 1988, sect. 14 and 15). Wilson (1981, sect. II) sketches an account similar to Curley's, simply setting it alongside the familiar voluntarist story without attempting to reconcile the two. On the other hand, her position in her book on Descartes (Wilson 1978a, 127) amounts to a qualified voluntarist interpretation. Arguing on quite different grounds, J.-M. Beyssade notes the "accent presque spinoziste" (1979, 124) of the doctrine of the creation of the eternal truths, particularly in the *Conversation with Burman*.

7 Gueroult (1968, II, 26–30) touched off this dispute, arguing for a class of "vérités premières situées en quelque sorte *au delà des vérités éternelles instituées par le libre arbitre divin*." These eternal truths possess a necessity that is "absolue et immanente à Dieu" as opposed to one that is "relative à moi et décrétée par Dieu" (ibid., II, 34, n. 27) – two types of necessary truths.

8 This class is assigned a very broad extension by Gueroult. It includes even what Bouveresse terms "les deux dogmes cardinaux de la physique cartésienne" (Bouveresse 1987, 327): the denials of atoms and of the void. Gouhier (1969, 286 and 291) embraces Gueroult's distinction between created and uncreated (or absolute) eternal truths, though he is more cautious about the extension of

this class. So too Rodis-Lewis (1971, chap. III, §5). Frankfurt flatly rejects the suggestion that some eternal truths are neither created nor alterable by divine omnipotence (1987b, sect. VII). This is also the view of Wilson (1978a) and J.-M. Beyssade (1981; 1979, 115ff.). Curley (1987, 365) cautiously endorses a distinction like that drawn by Gueroult, confining the extension of the uncreated eternal truths to "truths about God," while leaving undecided exactly what this does and does not include – presumably because it is undecidable on the available evidence. This is apparently Bouveresse's conclusion as well: "Il est probable que Descartes, sous peine de mettre en péril son propre système, a dû soustraire certaines vérités éternelles à la doctrine de la libre création, en particulier certaines vérités concernant Dieu lui-même" (1987, 331). Similarly Marion: "En fait, une seule vérité s'impose à Dieu ... – son existence. Mais il ne s'agit point là d'une nécessité logique ..., mais de l'instance qui instaure le code où se formulent seulement tous possibles et tous contradictoires" (1981a, 296–303, esp. 301). The whole controversy goes back to Boutroux (1927, 23ff. and 84).

9 Gueroult denies that the extension of this class of eternal truths coincides with that of those first principles perfectly immune from all (even metaphysical) doubt (1968, II, 31f.). Some of the uncreated among the eternal truths are immune from doubt, but others are not; the "privilege" of these latter, their certainty, "ne saurait venir, en tout cas, de ce qu'ils sont des vérités incréés, puisque ce privilège manque à certains d'entre elles." Gouhier anwers the question in the affirmative (1969, 286), seeing in this the means of avoiding a circle.

10 Bouveresse suggests a notion of absolute (*in se*) and relative (*quoad nos*) modality something like this: everything we clearly and distinctly conceive as *possible* (free of contradiction) really is so, since anything so conceivable can also be brought about by God (cf. AT VII 78: CSM II 54; AT VII 71: CSM II 50; AT VII 227: CSM II 160; AT VIII-1 28f.: CSM I 213; and AT VII 425: CSM II 287); however, our conceiving something as *im*possible or as *necessary* does not entail its impossibility or necessity in itself, i.e., for God, since a perfect being can both understand how it could be otherwise and could make it so if he wished. Thus, unlike eternal truths (1) about the possible and (2) about God himself, the "notions cartésiennes de nécessité et impossibilité sont essentiellement épistémiques" (1987, 309; cf. 317); they tell us something about the nature of human reason as freely created by God, not about what is necessary or impossible *in se*.

Taking this to mean that Descartes's concepts of necessity and impossibility tell us something about our contingent psychological make-up, Ishiguro (1987a, 1987b) rejects Bouveresse's epistemic account of Descartes's theory of modality: "what Descartes means by eternal truths having their seat in the mind seems closer to Kant's view on the a priori than it does to epistemic views like that of Hume" (1986, 463). The asymmetry established by Bouveresse between possibility on the one hand and impossibility and necessity on the other is pushed a step farther: for Ishiguro, the notion of impossibility alone is absolute, while necessity "is ... a conditional modality" (1987a, 337ff.; 1987b, 378), dependent on God's will in creating our minds as they are and *thereby* a world in which certain a priori truths obtain. Ishiguro thus redraws the boundary between relative and the absolute impossibility within the realm of logical or conceptual truths where Gueroult first drew it, but in a way having little to do with Gueroult (or, so far as I can see, with Descartes).

The shared assumption of Bouveresse and Ishiguro is that the eternal truths implanted there by God "have their seat in the mind" (Ishiguro 1987b, 375), i.e., *only* in the mind. Against this interpretation, see section 10.11 on the ontological status of mathematical objects (*vera et realia entia*) and of "true and immutable natures" generally.

11 Bouveresse (1987, 316) suggests that Descartes's strategy, unlike that of others similarly smitten by the mathematical ideal (e.g., Spinoza), was to assimilate his mathematics to the truths of physics rather than vice versa. The truths of mathematics thus possess the kind of necessity possessed by the basic laws of nature rather than the other way round. Ishiguro argues (1987a, 333 and more fully in 1987b, 374ff.) that there is a sharp division between the eternal truths of logic and mathematics and the truths of physics ("particular rules governing changes in the created world"). While this is no doubt correct for derivative laws, the case of the most basic laws of nature is much less clear. See, for example, Osler 1985. Certainly, "the seeds of truth" doctrine elaborated in the *Regulae* and the *Discourse* (and not usually considered as relevant to this issue – see section 18.9) suggests that these laws are innate and hence necessary in precisely the same sense as the simple truths of logic or mathematics.

The key passage from the *Discourse* dealing with the basic laws of physics reads: "Further, I showed [in *Le Monde*] what the laws of nature were, and without basing my arguments on any principle other than the infinite perfections of God, I tried to demonstrate all those laws about which we could have any doubt, and to show that they are such that, even if God created many worlds, there could not be any in which they failed to be observed" (AT VI 43: CSM I 132; cf. also AT XI 47: CSM I 97 and *Principles*, III, 47). Since these laws are true in 'all possible worlds,' it has seemed to commentators heavily influenced by Leibniz (Bouveresse among them) that they belong to the same category as the necessary truths of logic and mathematics. But it is not enough to dismiss this as "anachronistic" (Ishiguro). To understand this passage in Cartesian terms, the words "conceivable by us" must be inserted after "any." The laws of nature are indeed necessary in any world *we can conceive of*, given the nature of our minds as furnished with common notions and eternal truths by God, but not in any world *tout court*. (Marion [1981a, 264] seems to understand the passage in this way when he speaks of "tous les mondes *intelligibles* possibles" [my italics].) Though necessary 'for us,' we cannot deny that the divine mind can conceive and create other laws and other worlds of which we cannot conceive. Like the truths of logic and mathematics, then, the basic laws of physics are necessary and innate rather than contingent truths discovered through experience. Cf. also sections 15.7 and 18.9.

12 This is the answer given issue (5) above.

PART ONE: THOUGHT AND CONSCIOUSNESS

1 McRae made these points in an earlier essay as well (1972b), noting a few contexts in which the French *conscience* and *pensée* are indeed used synonymously. On this see also Radner 1988, 440, who proposes a distinction (found later in Brentano) between two uses of *conscientia* (ibid., 445ff.), C_1 and C_2. The first is a mode of thinking, the second an "ingredient" in modes of thinking but not itself a thought. On these two senses of *Bewußtsein* in Brentano, see Brentano 1973, 102 (Radner's C_1) and 126f. (her C_2). Despite the philosophical importance of the distinction, which is clearly prefigured in Descartes, the occurrences of *conscientia* in sense C_1 (see, for example, the passage from the Fifth Replies quoted in section 7.5 below) are so uncharacteristic and ambiguous that this manner of fixing the distinction terminologically seems unwarranted.

6: Descartes's Definition of 'Thought'

1 In the Seventh Replies (cf. AT VII 518: CSM II 352) Descartes includes "remembering" along with willing, imagining, and having sensory perceptions among the "properties of a thinking thing." In the *Regulae* he speaks of "four faculties" of cognition: "intellect, imagination, sense-perception, and memory" (AT X 411: CSM I 39; cf. also AT X 398: CSM I 32).

2 The full passage from which the words "operations of the soul" are taken reads: "if you take the word 'thought' as I do, to cover all the operations of the soul, so that not only meditations and acts of the will (*non seulement les meditations & les volontez*), but the activities of seeing and hearing and deciding on one movement rather than another, so far as they depend on the soul, are all thoughts ..." In this odd use, 'meditation' may stand for 'imagination' – as it quite clearly does in the following passage of the Sixth Meditation: "And since the ideas perceived by the senses were much more lively and vivid and even, in their own way, more distinct than any of those which I deliberately formed *through meditating* or which I found impressed on the memory ..." (AT VII 75: CSM II 52 e.a.). But Descartes uses the word in other ways as well.

3 We shall have occasion to return to this special use of *percipere, savoir*, and *idea* later (cf. sections 8.4 and 16.3). If the foregoing is correct, then the view that "there can be nothing within me which I am in no way conscious of" (AT VII 107: CSM II 77; cf. also AT VII 246: CSM II 171 and AT VII 107: CSM II 77) does *not* entail the so-called "evidence thesis" that being conscious of x involves knowing x. Cf. Radner 1988, 443f. on the thesis and its proponents. On consciousness, thought, and reflexion, cf. chapter 15 below.

4 Cottingham is reiterating a point already made by Kenny 1968, 69. Gassendi too may be unaware of what 'thought' covers when he writes (à propos of Descartes's claim that 'thinking' is an innate idea): "just as the mind can, from the idea of one town, construct the idea of another, so from the idea of one action such as seeing or tasting it can construct the idea of another action such as thought" (AT VII 281: CSM II 196). Similarly, Hobbes when he writes: "Even if we grant that fear is a thought ..." (AT VII 182: CSM II 128) – something Hobbes is plainly reluctant to do, presumably because it runs counter to established usage.

5 On nutrition, see the Seventh Replies (AT VII 477: CSM II 321): "one of the most notable points in my *Meditations* is that I refer nutrition to the body alone, not to the mind or to that part of man which thinks." Also the Fifth Replies: "the principle in virtue of which we [and other living things] are nourished is wholly different – *different in kind* – from the principle in virtue of which we think" (AT VII 356: CSM II 246 e.a.).

On sensation, which Descartes refers in one sense to the body, in another to the mind, see the distinction between "organic sensation" and sensation *praecise sic sumptum* in chapter 9 below. Of the latter Descartes remarks that it *nihil aliud est quam cogitare*.

On locomotion, see AT VII 351: CSM II 243. Regarding the Scholastic doctrine of the dependence of locomotion on the soul, Descartes comments in the Sixth Meditation: "I might consider the body of a man as a kind of machine equipped with and made up of bones, nerves, muscles, veins, blood and skin in such a way that, even if there were no mind in it, it would still perform all the same movements as it now does in those cases where movement is not under the control of the will, or consequently, of the mind" (AT VII 84: CSM II 58).

This leaves thinking or pure understanding in the Scholastic sense as a genuinely intellectual faculty or act in no way reducible to or dependent upon any bodily function. See above, chapter 1, n. 15. It alone is included under 'thinking' in Descartes's sense. On the locution *mens, sive animus, sive intellectus, sive ratio* in the Second Meditation (AT VII 27: CSM II 18), see sections 9.2 and 13.2 below.

6 Cf. the parallel passage from *The Search for Truth*. Having given the answer 'a man' and then been brought to recognize the obscurity into which the customary Scholastic definition of 'man' might lead him, Polyander explains that he was

speaking at the level of plain common sense when he answered Eudoxus's
question, "what are you – you who have doubts about everything but cannot doubt
that you yourself exist" (AT X 515: CSM II 410). He adds that he "was thinking
about the things we see, touch, perceive with our sense, and experience within
ourselves (*in nobismetipsis experimur*) – in a word, about things which even the
most simple-minded of men (*omnium simplicissimus hominum*) know just as well
as the greatest philosopher in the world. Undoubtedly I am a certain whole made up
of two arms, two legs, one head, and all the other parts which make up what we call
the human body, and which besides is nourished, walks, perceives by the senses
and thinks" (AT X 517: CSM II 412). While this is professedly a report of everyone's ordinary pre-philosophical experience, the point-by-point correspondence
with the Scholastic doctrine of the soul's functions is obvious.

7 On the uses of 'common sense' (*sensus communis*) in Descartes and on *bon sens*
(*bona mens*) as a special case of *sensus communis,* see sections 10.2 and 21.4. The
name 'Eudoxus' was no doubt selected as an echo of *bon sens* in the famous use of
the opening words of the *Discourse.* 'Polyander' ('everyman' or 'many men')
refers to that untutored pre-philosophical *sensus communis* that underlies the
"métaphysique du sensible" (Gilson) of the Scholastics. A third and separate use of
sensus communis, likewise found in Scholastic-Aristotelian philosophy, is docu-
mented in chapter 10, n. 10.

8 See section 21.4. On these two senses of *sensus communis* see previous note. On
the Scholastic-Aristotelian doctrine of the vegetative (nutritive), locomotive, and
sensitive-appetitive functions of the soul, cf. Aristotle 1961 (*de An.,* 413a 23ff. and
414a 32ff.) and Aquinas 1947–8 (*ST,* Ia.78.1). For a recent, illuminating account of
Descartes's redrawing of the boundary between the mental and the physical, see
Cottingham 1992b, the last section.

    The underlying principle of demarcation is set out in the *Passions of the Soul*:
"anything we experience as being in us [as human beings rather than minds], and
which we see can also exist in wholly inanimate bodies, must be attributed only to
our body" (AT XI 329: CSM I 329). This is then immediately applied to bodily
movement. For more on Descartes's identification of mind with that which thinks
and of both with reason, see section 9.2 below.

9 The now standard English translation of Descartes's works by Cottingham,
Stoothoff, and Murdoch renders *cogitare* by forms of the verb 'to think.' This was
already the practice of Haldane and Ross. It was defended by Kenny (1968, chap.
4), who followed it in his translations of Descartes's letters (now vol. III of CSM).
It is preferable to the innovations of Anscombe and Geach. *Conscientia* is usually
translated as 'awareness' by both Cottingham et al. and by Anscombe and Geach.
We shall retranslate it as 'consciousness.'

10 Cf. Radner 1988, 440 n. 5: "Descartes does not say that in having a thought of x I

am conscious of x; rather, he says that in having a thought of x I am conscious of the thought."

11 In the context of the remark to Caterus Descartes is explaining how the Third Meditation proof of God's existence differs from Aquinas's Second Way. The principal difference ("I preferred to use my own existence as the basis of my argument" rather than the infinite "succession of causes" among sensible things used – so Descartes believed – by St Thomas) is clarified in these terms: "in enquiring about what caused me, I was asking about myself, not in so far as I consist of mind and body, but only and precisely in so far as I am a thinking thing. This point is, I think, of considerable relevance. For such a procedure made it much easier for me [1] to free myself from preconceived opinions, [2] to attend to the light of nature, [3] to ask myself questions, and [4] to affirm with certainty that *there can be nothing within me which I am in no way conscious of*" (AT VII 107: CSM II 77 e.a.).

By the "questions" mentioned in [3] Descartes means: 'Can I myself be the cause of the idea of God which I find within me?' and 'Can I derive my existence from myself?' [4] is likewise elliptical, the full sense being: 'this procedure made it much easier to affirm that I am only a thinking and not also a corporeal thing, since I am conscious of nothing corporeal in me and *there can be nothing in me (qua mind) of which I am not conscious.*' So the point of this remark to Caterus is fairly close to that of the Fourth Replies.

Points [1] and [2], preconceived opinions and the natural light, will be touched on below and discussed in detail in sections 10.1 and 10.2.

12 Locke 1977, 36f. (*Essay*, 2.1.10.) Cf. also ibid., 41ff. (2.1.17ff.).

13 Cf. also AT X 524: CSM II 417, where Descartes expands on the same point. The view is clearly expressed as early as the *Regulae* (AT X 426: CSM I 48): "the learned are often inclined to be so clever that they find ways of blinding themselves even to facts which are self-evident and which every peasant knows. That is what happens whenever they try and explain things which are self-evident in terms of something even more evident: what they do is to explain something else or nothing at all." And AT X 442: CSM I 59: "the learned often employ distinctions so subtle that they disperse the natural light, and they detect obscurities even in matters which are perfectly clear to peasants."

14 Cf. the brief but violent diatribe against Scholastic definitions in *The Search for Truth* (AT X 516f.: CSM 410f.). For a helpful discussion of the distinction between real (or "essential") and merely nominal definitions in Descartes (the subject of the next section), see Gewirth 1968, sect. 6.

15 The parallel with ostensive definitions is developed by Descartes himself in *The Search for Truth*: "Thus, it would be pointless trying to define, for someone totally blind, what it is to be white: in order to know what that is, all that is needed is to

have one's eyes open and to see white. In the same way (*ita etiam*) in order to know what doubt and thought are, all one need do is to doubt or to think. That tells us all it is possible to know about them and explains more about them than even the most precise definitions" (AT X 524: CSM II 418). A related analogy between the primary colours entering into the "secondary or mixed colours" and the "simple natures" underlying the complex is drawn in Rule XIV of the *Regulae*.

16 Descartes's notion of a formal cause obviously has little at all to do with the traditional concept. Both causes mentioned here are, though different, at bottom efficient causes. Nevertheless, this is the notion of formal causality that Descartes is prepared to defend. Cf. the lengthy reply to Arnauld's "principal complaint" at AT VII 235ff.: CSM II 164ff. and the comments in chapter 22, n. 25 of the Conclusion on Descartes's "réduction de toutes les causalités à l'unique cause efficiente" (Marion).

17 Chisholm (1960, [4]) describes "intentionality" as *the* criterion of the psychological or mental for Brentano. On the medieval history of the concept *intentio* (chiefly within epistemology and logic), see Knudson 1992. Moreau (1961) traces it from its medieval and early modern sources to Husserl and Sartre.

Descartes's 'definitions' of thought actually focus on a different feature, touched on but left aside as unsuitable by Brentano in the first chapter of Book Two. Even when elaborated along Cartesian lines in the following chapter, this feature ('immediate presence to consciousness') is still not put forward as the criterion of the mental. The reasons for this cannot be gone into here.

7: Thought, Consciousness, and 'the *Cogito*'

1 Cf. also *Principles*, I, 10 (a passage to be interpreted more fully in section 15.2) for a similar distinction between "simple notions ... which on their own provide us with no knowledge of anything that exists" – 'principles' in the first sense – and principles like the *cogito*. On the notion of a principle, cf. the preface to the *Principles* (AT IX-1, 2 and 9: CSM I 177 and 183).

Clarke takes Descartes to be distinguishing here between the "object sense" of 'principle' ("a principle as a thing") and "a principle as a proposition" (1982, 80f.). Röd (1971, 107f.) offers a similar interpretation of the "fundamentale Doppeldeutigkeit von 'Prinzip'" ('Proposition' or 'Natur'), tracing it to the distinction between *principia cognoscendi* and *essendi* in the Aristotelian tradition, particularly Suarez. He sums up (ibid., 109): "Bald bedeutet dieser Terminus [1] einen Grundsatz [i.e., a proposition], bald [2] eine 'Ursache,' wobei dieser Ausdruck ['Ursache'] wiederum einen Doppelsinn aufweist, indem er bald [2a] eine Wirkursache ['efficient cause'], bald [2b] eine einfache Natur ['simple nature'] bedeutet." 2a and 2b correspond to the order of being (real dependence among things) and the order of knowing, respectively. Simple natures and common notions are (2bi) first 'in themselves' within the order of cognition, though not (2bii) first 'for us.' If (1) is further subdivided into (1a) existential propositions and (1b) propositions having no existential import, all uses of *principium* to be met with in Descartes are pretty well covered by this scheme.

In the cited passage from the letter to Clerselier it is the distinction between (1a) and (1b) that is uppermost in Descartes's mind. This is the distinction most pertinent to Scholz's 'Aristotelian question.' Descartes's clearest pronouncement on the subject is found in *The Search for Truth*, where he remarks on certain *cognitiones* ('I exist' and 'I am a thinking thing') "which are *even more certain and more useful* than those which we commonly build upon that great principle, as the basis to which they are all reduced, the fixed point on which they all terminate, namely, 'It is impossible that one and the same thing should exist and at the same time not exist'" (AT X 522: CSM II 416 e.a.). On this, cf. also J.-M. Beyssade 1979, 219 and 222f.

2 Cf., e.g., AT X 420: CSM I 45; AT VII 37: CSM II 26; and AT VII 56ff.: CSM II 39f. In question is formal truth (and falsity): "the falsity to be found in a judgment can only be *formal*" (AT VII 233: CSM II 163). By contrast, that found in ideas can only be *material*. Cf. ibid: "as far as ideas are concerned, provided they are considered solely in themselves and I do not refer them to anything else [in judgments], they cannot *strictly speaking* be false" (e.a.), i.e., they cannot be formally false. The distinction of formal and material truth and falsity is discussed at VII 43ff.: CSM II 30f. and VII 232ff.: CSM II 162ff. Cf. also Arnauld's interesting remarks at AT VII 206f.: CSM II 145f. The passage at AT VII 151: CSM II 107, on the other hand, is not relevant: "Although materially true, this argument is formally a sophism." Here neither ideas nor judgments but arguments are in question; 'materially true' accordingly means 'having true premises' as opposed to being logically valid. (The argument under examination involves, Descartes argues, an equivocation.) On "the perplexing concept of material falsity" (Wilson 1978a, 100), see Wells 1984, Normore 1986, and Menn 1995 198ff. for some of the Scholastic background, as well as Gewirth 1968, sect. 4, Ashworth 1972, 94, and Wilson's later analysis (1990).

3 Thus, (taking the *cogito* principle as an example) in Part Four of the *Discourse* Descartes writes: "cette vérité: *Je pense, donc je suis* ..." (AT VI 32: CSM I 127) and in the Second Meditation: "*hoc pronuntiatum*, Ego sum, ego existo ..." (AT VII 25: CSM II 17). In the letter to Silhon of March or April 1648 we read: "*hanc propositionem*, Je pense, donc je suis ..." (AT V 137f.: CSMK 331) and in *Principles*, I, 10: "*hanc propositionem*, ego cogito, ergo sum ..." And yet in the Second Meditation Descartes writes of the *deus malignus*: "let him deceive as much as he can, he will never bring it about that I am nothing so long as (*quandiu*) I think that I

424 Notes to pages 69–70

am something" (AT VII 25: CSM II 17). In the same place, he attaches the temporal proviso *quoties a me profertur vel mente concipitur* to "I am, I exist." In question here is thus the certainty of what is judged *while I am actually judging it*. So too in *Principles*, I, 49: "*Is qui cogitat, non potest non existere dum cogitat*." The other passages, therefore, are elliptical, the same proviso being understood. For more on the temporal proviso, see section 11.7.

4 Cf. the *Comments on a Certain Broadsheet* (AT VIII-2, 363: CSM I 307): "over and above perception, which is a prerequisite of judgement, we need affirmation and negation to determine the form of the judgement ... Hence I assigned the act of judging itself, which consists simply in assenting (i.e., in affirmation or denial) to the determination of the will rather than to the perception of the intellect." Also AT IX-1 204: CSM II 270: "a judgement is an act of will."

On the significance of this as a departure from the Thomistic conception of judgment as an act of the intellect, cf. Maritain 1937, sect. III.

5 Cf. *Principles*, I, 11 (AT VIII-1 8: CSM I 196): "the more attributes we discover in the same thing or substance, the clearer (*clarius*) is our knowledge of that substance." Also AT VII 147: CSM II 105: "Whenever we call a conception obscure or confused, this is because it contains something of which we are ignorant (*quod est ignotum*).

6 The complete awareness of everything belonging to a "simple nature" is, of course, a very different matter from grasping the remoter truths that can be demonstrated of it with the help of axioms or common notions; and it is different, too, from a completely adequate understanding of it such as only God can possess. Thus, just as the complete idea that the mathematical novice possesses falls far short of the idea of a triangle possessed by the geometer, so this in turn falls short of the perfectly adequate idea of the triangle in the mind of God. As with mathematical ideas like 'triangle,' 'square,' and 'circle,' so with simple metaphysical ideas like 'mind' and 'body.' On completeness and adequacy, see the First Replies (AT VII 113: CSM II 81), the Fourth Replies (AT VII 220ff.: CSM II 155ff.), Gewirth 1968, sect. 5, and section 10.8 below.

7 Gewirth (1968, 260) treats clarity, too, as having to do with judgment rather than simple consciousness, i.e., with the relation between the "direct [content] and interpretive content" (ibid., 264) of ideas. Consequently, there is for him only a single mark of distinctness: "an idea is clear if its direct content ... includes all that which is included in the interpretation ... and distinct if the direct content includes nothing other than this." This interpretation of distinctness corresponds to our condition (2) alone. The further distinction Gewirth employs, between the "explicit and implicit" (ibid.) contents of thinking, has to do with attention and hence both with clarity on the one hand and our condition (1) of distinctness on the other. Thus, all the elements of the present interpretation are present in Gewirth, who however puts them together differently.

Ashworth (1972, 97) distinguishes two kinds of clear ideas: ordinary empirical concepts like 'dog,' 'cat,' and 'table' are clear when we attend to them, while innate ideas (or 'pure concepts') like 'God,' 'thought,' and 'extension' are "clear even when not actually perceived or reflected upon." But while the latter are indeed always latent in our thinking according to Descartes (cf. chapters 9 and 18 below), they can only be made clear through a degree of attention and distinct through judgments that are strictly confined to what such reflexive attention discloses. For Descartes himself, then, the distinction between these two kinds of concepts – the empirical and the pure – is that between (1) ideas that are partially clear but incomplete and so capable of only a limited degree of distinctness, and (2) those complete ideas that are capable of being made entirely clear and maximally distinct. On completeness, see sect. 10.8.

8 Cf. *Principles*, I, 63 (AT VIII-1 31: CSM I 215): "A concept is not any more distinct because we include less in it; its distinctness simply depends on our carefully distinguishing [in our judgments] what we do include in it from everything else."

9 Cf. AT VII 368: CSM II 254: "we do not doubt that a novice at geometry has an idea of a whole triangle when he understands that it is a figure bounded by three lines."

10 Cf. AT VII 147: CSM II 105: "Whenever we call a conception obscure or confused, this is because it contains some element of which we are ignorant (*aliquid ... quod est ignotum*)." Only when clear *and* distinct is a judgment about one's own mental states strictly "incorrigible"; judgments about one's mental states are not eo ipso distinct. See above chapter 4, n.6 on the "incorrigibility thesis" and Radner 1988, 443f. for some different versions of it.

11 At a later stage of this study the terms 'explicitation' and 'precisification' will be used – owing to their awkwardness, sparingly – for the complementary 'actions' of attending to all (explicitation) and only (precisification) that which is immediately present to consciousness. Cf. section 13.4. The two are quite sharply distinguished in the penultimate sentence of the Fourth Meditation: "For I shall unquestionably reach the truth, if only I [1] give sufficient attention to all the things which I perfectly [i.e., clearly] understand, and [2] separate these from all the other cases where my apprehension is more confused and obscure" (AT VII 62: CSM II 43). The English 'unfold' (used in the epigraph to Part Three) translates the Latin *explicare* both literally and pleasingly, but without perhaps bringing out sufficiently the idea of 'rendering explicit.'

12 Cf. also AT VII 182f.: CSM II 128: "It is self-evident that seeing a lion and at the same time being afraid of it is different from simply seeing it. And seeing a man run is different from silently affirming to oneself [i.e., judging in thought] that one sees him." The difference between seeing and fearing or seeing and judging is perfectly evident to anyone who performs these acts.

13 Cf. also AT VII 236: CSM II 165: "since the inexhaustible power or immensity of the divine essence is as *positive* as can be ..." For this reason "the idea that I have of God [is] *the truest* and most clear and distinct of all my ideas" (AT VII 46: CSM II 32), regardless of God's existence. Having proved God's existence in the Third, Descartes begins the Fourth Meditation: "I have taken careful note of the fact that there is very little about corporeal things that is truly perceived, whereas much more is known about the human mind, and *still more* about God" (AT VII 52f.: CSM II 37 e.a.). This would appear to be a reference to the maximally positive nature of the idea of God's nature. However, Descartes is not perfectly consistent on this point. See chapter 3, n. 27.

Arnauld takes Descartes's point perfectly: "though I can pretend that such a being [God] does not exist, I cannot pretend that the idea of such a being does not represent anything real to me" (AT VII 206f.: CSM II 145). To represent something real or positive is to represent it as possible – as at least capable of existing in reality. Cf. Wilson (1978a, 107f.): "In fact, when Descartes asks whether or not his ideas are of 'certain things' [cf. *rerum quarundam ideae* at AT VII 43: CSM II 30] he is *not* raising the question whether they represent to him entities that actually exist. For he indicates very explicitly ... that what represents *res* and what does not, depends on a concept of reality that is not equivalent to existence ... [W]hen Descartes asks whether an idea represents something real, or *rem*, he is asking whether or not ... it gives him cognizance of a *possible* existent." More succinctly still, Normore (1986, 227): "While having reality does not entail existing it does entail possibly existing." Cf. the 'axiom' or 'common notion' in the *more geometrico* demonstrations of the Second Replies, to be interpreted more fully in sect. 10.7: "Existence is contained in the idea or concept of every single thing, since we cannot conceive of anything except as existing. Possible or contingent existence is contained in the concept of a limited thing, whereas necessary and perfect existence is contained in the concept of a supremely perfect being" (AT VII 166: CSM II 117). Also the First Replies: "even though our understanding of other things [than God] always involves understanding them as if they were existing things, it does not follow that they do exist, but merely that they are capable of existing" (AT VII 117: CSM II 83).

14 The words 'in the *Meditations*' are important, since Descartes's teaching in this regard seems to have undergone important changes in the *Principles*. See Wilson 1978a, chapt. III, 2: "Material falsity and objective reality." Also Wilson 1990.

15 Cf. Wilson 1978a, 102: "when Descartes speaks of ideas being '*tanquam rerum imagines*' he does *not* mean that every idea involves a mental picture with *visual* properties: an idea, in other words, can purport to bring something into cognitive ken without purporting to represent it visually. (In fact ... it need not purport to represent the thing via *any* sensory modality.)" Also Heidegger 1994, 132:

"Descartes charakerisiert den Begriff der cogitatio so, daß er ungefähr mit dem heute in der Phänomenologie gebrauchten Begriff des *intentionalen Erlebnisses* zusammenfällt."

16 Tlumak (1978, 40f.) makes a similar point when he speaks of Descartes's "representational theory of external consciousness and non-representational theory of internal consciousness." Later in the same paper he notes: "We do not represent representatives; representations are presented to us" (65). This seems precisely right. Markie, on the other hand, misses the point entirely: "His [Descartes's] general position seems to be that we think of substances by grasping ideas of them, and he never indicates that his thoughts about himself are an exception" (1992, 163). And: "He [Descartes] seems committed to the view that he thinks of himself by conceiving some concept of himself" (165). This is true of reflexive, but not of that pre-reflexive self-awareness (*conscientia*) that makes *reflexio* possible.

17 A standard reference whenever this first objection is raised (cf., e.g., Cottingham [CB, 84f.] and Kenny 1968, 58ff.) is Russell 1945b, 567: "the word 'I' is really illegitimate; [Descartes] ought to state his ultimate premiss in the form 'there are thoughts.' The word 'I' is grammatically convenient, but does not describe a datum." For an interesting discussion of Russell on the *cogito* principle, cf. Imlay 1985, sect. I.

Compare Hume's classic observation (1967, 252): "For my part, when I enter most intimately into what I call *myself*, I always stumble on some particular perception or other, of heat or cold, light or shade, love or hatred, pain or pleasure. I never can catch *myself* at any time without a perception, and never can observe any thing but the perception." Cf. also Scholz's "Kantian question" as described at the beginning of chapter 1.

18 Gassendi fails to understand that 'thing' (*res*) and 'substance' (*substantia*) are usually synonymous in Descartes, taking *res* to be roughly synonymous with *ens* (cf. AT VII 281: CSM 196) and opposite in meaning to *non res* (or *non ens*), i.e., nothing: "to say first of all that you are a 'thing' is not to give any information. This is a general, imprecise and vague word which applies no more to you than it does to anything in the entire world that is not simply a nothing. You are a 'thing'; that is, you are not nothing, or, what comes to the same thing, you are something. But a stone is something and not nothing, and so is a fly, and so is everything else" (AT VII 276: CSM II 192f.). Given Descartes's novel employment of 'thing' as a synonym for 'substance' this seems entirely beside the point. However, Descartes continues to use *res* in the manner described by Gassendi (see previous section) as well.

The synonymy of *res* and *substance* extends even to their adjectival forms. Thus, Descartes consistently misinterprets that talk of 'real accidents' as implying that these so-called accidents are in fact conceived as substances. Cf., e.g., AT VII 364:

428 Notes to pages 78–9

CSM II 251 and AT VII 417: CSM II 281 for two instances of this ubiquitous confusion. For a much fuller account, cf. Gilson 1951, pt. II, chap. 1.

19 It is presumably with reference to the preceding objections by Hobbes and Gassendi that the authors of the Sixth Objections write: "For no one [among the previous objectors (?)] has yet been able to grasp that demonstration of yours by which you think you have proved that what you call thought cannot be a kind of corporeal motion" (AT VII 412: CSM II 278). Descartes's reply to this "appeal to authority" (AT VII 424: CSM II 286) is interesting for its bearing on the reference to "detaching the mind from the senses" in the "Synopsis" (cf. below, chapter 10 *in initio* and sections 10.1f.): "My reply is that I am very certain of this point, but I cannot guarantee that others can be convinced of it, however attentive they may be. I cannot guarantee that they will be persuaded, at least so long as they focus their attention not on things which are objects of *pure understanding* but only on things which can be *imagined*. This mistake has obviously been made by those who have *imagined* that the distinction between thought and motion is to be understood by making divisions within some kind of rarefied matter" (AT VII 425: CSM II 287 e.a.).

For a recent endorsement of this perennial criticism of Descartes, see Cottingham 1992b, the section entitled "The Recurring Fallacy." A rebuttal of Cottingham's critique is attempted in section 13.4 below.

20 Cf. Descartes's response: "Nor do I see what more you expect here, unless it is to be told what colour or smell or taste the human mind has, or the proportions of salt, sulphur and mercury from which it is compounded" (AT VII 359: CSM II 248).

21 Cottingham, Stoothoff, and Murdoch translate *istud nescio quid mei*: "this puzzling 'I'."

22 Locke 1977, 295ff. (*Essay*, 2.23.2) e.a. Also ibid., 86 (*Essay*, 2.13.19): "They who first ran into the notion of *accidents*, as a sort of real beings that needed something to inhere in, were forced to find out the word *substance* to support them. Had the poor *Indian* philosopher (who imagined that the earth also wanted something to bear it up) but thought of this word *substance*, he needed not to have been at the trouble to find an elephant to support it, and a tortoise to support his elephant: the word *substance* would have done it effectually. And he that enquired might have taken it for as good an answer from an *Indian* philosopher that *substance*, without knowing what it is, is that which supports the earth, as we take it for a sufficient answer and good doctrine from our *European* philosophers that *substance*, without knowing what it is, *is that which supports* accidents." Cf. ibid., 305 (*Essay*, 2.23.15) "our *Idea* of Substance, is equally obscure, or none at all, in both [bodies and minds]; it is but a supposed, *I know not what*, to support those *Ideas*, we call Accidents" (e.a.).

While all Berkeley's irony is directed against the notion of corporeal substance,

Hume follows Locke in treating corporeal and mental substance alike: "The mind is not a substance, in which the perceptions inhere ... We have no idea of substance of any kind, since we have no idea but what is derived from some impression, and we have no impression of any substance either material or spiritual. We know nothing but particular qualities and perceptions. As our idea of any body, a peach, for instance, is only that of a particular taste, colour, figure, size, consistence, etc.; so our idea of any mind is only that of particular perceptions, without the notion of anything we call substance" (Hume 1990, 39f.; cf. also 1967, 252f.). Interestingly, Kant remarks (with no less confidence): "if we remove from our empirical concept of any object, corporeal or incorporeal, all properties which experience has taught us, we yet cannot take away that property through which the object is thought as a substance or as inhering in a substance ... Owing, therefore, to the necessity with which this concept of substance forces itself upon us, we have no option save to admit that it has its seat in our faculty of *a priori* knowledge" (Kant 1929, B6). This may well strike one as bravado in the face of the criticisms of Locke et al.

It is Descartes who first made 'incorporeal substance' the concept of a *nescio quid*, later interpreting corporeal substance in a parallel way. He thus laid the very concept of substance open to the scathing attacks that are still the stock-in-trade of anti-metaphysicians. Once divorced from the notion of a substantial form or nature, from the potentiality-actuality dichotomy, and the distinction of formal from efficient causality, the concept of substance either ceases to do any ontological 'work' or is assigned the curious role of an internal *efficient* cause. In the first case, it becomes superfluous and can be relegated to the scrap heap along with the accidental forms of Scholastic natural philosophy and metaphysics; in the latter, it can easily be shown to be 'occult.' It goes (one hopes) almost without saying that none of these strictures has the slightest force against the original Aristotelian or the later Scholastic use of 'substance.'

23 While a positive hindrance to the clear and distinct perception of "intellectual things," the imagination nevertheless has a very important role to play in the clear and distinct perception of "material things." Cf., e.g., Rule XIV of the *Regulae* (AT X 441ff.: CSM 58f.) and the discussion in section 20.3.

Compare with the passage from the Second Meditation just cited the rather different account of the same absurdity in the *Discourse*: "It seems to me that trying to use one's imagination in order to understand these ideas ['God' and 'the soul'] is like trying to use one's eyes in order to hear sounds or smell odours" (AT VI 37: CSM I 129).

24 On Gassendi's empiricism, see AT VII 280: CSM II 195 and AT VII 310: CSM II 216.

25 Kenny (1968, 185) is one of those who retreat from the interpretation altogether: "The propositions never called into question in Descartes's system are those that

report the contents of the mind, those that express the consciousness of its own thoughts and ideas." Thus, the premise *cogito* is certain in a way that *sum* (the assertion of the existence of a substance) is not. Against this Wilson rightly observes (1978a, 67): "if the *cogito* is to work at all, we must take 'I think' (and not merely 'there (or here) is thought') as its starting point. And perhaps if it is possible to treat the subjective unity of thought as a datum, 'I think' may be as justifiable a starting point as 'there is thought.'" What tells against the immediate givenness of the 'I,' she believes, are Descartes's remarks about knowing subjects only through their attributes. She concludes that "there is an irreconcilable conflict in Descartes's position as to whether 'I' expresses a datum or refers to an entity known only by inference" (ibid.). On the view taken here it is unquestionably a datum of sorts; on the other hand, the presence of the *ergo* implies that some sort of inference is involved. Is this an "irreconcilable conflict"? Not in the least. See chapter 17.

26 Cf. AT IX-1 206: CSM II 271: "The third objection [meant is the third of Gassendi's so-called counter-objections] ... is that thought cannot exist without an object, e.g. body. Here we must avoid the ambiguity in the word 'thought,' which can be taken to apply both to the thing which thinks [i.e., the mind or intellect] and also to the activity performed by that thing [its acts]. Now I deny that the thing which thinks needs any object apart from itself in order to exercise its activity (though it may also extend the scope of this activity to material things when it examines them)." This would be Descartes's reply to Furth as well.

27 For indications to the contrary, see the passages to be interpreted in section 8.4, "Some textual difficulties."

28 Curley (1975, 174) writes: "Though having an idea ... is always having an idea that something is so, it is also always appropriate to paraphrase this by saying that when we have an idea that *p*, then it seems to us that *p*. And it is quite possible for it to seem to us that *p* without our judging that *p*. We can withhold our judgement." While this establishes correctly that the term 'idea' may include what we should call 'propositions,' it nevertheless strays from Descartes's own use of 'it seems to me that' in the Second Meditation.

Curley mentions three things: (1) having the idea that *p*, which is an act of the intellect, and two different operations involving the will: (2) forthright assertion that *p* and (3) suspension of judgment as to whether *p*. Now the locution 'it seems to me that *p*' is supposed to be equivalent to (1), having an idea. But what Descartes has in mind when he writes "I see, or I think I see (I am not here distinguishing the two)" is not the difference between having the idea that *p*, i.e., perception, and a corresponding judgment (or act of suspending judgment). Nor is it the difference between two different propositional attitudes toward one and the same extra-mental state of affairs (forthright assertion on the one hand, cautious assertion on the other). It is rather *two altogether different assertions or judgments*, one about an extra-mental state of affairs, the other about one's own mental state of perceiving. "I see, or I think I see (I am not here distinguishing the two)" expresses the act of *judging that one is in a certain mental state*, a type of judgment not even mentioned by Curley. (Curley revises his position on statements of the form 'it seems to me that *p*' in 1978 190ff.)

29 Cottingham (1978b, 210) apparently holds a similar view: "though it is sometimes claimed that 'any conscious process will do as a premise for the *cogito*,' this seems inconsistent with Descartes's method. 'I want' is not indubitable in the sense in which 'I think' or 'I doubt' are ... the 'thinking being' of whose existence Descartes is apprised as his first step out of the morass of doubt is precisely that – a being that thinks, in the ordinary, strictly cognitive sense."

30 So already Frankfurt 1966, 343f., followed by Curley 1978, 75f., and Cottingham 1986, 39 (just to cite a few examples).

31 Thus, Spinoza's substitution (1994, 116 [EIIA2]), "Man thinks (*Homo cogitat*)," is no equivalent of Descartes's *cogito*. The gloss "or, to put it differently, we know that we think" in the Dutch translation (ibid.) is a slight improvement since 'we think (you and I)' at least entails 'I think.' However, construed as a conjunctive proposition, 'I think *and* he thinks' or 'I think *and* you think,' '*we* think' still lacks in one part of what it asserts the very thing that renders the other part absolutely certain: immediate presence to consciousness of the very mode of thinking asserted to exist.

32 Frankfurt (1966, 334) argues that the closest thing to the *cogito, ergo sum* to be found in the Second Meditation (roughly, 'I thought, therefore I existed') does not alter the significance of Descartes's principle "in any substantial way." But as he himself recognizes (cf. ibid., 346) 'I thought (in the past), therefore I exist (now)' *would* involve a crucial alteration. This no doubt has some bearing on the question of the reliability of memory, since thought about one's past mental states is – oddly – thought about an extra-mental object for Descartes, 'the mental' in the relevant sense being coextensive with thinking that is now actually occurring or the immediate object of consciousness. Cf. J.-M. Beyssade 1979, 155: "Sans doute le sujet de la *Seconde Méditation* est-il un sujet momentané, sinon instantané, et les modalités temporelles du passé ou de l'avenir restent-elles en dehors de la première certitude."

33 Cf. AT VII 172: CSM II 122; AT VII 352: CSM II 244; VIII-1 7: CSM II 194f.; AT II 37f.: CSMK 98.

34 Alternatively, (c) and (d) could be collapsed into a single statement-type: statements about material things, whether my own body, including my brain (c), or other bodies (d).

35 Cf. Putnam 1980, 115: "one can have a 'pink elephant hallucination,' but one cannot have a 'pain hallucination,' or an 'absence of pain hallucination,' simply

because any situation that a person cannot discriminate from a situation in which he himself has a pain *counts* as a situation in which he has a pain, whereas a situation that a person cannot distinguish from one in which a pink elephant is present does not necessarily *count* as the presence of a pink elephant." The phenomenological reduction restores the missing parity. Henceforth being in a mental state which *to me* is in all respects perfectly indistinguishable from the state describable as 'perceiving a piece of wax' simply *counts* as perceiving the wax in the phenomenologically reduced sense.

36 Of course, appearance talk can be misleading. Gassendi may have had in mind cautious as opposed to forthright judgments about extra-mental realities, whereas Descartes's locution, 'it appears to me that x,' stands for judgments, not about x, but about actually occurring mental states of perceiving, believing, judging, etc. that x (cf. n. 28 above).

For an interpretation of the *cogito* in appearance-reality terms that goes seriously astray, see Henry 1993 and Marion's enthusiastic endorsement (1993, 60): "With the aid of a dazzling analysis of an enigmatic Cartesian formula – 'Yet I certainly *seem* to see, to hear, and to be warmed' (AT VII 29, ll. 14–15: CSM II 19) – Michel Henry seeks to carry out a hermeneutic of Descartes's *cogito, ergo sum* that is nonreflexive because nonintentional, relying on the principle that 'Cartesianism is a phenomenology ... a material phenomenology."

On the *alleged* "aporias of interpretations of the *cogito, ergo sum* in terms of intentionality and representation," see the first section of Marion's essay (entitled "The *Ego Cogito, Ergo Sum* as the 'Transcendental Spectator'). Marion's textual grounds for rejecting the intentional interpretation pioneered by Husserl and Heidegger are mentioned briefly in the next chapter (n. 2); the architect-simile in the passage invoked as evidence by Marion is interpreted in a very different way in section 15.4. The question, whether the *ego* of Descartes's founding principle is empirical or pure (transcendental) will be discussed in sections 9.3 and 9.4.

37 Toward the end of the Fifth Meditation, Descartes speaks of the *regula generalis* (AT VII 35: CSM II 24) first formulated in the Third ("whatever I perceive very clearly and distinctly is true") as a *regula veritatis* (AT VII 70). Cottingham et al. translate with the phrase: "a rule for establishing the truth" (CSM II 110). Following the practice of a number of recent writers (e.g., Bennett and Loeb), we shall refer to it as 'the truth rule' throughout the present work.

38 Cf. AT V 146: CSMK 332 (and the interpretation in section 11.8 below) on the opposition between *a sensibus* and *per sensus*. Heidegger (1994, 233, 235) misinterprets the latter to mean: "unter Mitbeteiligung der sinnlichen Wahrnehmung" – a reference to "die mathematischen und geometrischen Wahrheiten, sofern sie auf Anschauungen bezogen sind."

39 These varieties of true propositions will be discussed in section 12.6.

8: The Structure of Thought

1 To be strictly accurate this needs to be qualified slightly. All acts in Husserl's sense are psychic experiences (*Erlebnisse*), namely *intentionally structured* experiences; certain psychic experiences, however – for example, *Empfindungen* or sense-data – are not themselves acts, but constituents of acts, and consequently intentionally directed upon objects only thanks to the intentional experiences that they go to make up. Cf. Husserl 1970, Investigation V, chap. 2, sect. 10. After the *Logical Investigations* Husserl modified this concept. Also Heidegger 1994, 55.

2 Marion's polemic against this interpretation of the *cogito* (1993, 58f.; cf. also 1981a, 391, n. 32) is vitiated by his failure to distinguish sharply between simple (pre-reflexive) consciousness and reflexion itself. In this he was preceded by his teacher, Alquié (cf. Alquié 1950, 187ff. and Marion 1993, n. 16). Both are on solid ground in rejecting a "redoublement réfléxif" within the *cogito*, i.e., any suggestion of "une opération réfléxive, séparant pensée pensante et pensée pensée" (Alquié, 1950, 189); for this involves taking thought as an object (of a second-order act of *thinking* rather than of consciousness) *over and above* the object ordinarily so called. Faced with the danger of such a 'reduplication' it is perfectly in order to insist on "une présence si intime de la conscience à elle-même que nulle réflexion, nul doute, nulle séparation, nulle subtilité logique ne sauraient, contre elle, prévaloir" (ibid.). But this non-representational being-immediately-present-to-consciousness of representational thinking (*conscientia cogitationis*) is itself 'reflexive,' namely *pre*-reflexive, the condition of the possibility of reflexion in acts of attention and of second- and higher-order acts of thinking about thinking. J.-M. Beyssade, too, muddies the waters through failure to distinguish sharply between thought and consciousness, i.e., between what is represented by the former and present to the latter. Cf., e.g., 1979, 248.

   As will be seen later (cf. section 20.2), Descartes sometimes uses *experior* and its cognates, especially *experiri apud se*, as a synonym for *conscium esse*. The closest he comes to the actual notation proposed here is perhaps this: "We cannot fail constantly to experience in ourselves that we are thinking (*non potest quin semper apud nosmetipsos experiamur nos cogitare*)" (AT VII 427: CSM II 288). Marion (1981b, n. 45) proposes a few other candidate passages.

3 In one important sense, 'idea' is simply (1) synonymous with 'thought' in Descartes. In another, an 'idea' is (2) an abstract 'moment' of a thought, its objective reality. In what we have termed the 'strict' sense, ideas are neither synonymous with thoughts nor abstract moments of thoughts but (3) a subclass of thoughts: the representational among them, e.g., the idea of "a man, or a chimera, or the sky, or an angel, or God" (AT VII 37: CSM II 25), which Descartes describes

434 Notes to page 89

(in view of their representational character) as *tanquam rerum imagines*. On these
and other senses of 'idea,' cf. section 16.1ff.

4 As far as the distinction between act and intentional object goes, witness the
testimony of Heidegger (1994, 309): "Descartes sagt, in der clara et distincta
perceptio sind absolut evident gegeben 1. die cogitationes und 2. die ideae. – Dies
ist der Ursprung der Bestimmung Husserls, daß im Umkreis des Bewußtseins (als
Bereich gefaßt) evident gegeben sind: 1. *Akte*, das Noetische, die Noesis, and 2. das
in den Akten selbst Gemeinte, die Noemata; sie sind die ideae im Sinne Descartes'.
Das Noetische sind die cogitationes qua operationes mentis."

5 As for the exception mentioned above, Descartes himself resorts to talk of two
objects in *The Search for Truth*: "Thus, I can state that as soon as I began to doubt,
I began to have knowledge which was certain. But my doubt and my certainty did
not relate to the same objects (*non ad eadem objecta mea dubitatio, meaque
certitudo referebantur*): my doubt applied only to things which existed outside me,
whereas my certainty related to myself and my doubting (*mea dubitatio circa eas
tantum versabatur res, quae extra me existebant; certitudo vero meam
dubitationem, meque ipsum, spectabat*" (AT X 525: CSM II 418).

Compare to these two senses of 'object' Husserl's discussion in the *Logical
Investigations* of a related equivocation in appearance talk: "We cannot too sharply
stress the equivocation which allows us to use the word *'appearance' both of the
experience in which the object's appearing consists* (the concrete perceptual
experience, in which the object itself seems present to us) and of *the object which
appears as such*" (Husserl 1970, II, 538). Things, for Husserl, appear. Their
'appearings' are 'experienced' (*erlebt, Erlebnisse*, 'lived through'); the appearings
do not themselves appear; nor are the things experienced, except in a loose,
improper sense, e.g., I 'experienced' the Franco-Prussian war of 1870–1 – to take
Husserl's example. But, of course, I cannot have 'experienced' in the strict and
proper sense a war or anything else that did not actually take place within my own
'stream of consciousness.'

It was on the strength of this distinction between what appears and what is 'lived
through' as an actually occurring experience that Husserl rejected the representationalist notion of two objects of perceptual consciousness: the act itself (first
object) and the object of the act (second object). Descartes obviously pioneered
Husserl's distinction by elaborating the basic difference between consciousness that
presents and acts that represent. Husserl, it appears, took this over indirectly, via
Brentano, who developed insights found earlier in Kant and Descartes. Cf. Moreau
1961.

With Husserl's remarks, compare Henry's turgid commentary on Descartes's
concept of thought (1993, 44): "Thoughts belong to appearing; they are its
crystallizations; it is here that they differ fundamentally from bodies, that is, from

being. But appearing appears only insofar as it appears to itself." What is being said here may be correct, but this way of putting it is surely unhelpful.

6 Cf. AT VII 518: CSM II 353: "For the premise ["I know for certain that no mountain exists without a valley"] ... implies that I clearly and distinctly perceive that no mountain exists without a valley, not that I have a concept of a mountain without a valley. Since *there is no such concept*, we do not have to possess it in order to perceive that no mountain exists without a valley" (e.a.).

7 To quote it once more: "whenever I express something in words, and understand what I am saying, this very fact makes it certain that there is within me an idea of what is signified by the words in question. Thus, it is not only the images depicted in the imagination that I call 'ideas'" (AT VII 160: CSM II 113).

8 Cf. Ishiguro (1987b, 378): "no thoughts which contain ideas that are contradictories of one another can be instantiated – ... they are not thoughts of anything, they are impossiblities. It is absolutely impossible that a contradiction be instantiated, and so the ideas made up of contradictory elements are not coherent ideas."
Her point seems to be that while they *are* ideas they are not ideas *of* anything. On the view taken here they are thoughts (ongoings in the mind and hence 'ideas' in the broadest sense only) but not ideas in the strict sense *because* they are not *of* anything. Or rather they are not ideas *in the human mind*; only God can frame such ideas.

For some interesting reflexions, pertinent to this section as a whole, on just how far Husserl had strayed from his original Cartesian orientation by the time of the *Cartesian Meditations* (1929), see Carr 1973–4.

9 On the fundamental differences in starting point and goal separating Descartes's from Husserl's reductive method, see Heidegger 1994, §46, Husserl 1960, von Herrmann 1971, sect. II, and section 9.3 below.

10 Cf. section 16.4 on Hoenen. Menn (1993) and Wells (1993) may be suspected of falling into anachronism of this kind. Cf. Menn, ibid., sections III and IV, on the Augustinian background of (a) Descartes's conception of God and (b) its employment as "the universal first principle of the sciences" (539); and Wells on the late-Scholastic antecedents of Descartes's concept of 'idea' taken formally and materially.

11 Citing the first passage in a footnote, J.-M. Beyssade (1979, 234) remarks that "pensée est identifié à perception et à conscience." Radner (1988, 440), too, cites this passage as telling against a sharp distinction between *cogitatio* and *conscientia*.

12 As *sive* does, notoriously, in Spinoza, and not infrequently in Descartes. Cf., e.g., the famous formulation: *sum igitur precise tantum res cogitans, id est, mens, sive animus, sive intellectus, sive ratio* (AT VII 27: CSM II 18), to be interpreted in sections 9.2 and 13.2 below.

13 See *Principles*, I, 32 and *Passions of the Soul*, I, 17.

14 The passage will be interpreted in detail in section 9.2. To quote it in part at least:
"He [Fromondus] supposes that I think that animals see just as we do, i.e. being
aware or thinking they see (*sentiendo sive cogitando se videre*) ... I explain quite
explicitly that my view is that animals do not see as we do when we are aware that
we see (*dum sentimus nos videre*), but only as we do when our mind is elsewhere.
In such a case the images of external objects are depicted on our retinas, and
perhaps the impressions they make in the optic nerves cause our limbs to make
various movements, although we are quite unaware of them (*nihil tamen prorsus
eorum sentimus*)" (AT I 413f.: CSMK 61f.).

All this evidence tells against an everywhere carefully observed terminological
distinction; but a terminological distinction there is, nonetheless, and it is vital,
from a philosophical perspective, to tighten up Descartes's sometimes lax usage.

9: Pure and Empirical Thought

1 Cf. Owens 1993a, 108: "The Platonic Ideas, as Aristotle saw them, were reached
from sensible things with the added note of eternal duration. For Plato himself they
existed in natural reality and not just in human thought. *Neo-Platonic commentators did distinguish intellectual knowledge as coming from within, in contrast with
sensation that came from without*" (e.a.).
2 The ideas are "usually" juxtaposed as 'innate' and 'adventitious' because in one
work (*Comments on a Certain Broadsheet*) Descartes suggests that even the latter,
indeed all ideas, are innate. On the anomaly, see, e.g., Edgley (1970, 6), McRae
(1972a, 51), O'Neill (1974, 76ff.), and Brown (1980, n. 34). McRae's work will be
discussed in detail in the treatment of Descartes's concept of innateness in chapter
18 below. For a fuller elaboration of the Lockean (at bottom, Platonic-Stoic-
Ciceronian) concept of innateness, see chapter 19, n. 16.
3 Cf. Price 1992, 169: "The act of human thinking [*ratiocinare* and *intelligere*) shares
[for Albertus Magnus] in the activity of separate substances, namely knowledge of
self (*se intelligere*)." This complete *reditio in se ipsum* of *substantiae intellectuales*
is developed by Aquinas in *de Veritate* (1953, 18 [*QDV*, 1.9]), who invokes the
Liber de Causis (and hence Aristotle) as source. Thomas distinguishes between the
degrees to which *sensus* and *intellectus* involve *reditio*. On this, cf. Heidegger
1994, 251.
4 Note the echo of Anselm's notion of 'something than which nothing greater can be
conceived' in the words: "It is only the will, or freedom of choice, which I experience within me to be so great that the idea of any greater faculty is beyond my
grasp" (AT VII 57: CSM II 40). Descartes is speaking of the unrestricted *scope* of
the will (AT VII 58: CSM II 40), i.e., its sheer inability to withhold assent to what it
perceives clearly and distinctly (liberty of spontaneity) as well as its ability to

withhold assent from all else (liberty of indifference). Both make the finite will of man relatively perfect, i.e., perfect "when considered in itself" (ibid.), though such freedom is different in kind from the absolute perfection of God's infinite will, i.e., his perfect liberty of indifference (which is simply the same as his perfect knowledge) in respect of *everything*.

5 Cf. AT VII 25: CSM II 17 and AT VII 578: CSM II 390. For present purposes we may leave aside the famous passage on "the difference between our soul and that of the beasts" (AT VI 1: CSM I 111) in Part Five of the *Discourse*, which provides empirical support for the claim that human reason cannot be explained by the functioning of bodily organs in the way that sensation and all the vital functions of animals can. On this see Cottingham 1992b, the final section. More to the present point is the subsequent paragraph in which Descartes argues "not merely that the beasts have less reason than men, but that they have no reason at all," i.e., "that they have no intelligence at all, and that it is nature which acts in them according to the disposition of their organs. In the same way," he concludes, "a clock, consisting only of wheels and springs, can count the hours and measure time more accurately than we can with all our wisdom" (AT VI 58f.: CSM I 140f.).

6 On the Scholastic definition, see, along with AT VII 25: CSM II 17, *The Search for Truth*, AT X 517: CSM II 411f.

7 Cf. also AT VII 426: CSM II 287f.: "But in fact the brutes possess no thought whatsoever ... Yet those who assert, as if they were present in the animals' hearts, that 'dogs when awake know that they are running, and in their dreams know that they are barking,' are simply saying something without proving it. My critics go on to say that they do not believe that the ways in which beasts operate can be explained 'by means of mechanics without invoking any sensation, life or soul' (I take this to mean 'without invoking thought'; for I accept that the brutes have what is commonly called 'life,' and a corporeal soul and organic sensation) (*sensus organicus*)."

On the distinction between organic sensation and sense-perception proper, see the Second Meditation, AT VII 29: CSM II 19, and *The Search for Truth*, AT X 521: CSM II 414f.

8 The momentousness of this shift or ambiguity in the meaning of 'sensation' is highlighted by Kennington (1972, 107f.): "that which thinks is called in *Meditations* II by a proliferation of terms from which the traditional *anima* is absent ... In Meditation II *we witness the death of a 2000-year tradition of the soul* as the single principle of both life and motion as well as awareness, discernment, and thinking" (e.a.). However, it is not enough to understand the shift merely negatively, emphasizing the complete immateriality (real distinctness) of mind. (So not just Kennington, but Alquié [1950, 183] as well: "c'est le souci de bannir de l'être qui pense tout reste de corporéité qui amène Descartes à substituer au mot *anima*, trop

pénétré de souvenirs scolastiques [*scil.* âme végétative, sensible, etc.], celui de *mens.*") As 'soul' (*anima*) was widely used for the 'life-principle' separating living from non-living things, so 'mind' (*mens sive animus*) for the rational soul or intellect. Descartes is just as sensible of this close association of *mens* and *animus* with *intellectus* as of the remnant of corporeity in the Scholastic notion of the *anima.*

Traditionally, the operations of the *mens* or *intellectus* are free of the 'taint' of corporeity adhering to sensation and imagination by virtue of the bodily sense organs and brain involved in the latter. (On "organic sensation," see the previous note.) If Descartes equates mind, soul, and intellect, placing sense and imagination among the faculties of the mind so understood, then he does so not only because mind or thinking cannot depend on anything corporeal, but also and principally because *all* thought, even sensation, involves something purely intellectual (*intellectio nonnulla*), namely consciousness of one's acts of thinking, as a structurally necessary concomitant. That is the (generally overlooked) positive content of the doctrine, to be discussed more fully in section 17.2 below.

9 Descartes attached little or no importance to the terminological questions involved. When Bourdin harangued him on matters of usage, he replied: "As for what should be termed 'body,' or 'soul,' or 'mind,' my discussion made no reference whatever to this. I gave an account of two things, namely that which thinks and that which is extended, and I proved that everything else may be referred to these two. I also established by my arguments that they are two substances which are really distinct from one another. However, I did call one of the substances 'mind' and the other 'body'; if my critic does not like these terms, he may employ others, and I shall not complain" (AT VII 487: CSM II 329).

10 Gueroult mentions Cousin, Hamelin, Laporte, and Thévenaz as proponents of the view he is combating. The precise references are Gueroult 1968, I, 80, 78, 54n, and 62, respectively. Alquié, for his part, alleges a fundamental 'ambiguity' (1950, 191ff.) in Descartes's position as between "un idéalisme empirique" and "un idéalisme intellectualiste," i.e., Berkeleyan and Kantian conceptions of the *ego*. (This is not to say that Descartes, for Alquié, is an idealist. Cf. ibid., 181, 197, 200.)

11 On the spectre of complete scepticism, cf. a related point made at AT VII 151: CSM II 107. In this context, Descartes mentions several different "common notions," some metaphysical, others mathematical, "he who is actually thinking exists" among them. If these are doubted, he argues, the "upshot will be that all human knowledge will be destroyed, though for no good reason."

12 There is no need to rehearse his arguments in detail. Of course, it is one thing to argue that the immediate intuition of one's thinking is non-sensuous in nature, another to infer from this that its *object* (the 'I' that thinks) must be a pure (transcendental) rather than empirical object. This is a *non sequitur* even for Kant. It is hard to say whether Gueroult is guilty of it.

PART TWO: CERTAINTY AND TRUTH

1 The act itself, its act-character, the 'I' who acts, and the intentional object of the act.
2 Or, equivalently, 'it seems to me that I am thinking x,' or 'I think that I am thinking x.'
3 Cf. Gueroult's distinction between 'the *cogito*' as an *intuition actuelle* and as a proposition *situé dans l'ensemble des connaissances* (1968, I, 155ff.). Also J.-M. Beyssade (1979, 15): "On dissociera par exemple le *Cogito* actualisé, pure intuition de l'esprit par lui-même, plus certaine que toute science et dispensée de la garantie divine, et un *Cogito* objectivé, dont la certitude cesse d'être absolue."
4 On the question of the point at which the truth rule is validated, cf. the "Synopsis of the six following Meditations," AT VII 15: CSM II 11.
5 Cf. Cottingham (1986, 69): "Descartes, throughout his writings, describes the meditator as, par excellence, the seeker after *truth*." In a similar vein, Etchemendy: "But the *Meditationes* is, throughout, an enquiry into truth" (1981, 28). Wilson (1978a, 61) declares Frankfurt's efforts to supply a truth-surrogate "quite hopeless." Yet Frankfurt no less decidedly pronounced it "hopeless to approach Descartes's argument with the presumption that its point is to provide a demonstration that its conclusion is true" – though he admits that the presumption has "a very high initial plausibility" (1978, 32f.) What is odd is perhaps that a matter like this should be seriously in dispute.

10: The Degrees of Certainty

1 The latter use of *praejudicia* was first drawn to my attention by Professor Graeme Hunter. Cf. the first of the rules in Part Two of the *Discourse*: "never to accept anything as true if I did not have evident knowledge of its truth; that is, carefully to avoid precipitate conclusions and preconceptions (AT VI 18: CSM I 120). Here *précipitation* and *prévention* correspond to (2) and (1).
  If prejudices owing to *précipitation* and *prévention* are opposed, then it is as errors directly opposite in nature: excessive confidence and excessive diffidence concerning the powers of unassisted human reason. Both spring from a single source: inattention to the legitimate scope and inherent limitations of the human cognitive faculty. How diffidence leads to failure to use one's reason and to reliance on the authority of others is described both in the *Regulae* (AT X 428: CSM I 50) and the *Discourse*: "The world is largely composed of two types of minds ... First, there are those who, believing themselves cleverer than they are, cannot avoid *precipitate* judgements ... Secondly, there are those who have enough reason or modesty to recognize that they are less capable of distinguishing the true from the false than certain others by whom they can be taught; such people should be

content to *follow the opinions of others*" (AT VI 15: CSM I 118 e.a.). On authority, see also Rule III and AT IX-1 208: CSM II 272f.

2 Cf. also the distinction drawn earlier in the Sixth Replies (AT VII 436ff.: CSM II 294f.) among "three degrees" or "grades" of sensation (*tres quasi gradus* [scil. *sensus*]). The first is "organic sensation," that is, "the movement of the brain" and the sense organs (on this, see the previous chapter, nn. 7 and 8). The second is sense-perception properly speaking, that is, as a mental act. Of the first and second grades, Descartes remarks: "no [formal] falsity can occur in them." This is obviously so, since the first is non-mental while the second is mental but still pre-predicative. The third degree corresponds to perceptual *judgments*, and it is here that falsity and error can occur. The examples given are judgments about the size, distance, and shapes of sensible objects. A subclass of these, namely *habitual* "judgements about things outside us which we have been accustomed to make from our earliest years," constitute the class of *praejudicia sensuum*.

3 It is a constant refrain in Descartes's writings that "all the mistakes made in the sciences happen ... simply because at the beginning we make judgements too hastily (*nimium festinanter*), and accept as our first principles matters which are obscure and of which we do not have a clear and distinct notion" (AT X 526: CSM II 419). This is a major criticism of the Scholastics, but it applies *mutatis mutandis* to pre-philosophical common sense as well. Cf. also AT X 367: CSM I 14: "The main reason why we can find nothing in ordinary [i.e., School] philosophy which is so evident and certain as to be beyond dispute is that students of the subject first of all are not content to acknowledge what is clear and certain, but on the basis of merely probable conjectures venture also to make assertions on obscure matters about which nothing is known."

4 The term *misologia* is coined by the Platonic Socrates in the *Phaedo* (89D–91B). In the Seventh Replies, to Bourdin, Descartes writes: "we should not suppose that sceptical philosophy is extinct. It is vigorously alive today, and almost all those who regard themselves as more intellectually gifted than others, and find nothing to satisfy them in philosophy as it is ordinarily practised, take refuge in scepticism because they cannot see any alternative with greater claims to truth" (AT VII 548f.: CSM II 374). He then goes on to characterize scepticism in terms that would fit not only classical 'academic' scepticism (cf. AT VII 130: CSM II 94) and traditional Pyrrhonism (cf. AT X 512: CSM II 408), but Hume's scepticism as well. So while the prevalence of 'misology' or sceptical distrust of philosophical reason is a frequently overlooked aspect of what Descartes understands by 'scepticism' in the "Synopsis," it is not the whole story either.

On the whole question of the influence of the Renaissance revival of the arguments of the ancient sceptics and its impact on Descartes, see the well-known work by Popkin (1979).

5 Cf. Rule VIII: "while it is the intellect alone that is capable of knowledge (*scientia*), it can be helped *or hindered* by three other faculties, *viz.* imagination, sense-perception (*sensu*), and memory" (AT X 398: CSM I 32 e.a.).

6 On Descartes's use of 'pure' see above section 5.1. The root sense is 'unhampered,' 'unadulterated,' 'uncorrupted' – whether it be sensory, material (i.e., pertaining to extended matter), historical, conjectural, or other 'impurities' that creep in, and whether through habit, the prejudices of the senses, prejudices of authority, or precipitancy. Thus, where, in the *Regulae*, Descartes remarks (speaking of the syllogisms of School logic) that "the cleverest sophisms hardly ever deceive anyone who makes use of his pure reason (*pura ratione vtentem*)" (AT X 405f.: CSM I 36), Cottingham et al. translate freely (but correctly): "anyone who makes use of his untrammelled reason." Cf. also the expression *mens pura et attenta*, which occurs twice in Rule III.

7 Cf. Thomasius's *Lectiones de praejudiciis* (1689–90) and the *Einleitung in die Vernunftlehre*, c. 13, §§39 and 40.

8 On Schleiermacher's distinction, cf. Gadamer 1960, 262 [*TM* 247].

  Nothing recognizably akin to the Greek distinction ever comes expressly to the fore in Descartes's writings. The dichotomy between *physis* and *nomos* re-emerges explicitly, however, in Leibniz's critique of Cartesian corporeal substance. Matter as extended mass (extended, figurable, and mobile substance, endowed only with a passive force of resistance) is an *ens nomo* for Leibniz (cf. 1989, 89), i.e., an *ens rationis* having no more than mental unity, unity in thought ('for us'), not in fact ('in itself'). Cf. ibid., 79 and 86. It was for Kant to show, in the context of a general 'Copernican Revolution' in philosophy, not just that a mind-bestowed unity need not therefore be conventional or arbitrary, but that and how synthetic principles, notwithstanding their 'subjective' origin in the human mind, could be objectively necessary features of nature itself as the total object of possible experience.

  While Descartes regards reason as possessing total mastery over custom and habit once the therapy of methodic doubt has overcome the prejudices of authority and custom, Hume sees it as inevitably undoing its own authority, and yet – fortunately – powerless against the influence of custom and the passions. Cf. Hume 1990, 39: "Philosophy would render us entirely Pyrrhonian, were not nature [i.e.,, custom and the passions] too strong for it." Also ibid., 54: "the abstruse philosophy, being founded on a turn of mind, which cannot enter into business and action, vanishes when the philosopher leaves the shade and comes into open day; nor can its principles easily retain any influence over our conduct and behaviour." Cf. also Hume 1967, Book I, Part IV, Section VII. On reason as "slave of the passions," see ibid., Book II, Part III, Section III (and related passages).

9 Descartes regards it as self-evident that, while "reason does not insist that what we … see or imagine is true, … it does insist that all our ideas or notions must have

some foundation of truth; for otherwise it would not be possible that God, who is all-perfect and all-truthful, should have placed them in us" (AT VI 40: CSM I 131).

10 In addition to *philosophical* common sense, Descartes uses *sensus communis* in the Scholastic-Aristotelian sense for the faculty of the mind that coordinates the data received from the five external senses (cf. Rule XII of the *Regulae*, AT X 414f.: CSM I 41f.; the *Discourse*, AT VI 55: CSM I 139; *Optics*, AT VI 109: CSM I 164 and AT VI 144: CSM I 173; *Treatise on Man*, AT XI 177: CSM I 105; the letter to Mersenne of 21 April 1641, AT III 361f.: CSMK 180; and the *Meditations*, AT VII 32: CSM II 22 and AT VII 86: CSM II 59).

11 Not every objector, nor even all theologians among them, needed to have this pointed out to them. Cf. Caterus in the First Set of Objections: "I know we are basing our argument on reason alone and not on appeals to authority" (AT VII 98: CSM II 70). On (4), authority as a form of *"experientia* indirecte," i.e., second- or third-hand 'experience' as opposed to "l'*experientia* directe" or intuition, cf. the interesting remarks of Marion 1975, 43f.: "le mépris cartésien de l'histoire de la philosophie appartient à la pensée fondamentale des *Regulae*. Le vrai ne s'ouvre donc qu'à une *experientia* sans histoire, présence du principe sans recours à un commencement passé, savoir qui s'engendre lui-même de lui-même : science sans généalogie, où le savant se produit sans père."

12 Cf. the remark in the *Discourse*: "In doing this ['uprooting from my mind any errors that might previously have slipped into it'] I was not copying the sceptics, who doubt only for the sake of doubting and pretend to be always undecided; on the contrary, my whole aim was to reach certainty" (AT VI 29: CSM I 125). Similarly, in the Fifth Replies: "the purpose here is to come to recognize that certain other things which cannot be rejected in this way are thereby more certain and in reality better known to us" (AT VII 351: CSM II 243). Arnauld saw this clearly. The purpose of the regimen of doubt, he writes, is "to facilitate the discovery of something so firm and stable that not even the most perverse sceptic will have even the slightest scope for doubt" (AT VII 215: CSM II 151).

13 Cf. Eudoxus's (Descartes's) description of his method in *The Search for Truth*: "to take nothing to be true if I am not as sure of it as I am of the certain fact that I exist, and am thinking, and am a thinking thing" (AT X 526: CSM II 419). The 'measure' of certainty is the success of the 'operation' of doubting.

For an instructive account of 'operationism,' see Feigl's classic article (1949b). The parallel with the modern notion of defining terms operationally is admittedly strained since the operations by which 'certainty' is linked to the data of experience by Descartes are not objectively describable mathematical, observational, or manipulatory (mensurational or experimental) operations, but logically private psychological acts of doubting or suspending belief. The operations being *inner* experiences of doubt or the impossibility of doubting, it can even be objected that

Descartes's procedure is directly contrary to the spirit of modern 'operationalism' as epitomized, for example, in Feigl's conclusion: "Concepts which are to be of value to the factual sciences must be definable by operations which are (1) logically consistent; (2) sufficiently definite (if possible, quantitatively precise); (3) empirically rooted, i.e., by procedural and, finally, ostensive links with the observable; (4) naturally and, preferably, technically possible; (5) intersubjective and repeatable; (6) aimed at the creation of concepts that will function in laws or theories of greater predictiveness" (ibid., 508). (3) is the main sticking point. Still, provided it is not pushed too far, the analogy may be at least somewhat helpful in understanding the aims of First Meditation doubt.

Marion (1975, 47f.) speaks in a similar vein of a "définition strictement opératoire" of *intuitus* in the *Regulae*.

14 The term 'moral' certainty (or 'assurance') is found at AT VI 561 = AT VI 37f.: CSM I 130; AT IX-2 323 = VIII-1 327f.: CSM I 289f. 'Metaphysical' certainty occurs at AT VI 561=AT VI 35: CSM I 130; AT VII 477: CSM II 321; and AT VII 352: CSM II 244. 'Absolute' is used synonymously with 'metaphysical' at AT IX-2 323: CSM I 289.

For present purposes we leave aside that highest degree of certainty attainable only through the supernatural light of divine grace, confining ourselves to certainty attainable by unassisted human reason. On the "inner light which comes from God" and by which we are "supernaturally illumined," see the Second Set of Replies (AT VII 148: CSM II 105), cited in section 3.4, and the *Regulae*, Rule III *in fine* (AT X 370: CSM I 15). On moral certainty, cf. Hume 1990, 144: "in our reasonings concerning matter of fact, there are all imaginable degrees of assurance, from the highest certainty to the lowest species of *moral evidence*" (e.a.). Buchdahl glosses 'morally certain' as "'certain for all practical purposes'" (1969, 120).

15 Kennington (1972, 100) conveniently labels these the "existence thesis" and the "similarity thesis."

16 In *The Search for Truth*, as in the Sixth Meditation, it is not only external circumstances like distance and size of the object but also disorders of the sense organs themselves that make the observation conditions less than ideal: "I am well aware that the senses are sometimes deceptive if they are in poor condition, as when all food seems bitter to a sick person; or if their objects are too far away, as when we look at the stars, which never appear so large to us as they really are; or, in general, whenever they do not act freely in accordance with their natural constitution" (AT X 510: CSM II 407).

17 The passage cited in the previous footnote continues in a similar fashion: "But such defects of the senses are all quite easy to recognize, and do not prevent me from being quite sure at present that I am seeing you, that we are walking in this garden, that the sun is shining on us, and in a word, that everything which appears in the

common manner (*communement*) to my senses is veridical (*veritable*)" (AT X 510: CSM II 407).

18 Again, it is worth citing the corresponding passage from *The Search for Truth*. Note the way in which the suggestion of madness (which must render the doubt "incurable," in Hume's words) is again dismissed with indignation. Interesting, too, is the suggestion, not found in (though sometimes read into) the *Meditations*, that the whole of life might be one continuous (lucid) dream. "So if I wish to make you fear that the senses are deceptive on occasions when you are unaware of the deception, it is not enough for me to tell you that the senses deceive you on certain occasions when you perceive the deception. I shall have to go further, and ask if you have never seen one of those melancholic individuals who think themselves to be vases, or take some part of their body to be enormous; they will swear that what they see and touch is just as they imagine it to be. To be sure, a good man (*un honneste homme*) would be indignant if you told him that his beliefs cannot have any more rational basis than theirs, since he relies, like them, on what the senses and imagination represent to him. But you cannot take it amiss if I ask whether you are not, like all men, liable to fall asleep, and whether you cannot think, while asleep, that you are seeing me, that you are walking in this garden, that the sun is shining – in brief, all the things of which you now believe you are utterly certain ... How can you be certain that your life is not *a continuous dream*, and that every-thing you think you learn through your senses (*par vos sens*) is not false now, just as much as when you are asleep?" (AT X 511: CSM II 407f. e.a.). Later Polyander remarks: "I shall apply my mind to the task of doubting whether I have not been dreaming *all my life*" (AT X 514: CSM II 409 e.a.).

19 Compare Descartes's remark in the *Meditations* concerning the Deceiving God: "How do I know that he has not brought it about that there is no earth, no sky, no extended thing, *no shape, no size, no place*, while at the same time ensuring that all these things appear to me to exist just as they do now?" (AT VII 21: CSM II 14). Similarly, in the review of the First Meditation at the beginning of the Second: "I have no senses. Body, shape, extension, movement and place are chimeras" (AT VII 24: CSM II 16).

20 That Descartes regarded the denials of such propositions as self-contradictory is reasonably clear from the *reprise* of the present passage within the Third Medita-tion: "he [God] will never ... bring it about that two and three added together are more or less than five, or anything of the kind in which I see a manifest contradic-tion (*in quibus scilicet repugnantiam agnosco manifestam*)" (AT VII 36: CSM II 25). Alexander (1972) mistakenly assumes that this applies not just to simple mathematical truths but to the *cogito* as well, concluding that the impossibility involved in the denial of the clearly and distinctly perceived is logical impossibility. *Repugnantia, implicantia* (cf. AT VII 152: CSM II 108), *(omnino) repugnat,*

contradictionem involvit or *implicat* (AT VII 151: CSM II 107) are used interchangeably by Descartes. On the equivalence of *repugnantia* and *contradictio*, cf.
the letter to More of 15 April 1649: "It conflicts with my conception, or, what is the
same, I think it involves a contradiction (*Repugnat conceptui meo, sive quod est
idem, puto implicare contradictionem*) that the world should be finite or bounded"
(AT V 345: CSMK 374).

21 In the Fourth Set of Objections, Arnauld speaks in Descartes's own idiom of
"mathematicians, who do not deal with the existence of the objects they study" (AT
VII 212: CSM II 149). Yet the passage begins in very un-Cartesian terms: "We look
for the efficient cause of something only in respect of its existence, not in respect of
its essence. For example, if I see a triangle, I may look for the efficient cause that is
responsible for the existence of this triangle; but I cannot without absurdity inquire
into the efficient cause of this triangle's having three angles equal to two right
angles." Arnauld seems unaware that this very "absurdity" is enshrined in the
Cartesian doctrine of the creation of the eternal truths.

Only at the end of the Fifth Meditation is immunity to the dreaming argument
extended from mathematical to *all* clearly and distinctly perceived (including
existential) truths: "Can one raise the objection I put to myself a while ago, that I
may be dreaming, or that everything which I am now thinking has as little truth as
what comes to the mind of one who is asleep? Yet even this does not change
anything. For even though I might be dreaming, if there is *anything which is
evident to my intellect*, then it is wholly true" (AT VII 71: CSM II 49 e.a.).

22 Hume's is another way. Cf. 1990, 71: "Propositions of this kind [i.e., of 'Geometry,
Algebra, and Arithmetic'] are discoverable by the mere operation of thought,
without dependence on what is anywhere existent in the universe. Though there
never were a circle or triangle in nature, the truths demonstrated by Euclid would
for ever retain their certainty and evidence." This is the prototype of most subsequent distinctions between 'factual' truths about the world and 'conceptual' truths
asserting nothing at all about extra-linguistic reality. How remote it is from
Descartes's understanding of the difference between contingent truths about objects
in rerum natura and the eternal truths of mathematics will become clearer presently.

Beyssade remarks on the equivalence of the expressions *extra cogitationem
meam existere* and *in rerum natura esse* in the *Conversation with Burman* (cf. J.-M.
Beyssade 1979, 225, n. 4).

23 Cf. Feigl 1949a, 14: "In mathematical knowledge truth amounts to accordance with
the formal (syntactical) definitions, the postulates, of the system." To say that such
'coherence' theories of truth belong (if anywhere) in formal sciences is not to
dispute the importance of a certain type of coherence consideration employed
outside mathematics and logic. Thus, coherence of various sorts among the
elements of a network of hypotheses or theoretical statements undoubtedly plays a

great role in the construction, assessment, and refinement of theories in the empirical sciences. But that is another matter.

On Frankfurt's ascription (later recanted) of the coherence theory of truth to Descartes, cf. nn. 6 and 26 to chapter 12. Chapters 12 and 13 deal with Descartes's conception of truth. On Descartes's understanding of mathematical truth in particular, see Gewirth 1987b and 1987c, sect. I, Kenny 1968 and 1970, and Brown 1980. On the alleged preference for the coherence theory of truth and 'rationalist' philosophies (like Spinoza's), cf. Hampshire 1951, 100ff. On Cartesian definitions, see above, section 6.3.

24 That the words "clearly and distinctly" are implicitly understood in the formulation of the quoted *axioma sive notio communis* has been shown convincingly by Brown 1980, sect. III, esp. 33. On the additional criterion of completeness (overlooked by Brown), see the next section.

On the distinction of the simple and complex mathematical ideas referred to under (a) and (b), cf. Rule XII of the *Regulae* at AT X 418 and 422: CSM I 44 and 46. The *locus classicus* of the distinction of both kinds of innate from the factitious ideas listed under (f) is the Third Meditation (AT VII 38: CSM II 26). As for (g), Descartes sometimes suggests that ideas involving patent contradictions cannot properly be said to be thought at all (cf. section 8.2); though at other times he suggests that they are the objects of obscure and confused ideas. (Cf. e.g., AT VII 152: CSM II 108.) As suggested earlier, he may not have held any completely settled view on this matter.

In the First Replies (AT VII 117: CSM 83), responding to a classical objection to the ontological argument, Descartes describes 'a triangle inscribed in a square' as "invented and put together by the intellect." This seems to imply that it is no more a "true and immutable nature" than 'a winged horse' or 'an actually existing lion' – with both of which Descartes immediately lumps it together. Yet in the next breath (AT VII 118: CSM 84) he expressly includes it among the *vera entia*. Neither Kenny (1968, 154) nor Cottingham (CB, 91f.) sees any prospect of resolving this "hopeless contradiction" (Cottingham). But Brown (1980, sect. 1) does just that, suggesting that Descartes is willing to put 'a triangle inscribed in a square' together with 'a winged horse' and 'an existing lion' at the outset, where he regards it merely as another instance of a complex idea made up of two ideas not bound together by any logical tie; later, however, he separates it as he turns his attention to this key difference: we are not able to draw out of the composite of the ideas 'horse' and 'winged' anything we have not expressly put into it; we may *remember* some feature, but we cannot properly be said to *discover* anything new. In the case of the 'triangle inscribed in a square,' on the other hand, we can properly be said to discover a new feature of the composite that we did not put into it when we created it: that the area of the square cannot be less than double that of the inscribed triangle. This explains satisfactorily how class (c) differs from class (f), such that its objects qualify as *vera et realia entia* even though "invented and put together by the intellect."

This is as far as Brown goes. It may perhaps be added that 'a supremely powerful being' differs from a pure fiction like 'a supremely perfect body' even more sharply than class (c) from class (f), since it is not "a fiction of the intellect" even in the first instance: "necessary existence is contained in the idea of a supremely powerful being, not by any fiction of the intellect, but because it belongs to the true and immutable nature of such a being that it exists" (AT VII 119: CSM II 85 e.a.). That is why it belongs under (b) as distinct from (c).

25 "Similarly we do not doubt that a novice at geometry has an idea of a whole triangle when he understands that it is a figure bounded by three lines, even though geometers are capable of knowing and recognizing in this idea many more properties belonging to the same triangle (*alia multa de eodem triangulo cognosci possint*)" (AT VII 368: CSM II 254).

26 Cf. Brown 1980, 31: "Our ideas of things like the horse consist in an amalgam of ideas of various properties, the essential bond of which we can never clearly and distinctly conceive. Because of this, we can never be sure that the properties that we come, on the basis of sense-perception, to associate with the being of a horse actually define, or pick out, a true and real entity. This is just another way of saying that our division of the world into natural kinds always, and of necessity, contains a element of factitiousness; and we can never be sure that we have not divided the world up in the wrong way – that is, in such a way that our divisions fail to correspond to the true and immutable essences that God has in fact created."

Are we unable to grasp the "essential bond" because no such bond exists, the connections between the ideas in the amalgam being purely contingent? Or does it in fact exist while remaining inscrutable to us? Brown apparently opts for the latter alternative (which was certainly Locke's and probably Descartes's view), while Bréhier (1968, 197) takes the former. The ideas of natural kinds, he writes, are "a mere human artifice of classification and not a means of disclosing essences" at all. For the Scholastics, of course, the division of entities into *genera* and *species* was neither conventional nor arbitrary, but ontologically grounded in the substantial natures of the things themselves. Having rejected substantial natures, Descartes could have no truck with any such classification system.

27 As for (1) clarity, cf. *Principles*, I, 46: "a perception ... cannot be distinct without being clear." Regarding (2) distinctness, cf. *Principles*, I, 55 (entitled, "How we can also have a distinct understanding of duration, order and number"): "We shall also have a very distinct understanding of *duration, order*, and *number*, provided we do not mistakenly tack on to them any concept of substance," i.e., do not conceive of them as entities capable of existing in their own right, apart from the substances

that endure and are ordered and numbered. That "can have" and "shall have" do not restrict the claim that these ideas *are* clear and distinct is plain from I, 54, where Descartes says exactly the same thing of our "notions of thinking substance and of corporeal substance, and also of God." As for (3) simple, cf. Rule XII of the *Regulae* (AT X 419: CSM I 45).

28 Cf. to Arnauld, 29 July 1648: "So by 'thought' I do not mean some universal which includes all modes of thinking, but *a particular nature*, which takes on those modes, just as extension is a nature which takes on all shapes" (AT V 221: CSMK 357). A *principal* attribute would appear to have two other features besides (1) being a nature in this sense: (2) everything else, i.e., all the other properties of (or truths about) that kind of substance depend upon it, and (3) it itself depends on nothing that is more basic. On existence as constituting the nature of God, see the next note.

29 A third, the loosest, sense of 'attribute' covers both uses of 'attribute' distinguished above *and* all modes properly so called. This use is found, for example, in the *Comments on a Certain Broadsheet* (AT VIII-2 348: CSM I 297). It corresponds to one of the uses of 'property' (*proprietas*) found the Fifth Set of Replies (AT VII 382f.: CSM II 263): "we take the word 'property' to stand for any attribute, or whatever can be predicated of a thing." From this broad sense of 'property' Descartes distinguishes "property in the strictest sense": that which forms part of the essence of a certain kind of substance and no other (ibid.). This sounds like a use of 'property' that corresponds to 'principal attribute' as constituting the 'true and immutable nature' of a substance. It is in this sense that existence is a property, i.e., the essence of God: "God *is* his own existence" (ibid.). This *sounds* remarkably like Aquinas. On the notions of existence and essence in Aquinas, Descartes, and Kant, see the Conclusion, section 22.3.

30 That is, 'essence' conceived abstractly and not either as the principal attribute of mental or material substance or as the essence of some particular being or natural kind.

31 The authors of the Second Set of Objections urge that "the idea of the unity and simplicity of one perfection that includes all others [i.e., the infinite perfection of God] arises merely from an operation of the reasoning intellect, in the same way as those universal unities which do not exist in reality but merely in the intellect (as can be seen in the case of generic unity, transcendental unity, and so on)" (AT VII 124: CSM II 89). In reply, Descartes remarks that it is "not important that the idea of the unity of all the perfections of God is said to be formed in the same way as the Porphyrian universals." There is "a crucial difference, in that the idea in question denotes a certain positive perfection peculiar to God, whereas generic unity *adds nothing real to the nature* of the single individuals concerned" (AT VII 140: CSM II 100 e.a.). A page later he points out that the objection takes the infinite "as a nonentity and hence as not having a real nature."

32 Cf. AT VII 112: CSM II 80: "For since we understand not only what is meant by existence but also what is meant by its negation ... etc."

33 On the identity of actual ideal existence (of *vera et realia entia*) and possible real existence, see below. As for the identity of "eternal truths" and the "essences" of things, cf. the letter to Mersenne of 27 May 1630: "For it is certain that he [God] is the author of the essence of created things no less than of their existence; *and this essence is nothing other than the eternal truths*" (AT I 152: CSMK 25 e.a.). In classifying ideas as adventitious, factitious, and innate in the letter to Mersenne of 16 June 1641, Descartes speaks of the latter as representing (*representant*) "true and immutable *and eternal* essences" like the ideas of God, the mind, body, and a triangle (AT III 383: CSMK 183 e.a.). So talk of the creation or existence of 'eternal truths' and of 'essences' means exactly the same thing.

34 This much is clearly recognized by Brown (1980, 35, esp. n. 48), who nevertheless goes on to assert that the existence of material things is irrelevant to the truth of physical science as well. This blurs the sharply drawn boundary between the dreaming and deceiving God hypotheses. For the truth of physical science, the conditions are (1) that a material world exist and (2) that it be constructed or "disposed" by God in an order that is precisely describable in statements describing law-like regularities or relations of invariance among mathematical quantities like extension, shape, and motion. (1) is irrelevant to the truth of pure mathematics.

In a footnote sharply critical of Gewirth (see next note), Sievert (1977, n. 3) similarly overlooks the difference between pure and applied mathematics (or between mathematics and mathematical physics). The truth of the latter indeed depends upon the existence of physical objects, of space, place, motion, etc.; not so, however, the truth of pure mathematics.

35 Quite apart from the fairly conclusive textual evidence against the "existential interpretation" (some of which was cited in the previous section), without at least some form of the "essential" version of the ontological interpretation it will be difficult to make sense of the idea that God might alter the eternal truths unbeknownst to us, so that the objects of pure mathematics no longer conform to what we remember having clearly and distinctly perceived about them in the past. Yet this idea is central to Cartesian metaphysics and to the whole structure of the argument of the *Meditations* in particular (cf. chapter 14). The same problem arises if the eternal truths depend exclusively on the existence and nature of the human mind, as Ishiguro holds (see next note).

If Gewirth's own analysis has a serious defect, it is the failure to distinguish complete concepts of *vera et realia entia* from universals (cf. Gewirth 1987c, 117f.).

36 On the independence of mathematical objects of (1) the existence of material things, cf. Brown (1980, 36f.): "*vera entia*, and mathematical objects in particular,

have a 'being' that is independent of their actual existence in (physical) space or time, and that is characterized by what Descartes calls 'possible existence,' or by what we may call, to borrow Yvon Belaval's term, an 'existence logique.'" (Belaval contrasts the 'existence logique' of mathematical entities with the 'existence réelle' of material things [1960, 509].) Following Kenny (1968, 155 and 165–9 and 1970, 696), Brown stresses the similarities between Descartes's and Meinong's conceptions of "pure objects." (See 1980, n. 38 and 52 for the precise references to Meinong's works, and Chisholm [1960, 76–117] for an English translation of one of them.) It is even more common to draw parallels between Descartes's conception of the objects of pure mathematics and that of Frege (cf., e.g., Larmore 1984, 61). However, given the absolute dependence of the eternal truths on the divine mind, the resemblance between Descartes and Meinong or Frege is at best superficial.

Brown does not mention (2) the independence of mathematical objects of the existence and nature of the human mind, though the "essential version" of the ontological interpretation assumes it. Against this Bouveresse (1987, 318f.) argues that "pour créer les vérités arithmétiques [for example], Dieu n'a pas eu besoin de créer, en dehors de notre esprit, un domaine de réalité spécial, un univers de choses arithmétiques dont sont vrais les énoncés arithmétiques." All God need do is create our minds in a certain way. "La notion cartésienne de nécessité semble purement épistémique" (ibid., 317). Ishiguro (1987a, 1987b) takes over this approach, making the eternal truths depend solely on the existence of minds having natures like that God bestowed on ours. "In creating our mind, he [God] creates the eternal truths ... They are there, in the language Kant was to use, as a priori forms of thinking" (1987b, 373).

On the view of the matter to be taken here, the 'ideal existence' of mathematical objects entails (a) existence in the mind of God. It entails also (b) existence in the human mind (as implanted there by God and hence at least *implicitly* present to consciousness at all times) *only if* any human minds exist. But it does not imply (c) existence *in rerum natura*. Thus, even if there were no human minds, "true and immutable natures" and "common notions" would exist independently of material things in the mind of God. However, Descartes is too chary of details to warrant any very confident assertion in this regard. For more on what is meant by the phrase 'implicitly present to consciousness' above, see chapter 18 on Descartes's concept of innateness.

37 Cf. Jaeger 1967, 381: "Aristotle considered it axiomatic that nothing universal possesses independent existence." Also Halper (1993, 131): "Aristotle's mathematical ontology can be stated, in broad terms, quite simply: mathematical objects exist as attributes of sensible things." Mathematicals like shapes and numbers exist in bodies as potential parts of those bodies (cf. ibid., 147). For Aquinas (1955 [*SCG*, I 65]) "universals are not subsistent things, but have being in singulars only."

38 Cf. Gerson 1994, for an interesting survey of the complete range of classical opinion on the ontological status of essences and eternal truths, from the "full-bodied exemplarism" (ibid., 149) of Plotinus through the intellectualism of Augustine and Aquinas and the voluntarism of Scotus (and Suarez) to the nominalism of Ockham.

39 Regarding (d), cf. the comment at AT VII 428: CSM II 289: "the less power the atheist attributes to the author of his being, the more reason he will have to suspect that his nature may be so imperfect as to allow him to be deceived even in matters which seem utterly evident to him." Also *Principles*, I, 5: "the less powerful we make the author of our coming into being, the more likely it will be that we are so imperfect as to be deceived all the time." On 'all the time' (*semper*), see below.

40 As is often supposed, most recently by Loeb (1992, 204).

41 Cf. Gewirth 1987b, n. 21 for a fuller list of those who have urged that "Descartes's hyperbolic doubt condemns him to intellectual suicide."

42 Kennington (1971) limits the malicious demon in such a way that neither the axioms of mathematics and logic nor the metaphysical axioms used to prove God's existence and veracity are subject to doubt, thereby obviating the problem of the validation of reason by reason at the outset. This would seem to be mistaken. I share with Kennington, however, the minority view that the malicious demon is finite and differs from the deceiving God. For the long list of those who have held the "equivalence thesis" (as Kennington calls it), see Kennington 1971, n. 1.

43 Cf. Beck 1965, 143: "The force of the hypothesis of the Malignant Spirit breaks on the rock of the *Cogito*. The recognition of one truth as indubitably true, and self-evidently so, gives a rational conviction which is sufficient to destroy the hypothesis once and for all." If this were so, one would expect the hypothesis to have been dispensed with by the fourth paragraph of the Second Meditation. Yet that is clearly not the case, as Tweyman (1972, 123f.) has noted. The interpretation offered here takes this objection into account. On the disclosure of what truth itself is through the *cogito* principle, see section 12.5 below.

44 On the distinctiveness of theological knowledge among the eternal truths, see chapters 12 and 14 below. The expression "the knowledge of God" is ambiguous. By 'theological knowledge' is meant 'our knowledge of God,' not 'God's knowledge of all things,' i.e., 'divine knowledge.' But theological knowledge includes *our* knowledge of *God's* knowledge as well as of his existence and essence. While we know God's existence and nature both clearly and distinctly (though not adequately), we lack knowledge of his intellect (knowledge) and will (purposes), these being one and the same thing in God. Cf. the doctrine of the *incomprehensibilitas Dei* at AT VII 55: CSM II 38f.

Thus, in keeping with Descartes's new emphasis on the order of knowing, a new emphasis accrues to the *objective* genitive. Cf., e.g., AT VII 429f.: CSM II 290: "we

must begin with knowledge of God, and our knowledge of all other things must
then be subordinated to this single initial piece of knowledge, as I explained in my
Meditations." Yet where, in the Fourth Meditation, Descartes first uses the
expression "the true God," he writes: "from this contemplation of the true God, *in
whom all the treasures of wisdom and the sciences lie hidden*, I think I can see a
way forward to the knowledge of other things" (AT VII 53: CSM II 37 e.a.). Here
the allusion to the *subjective* genitive of Romans 11:33 is patent ("O the depth of
the riches both of the wisdom and knowledge of God! how unsearchable are his
judgments, and his ways past finding out!"). But so is the ambiguity, given that our
knowledge *of* God (*genitivus objectivus*) is the "way forward."

45 As early as 1937, Gueroult charged Gouhier with committing a *husteron proteron*
"en conditionnant par la métaphysique achevée de Descartes une conception qui,
pour Descartes lui-même, n'est possible qu'à un moment des *Méditations* où cette
métaphysique n'est pas encore établie." In other words, Gouhier reads back into
the deceiving God of the First Meditation a conception of divine omnipotence
involving the creation of the eternal truths that, at that stage, has yet to be introduced. Cf. Gouhier 1937, and Gueroult 1938, 458f.

46 Returning to the same subject much later (1969, chap. IX), Gouhier mounts a
complex and powerful argument for the conclusion that "l'hypothese du Dieu
trompeur n'est possible comme supposition que par référence à un Dieu créateur
des vérités éternelles" (258). See ibid., 260 n. 91 for references to others of his
works and the works of other authors who have defended the same thesis.

47 This concedes *in part* the point of the objections of Cottingham (1976, 258) and J.-
M. Beyssade (1979, 94f.) against the widespread conviction that the deceiving God
or evil demon is introduced specifically in order to render the truths of mathematics
uncertain. Both suggest, however, that the doubt raised by the *malin génie* bears
"principally" (Cottingham) on the external world. This goes too far.

   This first reason for the introduction of the malicious demon corresponds in a
rough general way to what Tweyman calls the 'personification view': "the evil
demon can ... be regarded as merely personifying his [Descartes's] hyperbolic
doubt." The second reason (see below) takes the malicious demon in accordance
with Tweyman's 'postulation view,' on which "Descartes has postulated the evil
genius as existing independently of himself." Cf. Tweyman 1972, 124f. For a series
of interesting (but not entirely convincing) suggestions as to Descartes's reasons for
the switch, cf. J.-M. Beyssade 1979, 94ff.

48 And, in fact, in *The Search for Truth*, it appears that he does: "In particular, how
can you be certain of this [i.e., 'that your life is not a continuous dream'] when you
have learned [by teaching] that you were created by a superior being who, being
all-powerful (*tout puissant*), would have found it no more difficult to create us just
as I am describing than to create us as you think you are" (AT X 512: CSM II 408).

There is of course the possibility that *tout puissant* (two words in the original) merely means *summe potens* rather than *omnipotens*, but that is difficult to say.

49 'To be deceived' and 'to err' are therefore not the same thing. Error can be defined purely phenomenologically in terms of the misuse of the will in assenting to what is not clearly and distinctly perceived; being deceived on the other hand is assenting to what is false or denying what is true. Its definition thus involves reference to extra-mental states of affairs. On Descartes's phenomenological theories of truth and error, see chapter 12 below (on error, see chap. 12, n. 22).

50 This can be compared to a similar compilation in Cottingham 1986, 29f.

11: The Kinds of Certainty

1 That the "common notions" or axioms of the natural light are alluded to in this passage is pointed out by Kenny 1968, 183.

2 Cf. Kenny 1970, 686: "If these ['the perceptions employed in the demonstration of God's existence'] require the divine guarantee, then Descartes's argument is circular; if they do not, then he contradicts himself when he says that all perceptions require guarantee."

3 Regarding Descartes's steadfast refusal to acknowledge the force of this objection, cf. especially the disclaimer in the letter to Clerselier of 12 January 1646 (AT IX-1 211: CSM II 274), after the whole question had been thrashed out repeatedly in the Replies.

4 Cf. Marion (1975, 36f.) on "la réduction de la vérité à l'experience psychologique de la certitude" in the *Regulae*. Probability, he claims, is similarly reduced to "la connaissance psychologiquement éprouvée comme incertaine." On the difference between phenomenological interpretation and psychologistic reduction, see section 12.4 below.

5 That time figures as the distinguishing feature of two kinds of certainty has been pointed out in one way or another by a number of commentators, e.g., Doney (1955, 336): "By *certain* [in one sense] he meant, roughly, incapable of being doubted *at any time*." This is contrasted with another sense of 'certain' that applies to the clearly and distinctly perceived as long, and only as long, as one attends to the grounds of its truth. Cf. also Cottingham 1986, 70f. The point is acknowledged obliquely in certain studies, in which the talk is of (e.g.) "a state of mind that is in a certain sense immutable" (Kenny 1968, 192).

6 By 'dialectics' and 'dialecticians' Descartes means Scholastic logic and its practitioners. He generally characterizes them as concerned with the rules of syllogistic argument (e.g., AT X 405: CSM I 36) and as arguing from merely probable premises (AT X 363: CSM I 11), i.e., commonly made assumptions and widely held opinions. Cf. the reference (ibid.) to "the weapons of the Schoolmen,

probable syllogisms." This corresponds roughly to 'dialectical' arguments in
Aristotle. These are opposed to 'didactic,' 'peirastic,' 'eristic,' and 'apodictic'
arguments, the latter being those that begin from premises that are self-evidently
true. Cf. Aristotle 1965, 15 [*SR* 165a39 – b9]. On Descartes's at bottom ambivalent
attitude toward logic or dialectics, see section 15.5.

7 Cf. *Principles*, I, 54: "And certainly no one can deny that we possess such an idea
of God, unless he reckons that there is absolutely no knowledge (*notitia*) of God to
be found" (AT VIII-1 26: CSM I 211).

8 Cf. Markie 1992, n. 16: "Descartes later modifies this position [taken at the
beginning of the Third Meditation] so it does not contain this implication [that the
cogito principle is doubtful]." This view has a long history, beginning with all those
who have held that in passages like this Descartes "imperceptibly transferred the
doubt from clearness and distinctness to memory" (Stout 1929, 183). For the
catalogue of names, cf. Doney 1970, 394f. Of course, Markie is not defending the
memory thesis or anything like it, but his own "self-evident intuition / immediate
inference" interpretation of the *cogito* (Markie 1992, 143 and 155). This will be
discussed briefly in n. 10 of the next chapter.

9 When in the Seventh Replies (AT VII 505: CSM II 343) Bourdin takes it that
having certain knowledge of something (*certo scire*) entails perceiving it clearly
(*clare percipere*), Descartes scoffs openly (AT VII 519: CSM II 353), as though it
were perfectly obvious that this is not so: "It is one thing to perceive something
clearly [i.e., to have now actually occurring clear and distinct perception of it], and
another to know it for certain [because, namely, one has perceived it clearly and
distinctly and likewise perceived clearly that a veracious God exists]: there are
many things that we *now* know for certain, either through faith or because we
clearly perceived them *on an earlier occasion*, but which we do not *now* perceive
clearly" (e.a.). Given that Bourdin is by far the least gifted of his objectors, and
assuming Descartes wished to make himself understood, the reply is surprisingly
curt; it would hardly be intelligible to anyone without the italics and interpolations.
And nowhere in the *Meditations* and Replies is the matter made much clearer than
this. A possible exception is this, also from the Seventh Replies, the parenthesis
being Descartes's own: "until we know that God exists, we have reason to doubt
everything (i.e. everything such that we do not have a clear perception of it before
our minds [*de omni re cujus claram perceptionem animo suo praesentem non
habet*])" (AT VII 546: CSM II 373).

10 With this use of the verb *convertere* compare that in Rule V of the *Regulae*: "The
whole method consists entirely in ordering and arranging the objects on which we
must concentrate our mind's eye (*ad quae acies mentis est convertenda*)" (AT VI
379: CSM I 20). Also this from Rule III: "everyone can mentally intuit that he
exists, that he is thinking, that a triangle is bounded by just three lines, and a sphere

by a single surface, and the like. Perceptions such as these are more numerous than most people realise, disdaining as they do to turn their minds to such simple matters (*ad tam facilia mentem convertere*)" (AT X 368: CSM I 14).

11 Cf. the very similar wording of Part IV of the *Discourse* at AT VI 33: CSM I 127.

12 For further passages in which the proviso is expressed (or suppressed), cf. above, chapter 7, n. 3.

13 On the proviso, see also J.-M. Beyssade (1979, 135ff.), who is undoubtedly correct in insisting *contra* Alquié (1950, 189) and Gueroult (1968, 156) that "le présent de la pensée n'est pas un point dans le temps [i.e., an instant], il est une partie du temps ou un moment." It has a certain duration, the duration of an operation or act of thinking. Simultaneous with this is the 'movement of thought' that is the concomitant act, or rather "action," of reflecting on one's act. Cf. chapter 15 below. On the question of whether thinking is a necessary as well as a sufficient condition of existence, see also Tweyman 1993b, 153.

14 Leonard Miller (1965, 38) writes: "Descartes is puzzled by the nature of these [mathematical] propositions whose truth appears to be self-evident, for he is inclined to say both that we cannot possibly be mistaken about them provided that we apprehend them clearly and distinctly and that we can be deceived by the demon no matter how clearly and distinctly we perceive them." If the foregoing is correct, Descartes is not just inclined, but perfectly entitled, to say both these things; but he is *not* puzzled. It is his interpreters who are puzzled.

   Frankfurt (1970, 64) cites the Seventh Replies passage just quoted as evidence that Descartes "supposes the mathematical propositions he discusses in the First Meditation to be perceived only confusedly." But this is to mistake Descartes's emphasis when he speaks of "the First Meditation, in which I was supposing that I was not *attending* to anything that I clearly perceived." 'Perceiving clearly and distinctly without attention' not only does not entail, it entails the denial of, 'perceiving obscurely or confusedly.' For independent textual evidence against this reading, see Kenny 1970, 691f. For a different estimate, see Cottingham 1976, 264 on Frankfurt 1966.

15 As with the doubt about God, so with that about minds: it is only a certain traditional conception that is rejected as doubtful. Thus, reviewing all that the First Meditation has rendered doubtful, Descartes speaks at the outset of the Second of having convinced himself "that there is absolutely nothing in the world, no sky, no earth, *no minds*, no bodies" (AT VII 25: CSM II 16 e.a.). When Bourdin baulks at "no minds" (AT VII 468: CSM II 315), he explains: "At the outset, when I was supposing that I had not yet sufficiently perceived the nature of the mind, I included it in the list of doubtful things; but later on, when I realized that a thing that thinks cannot but exist, I used the term 'mind' to refer to this thinking thing, and said that the mind existed" (AT VII 473: CSM II 318). Rejected, then, is the existence of *any*

mind or soul *in the Scholastic-Aristotelian sense* (which coincides with that of everyday pre-philosophical usage; see section 6.1), *not* the existence of *other* minds as *res cogitantes* (*pace* Cook 1988). Cf. also AT VII 26: CSM II 17: "the first thought to come to mind ['whenever I used to consider what I was'] was that I had a face, hands, arms and the whole mechanical structure of limbs which can be seen in a corpse, and which I called the body. The next thought was that I was nourished, that I moved about, and that I engaged in sense-perception and thinking; *and these actions I attributed to the soul*" (e.a.). And AT VII 491: CSM II 332: "it is false that I asked whether I was a mind; for [at that point in the Second Meditation] I had not yet explained what I understood by the term 'mind.' What I did do was to enquire whether there were in me any of the features *which I had previously been in the habit of attributing to the soul as previously described by me*" (e.a.).

In the parallel passage within the *Principles* (I, 7), Descartes drops 'minds' from the list of doubtful things, perhaps to avoid having to explain himself as fully as he did to Bourdin: "it is easy for us to suppose that there is no God and no heaven and that there are no bodies, and even that we ourselves have no hands or feet, or indeed any body at all." That it is only the God of "long-standing belief" whose existence is doubted is not expressly stated here, perhaps because just two articles before Descartes had written: "*we have been told* that there is an omnipotent God who created us" (AT VIII-1 6: CSM I 194 e.a.) – which makes the point clearly enough.

In the corresponding part of *The Search for Truth*, Descartes has Polyander (whom Eudoxus has just led through the grounds of doubt) remark: "I shall be uncertain not only about whether you are in the world and whether there is an earth and a sun; but also about whether I have eyes, ears, a body, and even whether I am speaking to you and you are speaking to me. In short, I shall doubt everything (AT X 514: CSM II 409)." The 'you' to which Polyander refers is the man, person, human being, Eudoxus, in the pre-philosophical (and Scholastic-Aristotelian) sense. This is clear from the answer he gives when Eudoxus asks him, "But what are you – you who have doubts about everything but cannot doubt that you yourself exist?" Answer: "I shall say that I am a *man*" (AT X 515: CSM II 410). Cf. above chapter 6, n. 6.

16 Scholz (1931) commends Leibniz for pointing out the "hiatus" between the classic Aristotelian and Descartes's notion of a first principle or axiom. His characterization of Descartes's usage is as funny as it is just: "Ein singulärer Satz [Je suis] ein Axiom? Und ein Axiom der Metaphysik? Aristoteles würde sich bekreuzigt haben, wenn dieser Ausdruck des Entsetzens für ihn schon existiert hätte." Scholz could just as well have added: "A *contingent* proposition an axiom? Aristotle would have ... etc."

17 Rodis-Lewis (1979, 22) suggests misleadingly that this distinction is clearly in evidence in the *Meditations* themselves, citing AT VII 36 l. 14 and l. 29 and AT VII

68 l. 22 together with 69 ll. 12–15. She is undoubtedly right about what Descartes has in mind in these passages, though at most one of the pair is found along with various paraphrases of the other. The same is true of the passages in the Replies to which she adverts (ibid., 23f.). As for her comment, "Il faut noter que tous ces textes évoquent la possibilité d'une tromperie même dans ce qui (au présent) me *semble* très évident," this seems to fly in the face of the plain sense of the lot of them.

18 On first communicating his opinion on the eternal truths to Mersenne in the letter of 15 April 1630, Descartes writes: "Please do not hesitate to assert and proclaim everywhere that it is God who laid down these laws in nature." But he concludes by saying: "I do not want you to keep it a secret. On the contrary, I beg you to tell people as often as the occasion demands, provided that you do not mention my name" (AT I 145: CSMK 23 e.a.). The proviso may seem contemptibly timid. Consider, however, a passage near the beginning, which sets the tone of the entire letter: "If people are going to think about me, I am civilized enough to be glad that they should think well of me; but I would much prefer them to have no thought of me at all. I fear fame more than I desire it; I think that those who acquire it always lose some degree of liberty and leisure, which are two things I possess so perfectly and value so highly that there is no monarch in the world rich enough to buy them away from me" (AT I 136: CSMK 20f.).

12: The Modalities of Truth

1 Cf., e.g., Wilson 1978a, 59: "Descartes ... insist[s] on the distinction between the existence of a thought or experience, on the one hand, and the existence of things thought, imagined or 'sensed,' on the other hand."

2 Two quite similar versions are formulated by Kenny (1968, 197f.) and Flew (1971, 329). Most critics argue that Descartes embraced the first horn of the dilemma, but then inconsistently abandoned his purely introspective criterion of truth when he resorted to the divine guarantor. Cf., e.g., Gewirth 1968 and Ashworth 1972, 101ff., esp. 105.

3 The exception is Alexander 1972, who is practically alone in regarding *cogito* and *sum* as self-evident truths (*per se nota*), the denials of which are self-contradictory.

4 Some prominent commentators simply accept this as at least part, though usually not the whole, of the story. Cf. Marion 1981a, 380. Others, like Wilson (1978a, 70) and Kenny (1968, 43), reject it outright.

Instead of "existentially self-verifying" sentences, Hintikka at times speaks of "a performance through which an existentially inconsistent statement *defeats* itself" (1968, 130 e.a.). Tweyman's is apparently a variant of this 'performatory' interpretation: "the contradiction is not in the *Cogito*, or more precisely, in its denial. It is the *effort* or *activity of denial* which is self-contradictory. An effort or activity would be self-contradictory if seeking to engage in it resulted in engaging in the opposite effort or activity" (1993a, 16).

5 Williams offers a variant of this view that turns on the distinction between entailment and presupposition. Cf. Williams 1962, 96 (and passim). Curley (1978, 92) has long since pointed out the flaw in this approach.

6 Frankfurt 1966, 333: "It seems clear to me ... that Descartes regards his existence as something inferred. The purpose of the inference, however, is not to prove that *sum* is true ... Descartes's concern is not to decide whether or not he exists, or to offer a proof of *sum*, but to establish that his existence is in a rather unusual sense certain or indubitable." Gombay (1972, 71) distinguishes three claims in this passage: "(1) Descartes regards his existence as something inferred. (2) The purpose of the inference is not to prove that '*sum*' is true; (3) Descartes's concern is rather to establish that his existence is, in a rather unusual sense of 'indubitable,' indubitable." While it is (1) that interests Gombay (on this, see chapter 17), and although it is (3) that concerns us here, it may be worth commenting briefly on the shift in Frankfurt's thinking that led to Gombay's (2).

It is apparently the result of a shift from a 'coherence' to a 'correspondence' conception of truth. In the statement, "[Descartes] establishes truths by removing the grounds for doubting them rather than by proving their truth in a direct way" (Frankfurt 1970, 174), the first use of 'truth' implies a coherence theory. As Sievert (1977, 374f.) correctly observes, Frankfurt is "not denying that Descartes seeks truth; rather, he interprets the quest for truth as the quest for a proof of the consistency of reason." But truth is one thing, the consistency of reason another: "The contrast between discovering that a good God exists and reason's leading to the conclusion that a good God exists is that the former involves the existence of God whereas the latter merely implies that our best lights leave us 'persuaded' about God's existence and goodness. On the latter view, whether God actually exists is a further unanswered question" (Sievert, ibid., 381). Eight years later (1978, 36f.) Frankfurt was to acknowledge having ascribed a 'coherence' theory of truth to Descartes, admitting that there is no textual support for this and recanting explicitly: "whenever Descartes gives an explicit account of truth he explains it unequivocally as correspondence with reality." Given that *this* is what 'truth' means for Descartes, it becomes Frankfurt's considered view that it is not really truth he is after at all – the point stated by Gombay in (2). For more on this subject, cf. n. 26 below.

7 Gombay nuances the 'inference' option, distinguishing between 'inference' and 'argument' (1972, 75f.). Although he suggests (87f.) that the debate is "philosophically unexciting," his own interesting discussion of the issues involved suggests otherwise. See chapters 15 and 17 below.

8 In the present context all forms of indirect inference may be lumped together under

the title 'syllogism,' though one can certainly sympathize with the sentiment expressed by Kneale: "Since Aristotle is the originator of the theory of the syllogism, he is clearly entitled to say what is to be accounted a syllogism" (1949, 26). Katz opines that "the term 'syllogism' would have been used in Descartes's time to cover hypothetical forms like *modus ponens*" (1987, 176). This is confirmed by Curley (1978, 30).

In the contemporary literature the distinction between direct and indirect inference looms larger than that between the Aristotelian syllogism proper (as a form of reasoning that establishes its conclusion by means of a middle term) and other forms of deductive inference involving more than a single premise, though the enthymeme and the *modus ponens* form receive a certain play as interpretations of the *cogito* principle. Cf., e.g., Röd 1959–60, 177, Wilson 1978a, 54–61, and Cottingham 1986, 37.

9 Though it is not obvious that this is what Hamelin means. Hoenen certainly takes 'raisonnement' in Hamelin to mean 'raisonnement syllogistique' (1937, 468). Gewirth, too, thinks that Hamelin "seems to hold ... that for the *cogito* to be implicative [i.e., a *raisonnement*] is for it to be syllogistic" (1987a, n. 40). Röd concurs (1959–60, 180).

10 Versions of the thesis that *sum* involves an *immediate* (non-syllogistic) logical inference – a 'deduction' in the sense of the *Regulae* – have been defended by Marc-Wogau (1954), Williams (1962), Beck (1965, 86ff.), Rodis-Lewis (1971), Röd (1971, 51), and J.-M. Beyssade (1979, 237ff.). Wilson probably belongs here as well. Carefully detaching 'inference' from 'syllogism' (1978, 55), she interprets the *cogito* "as involving an inference from 'I think' to 'I exist'" (63), devoting her efforts principally to the rebuttal of objections against this "naïve" interpretation and to unmasking the flaws in the alternative approaches of Hintikka and Ayer. Hintikka's position had already been rejected by Kenny (1968, 53ff.), who attempted to "settle the debate about whether the *cogito* is an intuition or an inference" (55) by showing that the two main logical approaches are *both* right. The view of the inference that he endorses is close to Weinberg's and similarly based on the *Regulae*.

Recently, Peter Markie has derived from the same source a much fuller version of this interpretation, which he dubs the "self-evident intuition/immediate inference interpretation" (1992, 143, 155). As Markie initially portrays it, the *cogito, ergo sum* is an *immediate* inference. On the "modified" (ibid., 155) and "improved" (153) version he then develops, the *sum* is still an immediate inference from the self-evident intuition, *cogito*, but neither is strictly certain as opposed to just "very reasonable" (158). In order to explain why Descartes held his thought and existence to be certain, Markie turns from *de facto* considerations about what logically entails what to *de jure* deliberations about the conditions under which a hypothesis (the deceiving God) does and not does constitute *legitimate* grounds for doubting one's thought and existence. (It does not provide grounds for doubt when it in fact entails the truths in question.) So though his starting point is apparently a descriptive logical interpretation of necessity, not unlike Weinberg's and Kenny's, Markie ultimately endorses the normative interpretation of the *cogito, ergo sum* associated with Frankfurt.

11 Not unlike the appeal to the peculiar logic of speech-acts is Katz's attempt to identify a purely linguistic source of inference validity. The *cogito, ergo sum* is an example of "a class of inferences which are valid because the meaning of the premiss contains ... the meaning of the conclusion, so that the truth conditions of the premiss include those of the conclusion. Here validity would rest not on logical laws that bridge the gap from premiss to conclusion, and connect their separate truth conditions necessarily, but on the fact that the meaning of the premiss is such that there is no gap to be bridged" (1987, 180). This notion of the *cogito* as an instance of "analytic entailment" (ibid., 189) is much more fully developed in Katz's book (cf. ibid., n. 1).

12 Hintikka 1962, 122: "The relation which the particle *ergo* serves to express in Descartes' sentence is therefore rather peculiar." Just before this the relation was described as that of "a process to its product. The indubitability of my own existence results from my thinking of it almost as the sound of music results from playing it or ... light ... from the presence of a light source." Cf. also Ayer (1968, 81): "There was therefore no need for Descartes to derive '*sum*' from '*cogito*'; for its certainty could be independently established by the same criterion," i.e., both propositions have the same logical peculiarity that "their truth follows from their being doubted by the person who expresses them." This leads to a new form of the objection that the argument – assuming it is one – is circular. In a similar vein, Mittelstraß (1978, 190), following Scholz (1931): "In diesem Sinne handelt es sich hier also tatsächlich um einen korrekten Schluß, allerdings um einen Schluß, der nichts Neues liefern kann, weil die Existenz des sum schon zu den Voraussetzungen dafür gehört, daß 'cogito' schon eine sinnvolle Aussage ist. 'Cogito' is dann selbst schon ein *formal wahrer*, also sicher *evidenter* Satz." Mittelstraß regards himself as in basic agreement with Hintikka (1963, 190 n. 48). On this circularity charge, cf. Imlay 1985, sect. II.

13 Among the interpreters who have aligned themselves with Frankfurt on the question of the necessity of the *sum* are Curley and Tlumak. Echoing Frankfurt, Curley writes: "The status of 'I think' is not that of a premise in a proof, whose premises must be known to be true. Its status is that of a necessary element in any skeptical hypothesis which purports to provide a ground for doubting 'I exist'" (1978, 186; cf. also 86ff.).

Tlumak includes as the fourth among six basic "adequacy conditions" that *any* interpretation of Cartesian certainty will have to satisfy: that metaphysical certainty "is a standard-setting concept of epistemic appraisal" (1978, 43). Simply to lay this down as an "adequacy condition" may seem a short way with dissent. Of course, it does not escape Tlumak that the term 'certain' has a purely descriptive psychological force "in some contexts"; but it has normative force, he maintains, "in the context of the Cartesian problem" (ibid., 43). Descriptive psychological states "may be a causal consequence of certainty, but they are not to be identified with it" (ibid., 44).

14 The following passages appear to reflect Descartes's awareness of the logical features of the situation. "For it is a contradiction to conceive (*repugnat ut putemus*, nous avons tant de répugnance à concevoir) that what thinks does not, at the very time when it is thinking, exist. Accordingly, this inference (*conclusion* in the French) 'I think, therefore I exist,' is the first and most certain of all to occur to anyone who philosophizes in an orderly way" (AT VIII-1 7: CSM I 195). "For if I judge that the wax exists from the fact that I see it, clearly this same fact entails much more evidently (*multo evidentius efficitur*) that I myself also exist ... But when I see, or think I see (I am not distinguishing the two), it is simply not possible that I who am now thinking am not something" (AT VII 33: CSM II 22). Cf. also n. 2 in chapter 5 above for a full list of the logical terms used by Descartes in this regard.

It is possible, no doubt, to construe the connection between *cogito* and *sum* in normative or in neutral terms like Wilson's: "it is surely an important feature of the *cogito* reasoning that doubt and/or the supposition of deception *itself* is supposed to *lead to*, rather than undermine, the certainty of 'I exist'" (1978, 61; emphasis in original). But their straightforwardly logical force seems hard to deny.

15 For examples, see Tlumak 1978. According to Bennett the normative is "the lesser strand" (1990, 76), the psychological or "factual" notion of certainty being the main one. Cf. also ibid., 81: "We might be encouraged by this to think that the normative concept is what Descartes is seriously employing, and that the odd intrusions of the other are negligible slips. But this would be wrong. Even the milder judgement that the factual concept is the junior partner, being less intensively present in the text than the normative one, is mistaken. A good many passages that seem to involve justification and reasons turn out on closer scrutiny to invite a reading in terms of factual indubitability." This seems on the whole correct, except that Bennett insists that the psychological necessity of assenting to a proposition is one thing, its truth another – a familiar point that makes perfect sense in relation to the ordinary concept of truth, but none at all in relation to the sense of 'truth' relevant to the *cogito* principle. Cf. Larmore (1984) for another instance of the same confusion.

Some warrant for labelling interpretations of this type 'psychologistic' rather than 'psychological' is provided by Larmore's title ("Descartes' Psychologistic

Theory of Assent"). This family of interpretations (some of which have come to the fore quite recently) are the exception referred to in the earlier enumeration of five contending types of interpretation.

16 On the "chasm" of which Bennett speaks, and the possibility of constructing a solid theological bridge across it, see section 14.2.

Gewirth urges (1968, 277) that the deficiency of Descartes's 'subjective' or psychological orientation is actually remedied by a different orientation. Clarity and distinctness, he argues, "cannot in their essential nature be the same as truth" understood as "the relation of 'correspondence' or 'conformity' between the idea and the thing" (254). "It is only after the nature of clearness and distinctness has been determined, and the veracity of God demonstrated, that Descartes is able to assert that clear and distinct ideas are true" (256). "It is precisely because ideas are viewed by Descartes as being representative of things which are not themselves perceived directly [i.e., his 'representationalism'; cf. sections 4.1 and 21.1], that clearness and distinctness, characteristics emerging within these operations, are not in their immediate nature the same as the transcendental relation of conformity between ideas and things which Descartes calls 'truth,' so that the methodological orientation must be supplemented by a metaphysical one culminating in the divine guarantee" (274). This is, of course, the same "chasm" described in other terms.

17 On the Scholastic (or rather Thomistic) definition, see Phelan 1967, 133–54 and Boehner 1958, 174–200. This is probably not the only occasion in the present work when 'Scholastic' and 'Scholastic-Aristotelian' has been used where 'Thomistic' and 'Aristotelico-Thomistic' would have been more appropriate. As 'Thomistic' cannot be identified with 'Scholastic,' so 'Scholastic' is not to be equated with 'medieval.' For a good brief overview of *medieval* conceptions of truth, see Serene 1982.

18 Cf. the conversation with Burman (AT V 160: CSMK 344): "As to whether our perceptions are clear or not, this is something we will know best from our own inner consciousness (*ex propria conscientia optime sciemus*)."

19 Gewirth (1968, 258) suggests a different interpretation of clarity and distinctness when he writes that "the clearness and distinctness, or obscurity and confusion, of an idea are neither intrinsic to the idea nor explicable in terms of a simple relation between idea and perceptive act." But this proves to mean only that clarity and distinctness are a function, not just of ideas, but of how we "interpret" them (in judgments that either do or do not correspond exactly to what is immediately present to consciousness). Thus, Gewirth's account of clarity and distinctness is strictly phenomenological (or "intraideational," as he aptly puts it in one place [ibid., 275]).

As noted in chapter 1, n. 16, although 'direct' and 'immediate' 'indirect' and 'mediate' are here used synonomously, 'direct' might usefully be opposed to 'reflexive' knowledge. 'Phenomenological' would then be 'reflexive' rather than 'direct' knowledge: the product of directing attention inward or *back* upon thinking itself (as immediately present to consciousness) rather than outward upon the immediate objects of thought.

20 On the *imago Dei* doctrine in Descartes, see section 9.1 above. On the whole theological background of "die beiden Freiheitsbegriffe Descartes,'" the Augustinian and the traditional (Aristotelian), cf. Heidegger 1994, §27. Note also Heidegger's interesting observation (ibid., 201) that in the *Principles* (which he hoped to have adopted by the Jesuits for use in their philosophy courses) Descartes highlights the traditional concept of *libertas indifferentiae* promoted by the Jesuits rather than the Augustinian-Jansenist concept clearly favoured in the Fourth Meditation.

21 See the polemic against this definition in *Le Monde* (AT XI 39: CSM I 93f.). As for the knowledge of what truth is, see the *Regulae*: "those who really do possess knowledge (*vere sciunt*) can discern the truth with equal facility whether they have derived it from a simple subject or from an obscure one. For once they have hit upon it, they grasp each truth by means of a single and distinct act which is similar in every case" (AT X 401: CSM I 33).

22 On the nominal definition, cf. also Gassendi's definition of 'truth' at AT VII 281: CSM II 196 (*conformitas judicii cum re*), and Descartes's remark in the Third Meditation: "the chief and most common mistake which is to be found here consists in my judging that the ideas which are in me resemble, or conform to (*similes esse sive conformes*), things located outside me" (AT VII 37: CSM II 26). Gassendi defines 'error' in a similar way, rejecting Descartes's *phenomenological* description of error in the Fourth Meditation as "the incorrect use of free will": "the essence of error does not seem to consist in the incorrect use of free will, as you allege, so much as in the disparity between our judgement and the thing which is the object of our judgement. And it seems that error arises when our intellectual apprehension of the thing does not correspond with the way the thing really is" (AT VII 317: CSM II 220). The phenomenological account of error, by contrast, involves no reference to anything extra-mental.

23 Cf. Bennett (1990, §VIII: "The derivation of the 'truth rule'"), who attempts to reconstruct the "argument," deciding after a "series of disasters" to "walk out on it" (93). As candidates for what Descartes might have meant by that special feature of 'I am a thinking thing' that renders it certain, Bennett considers in turn (a) "factual [i.e., psychological] indubitability [in a sense that does not entail truth]" (92); (b) normative indubitability; (c) truth; and (d) "normative indubitability taken as entailing truth." His rejection of (c) is based on a sense of 'truth' that is not the primary one in Descartes, and he nowhere considers (e) 'factual indubitability taken as entailing truth,' presumably because, not having got hold of the relevant sense of 'truth,' it makes no sense to him.

24 Cf. *Principles*, I, 10, where certainty is listed among the "common notions," with
the passage in the Third Meditation where Descartes classifies his ideas into three
kinds, innate, adventitious, and factitious. In the latter place, Descartes gives as
examples of innate ideas, "what a thing is, what truth is, and what thought is (*quid
sit res, quid sit veritas, quid sit cogitatio*)." In the *Principles*, he places in roughly
similar juxtaposition "*quid sit cogitatio, quid existentia, quid certitudo.*" The
parallel between the two passages provides some (if not conclusive) support for the
claim that Descartes meant by *veritas* (as an innate idea) precisely what he meant
by *certitudo*. For a list of passages in which *certitudo* = *veritas* in the *Regulae*, cf.
Marion 1975, §4, n. 23.

25 Frankfurt (1987b, sect. VIII) bases his normative interpretation largely on this
passage (as well as its "echo" in the Sixth Replies, AT VII 436: CSM II 294): "As
[Descartes] conceives it, the aim of inquiry is just to arrive at beliefs which it would
be irrational for us to doubt because the assumption that they are false involves us
in contradiction. But we cannot be so bold as to claim that rational inquiry leads us
to the truth as God has created it." And in the next section: "The inquiry to which
Descartes devotes his *Meditations* is an exploration by reason of its own limits or
necessities. Its goal is, and can only be, to determine what it is reasonable for us to
believe – that is, what it would be irrational for us to doubt and not what is true in
the eyes of God and the angels." Cf. also 1968, 226 and 1970, chap. 15. Section X
of the same article indicates that this approach evolved as a response to Koyré's
worries (cf. Koyré 1922, 19ff.) about the possibility of science, a problem suggested to Frankfurt by his reading of Gewirth. Cf. Frankfurt's explicit acknowledgment of indebtedness to Gewirth in 1968, n. 21.

26 Cf. Gewirth (1968, n. 76, 1987a, n. 18, and 1987b, 87f.), whose conclusions are
endorsed by Kenny 1970, 686. Gaukroger examines the letter in even greater depth
(1986, 52f.), concluding: "I think there is now general agreement that, for
Descartes, it is *p*'s corresponding to reality that makes it true" (66). Brown (1980,
36) speaks of "Descartes's apparent adherence to a correspondence theory of truth."
Where a "coherence" theory is discussed in the literature, it is usually Frankfurt's
normative account of certainty in Descartes that is meant. (See, e.g., Sievert's
article "Frankfurt on Descartes's View of Truth," 1977.) But if the point of view of
our earlier survey of scholarly opinion is correct, what Frankfurt develops is not so
much a different theory of, as a surrogate for, truth. Cf. n. 6 above, where this
ambiguity of 'truth' is discussed.

27 Does the *fact* of radical scepticism as a philosophical posture belie Descartes's
claims regarding what we are and are not psychologically capable of believing?
Perhaps not, if the sceptic has simply not reflected sufficiently on what truth is,
even though the answer is immediately (if only implicitly) present to consciousness
as long as he thinks at all. On the other hand, a retort such as this makes Descartes's

position sheerly unassailable (thereby laying it open to the charge of question-begging), since the sceptic's refusal to acknowledge the point at issue would be taken as proof that he has not reflected adequately, since anyone who reflects adequately ... etc.

Cf. the related point of Ashworth regarding clear and distinct perception (1972, 101f.): "Descartes avoided the pitfall of introducing yet further criteria which would distinguish clear and distinct ideas from those seemingly so; but he did so by saying in effect that we can only be deceived when we have not looked hard enough, and that we have only looked hard enough when we cease to be deceived. The legitimacy of such a move is, at best, highly dubious."

When Gassendi (AT VII 279: CSM II 194f.) put forward a form of the same objection ("what you ought to be working on is not so much establishing this [truth] rule, ... but putting forward a method to guide us and show us when we are mistaken and when not, on those occasions when we think we clearly and distinctly perceive something"), Descartes replied by assigning the entire First and Second Meditations no other purpose than this: "I carefully provided such a method in the appropriate place, where I first eliminated all preconceived opinions and afterwards listed all my principal ideas, distinguishing those which were clear from those which were obscure or confused" (AT VII 362: CSM II 250). Apparently not satisfied with this response, Leibniz urged a well-known version of the same complaint (cf., e.g., 1875–90, IV, 329, 331, 363, etc.).

13: Truth and Correspondence

1 Gueroult 1968, I, 94: "Dans la science philosophique, toutefois, il adviendra qu'en un point de la chaîne une raison sera saisie: Dieu vérace, qui investira soudaine-ment d'une valeur objective les vérités obtenues selon l'ordre des raisons." Cf. also I, 63: "C'est grâce à la IIIe Méditation [i.e., the proof of God's existence] que *ma* science deviendra plus tard *la* science, et que les vérités de ma science pourront être tenues pour les vérités des choses." And II, 24: "Elles [les idées mathématiques] apparaissent maintenant comme les conditions de possibilité, non plus seulement de nos représentations des choses, mais de ces choses mêmes. En leur conférant par la démonstration du Dieu vérace la valeur objective qui leur manquait, ma science a transformé les vérités de l'entendement en vérités des choses." And so on through-out the work. On the questionable sense given "l'ordre des raisons" here and throughout, see Röd 1971, 55.

2 Cf. also J.-M. Beyssade 1979, vi: "Établir avec les premières vérités la possibilité de la vérité, la possibilité de la vraie et certaine science: voilà ce que Descartes appelle métaphysique, ou philosophie première."

Gueroult describes "les trois grands problèmes" of Descartes in remarkably

Kantian terms: "problème du *fondement de la vérité* (valeur objective des idées claires et distinctes), problème des *limites de notre intelligence* (erreur et conditions humaines de la vérité), problème du *fondement des sciences de la nature* (fondement du mécanisme, séparation des substances, existence des corps, union substantielle)" (Gueroult 1968, I, 25). These correspond, roughly speaking, to the transcendental deduction of the categories, the transcendental dialectic, and the metaphysical first principles of natural science, respectively.

    On metaphysics and epistemological critique in Descartes, see section 3.2f.

3 As Wilson (1978a, 80f.) rightly stresses against the objections of Burtt (1927, 117).

4 First, it seems, by Malcolm (1968, Summary), who distinguishes three arguments ("from doubt," "from clear and distinct ideas," and "from indivisibility") bearing on the real distinction between mind and body. These labels were taken over by Cottingham 1986, chap. 5. However, only the second of them involves a logical inference from premises, i.e., an argument in the usual sense of the term. The first, in particular, only makes explicit, positively and negatively, what is already implicit in the insight *cogito, ergo sum*. This will be shown in the following. Nevertheless, the customary titles will be retained for ease of reference.

5 There is no need to consider the details of Arnauld's objection, backed up with an illustration from geometry, which is usually regarded as very acute. For a good brief account of the geometrical illustration and its force against both arguments, see Cottingham 1986, 112 and 114.

6 Cf. AT VII 221: CSM II 156: "I took 'a complete understanding of something' and 'understanding something to be a complete thing' as having one and the same meaning." On adequate, complete, and abstract (or incomplete) concepts, cf. section 10.8 above.

7 Cf. the Replies to the Second Set of Objections: "Here ['in the Second Meditation'] I wanted to give the reader an express warning that at that stage I was not yet asking whether the mind is distinct from the body, but was merely examining those of its properties of which I have certain and evident knowledge" (AT VII 129: CSM II 93). And when in the Third Objections Hobbes charges that the thing that thinks "may be something corporeal," since the "contrary is assumed not proved" (VII 173: CSM II 122), Descartes replies: "I certainly did not assume the contrary ... I left it quite undecided until the Sixth Meditation" (AT VII 175: CSM II 123). Again, in the Seventh Replies, Descartes writes to Bourdin: "I deny that I in any way presupposed that the mind is incorporeal; though later on, in the Sixth Meditation, I did in fact *demonstrate* as much (AT VII 492: CSM II 333 e.a.).

8 Compare Cottingham's remark (1992b, 245) that the "gap between subjective cognition and essential reality [also: 'objective reality'] is bridged by proving God's existence" with the passages from Gueroult cited earlier. Of course, Cottingham is concerned only with the real distinction between body and soul,

while Gueroult speaks in much the same vein of the objective truth or certainty of the *cogito, ergo sum* as well.

9 Cf. Cottingham (1986, 113): "in the relevant part of the *Discourse* (and the same would go for the Second Meditation) Descartes is merely recording his subjective perceptions concerning his nature or essence; he is not claiming that these map onto what is objectively the case." In 1992b, however, Cottingham is much more sceptical about this – with good reason, as it seems.

10 Descartes's distinction among distinctions is a replica of that of Suarez (cf. Menn 1995, 193) and departs from St Thomas's notion of a real distinction (cf. Owens, 1985, 37). Wells (1993, 518) distinguishes these as the "*duae res*" and "*ex natura rei*" varieties of real distinction. Cf. AT IV 350: CSMK 281.

11 In this sense the *Regulae* are indeed an epistemological or methodological treatise, as the *Discourse* and *Meditations* are not. Marion is one who appears to underestimate the differences. Cf. section 3.2.

12 Cf. Röd 1971, 59: "Descartes hat zwar in den *Regulae* die Frage nach dem Verhältnis von Erkenntnis- und Seinsordnung ausdrücklich ausgeklammert; das heißt jedoch nicht, daß er nicht schon damals eine bestimmte Vorstellung vom Verhältnis beider gehabt hätte. Tatsächlich kann die Annahme eingeborener Prinzipien des Erkennens, die Descartes seit seinen philosophischen Anfängen und mithin auch in den *Regulae* machte, nur dazu dienen, die Konformität von Erkenntnis- und Seinsordnung zu begründen. Es ist allerdings richtig, daß der in den *Regulae* auf Schritt und Tritt vorausgesetzte Parallelismus der Ordnung einfacher Sätze und der Ordnung einfacher Naturen 1628/9 *noch nicht zum Problem geworden war, weshalb er ihn auch nicht zu beweisen versuchte*" (e.a.). With this the foregoing is in substantial agreement.

13 Malcolm points out some reasonable facsimiles of the same argument in *The Search for Truth*, at two places in the *Principles*, in the *Broadsheet*, the "Synopsis" of the *Meditations*, and in the letter to Picot that serves as preface to the *Principles*. Cf. 1968, sect. 11. To these might be added the various places in the Replies where Descartes restates the Argument from Doubt, e.g., AT VII 353: CSM II 244.

14 Cottingham 1992b, 242ff. Strong language for the usually more restrained Cottingham; but see Carnap (1959a, 73), who charges Descartes with having committed two gross logical blunders in the space of three words. See below, chapter 17, n. 5.

15 Malcolm 1968, sect. 7, cf. esp. 322: "Descartes gives here a wrong account of his intentions in the *Discourse*"; and n. 44: "Descartes's own misinterpretation of the *Discourse*."

16 Cf. Descartes's own paraphrase of the Argument from Doubt in the Seventh Replies: "'The knowledge of those things that I know to exist (*Notitia eorum quae novi existere*) does not depend on the knowledge of things of whose existence I am

as yet unaware (*nondum novi*); now I know that a thinking thing exists, but I do not
yet know that any body exists; therefore the knowledge of a thinking thing does not
depend on knowledge of the body (*non pendet a notitia corporis*)" (AT VII 521:
CSM II 354f.). This differs slightly from the summary just given, with which it
nonetheless shares an emphasis on what I *know* myself to be and the *order of
knowing* ("does not depend on") as opposed to what I in truth *am* or am not.
Kennington (1972, 112) accordingly speaks of "the *only* fallacy" by which
Descartes "infers from 'knows only' to 'is only,' from the *ordo cognoscendi* to the
ordo essendi." The *tantum* will be discussed shortly.

17 Cf. Curley 1978, 197: "I think the best view of the Second Meditation is that it is
supposed to provide us, not with conclusions we can later use as premises in further
arguments, but with clear and distinct ideas. If I practice the methodical doubt
properly, I will find myself compelled to assent to the propositions that I exist and
that I think but not to any other propositions about myself ... In particular, I will
find that I am not compelled to ascribe to myself any properties which involve
extension." And in the circumstances, to say that I am not compelled is to say that I
am not warranted. See next note.

18 Hamelin 1921, 127: "S'il dit qu'il est une chose qui pense, cela signifie qu'il n'est
pas autorisé pour le moment à se considérer que comme une chose qui pense."

19 As Gewirth (1987b, sect. I) has argued persuasively. Cf. AT VII 381: CSM II 262:
"they [geometrical truths] undoubtedly *conform to* the true natures of things
established by God. Not that there are *in the world* (*in mundo*) substances which
have length but no breadth, or breadth but no depth ... etc."

20 This may provide the solution to a puzzle first drawn to my attention by Mr Stefan
Rodde: If God makes the good good by choosing it, then, were he to be a deceiver,
deception would be good and in no way inconsistent with the perfection of God's
nature. The solution is that deception is one of those things that are *absolutely*
inconsistent with God's omnipotence as tending toward non-being.

21 Cf., e.g., Knudsen 1982, 490: "Objective ... in the medieval sense ... indicates the
conceptual content that apears to the intellect."

22 Clearly understood notably by Heidegger (1962, 80f.). Grossly misrepresented not
just in the type of 'encephalic subjectivism' to be discussed in the Conclusion (cf.
section 21.4) but in psychologistic readings of Descartes as well.
   On the use of *hypokeimenon*, *subjectum*, and *objectum* in ancient and medieval
philosophy, cf. Owens 1978, 36, n. 10. Scotus, Owens remarks, uses *subjectum* and
objectum as equivalents, though the latter is "the more proper term" for what we
today call 'the object' (ibid.). Suarez's usage corresponds to that of Scotus: *primum
omnium inquirendum nobis est huius doctrinae objectum seu subjectum* ... (Suarez
1965, 2). Here *seu* obviously means "or, in other words." Descartes's usage follows
that of Suarez. Cf., for example, the first paragraph of the *Regulae*, where Descartes

notes that the sciences are distinguished by their objects (*pro diversitate objectorum*), adding that "the sciences as a whole are nothing other than human wisdom, which always remains one and the same, however different the subjects to which it is applied (*quantumvis differentibus subjectis applicata*)" (AT X 360: CSM I 9). *Subjecta* and *objecta* are apparently used interchangeably.

Strictly speaking, nothing in Heidegger's treatment of the *ego* as "ein ausgezeichnetes Zugrundeliegendes – hypokeimenon, subjectum" implies that the subject is anything more than first in the order of knowing, the first 'object' of certain knowledge – the *subjectum* par excellence in the Cartesio-Scholastic sense of the word (cf. also section 21.4). That is, there is nothing to suggest a reversal in the order of being such that, with Descartes's reorientation of philosophy toward the human subject, the totality of what is is reduced to an object (in Kant's sense) for a thinking subject. Cf. also Röd 1971, 79: "Der in dem Satz 'Ich denke, also bin ich' mitgemeinte Vorrang der Erkenntnis des Subjekts gegenüber der Erkenntnis der Objekte ist ein Vorrang innerhalb der durch die Methode bestimmten Erkenntnisordnung, nicht ein ontologischer Primat des Subjekts gegenüber der objektiven Wirklichkeit." Similarly, Kennington 1972, 106.

On the change in the order of being from the Scholastics to Descartes, see the discussion of Cartesian dualism and Scholastic-Aristotelian hylomorphism in section 22.1 of the Conclusion.

23 'Representative realism' is, of course, not to be confused with 'representationalism,' i.e., the 'veil-of-perception' doctrine discussed in sections 4.1 and 4.2. On the various senses of 'realism,' see sections 21.1 and 21.3 of the Conclusion.

14: Certainty and Circularity

1 Cf. Ross (Aristotle 1949a, 38): "Now the essence of a *petitio principii* is that it assumes two propositions of which one or the other cannot be known unless the conclusion is already known."

2 A similar criticism can be levelled at the ontological argument, which employs as its first premise the truth rule 'whatever I perceive clearly and distinctly is true' (AT VII 65: CSM II 45). Cf. the form in which the ontological argument is recast at AT VII 115: CSM II 83.

3 For detailed refutations of the memory answer, see Levett (1937) and Frankfurt (1987a) as well as the excellent post-mortem by Etchemendy (1981).

4 For the precise works under reference, see Loeb 1992, n. 2. In the next note, Loeb points out that Cottingham (1986, 69 and esp. n. 23) takes Frankfurt's (1970) to be an instance of the psychological interpretation, while Markie (1986) takes the interpretations of both Curley (1978) and Gewirth (1941) to be psychological. Cottingham too remarks on the fact that Curley was "strongly influenced" (ibid.,

77, n. 23) by Frankfurt: "although Curley 'subjectivizes' Descartes less than Frankfurt, his interpretation still appears to do insufficient justice to Descartes's central and highly ambitious goal of achieving '*knowledge of the truth* by means of first principles.'" This judgment is confirmed by Curley's most recent foray into the debate (1993, esp. 24, 27f.), a critical notice making many telling criticisms of Markie 1986. For all the attention given psychological certainty, Curley's own interpretation still seems to belong to the normative variety. In short, the "interpretation and classification of positions in the literature is itself a difficult matter" (Loeb 1992, n. 4). Fortunately, there is no need to enter into questions of secondary and tertiary criticism here.

5 Interpretations that appear to be examples of the 'limitation' strategy are found in Gewirth (1987b), Kenny (1968 and 1970), Schouls (1987), Van Cleve (1987), and J.-M. Beyssade (1979, 15f.). (For further candidates among those writing in English, see the review article of Hughes 1978, sections 3 and 4.) One key element of such interpretations is well expressed in Kenny's conclusion: "There is [in Descartes] no *single* faculty, or *single* exercise of a faculty, that is vindicated by its own use" (1968 198, e.a.). Another consists in making the vindicating faculty immune from metaphysical doubt, i.e., a source of *truth* even without the knowledge of God's existence and veracity. (It is this that makes Gewirth's and Kenny's adoption of a limitation strategy doubtful.) Schouls undertakes "an examination of what Descartes means by reason" (ibid., 308; cf. n. 4) that leads to a distinction between "intuition$_1$ and intuition$_2$." This is directly inspired by Kenny's distinction between first- and second-order doubt, which in turn represents an important advance on Gewirth's distinction between psychological and metaphysical certainty. Cf. Etchemendy's rather different portrayal and criticism of Kenny's solution (1981, sect. 4 and 5), based largely on Kenny 1970 rather than 1968.

Obviously, the distinction between *persuasio* and *scientia* belongs to the same family of solutions. J.-M. Beyssade (1981, 103f.), who also invokes it, asserts that this distinction "rejoint exactement" Kenny's distinction between first- and second-order doubt. This seems mistaken.

Of course, there are other classification schemes as well. Hughes (1978, 286) describes that of Markie (in his unpublished dissertation) in terms that suggest a division between what Doney calls the 'limitation thesis' and 'other' interpretations. Hughes himself modifies a classification devised by Bidgwood. See Hughes for exact references, a useful bibliography, and insightful (if terse) criticism of a decade of literature, mostly in English.

6 Cf. Loeb 1992, 202f.: An "unshakable belief is one that cannot be dislodged by argument. Whether or not a belief is unshakable is a question of descriptive psychology ... Knowledge, in the strict sense of scientific knowledge, is identified with unshakable belief, and hence itself has a psychological characterization."

7 It is not always convenient to note expressly that an actual act of remembering is not required in order for the knowledge of God to function as the guarantee of other clear and distinct perceptions, though I have generally tried to acknowledge what I take to be Loeb's point by speaking of 'being able to remember' or 'to recall' rather than 'remembering' or 'recalling.'

8 Little wonder, then, that he concludes his essay with the remark: "Many commentators ... have sought to attribute to Descartes some line of thought in which factual indubitability is intelligibly related to justification and/or to truth. They have usually admitted that the line of thought, whatever it is, is flawed; but the aim has been to find it – to point to some prima facie plausible set of considerations and to say '*That* is how Descartes thought he could interrelate the subjectivist [i.e., psychological] and objectivist strands of his thinking [i.e., the *truth* project].' Attempts to present Descartes in this light have all failed. They had to. The interrelating structure is just not there; nor is any plausible simulacrum of it" (1990, 108). For a reply to this (that the link is there, at least, not that it is not flawed), see the previous chapter.

That clear and distinct theological knowledge differs from all other clear and distinct ideas in some important way is another piece of "common property." Cf. Frankfurt 1970, chap. 15. A somewhat different interpretation from Frankfurt's of the crucial difference between theological and other 'eternal truths' will be offered below.

9 Cf. Descartes's remark to Gassendi in another context: "you cannot give a fair account of what I have to say on any topic unless you go into everything I wrote about all the other related issues" (AT VII 379: CSM II 261).

10 Note Miller's manner of conveying the representational or perceptual *and* volitional aspects of God's creation of the eternal truths: "God produced them [the eternal truths] by willing them or by willing-thinking them" (1965, 47).

11 Bouveresse (1987, 320f.) suggests initially that neither horn of the Euthyphro dilemma can be chosen by Descartes since God's intellect and will are the same; but he goes on to acknowledge that Descartes only excludes one horn as blasphemous. For a nice juxtaposition of Descartes's own with Suarez's and Vasquez's formulations of what is essentially the Euthyphro dilemma, cf. Marion 1981a, 59.

12 For a nest of references from Ockham, see Marion (1981a, 43, n. 1), who underscores the restriction of the doctrine to the moral domain. Marion questions the ascription of voluntarism to Scotus (ibid., 60 n. 21), as to Descartes (see next note).

13 Cf. also *Principles*, I, 23 and Gouhier's word of caution (1969, 239 and n. 29) concerning the context of the quotation from St Augustine. Marion rejects the designation 'voluntarism' outright (1981a, 283f.) on the grounds that it suggests a reversal of the traditional order of intellect and will in God: "Descartes n'inverse pas la hiérarchie thomiste des facultés en Dieu; il en récuse la possibilité: à la

racine, tout volontarisme devient impensable" (ibid.). Though true, this constitutes no insuperable objection to all uses of the word 'voluntarism' in connection with Descartes's doctrine. Marion, after all, acknowledges the prominent role assigned God's will in Descartes's discussion of the eternal truths (ibid., 292f.), even if the word *voluntas* only actually occurs once (295); he even speaks of a "quasi-priority of the will" (ibid.), although the 'indistinction' of the divine intellect and will, and the equivocity of the very terms 'intellect' and 'will' when applied to God and humans, render the talk of the divine will (so Marion) little more than a code of sorts for 'divine omnipotence.'

14 As Gouhier aptly observes (1969, 238): "S'il ne faut point parler de Dieu comme d'un Jupiter ou d'un Saturne assujetti au Styx et aux destinées [see below], il ne faut pas davantage en parler comme d'un satrape aveugle ou capricieux. Lorsque Descartes déclare que les vérités éternelles dépendent de la volonté de Dieu, *n'oublions pas que cette volonté est intelligence*" (e.a.). Similarly Marion (1981b, 275): "Sans aucun doute faut-il bien parler d'un arbitraire divin, mais, sans aucun doute non plus, il faut éviter même le soupçon d'un irrationalisme." Osler is another who criticizes Frankfurt from a similar perspective. Cf. 1985, n. 30. On this question, see also Menn 1990, 229: "Descartes's voluntarism is not irrationalism: God's laws are not tyrannical whims, but rational truths, proceeding from a God who is the source of truth and rationality."

15 Cf. Owens 1985, 136 on the Thomistic doctrine: "The first cause creates through free choice, not through necessity of nature. It has to know and choose what it creates. This means that the essences of things exist eternally in its knowledge. There the essences have being, but their being is the being of the first cause. There they are not creatures, but the creative essence." It follows that there can be no question of a distinction in Aquinas such as Descartes draws between created and uncreated eternal truths. Only the latter are truths about God's own nature or existence for Descartes; for Aquinas *all* eternal truths belong to God's creative essence. God, therefore, can no more change them than his own nature. On this, see Aquinas 1947–8, 233f. [*ST*, Ia.45.2]). The first objection Aquinas considers urges that it is "a commonly received axiom that *nothing is made from nothing*. But the power of God does not extend to the contraries of first principles; as for instance, that God could make the whole to be less than its part, or that affirmation and negation are both true at the same time." In his reply, Thomas concedes that God's power does not extend to the negation of such logical, metaphysical, and mathematical first principles.

For Descartes, as noted above, only the *un*created among the eternal truths belong to God's creative essence or nature. This would appear to include the principle just mentioned ('something cannot come from nothing') and perhaps others (e.g., the principle 'nothing has no properties'), though probably *not* the mathematical first principle mentioned by Thomas or the simple truths of arithmetic and geometry. The exact boundary between these and the created eternal truths is hard to fix.

Would Descartes perhaps have gone so far as to say that God creates *all* the eternal truths, some freely by an act of will, others, the absolutely eternal truths, by (to use Owens's phrase) "the necessity of his own nature"? There are certainly Neoplatonic models for such a move (of which Thomas is aware.) But there is no evidence at all that Descartes even toyed with the idea of explaining how certain metaphysical axioms or truths might "follow" from God's own nature along these lines.

Nevertheless, Spinoza may have seen something of the kind as latent in Descartes's distinction between two kinds of eternal truth. Fusing God's intellect, will, and creative power, he absorbed all the eternal truths of the former kind, including the most basic laws of nature, into those of the latter kind. Thus, Spinoza's God acts exclusively from the necessity of his own nature. Cf. Spinoza 1994, 97 (EIP16f.). There is no need to point out how remote this is from orthodox Christian theology; that the inspiration may have been partly Cartesian is, of course, speculation.

16 Cf. the frequently cited passage (e.g., Gueroult 1969, 241f. and Curley 1978, 355) from Aquinas 1947–8, vol. I, 94f. [*ST*, Ia.16.7]): "Hence, if no intellect were eternal, no truth would be eternal. Now because only the divine intellect is eternal, in it alone truth has eternity. Nor does it follow from this that anything else but God is eternal, since the truth of the divine intellect is God himself."

Frankfurt suggests (ibid.) that Descartes tacitly rejected alternative (3), held by "Scholastic Philosophers such as Suarez and Aquinas" (39), on the grounds that it introduced an invidious distinction (at least *rationis*) between God's intellect and will. Another explanation has it that he was quite unaware of "the authentic Thomist doctrine ... pure and undefiled," having known only its "corrupt and watered-down version as professed by [his] Jesuit preceptors" at La Flèche (Wells 1987, 56, summarizing Garin 1932).

Although createdness entails dependence, dependence of the eternal truths on God is in fact consistent with createdness, as in (1), *and* with uncreatedness, as in (3). Descartes may have mistaken the entailment for reciprocal and regarded (3), eternal truths that are uncreated *and* dependent, as self-contradictory. And self-contradictory it is on the assumption of a single type of dependence, dependence in the order of efficient causality: "God ... established the eternal truths ... by the same kind of causality as he created all things, that is to say, as their efficient and total cause" (AT I 151f.: CSMK 25). Thus, Descartes could *both* have correctly understood the authentic Thomistic position and still repudiated (3), *un*created yet dependent eternal truths, owing to the deliberate rejection of any form of causality apart from efficient (notably, exemplar causality). This is after all a fundamental feature of the new guiding idea of being in Descartes's philosophy (see section 22.3); the doctrinal reason suggested by Frankfurt, the identity of God's intellect and will, is ultimately only a corollary of Descartes's conception of causality (cf. n. 25 below). On the reduction of exemplar to efficient causality by some the late-Scholastic philosophers, see the article of Wells (1993, n. 12).

As for (2), i.e., eternal truths both uncreated and *in*dependent of God, this Descartes clearly rejected as a lapse into pagan Greek notions of divinity. Whether or not Descartes took St Thomas and Suarez to be among those who espoused this doctrine is probably undecidable. He certainly speaks of it as though it were the only, or at least the chief, alternative to his own view, (1); but that too may be explained by the tacit rejection of all but efficient causality. Of course, even without Aquinas there are still plenty of influential candidates for the distinction of having held (2). Cf. the references to Marion in chapter 5, n. 4 above.

17 Cf. Descartes's characterization of God in *Principles*, I, 22: "eternal, omniscient, omnipotent, *the source of all goodness and truth*, the creator of all things" (e.a.). Neither description in the Third Meditation (AT VII 40: CSM II 28 and AT VII 45: CSM II 31) includes the highlighted feature.

18 Cf. Kenny 1970, 690: "The clear and distinct perceptions used in the proof of God's existence are perceptions of particular propositions, ... The veracity of God is used to establish not any particular clear and distinct perception, but the general proposition that whatever I clearly and distinctly perceive is true." Substitute for the particular-general the *persuasio-scientia* distinction, and the result is the solution developed here. For detailed criticism of Kenny's position, see Gewirth (1987c), and Feldman and Levinson (1987), along with Kenny's response to the latter (1971). Kenny's solution (first developed in Kenny 1968) is more fully elaborated in his response to Gewirth (Kenny 1970).

19 In an influential paper on "Descartes's Conception of Perfect Knowledge," Doney criticized Bréhier's "ingenious" (1970, 396) suggestion that the doubt standing in the way of "perfect knowledge" arises from the mutability of the eternal truths. Doney argues (cf. ibid., 398): suppose that someone had once become convinced by the ontological argument that a veracious God exists forever. He would then know that the conclusion of the ontological argument is *always* true. But only remembering the conclusion, he can be certain only that what he clearly and distinctly perceived *at that time* was always true *when he so perceived it*, not that it is always true when he only remembers it. The uncertainty is thus only postponed; the very doubt that the knowledge of God was to dispel arises regarding the knowledge of God itself. The solution to this puzzle is the doctrine of divine immutability.

20 The foregoing solution to the problem of the circle is obviously not far removed from the 'continuing truth' answers provided by Kemp Smith and Etchemendy.

Smith touches on all the elements of the solution offered here: "this [clear and distinct apprehension *now*] suffices only for persuasion, not for science, i.e., it suffices for certainty as to what is present to the mind at the instant, not as yielding assurance that it will continue to be so apprehended at other instants. All instants of time are independent of one another. Until we have refuted the hypothesis that we are being deceived in all our thoughts, even in those which are distinct as well as clear, we have no right to conclude that what is true for us at one instant will hold true at other instants. For this we require proof of the goodness and consequent immutability of God" (1952, 273). However, the immediately following section, entitled "Descartes' manner of meeting the charge of circular reasoning," does a disappointing job of putting these pieces of the puzzle together.

In designating it a *circulus ex tempore*, Etchemendy rightly stresses the temporal dimension of the distinction between *persuasio* and *scientia* – without however bringing that particular distinction into play. In this he follows Bréhier, unlike whom he recognizes a distinction between two kinds of eternal truths, theological knowledge alone being strictly immutable. This meets Doney's objection to Bréhier's solution (see preceding note). Like Gueroult (1968, 26ff.), Etchemendy tends to make God's power (omnipotence) and uniqueness rather than the immutability of his nature do the work of forestalling a second circle (cf. 1981, 34f.).

Gouhier, too, presses a distinction between two classes of "eternal truths" or "common notions," the created and the uncreated (cf. 1969, 282: "les « notions communes » ou « vérités éternelles » ne peuvent être prises en bloc. Toutes ne tremblaient pas sous la menace du Dieu trompeur : elles ne sont peut-être pas toutes également des créatures"). Instead of treating the theological as a subclass of metaphysical eternal truths, as we have here, Gouhier treats *all* the axioms or common notions of metaphysics ('nothing comes from nothing,' 'nothingness has no properties,' etc.) as uncreated, even as "coinciding" with (or "a variant" of) (291) the "most eternal of all truths." This may be hard to square with the talk of God's existence as "the first and most eternal of all possible truths and the *one* from which alone *all* others proceed" (AT I 150: CSMK 24 e.a.), which clearly suggests some sort of derivation, though the details are obscure. On the other hand, it provides an apt reply to the charge of circularity, which Gouhier considers in the form in which Burman posed it (that is, the proof proceeds *per axiomata*; yet the truth of the axioms depends upon the very knowledge of God's existence and veracity which they are supposed to prove). Thus, even if knowledge of the metaphysical axioms depends on that of God, since, from Gouhier's perspective, all such axioms are strictly immmutable, the circle can be avoided.

Of all interpreters J.-M. Beyssade (1979) makes most of the temporal dimension in Descartes's thought, employing it to solve various standard puzzles, including both the problem of the circle and sense of the *ergo*.

21 The letter to More of 5 February 1649 makes the same point: "I say that it involves a contradiction that there should be any atoms which are conceived as extended and at the same time indivisible. Though God might make them such that they could not be divided by any creature, we certainly cannot understand that he might deprive himself of the power of dividing them" (AT V 273: CSMK 363).

22 In a letter to Gibieuf of 19 January 1642 Descartes treats the divisibility of matter and the separateness of mind and body together.

23 Cf. *Principles*, II, 36: "we understand that God's perfection involves not only his being immutable *in himself*, but also *his operating* in a manner that is always utterly constant and immutable" (AT VIII-1 62: CSM I 240 e.a.). In question here are the most universal laws of nature and only these: from God's immutability as the "universal and primary cause – the general cause of all the motions in the world" – follow "certain rules or laws of nature, which are the secondary and particular causes of the various motions which we see in particular bodies" (ibid.). These most basic laws are necessary or "eternal truths," while particular laws (of conservation or collision, for example) are contingent. For two opposed positions on this question, see Ishiguro 1987a and 1987b and Osler 1985. In sections 5.2 above and 18.9 below we side with Osler on the necessity of the most basic laws of nature.

24 Cf. Normore 1986, 231: "Philo of Alexandria ... moves the Forms into the Divine Mind and there through the influence of Clement of Alexandria and others they are firmly lodged by the time of Augustine." And Kenny 1970, 697: "ever since Augustine had identified the Platonic ideas with archetypes in the divine mind, no orthodox scholastic had ever admitted the existence of anything eternal except God and God alone." For 'orthodox' read 'Thomistic.' On the rampant unorthodoxy of the *minores* and the late-Scholastic period, see Marion 1981b, §§5 and 6.

25 This, according to Kenny, is one of the "two principal ways in which Descartes's doctrine of the creation of the eternal truths differs from that of any scholastic he is likely to have read. The first is its Platonic aspect: the mathematical essences are distinct from the essence of God. The second is its voluntarist aspect: the mathematical essences are under the control of God's will" (1970, 695).

Voluntarism – in a sense that neither obliterates the distinction between necessary and contingent truth nor makes God's decrees irrational (see above section 14.4) – may just be the consequence of Descartes's unprecedented identification of God's intellect and will. In this he was to be followed by Spinoza, who also brought God's power into the equation (cf. Bréhier 1937, sect. VI). However, the identification of God's intellect and will is itself a consequence of the rejection of any notion of a special causality (say, 'exemplar causality') for the creation of essences (see above, n. 16). This sets Descartes apart even from those unorthodox Scholastics (e.g., Henry of Ghent) who held a doctrine superficially, at least, not unlike his.

On 'exemplarism,' see Marion 1981a, §§3 and 4. On the rejection of all forms of causality other than efficient, see section 22.3 of the Conclusion, especially n. 25.

26 J.-M. Beyssade (1981, 87) argues that there is a standard method of reconciling logically irreconcilable conclusions in Descartes "en les hiérarchisant dans une succession réglée des attitudes (qui *se contrarient*)." Descartes certainly resorts to some method of the kind in the two letters to the Princess Elizabeth of May and June 1643 regarding the interaction of a mental and material substance in volition. Similarly with the difficulty of bringing human freedom into accord with divine preordination (cf. *Principles*, I, 40–1). The same may be true of the problem of conceiving how a free act of creation could create something not contingent.

Maritain (1937, 42) speaks with good reason of an "aspect d'agnosticisme qui passe à certains moments comme une ombre rapide sur le rationalisme cartésien," instancing the exchange with the Princess Elizabeth on mind-body union and the doctrine of the creation of the eternal truths.

27 On Descartes's exchange with Elizabeth, see Miles 1983, sect. IV. Far from showing that there is no problem about God's ability to alter the eternal truths, Descartes's conclusion implies that the problem is not obviously *more* intractable than others his system faced; and as Descartes remained stubbornly unperturbed by fairly obvious incongruities of his position on mind-body union and interaction, he never seriously wavered on the question of God's ability to alter the eternal truths, no matter what the apparent absurdities involved.

28 God's necessary existence has a unique sense in Descartes: the "power to create itself or maintain itself in existence" (AT VII 118: CSM II 84). On this shift in emphasis from formal to efficient causality, see section 22.3 of the Conclusion, especially n. 25. Obviously, this has a direct bearing on whether even God's necessary existence should be construed as *logical* necessity, though this question cannot be pursued here.

On the quite different sense in which, for St Thomas, the human soul, too, is a 'necessary being,' cf. Owens 1985, 324f. Very briefly: As a subsistent form capable, qua pure intellect, of *operating* without matter, the human soul is also capable of *existing* without matter. Cf. Aquinas 1947–8, I, 364 (*ST*, Ia.75.2): "Therefore the intellectual principle which we call the mind or the intellect has an operation *per se* apart from the body ... [But] a thing *operates* according as it *is* ...," i.e., as it receives the form of operating, so it receives the form of being. The soul, accordingly, receives the act of existence directly, not as the form of a material composite, the human being. As pure form, moreover, it has no principle of change and corruption in itself and so can neither come to be nor perish (by any natural means, i.e., otherwise than through an act of creation or of annihilation). Cf. ibid., 368 (*ST*, Ia.75.6): "the human soul could not be corrupted unless it were corrupted *per se*. This, indeed, is impossible, not only as regards the human soul, but also as regards anything subsistent that is a form alone. For it is clear that what belongs to a thing by virtue of itself is inseparable from it; but existence belongs to a form, which is an act, by virtue of itself. Wherefore matter acquires actual existence as it acquires the form; while it is corrupted so far as the form is separated from it. But it is impossible for a form to be separated from itself; and therefore it is impossible for a subsistent form to cease to exist."

As for the necessary being of other spiritual substances and of the Aristotelian heavenly bodies, see the references in Owens, ibid., 149, n. 10, who concludes: "In later Scholastic tradition, however, all beings other than subsistent being [i.e., God] have been regarded as contingent." This is already the standard orthodoxy by Descartes's time.

Kant understands 'necessary being' differently again when he argues that the *cogito, ergo sum* cannot be a syllogism: "The 'I think' is ... an empirical proposition, and contains within itself the proposition 'I exist.' But I cannot say 'everything which thinks, exists.' For in that case the property of thought would render all beings which possess it necessary beings" (Kant 1929, B422n.).

Could Kant have confused 'Necessarily, whatever thinks exists' with 'Whatever thinks, exists necessarily'? For an analysis that presumes such a misplacement of the modal modifier, see Williams 1968, 94. Scholz (1931, 133) sees Kant as rejecting the major on the grounds that it presupposes (contrary to the well-known Kantian dictum to be discussed in section 22.3 of the Conclusion) that existence is a real predicate. But his grounds are unclear and, in any case, Scholz's is not the obvious construction to put on Kant's words.

29 Cf. Gewirth 1987a, 1987b; Frankfurt 1968, 1970, 1978, 1987b. In 1987b, sect. VII Frankfurt considers and rejects the possibility of a limited autonomy of human reason in respect of the uncreated among the eternal truths (cf. Gueroult 1968, II, 26ff.). He then develops, in sect. XI, the conception of the "liberation of human reason" and rational autonomy that follows from his own view of the aims of rational enquiry as Descartes understood them.

30 Cf. AT IX-1 204: CSM II 270: "before we can decide to doubt, we need some reason for doubting."

PART THREE: REFLEXION AND INFERENCE

15: Consciousness, Thought, and Reflexion

1 Cottingham et al. translate the second sentence, *Non quod ad hoc requiratur scientia reflexa, vel per demonstrationem acquisita, & multo minus scientia scientiae reflexae ...,* as follows: "But this does not require reflexive knowledge, or the kind of knowledge that is acquired by means of demonstration; still less does it

require knowledge of reflexive knowledge." This suggests that the force of *vel* is "or, if you wish," "or, in other words." Though this is a natural reading of the Latin, the following interpretation of the four main responses maintains a distinction between (1) second- and higher-level acts of reflexion on what is immediately present to consciousness (*scientia reflexa*); (2) discursive acts, including those involved in logical definitions and deductions; and (3) that pre-reflexive and pre-discursive intuition of first principles that (for Descartes as for "the dialectitians") is not *scientia* at all. If it is correct to do so, then the sense of the Latin comes very near to "not reflexive knowledge, *nor yet* (*vel*) knowledge acquired by demonstration, much less knowledge of reflexive knowledge." That this is not the most natural way to read the Latin is conceded; but that it can bear this interpretation is at least arguable.

2 Gassendi also raised a form of the objection considered first: "The second objection ... is that in order to know that I am thinking I must know what thought is; and yet ... I do not know this at all, since I have denied everything" (AT IX-1 206: CSM II 271). This is taken up in the letter to Clerselier that forms the *Appendix to the Fifth Set of Objections and Replies*: "in order to know that I am thinking I must know what thought is; and yet ... I do not know this at all, since I have denied everything" (ibid.). To this Descartes replies: "But I have denied only preconceived opinions (*les préjugez*, i.e., *praejudicia*) – not notions like these, which are known without any affirmation or denial" (ibid.). Here Descartes contrasts immediate intuition of the meanings of concepts or ideas not with the reflexive or discursive operations of the mind but with *judgments* (affirmation and denial).

3 'Discursive' and 'discursive reasoning' are used here for *logical* reflexion generally, whether inter-propositional as in deductive *inference* ('ratiocinative' in our use of the term) or intra-propositional as in "logical *definitions*" by genus and specific difference. This is significantly narrower than Descartes's own usage, which appears to cover all certain knowledge arrived at by a process or *progress of the mind*, i.e., all but relatively *simple* intuitions. In Rule III of the *Regulae* Descartes writes: "The self evidence and certainty of intuition is required not only for apprehending single propositions, but also for any train of reasoning whatever (*quoslibet discursus*)" (AT X 369: CSM I 14f.). Cf. also Rule XVII: "we shall be carrying out everything this Rule prescribes if, recognizing that the unknown is determined by the known, we reflect on the terms that occur to us first and count the unknown ones among the known, so that by reasoning soundly step by step (*gradatim et per veros discursus*) we may deduce from these all the rest (*caetera omnia ... deducamus*)" (AT X 461: CSM I 71; cf. also the heading of the Rule in question at AT X 460: CSM I 70). Note also Descartes's use of *discursus* in the fifth of the "Postulates" in the *more geometrico* arguments at the end of the Second Replies: "For there are certain truths which some people find self-evident (*per se*

nota), while others come to understand them only by means of reasoning (*non nisi per discursum*) (AT VII 164: CSM II 115). Finally, in a letter (to Silhon or Newcastle) of March or April 1648, Descartes writes: "Whatever we can know of God in this life, short of a miracle, is the result of reasoning and discursive enquiry (*raisonnement & progrez de notre discours*)" (AT V 136f.: CSMK 331).

This sense of 'discursive' obviously has nothing to do with Gaukroger's narrower use of the term (roughly, 'arguing by question and answer') in contrasting discursive and facultative conceptions of inference. Cf. Gaukroger 1986, esp. 31f. The boundary between intuition and discursive thought is discussed in section 20.1.

4 Cf. Williams 1962, 91: "Does this passage contradict the one I quoted before? Burman thought that it did." On the other hand, McRae 1972b, 39: "Burman asks whether this [passage from the Second Replies] is consistent with what Descartes says in *Principles*, I, 10. Plainly it does seem contrary." Gombay (1972, 83f.) attempts to reconcile them by means of a distinction between the 'personal' and the 'impersonal' mode of speech (cf. ibid., 77 on this distinction).

5 This manner of reconciling the passages in which Descartes speaks of the knowledge of universal principles, now as prior to that of particular instances, now as posterior, seems preferable to Wilson's suggestion that Descartes "simply could not make up his mind" (Wilson 1978a, 57).

The preceding account of the progress of the mind from (1) to (3) serves to confirm the view of McRae (1972b, 38) and Curley (1977 and 1986, n. 10) that the primary sense of 'innateness' in Descartes has little to do with the meanings given the term by Aristotle and Locke, and much to do with the sort of direct grasp of universal truths through analysis of single instances that, in discussions of Aristotle's *Posterior Analytics*, is referred to as 'intuitive induction.' Cf. above, chapter 5, n. 3, on the different senses of 'induction' in Aristotle. Oddly, the same Curley likens Descartes's analytical method of discovery to "the dialectical method" as an "essentially Platonic procedure" (Curley, 1986, 157). Cf. also n. 22 to this chapter.

The point about intuitive induction is duly emphasized, not just by McRae and Curley, but by Hoenen (1937, §10) and Clarke (1982, 201) as well. Yet they too overestimate the extent of the affinity with Aristotle. Some important differences between Aristotle and Descartes will be discussed in section 20.5.

6 Markie (1992, 170) simply discounts this distinction, remarking of the passage from the conversation with Burman: "The difference between explicit and implicit knowledge escapes me" (ibid.). Wilson clearly recognizes that it coincides with the distinction between reflexive knowledge and consciousness or "internal cognition" (1978a, 160). Another interpreter who recognizes its fundamental importance is Röd (1959–60, sect. IV). He employs it not so much to reconcile the statements in the Second Replies and *Principles*, I, 10 as to overcome the basic "dilemma" posed by the *cogito, ergo sum*: "Folgerung oder Erstes Prinzip." Nevertheless, Röd

misconstrues the process of 'explicitation' as "logische Explikation" and "logische Enfaltung," i.e., as a discursive operation. Cf. also Röd 1971, 51 on the fluidity of the boundary between intuition and deduction. While the latter is sharply distinguished from syllogistic reasoning, Röd's view of the logical character of the inference remains essentially unchanged.

Heidegger speaks in a similar vein of "eine unmittelbare Explikation des Gegebenen" (1994, 314), although the nature of the operation involved is not entirely clear. He goes on to identify "der Satz des Widerspruchs" as "die Kontrolle" used by Descartes. This certainly suggests "logische Explikation," as in Röd. But the sentence that reads, "Dieser Satz des cogito hat für Descartes den Charakter eines formal-logischen Satzes" (ibid., 248) is almost certainly a misprint for "formal-ontologischen" (ibid., passim). By *'formal*-ontological' Heidegger means that Descartes establishes this first truth regarding the being of a substance without having understood or enquired into the *specific* ontological sense of 'being' in the case of *ego sum* – a familiar theme in Heidegger (cf. Heidegger 1977, 33).

Interpreting the passage from the Second Replies, Gombay (1972, 80f.) points out that the French translation of the Latin employs the verb *conclure*: "& losque quelqu'un dit : *Ie pense, donc ie suis, ou i'existe, il ne conclut pas son existence de sa pensée comme par la force de quelque syllogisme, mais comme une chose connuë de soy*" (AT IX-1 110). (On the ambiguities of the Latin *conclusio* and the French *conclusion*, see chapter 5, n 2.) "What is contrasted," remarks Gombay (81), is not "(a) concluding and (b) recognizing as self-evident" but rather "(a) coming to a conclusion by syllogism and (b) coming to a conclusion by simple mental intuition." This much is borne out by Röd's no less than the foregoing interpretation, even if Gombay's subsequent employment of the personal-impersonal (77) and the analytic-synthetic distinction (85ff.) does not coincide with the implicit-explicit distinction employed here.

7 For an interpretation of the *cogito* that sees the solution to the difficulty raised by Burman in the difference between "simple notions" having no existential import and existential propositions, see Williams 1962, 92.

8 An apparently similar objection is raised by Hobbes: "For although someone may think that he *was* thinking (for thinking is nothing but remembering), still it is quite impossible for him to think that he *is* thinking (*quamvis enim aliquis cogitare potest se cogitasse [quae cogitatio nihil aliud est quam meminisse] tamen omnino est impossibile cogitare se cogitare*)" (AT VII 173: CSM II 122f. e.a.). However, Hobbes has in mind the danger of an infinite regress (see below), which would not appear to be Burman's worry.

Descartes responds to Hobbes's point in the Replies to the Sixth Objections (AT VII 422: CSM II 285), where it crops up again. Although they are different, the reply to Burman's difficulty will be seen to take care of Hobbes's problem as well.

Leibniz, as we shall see later in this chapter, followed Hobbes in construing self-consciousness as a form of memory. But he called it 'intellectual memory,' sharply distinguishing it from the sort of empirical memory that he ascribed even to beasts. Arnauld might be supposed to have held the same theory. In a letter of 29 July 1648 to Arnauld Descartes writes: "Being conscious of our thoughts at the time when we are thinking is not the same as remembering them afterwards" (AT V 221: CSMK 357). But Arnauld's point in the letter to which Descartes here replies was in fact different, almost Lockean (see above, section 6.2), in intent: "Since it is the nature of thought (*cogitationis*) that we are always conscious (*conscij*) of it, if we are always actually thinking, we ought always to be conscious that we are thinking (*debemus semper esse conscij nos cogitare*); but this seems contrary to experience, particularly in the case of sleep" (AT V 214). Accordingly, Descartes continues: "Thus, we do not have any thoughts in sleep without being conscious of them at the moment they occur; though commonly we forget them immediately" (AT V 221: CSMK 357).

9 An important point made by McRae 1972b, 67 and Wilson 1978a, 159. Cf. also Heidegger: "Solange man aber das innere Bewußtsein als eine Begleiterscheinung faßt, *die fehlen und auch nicht fehlen kann*, hat man das Moment nicht gesehen, das für Descartes entscheidend ist" (1994, 250 e.a.). Later (255) he calls it "ein konstituierendes Moment." It is, of course, *reflexio*, not *conscientia*, "die fehlen und auch nicht fehlen kann." Cf. also J.-M. Beyssade 1979, viii: "La réflexion est un acte supplémentaire, d'entendement pure, qui peut ou non s'ajouter à la conscience." Cottingham (1978a, 555) takes Descartes to be "defining" *conscientia* as reflection in the passage in question, whereas I take this particular use of *conscium esse* in the sense of *reflectere* to be anomalous – and perhaps due to Burman's faulty memory. See following note.

10 Alternatively, the anomaly may be explained by the fact that the conversation with Burman is only the latter's recollection of Descartes's words. Acknowledging the possibility of a slip of this sort is perfectly consistent with attaching great importance and ascribing a very high degree of reliability to the *Conversation with Burman* (as has been done throughout the present work). For two contrasting views of this text as a source of Descartes's thought, see Alquié (ALQ, 1963–7, 765ff.) and Cottingham (CB, xvi ff.). Cottingham's is surely the more reasonable estimate.

11 For a diametrically opposed view of the *Discourse* passage, cf. Curley 1978, 177: "This text is particularly interesting in the reason it assigns for our ignorance of our beliefs, namely, that knowledge of a mental act is a distinct act of thought from the mental act which is its object." Similarly, J.-M. Beyssade 1979, viii: "Première thèse : *penser et penser que l'on pense font deux*." Both Curley and J.-M. Beyssade make no distinction between *acte* and *action*.

12 It follows that consciousness and reflexion differ in degree rather than kind. And as these functions *of the intellect* (at bottom, intuition and a certain kind of

deduction – see the final sentence of this note) differ from one another, so the intellect or reason differs from ordinary sensory experience. That is, for Descartes, much as for the *Schulmetaphysik* of the eighteenth century, the senses and the understanding differ in degree rather than kind. In other words, they differ in respect of the degree to which all that is contained in each is clearly and distinctly perceived. 'The understanding represents things clearly and distinctly, the senses obscurely and confusedly' is a favourite way of Kant's of presenting what he considers a fundamental error about the nature of intuition and thought. Cf. Buchdahl 1969, 135 and 174. Also Miles 1978, §§7–9. In his treatment of "Experience versus reason," Clarke completely overlooks this fundamental feature of Descartes's thought (1992, 70ff.).

The identity of consciousness with *experientia*, i.e., *inner* experience (*testimonium internum*) and with intuition will be discussed more fully in chapter 20. In the last two sections below (and later in section 20.1) it will be shown that reflexion is one key sense of *deductio* and that it coincides with the 'analytic method of discovery' in Descartes.

13 For a lucid account of the reasoning involved cf. Brentano 1973, 121f.: "no mental phenomenon is possible without a correlative consciousness [of that phenomenon]; along with the presentation (*Vorstellung*) of a sound we have a presentation of the presentation of this sound at the same time. We have, therefore, *two* presentations, and presentations of very different sorts at that. If we call [1] the presentation of a sound 'hearing,' we have, in addition to the presentation of this sound, a [2] presentation of the hearing, which is as different from the hearing as hearing is from sound.

"But this is not the end of it. If every mental phenomenon must be accompanied by consciousness, [2] the presentation of hearing must also be accompanied by a consciousness, just as the presentation of sound is. Consequently, there must be [3] a presentation of it [i.e., of 2]. In the hearer, therefore, there are three presentations: [1] a presentation of the sound, [2] a presentation of the act of hearing, and [3] a presentation of the presentation of this act. But this third presentation cannot be the last one. Since it too is conscious, it is present in the mind and in turn its presentation is also presented. In brief, the series will either be infinite or will terminate with an unconscious presentation. It follows that those who deny the existence of unconscious mental phenomena must admit an infinite number of mental activities in the simplest act of hearing."

On Aquinas, see Brentano's long footnote, ibid., 125f.

14 For fuller documentation of these views see Kulstad 1991, chap. 2. In his interpretation of Leibniz, Kulstad draws on the work of McRae (1976), in interpreting St Thomas, on Brentano (1973).

I would, however, propose this correction of Kulstad's portrayal of the relationship of Leibniz to Descartes. As Kulstad notes (62 n. 27 *in fine*), there are two elements to Leibniz's theory: (1) "making consciousness a matter of having a thought about a thought, with the thoughts being distinct acts of the mind"; and (2) "putting the higher level thought after the original." Descartes, he claims, is committed to (1) but not (2). But on the interpretation given here, Descartes held neither (1) nor (2), so that Leibniz departed from the Cartesian theory of the mind on both counts, preferring to follow Hobbes.

15 On logic as 'dialectics' see above, chapter 11, n. 6. This Descartes distinguishes from "the kind of logic which teaches us to direct our reason with a view to discovering the truths of which we are ignorant" (AT IX-1 13f.: CSM I 186), i.e., the study of method or (as we may say, adapting a phrase of Popper's) the 'logic of discovery.' Cf. also Tweyman (1993a, 2), who also uses this expression.

For an interesting historical sidelight on Descartes's attitude toward formal logic, see Marion's account (based on Baillet) of his alleged remarks on 'dialectic' at the meeting with the Papal Nuncio, Cardinal de Bérulle, M. de Chandoux, and others (including Mersenne) in 1627(?). Marion 1981a, §8, esp. 154f. and n. 21. (Baillet's account is translated by Kemp Smith [1953] as appendix B to the first chapter.)

For a similar perspective and some useful bibliographical references, see also Popkin's description of the same meeting (1979, 174ff.). Descartes refers to the meeting in a letter to Villebressieu, who was also present (AT I 213: CSMK 32). Gouhier (1972, chap. I, sect. IV) treats of it at some length.

16 Cf. also the comment in the Seventh Replies: "his [Bourdin's] apparent intention is to persuade people that I do not approve of syllogistic patterns of argument, and hence that my method is not a rational one. But this is false, as is clear enough from my writings where I have always been prepared to use syllogisms when the occasion required it" (AT VII 522: CSM II 355).

17 Kemp Smith (1952, 67f.) is characteristically acute on this point. Descartes's principle that "'Things that are the same as a third thing are the same as each other'" (AT X 419: CSM I 45) (symbolically: If $A = B$, and $B = C$, then $A = C$) is employed as the major of the following syllogism: All things equal to the same thing are equal to one another; A and C are things equal to the same thing, B; hence A and C are equal to one another. Descartes allows, Smith observes, that this syllogism states the conditions on which the truth of the conclusion rests. But what he wishes to emphasize is that "in taking this roundabout path it is all too apt to *conceal from view the path by which alone the conclusion can have been reached*" (e.a.).

This captures the source of Descartes's dissatisfaction with the syllogism well enough. But is the path thus concealed the very path or progress of the mind described in the *Conversation with Burman*? Everything in Smith's analysis suggests that it is. Expressed in the minor premiss of the syllogism, he writes, is

"the material condition ... that *A* and *C* are both equal to the same third thing, *B*."
This "is the whole of the inference": to know this minor, i.e., to intuit the simple
natures for which *A*, *B*, and *C* stand and the relations among them is indeed "to
know the whole matter." Yet *how* the minor is known is not only not explained, but
actually obscured, by the syllogistic form. That is Descartes's complaint. As for
"the formal condition expressed in the major premiss," concrete particular truths do
not require to be deduced from abstract universal ones since they possess "the same
intrinsic underived validity" (ibid.). It is one and the same process of intuition by
which we both know particular truths and "apprehend the corresponding
universals" (ibid.). Thus, that "two plus two and three plus one are both equal to
four, and therefore to one another, are truths as certain as the axiom that things
equal to the same thing are equal to one another; and as [Descartes] further
contends, we must intuitively apprehend the particular truths if we are to be in a
position to discern and approve the wider, general truth" (ibid.). The parallels with
the *Conversation with Burman* are unmistakable.

    See also Curley's treatment of the same example (1978, 29ff.).

18 Cf. the Letter to Voetius (AT VIII-2 43: CSMK 222): "those who seek learning from
these sources ['by appeal to authority or by short summary syllogisms'] ... lose the
use of their natural reason and put in its place an artificial and sophistical reason."

    For a more formalistic interpretation of Descartes anti-formalism in the *Regulae*,
cf. Curley 1978, 26ff. His interpretation of the passage just cited is found at ibid.,
31f.

19 Cf. Hintikka 1978, 85: "A number of Descartes's general methodological ideas ...
become clearer when we realize that he is thinking in terms of a network of
functional dependencies between the known and the unknown, not in terms of a
linear sequence of inferences." In the letter to Voetius (partially cited in the
previous note), Descartes goes on to say that "the true use of reason, which is the
basis of all education, all intelligence and all human wisdom, does not consist in
isolated syllogisms, but only in the scrupulous and careful inclusion of everything
required for knowledge of the truths we are seeking. This can almost never be
expressed in syllogisms, *unless many of them are linked together*; so it is certain
that those who use only *isolated* syllogisms will almost always leave out some part
of what needs to be looked at as a whole, and thus grow careless and lose the use of
a mind that is in good order" (AT VIII-2 43: CSMK 222 e.a.). When in Rules VI
and VII Descartes speaks of a *contextus consequentiarum*, i.e., a 'web' of interde-
pendent propositions all dependent on the "primary and supremely simple
proposition" (AT X 383: CSM I 22; cf. AT X 387: CSM I 25), Cottingham et al.
translate misleadingly: "the chain of inferences." This will do for *conclusionum
intermediarum catenatio* (AT X 388: CSM I 25) or *catena* (AT X 390) CSM I 26),
but it is less satisfactory as a translation of *contextus*. For a 'linear' interpretation of

the linking together, cf. Cottingham 1988, 45f. (and the criticisms of Tweyman 1993b).

20 Tweyman (1993a, 31) denies that the interdependence and interconnectedness of the sciences (cf. Rule I of the *Regulae*) "are logical in nature, as in a deductive or axiomatic system"; yet within the confines of the mathematical sciences, whose method is "synthetic," they are just that: "When applied to the *Regulae* and the geometric-type method developed in that work, 'demonstration' is what we know as deductive reasoning. In the Replies to Objections II, this method of proof is called 'synthesis'" (ibid., 9).

21 Cf. Edgley 1970, 14 on "the temptation to suppose that everything implied by what someone knows to be true he must also know to be true." Also Curley 1978, 28: "the principle 'If p entails q, then (a knows that p) entails (a knows that q)' is a very tempting one in cases where the inference from p to q is obvious."

22 Cf. AT VII 464: CSM II 312: "My principal aim has always been to draw attention to certain very simple truths which are innate in our minds, so that as soon as they are pointed out to others, *they will not consider that they were ever ignorant of them* (*non putat se illas unquam ignorare*)" (e.a.). Or, as Cottingham et al. translate, somewhat more freely: "so that ... they will consider that they have *always known them*" (e.a.). Imlay (1985, 84) burdens Descartes with contradiction for holding that "principles both are and are not known before their particular applications," suggesting that the only way out of this contradiction is to abandon one of the two. From the foregoing it seems clear that this is not so.

    Hintikka (1978, 86) regards the "characteristic feature of Cartesian analysis as a kind of *conceptual* analysis" or "conceptual clarification." While this too overlooks what is distinctive about this process of rendering explicit the implicitly known, it is hard to disagree with Hintikka's conclusion that "the usual logico-deductive methods have contributed relatively little to our understanding of [Descartes's] way of thinking and arguing" (ibid., 87). Curley's substitution of a "dialectical" procedure (characterized as "Platonic," but having some of the earmarks of hypothetico-deductive method) is no doubt an improvement, while his earlier appeal to the Aristotelian notion of intuitive induction is (as will be shown in due course) still more apt. Cf. Curley 1986, 157, and n. 5 of the present chapter.

23 The rest are synthetic. While synthetic a posteriori judgments can be justified by straightforward appeal to observation and experience, the *Critique* as a whole is devoted to the elaboration of the transcendental method of demonstrating synthetic a priori truths. The relationship of Descartes's analytic method of discovery to Kant's transcendental method cannot be pursued here. Some relevant considerations are found in the text to n. 34 below and in the note itself.

24 The distinction between the methods of doubt and discovery sheds an interesting light on Röd's question (1971, 93) whether the all-embracing doubt of the First Meditation makes an exception of certain rules of method. So too on the question

(cf. Tweyman, 1993a, Introduction) whether the analytic method of the *Meditations* is (or is akin to) the method first elaborated using the model of the mathematical sciences in the *Regulae* (and further clarified in Part II of the *Discourse*), or whether it is a different method without " 'analog [*sic*] or counterpart' in [pure] mathematics" (ibid., 2).

The method of doubt is not just the means of discovering a first and indubitable truth about the existence of a substance, thus laying an unshakeable metaphysical foundation for human knowledge; it serves also to discover and to secure against doubt the sole and unique method of grasping that starting point explicitly and then advancing safely from the first principle of knowledge to the explicit knowledge of other truths implicit in it. Like the truths it discloses, the analytic method of discovery is itself discovered through reflexion on the *cogito, ergo sum*; it is no more presupposed as valid than the principles of the natural light are presupposed as true. Like those truths to the discovery of which it leads, the analytic method must *already* have been known, though only implicitly. It is accordingly "innate." Cf. the remarks in Rule IV on "the innate (*ingenitis*) principles of this method," i.e., analysis (AT X 373: CSM I 17), the first mention in the *Regulae* of the "seeds of truth" doctrine. The regimen of doubt through which the analytic method comes to be explicitly and definitively known, i.e. *validated*, is thus a meta-methodological device – though Descartes's first thoughts on the analytic method in the *Regulae* antedate by many years his use of methodic doubt and decision to work the question of method into an over-arching *metaphysical* framework.

That is the answer to Röd's question. On Tweyman's, see the next two notes.
25 Tweyman (1993a, 8 and passim) overlooks the bidirectionality of the method, simply equating analysis with the 'upward' movements to first principles: "Metaphysical truths for Descartes are first principles ... First principles cannot be the conclusions of geometric-type demonstrations." This much is true. But he continues: "Accordingly, Descartes correctly sees that the methodology developed in the *Regulae* ... would not serve his purpose in the *Meditations*." From the foregoing it appears that the 'reductive' process leading to the simple, the easy, the cause, the primitive or absolute is only the first phase of the analytic method; analysis also comprises the upward path to the complex, the more difficult, the effect, the derivative or relative – partly, no doubt, through logical deduction, but principally through a further process of reflexion on all that is implicit in the starting points.

The distinction between the upward and downward progress of the mind ('resolution' and 'composition,' according to Röd) goes right back to Rule IV of the *Regulae* (AT X 378f.: CSM I 20), where it is identified with universal mathematics itself: "I have resolved in my search for knowledge of things to adhere unswervingly to a definite order, always [a] starting with the simplest and easiest things and [b] never going beyond them *till there seems to be nothing further which is worth achieving where they are concerned.* Up to now, therefore, I have devoted all my energies to *this universal mathematics (mathesis universalis)"* (e.a.). This is expanded in Rule V: "The whole method consists entirely in the ordering and arranging of the objects on which we must concentrate our mind's eye if we are to discover some truth." Here the allusion to the analytic process of reflexion is clear enough. Next, the description of its dual aspect: "We shall be following this method exactly if we first reduce (*reducamus*) complicated and obscure propositions step by step to simpler ones, and then, starting with the intuition of the simplest ones of all, try to ascend (*ascendere*) through the same steps to the knowledge of all the rest" (AT X 379: CSM I 20). The same distinction is found, essentially unaltered, in the second rule of the *Discourse* (AT VI 18f.: CSM I 120), and expanded in the other rules: "[a] to direct my thought in an orderly manner, by beginning with the simplest and most easily known objects in order [b] to ascend little by little, step by step, to knowledge of the most complex." On the parallels between the rules of the *Regulae* and the *Discourse*, see Curley 1978, 21f. and Beck 1952, 149f.

26 For a list of occurrences of 'analysis' and 'synthesis' as "technical terms ... in mathematical contexts," see Garber and Cohen 1993, n. 1. There is only one such occurrence in the *Regulae* (AT X 373: CSM I 17). Similarly, the *only* use of 'analysis' with reference to the method of the *Meditations* is that of the Second Replies (cited above). The question is, then, whether that analysis and this are the same.

Tweyman (1993a, 2) tries to insert a wedge between the analytic method of the *Meditations* and the 'logic of discovery' described in the *Regulae*. Among those who take the latter to be fundamentally the same as the method described in Part Two of the *Discourse* and employed in the *Meditations* are Roth (1937, 64) and Beck (1952, 1–8). For mildly dissenting views, see Gilson 1947a, 290 and Kemp Smith 1953, 80ff., both of whom do not "go far enough" for Curley (1978, 43). Tweyman situates himself between Beck and Curley. On his "third interpretation," the *Regulae* "expresses Descartes' method for philosophy, although it is not applicable to metaphysics" (1993a, 11) as the science of "first principles" (see preceding note). On this distinction between metaphysics and philosophy, see n. 33 below.

The difficulties fuelling this controversy – notably, Descartes's complete confidence in mathematical certainty in the *Regulae* and extreme diffidence afterwards – have to do either with the device of systematic doubt first introduced in the *Discourse* or with the still earlier doctrine of the divine creation of the eternal truths; they vanish, accordingly, when one distinguishes the method of doubt from the analytic method of discovery. The former is indeed absent from the *Regulae*. While references to "what is perfectly known and incapable of being doubted" (AT X 362: CSM I 10) figure prominently in the rejection of "merely probable cognition" (ibid.) in the *Regulae*, the *method* of doubt "properly understood" is, as

Curley rightly observes (ibid., 44), "not merely a resolution to accept only what cannot be doubted but also a resolution to attempt to doubt all previous beliefs by searching for grounds of doubt." This makes its appearance only "sketchily" (ibid.) in the *Discourse*, emerging fully formed in the *Meditations* for the first time. The final stage, in particular the deceiving God (and evil demon), is an innovation of the latter work.

In short, all that suggests *abandonment* of the method described in the *Regulae* can be shown to be due to *its supplementation* by the meta-methodological device of systematic doubt (see n. 24). Of course, the deceiving God and evil demon are prepared for by the doctrine of divine creation of the eternal truths. It is this that Descartes has in mind when, in 1630, shortly after abandoning work on the *Regulae*, he writes to Mersenne: "I think that I have found how to prove metaphysical truths in a manner which is more evident than the proofs of geometry" (AT I 144: CSMK 22). In taking this passage to be a direct reference to the method of the *Regulae*, Beck is overlooking a key point (1952, 9); yet Tweyman overstates the case by maintaining that "the letter to Mersenne is *in no way* referring to [the method of] the *Regulae*" (1993a, 12 e.a.). The doctrine of the divine creation of the eternal truths explains both Descartes's diffidence about the method of the *Regulae* as applied in the mathematical sciences and his new-found confidence in *that very method* when applied outside the domain of mathematics, in metaphysics (or philosophy). The method of doubt simply clinches the matter for him. To quote Curley again: "It is no accident that the letter in which Descartes first states the doctrine of the creation of the eternal truths is also the letter in which he first claims to be able to attain a certainty greater than the certainty of mathematics by seeking knowledge of God and the self."

Hence, Beck's thesis stands: "The object of Cartesian methodology is to extend the method used in the mathematical sciences to all other branches of knowledge, including, of course, metaphysics and the other philosophical sciences" (1952, 13). But (*pace* Beck) "the method used in the mathematical sciences" has more to do with the analytical method of reflection than with *logical* deduction from definitions and axioms. This is just the question (see above), whether the two analyses – the mathematical and the metaphysical – are the same. It will be dealt with in the next section.

27 Cf. Röd 1971, 49: "Unmittelbare Folgebeziehungen werden daher ebenso wie einfache Naturen entweder adäquat oder gar nicht erfaßt." That more complex operations are indeed subject to error Descartes himself points out in the *Discourse*: "since there are men who make mistakes in reasoning, committing logical fallacies concerning the simplest questions in geometry, and because I judged that I was as prone to error as anyone else ... etc." (AT VI 32: CSM I 127). So too in the *Meditations*: "since I sometimes consider that others go astray in cases where they think they have the most perfect knowledge" (AT VII 21: CSM II 14). And in

Principles, I, 5: "we have sometimes seen people make mistakes in such matters [i.e., 'the demonstrations of mathematics']."

28 Cf. Rule XIII: "the human mind is liable to go wrong in one or other of two ways: it may assume something beyond the data ..., or on the other hand it may leave something out" (AT X 435: CSM I 54). The former of these errors is mooted already in Rule III: "we would be well advised not to mix any [merely probable] conjectures into the judgements we make about the truth of things" (AT X 367: CSM I 14). These two sources of error are a constant in Descartes's thought right down to the definitions of 'clear' and 'distinct' in the *Principles* (see section 7.1 and the remarks on the complementarity of 'precisification' and 'explicitation' in section 13.4 above).

29 As mentioned already (chapter 1, n. 9), Descartes's analytic/synthetic distinction has been invoked to clear up two puzzling differences between the *Meditations* and the *more geometrico* proofs of the Second Replies (as well as the *Principles*), notably by Gueroult (e.g., 1968, 26f.), McRae (1961, 145f.), and Curley (1977 and 1986). McRae points out that the existence of God stands as 'first principle' in the *more geometrico* proofs, where the *cogito, ergo sum* does not even figure. That is the first puzzling anomaly. The other concerns the altered sequence of the a priori and a posteriori proofs of God's existence, not just in the *more geometrico* proofs, but in the *Principles* as well (cf. Gueroult, ibid., 22 and 357ff.). Both difficulties are explained by the fact that the *Meditations* employ the analytic method of discovery, while the other two works are cast in synthetic form.

Garber and Cohen (1993) dispute the relevance of this distinction and the underlying assumption (based only on Burman's testimony) that the *Principles* are synthetic. As for the distinction, it is indeed the key to both puzzles; the problem is that Gueroult misinterprets it. In his view, the analytic method of discovery reflects the order of knowing (*ratio cognoscendi, vérité de la science*), while the synthetic corresponds to the order of being (*ratio essendi, vérité de la chose*), i.e., the real order of dependence among things themselves. Accordingly, the *cogito, ergo sum* and the a posteriori proof precede the a priori proof of God's existence in the analytic *Meditations*; in the *Principles* and *more geometrico* proofs, however, God's existence comes before the soul's and the a priori proof precedes the a posteriori or causal proof based on the existence of the idea of God in the human mind.

So Gueroult. However, from the foregoing it appears that the analytic method of discovery proceeds from the particular, from what is first for us (the knowledge of our own existence as immediately given in inner experience), to the general principles implicit in such knowledge and really prior to it, i.e., to that which is prior 'in itself' *within the order of knowing*. The synthetic method of the *Principles* and the *more geometrico* proofs just reverses the order, beginning from what is first in itself *in the order of cognition*: general definitions and axioms or "common notions." The order of being does not enter into it.

Thus, Gueroult is wide open to attack, even though the analytic/synthetic
distinction (rightly understood) is indeed the key to both puzzles. Curley's use of it
is faulted for relying on Burman in taking the *Principles* to be synthetic (cf. Garber
and Cohen 1993, 140ff. and Curley's apt rejoinder, 1986, n. 13). Yet Burman is a
vital source of information regarding analytical reflexion, which is the key to the
analytic method of discovery. Curley's analysis therefore retains its force, in
particular his observations on the use of "formal definitions" in the synthetic
Principles for "important concepts" introduced by examples in the analytic
Meditations (1977, 136f.). Cf. n. 22 above and section 6.3 ("Cartesian definitions").

30 Cf. Ferejohn 1992. Aristotle refers to the paradox at the beginning of the *Posterior
Analytics* (1949a [*An. Post.*, I, 1, 71a 29ff.]), remarking (71b 6ff.) that "there is no
reason why a man should not in one sense know, and in another not know, that
which he is learning. The absurdity consists not in his knowing in some qualified
sense (*pōs*) that which he learns, but in his knowing it in a certain particular sense,
viz. in exactly the same way and manner in which he learns it." Descartes skirts this
absurdity by distinguishing between *conscientia* and *reflexio* (or *perspicacitas* and
sagacitas), just as he avoids the charge of circularity by the distinction between
persuasio and *scientia*.
   Meno's paradox and Plato's solution, the *anamnēsis* theory, are alluded to in the
opening paragraphs the Fifth Meditation (see below, chapter 18, esp. n. 22). Cf. also
the letter to Voetius of May 1643 quoted in n. 36 below (AT VIII-2 167: CSMK
222f.).

31 As Röd (1971, 12) remarks: "die Meinungen über die Anwendbarkeit der Regeln der
Resolution und der Komposition [gehen] auseinander. Vor allem wurde bezweifelt,
ob die Erste Philosphie als Anwendungsfall ... [for the rules in the *Discourse*] gelten
könne." He surmises that there is "eine gewisse Wahrscheinlichkeit" that they can be
so applied, though the matter must remain "bei bloßen Vermutungen." In fact,
however, the textual evidence seems pretty clear. See n. 33 below.

32 On perfectly understood problems, cf. Rule XII *in fine*. Regarding the use of
mathematical examples, Descartes's own comment on this in Rule IV is instructive:
"I would not value these Rules so highly if they were good only for solving those
pointless problems with which arithemeticians and geometers are inclined to while
away their time, for in that case all I could credit myself with achieving would be to
dabble in trifles with greater subtlety than they. I shall have much to say below
about figures and numbers, for no other disciplines can yield *illustrations as
evident and certain as these* (AT X 373f.: CSM I 17 e.a.).

33 In a letter to Mersenne of 27 February 1637 regarding the *Discourse* and the
attached essays, Descartes states: "I have also inserted a certain amount of *metaphysics*, physics and medicine in the opening *Discourse* in order to show that my
method extends to topics *of all kinds* (AT I 349: CSMK 53 e.a.), i.e., even to metaphysics. This is at least implied at AT VI 21: CSM I 121f. of the *Discourse* as well:

"and since I did not restrict the method to any particular subject-matter, I hoped to apply it as usefully to the problems of the other sciences as I had to those of algebra ... But observing that the principles of these sciences [e.g., physics, astronomy, and medicine] must all be derived from philosophy ... I thought that first of all I had to try to establish some certain principles in philosophy," i.e., apply the method to *it*.

There is no appreciable difference between 'metaphysics' and 'philosophy' in these two passages. (Cf. also the remark to Burman quoted in n. 36 below.) This is not to question the existence of a distinction between 'first philosophy' and 'philosophy' (cf. the Preface of the *Principles*), but rather Tweyman's use of it to restrict the scope of the analytic method of discovery.

34 The examples of the 'absolute' and 'relative' given in Rule VI are instructive. Absolute: "whatever is viewed as being independent, a cause, simple, universal, single, equal, similar, straight, and other qualities of that sort." Relative: "what shares the same nature, or at least something of the same nature, in virtue of which we can relate it to the absolute and deduce it from the absolute in a definite series of steps. The concept of the 'relative' involves other terms besides, which I call 'relations': these include whatever is said to be dependent, an effect, composite, particular, many, unequal, dissimilar, oblique, etc." (AT X 381f.: CSM I 21). While some of these terms, e.g. 'equality,' presuppose quantity, most are, like 'simple,' 'universal,' etc., more generic. In the next paragraph Descartes remarks: "Thus a species is something absolute with respect to particulars, but with respect to the genus it is relative; and where measurable items are concerned, extension is something absolute, but among the varieties of extension length is something absolute etc." This certainly implies that "measurable items" are not *always* concerned – an important point in the present context.

35 McRae (1961, 62f.) suggests that *mathesis universalis* should be regarded as "the science of 'order and measurement,'" while the still more universal method common to all sciences is the science of 'order'." Thus, for *all* sciences constituting *scientia* (*sapientia*) *univeralis*, "that element by virtue of which they are sciences will be simply the investigation of problems of order, in no matter what kind of objects they arise" (ibid.), while for the mathematical sciences it is order *and* measure. Certainly, some such interpretation is indicated if *mensura* is taken in the proper sense as (roughly) 'that by which the *quantity* of something is determined,' i.e., measurement. But it is difficult to see how there can be any order without some measure in the transferred sense of a *standard* (whether an ideal or a unit) in relation to which the items are ordered or 'priorized.'

On the proper and transferred sense of *mensura*, see Mahoney's (1982, 169) paraphrase of a passage from St Thomas's early *Scriptum super libros Sententiarum* (circa 1256): "A measure (*mensura*) in the proper sense of the word is that by which the quantity of a thing (*quantitas rei*) becomes known. In the genus of quantity it is the minimum of the genus – namely, the unit – which provides the measure. However, the term 'measure' (*mensura*) has been transferred (*transumptum*) to all genera, so that what is first, simplest, and most perfect in each genus is said to be the measure of everything else in that genus." A similar distinction is then traced through a variety of other medieval and Renaissance thinkers. Thus, there is some precedent for the double usage ascribed to Descartes here.

36 Cf. his remark to Burman: "A study of mathematics ... is a prerequisite for making new discoveries both in mathematics itself *and in philosophy* ... since reasoning (*ratiocinatio*) is exactly the same in every subject" (AT V 177: CSMK 351f.). This recalls the opening gambit of the *Regulae* just cited. That Descartes means by 'wisdom' there what he elsewhere calls 'reason,' *bons sens*, 'the natural light' is borne out by the phrase "*de bona mente, sive de hac universali Sapientia*" later in the same passage.

For a parallel treatment of mathematical and philosophical topics, see the letter to Voetius of May 1643: "all those things whose knowledge is said to be naturally implanted in us are not for that reason *expressly* known by us; they are merely such that we come to know them by the power of our own native intelligence, without any sensory experience." This seems a fair description of the implicit knowledge rendered explicit by the process of analytical reflexion. Descartes goes on to illustrate it, first with reference to geometry, then to metaphysics: "All geometrical truths are of this sort – not just the most obvious ones, but all the others, however abstruse they may appear. Hence, according to Plato, Socrates asks a slave boy about the elements of geometry and thereby makes the boy able to *dig out certain truths from his own mind which he had not previously recognized were there*, thus attempting to establish the doctrine of reminiscence. *Our knowledge of God is of this sort*" (AT VIII-2 167: CSMK 222f. e.a.). Here mathematical knowledge and the metaphysical knowledge of God are treated on exactly the same footing.

That the key factor in both types of knowledge is the process of analytical reflexion is borne out by Descartes's response to Gassendi's objection to the primitiveness of the *cogito, ergo sum*. No sooner does he admonish Gassendi that "we must always begin with particular notions in order to arrive at general ones later on (though we may also reverse the order and deduce other particular truths once we have discovered general ones)," than he resorts to mathematical examples: "Thus when we teach a child the elements of geometry we shall not be able to get him to understand the general proposition 'When equal quantities are taken from equal amounts the remaining amounts will be equal,' or 'The whole is greater than its parts,' unless we show him examples in particular cases" (AT IX-1 206: CSM II 271). The transition from the *cogito* to mathematics is smooth and seamless.

37 Yet Buchdahl has misgivings: "It is very difficult to attribute a sense to their

possessing a third alternative status" (1969, 159). It is perhaps not so difficult if we take into account Descartes's theory of innate ideas and the doctrine of divine creation of the eternal truths. Maybe Buchdahl is speaking elliptically. If he means, 'a sense that one could defend philosophically, given that transcendental arguments are unavailable,' his point is well taken. For his part, Röd has little hesitation in ascribing to Descartes a significant anticipation of Kant's transcendental method in the sphere of first philosophy. He accordingly sees a "Vorstufe von Kants transzendentaler Deduktion" in one of the many senses of *deductio* in the *Regulae* (cf. 1971, 53ff.). It is of course true that the 'subjective turn' or 'Cartesian revolution' is a necessary condition of the later 'transcendental turn' or 'Copernican revolution'; but the distance between them should not be diminished. See the Conclusion.

Miller (1957, 40ff.) sees indeed analogies but no analysis to support a theory of synthetic *a priori* knowledge in Descartes: "according to Descartes, the necessary connections between simple concepts must be revealed by some mental operation which involves more than grasping their meanings. But how does this capacity operate, and exactly what does it mean to say that certain simples are necessarily related to each other in certain manners? Unfortunately, Descartes does not give an analysis. Instead, adopting an analogy with vision, he simply reiterates again and again that the necessity is revealed by the 'eyes of the mind,' 'mental vision,' 'spiritual illumination,' or the 'natural light.' It is quite clear that the natural light is the light of reason and that this light is cast upon the simples, thus revealing the necessary relations between them, but the exact manner in which reason inspects its objects and the exact nature of the relations it observes remain obscure" (ibid., 43).

If Röd errs on the side of generosity, this is surely somewhat unfair to Descartes given all that he in fact has to say on the subject of that distinctly analytical reflexion that provides the key to his theory of the mind. On the other hand, it *is* fair to say that the analysis Miller seeks is not elaborated clearly in Descartes's *published* writings. In this chapter the attempt has been made to coax it out of the various (in some cases obscure) sources in which it is actually found.

38 The same goes for McRae's distinction (1961, 51) between the unity of the mind in knowing and the unity of what is known by the mind. We may wish to distinguish these for various purposes, but Descartes probably did not.

39 On the question whether *mathesis universalis* is strictly universal or restricted to the mathematical and mathematizable sciences, see also the definition of 'method' in Rule IV: "By 'a method' I mean reliable rules which are easy to apply and such that if one follows them exactly, one will never take what is false to be true or fruitlessly expend one's mental efforts [on that which is beyond one's ken], but will gradually and constantly increase one's knowledge (*scientia*) till one arrives at a true understanding of *everything* within one's capacity (*omnium quorum erit capax*)"

(AT X 371f.: CSM I 16). On the strength of this, Vollrath (1962, 280, 282) describes Descartes's *mathesis universalis* as a *cognitio omnium.*

40 Detailed consideration of the similarities and differences between the analytic-synthetic distinctions found in the Greek mathematicians, Aquinas (see section 2.3), Galileo, Descartes, Newton, and Kant is beyond the scope of this study. So too the uses of 'analysis' in the writings of Descartes's contemporaries and in modern mathematics. Some helpful pointers are found in Röd 1971, 25ff., Hintikka 1978, and Mittelstraß 1979, 599.

41 Cf. McRae 1961, 63: "To say ... that universal mathematics provides a model for a universal science or method is not to say that Descartes borrowed his conception of this method from mathematics. It is to say, rather, that he constructed the particular model in the light of his universal science. The method was not derived from mathematics but applied to mathematics." It is hard not to agree with Mittelstraß's rejoinder (1979, 600): "in the description of *mathesis universalis* Descartes directly orients himself with the help of mathematical procedures." And ibid., 603: "First, the pattern of the 'analysis of the old' and the 'algebra of the modern' leads him to the conception of a *mathesis universalis*. Second, this *mathesis universalis* is regarded as the *organum* of a universal science still to be elaborated. Third, the rules of this *organum* Descartes outlines in the *Discours* in the sense of a general theory of philosophical method. (Unchanged from Mittelstraß 1978, 186 and 191). This seems correct, as far as it goes. But from here it is a further and important step to the image of the sciences found in the Preface to the French translation of the *Principles*.

16: Idea and Object

1 Cf. Yolton 1975a, 149: "What was the contrast between formal and objective, in the vocabulary of the *Meditations*, becomes, in his reply to Arnauld, the difference beween material and formal."

2 Gilson 1947a, 319f. Cf. also Gouhier 1969, 234 (and the references to St Thomas there), Kenny 1968, 96, Ashworth 1972, 91, and Marion 1981a, 34ff. Normore (1986, 235) calls attention to an early step in this direction, well before Descartes, but confirms (236) the general point about traditional Scholastic usage.

3 Cf. Gilson 1947a, 319f. and Owens 1985, 358: "God accordingly in knowing his essence perfectly knows all finite essences. He knows them not primarily in themselves but properly in his own essence. Insofar as he knows his essence as imitable by some creature, he knows it as the idea or prototype of that creature. In this way the divine ideas are many though the essence is one. The ideas serve as the exemplars according to which all things in the created universe are produced." Cf. Aquinas 1947–8, vol. I, 87f. (*ST*, Ia.15.2).

4 So too Ashworth 1972, 91: "Descartes took the word 'idea' and applied it to the
contents of the human mind because he wanted to escape the suggestion that these
contents must be in some sense dependent on the external world as a causal agent."
For a different interpretation, see Curley 1986, 163: "Since God's thought is free of
images, we use a term originally deployed in connection with his thought to express
the fact that our thought can be without images." On the difference between ideas
and images, see section 4 of the present chapter.

   Contrast with this the interpretation of the Kneales (1962, 310), which accords in
the main with Gilson's: "In the Middle Ages the word *idea* was still reserved for a
form as that was understood in the Christian Platonism of St Augustine, i.e., for an
archetypal concept in the mind of God ... At that time the forms that were supposed
to exist in human minds were described as *species* or *intentiones*, and there were
debates between philosophers who followed Aristotle in thinking that *species
intelligibiles* were all derived by abstraction from *species sensibiles* and others who
followed St Augustine in thinking that *species intelligibiles* could be acquired only
by divine illumination ... When Descartes and Locke used it as a substitute for the
medieval *species* and *intentio*, their chief purpose was no doubt to free themselves
from medieval entanglements, but Descartes had in mind also the Augustinian
precedent. For in reply to Hobbes he declares: 'I employed this term because it was
the term commonly used by philosophers for the forms of perception in the divine
mind.' That is to say, by his doctrine of innate ideas he deliberately assimilated the
human mind to the divine mind as that was described by theologians in the
Augustinian tradition." On the clash of the Augustinian and Aristotelian traditions,
cf. also Serene 1982.

   In the remark to Hobbes, Descartes is not speaking of innate ideas only; the
assimilation of the human to the divine mind applies to *all* ideas generally. It would
be rash to take the 'assimilation thesis' in its universal form much further than does
Ashworth. As for innate ideas in particular, the Augustinian precedent is no doubt
very much on Descartes's mind (cf. Menn 1993), though that did not prevent him
from distinguishing sharply between the natural light of human reason (which
includes innate ideas and principles) and the supernatural light of divine revelation
or illumination (see section 3.4 and the table at the end of chapter 12). The two
accounts should be taken as complementary rather than competing explanations of
Descartes's use of 'idea.'

   For a sensitive reading of the leading passages in St Thomas dealing with the
ideas of possibles and the divine mind, cf. Dewan 1979 (esp. 84f.) and 1991.
5 While the representationalism of Locke (cf. Yolton 1975a, n. 2 for references) and
Malebranche (cf. Nadler 1992, appendix) are somewhat controversial, the passage
from Hume (1967, 239) quoted earlier (chapter 4, n. 2) has strong claims to be the
classic statement of the 'veil-of-perception' doctrine mistakenly ascribed to

Descartes, who is supposed to have escaped scepticism and extended certainty beyond the immediately given only by the desperate expedient of the divine guarantor (cf. sections 4.1, 9.3, and 13.5).

To say of a philosopher that he generated a serious confusion without having participated in it is perhaps less odd than it seems. Speaking of the confusion surrounding the 'verificationist' and 'falsificationist' criteria of meaning, Popper takes full responsibility for the muddle, since it arose from something he had written about the demarcation of science from pseudo-science. He himself, however, was never in the slightest doubt about the difference between the two criteria. Cf. Popper 1962, 40f.

6 On the distinction implicitly drawn here between the object intended in an act and the object *as* it is intended, cf. Husserl 1970, vol. 2, 578. It has a close parallel in Anscombe's distinction between different "descriptions under which" one and the same object may be desired. Cf. Anscombe 1957, 65. Did Descartes grasp this distinction? It is at least suggested by the example he gives in the second part of his definition of 'idea' in the Second Replies, so that the question may best be taken up in the context of the interpretation of that passage.

7 On the interpretation of the locution 'it seems to me that ...,' see also chapter 7, n. 28 above.

8 For a detailed account of the formation of 'corporeal ideas' upon the inner superficies of the brain, cf. *Le Monde*, AT XI 174ff. (abbreviated in CSM I 105f.). On the corporeal imagination, cf. AT VI 55: CSM I 139.

9 As already noted, McRae (1965) traces three of these senses through seventeenth-century philosophy and ultimately to Descartes: (3) idea as object, (1) idea as act, and (7) idea as disposition. Hereby, (3) is so interpreted as to yield a 'dual-object' or representationalist theory.

10 In the second section of the definition Descartes writes that merely understanding a verbal "expression" *entails* having in one's mind the idea of "that which is signified by those words": from the former (*ex hoc ipso*) the latter follows (*certum est ...*). Apparently, the type of verbal expression he has in mind does not merely intend, it asserts something *about*, an object. Thus, simply having in mind the very same intentional object to which a particular expression refers is not yet to understand the expression; the idea in the mind must intend the object *in the same way* as the proposition expressed. It must, in other words, not only have the same referent, but intend it in a way that corresponds to the ideal sense of the proposition expressed in the judgment. It seems, then, that Descartes did in fact distinguish between the object intended in an act and the object *as* it is intended – though not explicitly. See above, n. 6.

11 Gilson quotes the definition in full, remarking that the term "*forme*, qui est le plus caractéristique de cette définition, peut prêter à confusion" (Gilson 1947a, 319). In

Scholastic usage 'form' designates "la forme sensible de la chose même, qui, rendue intelligible par la pensée devient le principe de notre connaissance" (ibid.). This concept of form undergoes a decisive transformation in passing into the Cartesian system. Predictably, all reference to an actually existing extra-mental *res* is suppressed. What remains of the specifically Scholastic notion of abstracting intelligible forms from sensible species is its purely phenomenological aspect alone: the *representative* character of forms. Cf. also the quotation from Heidegger in n. 14 below.

12 Cf. Kenny 1968, 110: "By calling ideas 'forms' Descartes seems to mean simply that they are nonmaterial *representations* of things" (e.a.). Nevertheless, when Descartes speaks (as he will in the Third Meditation passage to be interpreted presently) of "additional forms," these are non-representational despite the designation 'form.'

13 Cf. the passage cited earlier (chapter 7, n. 12): "It is self-evident that seeing a lion and at the same time being afraid of it is different from simply seeing it. And seeing a man run is different from silently affirming to oneself [i.e., judging] that one sees him" (AT VII 182 f: CSM II 128).

14 Cf. Heidegger's warning: "An den Terminus *imago* hat sich ein ganzer Knäuel von Irrtümern gebunden, insofern man nun die Vorstellungen als Bilder von Äußerem nahm. Imago rei muß jedoch viel formaler in dem Sinne gefaßt werden, daß idea etwas als imago rei ist. Sie gibt etwas für das Sehen, *stellt etwas dar*. Das Repraesentieren ist die Grundfunktion der idea" (1994, 136). This makes phenomenologically the point that Gilson makes historically.

15 Cf. Kenny 1968, 99: "when I notice a spider, that is a change in me, not in the spider." On the difference between an 'extrinsic denomination' (e.g., the knowledge of Socrates that exists in Plato) and a 'relation of reason' (Socrates's 'knownness' by Plato), cf. Menn 1995, 190f.

16 Kenny 1968, 115f. thinks Descartes actually contradicts himself in his response to Caterus.

17: The Inferential Import of the *Ergo*

1 Cf. also AT VII 222: CSM II 156: "We do not have immediate knowledge of substances, as I have noted elsewhere. We know them only by perceiving certain forms or attributes (*formas sive attributa*) which must inhere in something if they are to exist; and we call the thing in which they inhere 'substance.'" And AT IX-1 216: CSM II 277: "In *distinguishing* a substance from its accidents we must consider both the one and the other, and this is very useful in helping us to gain knowledge of a substance. But if we merely separate the substance from its accidents by *abstraction*, i.e., consider it all on its own without thinking of the

accidents, *this prevents our being able to gain sound knowledge of it, because it is by means of the accidents that the nature of substance is revealed"* (e.a.). See also the discussion of this point in section 2.2 above.

2 In a letter a month earlier (4 June 1648) Descartes identifies this "reflexive act of the intellect" with "intellectual memory" (AT V 193: CSMK 354). This calls to mind Leibniz's different but related doctrine (see section 15.4). In the *Regulae* Descartes does not mention intellectual memory explicitly, though he does speak of its counter-concept, 'corporeal' memory: "memory is no different from imagination – at least the memory which is corporeal and similar to the one that animals possess" (AT X 416: CSM I 43).

3 For more on innateness, see chapter 18 below. Kenny (1968, 71f.) recognizes the close connection between *intellectio* and *conscientia*, but takes Descartes to be thoroughly confused (or at least "ambiguous") about the relationship of thought and consciousness. McRae (1972b, 64ff.) regards the thesis that "there are no perceptions, appetites, emotions, or sensations of which we are not conscious" as the conclusion of an argument whose premises he describes in this way. "The first is that there is no *intellection* of which we are not conscious ... The second premise is that all perceptions, appetites, emotions and sensations involve intellection" (66). In respect of the first premise, he notes that "Leibniz goes beyond Descartes, and makes consciousness a condition of the very possibility of intellection or rationality." But this is precisely what Descartes, for whom reflexion presupposes prereflexive consciousness, had done already. Cf. chapter 15, n. 12 above on the parallel between the relation of thought to consciousness and of understanding to the senses.

4 As far as I am aware, the only recent commentators writing in English to have insisted on the pivotal role of the metaphysical principle of the natural light 'nothing has no properties' are Sievert (1975) and Curley (1978, 92f.), though one, Markie (1992, 160), has expressly pronounced both *Principles*, I, 52 and the reply to Hobbes "irrelevant to the logic of Descartes' *Cogito* inference." Wilson (1978a, 66 and n. 26) is similarly adamant on this point, though Kenny (whom she is criticizing at this stage) underplays, if anything, the role of this principle (cf. Kenny 1968, 50 and 60). Cottingham (1986, 36ff.) mentions the principle, though as a candidate for the role of missing premise in an argument of *modus ponens* form; as such he rightly rejects it. He adds that "it is highly implausible to suppose that [Descartes] is relying on this maxim when he infers his own existence in the Second Meditation. For he explicitly asserts, later in the *Meditations*, that there are objects (e.g., triangles) to which we can assign properties *without committing ourselves to their actual existence* ... So the maxim 'Nothingness has no attributes' cannot entail that all property attribution presupposes an actually existing subject." This is true as far as it goes. But if an attribute is asserted to exist actually (as in the

proposition *cogito*, though not in mathematical truths), then, according to the principle, there must be some actually existing subject for it to inhere in. To this there are no exceptions.

Schopenhauer (1969, II, 32) already sketched an argument along the right lines. Both Alquié (1950, 182) and J.-M. Beyssade (1979, 238 n.3) suggest that this principle of the natural light plays a crucial role in the 'movement' of thought from *cogito* to *sum*. The latter provides the fullest account to be found anywhere of the temporal character of the 'movement of thought.' Apart from Hoenen (1937), whom he cites at a couple of points in his analysis, Gouhier (1969, 281) is perhaps the author who gives the principle greatest prominence. Though he develops his account of the *ergo* in a very brief space (it was treated more fully in Gouhier 1950), it appears to coincide in the essentials with that given here. Cf. 1969, 283: "L'intuition du *cogito* a saisi une *res* dont l'existence échappe à toute tromperie même transcendante, et ceci dans *une expérience qui décèle l'axiome métaphysique* [*ex nihilo nihil fit*] sous une autre formule : « le néant n'a point de propriétés »" (e.a.). Gouhier suggests (cf. ibid., 285, n. 85) that Malebranche and Fénelon proceed entirely in the spirit of Descartes in taking the certainty of 'nothingness has no properties' as founding the *cogito* (cf. also J.-M. Beyssade 1979, 247, n. 6); Gueroult, on the other hand, is cautious on this point (cf. 1968, II, 31).

All of the authors just mentioned tend to treat the innate principle as an inference licence rather than as operative in a process of analytical reflection.

5 The view that the *ergo* signifies an immediate inference "from a predicative to an existential proposition" has been defended by Williams (1962, 95), who follows in this Rodis-Lewis (1950, 96). J.-M. Beyssade takes essentially the same view (1979, 229).

Against this Marion (1981a, 378f.) rightly insists on the existential import of the *cogito*: "le *cogito* n'aboutit pas tant à l'existence à partir de raisons, qu'il ne commence par l'existence, expérimentée dans la raison ... [I]l ne faudrait point objecter, puisque cette existence s'experimente dans la pensée, que le *cogito* va de la pensée – première – à un résultat et terme – l'existence." The objection is invalid because "la *cogitatio* n'ouvrirait sur aucune existence si elle ne s'éprouvait elle-même d'emblée comme une existence." In a footnote (ibid.), Marion attributes this objection to Brunschvicg, Alquié, and Gouhier as well as J.-M. Beyssade (for references, see Marion, ibid., n. 15).

Carnap (1959a, 73f.) is another who takes the *cogito* to be predicative, faulting the inference to what is clearly an existential *sum*. Thus, Descartes figures among those metaphysicians who have "allowed themselves to be seduced into pseudo-statements" (such as 'I am' and 'God is') by the fact that the existential use of 'to be' "feigns a predicate where there is none. To be sure," he notes, "it has been known for a long time that existence is not a property (cf. Kant's refutation of the ontological proof for the existence of God). But it was not until the advent of modern logic that full consistency on this point was reached: the syntactical form in which modern logic introduces the sign for existence is such that it cannot, like a predicate, be applied to signs for objects, but only to predicates" (ibid.). Thus, there are "two essential logical mistakes" in Descartes's founding principle. The "I am," which employs the verb 'to be' in the sense of existence, "violates the ... logical rule that existence can be predicated only in conjunction with a predicate, not in conjunction with a name. An existential statement does not have the form '*a* exists' (as in 'I am,' i.e., 'I exist') but 'there exists something of such and such a kind'" (ibid.).

Now, of course, *sum, existo* can be correctly paraphrased as 'there exists an x, such that x is t (i.e., thinking).' So this alleged mistake is nothing to worry about. It is the other that is relevant at this point in our interpretation. It has to do not with the *sum* but with the derivation of *sum* from *cogito*. Here, Carnap alleges, an existential statement is deduced from a predicative statement, 'P(a)' ('a has the property P'). But logically the conclusion "can assert existence only with respect to the predicate P, not with respect to the subject *a* of the premise. What follows from 'I am a European' is not 'I exist,' but '*a* European exists.' What follows from 'I think' is not 'I am' but 'there exists something that thinks'" (ibid.). But for one thing, Descartes's premise, *cogito*, is itself an existential statement; and for another the conclusion is not logically deduced but derived by the non-logical process described here as 'analytical reflexion.'

Kant's dictum that "Being is obviously not a real predicate ... etc." is considered in relation to Aquinas and Descartes in section 22.3 of the Conclusion.

6 Although 'gropings and guessings,' however appropriate to Aristotle's discussion of attempts to spot real causal connections (as, say, between bile and longevity in Aristotle's notorious example), hardly fits the paradigmatic cases of intuitive induction in the exact (mathematical) sciences.

7 Cf. Ross's reply (on Aristotle's behalf) to the charge of *petitio principii* traditionally brought against the syllogism: "To this Aristotle would have replied by a distinction between potential and actual knowledge. In knowing premises we potentially know the conclusion; but to know anything potentially is not to know it, but to be in such a state that given one further condition we shall pass immediately to knowing it. The condition that is needed ... is the seeing of the premises in their relation to each other ... *[I]nference is a real process, an advance to something new ... the making explicit of what was implicit.*" (Aristotle 1949a, 39f. e.a.). This too is 'explicitation,' though of a very different sort than that implied by the presence of the *ergo* in Descartes's founding principle. So is the act of judgment for St Thomas. Cf. next note.

8 "Pour Saint Thomas," writes Hoenen (1937, 468), "le jugement de l'esprit humain,

tout jugement, est, tout comme le raisonnement, une transition de la puissance à l'acte, et le mouvement qu'il découvre ainsi dans les deux opérations [judgment and reasoning] a la même racine: l'imperfection de l'esprit humain qui ne voit pas d'un seul coup d'oeil toutes les richesses de ses données." But what then are these *données* that the weakness of the *lumen intellectuale in nobis* forces us to elaborate gradually in a judgment that is "virtuellement multiple"? Hoenen's examples (ibid., 469) leave no doubt whatsoever: the objects of ordinary non-reflexive sensory experience.

18: Reflexion and Innateness

1 Cf. the Third Meditation: "Again, I perceive that I now exist, and remember that I have existed for some time; moreover, I have various thoughts which I can count; it is in these ways that I acquire the ideas of duration and number which I can then transfer to other things" (AT VII 44f.: CSM II 30f.). On 'duration' cf. also the letter to Arnauld of 29 July 1648: "earlier and later in any duration are known to me by the earlier and later of the successive duration which I detect *in my own thought*" (AT V 223: CSMK 358 e.a.). To 'duration' the *Regulae* add, as further "common notions" derived from the same source, 'existence,' and 'unity' (AT X 419: CSM I 45), while in the *Principles* (I, 47–8) Descartes includes among the "simple notions which are the basic components of our thoughts" (AT VIII 22: CSM I 208) "*substance, duration, order, number* and any other items of this kind which extend to all classes of things" (AT VIII-1 22f., CSM I 208). See above, section 10.9, on the universals.

2 McRae takes the first part of Descartes's reply to Gassendi to be "a denial that the idea of extension is innate," but concedes that the subsequent use of 'often' "seems to leave open the possibility of an alternative origin" of that idea, i.e., its innateness (cf. McRae 1973b, 43). On the most cautious estimate, the reply neither asserts nor denies anything concerning the origin of the idea of extension; it only suggests that there *may* be *another* idea of body derived from a source different from that of the sensible ideas of body employed in the proof of the existence of material things. See the sixth section below.

3 As McRae acknowledges. Apart from the letter to Elizabeth, to be discussed presently, McRae (1972a, 44) cites *Principles*, II, 3: "sensory perceptions are related exclusively to this combination of the human body and mind. They normally tell us of the benefit or harm that external bodies may do to this combination, and do not, except occasionally and accidentally, show us what external bodies are like in themselves. If we bear this in mind we will easily lay aside the preconceived opinions acquired from the senses, and in this connection make use of the intellect alone, carefully attending to the *ideas implanted in it by nature*" (AT VIII-1 41f.: CSM I 224 e.a.). Elsewhere (1978, 99) McRae quotes the letter to Mersenne of June 1641: "I use the word 'idea' to mean everything which can be in

our thought, and I distinguish three kinds. Some are adventitious ..., others are constructed or made up ... and others are innate, such as the idea of God, mind, *body*, *triangle*, and in general all those which represent true, immutable and eternal essences" (AT III 383: CSMK 183 e.a.). Relevant here, but not cited by McRae, is this from the Sixth Replies: "But at that age the mind employed the bodily organs less correctly than it now does, and was more firmly attached to them; hence it had no thoughts apart from them and perceived things only in a confused manner. Although it was aware (*conscia*) of its own nature and *had within itself an idea of thought as well as an idea of extension*, it never exercised its intellect on anything without at the same time picturing something in the imagination" (AT VII 441: CSM II 297 e.a.)

Regarding McRae's argument that the adventitious character of the idea is indispensable to the proof of the existence of the external world, see the exchange published in *Dialogue* (Miles 1988a, 1988b, McRae 1988).

4 This interpretation may be hard to square with a similar use of 'innate' in the letter to Mersenne of 22 July 1641: "Altogether, I think that all those [ideas] *which involve no affirmation or negation* are *innatae* [Latin in original] in us; for the sense-organs do not bring us anything which is like the idea which arises in us on the occasion of their stimulus (*se réveille en nous à leur occasion*), and so this idea must have been in us before" (AT III 418: CSMK 187 e.a.). Here Descartes makes it quite clear that he is *not* talking about judgments.

5 Thus, in the *Regulae* Descartes speaks of "figures or ideas which come, *pure and without body*, from the *external senses*" (AT X 414: CSM I 41 e.a.). 'Pure' here means "without body," i.e., purged of matter, not "corporeal ideas" (as material entities in the brain), but purely mental entities. But it obviously cannot mean 'without sensory elements' since Descartes refers explicitly to the "external senses." In the expression *intellectio pura*, by contrast, 'pure' means again purged of matter (cf. AT VII 387: CSM II 265: "the pure understanding both of corporeal and incorporeal things occurs without any corporeal semblance") and of sensory elements as well.

6 In a valuable study of the whole question of innateness, Edgley distinguishes "the dominant and the recessive doctrine" of innate ideas in seventeenth-century thought: "The dominant doctrine is that some of our ideas are derived from experience and some are innate, and these innate ideas constitute knowledge of reality. The recessive doctrine is that all of our ideas are innate, and these ideas constitute 'habits, dispositions, or powers.' I call this the recessive doctrine because in maintaining the strong thesis that not just some but all of our ideas are innate it weakens the notions of innateness and of ideas to the point at which empiricism can agree – but without much enthusiasm, because this is the point at which triviality sets in" (Edgley 1970, 6).

Descartes's doctrine *cuts across* this distinction (for which, in any case, no claim to historical accuracy is made). What Edgley calls "the dominant theory" is weak (applies to some ideas only) and non-dispositional, while his "recessive theory" is dispositional and strong, i.e., applies to all ideas, becoming for that very reason trivial. Now according to what will be seen to be Descartes's dominant theory, only some, not all ideas are innate, whereby 'innate' is understood in a *dispositional* sense; moreover, these ideas alone furnish "knowledge of reality." The sense in which *all* ideas can be (and are, in the *Broadsheet*) said to be innate is different from this *but again dispositional*; it is indeed trivial, however, since it contains nothing the most hard-bitten empiricist would be unwilling to grant.

On Descartes's dominant concept of innateness, cf. Röd 1959–60, 185: "Gewiß darf das Angeborensein im Descartesschen Sinne nicht als Vorhandensein fertiger Denkformen im Bewußtsein gedeutet werden, vielmehr heißt eine Wahrheit dann angeboren, wenn ihre Wahrheit allein aus dem Denken eingesehen werden kann." Although applicable in this form only to innate axioms or propositions the *truth* of which is grasped in reflexion upon thinking, this nevertheless captures the root sense of innateness; it could easily be extended to innate concepts or ideas acquired through such reflexion. Especially noteworthy in Röd's formulation is the way in which it sets Descartes's apart from Kant's concept of the *a priori* (assuming that this is the point of the talk of "fertige Denkformen").

7 For more on this theory, cf. chapter 19, n. 16 below. Calling the theory of the *Broadsheet* the 'recessive theory' of innateness, as Edgely suggests (see previous note), would leave one with the problem of what to do with the non-dispositional 'Platonic-Stoic-Ciceronian' theory of innateness (see above, chapter 9, n. 2; also next section), to which Descartes reverts in a variety of contexts. It is therefore perhaps better treated as an aberration of the *Broadsheet*, interesting in relation to Descartes's theory of perception perhaps, but not for purposes of determining the extent of his 'rationalism.' In the final analysis, Edgley's manner of distinguishing dominant and recessive theories simply does not apply to Descartes, though there are dominant and recessive strands within the reflexive-dispositional theory.

8 The distinction drawn here between the metaphysical principles of the natural light and the principles of logic, while not one Descartes would have drawn, is not therefore anachronistic either (see section 8.3). A useful compilation of "common notions" is found in Gouhier 1969, 272f. If Descartes regards these principles as belonging to separate disciplines, there is certainly no indication that this is so in the hodge-podge of *Principles*, I, 49 (AT VIII-1 23: CSM I 209).

9 Owing to this passage, the proof of God's existence earlier in the same Meditation has been dubbed the "Trademark Argument" by Cottingham (1986, 48ff.) and others. Cf. also AT VII 105: CSM II 76: "Because the idea of God is implanted in the same way in the minds of all, we do not notice it coming into our minds from any external source, and so we suppose it belongs to the nature of our own intellect."

10 Cf. Hume 1990, 65: "The idea of God, as meaning an infinitely intelligent, wise, and good Being, arises from reflection on the operations of our own mind, and augmenting, without limit, those qualities of goodness and wisdom."

11 J.-M. Beyssade (1981, 4) discerns a "double mouvement" in the acquisition of the idea of God, corresponding to the two types of divine attributes: those like intellect, will, and power, of which "we recognize some traces in ourselves," and God's "absolute immensity, simplicity and unity which embraces all other attributes and has no copy in us" (AT VII 137: CSM II 98f.). The one 'movement' proceeds "du créé à l'incréé, de l'exemple ou vestige (fragmentaire) à un infini en son genre que l'on appellera aussi bien indéfini ... L'autre descend de l'idée (sans vestige ou exemple) de l'unité absolue, de l'Infini au sens fort."

In the present context, it is worth noting that (as Descartes suggests to both Hobbes and Gassendi) the former 'movement' presupposes possession (at least implicit awareness) of the idea of divine perfection, as the unity of all his attributes. It is unclear whether there is any other 'movement' involved than the temporal process of gradually rendering explicit what is at first only implicitly understood. We can indeed focus our attention first on that which we can comprehend, namely our own nature, proceeding thence to that which we can understand but never comprehend; or we can focus attention immediately upon the latter in order the better to understand our own finite nature.

12 Cf. *Phaedo*, 74d–77a and *Republic*, 504c ("Nothing imperfect is a measure of anything"). Compare this with Descartes's use of *mensura* as interpreted in section 15.7. On the extent of the parallel with Plato, see also the remarks on Descartes and the Platonic theory of *anamnesis* in section 20.5 below.

For precedents in Aristotle, Augustine, Anselm, and Aquinas, cf. Owens 1985, 348, n. 44. On Augustine, in particular, cf. Menn 1993, 546 and (explicitly) 558. Apart from the conversation with Burman (AT V 153: CSMK 338), Descartes uses the expression 'falls short of' also at AT VII 42: CSM II 29: "So it is clear to me, by the natural light, that the ideas in me are like <pictures, or> images which can easily fall short of the perfection of the things from which they are taken, but which cannot contain anything greater or more perfect."

13 Cf. the Second Set of Objections, the authors of which urge that "we can find simply within ourselves a sufficient basis for our ability to form the said idea [of God], even supposing that the supreme being did not exist, or that we did not know that he exists and never thought about his existing" (AT VII 123: CSM II 88). That basis is provided by first observing different degrees of perfections of various kinds, and then "positing higher and higher degrees of perfection up to infinity" (ibid.) by means of the imagination.

In reply, Descartes concedes that "we can find simply within ourselves a sufficient basis for our ability to form the said idea," since the idea is really "'innate in me' – in other words, ... comes to me from no other source than myself" (AT VII 133: CSM II 96), i.e., *since God himself has placed it in me*. He thus grants that we could have it even supposing "we did not know that he exists and never thought about his existing," but denies that we could have the idea "even supposing that the supreme being did not exist." This reply simply begs the questions that Descartes answered clearly in the conversation with Burman and the other passages cited.

14 The above portions of the *Broadsheet* clarify the dispositional sense in which the idea of God, *like the other metaphysical ideas and common notions*, is acquired through reflexion due to an innate disposition of the mind. The comments on article fifteen, on the other hand, treat of Regius's attempted refutation of Descartes's proofs of God's existence. They highlight an important sense in which the idea of God is *unlike* other innate ideas and principles. To this we must return.

15 The fullest account of the state of an infant's mind and the stages of its development is found at *Principles*, I, 71 (cf. also the passage at AT VII 441: CSM II 297 quoted partially already in section 10.1). It will be discussed briefly in the context of the treatment of mathematical axioms below. Here we may quote from the Fifth Set of Replies Descartes's response to Gassendi's query, what sort of idea of God he would have had without the use of the external senses: "I do not doubt that the mind – provided we suppose that in thinking it received not just no assistance from the body *but also that it received no interference from it* – would have had exactly the same ideas of God and itself that it now has, with the sole difference that they would have been much purer and clearer. The senses often impede the mind in many of its operations, and in no case do they help in the perception of ideas. The only thing that prevents all of us noticing equally well that we have these ideas is that we are too occupied with perceiving the images of corporeal things" (AT VII 375: CSM II 258 e.a.).

16 Regarding (1), cf. AT V 149: CSMK 336, where Burman takes up Arnauld's objection: "The author of these objections [i.e., Arnauld] conjectured that it would follow from this that the mind must always be thinking, even in the case of infants." Descartes confirms that this is conceded in his reply: "The author [of the Replies] agreed." Similarly, to Gassendi's question, "whether in saying that thought cannot be separated from you, you mean that you continue to think indefinitely so long as you exist" (AT VII 264: CSM II 184), Descartes replies: "But why should it [the mind] not always think, since it is a thinking substance? It is no surprise that we do not remember the thoughts that the soul had when in the womb or in a deep sleep, since there are many other thoughts that we equally do not remember, although we know we had them" (AT VII 356: CSM II 246f.)? For further unequivocal statements on the subject, see the letters to Gibieuf of 19 January 1642 (AT III 478f.: CSMK 203) and to Hyperaspistes of August 1641 (AT III 422: CSMK 189), cited above.

17 Compare the similar wording in Descartes's own gloss on 'innate' at AT VII 133: CSM II 96: "that this idea [God] is 'innate in me' – in other words, that it comes to me from no other source."

18 Compare the following two passages at AT VII 45: CSM II 31: "As for all the other elements which make up the ideas of corporeal things, namely extension, shape, position and movement, these are not formally contained in me, since I am nothing but a thinking thing; but since they are merely modes of a substance, and I am a substance, it seems possible that they are contained in me eminently." And: "It is true that I have the idea of substance in me in virtue of the fact that I am a substance; but this would not account from my having the idea of infinite substance, when I am finite."

19 The form in which the proof of the existence of 'body' or 'matter' was recast in the *Principles* (II, 1) provides somewhat better support for McRae's claim that the idea of extension is adventitious: "But we have sensory awareness of, or rather as a result of sensory stimulation we have a clear and distinct perception of, some kind of matter (*sive potius a sensu impulsi clare ac distincte percipimus, materiam quandam*), which is extended in length, breadth and depth, and has various differently shaped and variously moving parts which give rise to our various sensations of colours, smells, pain and so on." However, the translation of *a sensu impulsi* by "as a result of" may be misleading. The verb *impello* suggests that sense is only the accidental and remote cause or occasion of our becoming reflexively aware of an idea already present to consciousness, though only implicitly grasped. Nevertheless, it must be admitted that the matter is less clear-cut here than in the Sixth Meditation version of the proof. See the references to the exchange with McRae on this point in n. 3 above.

20 The imagination is defined at AT VII 28: CSM II 19 as "contemplating the shape or image of a corporeal thing" and described at AT VII 387: CSM II 265 as having "only corporeal things as its object."

21 That a turning toward the body or brain is involved in corporeal memory is attested also by this passage from the Fifth Replies: "So long as the mind is joined to the body, then in order for it to remember thoughts which it had in the past, it is necessary for some traces of them to be imprinted on the brain; *it is in turning to these, or applying itself to them*, that the mind remembers" (AT VII 357: CSM II 247 e.a.).

22 Here, incidentally, is the most overt reference to *anamnesis* and the heuristic paradox of the *Meno* to be found anywhere in Descartes's writings. Cf. above, chapter 15, n. 30. McRae alleges that where Descartes invokes the simile he is not "referring to ideas which are got by reflecting on his own nature as he does in the first four *Meditations*. Nor is the simile of reminiscence appropriate to that earlier account of innateness" (1972a, 46). This would appear to be mistaken.

23 Thus, the ontological argument does not conclude in some such way as: 'Therefore, God exists (actually and necessarily)'; rather, it concludes: "I ought ... to regard the existence of God as having *at least the same level of certainty as I have hitherto attributed to the truths of mathematics* which concern only figures and numbers" (AT VII 65f.: CSM II 45, e.a., the last six words being added in the French text at AT IX-1 52). Were it not for the parallel with mathematics, the obvious place to treat of "the essence of material things" would have been in the Sixth Meditation, where their existence is proved.

24 Cf. the remark to Burman, cited earlier: "the idea of God and ourselves, *which never were in the senses*" (e.a.).

25 Gassendi acknowledges no difference, or at most a difference of degree, between intellect and imagination. Cf. AT VII 329f.: CSM II 228f. and again at AT VII 331: CSM II 230. This is something for which Descartes continually castigates him.

26 Despite this difference between the two, Gassendi obviously makes no distinction such as Aquinas draws in separating *abstractio totius* and *abstractio formae*. In the former, abstraction is from the many particular individuals and their accidental features (taken as 'parts' of a whole), but not from the substantial form and the matter (both considered in general) that make up the substantial nature of the thing. This is the procedure followed in natural philosophy; it leads to generic concepts like 'man,' 'animal,' etc. In the *abstractio formae*, by contrast, abstraction is from all the sensible properties in the nine secondary categories. This type of abstraction characterizes the mathematical sciences (for example, the formation of the mathematical concept 'triangle'). On the distinction of *abstractio totius* from *abstractio formae*, cf. Maurer's introduction to Aquinas 1986, xx f.

Of course, Descartes's own account of mathematical concepts is hardly more in accord with Thomas's than is Gassendi's. As Gouhier (1969, 210) has remarked: "*Abducere mentem a sensibus* ne signifie nullement extraire l'intelligible du sensible" for Descartes, at it does for Thomas, "mais se détourner des choses sensibles pour se tourner vers l'esprit qui porte en soi les intelligibles." (Cf. above section 10.1 for some pertinent texts dealing with 'leading the mind away from the senses.') Nothing could be further from Aquinas. Where Descartes does provide an example of something resembling *abstractio formae*, in the wax example of the Second Mediation, it leads to the discovery of the *metaphysical or substantial* (!) nature of body – precisely what, for Thomas, is inaccessible in the mathematical *abstractio formae*. This is symptomatic of a radical change in the metaphysical understanding of 'essence' or 'nature.' Cf. the highly pertinent quotation from Gouhier in the next note and the discussion of "the old and the new metaphysics" in chapter 22 of the Conclusion.

27 Cf. Gouhier 1969, 210: "Le mathématicien Descartes a toujours cru que les figures et les chiffres dessinées sur le papier étaient les signes sensibles de réalités non

sensibles, et, par suite, présentes dans l'esprit indépendamment de l'exercice de la puissance sensitive. Il y a des idées qui sont nées avec moi." This last formulation unfortunately mistakes the sense of innateness in Descartes (i.e., 'born of reflexion on my own thinking, of inner experience,' etc.); but apart from this, Gouhier's comment is instructive.

28 Descartes dismissed the question earlier: "The points you go on to make against the universals of the dialecticians do not touch me, since my understanding of universals is not the same as theirs" (AT VII 380: CSM II 261). On Descartes's theory of universals, see section 10.9.

29 Rapidly sketching this argument, Buchdahl remarks that it "has a noble ancestry stetching back to Plato." Though possibly true, this is still to read a great deal into the sketchy discussion of Equality in the *Phaedo* (74a ff.) that is simply not in the text. Still, Buchdahl's whole treatment of the argument is interesting. Cf. Buchdahl 1969, 110–18.

30 Cf. Clarke 1982, 189: "The reference to reflection in this passage [AT VI 41: CSM I 131] should not be misunderstood as an intuition of first principles through some kind of purely intellectual reflection ... [W]hat is at issue here is the role of ordinary experience, critically evaluated by reflection, in determining both the basic explanatory concepts and the fundamental principles of any scientific explanation."

31 Cf. Gilson 1947a, 373: "les lois les plus universelles de la nature se trouvent en nous à l'état de connaissances innées, en ce sens qu'il nous suffit d'être attentifs au contenu de notre pensée pour les y découvrir." This captures the sense of 'innate-ness' in Descartes perfectly, yet without betraying the slightest uneasiness about bringing under it the most basic laws of the material universe. Also ibid., 453: "La déduction *a priori* de la physique est rendue possible par le caractère innée de l'idée de Dieu et des principes premiers dont elle découle tout entière." Gilson is in no doubt about the innateness of the idea of extension either. Cf. 433. There is plenty of evidence in *Le Monde* (cf. AT XI 47: CSM I 97), the *Discourse* (AT VI 43: CSM I 132), and the *Principles* (IV, 199–206) that the basic truths of physics are expressly assimilated to the eternal truths of mathematics – or vice versa (see chapter 5, n. 11). From here it is but a small step (though decidedly a step rather than a logical inference) to the conclusion that they were conceived as innate in precisely the same way.

32 The italicized word is important. Röd who, like Gilson, understands the relevant sense of innateness in Descartes correctly, remarks (1959–60, 185): "Auch für Descartes gilt der Kantische Satz: 'Wenn aber gleich alle unsere Erkenntnis *mit* der Erfahrung anhebt, so entspringt sie darum doch nicht eben alle *aus* der Erfahrung.'" However, Kant means by 'Erfahrung' phenomenologically unreduced 'outer experience' of a material universe (nature): no knowledge is temporally prior to, though not all knowledge derives from, experience so understood. Descartes

understands 'experience' differently, so that a certain ambiguity creeps in when Kant's dictum is extended to Descartes in this way. On Descartes's concept of experience, see chapter 20.

19: The Model of the Mind

1 Locke certainly describes reflection in such terms in 2.1.4 of the *Essay* (1977, 34), employing his account throughout much of the remainder of Book Two to explain how the ideas traditionally regarded as innate (by Descartes and others) originate, if not in "internal sense" or "reflection," then at least in internal and external sense together.
2 In *The Search for Truth* it is the paragon of Scholastic learning, Epistemon, who invokes the *tabula rasa* model (cf. AT X 507: CSM 405). Descartes's spokesman, Eudoxus, suggests wiping the slate clean with a sponge (radical doubt). Having done so, a man must then "begin in earnest to form new ideas, applying all the strength of his intellect so effectively, that if he does not bring these ideas to perfection, at least he will not be able to blame the weakness of the senses or the irregularities of nature" (AT X 508: CSM II 406).
3 Cf. Edgley 1970, 13: "Sometimes, indeed, the debate seems to take a fairly innocuous form about whether both elements are necessary and if so which is the more important."
4 In the *Discourse* Descartes formulates the same maxim in this way: "At the beginning [of the advance of knowledge], rather than seeking those [observations (*expériences*)] which are more unusual and highly contrived, it is better to resort only to those which, presenting themselves spontaneously to our senses, cannot be unknown to us if we reflect even a little. The reason for this is that the more unusual observations (*expériences*) are apt to mislead us when we do not yet know the causes of the more common ones, and the factors on which they depend are almost always so special and so minute that it is very difficult to discern them" (AT VI 63: CSM I 143).
5 Cf. the parallel comments about the Scholastic definition of place as 'the surface of the surrounding body' and as "the simple and self-evident nature in virtue of which something is said to be here or there. This nature consists entirely in a certain relation between the thing said to be at the place and the parts of extended space" (AT X 433: CSM I 53).
6 Cf. the *Opticks* (Newton 1974, 174): "The *vis inertiae* is a *passive* principle by which bodies persist in their motion or rest [according to the first of Newton's three laws of motion], receive motion in proportion to the force impressing it [according to the second law], and resist as much as they are resisted [according to the third law]."

7 On 'occultation,' cf. AT VII 163: CSM II 115: "exercising the intellectual vision (*perspicuitatem intellectus*) ... in the pure form which it attains when freed from the senses; for sensory appearances generally interfere with it and *darken it to a very great extent*" (e.a.). Of course, the bodily senses (*praejudicia sensuum*) are not the only source of occultation; prejudices due to authority (*praejudicia auctoritatis*) are another. They lead men to adopt the traditional methods of their Scholastically trained teachers. Thus, Descartes remarks in the *Regulae* that without his method "the pursuit of learning would ... be more harmful than profitable" (AT X 373: CSM I 17): the traditional "operations which dialectic claims to direct ... are of no use ... or rather should be reckoned *a positive hindrance*, for nothing can be added to the pure light of reason which does not in some way dim it (*nihil puro rationis lumini superaddi potest, quod illud aliquo modo non obscuret*)" (e.a.). Later in the *Regulae* Descartes remarks that solving problems by "random and unmethodical guesses" can "*dim the light of the mind* and make it become habituated to childish and futile pursuits" (AT X 405: CSM I 36 e.a.). The fact that prejudices of both kinds, as well as the use of merely probable premises, cannot come into play in the mathematical sciences is the chief reason for their superior progress in relation to philosophy "in which greater obstacles tend to stifle progress" (AT X 373: CSM I 17).

   For some interesting parallels in seventeenth-century English thought – notably the talk of "an Intellectual Lamp" and "the Candle of the Lord, which God has lighted up for the discovery of his own Lawes," etc., see Yolton 1956, 41. Cf. also Popper's interesting observations on the epistemological optimism of the "truth is manifest doctrine" that began in the Renaissance (Popper 1962, 5ff.). And Heidegger's intriguing comment (the theological background of which we cannot stop to consider here), that Descartes's position represents "ein extremer Pelagianismus des theoretischen Erkennens" (Heidegger 1994, 228).

8 Also in Book I of the same work and in the *Meditations on Knowledge, Truth, and Ideas* (1684). Cf. Leibniz 1875–90, V, 77 and IV, 426.

9 Cf. Yolton 1956, 56: "For Locke there were just two alternatives. Either ideas and principles are innate in the sense of full-blown and perfect ideas, or they can be only tendencies which arise with experience. The former is absurd and false, the latter trivial and of no consequence."

10 For detailed analyses of the issues presented in rapid overview here, cf. Jalabert (1946), Naërt (1961), Belaval (1976), McRae (1976), and Kulstad (1991). For more argument on points that may seem controversial in what follows, see my critical notice of Kulstad (Miles 1994b).

11 Thus, *s'apercevoir de* ... can at times designate the sense-perception of external objects or (equivalently, for Leibniz) of sensory images of those objects, i.e., the sensations of which both men and beasts are capable. Cf., e.g., *New Essays*, 2.21.5

(Leibniz 1875–90, V, 159) and the preface to that work, where Leibniz comments that, at death, perception is "reduced to a state of confusion in animals which suspends [their] apperception." From this it is clear that animals too apperceive in this non-technical sense.

12 *Pace* McRae, who, overlooking the non-technical use, holds that consciousness, reflexive knowledge, and apperception are, "in all instances of their use, equivalent" (1976, 31ff.).

13 Cf. *New Essays*, 2.21.5 (Leibniz 1875–90, V, 159): "intellection, qui est une perception distincte jointe à la faculté de réfléchir ... Toute perception jointe à cette faculté est une pensée."

14 In apperceiving the mind itself "adds something to the objects" of those perceptions that it raises to the level of thought. Hence the choice of the term 'apperception' (from *ad-percipere*) for this technical usage. Cf. Leibniz 1989, 188: "The thought of *myself* who perceives sensible objects, and the thought of the action of mine that results from it, *adds something* to the objects of the senses" (e.a.). Leibniz goes on to enumerate the various metaphysical concepts ("substance in general ... cause, effect, action, similarity, etc.") furnished by the mind through apperception. In the preface to the *New Essays*, he produces the following catalogue of metaphysical concepts: "being, unity, substance, duration, change, action, perception, pleasure, and a thousand other objects of our intellectual ideas" (Leibniz 1989, 294). For reasons that should be obvious in the light of Descartes's concept of innateness (cf. chapter 9, *in initio*), the inclusion of a sensation like pleasure in this list is particularly interesting.

15 On enthymemes, see *New Essays*, 1.1.4 and 1.1.19 (Leibniz, 1895–90, V, 73 and 69). For the reference to the *Meno*, see *Discourse on Metaphysics*, sect. 26 (ibid., IV, 51) and the letter to Queen Sophie Charlotte of Prussia (ibid., VI, 506). On Descartes and the *Meno*, see above, chapter 15 n. 30 and chapter 18 n. 22. Interestingly, both Leibniz, the formalist, and Descartes, the intuitionist, see their own doctrines prefigured in the *Meno*.

16 Locke 1977, 5f. (*Essay*, 1.2.2), quoted by McRae 1972b, 32. Cf. ibid., 33 (*Essay*, 2.1.1): "native *ideas* and original characters stamped upon their minds in their very first being," and 2.9.6: "original characters impressed upon it [the mind] at the very first moment of its being and constitution." What Edgley (1970, 1) calls "the rationalist doctrine of innate ideas" coincides at bottom with this doctrine "that some at least of our ideas and knowledge of things are not derived from outside the mind, through experience, but are present from birth in the mind itself and thus represent the mind's own contribution to our understanding of reality."

On Cicero and the Stoic doctrine of *prolepsis*, especially their influence on Locke's contemporaries, including his great antagonist, Stillingfleet, see Yolton 1956, chap. II, esp. 36f. Yolton distinguishes "a naive form" (ibid., 29) of the doctrine of innateness from the "dispositional doctrine of innate knowledge" (39,

48 etc.). He has frequent occasion to remark that even where the *language* used is that of the naive theory, the actual doctrine is often the more sophisticated dispositional one.

This is true of Descartes as well. Yet Descartes's distinctive conception of what it is for innate ideas to be in the mind *potentiâ* does not appear to have been defended by any of the figures examined by Yolton: not (here I rely on Yolton's account rather than first-hand knowledge) by Sclater, More, Culverwel, Charleton, Ferguson, Parker, Burthogge, or any of those who reacted critically to Locke's attack. And this despite the fact that references to 'reflection' and 'attention' are not uncommon in the period (cf., e.g., the quotation from Parker, ibid., 45, or from King, ibid., 50). There may well be affinities with Leibniz's dispositional theory in authors like Henry Lee (cf. ibid., 58), but nothing like a clear analogue of Descartes's theory.

20: Experience and Induction

1 So too Röd (1971, 102): "Descartes untershied zwei Arten von Erfahrungsinhalten: solche, die auf Grund äußerer Reize, und solche, die durch Reflexion des Intellekts auf such selbst gebildet werden." Gewirth (1941, 185ff.) likewise speaks of "a division of experience into two kinds, sensitive or external, and reflective, or internal ... The general problem of experience [in the *Regulae*]," he suggests, "is ... whether there are any objects for the knowledge of which the pure understanding [alone] is not sufficient," i.e., for which experience (sense and imagination) is required.

Like Clarke and others, Gewirth is reacting to the "completely deductive and non-empirical" (ibid., 190) model of scientific method ascribed to Descartes by certain older commentators (in this case, the study by Roth 1937). For Clarke, it is Randall (1940, I, 384f.) who furnishes the target. On *deductio* and *experientia* (or *experimenta*), cf. above, sections 15.6 and 15.7, and section 20.1 below.

2 Cf. section 9.4 *in fine*. What is nowadays called 'introspection' or 'inner sense' is *not* among the senses of *experientia* in Descartes. As for 'experience' in the sense of ordinary external, sensory experience, this is no doubt present in Descartes's writings (e.g., AT X 502f.: CSM II 403; AT X 371: CSM I 16; AT VIII-2 358f.: CSM I 304, and AT X 526: CSM II 419, to give only a few examples); but it figures only as the source of *adventitious* ideas (including the adventitious idea of body). Although intellectual ideas of corporeal things like 'extension,' 'shape,' and 'motion' have their origin in experience, it is neither experience in this everyday reach-me-down sense nor introspection that is the proper source of such ideas, but *inner* experience in the uniquely Cartesian sense to be described in what follows.

3 Descartes does, of course, distinguish between the 'internal and external senses'

(*sensus interni et externi*). By means of the inner sense, examples of which are emotions and appetites, we are aware only of the condition of our own bodies, while the external senses make us aware of bodies other than our own as well. Cf. *Principles*, IV, 190–1 (AT VIII-1 316ff.: CSM I 280ff.) and the reference to "ideas which arise from the sensations of appetite" (*ideis quae ab appetitu sensitivo oriuntur*) at AT VII 234: CSM II 164). This distinction coincides with none of those later distinctions just mentioned. Cf. also Leibniz's distinction between internal and external sense, which is again *sui generis* (Leibniz 1989, 187).

4 The following from Rule XIV gives a fair idea of the extreme latitude Descartes permits himself in the use of *deductio*: "if someone at some time has seen the primary colours, though not the secondary or mixed colours, then by means of a deduction of sorts (*deductionem quandam*) it is possible for him to form images even of those he has not seen, in virtue of the similarity to those he has seen" (AT X 438: CSM I 56f.). Hume (1990, 66) employs a similar example (differing hues of the same colour) to illustrate an anomaly: an idea actually formed by the mind rather than 'copied' from antecedent impressions. Here Descartes designates this particular use of the imagination *deductio* because of the affinity between *deductio* and *inductio* or *enumeratio* involving imagination or memory (see below).

On the use of *deductio* to designate a fairly straightforward instance of hypothetico-deductive method, see Rule X: "the method usually consists simply in constantly following an order, whether it is actually present in the matter in question or is ingeniously read into it (*vel in ipsa re existentis, vel subtiliter excogitati*). For example, say we want to read something written in an unfamiliar cypher that lacks any apparent order: what we shall do is to *invent an order* so as to *test* every *conjecture* we can make about individual letters, words, or sentences, and to arrange the characters in such a way that by an enumeration we may discover what can be deduced from them" (AT X 404f.: CSM I 35f. e.a.). On the applicab*ility* of hypothetico-deductive method (*deductio*) to scientific questions (as something other than a *pis aller*), cf. McRae 1961, 65f. For concrete scientific examples of its use, cf. Buchdahl 1969, chap. III *passim*. For a description of this method in the later work, see the *Discourse* at AT VI 76f.: CSM I 150 and *Principles*, III, 42. Buchdahl regards scientific reasoning of this kind as one sense of 'analysis' (he terms it "analysis$_h$"). What we have termed 'analytical reflexion' corresponds in a rough way to Buchdahl's "analysis$_r$" ("intuition of basic structure"), while his "analysis$_m$" designates one particular mode of mathematical reasoning ('from the unknown to the known'). As one might expect, these different analyses (and other operations besides) are all among the senses of *deductio* in Descartes as well.

As for induction in the contemporary sense, there seems (*pace* Clarke 1982, 70) to be no straightforward example in the *Regulae* of either *deductio* or *inductio* in this particular use ("induction over members of a class"), though the talk of "probable conjectures" in various contexts may cover this along with hypothetico-deductive patterns of inference. An apparent exception will be discussed presently.

5 On *compositio*, cf. AT IX 424: CSM I 47, to be interpreted in section 20.3 below.

6 Cf. also AT X 389: CSM I 26: "if we have deduced one fact from another immediately, then provided the inference is evident, it already comes under the heading of true intuition."

7 Cf. also AT X 369: CSM I 14f.: "The self-evidence and certainty of intuition is required not only for apprehending single propositions, but also for any train of reasoning whatever. Take, for example, the inference that 2 plus 2 equals 3 plus 1: not only must we intuitively perceive that 2 plus 2 make 4 and that 3 plus 1 make 4, but also that the original proposition follows necessarily from the other two [in accordance with the principle of the natural light: 'things equal to the same thing are equal to each other']." Thus, $2 + 2 = 3 + 1$ could be said to be known by deduction *or by intuition*, the inference or movement of thought being *immediate* and hence such as can be easily encompassed within a single intuition. Curiously, J.-M. Beyssade (1979, 148) suggests that conclusions like this can strictly be called *neither*. Many puzzles ensue.

   On whether the derivation of the conclusion in mathematical *deductio* is *logical* deduction, see section 15.7.

8 On enumeration as "eine Unterart der Deduktion" cf. Röd 1971, 57.

9 The metaphysical example runs as follows: "if I wish to show in the same way [i.e., by enumeration of the kinds of corporeal entity there are] that the rational soul is not corporeal, there is no need for the enumeration to be complete; it will be sufficient if I group all bodies together into several classes so as to demonstrate that the rational soul cannot be assigned to any of these." This is again a matter of 'grasping the universal in the particular.'

10 Even the term Descartes employs here, *perlustrare*, 'to wander through,' 'to roam afield,' is, in its literal use, evocative of *discursus* and its cognates, used elsewhere (cf. section 15.1, n. 3). However, Descartes uses the same term in the famous 'basket-of-apples' metaphor (AT VII 481: CSM II 324; cf. also AT VII 512: CSM II 349) for the process of going through the contents in an orderly way, so that it would be unwise to place too much emphasis on the choice of this word.

11 In this passage, too, the link between *conscientia* and the intellectual faculty (see above, sections 9.2 and 17.2) is at least alluded to.

12 Gewirth is more ambivalent than Clarke on this point. Cf. 1941, 187: "Descartes's method provides a place for experience as putting the understanding in direct contact with the objects of physical science, as a source of truth, as a necessary aid to the understanding. *This does not mean, however, that some knowledge even of 'material' objects is not possible without specific reference to sense or imagination*" (e.a.). On the other hand, "experience is for Descartes the source of the basic

concepts and principles of all physical science" (195). While similarly opposed to Roth's interpretation of Descartes's alleged 'deductivism' on the model of a formal axiomatized system, these passages suggest that Gewirth is slightly more receptive than Clarke to a fairly robust form of nativism. But he is obviously uneasy about it.

13 We say "from each of *two* sources" because A1 and A2 are taken together as a single source. This seems to be Descartes's own manner of treating them in the final sentence.

14 Though the two mean the same. Back in Rules II and III, Descartes first notes that "there are two ways of arriving at a knowledge of things – through experience and through deduction" (AT X 365: CSM I 12) – and then, a bare two pages later, that he recognizes "only two actions of the intellect (*intellectus nostri actiones*) by means of which we are able to arrive at a knowledge of things with no fear of being mistaken: ... intuition and deduction" (AT X 368: CSM I 14). The switch is not surprising if *intuitus* can be understood in a broad sense that encompasses *experientia*. Yet two senses of 'intuition' are only sharply distinguished in Rule XII.

15 The idea of God does not figure in the *Regulae*, though its composite nature as involving the ideas (a) infinite, (b) thinking, (c) substance is obvious. Cf. the 'recipe' of the *Discourse* for forming the idea of the *deus philosophorum* as *omnitudo realitatis*: "in order to know the nature of God, as far as my own nature was capable of knowing it, I had only to consider, for each thing of which I found in myself some idea, whether or not it was a perfection to possess it; and I was sure that none of those which indicated any imperfection was in God, but that all the others were" (AT VI 35: CSM I 128).

On the complex nature of 'triangle,' cf. the fifth of the "assumptions" set out in Rule XII: "Indeed it is often easier to attend at once to several mutually conjoined natures than to separate one of them from the others. For example, I can have knowledge of a triangle, even though it has never occurred to me that this knowledge involves knowledge also of the angle, the line, the number three, shape, extension, etc. But that does not preclude our saying that the nature of the triangle is *composed* of these other natures and that they are better known than the triangle, for it is just these natures that we understand to be present in it" (AT X 422: CSM I 46 e.a.). Descartes earlier (AT X 418: CSM I 44) says much the same of 'body' (cited and interpreted in section 13.3).

16 The reference is to Aristotle 1949b [*Post. An.*, 81a38–b9].

17 For a perceptive account of "acquaintance with (immanent) universals" in *aisthēsis*, cf. Ferejohn 1992, sect. II.

CONCLUSION

1 Russell 1900, xif. The point of view adopted in this Conclusion was first elaborated

in two comparative seminars on ancient and early modern philosophy offered
jointly by the author and Professor Martha Husain. Many of the ideas and certain of
the formulations are the product of collaborative efforts inside and outside the
classroom.

2 Cf. also Spinoza's reformulation (1963, 16): "Therefore, *cogito, ergo sum* is a
unique proposition equivalent to 'I am a thinking thing' (*cogito ergo sum est
propositio quae huic, ego sum cogitans, aequivalet*)."

Hoenen alleges (1937, 459f.) that Spinoza's gloss reduces *(ego) cogito, ergo sum*
to *cogito*. But far from suppressing either the *sum* or the *ego*, Spinoza's reformulation expressly includes both. The *ergo*, on the other hand, *is* suppressed – a clear
indication of Spinoza's recognition that the *cogito* principle is no inference in the
usual sense, certainly not a syllogism. Others who similarly suppress the *ergo*,
probably for the same reason, are Heidegger (who regularly speaks of Descartes's
cogito sum), Heimsoeth, Thouverez, and Buchenau. For references, cf. Scholz
1931, 134f., who dismisses the lot of them in the same breath with Spinoza.

According to Hoenen, Hamelin assumes that Spinoza does away with the *ergo*
because he understands the *cogito* principle as a judgment rather than an inference
(cf. Hoenen, ibid.). This interpretation Hamelin finds unsatisfactory owing to the
difficulty of classifying this judgment as either analytic or synthetic. (On this, cf.
section 15.6 above). Yet Hoenen, for his part, agrees with Spinoza that it is a
judgment, dismissing the Kantian puzzle ("pourquoi ne pas chercher ailleurs un
terme de comparaison") and directing attention to the source in Aristotle's *Posterior
Analytics* of the Stoic doctrine of the causal proposition (cf. section 17.4).

If the interpretation of the immediately preceding chapter is correct, the *cogito*
principle is at least not a judgment *as distinct from* either intuition or inference, but
rather a progress of the mind within intuition itself. (This much Hoenen well
understands.) The right place to look for a suitable comparison may therefore be the
doctrine of intuitive induction found in the same work of Aristotle. The only
question is, to what extent Spinoza and the others just mentioned may have
recognized this as the reason for suppressing the *ergo*. It seems doubtful that in
addition to the negative justification ('not a syllogism'), the positive reasons for
eliding the *ergo* (cf. chapter 17) have been clearly understood.

21: Realism, Subjectivism, and Transcendence

1 Cf. the first paragraph of this Conclusion, section 4.2, and section 10.5. In section
10.5 it is pointed out that the view to which representationalism is opposed
frequently goes by the name 'naive realism' today, though Descartes himself
regarded not this, but the combination of causal and representational realism as
'naive.' Thus, the contemporary sense of 'naive realism' would in itself dictate that

518 Notes to pages 365–7

representationalism be treated as a form of epistemological 'idealism.' The same may be said of the anti-realist tenets under (2) and (3), while (4) can be correctly described as a form of metaphysical idealism. More will be said of metaphysical idealism, including (4), in section 21.3.

2 *Semel in vita* occurs at AT VII 17: CSM II 12; AT III 695: CSMK 228; AT V 165: CSMK 346; and AT X 395 and 396: CSM I 30. Cf. also AT II 35: CSMK 97.

3 Cf. Röd 1971, 140: "Der scheinbare Subjektivismus bzw. sogar Solipsismus der ersten Phase ist lediglich provisorisch, seine Verselbständigung mithin unstatthaft. Nur wenn das Verfahren ... vorzeitig abgebrochen wird, kann der Eindruck einer subjektivistischen Position, die Descartes wenigstens zeitweise als definitives Resultat betrachtet hätte, entstehen."

4 See above, section 4.2. The point – made by Curley (1978, 172ff.), for example – that Descartes's *mens notior corpore* doctrine had important antecedents in Augustine and Montaigne hardly diminishes his stature as the great innovator who brought about a radical reversal in the order of knowing in the transition from medieval to modern philosophy.

5 Cf. Leibniz 1989, 128: "the middle way ... is best. That is, we acknowledge that all corporeal phenomena can be derived from efficient and mechanical causes, but we understand that these very mechanical laws as a whole are derived from higher reasons. And so we use this higher efficient cause only in establishing general and distant principles. But once these principles have been established, then afterwards, whenever we deal with the immediate and specific efficient causes of natural things, we should take no account of souls or entelechies, no more than we should drag in useless faculties or inexplicable sympathies." This "middle way" leads neither to idealism nor phenomenalism in the contemporary sense (cf. section 1.2, n. 18, 19.5, and n. 11 below) but to a realism regarding both the existence and knowability of sensible things that is set squarely within the framework of a two-world metaphysics quite unlike Plato's. Cf. n. 8 below. On "natural machines," see, for example, ibid., 142. They are called "divine machines" in the *Monadology*, sect. 64.

6 Aside from the (1) ontological and (2) methodological varieties, 'monism' and 'pluralism' are nowadays frequently spoken of in the context of the controversy as to whether 'facts' exist and are available for purposes of theory-evaluation even without consideration of alternative theories to that under examination. For an interesting critique of such 'theoretical monism,' i.e., (3) the view that theories can be tested in isolation from competing theories, and a spirited defence of the claims of 'theoretical pluralism,' cf. Feyerabend 1980 (and related writings).

7 On Aristotle, see Cardinal Newman's comment (Newman 1960, 83): "While we are men, we cannot help, to a great extent, being Aristotelians, for the great Master does but analyze the thoughts, feelings, views, and opinions of human kind." And

Gilson (1952, 42): "The metaphysics of Aristotle is the normal philosophy of all those whose natural trend of mind or social vocation is to deal, in a concrete way, with concrete reality." As for Hume, it is worth citing his remark that "philosophical decisions are nothing but the reflections of common life, methodized and corrected" (Hume 1990, 192). Oddly enough, the same Hume realized full well how totally at odds the 'veil-of perception' doctrine of philosophy was with common sense (cf. above, chapter 4, n. 2). On Heidegger, see section 22.2; on Quine see Hesse's comment, quoted in chapter 22, n. 11 below. On Leibniz's philosophy as a philosophy of transcendence, see the next note.

8 Like Descartes, Leibniz (see n. 5 above) is a methodological dualist at the physical, scientific, or phenomenal level; but in contrast to Descartes he is a *methodological* monist at the ultimate metaphysical or noumenal level of explanation. Leibniz, that is, accepts Descartes's vertical cleavage between two realms, mind and matter, each with its own principles of explanation, as the correct scientific view. But he introduces a further horizontal cleavage in addition to that on which Descartes insists: Descartes posits a sharp division between (1) material things as they are known through the senses and (2) those same things as known through the intellect aided by the imagination, i.e., as extended mass (figurable, mobile, impenetrable Cartesian matter), *res extensa*, the total object of mathematical physics; to this Leibniz adds the divide between (2) and (3), those same things considered as the monadically structured objects of pure intellection or metaphysics. At this ultimate metaphysical level of explanation, even material things exhibit the same basic structure and are intelligible in accordance with the same first principles as *res cogitans*.

Underlying the methodological monism of this "middle way" is an almost bizarrely hybrid *metaphysical* outlook. The Aristotelian substantial or hylomorphic principles (see chapter 22, n. 23), matter and form, are curiously transmogrified with the help of the Cartesian analysis of mind. The material principle in substances becomes a primitive passive power of perception, while form is construed as appetition and as a primitive active force. These principles are applicable exclusively to the supersensible, i.e., the substantial, ultimately monadic, reality underlying the sensible appearances of things, while the principles of Cartesian natural philosophy are applied by Leibniz to the same entities considered as sensible beings.

Though logically incompatible, both accounts, the physical and the metaphysical, are reconciled by the expedient of a new type of two-world metaphysics. For Leibniz, the *mundus intelligibilis* is not a reality 'beyond' the sensible particulars, as in Plato's horizontal divide (the many particulars *ici bas* and the one Form 'above' or 'beyond'); nor is it, as for the pre-critical Kant, a noumenal reality *ici bas* but 'behind' the sensible appearances, accessible only to the pure intellect. If the recurrent metaphor of "metaphysical points," clearly borrowed from contemporary atomism, signifies anything, it is a part-whole ('mereological') dichotomy of 'true being' (*mundus intelligibilis*) and sensible being or being 'by convention' (*nomo*), that is at work, yet with genuine knowledge (science) possible even of the *mundus sensibilis*. So at least as far as the 'ultimate constituents of reality' are concerned.

So much for metaphysics. *Epistemologically*, finally, the situation is this. Not only is (1) the scientific account of things incompatible with (2) the deliverances of ordinary, pre-philosophical experience, as in Descartes; it is similarly at odds with (3) the purely intellectual understanding of the true natures of those and all other objects as substantial or merely accidental aggregates of "metaphysical points" or true monadic substances. If science subverts ordinary pre-scientific experience, as in Descartes, metaphysical reflexion, Leibniz holds, overturns Cartesian dualism as a mistaken metaphysical doctrine of the being of beings, i.e., the substantiality of substances.

In sum: despite subscribing (at one level) to the methodological monism earlier said to be charactistic of 'pure' philosophies of immanence and transcendence, Leibniz, in the end, takes up a highly eclectic stance that is perhaps best described as a 'mixed' philosophy of transcendence, like Descartes's, though (despite borrowings from Aristotle and atomism) even more akin to Plato than is Cartesianism.

9 However conservative, this is still preferable to Whitehead's notorious *bon mot*, "a series of footnotes to Plato" – unless this description is made to fit Aristotle himself. So understood it boils down to an enigmatic way of saying the same thing.

10 Berkeley launches a whole battery of criticisms against both the 'vulgar' or common-sense notion as well as the Lockean, philosophical notion of 'material substance.' (References are to the paragraph numbers of the *Principles* [Berkeley 1965].)

The concept of material substance is (a) 'unintelligible' in the strict logical sense of 'self-contradictory' (4, 9); (b) 'unintelligible' in the looser epistemic senses of 'unimaginable' ('unrepresentable') or 'without any distinct meaning,' i.e., 'obscure and confused' (10, 16, 17); and (c) 'unintelligible' in the quite loose sense of being without any empirical or rational justification, having no explanatory force whatever, even fostering the very atheism and scepticism against which it is supposed to be a bulwark. In short: groundless, useless, and self-defeating (cf. 19, 20).

The criticism in (a) applies both to the 'vulgar' conception of substance or 'thing' and to the philosophical notion of a *substratum*. (b) applies to the philosophical notion of a *substratum*, whether conceived as having certain determinations (these are said to be 'unimaginable' or 'obscure') or as having no determinations at all (hence: 'no *distinct* meaning'). (c) applies to the other philosophical notion of material substance found in Locke: substance as 'real essence.'

11 More common nowadays than 'idealism' is the talk of 'phenomenalism' in discussions of Berkeley. The term 'phenomenalism' first came into use in the context of the mid-twentieth-century debate concerning (a) the meaning of scientific statements and (b) the structure of scientific knowledge, only later to be applied retroactively to the metaphysical idealism of Berkeley. In the philosophy of science it is generally used to characterize the view that the basic or elementary sentences of science are 'reports' (*Konstatierungen*) about the experiences of observers. Opposed to this is the view (known as 'physicalism') that those *Elementar-* or *Protokoll-Sätze* are rudimentary statements about extra-mental (material) things rather than about 'sensa' or sense-data in the mind. What both views have in common is a certain 'foundationalist' conception of science, according to which the whole fabric of (scientific) knowledge consists of "logical constructions" upon simple observation statements of the one sort or the other; that, in other words, it does *not* rest on self-evident first principles or axioms, as in the very different 'foundationalisms' of Aristotle and Descartes.

As far as the theory of meaning goes, 'phenomenalism' may be crudely sketched as a theory that any meaningful material-thing-statement whatever can be reduced *without remainder* to some set of statements about actual and possible perceptions or perceptual states of a hypothetical observer. The meaning of such statements is thus identical with the process of their verification (hence the talk of 'verification-ism'). At the same time the theory furnishes a criterion of meaningfulness, i.e., a test or means of distinguishing meaningful from meaningless statements and utterances. On this see chapter 22, n. 17 below.

From here it is a short step to Berkeley's position on what it is for something to exist and be known to exist – or what it means to say that something exists and is known to exist (Berkeley is systematically ambiguous about the difference) – outside the mind as a real thing rather than a figment of the imagination, hallucination, and illusion, etc. Thus, the term 'phenomenalism' has largely replaced 'subjective idealism' in discussions of views like Berkeley's, including Mill's and Leibniz's. (See n. 5 above for references to the debate concerning Leibniz.) Still, it is helpful to be as clear as possible about the boundaries between the theory of knowledge (science), the theory of meaning, and primarily metaphysical theories about the order of being like Berkeley's.

12 On God, cf. Owens 1993b, 39: "Aristotelian metaphysics reasons from the eternity of the cosmic processes and animated heavens to separate and immobile substance as final cause." As for Thomistic metaphysics, it is to God as efficient cause of the becoming, being, and activity of all creatures that the metaphysician reasons. Cf. Wippel 1993, 87: "In the case of philosophy [as opposed to the order to be followed

in the teaching based on faith] one considers created reality in itself and moves from an examination of reality to a knowledge of God." ·

On the mind, see again Owens, ibid., 53: "Common to both Aristotle and Aquinas is the tenet that all naturally attainable knowledge originates in external sensible things. By their efficient causality, transmitted through the appropriate media, the external things impress their forms upon the human cognitive faculties, and thereby make the percipient be the thing perceived in the actuality of cognition. The awareness is directly of the thing itself, and only concomitantly and reflexively of the percipient and the cognitive acts. The external things remain epistemologically prior." Also Doig 1974, 71: "after having known external, material objects, the soul returns to itself and discovers what are the necessary characteristics of the soul which are presupposed for knowledge of external material objects."

13 Cf. Heidegger 1962, 81: "Daß das » Ich « zu der Kennzeichnung dessen kommt, was für das Vorstellen das eigentliche im vorhinein schon Vor-liegende (das » Objektive « im heutigen Sinne) ist, das liegt nicht an irgendeinem Ichstand-punkt oder an einem subjektivistischen Zweifel ... Bis zu Descartes galt als » Subjekt « jedes für sich vorhandene Ding; jetzt aber wird das »Ich« zum auge-zeichneten Subjekt." See Marion's distorting echo of this passage (Marion 1975, 188), which is apt to foster a 'subjectivist' misinterpretation of Descartes after all.

14 I am indebted to my colleague Dr Martha Husain for having drawn this out-of-the-way source to my attention.

15 They are conflated by Kennington (1972, passim), for example.

16 On "the confused ideas of gods which are concocted by idolaters," cf. AT VII 233: CSM II 163.

22: The Old and the New Metaphysics

1 The talk of 'the old and the new metaphysics' is patterned after an essay entitled "The Old and the New Logic" by Carnap (1959b), one of the self-appointed undertakers of metaphysics in the earlier part of this century. Similar language was used by Voetius, the Rector at Utrecht, who managed to have the "new philosophy" of Descartes condemned by the University Senate. Of course, Descartes's own view of the matter was quite different (and "paradoxical" as he acknowledged). See the Letter to Father Dinet, quoted partially already in section 20.1: "Everything in peripatetic philosophy, regarded as a distinctive school that is different from others, is quite new, whereas everything in my philosophy is old. For as far as principles are concerned, I only accept those which in the past have always been common ground among all philosophers without exception, and which are therefore the most ancient of all. Moreover, the conclusions I deduce (*deduco*) are already contained and implicit in these principles, and I show this so clearly as to make it apparent

that they too are very ancient, in so far as they are naturally implanted in the human mind. By contrast the principles of the commonly accepted philosophy – at least at the time when they were invented by Aristotle and others – were quite new, and we should not suppose that they are any better now than they were then" (AT VII 580f.: CSM II 391f.).

If this means that 'Platonic' philosophy is old and true because founded on principles of natural human reason, while the peripatetic was (in its day) 'new' and mistaken because it followed the testimony of the senses rather than the innate principles of reason, there is perhaps nothing particularly "paradoxical" about this after all. If not, it is hard to say what it can mean.

2 Or Ideas. Regarding Platonic Idealism, the distinction of 'the Gods' from 'the Giants' (materialists) was first elaborated by Plato in the *Sophist* (246a–249d), while the varieties of modern idealism seem to have been worked out first by Kant (see section 21.3). Interestingly, the Platonic *gigantomachia* is invoked by the authors of the Second Set of Objections to the *Meditations*, who commend Descartes as follows: "The task of defending the Author of all things against a new race of giants [i.e., atheists and materialists], and of demonstrating his existence, is one which you have undertaken ... etc." This suggests that Descartes's affinities with Platonism were recognized from the start (and usually exaggerated). On the early modern history of the "Battle of the Gods and Giants," see Lennon's work of the same name (1993).

3 At least in the broad sense just described. There is, however, a special ontological usage that is even more prevalent today (see n. 9); and, of course, there is Lovejoy's epistemological usage (see section 21.3).

4 Apart from those discussed by Margaret Wilson 1978a. Wilson shows that historical Cartesian dualism was a much more "robust" affair than that which passes for "Cartesian dualism" among philosophical psychologists today. To this robustness there are two aspects. First, purely mental conception both occurs without any concomitant physical event in the brain and is clearly and distinctly conceivable apart from the conception of any such event. The denial of any psycho-physical correlation in the case of purely intellectual processes is Wilson's main point. She is rightly more tentative about a second difference: sensation and the passions cannot be clearly and distinctly conceived apart from their physical correlates. On balance (see chapter 6 and section 7.5), Descartes appears to take the view that *any* mental act whatever, even sensation, is, qua mental, clearly and distinctly conceivable apart from *anything* material. What clouds the issue is perhaps his choice of examples like knowledge (or doubt) and volition in *The Search for Truth*; but as noted in chapter 6, sensation figures pretty prominently in various other contexts as an example of a mental act clearly and distinctly conceivable apart from anything of a physical nature.

5 Spinoza is an obvious exception, having anticipated the eighteenth-century attacks on the second component.

6 In the famous letter of 15 April 1630 to Mersenne, Descartes begs his friend "to tell people as often as the occasion demands" about his doctrine of God's creation of the eternal truths "provided you do not mention my name. I should be glad to know the objections which can be made against this view" (AT I 146: CSMK 23).

7 Cf. AT IX-1 206: CSM II 271f.: "Now I deny that the thing which thinks needs any object apart from itself in order to exercise its activity (though it may also extend the scope of this activity to material things when it examines them)." Descartes is speaking of "the thing which thinks" in its *present* condition in this life. St Thomas envisages a condition of the soul in which it is not dependent on the body in order to know, but that is not its present condition. Historically, it is a matter of debate whether this is also Aristotle's position. The assumption made here is that it is not.

8 Cf. the similarly titled article by Richardson 1982.

9 Cf. Cottingham 1986, 119: "By 'Cartesian dualism' is meant the thesis that man is a compound of two distinct substances – *res cogitans*, unextended thinking substance, or mind, and *res extensa*, extended corporeal substance, or body."

10 By Arnauld, for example (cf. AT VII 203: CSM II 143). For a fuller treatment of this theme see Miles 1983.

11 Historically, the former stems from Wittgenstein and the Vienna Circle (cf., e.g., Ayer 1959, Editor's Introduction), the latter from Duhem and Quine. Cf. Hesse's interesting discussion of Quine's manner of taking up Duhem's revisions of classical empiricism, especially the way in which (according to Quine's famous dictum) 'our statements about the external world face the tribunal of sense experience not individually but only as a corporate body.' Remarks Hesse: "how they face it has come in [Quine's] recent writings [especially *Word and Object*] to be a question for a stimulus-response psychology" (1970, 194f.).

12 See Cardinal Newman's and Gilson's comments, quoted in chapter 21, n. 7 above. In the next section it will be suggested that the continuity is even greater in Heidegger.

13 Cf. Owens 1993a, 120: "Aristotle makes clear how one can honestly and consistently meld one's philosophic life with the real life one is daily living in common with the non-philosophical public." The expression "think with the learned and speak with the vulgar" is found in Berkeley (1965, §51), who may have borrowed it from Francis Bacon, *De Augumentis Scientiarum* (London, 1623), bk. V, chap. 4: "Loquendum esse ut vulgus, sentiendum ut sapientes."

14 For a critical survey of recent efforts to resolve this problem, see Miles 1990.

15 When Quine writes, "Science is a continuation of common sense, and it continues the common-sense expedient of swelling ontology to simplify theory" (1953, 45), it is well to remember that physical objects encountered in ordinary sense-experience

are for him no less conventional (cultural) posits than the entities of microphysics. It is in this respect, then, that science is continuous with common sense: both "swell ontology" with theoretical constructs in order to render an otherwise intractable welter of experiences conceptually more manageable. Yet *what* science on the one hand and common sense on the other posit as constituting the nature of physical objects could hardly be more disparate. Cf. the famous "two tables" of Eddington, the everyday object and the "scientific table" (Eddington 1928, xiff.).

In a similar vein, Sellars (1980, 104f.) writes: "[S]cientific discourse is but a continuation of a dimension of discourse which has been present in human discourse from the very beginning." This too is misleading. Sellars's point is that the "framework of categories of the common-sense picture of the world," though very different from the "scientific picture," has at least this in common with the latter: it too is just "a dimension of discourse," that dimension of which the scientific enterprise is (so Sellars) "the flowering." Continuity of *this* sort, however, *subverts* the "manifest image" of the world in everyday experience, as Sellars himself notes (adapting Protagoras's famous dictum): "in the dimension of describing and explaining the world, science is the measure of all things, of what is that it is, and of what is not that it is not." Thus, "the scientific picture of the world *replaces* the common-sense picture; ... the scientific account of 'what there is' *supersedes* the descriptive ontology of everyday life ... *[S]peaking as a philosopher*, I am quite prepared to say that the common-sense world of physical objects in Space and Time is unreal – that is, that there are no such things" (1980, 105 e.a.).

Presumably, 'speaking as a philosopher' (or "lay physicist" [Quine 1953, 44]) is opposed to 'speaking as an ordinary human being' here. As philosophy is to ordinary experience in the view of Aristotle, so philosophy is, not to ordinary experience, but to the scientific conception of the world in the view of Sellars and Quine. This sort of continuity is not just remote from what was meant earlier in speaking of 'philosophies of immanence' as continuous with pre-philosophical experience, of which Hume's was the paradigm; it is the exact opposite, its inspiration unmistakably Cartesian, though the details of its understanding of science are more up-to-date.

16 Now, at least, though perhaps not during the first 150 years of the existence of the theory. Cf. Feyerabend (1980b, n. 1).

17 Cf. Russell 1945a, 243: "Whatever knowledge is obtainable, must be obtained by scientific methods; and what science cannot discover, mankind cannot know." This is moderate by comparison with Carnap and those early positivists for whom metaphysics is beyond the pale, not just of knowledge, but of meaningful discourse (intelligibility). Cf., e.g., Carnap 1959a, esp. 76 (and other essays in the same volume): "meaningful metaphysical statements are impossible. This follows from the task which metaphysics sets itself: to discover and formulate a kind of knowl-

edge which is not accessible to empirical science." Quine and Sellars (cf. above, n. 15) echo Russell's rather than Carnap's outlook. With Feyerabend (1980, 189) things have come full circle: "Elimination of all metaphysics, far from increasing the empirical content of the remaining theories, is liable to turn those theories into dogmas." The allusion to Carnap 1959a ("The Elimination of Metaphysics through Logical Analysis of Language") is unmistakable.

18 Cf. Owens 1993a, sect. II; also 1993b, sect. V. This division itself is quite old. Deriving originally from Aristotle (1949b [*de Int.* 16a 3–8]), it is taken up in the medieval teaching (met with in Cajetan and St Thomas, for example) that a thing may be considered in three ways: as it is *in se*, or *in intellectu nostro*, or *in nostro ore*. On the doctrine of the three 'orders' (*essendi, cognoscendi, significandi*), cf. Phelan 1967, 95, n. 3.

19 Cf. Carnap 1980, Quine 1953, and Sellars 1980 for a representative sampling of the latter type of linguistic philosophy, which is obviously of far greater philosophical significance than either postmodernism or linguistic analysis. On linguistic analysis, cf. Feyerabend's scathing comment in 1980, nn. 2 and 22. It is difficult to understand why Owens ascribes the importance he does to postmodernism. Is it because he regards it as stemming from Heidegger via Gadamer, i.e., from hermeneuticism, and as therefore a philosophical force to be reckoned with?

20 'Discernible' not through simple apprehension but through judgment. Cf. Owens 1993b, 51 and Wippel 1983, chap. 4 and 1993, 88. On the absolute priority of (the act of) existence to essence, finite form, or quiddity – in a word, the 'existentialism' of St Thomas – cf. Owens 1993b, chap. 5, esp. 73ff. This is indeed "one of the most difficult points in the whole problem of being" (ibid.): a predicable accident that is yet prior to the substance whose accident it is. The priority of existence extends equally to matter. Cf. ibid., 47: "Efficient causality now bears on the whole of the finite thing and extends to the production of both matter and form through a creative act." This is what the idea of creation *ex nihilo* involves. Whether such a priority of existence to finite form and matter is ultimately intelligible or not is hard to say.

21 Cf. Owens 1985, 323, n. 1: "For Aristotle the form is 'the primary entity' [*hē protē ousia*] (*Met.* Z 7 1032b 1–14; 11, 1037a 28), that is, the primary instance of being in the composite thing, and in this way the 'cause of being' (*Met.*, Z 17, 1041b 26–8; H 2, 1034a 2–4) without requiring any further actuation by a more primal act." The concluding phrase, "without requiring any further actuation by a more primal act," reflects the Neo-Thomistic perspective of Owens's work: for St Thomas, that "more primal act" is precisely the act of existence as received by the finite form.

The role of form in Aristotle's metaphysics is quite opaque apart from the Parmenidean idea of being as one, whole, complete, perfect, eternal, unchanging, etc. Of the Aristotelian principles, form satisfies these requirements best. And as in the *Metaphysics*, so in the *Physics*. "What populates the Aristotelian universe," remarks Kuhn (1980, 197), "is immaterial 'natures' or 'essences'; the appropriate parallel for the contemporary periodic table is not the four Aristotelian elements, but the quadrangle of four fundamental *forms*" (e.a.).

22 If this is correct, then the commonly held opinion that major shifts in philosophical outlook come as a result of crises precipitated by scientific revolutions is at best partially true of *some* changes.

23 On the distinction between the "substantial" and "entitative" principles, cf. Owens 1985, 302f. It may be preferable to refer to these as the 'hylomorphic' and 'onto-logical' principles, respectively. The problem is that 'substantial principle' and 'entitative principle' suggest that the principles themselves are substances or entities – when what is meant is precisely that they are *not* substances or entities, but rather co-constitutive either of substances (the 'substantial principles') or of entities generally (the 'entitative principles'). Were it not for the fact that form and matter are *non*-substantial and *non*-entitative 'causes' or principles of substance rather than themselves substances or entities, they would belong to the same 'order' as those things whose causes and principles they are. The appeal to such principles would accordingly be 'circular,' as in 'transcendental realism.' On transcendental realism, cf. section 9.3.

Menn insists that "a substantial form is a form that is a substance" (1995, 187) for Descartes as for his Scholastic predecessors (cf. ibid., n. 7: "Descartes is correctly following Scholastic usage in saying that a substantial form is form that is a substance"). But this is Descartes's *mis*understanding of the Thomistic doctrine (in which he may have been preceded by some late Scholastics), as Gilson (whom Menn is correcting here) and Hoenen argued convincingly long ago. See above, chapter 4, n. 5.

24 Cf. above, chapter 4, n. 5. According to Menn (1995, 187), it was a "common stance" among seventeenth-century philosophers to retain forms of various sorts while rejecting substantial forms and real qualities: "Most discussions of Descartes's 'rejection of hylomorphism,'" he writes, "are impeded by a tendency to take 'substantial' form and 'real' quality and 'prime' matter as pleonastic expres-sions for the Scholastic conceptions of form, quality, and matter." As a conse-quence, the rejection of the former is taken for the rejection of form, quality, and matter *tout court*.

Of course, it is true that the *word* 'form' continues to enjoy wide currency even in seventeenth-century natural philosophy; in *Le Monde*, for example, Descartes applies it to the modes of extension, 'motion,' 'size,' and 'shape' (cf. AT XI 26: CSM I 89). The question, however, is whether it figures in the same substance-accident ontology, or whether an altered metaphysical schema has been substituted for the old Scholastic-Aristotelian framework.

It is hard to mistake Descartes's intention to eliminate the qualities and forms of Scholastic metaphysics, or the reductivist thrust of his treatment of sensible qualities generally. Buchdahl has traced it on three distinct levels: the logical, physical, and metaphysical (1969, 102).

On the theological worries occasioned by Descartes's view that (as Arnauld put it) "there are no sensible qualities, but merely various motions in the bodies that surround us which enable us to perceive the various impressions which we subsequently call 'colour,' 'taste,' and 'smell'" (AT VII 217: CSM II 153), see Descartes's reply to Arnauld regarding the doctrine of transubstantiation (AT VII 248ff.: CSM II 173ff.). Of course, Descartes was never particularly worried by any problem that he regarded as no more acute for his than for the officially sanctioned philosophy of 'the Schools.' Given that, for the traditional philosophy, every real accident depends on a substance in which to inhere, it seemed to him equally unintelligible that the accidents of the bread and wine of the sacrament are supposed to continue to exist without inhering in any substance, whether they be so-called real accidents or merely the effects of motion as a mode of extended substance. (On this see also Menn 1995, 192.) In fact, Descartes believed the difficulties *less* in his own case, and the Scholastic solutions mired in contradictions, inconsistent with revealed theology, and constrained to posit a further miracle additional to that of transubstantiation ("irrational, incomprehensible, and hazardous for the faith," as Descartes puts it at AT VII 255: CSM II 177). The reasons for this are beyond the scope of this study.

25 Cf. *Principles*, II, 23: "All the properties which we clearly perceive in it [matter] are reducible to its divisibility and consequent mobility in respect of its parts, and its resulting capacity to be affected in all the ways which we perceive as being derivable from the movement of its parts." And passim in the *Principles*, and *Le Monde*.

On the "réduction de toutes les causalités à l'unique cause efficiente," see Marion 1981, 286ff.

Of course, outside natural philosophy matters stand rather differently. When it comes to the manner in which God is the 'cause of himself' or the soul the substantial form (and hence formal cause) of the body, Descartes is still prepared (though doubtfully entitled) to speak favourably of formal causes. Cf. the Fourth Replies (AT VII 238ff.: CSM II 166ff.) on God's nature as the *formal* cause of his existence, and the letter to Regius of January 1642 (AT III 505: CSMK 208) on the soul as substantial form of the body. Still, in the former context, formal is treated as a limiting case of efficient causality in a special, loose sense, so that Descartes has to resort to a mathematical parallel to justify his usage: "just as no one criticizes these proofs [of the mathematicians], although they involve regarding a sphere as similar to [i.e., a limiting case of] a polyhedron, so I am not open to criticism in this context for using the analogy of efficient cause to explain the features which in fact belong to a formal cause, that is to the very essence of God" (AT VII 231: CSM II 168). But he also backs it up with a metaphysical argument: since the efficient is cause of the existence, the formal of the essence of things, and since in God existence and essence are one and the same, "the formal cause will be strongly analogous to an efficient cause, and hence can be called *something close to an efficient cause*" (AT VII 243: CSM II 170 e.a.).

26 Even where Descartes explicitly distinguishes between the "causes of being" and the "causes of coming into being" (AT VII 370: CSM II 255), the former have nothing to do with formal causality in anything resembling the Aristotelian sense, but refer to the efficient causality of the conserving (as opposed to the originative) creative cause.

27 Whatever the merits or drawbacks of competing classificatory schemes, there is probably no compelling reason to revise the customary periodization of philosophy into ancient, medieval, and modern. Although the historical continuum of change can be segmented in different ways, these broad divisions seem to reflect pretty well the most important discontinuities in the process. However, if the view of the matter just developed is correct, greater care should be taken not to elide important differences between pre- and post-Kantian modern thought, as has been done consistently in the Descartes scholarship of this century. This is the principal consideration in favour of at least four "great types."

References

Descartes's writings

References to Descartes's works and letters, inserted parenthetically into the running text, are to volume and page of the definitive Franco-Latin edition of C. Adam and P. Tannery (*Oeuvres de Descartes*, 11 vols, Paris, 1897–1913, nouvelle présentation par P. Costabel et B. Rochot, Paris, Vrin-CNRS, 1964–76), followed by volume and page of the now standard English translation by Cottingham, Stoothoff, and Murdoch (*The Philosophical Writings of Descartes*, 3 vols, Cambridge, Cambridge University Press, 1984–91), e.g., AT VII 121: CSM II 86. (CSMK refers to volume III of CSM, by the same translators and Anthony Kenny.) The translations have not infrequently been modified. Square brackets in the text of a quotation indicate interpolations by the author, while 'e.a.' after a reference stands for 'emphasis added.' Where, other than in quoted passages, Latin terms are mentioned rather than used, the customary inverted commas have been omitted.

Abbreviations used in referring to other editions

ALQ Alquié, F. *Descartes. Oeuvres Philosophiques*. Edited by F. Alquié. 3 vols. Paris: Garnier, 1963–7.
A/G Anscombe and Geach. *Descartes. Philosophical Writings*. A selection translated and edited by Elizabeth Anscombe and Peter Thomas Geach with an introduction by André Koyré. London: Nelson, 1966.
CB Cottingham, ed. *Descartes' Conversation with Burman*. Translated with an introduction and commentary by John Cottingham. Oxford: Clarendon Press, 1976.

Other philosophical works cited or referred to in the text and notes

Other major philosophical works have been cited by author, year of publication, and (wherever possible) page number of the edition or translation used, followed in square brackets by the standard mode of reference. Thus '(Aquinas, 1948–9, 364 [*ST*, IaIIae.75.2])' stands for the first part of the second part, question 75, article 2 of the *Summa Theologiae*, the edition used being the translation of the Dominican Fathers.

Aquinas, Thomas. 1947–8. *Summa Theologica*. 3 vols. Translated by the Fathers of the English Dominican Province. New York: Benziger Brothers Inc. (*ST*)

– 1950. *In duodecim libros Metaphysicorum Aristotelis expositio*. Edited by Cathala and Spiazzi. Turin and Rome: Marietti. (*In Metaph.*)

– 1953. *Questiones Disputatae. Volumen I. De Veritate*. Edited by R. Spiazza. Turin and Rome: Marietti. (*QDV*)

– 1955. *Summa contra Gentiles*. Translated by A. Pegis. New York: Doubleday Image Paperbacks. (*SCG*)

– 1959. *Expositio super librum Boethii de Trinitate*. Edited by B. Decker. E.J. Leiden: Brill. (*BDT*)

– 1961. *Commentary on the Metaphysics of Aristotle*. Translated by John P. Rowan. Chicago: Henry Regnery Co. (*In Metaph.*)

– 1986. *The Division and Methods of the Sciences*. Questions V and VI of his Commentary on the *De Trinitate* of Boethius, translated with introduction and notes by Armand Maurer. Toronto: Pontifical Institute of Mediaeval Studies. (*BDT*)

Aristotle. 1924. *Metaphysics*. A revised text with introduction and commentary by W.D. Ross. Oxford: Oxford University Press. (*Met.*)

– 1949a. *Prior and Posterior Analytics*. A revised text with introduction and commentary by W.D. Ross. Oxford: Oxford University Press. (*An. Post.*)

– 1949b. *Categoriae et Liber de Interpretatione*. Edited by L. Minio-Paluello. Oxford: Oxford University Press. (*Cat.* and *de Int.*)

– 1955. *Parva Naturalia*. A revised text with introduction and commentary by Sir David Ross. Oxford: Oxford University Press. (*PN*)

– 1961. *De Anima*. Edited, with introduction and commentary, by Sir David Ross. Oxford: Oxford University Press. (*de An.*).

– 1962. *The Nichomachean Ethics*. With an English translation by H. Rackham. London: Harvard University Press. (*EN*)

– 1965. *On Sophistical Refutations. On Coming-to-be and Passing Away*. Translated by E.S. Forster. *On the Cosmos*. Translated by D.J. Furley. Cambridge, Mass.: William Heinemann Ltd., Harvard University Press. (*SR*)

Baumgarten, A. 1963. *Metaphysica*. Reprografischer Nachdruck der Ausgabe Halle 1779. Hildesheim: Georg Olms Verlagsbuchhandlung.

Berkeley, G. 1965. *Principles, Dialogues, and Philosophical Correspondence*. Edited, with an introduction, by Colin Murray Turbayne. Indianapolis: Library of Liberal

Arts, Bobbs-Merrill Educational Publishing. (Cited also by part and section number.)

Gadamer, H.-G. 1960. *Wahrheit und Methode*. Tübingen: J.C.B. Mohr (Paul Siebeck). References are to the German edition, followed by *TM* and the page number of the English translation (New York: Crossroads Publishing, 1984).

Heidegger, M. 1957. *Identität und Differenz*. Pfüllingen: Günter Neske Verlag. (References to Heidegger's German works are either to the *Gesamtausgabe* [*GA*] or to the separate editions.)

‒ 1961. *Nietzsche*. 2 vols: Pfullingen: Günther Neske Verlag. Re-edited within the *Gesamtausgabe* as volumes 43 and 44.

‒ 1962. *Die Frage nach dem Ding. Zu Kants Lehre von den Transzendentalen Grundsätzen*. Tübingen: Max Niemeyer Verlag.

‒ 1973. *Kant und das Problem der Metaphysik*. Frankfurt am Main: Vittorio Klostermann Verlag.

‒ 1977. *Sein und Zeit*. Frankfurt am Main: Vittorio Klostermann Verlag. (*GA*, Bd. 2)

‒ 1983. *Die Grundbegriffe der Metaphysik. Welt ‒ Endlichkeit ‒ Einsamkeit*. Frankfurt am Main: Vittorio Klostermann Verlag. (*GA*, Bd. 29/30)

‒ 1994. *Einführung in die Phänomenologische Forschung*. Frankfurt am Main: Vittorio Klostermann Verlag. (*GA*, Bd. 17)

Hobbes, T. 1994. *Leviathan*. Edited with an introduction by E.M.Curley. Indianapolis: Hackett Publishing Co.

Hume, D. 1967. *A Treatise of Human Nature*. Edited by L.A. Selby-Bigge. Oxford: Oxford University Press.

‒ 1990. *An Enquiry Concerning Human Understanding*. Edited by Antony Flew. Lasalle, Ill. Open Court.

Husserl, E. 1960. *Cartesian Meditations*. Translated by Dorion Cairns. The Hague: Martinus Nijhoff.

‒ 1964. *Paris Lectures*. Translated by Peter Koestenbaum. The Hague: Martinus Nijhoff.

‒ 1970. *Logical Investigations*. Translated by J.N. Findlay. London: Routledge and Kegan Paul.

Kant, I. 1929. *Critique of Pure Reason*. Translated by Norman Kemp Smith. London: Macmillan. (Cited in the standard manner, according to the pagination of the original A and B editions.)

‒ 1972. *Briefwechsel*. Hamburg: Felix Meiner Verlag (Philosophische Bibliothek).

Leibniz, G.W. 1875‒90. *Die Philosophischen Schriften von Gottfried Wilhelm Leibniz*. Edited by C.I. Gerhard. 7 vols. Repr. Hildesheim: Georg Olms Verlags-buchhandlung, 1965.

‒ 1989. *Philosophical Essays*. Translated by Roger Ariew and Daniel Garber. Indianapolis: Hackett Publishing Co.

Locke, J. 1977. *An Essay Concerning Human Understanding*. Abridged and edited with an introduction by John W. Yolton. London: Dent. (Cited also by book, chapter, and paragraph number.)

Newman, J.H. 1960. *The Idea of a University. Defined and Illustrated*. Edited by Martin J. Svaglic. New York: Holt, Rinehart and Winston.

Newton, I. 1974. *Newton's Philosophy of Nature. Selections from His Writings*. Edited and arranged with notes by H.S. Thayer. New York: Hafner Press.

Schopenhauer, A. 1969. *The World as Will and Representation*. Translated from the German by E.F.J. Payne. 2 vols. New York: Dover Publications.

Spinoza, B. 1963. *Earlier Philosophical Writings. The Cartesian Principles and Thoughts on Metaphysics*. Translated by Frank A. Hayes. Indianapolis: Bobbs-Merrill Co. Inc.

– 1994. *A Spinoza Reader. The Ethics and Other Works*. Edited by E.M. Curley. Princeton: Princeton UP. (The *Ethics* is cited also in the usual manner, e.g., 'EIP15S' for *Ethics*, Part I, Proposition 15, Scholium.)

Suarez, F. 1965. *Disputationes Metaphysicae*. Reprografischer Nachdruck der Ausgabe Paris 1866. Hildesheim: Georg Olms Verlag.

Wittgenstein, L. 1971. *Tractatus Logico-Philosophicus*. German text of *Logisch-philosophische Abhandlung* with a new edition of the translation by D.F. Pears and B.F. McGuinness, with an introduction by Bertrand Russell. (Cited also as *Tractatus* by section number.)

Interpretive literature and other works cited or referred to in the text and notes

Note: Where articles are listed as reprinted and/or translated in an anthology, references are to the pagination of the reprint.

Alexander, R.E. 1972. "The Problem of Metaphysical Doubt and Its Removal." In Butler 1972.

Allison, H. 1983. *Kant's Transcendental Idealism*. New Haven: Yale University Press.

Alquié, F. 1950. *La Découverte métaphysique de l'homme chez Descartes*. Paris: Presses Universitaires de France.

Anscombe, G.E.M. 1957. *Intention*. Oxford: Basil Blackwell.

Ariew, R. 1992. "Descartes and Scholasticism." In Cottingham 1992a.

Ariew, R., and M. Grene. 1995. *Descartes and His Contemporaries: Meditations, Objections, and Replies*. Edited by Roger Ariew and Marjorie Grene. Chicago: University of Chicago Press.

Ashworth, E.J. 1972. "Descartes's Theory of Clear and Distinct Ideas." In Butler 1972.

Aubenque, P. 1962. *Le Problème de l'être chez Aristote*. Paris: Aubier.

Ayer, A.J. 1968. "I think, therefore I am." In A.J. Ayer, *The Problem of Knowledge* (New York: St Martin's Press, 1956). In Doney 1968.

– 1959. *Logical Positivism*. New York: The Free Press.

Beck, L.J. 1952. *The Method of Descartes. A Study of the* Regulae. Oxford: Oxford University Press.

– 1965. *The Metaphysics of Descartes*. Oxford: Oxford University Press.

Belaval, Y. 1960. *Leibniz critique de Descartes*. Paris: Gallimard.

– 1976. *Études leibniziennes. De Leibniz à Hegel*. Paris: Gallimard.

Bennett, J. 1965. "Substance, Reality, and Primary Qualities." *American Philosophical Quarterly* (2)1. In Engle and Taylor 1968.

– 1990. "Truth and Stability in Descartes's *Meditations*." In Copp 1990.

Beyssade, J.-M. 1979. *La Philosophie première de Descartes*. Paris: Flammarion.

– 1981. "Création des vérités éternelles et doute métaphysique." *Studia Cartesiana* 2.

– 1993. "On the Idea of God." In Voss 1993.

Beyssade, M. 1993. "The *Cogito*: Privileged Truth or Exemplary Truth?" In Voss 1993.

Blanchet, L. 1920. *Les Antécédents historiques du « je pense, donc je suis »*. Paris: Alcan.

Bochenski, I. 1963. *Ancient Formal Logic*. Amsterdam: North Holland Publishing Co.

Boehner, T. 1958. *Collected Articles on Ockham*. Edited by E.M. Buytaert. St Bonaventure, NY: The Franciscan Institute.

Boutroux, É. (1927. *De veritatibus aeternis apud Cartesium*. Translated by G. Canguilhem. Paris: Alcan.

Bouveresse, J. 1987. "La Théorie du possible chez Descartes." In Doney 1987.

Bréhier, É. 1968. "La Création des verités éternelles dans le système de Descartes." *Revue Philosophique de la France et de l'Étranger* 93, nos. 5–6, 7–8 (May–August) included in *La Philosophie et son passé*, by Émile Bréhier (Paris: Alcan 1940). Translated in Doney 1968.

– 1943. « Une Forme archaïque du 'Cogito ergo sum' ». *Revue Philosophique* 1943/2.

Broad, C.D. 1975. *Leibniz: An Introduction*. Edited by C. Lewy. Cambridge: Cambridge University Press.

Brentano, F. 1973. *Psychology from an Empirical Standpoint*. Edited by Oskar Kraus; English edition edited by Linda L. McAlister. New York: Humanities Press.

Brown, G. 1980. "*Vera Entia*: The Nature of Mathematical Objects in Descartes." *Journal of the History of Philosophy* 18.

Buchdahl, G. 1969. *Metaphysics and the Philosophy of Science. The Classical Origins: Descartes to Kant*. Cambridge: MIT Press.

Burtt, E.A. 1927. *The Metaphysical Foundations of Physics*. New York: Harcourt, Brace & Co.

Butler, R.J. 1972. *Cartesian Studies*. Edited by R.J. Butler. Oxford: Basil Blackwell.

Butterfield, H. 1950. *The Origins of Modern Science 1300–1800*. London: Bell and Sons Ltd.

Caton, H. 1973. *The Origin of Subjectivity: An Essay on Descartes*. New Haven: Yale University Press.

Carnap, R. 1959a. "The Old and the New Logic." In Ayer 1959.

- 1959b. "The Elimination of Metaphysics through Logical Analysis of Language." In Ayer 1959.
- 1980. "Empiricism, Ontology, and Semantics." In Morick 1980.

Carney, J. 1962. "*COGITO, ERGO SUM* and *SUM RES COGITANS.*" *Philosophical Review* 71.

Carr, D. 1973–4. "The 'Fifth Meditation' and Husserl's Cartesianism." *Philosophy and Phenomenological Research* 34.

Chisholm, R. 1960. *Realism and the Background of Phenomenology*. Glencoe: The Free Press.

Clarke, D.M. 1982. *Descartes' Philosophy of Science*. University Park: Pennsylvania State University Press.

Cohen, M., and E. Nagel. 1934. *An Introduction to Logic and Scientific Method*. New York: Harcourt, Brace & World.

Conze, E. 1928. *Der Begriff der Metaphysik bei Franciscus Suarez. Gegenstands-bereich und Primat der Metaphysik*. Naumburg (Saale): Lippert & Co.

Cook, M. 1988. "Descartes' Doubt of Minds." *Dialogue* 27.

Copp, D. 1990. *Canadian Philosophers: Celebrating Twenty Years of the CJP*. Calgary: University of Calgary Press.

Cotgrave, R. 1970. *A Dictionarie of the French and English Tongues*. Hildesheim: Georg Olms Verlag.

Cottingham, J. 1976. "The Role of the Malignant Demon." *Studia Leibnitiana* 8(2).
- 1978a. "'A Brute to the Brutes?': Descartes' Treatment of Animals." *Philosophy* 53.
- 1978b. "Descartes on Thought." *Philosophical Quarterly* 28.
- 1986. *Descartes*. Oxford: Basil Blackwell.
- 1988. *A History of Western Philosophy, 4. The Rationalists*. Oxford: Oxford University Press.
- 1992a. *The Cambridge Companion to Descartes*. Edited by John Cottingham. Cambridge: Cambridge University Press.
- 1992b. "Cartesian Dualism." In Cottingham 1992a.

Cover, J., and M. Kulstad. 1990. *Central Themes in Early Modern Philosophy*. Essays presented to Jonathan Bennett. Indianapolis: Hackett Publishing Co.

Cronin, T. 1987. "Eternal Truths in the Thought of Descartes and His Adversary." *Journal of the History of Ideas* 3. In Doney 1987.
- 1966. *Objective Being in Descartes and Suarez*. Rome: Gregorian University Press.

Curley, E.J. 1975. "Descartes, Spinoza and the Ethics of Belief." In Mandelbaum and Freeman 1975.
- 1977. "Spinoza as an Expositor of Descartes." In Hessing 1977.
- 1978. *Descartes Against the Sceptics*. Cambridge, Mass.: Harvard University Press.
- 1986. "Analysis in the *Meditations*." In Rorty 1986.
- 1987. "Descartes on the Creation of the Eternal Truths." In Doney 1987.

– 1988. *Behind the Geometrical Method: A Reading of Spinoza's* Ethics. Princeton: Princeton University Press.

– 1993. "Certainty: Psychological, Moral, and Metaphysical." In Voss 1993.

Dewan, L. 1979. "St. Thomas and the Possibles." *The New Scholasticism* 53(1).

– 1991. "St. Thomas, James Ross, and Exemplarism: A Reply." *Proceedings of the American Catholic Philosophical Association* 65.

Doig, J. 1974. *Aquinas on Metaphysics: A Historico-Doctrinal Study of the* Commentary on the Metaphysics. The Hague: Marinus Nijhoff.

Doney, W. 1955. "The Cartesian Circle." *Journal of the History of Ideas* 3. In Doney 1987.

– 1968. *Descartes: A Collection of Critical Essays.* Edited by Willis Doney. Notre Dame: University of Notre Dame Press.

– 1970. "Descartes's Conception of Perfect Knowledge." *Journal of the History of Philosophy* 8. In Doney 1987.

– 1987. *Eternal Truths and the Cartesian Circle: A Collection of Studies.* Edited by Willis Doney. New York: Garland Publishing, Inc.

Düring, I. 1966. *Aristoteles. Darstellung und Interpretation seines Denkens.* Heidelberg: Winter.

Eddington, A. 1928. *The Nature of the Physical World.* Cambridge: Cambridge University Press.

Edgley, R. 1970. "Innate Ideas." In *Knowledge and Necessity*, Royal Institute of Philosophy Lectures, vol. III. London: Macmillan and Co., St Martin's Press.

Engle, G., and G. Taylor. 1968. *Berkeley's* Principles of Human Knowledge: *Critical Studies.* Belmont: Wadsworth Publishing.

Etchemendy, J. 1981. "The Cartesian Circle: *circulus ex tempore.*" *Studia Cartesiana* 2.

Feigl, H. 1949a. "Logical Empiricism." In Feigl and Sellars 1949.

– 1949b. "Operationism and Scientific Method." In Feigl and Sellars 1949.

Feigl, H., and W. Sellars 1949. *Readings in Philosophical Analysis.* New York: Appleton-Century-Crofts Inc.

Ferejohn, M. 1992. "Meno's Paradox and *De Re* Knowledge in Aristotle's Theory of Demonstration." In Preus and Anton 1992.

Feldman, F., and A. Levinson. 1987. "Anthony Kenny and the Cartesian Circle." In Doney 1987.

Feyerabend, P. 1980. "How to Be a Good Empiricist." In Morick 1980.

Flew, A.G.N. 1971. *An Introduction to Western Philosophy: Ideas and Arguments from Plato to Sartre.* London: Thames and Hudson.

Frankfurt, H.G. 1966. "Descartes's Discussion of His Existence in the Second Meditation." *Philosophical Review* 75(3).

– 1968. "Descartes' Validation of Reason." *American Philosophical Quarterly* 2(2) (1965). In Doney 1968.

- 1970. *Demons, Dreamers, and Madmen: The Defense of Reason in Descartes's Meditations*. Indianapolis: Bobbs-Merill Co.
- 1972. *Leibniz: A Collection of Critical Essays*. New York: Doubleday.
- 1978. "Descartes on the Consistency of Reason." In Hooker 1978.
- 1987a. "Memory and the Cartesian Circle." *Philosophical Review* 71 (1962). In Doney 1987.
- 1987b. "Descartes on Eternal Truths." *Philosophical Review* 86(1) (1977). In Doney 1987.

Fritz, K. von. 1964. *Die ἐπαγωγή bei Aristoteles*. Verlag der Bayerischen Akademie der Wissenschaften. Munich: C.H. Beck Verlagsbuchhandlung.

Furth, Montgomery. 1972. "Monadology." *Philosophical Review* 76 (1967). In Frankfurt 1972.

Garber, D. 1992. *Descartes' Metaphysical Physics*. Chicago and London: University of Chicago Press.

Garber, D., and L. Cohen. 1993. "A Point of Order: Analysis, Synthesis, and Descartes' Principles." In Tweyman 1993a.

Garin, P. 1932. *Thèses cartésiennes et thèses thomistes*. Paris: Desclée de Brouwer.

Gaukroger, S. 1986. *Cartesian Logic: An Essay on Descartes's Conception of Inference*. Oxford: Oxford University Press.

Geach, P. 1987. "Omnipotence." In Doney 1987.

Gerson, L. 1994. "Eternal Truths: Plotinus, Aquinas and James Ross." *Proceedings of the American Catholic Philosophical Association* 67.

Gewirth, A. 1941. "Experience and the Non-Mathematical in the Cartesian Method." *Journal of the History of Ideas* 2(2).
- 1968. "Clearness and Distinctness in Descartes." In Doney 1968.
- 1987a. "The Cartesian Circle." *Philosophical Review* 1(4). In Doney 1987.
- 1987b. "The Cartesian Circle Reconsidered." *Journal of Philosophy* 67. In Doney 1987.
- 1987c. "Descartes: Two Disputed Questions." *Journal of Philosophy* 69. In Doney 1987.

Gibson, B. 1932. *The Philosophy of Descartes*. London: Methuen & Co.

Gilson, E. 1947a. *Discours de la Méthode, commentaire*. Paris: Vrin.
- 1947b. *The Unity of Philosophical Experience*. New York: Scribners.
- 1947c. *Réalisme Thomiste et Critique de la Connaissance*. Paris: Vrin.
- 1951. *Études sur la rôle de la philosophie médiévale sur la formation du système cartésien*. Paris: Vrin.
- 1952. *Being and Some Philosophers*. Toronto: Pontifical Institute of Medieval Studies.

Gombay, A. 1972. "'Cogito, ergo sum': Inference or Argument?" In Butler 1972.

Gouhier, H. 1937. *Le Grand Trompeur et les significations de la métaphysique cartésienne. IXe Congrès international de philosophie*, 1937, I.

– 1950. "Les Exigences de l'existence dans la métaphysique de Descartes." *Revue internationale de philosophie* 4.

– 1969. *La Pensée métaphysique de Descartes.* Paris: Vrin.

Grene, M. 1979. *Spinoza: A Collection of Critical Essays.* Edited by Marjorie Grene. Notre Dame: University of Notre Dame Press.

Gueroult, M. 1938. "Descartes au Congrès Descartes." *Revue de métaphysique et de morale,* 1938. In Rodis-Lewis 1987.

– 1968. *Descartes selon l'ordre des raisons.* 2 vols. Paris: Aubier.

Hager, F.-P. 1979. *Wege der Forschung.* Vol. 206. Edited by Fritz-Peter Hager. Darmstadt: Wissenschaftliche Buchgesellschaft.

Halper, E. 1993. *Form and Reason: Essays in Metaphysics.* Albany: State University of New York Press.

Hamelin, O. 1921. *Le Système de Descartes.* 2nd ed. Paris: Librarie Félix Alcan.

Hampshire, S. 1951. *Spinoza.* Harmondsworth: Penguin.

Harman, G. 1974. *On Noam Chomsky: Critical Essays.* New York: Anchor Press/ Doubleday.

Hatfield, G. 1992. "Descartes' Physiology and Its Relation to His Psychology." In Cottingham 1992a.

Henry, M. 1993. "The Soul according to Descartes." In Voss 1993.

Herrmann, F.-W. von. 1971. *Husserl und die Meditationen des Descartes.* Frankfurt a. M.: Vittorio Klostermann Verlag.

Hesse, M. 1970. "Duhem, Quine and a New Empiricism." In *Knowledge and Necessity,* Royal Institute of Philosophy Lectures, vol. III. London: Macmillan and Co., St Martin's Press.

Hessing, S. 1977. *Speculum Spinozanum.* Edited by S. Hessing. London: Routledge and Kegan Paul.

Hintikka, J. 1962. "Cogito, Ergo Sum: Inference or Performance." *Philosophical Review* 71(1). In Doney 1968.

– 1963. "*Cogito, ergo sum* as an Inference and a Performance." *Philosophical Review* 72(4).

– 1978. "A Discourse on Descartes' Method." In Hooker 1978.

Hoenen, P. 1937. "Le 'cogito, ergo sum' comme intuition et comme mouvement de la pensée." In *Cartesio nel terzo Centenario del « Discorso del metodo ».* Milan: Società editrice "Vita e pensiero."

– 1968. "Descartes's Mechanicism." In Doney 1968.

Hoffman, P. 1986. "The Unity of Descartes's Man." *Philosophical Review* 95.

Hooker, M. 1978. *Descartes: Critical and Interpretive Essays.* Edited by Michael Hooker. Baltimore: Johns Hopkins University Press.

Hughes, R.D. 1978. "Le Cercle des *Méditations*: Un état des recherches récentes." In Rodis-Lewis 1987.

Imlay, R. 1985. "Descartes, Russell, Hintikka and the Self." *Studia Leibnitiana* 17(1).

Ishiguro, H. 1987a. "Reply to Jacques Bouveresse." In Doney 1987.

– 1987b. "The Status of Necessity and Impossibility in Descartes." First published in Rorty 1986. In Doney 1987.

Jaeger, W. 1967. *Aristotle: Fundamentals of the History of His Development*. London: Oxford University Press.

Jalabert, J. 1946. "La Psychologie de Leibniz. Ses caractères principaux." In *Revue Philosophique de la France et de l'Etranger* 136(10–12).

Jolley, N. 1986. "Leibniz and Phenomenalism." *Studia Leibnitiana* 18(1).

– 1995. *The Cambridge Companion to Leibniz*. Cambridge: Cambridge University Press.

Katz, J. 1987. "Descartes's Cogito." *Pacific Philosophical Quarterly* 68.

Keeling, S. 1968. *Descartes*. Oxford: Oxford University Press.

Kennington, R. 1971. "The Finitude of Descartes' Evil Genius." *Journal of the History of Ideas*, 32. In Doney 1987.

– 1972. "The 'Teaching of Nature' in Descartes' Soul Doctrine." *Review of Metaphysics*, 26.

Kenny, A. 1968. *Descartes: A Study of His Philosophy*. New York: Random House.

– 1970. "The Cartesian circle and the eternal truths," *Journal of Philosophy*, 67.

Kneale, W. 1949. *Probability and Induction*. Oxford: Oxford University Press.

Kneale, W., and M. Kneale. 1962. *The Development of Logic*. Oxford: Oxford University Press.

Knudsen, C. 1982. "Intentions and Impositions." In Kretzmann, Kenny, and Pinborg 1982.

Koyré, A. 1922. *Essai sur l'idée de Dieu et les preuves de son existence chez Descartes*. Paris: Vrin.

Kretzman, N., A. Kenny, and J. Pinborg. 1982. *The Cambridge History of Later Medieval Philosophy*. Cambridge: Cambridge University Press.

Kretzman, N., and E. Stump. 1993. *The Cambridge Companion to Aquinas*. Edited by Norman Kretzman and Eleonore Stump. Cambridge: Cambridge University Press.

Kuhn, T. 1980. "Incommensurability and Paradigms." In Morick 1980.

Kulstad, M. 1991. *Leibniz on Apperception, Consciousness, and Reflection*. München: Philosophia Verlag.

Laporte, J. 1950. *Le Rationalisme de Descartes*. Paris: Presses Universitaires de France.

Larmore, C. 1984. "Descartes' Psychologistic Theory of Assent." *History of Philosophy Quarterly* 1(1).

Lennon, T. 1993. *The Battle for the Gods and Giants: The Legacies of Descartes and Gassendi 1655–1715*. Princeton, NJ: Princeton University Press.

Levett, M. 1937. "A Note on the Alleged Cartesian Circle." *Mind* 46.

Loeb, L. 1981. *From Descartes to Hume: Continental Metaphysics and the Development of Modern Philosophy*. Ithaca: Cornell University Press.

- 1986. "Is There Radical Dissimulation in Descartes's *Meditations*?" In Rorty 1986.
- 1992. "The Cartesian Circle." In Cottingham 1992a.

Lovejoy, A.O. 1923. "Representative Ideas in Malebranche and Arnauld." *Mind* 32.

- 1960. *The Revolt Against Dualism*. Lasalle, Ill: Open Court Publishing.

MacIntosh, J.J. 1970–1. "Leibniz and Berkeley." *Proceedings of the Aristotelian Society*.

McRae, R. 1961. *The Problem of the Unity of the Sciences: Bacon to Kant*. Toronto: University of Toronto Press.

- 1965. "'Idea' as a Philosophical Term in the Seventeenth Century." *Journal of the History of Ideas* 26.
- 1972a. "Innate Ideas." In Butler 1972.
- 1972b. "Descartes' Definition of Thought." In Butler 1972.
- 1976. *Leibniz: Perception, Apperception, and Thought*. Toronto: University of Toronto Press.
- 1988. "Reply." *Dialogue* 27(1).

Mahoney, E. 1982. "Metaphysical Foundations of the Heirarchy of Being According to Some Late-Medieval and Renaissance Philosophers." In Morewedge 1982.

Malcolm, N. 1968. "Descartes's Proof That His Essence Is Thinking." *Philosophical Review* 74(3). In Doney 1968.

Mandelbaum, M., and E. Freeman. 1975. *Spinoza: Essays in Interpretation*. La Salle, Ill.: Open Court Publishing.

Mansion, A., 1958. "Philosophie première, philosophie seconde, et métaphysique chez Aristote." *Revue philosophique de Louvain* 56. Repr. in German translation in Hager 1979.

Marc-Wogau, K. 1954. "Der Zweifel Descartes' über das *Cogito ergo sum*." *Theoria* 20.

Marion, J.-L. 1975. *Sur l'ontologie grise de Descartes: Science cartésienne et savior aristotélicien dans les* Regulae. Paris: Vrin.

- 1981a. *Sur la théologie blanche de Descartes*. Paris: Presses Universitaires de France.
- 1981b. "L'Ambivalence de la métaphysique cartésienne." In Marion 1975 (2nd edition, 1981).
- 1986. *Sur le prisme métaphysique de Descartes*. Paris: Presses Universitaires de France.
- 1993. "Generosity and Phenomenology: Remarks on Michel Henry's Interpretation of the Cartesian *Cogito*." In Voss 1993.

Maritain, J. 1937. "Le Conflit de l'essence et de l'existence dans la philosophie cartésienne." *IXe Congrès Internationale de Philosophie (Congrès Descartes)*, ed. Raymond Bayer. Vol. I. Paris: Herman.

Markie, P. 1986. *Descartes' Gambit*. Cornell University Press: Ithaca.

- 1992. "The Cogito and Its Importance." In Cottingham 1992.

Marx, W. 1972. *Einführung in Aristoteles' Theorie vom Seienden*. Freiburg i. Br.: Rombach.

Menn, S. 1990. "Descartes and Some Predecessors on the Divine Conservation of Motion." *Synthese*, 83.

– 1993. "The Problem of the Third Meditation." *American Catholic Philosophical Quarterly* 67(4).

– 1995. "The Greatest Stumbling Block: Descartes's Denial of Real Qualities." In Ariew and Grene 1995.

– In press. *Augustine and Descartes*.

Merlan, P. 1960. *From Platonism to Neoplatonism*. 2nd. ed. The Hague: Martinus Nijhoff.

Miles, M. 1978. *Logik und Metaphysik bei Kant*. Frankfurt am Main: Vittorio Klostermann Verlag.

– 1983. "Psycho-physical Unity: The Problem of the Person in Descartes." *Dialogue* 22(1).

– 1986. "Kant and the Synthetic *A Priori*." *University of Toronto Quarterly* 55(2).

– 1988a. "The Idea of Extension: Innate or Adventitious? On R.F. McRae's Interpretation of Descartes." *Dialogue* 27(1).

– 1988b. "McRae on Innate Ideas: A Rejoinder." *Dialogue* 27(1).

– 1989. "Heidegger and the Question of Humanism." *Man and World* 22.

– 1990. "Some Recent Research on the Mind-Body Problem in Descartes." *Manuscrito. Revista Internacional de Filosofia* 13(2).

– 1994a. "Leibniz on Apperception and Animal Souls." *Dialogue* 33(2).

– 1994b. "Fundamental Ontology and Existential Analysis in Heidegger's *Being and Time*." *International Philosophical Quarterly* 34(3).

Miller, L. 1965. "Descartes, Mathematics, and God." *Philosophical Review* 66. In Sesonske and Fleming 1965.

Mittelstraß, J. 1978. "Die Idee einer Mathesis Universalis bei Descartes." *Perspektiven der Philosophie* 4.

– 1979. "The Philosopher's Conception of *Mathesis Universalis* from Descartes to Leibniz." *Annals of Science* 36.

Moreau, J. 1961. "The Problem of Intentionality and Classical Thought." *International Philosophical Quarterly* 1.

Moreno, A. 1966. "The Nature of Metaphysics." *The Thomist* 30.

Morewedge, P. 1982. *Philosophies of Existence*. New York: Fordham University Press.

Morick, H. 1980. *Challenges to Empiricism*. Indianapolis: Hackett Publishing Co.

Murchland, B. 1974. "The Myth of Alienation." *Diotima* 2.

Nadler, S. 1992. *Malebranche and Ideas*. New York: Oxford University Press.

Naërt, E. 1961. *Mémoire et conscience de soi selon Leibniz*. Paris: Vrin.

Normore, C. 1986. "Meaning and Objective Being: Descartes and His Sources." In Rorty, 1986.

Norton, D. 1968. "Descartes on Unknown Faculties: An Essential Inconsistency."
    Journal of the History of Philosophy 6(3).
O'Neil, B. 1974. *Epistemological Direct Realism in Descartes' Philosophy.*
    Albuquerque: University of New Mexico Press.
Osler, M. 1985. "Eternal Truths and the Laws of Nature: The Theological Foundations
    of Descartes's Philosophy of Nature." *Journal of the History of Ideas* 46(3).
Owens, J. 1966. "Aquinas and the Proof from the 'Physics.'" *Medieval Studies* 28.
–   1978. *The Doctrine of Being in the Aristotelian Metaphysics.* 3rd ed. Toronto:
    Pontifical Institute of Mediaeval Studies.
–   1985. *An Elementary Christian Metaphysics.* Houston: Center for Thomistic Studies,
    University of St. Thomas.
–   1993a. "Aristotle and Aquinas on Cognition." *Canadian Journal of Philosophy*
    Supplementary volume 17.
–   1993b. "Aristotle and Aquinas." In Kretzman and Stump 1993.
Patzig, G. 1960. "Theologie und Ontologie in der 'Metaphysik' des Aristoteles."
    Kantstudien 52.
Phelan, G. 1967. *Selected Papers.* Edited by Arthur G. Kirn, C.S.B. Toronto: Pontifical
    Institute of Mediaeval Studies.
Popkin, R. 1979. *The History of Scepticism from Erasmus to Spinoza.* Berkeley:
    University of California Press.
Popper, K. 1945. *The Open Society and Its Enemies.* 2 vols. London: Routledge.
–   1962. *Conjectures and Refutations: The Growth of Scientific Knowledge.* New York:
    Basic Books.
Price, B. 1992. *Medieval Thought: An Introduction.* Oxford, UK: Blackwell.
Preus, A., and J. Anton. 1992. *Essays in Ancient Greek Philosophy V: Aristotle's
    Ontology.* Albany: State University of New York Press.
Putnam, H. 1980. "Brains and Behaviour." In Morick 1980.
Quine, W. 1953. *From a Logical Point of View.* New York: Harper Torchbooks.
–   1980. "Meaning and Translation." In Morick 1980.
Radner, D. 1988. "Thought and Consciousness in Descartes." *Journal of the History of
    Philosophy* 26(3).
Randall, J.H. 1940. *The Career of Philosophy.* New York: Columbia University Press.
Reiner, H. 1954. "Die Entstehung und ursprüngliche Bedeutung des Namens
    Metaphysik." *Zeitschrift für Philosophische Forschung* 8. In Hager 1959.
Richardson, R. 1982. "The 'Scandal' of Cartesian Interactionism." *Mind* 91.
Robinson, T. 1991. *Heraclitus. Fragments.* Text and translation with a commentary by
    T.M. Robinson. Toronto: University of Toronto Press.
Röd, W. 1959–60. "Zum Problem des Premier Principe in Descartes' Metaphysik."
    Kantstudien 51.
–   1964. *Descartes: Die innere Genesis des Cartesianischen Systems.* München:
    Reinhardt.

- 1971. *Descartes' Erste Philosophie: Versuch einer Analyse mit besonderer Berücksichtigung der Cartesianishen Methodologie.* Bonn: Bouvier Verlag Herbert Grundmann.
- 1979. "Einige Überlegungen zur Debatte über das 'Cogito ergo sum' in der Philosophie des 20. Jahrhunderts." *Studia Cartesiana* 1.

Rodis-Lewis, G. 1950. *L'individualité selon Descartes.* Paris: Vrin.
- 1971. *L'oeuvre de Descartes.* Paris: Vrin.
- 1979. "Note sur le «cercle» cartésien." In Rodis-Lewis 1987.
- 1987. *Méthode et métaphysique chez Descartes: Articles en français.* Edited by Geneviève Rodis-Lewis. New York: Garland Publishing.

Rorty, A.O. 1986. *Essays on Descartes' Meditations.* Edited by Amélie Oksenberg Rorty. Berkeley: University of California Press.

Roth, L. 1937. *Descartes' Discourse on Method.* Oxford: Oxford University Press.

Rubin, R. 1977. "Descartes's Validation of Clear and Distinct Apprehension." *Philosophical Review* 86.

Russell, B. 1900. *A Critical Exposition of the Philosophy of Leibniz.* London: George Allen and Unwin.
- 1945a. *Religion and Science.* London: Oxford University Press.
- 1945b. *A History of Western Philosophy.* New York: Simon and Schuster.

Rutherford, D. 1995. "Metaphysics: The Late Period." In Jolley 1995.

Scholz, H. 1931. "Über das Cogito, ergo sum." *Kantstudien* 36.

Schouls, P. 1987. "Descartes and the Autonomy of Reason." In Doney 1987.

Schul, J.-P. 1948. "Y-a-t-il une source aristotélicienne du «Cogito»." *Revue Philosophique* 1948/1.

Sellars, W. 1980. "Empiricism and the Philosophy of Mind." In Morick 1980.

Serene, E. 1982. "Demonstrative Science." In Kretzmann, Kenny, and Pinborg 1982.

Sesonske, A., and N. Fleming. 1965. *Meta-meditations: Studies in Descartes.* Belmont, CA: Wadsworth Publishing Co.

Shaney, B. 1996. "St. Thomas Aquinas, Onto-theology, and Marion." *The Thomist* 60(4).

Sievert, D. 1975. "Descartes' Self-Doubt." *Philosophical Review* 84.
- 1977. "Frankfurt on Descartes' View of Truth." *New Scholasticism* 51.

Smith, N.K. 1952. *New Studies in the Philosophy of Descartes.* London: Macmillan.

Sosa, E. 1987. *Essays on the Philosophy of George Berkeley.* Dordrecht: D. Reidel Publishing Co.

Stout, A.K. 1968. "The Basis of Knowledge in Descartes." *Mind* 38. In Doney 1968.

Thomas, D. 1964. *Collected Poems, 1934–1952.* London: J.M. Dent & Sons.

Tlumak, J. 1978. "Certainty and Cartesian Method." In Hooker 1978.

Tweyman, S. 1972. "The Reliability of Reason." In Butler 1972.
- 1993a. *René Descartes. Meditations on First Philosophy in focus.* Routledge: London.

– 1993b. "Professor Cottingham and Descartes' Methods of Analysis and Synthesis."
   In Tweyman 1993a.

Van Cleve, J. 1987. "Foundationalism, Epistemic Principles, and the Cartesian Circle."
   In Doney 1987.

Vollrath, E. 1962. "Die Gliederung der Metaphysik in eine Metaphysica Generalis
   und eine Metaphysica Specialis." *Zeitschrift für Philosophische Forschung* 16(2).

Voss, S. 1993. *The Philosophy and Science of René Descartes.* Edited by Stephen Voss.
   New York: Oxford University Press.

Watson, R. 1987. *The Breakdown of Cartesian Metaphysics.* Atlantic Highlands, NJ:
   Humanities Press International.

Weinberg, J.R. 1963. "*Cogito, Ergo Sum*: Some Reflections on Mr. Hintikka's Article."
   Philosophical Review 71(1).

Weisheipl, J. 1963. *Friar Thomas D'Aquino: His Life, Thought, and Works.* Washington: Catholic University of America Press.

– 1965. "The Classification of the Sciences in the Middle Ages." In Weisheipl
   1985.

– 1985. *Nature and Motion in the Middle Ages.* Edited by William E. Carroll. Washington: Catholic University of America Press.

Wells, N. 1984. "Material Falsity in Descartes, Arnauld, and Suarez." *Journal of the
   History of Philosophy* 22.

– 1987. "Descartes and the Scholastics Briefly Revisited." *New Scholasticism* 2
   (1961). In Doney 1987.

– 1993. "Descartes' *Idea* and Its Sources." *American Catholic Philosophical Quarterly*
   67(4).

Williams, B. 1962. "The Certainty of the *Cogito.*" Translation of a paper published in
   French in *Cahiers de Royaumont, Philosophie no IV: La Philosophie Analytique*
   (Paris: Les Éditions de Minuit). In Doney 1968.

Wilson, M. 1978a. *Descartes.* London: Routledge and Kegan Paul.

– 1978b. "Cartesian Dualism." In Hooker 1978.

– 1981. "Leibniz's Dynamics and Contingency in Nature." In Woolhouse 1981.

– 1987. "The Phenomenalisms of Leibniz and Berkeley." In Sosa 1987.

– 1990. "Descartes on the Representationality of Sensation." In Cover and Kulstad
   1990.

Wippel, J. 1983. *Metaphysical Themes in Thomas Aquinas.* Washington: Catholic
   University of America Press.

– 1993. "Metaphysics." In Kretzman and Stump 1993.

Wolz, H. 1950. "The Universal Doubt in the Light of Descartes's Conception of Truth."
   Modern Schoolman 27(4).

Woolhouse, R. 1981. *Leibniz: Metaphysics and Philosophy of Science.* Edited by R.S.
   Woolhouse. Oxford: Oxford University Press.

– 1993. *Descartes, Spinoza, Leibniz: The Concept of Substance in Seventeenth-Century Philosophy*. London: Routledge.

Yolton, J. 1956. *John Locke and the Way of Ideas*. Oxford: Oxford University Press.

– 1975a. "Ideas and Knowledge in Seventeenth-Century Philosophy." *Journal of the History of Philosophy* 13.

– 1975b. "On Being Present to the Mind: A Sketch for the History of an Idea." *Dialogue* 14(3).

– 1984. *Perceptual Acquaintance: From Descartes to Reid*. Minneapolis: University of Minnesota Press.

Zimmermann, A. 1965. *Ontologie oder Metaphysik? Die Diskussion über den Gegenstand der Metaphysik im 13. und 14. Jahrhundert*. Leiden: E.J. Brill.

Index

absolute 492

abstraction 93, 131, 133–4, 188, 190, 200

action 57, 267, 270, 455; three meanings of 239–40, 242, 284

acts 57, 73, 84, 86, 173; act-character of 73, 87; criterion of mental 57–8, 67, 93, 100, 304; discursive xvi, 49, 105, 218, 230–4, 237–9, 245, 248–9, 288, 332, 340–2, 349, 354, 479–80, 515 (*see also* definitions, Scholastic; inference, logical); first-order 40, 42, 87; founding and founded 268, 270–6; intentional object of 39–40, 75–6, 79–80, 87–8, 229; performatory (*see* performance); ratiocinative xvi, 49, 218, 230–4, 237–9, 245–9, 288, 332, 340–2, 349, 479 (*see also* demonstrations; inference, logical); second- and higher-order 40, 42, 87, 231–4, 263, 479; speech-acts 85, 160, 169, 460; thought-acts 85, 160, 169, 173

Adam ii

Adam, C. 408

Aegidius Romanus. *See* Giles of Rome

Albertus Magnus 14, 17, 18, 436

Alexander, R. 171, 444, 457

Alexander of Aphrodisias 18

Alexander of Hales 18

Alquié, F. 40, 408, 433, 437, 438, 455, 500

anachronism 45, 86, 91–3, 264, 413, 435, 504

analogia entis 17–19, 397–8, 401–2

anamnēsis 357–8, 491, 493, 505, 507

anima, as distinct from *animus* 437–8. *See also* mind

animism 306, 387, 412

Anscombe, E. 420, 497

Anselm, St 388, 436, 505

apperception. *See* Leibniz, on consciousness

Aquinas, St Thomas 4, 61, 214, 217, 244, 287, 289–90, 330, 381, 385–90, 397, 400, 403, 436, 448, 450, 451, 472, 473, 474, 476, 477–8, 483, 505, 521–2, 524, 526; on abstraction 508; ambiguity of 'measure' in 492–3, 505; on analytic and synthetic method 20–1, 495; on certainty 20; conception of metaphysics 14–23; *distinctio realis* in 467; existentialism of 526; guiding idea of being of

109, 209, 158–9, 215; unassisted 131,
182, 439, 443; validation of 47–8
recollection. *See anamnēsis*
reduction. *See epochē*
Reiner, F. 396
reflexion xvi, 47, 66, 96–101, 104–5,
180, 229–30, 297–8, 395 (*see also*
attention); analytical (or reflexive
analysis) xvi, 49, 177, 196, 229–30,
239, 248–54, 256–61, 281–2, 286–7,
291, 296, 301–8, 337–42, 354,
357–8, 493, 494, 500, 501, 514;
discursive (*see* acts, discursive);
distinguished from consciousness
239–45, 433, 482, 491; distinguished
from thought 243–5; faculty of 97,
99, 301–8 (*see also* potentiality)
Regius, H. 152–3, 155–7, 181, 216, 283,
301–2, 306, 352, 506, 528
Reid, T. 264
relative 492
relativism 113, 374–5
relaxation thesis. *See* thesis, relaxation
reminiscence. *See amamnēsis*
Reneri, H. 82, 413
representation 74–6, 87–8, 90
representationalism xv, 9–10, 41–4, 49,
94–5, 122–3, 263–4, 268–9, 364–5,
371, 372–3, 410–11, 412, 462, 469,
497, 517
revelation 131–2, 183, 352
Richardson, R. 524
Robinson, T. 92
Röd, W. 391, 393–4, 406, 407, 408, 413,
422, 459, 465, 467, 469, 480–1,
486–7, 489, 491, 494, 495, 504, 509,
513, 515, 518
Rodde, S. 468
Rodis-Lewis, G. 415, 456–7, 459, 500
Ross, W.D. 356–7, 396, 413–14, 469, 501

Roth, L. 402, 488, 513, 516
Rubin, R. 172, 207
Rubius, A. (Rubio, Ruvio) 396
Russell, B. xvii, 50, 76, 363, 383, 386,
402, 427, 516, 525–6
Rutherford, D. 395
Ryle, G. 402

sagacity 254, 350, 491. *See also* attention; reflexion, analytical
sapientia universalis. *See mathesis
universalis*
Sartre, J.-P. 76, 422
scepticism 41–2, 102, 125, 179, 215,
225, 226–7, 236, 269, 364, 438, 440,
442, 464, 497 (*see also* relativism;
misology); of the Ancients 113, 118,
440; and Cartesian doubt 111, 365; of
Hume 9, 370, 440; of Locke 9,
520–1; of the Renaissance 246, 440
Schleiermacher, F. 115, 441
Scholastics. *See under* acts; certainty;
definitions; freedom; metaphysics;
mind; truth
Scholz, H. 3, 391, 413, 460, 478, 517;
"Aristotelian question" of 3, 68, 423,
456; "Augustinian question" of 3–5;
"Kantian question" of 3, 427
Schopenhauer, A. 3, 500
Schouls, P. 470
Schulphilosophie 17, 27, 28, 403
scientia: as a kind of certainty distinct
from *persuasio* 47–8, 107–9, 151–64,
491; –, the temporal axis of the distinction 153, 156, 159–61; *reflexa*
(*see* acts, second- and higher-order);
universalis (*see mathesis universalis*);
vera & certa 47–9, 107, 142, 157,
162, 180–1, 185, 200–1, 205, 216, 382
Sclater, W. 513